THE ANALYTICAL CHEMISTRY OF SYNTHETIC DYES

The Analytical Chemistry of Synthetic Dyes

Edited by

K. VENKATARAMAN

**National Chemical Laboratory
Poona, India**

A WILEY-INTERSCIENCE PUBLICATION

JOHN WILEY & SONS, New York • London • Sydney • Toronto

Library of Congress Cataloging in Publication Data:

Venkataraman, Krishnasami, 1901-
 The analytical chemistry of synthetic dyes.

 "A Wiley-Interscience publication."
 Includes bibliographical references.
 1. Dyes and dyeing—Chemistry. I. Title.

TP910.V46   547′.86   76-39881
ISBN 0-471-90575-5

Printed in the United States of America

10 9 8 7 6 5 4 3 2 1

Contributors

JOHN E. BAILEY, Food and Drug Administration, Washington, D.C.

SANDRA J. BELL, Food and Drug Administration, Washington, D.C.

T. E. BEUKELMAN, Organic Chemicals Department, Research and Development Division, E. I. du Pont de Nemours & Company, Wilmington, Delaware

JOHN F. CORBETT, Clairol Research Laboratories, Stamford, Connecticut

ELIZABETH A. COX, Food and Drug Administration, Washington, D.C.

ANTHONY FORIS, Organic Chemicals Department, Research and Development Division, E. I. du Pont de Nemours & Company, Wilmington, Delaware

CHARLES E. GARLAND, Organic Chemicals Department, Research and Development Division, E. I. du Pont de Nemours & Company, Wilmington, Delaware

J. GASPARIČ, Research Institute of Organic Syntheses, Pardubice-Rybitvi, Czechoslovakia

CHARLES GRAICHEN, Food and Drug Administration, Washington, D.C.

ERIK KISSA, Organic Chemicals Department, Research and Development Division, E. I. du Pont de Nemours & Company, Wilmington, Delaware

ROLAND M. LANZARONE, Produits Chimiques Ugine Kuhlmann, Dyes Division, Oissel, France

ADRIAN B. LEATHERMAN, Food and Drug Administration, Washington, D.C.

R. K. MILLER, Organic Chemicals Department, Research and Development Division, E. I. du Pont de Nemours & Company, Wilmington, Delaware

v

LOUIS J. PAPA, Organic Chemicals Department, Research and Development Division, E. I. du Pont de Nemours & Company, Wilmington, Delaware

M. SCHRIER, Otto B. May, Inc., Newark, New Jersey

H. SCHWEPPE, BASF AG, Ludwigshafen am Rhein, Germany

MANJEET SINGH, Food and Drug Administration, Washington, D. C.

JIRI ŠRÁMEK, Research Institute of Textile Finishing, Dvůr Králové nad Labem, Czechoslovakia

J. THOMSON, Pigments Division, Ciba-Geigy (U.K.) Ltd., Paisley, Scotland

K. VENKATARAMAN, National Chemical Laboratory, Poona, India

PERCY M. WATLINGTON, Food and Drug Administration, Washington, D.C.

A. WHITAKER, Department of Physics, Brunel University, Middlesex, England

M. S. YLLO, Physical & Analytical Division, E. I. du Pont de Nemours & Company, Wilmington, Delaware

Preface

No book on the analytical chemistry of synthetic dyes published so far compares in scope with this volume, although synthetic dyes constitute one of the largest and most important of the organic chemical industries. The third edition of A. G. Green's *The Analysis of Dyestuffs* was published in 1920; E. Clayton's *Identification of Dyes on Textile Fibers* (Society of Dyers and Colourists, 1963, 39 pp.) consists mainly of a series of tables representing a modification of Green's original scheme. A 50-page chapter was devoted to the "Identification, Analysis and Evaluation of Dyestuffs" in the *Chemistry of Synthetic Dyes*, Vol. II, 1952. Since that time other books (e.g., on chromatography) and encyclopedias have included chapters on the analysis of dyes; many useful papers dealing with isolated aspects have also appeared. This book is the first attempt to survey the entire field; a glance at the Contents and the list of contributors will show the comprehensive and authoritative coverage.

The introductory chapter, which presents a classification of dyes and other background material, is followed by chapters on various chromatographic techniques useful for the separation and identification of dyes. The well-established UV–visible and IR spectroscopy and the newer NMR and mass spectrometry are discussed in four chapters. Basic knowledge of theory and practice in all these areas, as well as familiarity with the chemistry of synthetic dyes, is assumed; the approach throughout is the specific application of these techniques to the analysis of synthetic dyes.

A brief chapter on X-ray powder diffraction is included because of its importance in the characterization of pigments. Limitations of space have resulted in the exclusion of nearly all the tables of remeasured and recalculated data, which may be obtained from the author.

Chemical degradation methods, supported by chromatography, continue to be useful in determining the structures of water-soluble azo dyes in particular, as described in Chapter 11. The integrated application of all the methods discussed in the earlier chapters is illustrated in Chapters 12–14 by numerous examples in which the structures of synthetic dyes are determined. It is relevant to note in this connection that Japanese Government regulations require the disclosure of the exact chemical structures of all dyes and the composition of the commercial products.

Detailed procedures for identifying dyes on textile fibers and other substrates are presented in two chapters. Analyses performed by the Food and Drug Administration in the United States on each batch of color additive submitted for certification are described in detail by members of the FDA staff in Chapter 17. Dyes and intermediates in hair-coloring products receive separate treatment because they are used only in the dyeing of fur and human hair. Quantitative dye analysis, with special reference to dissolution and extraction methods for dyes in fibers, is discussed in Chapter 19.

As stated in the first sentence of the final chapter, "The deterioration of environmental quality and the disturbance of the ecological balance have aroused international concern in recent years." From this point of view, analytical techniques for ecological and toxicological monitoring are of great importance, and this book as a whole acquires special significance.

I am deeply indebted to Dr. J. R. Martin of the Du Pont Company at Wilmington for his invaluable help in organizing this volume. Eight of the 20 chapters have been written by his colleagues in the Organic Chemicals Department, Research and Development Division in which Dr. Martin is a Division Head, and he has been involved in much of my correspondence with the authors, beginning with the assignments of the topics. I am equally indebted to all the authors for their cooperation in my endeavor to present a balanced and coordinated account of a complex and many-sided subject.

Thanks are due to Dr. P. M. Nair, Dr. K. G. Das, Dr. C. I. Jose, and Dr. N. R. Ayyangar for useful suggestions; to Mr. S. A. Nair for typing extensive correspondence and parts of the manuscript; and to Mr. G.V. Kulkarni for checking literature references.

I am very grateful to Dr. B. D. Tilak, Director of the National Chemical Laboratory, and Dr. Y. Nayudamma, Director-General of Scientific and Industrial Research, for providing me with excellent facilities, which have enabled me to work for 10 years after official retirement.

K. VENKATARAMAN

Poona, India
December 1976

Contents

Notes

Spectral Data

Infrared absorption bands are given in cm^{-1}.
Chemical shifts in NMR (PMR) spectra are δ values (ppm downfield from tetramethylsilane). Coupling constants (J) are in Hz. The following abbreviations are used: s = singlet; d = doublet; t = triplet; q = quartet; qn = quintet; m = multiplet; br = broad; o, m, and p = *ortho*, *meta*, and *para* couplings $(J = 7–10, 1–3,$ and <1 Hz, respectively). **Temperatures** are in °C.

Abbreviations

Ac	Acetyl
Ar	Aryl
CMR	Carbon-13 magnetic resonance
DMF	Dimethylformamide
DMSO	Dimethyl sulfoxide
DNPH	2,4-Dinitrophenylhydrazone
DP	Degree of polymerization
EDTA	Ethylenediaminetetraacetic acid
Et	Ethyl
GC	Gas chromatography
GLC	Gas–liquid chromatography
HPLC	High-pressure liquid chromatography
HRMS	High-resloution mass spectrometry
IR	Infrared

M	Molecular weight
M·+	Molecular ion in the mass spectrum
Me	Methyl
m.p.	Melting point
MS	Mass spectrum; mass spectra; mass spectrometry
NMR	Nuclear (generally proton) magnetic resonance
OEt	Ethoxyl
OMe	Methoxyl
owf	On weight of fiber
PC	Paper chromatography
Ph	Phenyl
PLC	Preparative layer chromatography
PMR	Proton magnetic resonance
R	Alkyl or aralkyl
TFA	Trifluoroacetic acid
THF	Tetrahydrofuran
TLC	Thin-layer chromatography
UV	Ultraviolet

Journals and Books

Abbreviations of names of journals follow *Chemical Abstracts Service Source Book*, 1975.

CA	*Chemical Abstracts*
CI	*Colour Index*, 3rd ed., 1971
CI AA	*Colour Index, Additions and Amendments*
CSD I–VII	*The Chemistry of Synthetic Dyes*, Academic Press, New York

Colorant Manufacturers

CI code letters are used.

Patents

BP	British patent
CP	Canadian patent
DBP	Deutsche Bundespatente
DRP	Deutsche Reichspatente
Ger. Offen.	Deutsche Offenlegungsschrift (DOS)
JP	Japanese patent
USP	United States Patent

THE ANALYTICAL CHEMISTRY OF SYNTHETIC DYES

CHAPTER ONE

Introduction

K. VENKATARAMAN

A dye to be identified may be available either in substance or on a textile fiber or other substrate. If the dye sample carries the manufacturer's label, the name usually shows the application class; the relevant pattern card provides information on methods of application and properties of the colored material. Then the analyst may merely be required to compare the sample with a standard product for homogeneity, concentration, and other criteria. If the dye is listed in the *Colour Index*, its chemical class is usually mentioned; the complete structure may also be disclosed, but generally not for the more recent dyes. A dye with desirable properties may be of sufficient interest to a competitive firm for its research department to undertake structure determination and confirmation by synthesis.

The examination of an unknown dye involves first (*a*) the determination of its application class, (*b*) paper or thin-layer chromatography (PC or TLC) to check its homogeneity, (*c*) separation of the constituent dyes if the sample is a mixture, and (*d*) determination of the chemical class by color reactions or "spot tests" (conc. sulfuric and nitric acids; aqueous sodium hydroxide; neutral, acidic, and alkaline reduction and reoxidation; tests for Cu, Cr, and Co). The next and much more difficult stage is to match the dye with a dye having a CI generic name. Since a direct comparison in terms of chromatography, color reactions, and UV and IR spectra is both the most rapid and most dependable procedure for proving identity, the larger the collection of dyes (commercial and chemically pure) and data catalogues at the disposal of the analyst, the easier his task.

1

1 COLOUR INDEX

The second edition of *Colour Index* (1956) and the Supplement (1963) were reviewed in *CSD* III. The third edition appeared in 1971. According to the foreword the need for this revised and enlarged edition "was made evident by the increase in the number of generic names of individual dyes and pigments from 6047 in the second edition and Supplement to 7895 in the third edition." The generic names of reactive dyes increased from 88 to 361. The value of the third edition is mainly in the correlation of commercial names with generic names because of the "marked tendency for alternative names to be given to existing dyes to indicate their suitability for use" on the newer fibers or other substrates. The data provided on dyeing and fastness properties are useful, but they must be supplemented by the pattern cards, manuals, and leaflets issued by dye manufacturers.

1.1 Generic Names

The separate treatment of dyes grouped according to (*a*) usage classes and hue and (*b*) chemical constitution, adopted in the second edition, has been followed in the third with one difference. Volumes 1, 2, and 3 list generic names indicating usage class and hue (such as Acid Yellow 163 and Basic Blue 56), together with the dyeing and fastness properties on textile fibers as well as nontextile substrates; but commercial names arranged alphabetically under each generic name are given separately in Volume 5, which begins with the names, addresses, and code letters of dye and pigment manufacturers and ends with an alphabetical index of commercial names. The number of manufacturers of a dye with a particular generic name is an indication of its popularity and the quantities in demand.

Table 1.1 (cf. Table II, *CSD* III, p. 7) lists the number of CI dyes (including those in *CI AA* 1–18) in each usage class subdivided according to hue; the second and third numbers under each head represent the dyes of known chemical class and the dyes of known structure, respectively. The actual numbers of dyes in each usage class are without doubt considerably smaller because (*a*) some dyes have more than one generic name representing alternative uses; and (*b*) many dyes with generic names, although they are not marked as discontinued, are in fact not manufactured now. It is common experience to write to a firm for a dye listed in CI and find that it is no longer manufactured.

In addition to the dyes in Table 1.1, CI generic names cover the following.

CI Food Dyes represent the permitted lists of the United Kingdom, United States, West Germany, and the European Economic Community.

Table 1.1   Dyes in CI and CI AA (1–18, up to January 1976)[a]

Dye Type	Yellow	Orange	Red	Violet	Blue	Green	Brown	Black
Acid	172	126	273	84	233	79	280	298
	148	106	253	70	211	73	224	128
	46	43	101	31	73	23	33	31
Basic	63	41	87	44	108	13	11	7
	63	41	85	42	102	12	11	6
	10	11	14	15	21	3	5	3
Direct	113	73	161	51	184	62	135	107
	91	53	143	43	167	57	103	96
	35	39	81	24	78	20	47	33
Disperse	157	115	245	68	251	3	18	19
	125	110	240	68	248	3	17	18
	19	8	15	8	15	0	1	5
Mordant	35	22	42	26	35	21	49	55
	26	16	35	24	31	18	41	41
	18	10	23	17	20	11	24	18
Pigment	93	39	158	32	30	16	12	7
	93	39	158	32	30	16	12	5
	34	22	90	19	22	14	8	1
Reactive	117	81	160	31	154	18	26	33
	116	80	159	31	151	18	26	33
	3	2	12	3	7	—	1	2
Solvent	114	68	153	29	102	18	37	34
	94	61	125	27	92	17	31	24
	28	17	41	11	28	5	7	5
Sulfur	12	4	10	4	15	29	57	13
Vat	29	19	39	16	41	31	46	37
	24	9	37	14	40	29	42	34
	15	2	22	13	31	12	15	12

[a] Discontinued generic names and those for which there is "no known maker" have been excluded. The first number is the total, the second the number of dyes of known chemical class, and the third the number of dyes of known structure (dyes with constitution number).

All the CI Food Dyes are of known structure, and the commercial products have to conform to prescribed standards of purity (see Chapter 17). CI also lists Drug Dyes, Drug and Cosmetic Dyes, and Cosmetic Dyes permitted in the United States (see also Chapter 17).

CI Leather Dyes are a separate list of acid, mordant, and direct dyes, that have important leather usage.

CI Azoic Colorants comprise (a) (1) CI Azoic Coupling Components (arylamides of 2-hydroxy-3-naphthoic acid and four similar acids for red to black shades, and bis-acetoacet-o-tolidide and three analogues for yellow shades) and (2) CI Azoic Diazo Components (primary aromatic amines or the stabilized diazonium salts), which are used to produce insoluble azo dyes usually on a textile substrate, in particular, cotton; and (b) CI Azoic Compositions, which contain both diazo and coupling components in suitable forms for development, after printing, by neutral steaming or other treatment. The structures of nearly all the azoic coupling and diazo components are known, and recent developments are concerned mainly with stabilization techniques for azoic compositions.

CI Ingrain Dyes are all dyes formed in the substrate and should therefore include azoics and oxidation colors, but the CI list is restricted to products (14 Ingrain Blues, 6 Greens, and 1 Brown) yielding phthalocyanines; one exception is Ingrain Yellow 1, an isothiuronium salt of chloromethylated azodehydrothiotoluidine (CSD IV, p. 166). Ingrain Blues 1, 3, 4, and 8 and Ingrain Greens 1 and 2 are similar cationic dyes (Alcian dyes, ICI) soluble in aqueous acetic acid and rendered insoluble on the fiber by alkali (in dyeing) or steaming (in printing). The other Ingrain Blues (CSD V, pp. 307–309) are phthalocyanine precursors: (a) Cu, Ni, or Co complexes of dehydrophthalocyanine; and (b) 1-amino-3-iminoisoindolenine derivatives and their mixtures with Cu, Ni, and Co donors and with "developers" for modifying the shades. Ingrain Green 3 is a precursor for copper tetraphenylphthalocyanine.

CI Developers are components for coupling on the fiber with dyes containing a primary amino group that is diazotized. Many direct cotton dyes and a few disperse dyes on cellulose acetate are suitable for this purpose. Common developers are 2-naphthol, 2-hydroxy-3-naphthoic acid, and m-phenylenediamine. The CI list includes one amine for diazotization (p-nitroaniline).

CI Fluorescent Brighteners are colorless compounds that absorb UV radiation from sunlight and emit visible (mostly blue) light.[1] They are used in detergent mixtures, on paper and textiles, and in plastics and oils. Only 14 of 245 bear constitution numbers. About 80% are stilbene derivatives. The water-soluble compounds contain SO_3Na or NH_4 salt groups.

CI Oxidation Bases are mostly primary aromatic amines that undergo oxidation on the fiber to intensely colored (mainly brown and black) insoluble compounds, but several phenols and naphthols are included. Fe, Cr, Cu, and Al salts may be used for mordanting. Except for Aniline Black on cotton, they are used mainly for dyeing fur.

CI Reducing Agents, used in dyeing and printing and as stripping agents, are included, although "they may seem to be a little out of place at first sight."

The Sections on Natural Dyes and Pigments in Volumes 2 and 4 should be completely ignored. They are not merely irrelevant, but also provide hopelessly inaccurate information (cf. *CSD* III, p. 14).

1.2 Chemical Constitution

The constitution numbers of the second edition are retained, and new numbers interposed in the appropriate positions for new structural disclosures, which are relatively few. In fact, there is only a marginal addition in the new edition to our knowledge of the chemistry of commercial dyes; but more structures are being disclosed in *CI AA*.

The dyes mentioned in this book carry both the CI generic names and constitution numbers (e.g., CI Acid Blue 17; CI 42625); the absence of the latter indicates that the structure has not been published.

2 SOLUBILITY, DYEING PROPERTY, HUE, AND CHEMICAL CLASS

For our present analytical purposes dyes may be divided first into *water-soluble*, anionic and cationic, and *water-insoluble;* and then into usage classes as follows, incidentally recalling certain definitions.

Water-soluble
Anionic: acid dyes, acid-mordant dyes, direct cotton dyes, reactive dyes, solubilized vat dyes, solubilized and "condense" sulfur dyes, and leuco sulfur dyes
Cationic: "basic dyes"

Water-insoluble
Mordant dyes, disperse dyes, solvent dyes, pigments, vat dyes, and sulfur dyes

In the following elaboration of this classification, broad correlations of chemical constitution with hue and dyeing properties will also become apparent.

2.1   Water-Soluble Dyes

It is common practice to classify a water-soluble dye by examining the behavior of a multifiber fabric (e.g., containing cotton, wool, nylon, acetate, polyester, and acrylic fiber) toward a boiling aqueous solution of the dye with the addition of sodium chloride, acetic acid, or sulfuric acid.

2.1.1   Anionic. *Acid Dyes.* Nearly all contain one or more SO_3Na or SO_3H groups. Acid dyes containing O—SO_3Na and CH_2SO_3Na groups should also be looked for, especially among dyes for nylon; several of the Solacets (ICI), water-soluble dyes containing O—SO_3Na groups, which were developed originally for cellulose acetate, are now marketed as Nylomine A dyes for nylon.[2] Neutral-dyeing Cr and Co complexes may contain only SO_2NH_2 groups (e.g., CI 13906; CI 18732). A few acid dyes (such as fluorescein and its derivatives) are carboxylic acids.

Acid dyes dye wool, silk, nylon, modified acrylic fibers, and leather from acidic or neutral baths; they do not dye cotton. Nearly all the yellows, oranges, reds, browns, and blacks are azo. An old and widely used yellow is sodium or potassium 2,4-dinitro-1-naphthol-7-sulfonate (CI Acid Yellow 1; CI 10316), and an exceptional type is an *N*-phenylnaphthalimide (CI 56205; *CSD* II, p. 1188). A few reds are anthraquinones, and there are several fluorescein derivatives. Although azo dyes constitute the great majority, there are among the important violets, blues, and greens many anthraquinones and triphenylmethanes. A few blues are phenazines. A few browns and blacks are anthraquinones. Several browns (mainly leather dyes) are nitrodiphenylamines.

CI Acid Dyes include 1:1 and 2:1 dye–metal (mostly Cr and a few Co) complexes of azo dyes containing *o,o'*-dihydroxy or (rarely, but as in the important CI Acid Green 12; CI 13425) *o*-hydroxy-*o'*-amino groups. An old and still important green is the Fe complex of 1-nitroso-2-naphthol-6-sulfonic acid (CI Acid Green 1; CI 10020).

Acid-Mordant Dyes. These are acid dyes with the additional property that the washfastness is improved, frequently with simultaneous deepening of color, by treatment with a metallic mordant, mostly a Cr salt. Their main use is in wool dyeing and the word "chrome" often occurs in the commercial names. Structurally, they are mostly *o*-hydroxyazo compounds with OH or NH_2 or COOH in the *o'*-position or azosalicylic acids (notably CI Mordant Yellow 1; *m*-nitroaniline → salicylic acid). There are some triphenylmethanes containing one to three salicylic acid groups (e.g., the important CI Mordant Blue 1; CI 43830), one alizarin derivative (the 3-sulfonic acid), and three phthalocyanines (one an "azo phthalocyanine"). Nearly all CI Mordant Dyes are acid-mordant dyes.

Direct Cotton Dyes. CI Direct Dyes are closely related to acid dyes, the distinguishing property being substantivity to cellulose in the presence of sodium chloride or sulfate. Nearly all are azo dyes; the few exceptions are dioxazines and phthalocyanines. The relatively few monoazo dyes are derived from Primuline or dehydrothiotoluidine or J-acid. Disazo dyes (especially of the type $E^1 \leftarrow D \rightarrow E^2$) are the most numerous. Trisazo and polyazo dyes are mostly blue, green, brown, and black; some are useful for leather. Dyes with four or five azo groups are mixtures and very few are current. Yellow to brown dyes of indeterminate structure are derived from 4,4′-dinitrostilbene-2,2′-disulfonic acid. Direct dyes include Cu complexes (e.g., CI Direct Blue 98; CI 23155) and a few dyes (derived, for instance, from 8-hydroxyquinoline) that are coppered on the fiber for improving wash- and lightfastness.

Reactive Dyes. These are structurally similar to acid dyes with the important difference that they contain labile Cl or O—SO₃Na as a leaving group, enabling the dyes to form covalent bonds with fibers (primarily cellulose).[3] In the Basazols (BASF), fixation involves a cross-linking agent between fiber and dye.[3]

In addition to the reactive systems of commercial dyes tabulated in *CSD* VI, pp. 2, 3, the following are mentioned in the *CI* preamble: 2,4-dichloropyrimidinyl, 1,4-dichlorophthalazine-6-carbonyl, β-chloroethyl-sulfonyl, and β-sulfatopropionamido. However, the generic names cover only four reactive systems: mono- or dichloro-*s*-triazine, trichloropyrimidine, 1,4-dichlorophthalazine, and vinyl sulfone (equivalent to $SO_2CH_2CH_2$—O—SO_3-Na). Among CI Reactive Dyes, nearly half are mono- or dichloro-*s*-triazines; the remainder are about equally divided between trichloropyrimidines and vinyl sulfones. A few derivatives of 1,4-dichlorophthalazine-6-carboxylic acid are mentioned, but this type is probably obsolete.

Nearly all the yellow, orange, red, violet, brown, and black dyes are azo, but the blues consist of almost equal numbers of azo, anthraquinone, and phthalocyanine derivatives; the greens are mainly anthraquinones and phthalocyanines, but there are a few azo dyes including one formazan. Some of the azo dyes are Cu complexes; a few browns and blacks and most of the reactive dyes for wool are Cr and Co complexes.

Solubilized Vat Dyes. These dyes (which appear in *CI* immediately after each parent vat dye) contain O—SO₃Na groups; they are prepared from vat dyes by sulfation of the leuco derivatives. The aqueous solutions are oxidized back to the parent vat dyes by treatment with sodium nitrite and acid. The main use is for pale shades on cotton and rayon. Fewer than one-fifth of the commercial vat dyes are marketed in the solubilized form. A few vat dyes are marketed only as the solubilized dyes. The waning interest in this group is shown by the very small number of new and recently marketed dyes.

Solubilized and Condense Sulfur Dyes. Both types contain S—SO$_3$Na groups. The former are prepared by heating sulfur dyes with aqueous sodium sulfite or bisulfite, and the latter (Bunte salt dyes; *S*-alkyl or *S*-aryl thiosulfates) by synthetic methods from intermediates containing an S—SO$_3$Na group.[4] Of the 17 CI Condense Sulfur Dyes, the three blues are anthraquinone derivatives, and the green is a phthalocyanine; the others are azo dyes. Only one has a constitution number (CI 18790). Insoluble products are obtained by reduction with sodium sulfide and subsequent air oxidation.

Leuco Sulfur Dyes. These sulfur dyes are reduced with sodium sulfide, and therefore contain SNa groups. Air oxidation regenerates the insoluble sulfur dyes. CI Solubilized Sulfur Dyes and CI Leuco Sulfur Dyes follow immediately in CI after each parent CI Sulfur Dye.

2.1.2 Cationic. CI Basic Dyes are ammonium, sulfonium, or oxonium salts; solubility in water is improved by the addition of acetic acid. At the present time their main use is for acrylic fiber.[5] The older dyes are used for paper coloration, and some for very bright shades in dyeing and printing of tannin-mordanted cotton; but a few (such as Basic Blues 1, 3, and 5) are useful for acrylic fiber. An important application is for conversion into pigments. For these purposes dyes such as Chrysoidine, Bismarck Brown, Thioflavine, Auramine, Malachite Green, Magenta and its derivatives, Rhodamines, Safranine, Meldola's Blue, and Methylene Blue are made by many firms. Their chemistry is well-known, and they are easy to identify. Structures have been disclosed for only a fourth of CI Basic Dyes (and only a tenth of the 130 or more marked as "azo"), and most of them are classical dyes. Minor modification of the substituents in triphenylmethanes and oxazines has led to some commercial dyes for synthetic fibers. Only one of the 17 anthraquinones has a constitution number (CI 61111). Out of more than 50 cyanine dyes, 12 or more are derivatives of 3,3-dimethylindolenine. Several of them (Astrazon colors for cellulose acetate) were made by the IG from Fischer's base or aldehyde and later found to be suitable for acrylic fiber. Among the CI Basic Dyes marked as dyes for acrylic fiber, dyes made by a single manufacturer and of undisclosed structure represent a large proportion, indicating recent development and patent protection.

Except for a few amine salts (such as Chrysoidine), cationic dyes can be classified as follows for identification and structure determination.[5]

Dyes with a pendant cation include (1) azo dyes; (2) anthraquinone derivatives; (3) styryl dyes, quinophthalones, etc. Dyes with a delocalized cation are (1) diphenylmethanes and triphenylmethanes; (2) 9-phenylxanthenes (phthaleins); (3) acridines; (4) 9-phenylphenazinium chlorides; (5) phenoxazines; (6) phenothiazines; (7) cyanine dyes, defined as dyes in which a cationic charge resonates between the N atoms of two heterocyclic rings connected by a conjugate chain of C atoms (in which one or more methine groups may be replaced by N), and customarily including dyes in which one tertiary N is attached to a benzene ring or an alkene group (and other related types).[6] A discussion of the cyanines as photographic sensitizers is outside the scope of this book. Cyanine dyes for synthetic fibers[5] are mainly of the following types: (a) stilbene analogues with one or both benzene rings replaced by heterocyclic rings (e.g., CI 48015; CI 48035); (b) azo dyes in which one or both benzene rings are replaced by heterocyclic rings (e.g., CI 11055; CI 11460); and (c) aza- or diazatrimethinecyanines.

2.2   Water-Insoluble Dyes

Mordant Dyes.   The few dyes of this type are 1-nitroso-2-naphthol, alizarin, anthragallol, and gallocyanine and its derivatives, which are soluble in aqueous sodium carbonate or bisulfite.

Disperse Dyes.   Disperse dyes are applied to cellulose acetate and polyester fiber as aqueous dispersions, anionic dispersing agents mainly being used. Dyes for polyester fiber are now outstandingly important, and selected dyes are applicable to nylon. In the absence of dispersing agents, dyes with poor sublimation fastness are used for transfer printing.

Nearly all disperse dyes are azo (mostly monoazo) dyes or anthraquinones, substituted by NH_2 or NR_1R_2, in which R_1 and/or R_2 are CH_2-CH_2OH, CH_2CH_2CN, and similar groups designed to balance hydrophobic and hydrophilic character. Azo dyes containing NH_2 groups can be diazotized on the fiber and developed with suitable components, usually for producing blacks (such as the largely used CI Disperse Black 1; CI 11365). Some of the blacks are azoic compositions. Among the yellows there are several nitrodiphenylamines (such as the largely used Yellow 42; CI 10338), styrene derivatives (such as condensation products of N-alkyl or aryl derivatives of p-aminobenzaldehyde with cyanoacetic ester or malononitrile), and quinophthalones (e.g., CI 47020, 47023). Nearly all the oranges and reds are azo, but a few are simple anthraquinone derivatives, and one (CI Disperse Red 196; CI 48310) is the condensation product of naphthostyril with ethyl 5-pyrazolone-3-carboxylate. Azo dyes and anthraquinones are equally represented in the violets. The blues are predominantly anthraquinones, but there are 50 or more azo dyes, nearly all of undisclosed structure. Four very popular anthraquinones have the following substituents: $1,4,5,8$-$(NH_2)_4$; 1-$NHMe$-4-$NHCH_2CH_2OH$; $1,4$-$(OH)_2$-$5,8$-$(NHCH_2$-$CH_2OH)_2$; Cl- or Br-$1,5$-$(NH_2)_2$-$4,8$-$(OH)_2$. These are typical of the more than 100 dyes, although the structures of fewer than 20 have been disclosed. Only four of the eight greens are current; one is a mixture of $1,4$-diarylaminoanthraquinones (see Chapter 14). Only one of the 10 browns (all azo) is of known structure (CI 11152).

Solvent Dyes. Solvent dyes are soluble in organic solvents (such as alcohols, esters, hydrocarbons, chlorinated hydrocarbons, and fats), but they may be incorporated directly into the product to be colored. Yellows, oranges, browns, and reds are mostly azo, but there are several anthraquinones and the bright reds are xanthenes; blues and greens are mostly anthraquinones, together with some triphenylmethanes, phenazines, phenothiazines, and phthalocyanines; blacks are mainly azo, but important blacks are made from Nigrosine (CI 50415). The bases of cationic dyes may be directly solvent-soluble or can be dissolved in fatty acids. Sulfonic acids (infrequently used) are solubilized as salts of diarylguanidine, dicyclohexylamine, and diisoamylamine.

Pigments. CI Pigments[7] include the following. (*a*) Water-insoluble organic compounds, such as azoics (yellow to red, the most numerous), azamethines (including Cu and other metal chelates, yellow to violet and brown), Aniline Black, dioxazines (violet), phthalocyanines (blues and greens), quinacridones (reds and red-violets), and vat dyes. (*b*) "Toners" of two types: (1) Ba, Ca, Sr, and other insoluble salts of acid dyes, the widely used Pigment Red 49 (Tobias acid → 2-naphthol) being a very sparingly soluble Na salt; widely used red toners are made from monoazo dyes using 2-hydroxy-3-naphthoic acid as coupling component, which are not textile dyes. CI Pigment Greens 8 and 12 are Fe complexes of 1-nitroso-2-naphthol and its 6-sulfonic acid. (2) Insoluble salts of basic dyes with acids such as phosphotungstomolybdic acid or phosphomolybdic acid or complexes with copper ferrocyanide. Water-insoluble salts of textile dyes used as pigments are listed in *CI* in an appendix. (*c*) Lakes, which are similar to toners, but obtained by precipitation in presence of a substrate; Al and Ca lakes from alizarin, quinizarin, and their sulfonic acids are examples. Except for CI Pigment Blue 24 and a few red lakes, inorganic substrates have declining use, but fluorescent dyes (notably the Rhodamines) precipitated on synthetic resins find increasing use. (*d*) Extended pigments, obtained by dilution with alumina, lithopone, and inorganic substrates. (*e*) Inorganics.

Vat Dyes. The "vat," obtained by treatment with aqueous sodium hydroxide and dithionite, has affinity for cotton, and the insoluble dye is regenerated by air oxidation. Anthraquinonoids constitute the great majority, but there are about 20 indigoids and thioindigoids. The anthraquinonoids give deeply colored vats, and the indigoids pale yellow or pale brown vats. The anthraquinonoids can be classified into anthraquinone and anthrone derivatives. There is a third small group of derivatives of naphthalene and perylene *peri*-carboxylic acids.[8] In addition there are a few sulfurized vat dyes (notably CI Vat Blue 42, 43, 47, the Hydron Blues) and one or two phthalocyanines (CI Vat Blue 29, 57).

Sulfur Dyes. The solution in aqueous sodium sulfide is substantive to cotton, and the dye is regenerated by air oxidation. In *CI* each sulfur dye made from a known intermediate or mixture of intermediates has a constitution number, although the structures of the dyes themselves are unknown.

3 PURITY OF COMMERCIAL DYES

Commercial dyes are products standardized for their end use, not homogeneous chemical compounds, although many vat dyes, disperse dyes, cationic dyes, and anthraquinonoid acid dyes are of high purity (except for colorless diluents or dispersing agents) and can be readily purified further by appropriate isolation procedures and crystallization. Rigid standards of purity are specified for permitted food colors.

Anionic azo dyes, especially those prepared by several coupling reactions and containing several sulfonic groups, are difficult to isolate in the pure state. So simple a dye as Orange I (CI Acid Orange 20; CI 14600; sulfanilic acid → 1-naphthol) has been found by gel chromatography on Sephadex G-25 to yield six colored bands in addition to the expected dye.[9] Column chromatography[10] of an aqueous ethanol solution of CI Direct Green 6 (CI 30295) on alumina shows the presence of five dyes with λ_{max} 388, 644, 534, 640, and 556 nm.

In connection with the histochemistry of Alcian Blue 8GX (CI Ingrain Blue 1; CI 74240) Scott found that commercial samples contained 40–50% boric acid, removable by precipitation of the dye by acetone from an aqueous solution.[11] He has stated that "the main manufacturers refused to divulge structural details, which would permit reliable interpretations in molecular biological terms of histochemical experiments. The reasons are hard to see." In a review of laser dyes Drexhage[12] has stated that "organic dyes are often sold under false names." He observed that several commercial samples were "incorrectly labeled." These are extreme examples cited from very special points of view, but they illustrate the need for the analysis of commercial dyes by methods designed for specific purposes.

A general method for isolating acid, acid-mordant, direct, and reactive dyes containing SO_3Na groups from commercial products containing sodium chloride, sulfate, and other inorganic diluents, is to dissolve the dye in DMF, filter, and precipitate with acetone or chloroform.[13]

TLC and PC are discussed in Chapters 2 and 3. TLC has the advantage of the availability of several adsorbents, and it provides the basis for isolation by PLC or column chromatography. PC is particularly useful for obtaining reproducible R_F values. Adsorption chromatography on Sephadex gels has been used to separate azo dye sulfonates from colored impurities not removable by crystallization.[9] High-pressure liquid chromatography, especially valuable for dyes containing SO_3H or SO_3Na groups, is described in Chapter 4. A recent application is reverse-phase HPLC of ion pairs, by which Tartrazine has been separated from the intermediates, sulfanilic acid and 1-(p-sulfophenyl)-5-pyrazolone-3-carboxylic acid.[14] A solution of the dye in water–methanol is injected into the chromatographic system, and the mobile phase consists of methanol, water, formic acid, and a quaternary amine (e.g., tetrabutylammonium hydroxide) or a tertiary amine (e.g., tridecylamine).

Methods for the quantitative analysis of dyes are discussed in Chapter 19. Chemical methods, such as the reduction of azo dyes with titanous or chromous chloride, oxidation of solubilized vat dyes or other oxidizable compounds with ceric salts, or titration of cationic dyes with anionic dyes, can be used only for determining a functional group or for quantitatively estimating a dye in a mixture containing no other dye or product capable of reacting with the same reagent. When the pure authentic dye or a commercial dye suitable as a standard is available, the simple and generally applicable method is visible absorption spectrophotometry.

4   IDENTIFICATION OF DYES IN SUBSTANCE AND ON SUBSTRATES

The hue, solubility, dyeing properties, a few color reactions, and PC or TLC are usually adequate for identifying a dye in terms of both the application and chemical classes. A separate chapter has not been devoted to the identification of dyes in substance in this book, but the methods described in Chapter 15 for the identification of dyes on textile fibers are applicable; the test reactions can be carried out in solution or after taking up the dye on cotton, wool, or a synthetic fiber. Dyeing experiments ("dye trials"),[15] carried out with manufacturers' pattern cards and standard dyeings prepared from known dyes for comparison, are useful not only for the practical evaluation of the shade, strength, and fastness properties of dyes, but also for their identification. When authentic samples are available for direct comparison, precise identification as a dye with a CI generic name or a dye of known structure is possible by TLC, PC, and the determination of visible and IR absorption spectra (see Chapters 2, 3, 6, 7, and 16).

5 STRUCTURE DETERMINATION

The structure of a dye may be known to one or more firms, but a prospective rival manufacturer or a scientist for research purposes has to find it for himself. Incidentally, it is unsafe to assume that dyes listed in *CI* under the same generic name are identical in chemical constitution; often the differences may be minor, such as a difference in the number or position of halogen, but the possibility of more serious discrepancies cannot be ignored. More challenging to the organic chemist is the investigation of the structures of dyes that are unknown even to the producer, such as sulfur dyes as a class, prepared by thionation processes.

Many examples of structure determination by the integrated use of spectroscopic methods, supported if necessary by chemical degradation, are given in Chapters 12–14; the individual techniques are discussed in Chapters 6–9 and 11. A few disjointed observations and examples, as an extension of Chapter 12, are given below.

The first steps are to isolate the dye in the pure state by chromatography and crystallization, establish the molecular formula, record the UV–visible and IR spectra, and carry out a few color reactions, of which perhaps the most important is the behavior on reduction and reoxidation. NMR and MS can then be used for determining the precise structure, shortcuts being provided by a knowledge of the structures of related dyes and the patent literature.

5.1 Deamination of Aromatic Amines via the Diazonium Salts

The replacement of an aromatic NH_2 group by H via the diazonium salt is useful for determining the structures of Fast Bases and Salts, as well as other purposes. A convenient procedure is to warm the diazonium fluoroborate with DMF until nitrogen evolution ceases. Thus *p*-aminoazobenzene gives azobenzene in about 70% yield, and 4,8-diaminoanthrarufin gives anthrarufin in greater than 50% yield.[16,17] 2,4,6-Trichloroaniline gives tri-chlorobenzene in greater than 95% yield when the diazonium fluoroborate in dioxane is treated with 1,4-diazabicyclo[2.2.2]octane (DABCO) at 25–30°. Leuco Malachite Green is converted to Malachite Green by diazonium salts.

When the blue dyes (1) and the 2-anisyl isomer were deaminated by the action of DMF on the diazonium salt, and the two OH groups were methyl-ated, the appearance of four H as a *m*-coupled or *o*-coupled *d* in the NMR spectra of the products was adequate to show the positions of the anisyl substituent, which are the reverse of those mentioned in the relevant pat-ents on the *C*-arylation of CI Acid Blue 45 (CI 63010) and 4,8-dinitro-1,5-dihydroxyanthraquinone.[18] TLC of two commercial dyes listed in CI as Disperse Blue 73 showed that one had the structure (1). The other was an approximately 1:1 mixture of (1) with the analogue from phenol, as shown by the relative intensity of the methoxyl resonance in the NMR spectrum of the dye in comparison with (1) in TFA.[19a]

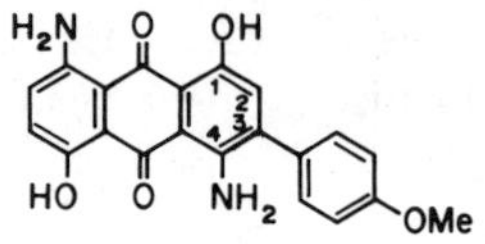

CI Disperse Blue 73 (1)

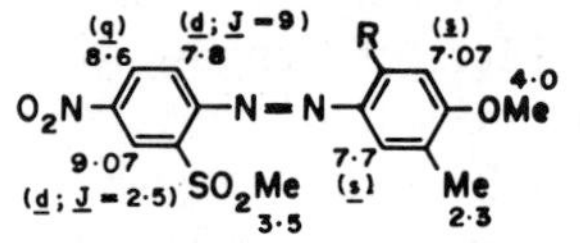

Fast Olive Salt BR (R = N_2^+)

(2 ; R = Cl)

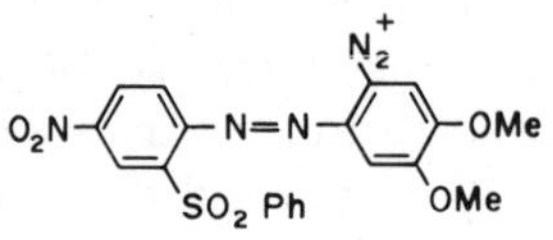

Fast Green Salt GT

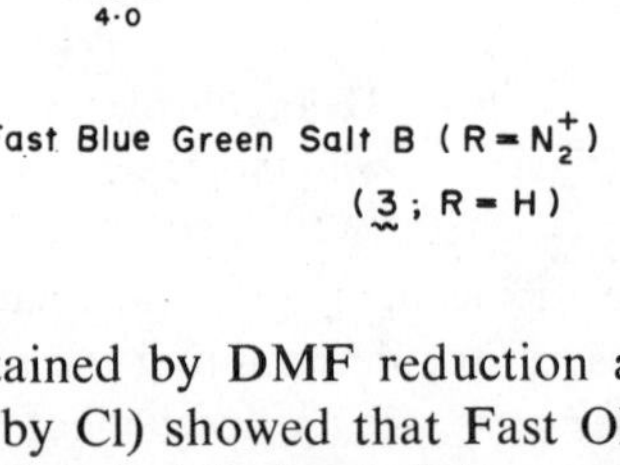

Fast Blue Green Salt B (R = N_2^+)

(3 ; R = H)

The NMR and MS of the products obtained by DMF reduction and by the Sandmeyer reaction (replacing N_2^+ by Cl) showed that Fast Olive Salt BR, Green Salt GT, and Blue Green Salt B (CI Azoic Diazo Com-ponents 125, 134, and 118) have the indicated structures. NMR data for (2) and (3) are summarized in the formulas.[16]

5.2 Azoic Diazo Components for Green and Brown Shades[19b]

Azoic Diazo Components 135, 138, 136, and 137 are listed in *CI* 5 as the Co and Cu complexes of Variogen Base I and the Cu complexes of Base II and III, respectively; but in *CI* 1 they are mentioned as bases or salts suitable for metal complex formation. Variogen Base I yields deep olive green and the other two yield brown azoic dyeings when they are aftertreated with Co or Cu salts.

All three commercial products were found to be the free bases, crystallizable from ethanol. Variogen Base I, $C_7H_6N_3Cl$ (M·+ 167), shows in its NMR spectrum (in DMSO) three aromatic H in the 1, 2, and 4 positions (*o*-coupled *d* at 7.7; *m*-coupled *d* at 7.3, and a q at 6.87). By refluxing with acetic anhydride a triacetyl derivative is obtained. The patent literature[20] suggests the structure 3-amino-6-chloroindazole.

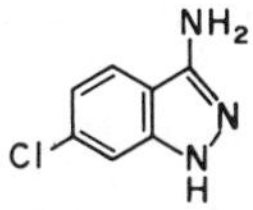

Variogen Base I

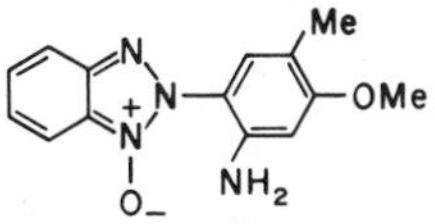

Variogen Base II

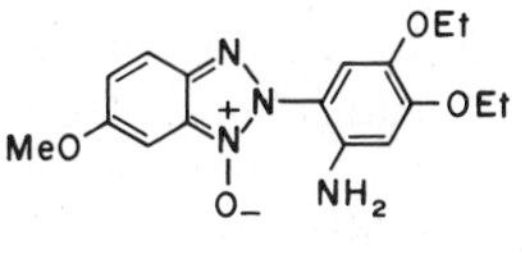

Variogen Base III

Variogen Base II, $C_{14}H_{14}N_4O_2$ (M·+ 270), contains one OMe, one aromatic C—Me, and six aromatic H (five H *m* at 7.8; and one H *s* at 7.3) as shown by the NMR spectrum in TFA. An *N*-oxide is indicated by the loss of 16 mass units from M·+, and the probable structure follows from a patent.[21]

Variogen Base III was obtained as greenish yellow needles from benzene after silica gel chromatography, $C_{17}H_{20}N_4O_4$ (M·+ 344). It is an *N*-oxide. The NMR spectrum (CDCl₃) shows one OMe, two OEt, one NH₂ (six H as a complex *m* at 3.93–4.33 for two CH₂ + one NH₂), and five aromatic H (two *s* at 6.40 and 7.55; an *o*-coupled *d* at 7.63; and two H *m* at 6.83–7.34). The indicated structure is in agreement with the available data.[21]

The three bases were conveniently characterized as the *N*-picryl derivatives, which also yield useful NMR spectra.

5.3   Azo Dyes

Chromatography on polyamide, prepared, for instance, from nylon 6 by treatment with hydrochloric acid and widely used for plant phenolics, is useful for the isolation of azo dyes (acid, direct, and reactive dyes) from aqueous or DMF solution mixed with the appropriate amounts of ethanol, acetone, or chloroform.

The main procedure for structure determination continues to be reduction and identification of the products (see Chapter 11). The older techniques of derivatization of the products (N-acylation, condensation with phenanthraquinone, arylamine and S-benzylthiuronium salt formation from sulfonic acids) are still useful, but PC and TLC followed by color reactions or spectroscopy have facilitated the identification process. N-Picryl derivatives, prepared by the action of picryl chloride or 2,4,6-trinitrobenzenesulfonic acid (which attacks NH_2 but not OH)[22] and sodium acetate, have the advantage that they are colored for chromatography and are usually soluble in DMSO for NMR study.[19b]

When azo dyes are reduced in DMF solution with sodium formaldehyde sulfoxylate (Rongalite C; Formosul), the products can be precipitated by chloroform as filterable solids available for further treatment.[19b]

5.4   Cationic Dyes

The chlorides, iodides, and picrates are usually crystallizable. The behavior on reduction in aqueous, methanolic, or DMF solution with sodium borohydride (SBH) and the ease of isolation or oxidizability of the product are useful for distinguishing between cationic dyes of the various classes listed in Section 2. Many of the cationic dyes are directly amenable to NMR study, but the MS can be interpreted only after examining a large number of dyes of known structure. SBH reduction of the dyes derived from Fischer's base or aldehyde yields dequaternized products suitable for analysis by both NMR and MS.[23] Oxazines, phenazines, and thiazines can be reduced by dithionite and the leuco bases stabilized by acetylation or benzoylation.[16]

A commercial sample of CI Basic Red 22, examined as a model for certain experiments, proved to be the diethylaniline homologue of CI 11055. The NMR spectrum of the picrate in TFA shows the NEt_2 group (four H q at 3.9 and six H t at 1.4) in addition to the expected signals.[19c]

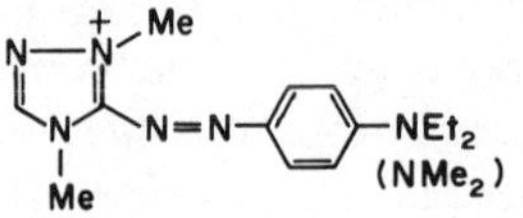

CI Basic Red 22;
CI 11055

Two CI Basic dyes (Orange 25 and 24) gave dinitrophenylhydrazones (cf. *CSD* IV, p. 167).

CI Basic Orange 25, $C_{18}H_{23}N_4OCl$, shows ν_{max} 3150, 3050 (d; NH_2), 1670 (C=O); δ(TFA) 2.66 (s; aromatic C–Me), 3.53 (s; $^+NMe_3$), 5.06 (s; CH_2), 7.0 (m; two aromatic H), 8.0 (m; five aromatic H). The data led to structure (**4**), confirmed by chemical tests (diazotization and coupling; reduction of CO to CHOH by SBH; reduction by dithionite to *p*-toluylenediamine and a water-soluble amine) and the MS fragmentation: m/e 296 ($C_{17}H_{20}N_4O$, loss of CH_3 from the dye cation), base peak at 253 (296 − 43, loss of CH_2=N—CH_3), and a peak at 210 (253 − 43; further loss of HO—C= CH_2).[19c]

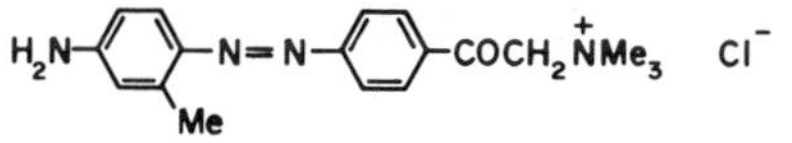

CI Basic Orange 25

(**4**)

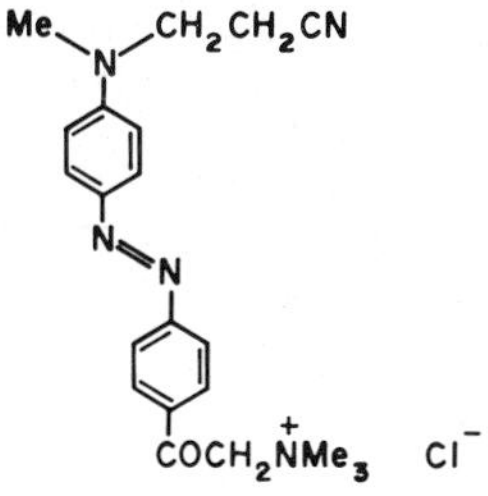

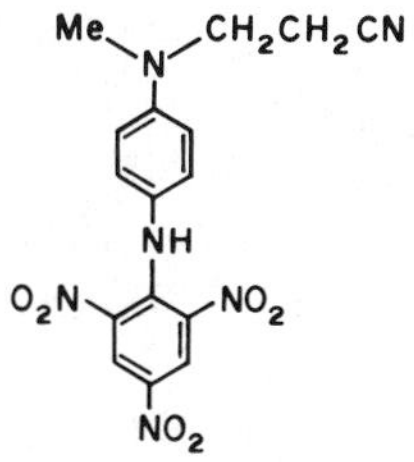

CI Basic Orange 24 (**5**)   (**6**)

CI Basic Orange 24 has ν_{max} 1690 (C=O), 2200 (CN); δ(TFA) 4.20 (t) and 3.16 (t) (two H each; N–CH_2CH_2CN), 3.60 (s; $^+NMe_3$), 3.70 (s; NMe), 5.13 (s; CH_2), 7.25 (br; two aromatic H), 7.93 (m; six aromatic H). In conjunction with chemical tests, structure (**5**) can account for the IR and NMR data.[19c]

In the NMR spectrum of the SBH reduction product the CH_2 and Me protons appear in approximately the same positions as in the parent dye, but there is an additional one-H q (–CH—OH) and the eight aromatic H show up as four clear d ($J = 10$) at 7.23, 8.16, 7.63, and 7.9. The MS confirms the secondary alcohol corresponding to (**5**); m/e 351 ($C_{20}H_{25}N_5O$, loss of CH_3Cl from the molecule), 306 (loss of $HNMe_2$), 266 (loss of CH_2CN), 252, and 238 (successive loss of CH_2).

Reduction of the dye with dithionite and condensation of the ether-soluble product with picryl chloride yielded a derivative, $C_{16}H_{14}N_6O_6$, $M\cdot^+$ 386; the two-H s at 9.2 of the picryl group and the NH at 10.3 in the NMR spectrum were useful for characterizing it as (**6**).

5.5   Disperse Dyes

When the commercial product is heated for a few minutes with saturated brine, the dye separates from the dispersing agent and can usually be purified by crystallization, after running through a short silica gel column if necessary. The azo compounds are relatively easy to identify from the elemental analysis, NMR, and MS data; IR absorption shows the CN group at about 2230, the sulfone (including the SO_2—N) group at about 1340 and 1150, and the sulfonate group at about 1370 and 1170.

CI Disperse Yellow 68, $C_{18}H_{14}N_4O_2$, is a phenol that crystallized from nitrobenzene. The NMR spectrum (TFA) shows four H s at 8.22 (middle benzene ring); d ($J = 9$) at 7.33 for four H adjacent to OH; and d ($J = 9$) at 8.30 for the remaining four H.[19a]

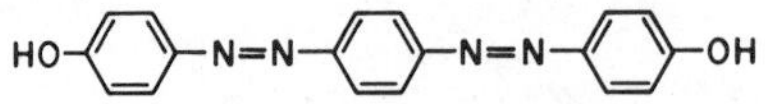

CI Disperse Yellow 68

CI Disperse Orange 30, $C_{19}H_{17}N_5O_2Cl_2$, $M \cdot^+$ 449, shows in the MS fragments for the loss of CH_2CN (m/e 409), loss of AcOH (m/e 389), loss of CH_2OAc (m/e 376), and loss of $C_6H_2N_3O_2Cl_2$ (m/e 231).

The NMR spectra of Disperse Orange 30, Red 73, and Yellow 92 were taken in two solvents, pyridine (for the 0–5 region) and DMSO (for the lower region).[16] TFA was the solvent used for Red 88, Red 86, Blue 183, and Yellow 77.[19a]

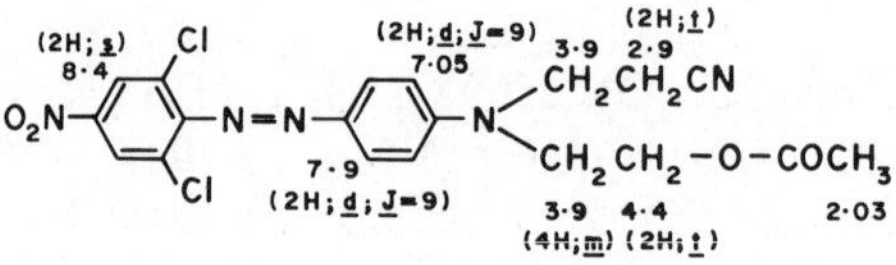

CI Disperse Orange 30

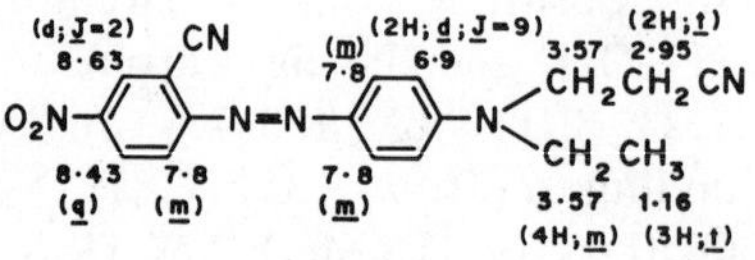

CI Disperse Red 73

CI Disperse Red 88, $C_{19}H_{21}N_5O_4S$, crystallized from ethanol after chromatography on silica gel (benzene–acetone). The MS shows $M \cdot^+$ 415 and m/e for loss of Me and two Me, CH_2CN, $C_{12}H_{15}N_2$, and $C_7H_6NO_4S$.[19a]

CI Disperse Blue 183, $C_{20}H_{21}N_6O_3Br$, crystallized from benzene. The MS was useful only for $M \cdot^+$ 472.[19a]

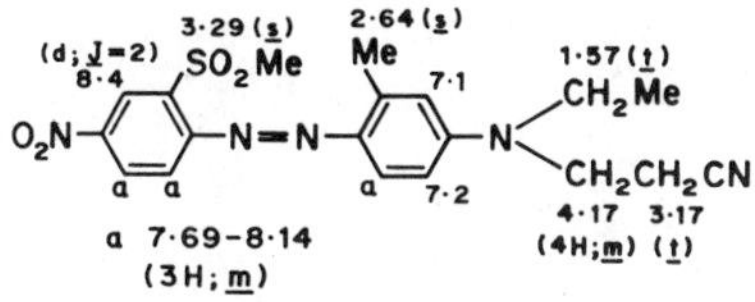

CI Disperse Red 88

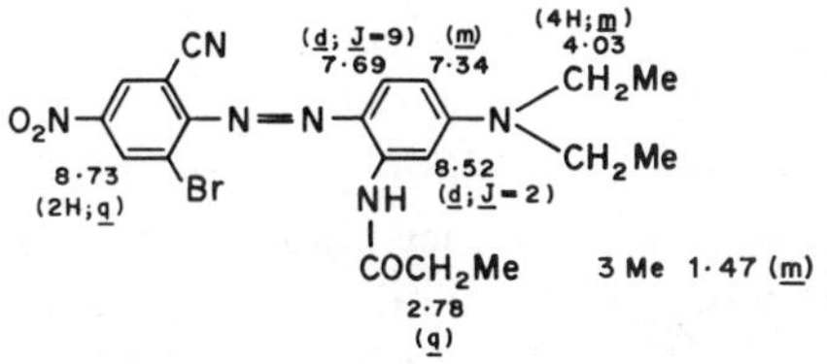

CI Disperse Blue 183

Four of the disperse dyes examined proved to be anthraquinone derivatives.

CI Disperse Yellow 92, $C_{23}H_{22}N_4O_6$, crystallized from toluene. The IR spectrum shows $C=0$ at 1640 and 1660, and strongly bonded NH at 3100. 1-Aminoanthraquinone was obtained by refluxing the dye with 40% hydrobromic acid. The NMR data and the characteristic MS fragmentation are shown in Figure 1.1.[16]

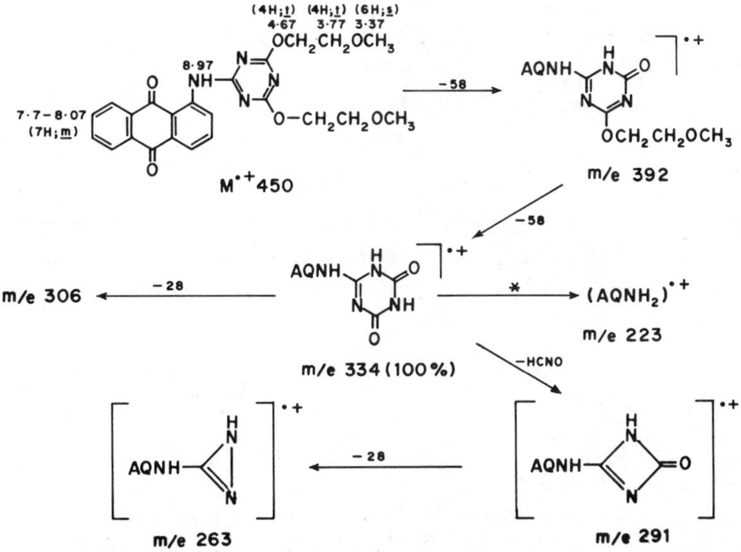

Figure 1.1   NMR data and MS fragmentation of CI Disperse Yellow 92.

CI Disperse Red 86, $C_{22}H_{18}N_2O_5S$, crystallized from ethanol. The MS shows M·+ 422 and m/e 252 (loss of NH—SO_2—C_6H_4—CH_3), 224 (loss of CO) and 196 (loss of CO).

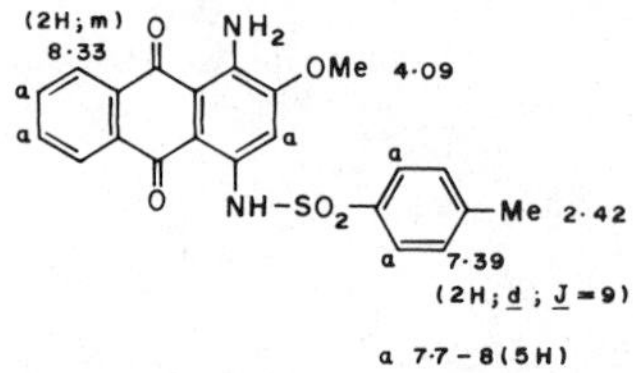

CI Disperse Red 86

CI Disperse Green 5, $C_{26}H_{18}N_2O_4$, was identified as 5,8-dianilinoquinizarin,[19a] confirmed by comparison with the product obtained by heating leuco 1,4,5,8-tetrahydroxyanthraquinone with aniline in the presence of boric acid.[24] It did not have adequate solubility in any NMR solvent, but the NMR spectrum of the diacetyl derivative in DMSO shows a m at 7.33 (10 H) and two two-H s at 7.49 and 7.52 for four β-H of anthraquinone.

CI Disperse Yellow 77, $C_{23}H_{12}N_2O_2$, crystallized from DMF. The MS shows M·+ 348 and m/e 320, 292 (successive loss of CO), 291, 290 (successive loss of H), 265, and 264 (loss of C_2H_2 from 291 and 290). Fragments for corresponding doubly charged ions are also seen. The IR spectrum shows C=O at 1705 and 1680. At least eight isomeric compounds are known which are in broad agreement with the NMR data.

3 multiplets
a 9·88 (1H)
b 8·33 – 8·93 (5H)
c 7·68 – 8·33 (6H)

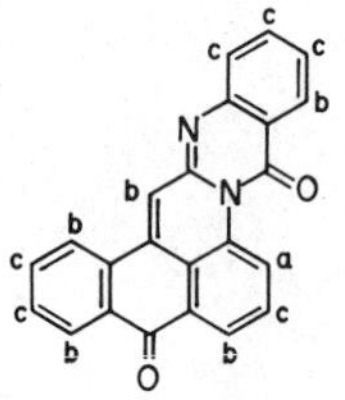

Disperse Yellow 77

A literature search suggested the probability of Yellow 77 being identical with the product obtained by heating 1-acetamidoanthraquinone with anthranilic acid, acetic anhydride, and zinc chloride.[25] Synthesis and direct comparison confirmed the identity.[19a]

REFERENCES

1. For a detailed account of the chemistry of fluorescent brighteners, including analytical methods, see H. Gold in *CSD* V.
2. J. D. Rigg, *J. Soc. Dyers Colour*, **91**, 17 (1975). See also Toms River Chem. Corpn., *BP* 1,370,971; FH, *BP* 1,370,560; CGY, *BP* 1,368,485; FBy, *BP* 1,380,677.

3. E. Siegel, in *CSD* VI; W. F. Beech, *Fiber-reactive Dyes*, Logos Press, London, 1970.

4. D. G. Orton and C. D. Weston, in *CSD* VII.

5. D. R. Baer, in *CSD* IV.

6. See G. E. Ficken, in *CSD* IV, p. 212.

7. For a detailed account of the chemistry, properties, and evaluation of pigments, see J. Lenoir, in *CSD* V, pp. 314-474.

8. For a detailed classification, see *CSD* II, p. 864; V, p. 131.

9. R. L. Reeves, *J. Am. Chem. Soc.*, **97**, 6019 (1975); R. L. Reeves, R. S. Kaiser, and K. T. Finley, *J. Chromatogr.*, **47**, 217 (1970).

10. P. Rabin, *Nature*, **199**, 596 (1963).

11. J. E. Scott, *Histochemie*, **29**, 129 (1972).

12. K. H. Drexhage, in *Topics in Applied Physics*, F. P. Schäfer, Ed., Springer, Berlin, 1971, p. 178.

13. Cf. H. U. Mehta, M. R. Ravikrishnan, and A. G. Chitale, *J. Soc. Dyers Colour.*, **78**, 552 (1962); C. D. Mehta and K. H. Shah, *Indian J. Appl. Chem.*, **29**, 123 (1966).

14. D. P. Wittmer, N. O. Nuessle, and W. G. Haney, Jr., *Anal. Chem.*, **47**, 1422 (1975).

15. *CSD* I, p. 276; *CSD* II, p. 1349; C. H. Giles, *A Laboratory Course in Dyeing*, 3rd ed., Society of Dyers and Colourists, Bradford, 1975.

16. V. Parameswaran, Ph.D. Thesis, University of Bombay, 1974.

17. Cf. CFM, *DBP* 901,175; 905,014.

18. E. D. Pandhare, V. B. Patil, A. V. Rama Rao, and K. Venkataraman, *Ind. J. Chem.*, **9**, 1060 (1971).

19. Unpublished work of (*a*) K. G. Das, P. M. Nair, and D. R. Wagle; (*b*) R. J. Deshpande, K. Muralidhar, and P. M. Nair; (*c*) K. G. Das, I. K. Khanna, A. R. Mehendale, and P. M. Nair.

20. FH, *DBP* 1,086,832; *BP* 924,319.

21. FH, *DBP* 1,126,545; *BP* 951,452.

22. T. Okuyama and K. Satake, *J. Biochem. (Tokyo)*, **47**, 454 (1960).

23. V. Parameswaran, A. V. Rama Rao, and K. Venkataraman, *Indian J. Chem.*, **12**, 785 (1974).

24. K. Zahn and P. Ochwat, *Justus Liebigs Ann. Chem.*, **462**, 72 (1928).

25. R. Lesser, G. Gad, and IG, *DRP* 536,448. Cf. S. I. Popov, T. H. Kudryumova, and N. S. Dokunikhin, *Khim. Geterotsikl Soedin*, *Sb. 1; Azolsoderzhashchie Geterotsikly*, 314 (1967); *CA*, **70**, 87741 (1969).

CHAPTER TWO

Thin-Layer Chromatography

H. SCHWEPPE

1 INTRODUCTION

Thin-layer chromatography (TLC) was more or less neglected until Stahl[1] found a convenient method of producing uniform layers, combined the individual items of equipment into one basic unit, standardized the adsorbents and chromatographic conditions, and established a wide range of application of the method by investigating a variety of classes of substances. Detailed information on the theory and practice of TLC is provided in refs. 2–8. In addition, there are some comprehensive publications on the TLC of synthetic dyes.[9–13]

2 DESCRIPTION OF THE PROCESS

2.1 Apparatus

The basic equipment for TLC is simple and inexpensive, the method is highly versatile in application, and the time involved is short. The following apparatus is needed.

1. A tank for development. This may be a glass vessel fitted with a cover in which the plates can be installed in an almost vertical position. Preserving jars, closable vessels, and special "sandwich chambers" may be employed. Commercial tanks are designed to accommodate 20-cm TLC plates.

2. TLC plates. These may be made of glass, aluminum, or polyester film, and are coated with a thin, uniform layer of substrate. Silica gel, cellulose, alumina (aluminum oxide), or polyamide substrates are usually employed for the chromatography of dyes, but substances such as acetyl cellulose, kieselguhr, and others can also be used. Until very recently it was customary to prepare one's own TLC plates with a spreading device (see Stahl,[2] pp. 52–59; Stahl,[3] pp. 53–60). Now there are numerous manufacturers of prepared plates,[14] which mainly consist of thin aluminum or polyester sheet coated with the usual substrates in which a binding agent, such as gypsum, starch, or a polymer, is incorporated. The advantage of these sheets over glass is that they can easily be cut to any desired size. Furthermore, they can be attached to paper or board and covered with transparent, UV-stabilized, self-adhesive film[15] for archival purposes. As compared with self-prepared TLC plates, commercial plates also offer superior reproducibility of results, easier storage, and greater mechanical stability.

3. Applicators. Solutions of substances to be separated may be applied with thin glass rods, platinum loops, glass capillaries, micropipettes, or microsyringes. There are also devices, some of them automatic, for the application of streaks.[2]

4. Spray devices. Throat sprays, compressed-air atomizers, and aerosol sprays are some of the devices used for applying prepared reagents for detecting colorless substances in thin-layer chromatograms. In many cases it is also possible to immerse the plate in a reagent solution.

5. Spreading devices are used for coating glass plates for TLC. "Do-it-yourself" equipment is seldom used any more. Some of the commercial machines now available are as follows: (a) Desaga Stahl-type coater,[16] which has a traveling coating trough and enables the production of layers 0–2 mm thick; (b) Camag coater, of the Mutter and Hofstetter type,[17] with a fixed trough. The plates are passed one after the other under the trough. Plates 5, 10, and 20 cm wide can be coated in various thicknesses; (c) Shandon Scientific Company coating machine[18] can also be adjusted to producing various thicknesses of coating and has a special leveling device.

6. Frame. The frame, usually of light metal, is used for drying and storing 10–12 coated plates (for manufacturers, see refs. 16–18).

7. UV lamps. These detect substances that fluoresce under UV light. Fluorescent indicators can also be incorporated in the substrate (as well as in commercial plates). When such plates are irradiated with UV light, nonfluorescent substances appear as dark spots on a fluorescent background.

2.2   Experimental

Before a TLC separation is undertaken, three fundamental factors must be considered if optimal resolution is to be achieved: the substrate or stationary phase, the sample to be analyzed, and the moving phase.

2.2.1   Substrate. Of the substrates used, silica is the most frequently employed, since it is capable of effecting the separation of substances in most chemical classes. Rettie and Haynes[10] give a comprehensive account of its use in distinguishing dyes, and McClure et al.[19] and Schlegelmilch and Kuss[20] describe the separation of organic pigments on this medium.

The adsorption properties of silica gel are determined by the number of hydroxyl groups at the surface. Siloxane groups are also present, but their adsorption power is much lower, since a strong hydrogen bond exists between water and their OH groups and prevents the adsorption of less polar compounds. Adsorbed water can be driven off by heating the gel to 150°, and the plates can then be stored in their activated form in a desiccator ready for use. As soon as such a plate is removed from the desiccator it begins to take up moisture from the atmosphere. Determinations made by Dallas[21] show that, at 50% relative humidity, about 60% of the previously removed water is replaced within 5 minutes, and about 80% within 10 minutes. Thus the activity of a silica gel plate is mainly affected by the atmospheric humidity of the laboratory, and it is absolutely essential to wait until equilibrium with the ambient air has been established if reproducible separations are to be obtained.

The separating power of a substrate can be modified by spraying or impregnating with a suitable reagent. Acidic silica gel layers can be produced by treating with 0.5 N acetic or oxalic acid, and a saturated soda solution or a 0.2 N sodium hydroxide solution can be used to render the layer alkaline. Acidic layers can be employed for dealing with phenols and acids, and alkaline layers can be employed for amines.

Though silica gel layers are not modified in the majority of cases, such a modification sometimes improves their effectiveness. For instance, Sweeny[12] was able to separate 1-amino-2,4-dichloroanthraquinone and 1-amino-2-chloro-4-hydroxyanthraquinone on silica gel layers previously soaked with a saturated soda solution, using benzene–acetone (9:1) as the solvent; such a separation is not possible on neutral or acidic silica gel layers.

2.2.2   Analysis Sample.   The concentration of the dye solution should be of the order of 1% for TLC. Sparingly soluble components of a mixture can cause difficulty because of incomplete solution, so that a component may be partially, or even entirely, lost by being filtered out.

When the dyes to be investigated are on fabrics, the procedure becomes somewhat more laborious than with samples of the dye itself. If the dyed material consists of one type of fiber only, the dyes can be brought into solution by one of the numerous solvent and extraction procedures described in the literature.[12,22–24] Fabrics made of different fibers in warp and weft can be split mechanically into their components before proceeding with extraction. Table 2.1 lists solvents recommended by Sweeny[12] for extracting dyes from a blend of fibers. Some solvents in this table dissolve dyes of only one or very few types, so that it is often possible to strip each kind of fiber present separately. For instance, in a polyester–wool blend material, the wool component can first be stripped with pyridine–water (53:47) before removing the dyes on the polyester fiber with nitrobenzene. One disadvantage of this procedure is that a dye released from one of the component fibers may go on to the other, a frequently observed phenomenon.

Another way of isolating dyes from fiber blends for separation by TLC is to extract them with solvents that dissolve the dyes from all the fibers

Table 2.1   Solvents Useful for Extraction of Dyes from Fibers[12,a]

Solvent	Acetate	Cotton (direct)	Cotton (vat)	Nylon	Polyester	Wool
Chlorobenzene	G	No	No	No	No	No
Chlorobenzene–acetic acid (50:50)	D	No	No	G	F	F
DMF	D	G	F–B	No	F	F
DMSO	D	G	F–B	G	G	G
1-Methyl-2-pyrrolidone, 25% aq.	F	F	No	No	No	No
Nitrobenzene	D	F	F–B	G	G	No
Pyridine	D	F	F–B	No	No	No
Pyridine–water (53:47)	F	G	No	G	No	G

[a] At 25° unless otherwise stated.
Code: B = boil; D = dissolved fabric; F = fair; G = good; No = little stripped, if at all.

at the same time.[12] DMSO is suitable for this. If components of the fibers themselves also dissolve, they can be precipitated by adding a second solvent. The dye solutions are concentrated by evaporation in a rotary vacuum dryer; 2–5 μl of the concentrated solution is then placed on the starting line of a thin-layer chromatogram and allowed to dry. The diameter of the spot should be less than 4 mm. If the concentration of the dye is too low, the application is made several times, a hair dryer or IR lamp being used for drying out between each application to prevent any increase in the size of the spot. The distance of the starting line from the edge should be about 20 mm, and the spots should be at least 10 mm apart.

When all the spots are dry the thin-layer plate is placed, with the starting line at the lower end, vertically into a developing chamber that contains a suitable solvent to a depth of about 1 cm. Three of the walls of the chamber are lined with filter paper soaked with the solvent to saturate the interior with solvent vapor; naturally, such a lining is unnecessary when using a "sandwich chamber."

2.2.3 Eluent. The selection of a suitable eluent, or solvent, is important for successful separation. It must be capable of dissolving the dye to a certain degree, thereby effecting migration on the substrate. The ability to bring about migration is a function of the eluting power of a solvent, and this in turn depends on its polarity. These relationships were first described for column chromatography by Trappe[25] and Strain,[26] and later applied by Stahl,[2,3] and Randerath[4] to TLC. These authors arranged the solvents in order of increasing eluting power, or polarity, i.e., in "eluotropic series." The more important solvents are thus arranged in the following eluotropic series: hexane, cyclohexane, carbon tetrachloride, benzene, the chlorobenzenes, chloroform, ether, ethyl acetate, dioxane, pyridine, acetone, ethanol, methanol, and water.

In most cases, mixtures of solvents produce better separations than single solvents. Nevertheless, such a mixture should be made as simple as possible, not only to ensure better reproducibility, but also because multicomponent systems tend to form a second solvent front during the chromatographic process.

A microcircular technique devised by Stahl[1] can be used to arrive at a suitable solvent. A drop of the dye solution being investigated is placed on a horizontal silica gel plate and dried. A ring chromatogram about 2 cm in diameter is developed by adding a few drops of solvent.

When separating on cellulose layers, one should try the solvents that have proved effective in paper chromatography.

A known dye mixture or individual dyes can be applied to the same thin-layer plate to assist in identifying unknown dyes. However, it must be remembered that although like rates of migration and spots with the same shade can mean that the dyes are identical, this is not necessarily so. On the other hand, a divergence in one of these characteristics definitely means that the dyes are different. Comparison solutions applied in parallel serve simultaneously as a check on the suitability of an eluent system and as an internal standard for comparison with other plates.

2.2.4 R_F Values. Another method of establishing the distance traveled by a substance under the influence of a given solvent system is provided by the R_F value: the ratio of the distance traveled by a substance to that covered by the solvent, as measured from the starting line. By definition, R_F lies between zero and unity. Absolute R_F depends on many experimental conditions, such as temperature, moisture, and the equilibrium state of the system (including the environment), so reference samples should be used for comparison. hR_F values are R_F values multiplied by 100 and therefore are whole numbers when only the first two digits are taken into account.

2.2.5 Faults. If the concentration of the dye solutions applied to the plate is too high, "tailing" can occur. To prevent this, either the concentration of the dye solution can be reduced or—if this does not help—another solvent system can be used.

3 ACID DYES

In general, acid dyes contain one or more sulfonic groups. The only dyes that contain a carboxyl group as an anion are fluorescein (CI Acid Yellow 73; CI 45350; *CSD* II, 747) and its halogen derivatives, as also some azo dyes.

3.1 Acid Dyes for Dyeing

Table 2.2 lists numerous papers on the TLC of acid dyes and summarizes the relevant experimental conditions. It can be seen that silica gel G has been used in most cases. Only Meckel et al.[27] use "reactive layers" in their separation of three azo wool dyes. These reactive layers consist of alkalized silica gel G or alumina G first proposed by Stahl.[28] In the preparation of the spreading composition, the adsorbent is made into a slurry with a 2.5% sodium carbonate solution instead of water. The separations are more sharply defined on alkalized silica gel G layers than on the corresponding alumina G layers. Rettie and Haynes[10] used cellulose layers for the TLC of acid dyes and separated dyes of the anthraquinone class on these layers

Table 2.2   Eluents for the TLC of Acid Dyes on Silica Gel G Layers

Eluent System	Ref.
1. Ethanol (95%)	30
2. n-Butanol–acetic acid–water (20:10:50) (upper phase)	31
3. n-Butanol–acetic acid–water (40:10:50) (upper phase)	29
4. n-Butanol–ethanol–water–acetic acid (60:10:20:0.5)	10
5. Benzene–dioxane–acetic acid (90:25:4)	29
6. Chloroform–acetic acid (90:10)	32
7. Benzene–acetic acid (90:10)	32
8. Toluene–acetic acid (65:35)	33
9. Benzene–propionic acid (80:20)	10
10. Benzene–chloroform–propionic acid (40:40:20)	10
11. Benzene–isopropanol–acetic acid (60:40:1)	10
12. Ethyl acetate–pyridine–water (60:30:10)	10
13. Amyl alcohol–ethanol–ammonia (conc.) (50:45:5)	10
14. n-Butanol–ethanol–ammonia (conc.)–pyridine (40:10:30:20)	9
15. n-Butanol–acetone–water–ammonia (conc.) (5:5:1:2)	9
16. Methyl ethyl ketone–acetone–water (2:4:1:1)	11
17. Propanol–acetone–water–acetic acid (5:5:3:1)	12
18. Propanol–ammonia (conc.) (1:1)	12
19. n-Butyl acetate–pyridine–water (40:40:20)[a]	10
20. n-Butyl acetate–pyridine–water (30:45:25)[b]	26

[a] Or on cellulose.
[b] Silica gel G or alumina G + 2.5% Na_2CO_3.
Note: Our own checks revealed that Eluents 2, 3, 4, and 20 (silica gel G) give the best separation of acid dyes containing sulfonic groups, whereas Eluents 7, 8, 10, 12, 13, 14, and 15 are best for separating acid dyes containing carboxyl groups.

with the help of an n-butyl acetate–pyridine–water (40:40:20) eluent system. Various acid dyes of the triarylmethane class used for preparing inks have been separated by Jamieson,[29] who used silica gel G and an n-butanol–acetic acid–water (40:10:50) solvent system. Druding[30] separated some ink dyes on silica gel with 95% ethanol. n-Butanol–ethanol–water–acetic acid (60:10:20:0.5) is a useful solvent system for separating blue ink dyes on silica gel.[10] Good resolution of colored secondary components in a number of acid dyes was effected by Logar et al.[31] using n-butanol–acetic acid–water (20:10:50). Walker and Beroza[32] used alternative solvent systems to separate fluorescein and its halogen derivatives: benzene–acetic acid (90:10) and chloroform–acetic acid. Such separations were achieved by Naff and Naff,[33] who employed toluene–acetic acid (65:35), whereas Rettie and Haynes[10] recommend benzene–propionic acid (80:20) and benzene–chloroform–propionic acid (40:40:20) for the same purpose; the last-mentioned system is particularly suitable for resolving mono- and dihalogen derivatives of fluorescein. Jamieson[29] favors the use of a 90:25:4 benzene–dioxane–acetic acid system for the TLC of these dyes.

3.2 Acid Indicator Dyes

Investigations by Rettie and Haynes[10] revealed that acid–base indicators of the sulfophthalein class of compounds, e.g., Thymol Blue, Phenol Red, and Bromophenol Blue, can be separated on silica gel G by using benzene–isopropanol–acetic acid (60:40:1), ethyl acetate–pyridine–water (60:30:10), or amyl alcohol–ethanol–ammonia (conc.) (50:45:5) solvent systems.

Waldi[34] established hR_F values for the identification and purity determination of indicator dyes under standardized conditions. He used 1:1 alumina G–silica gel G layers and a 60:30:10 ethyl acetate–methanol–5 N ammonia solution solvent system; the hR_F values are given in Table 2.3.

Table 2.3 Guiding hR_F Values for Indicator Dyes on Alumina G–Silica Gel G (1:1) Layers[34]

Indicator Dye	hR_F	Color of Spots
1. Chlorophenol Red	27 (78)[a]	Violet (yellow)[a]
2. Bromocresol Purple	40 (0)	Violet (yellow-brown)
3. Cresol Red	42 (60; 77)	Orange-yellow (pale red and yellow)
4. Metacresol Purple	43 (71)	Orange-yellow (yellow)
5. Bromophenol Blue	48 (39)	Blue-violet (red-violet)
6. Bromochorophenol Blue	48	Blue-violet
7. Bromothymol Blue	65	Green-brown
8. Benzyl Orange	67	Yellow
9. Methyl Orange	67	Yellow-orange
10. Thymol Blue	74	Orange-yellow
11. Phenolphthalein	83	Colorless, red with alkali
12. p-Ethoxychrysoidine	84	Orange

[a] The hR_F values and colors of the accompanying dyes are given in parentheses; 2 mm^3 samples of the 0.25% solutions in methanol were applied.

Pastuska and Trinks[35] reported on the thin-layer electrophoresis of indicator dyes.

4 DIRECT COTTON DYES

This class of dyes comprises mainly disazo and polyazo dyes of relatively high molecular weight and containing sulfonic groups. It is possible to separate substantive dyes (CI Direct Dyes) by TLC under conditions similar to those of acid dyes. The difficulties of tailing, so frequently encountered in PC because of the substantivity of the dyes for cellulose, are less frequent in TLC. Methods for the TLC of substantive dyes are given in Table 2.4, together with details of the conditions.

Table 2.4 TLC of Direct Dyes

Layer	Eluent	Ref.
1. Alumina	Ethanol–water (various amounts)	36
2. Silica gel G	n-Propanol–ammonia (60:30)	37
3. Silica gel G	n-Amyl alcohol–pyridine–ammonia (30:30:30)	37
4. Silica gel G	n-Butanol–acetone–water–ammonia (conc). (50:50:20:20)	9
5. Silica gel G	n-Butanol–ethanol–ammonia–pyridine–water (40:15:20:20:15)	9
6. Silica gel G	n-Butanol–methanol–ammonia–pyridine (40:10:30:20)	38
7. Silica gel G	Propanol–acetone–water–acetic acid (50:50:30:10)	12
8. Silica gel G	Butyl acetate–pyridine–water (50:50:20)	12
9. Silica gel G	Butanol–acetone–water (50:50:30)	12
10. Silica gel G	n-Butanol–water–ammonia (20:10:10) (upper phase)	12
11. Silica gel G[a] or alumina G[a]	n-Butyl acetate–pyridine–water (30:45:25)	26
12. Alumina G[a]	Ethylene glycol monoethyl ether–ammonia (2%) (80:20)	39
13. Silica gel–kieselguhr	Methyl ethyl ketone–diethylamine–ammonia (25%) (50:10:10)	40

[a] With addition of 2.5% Na_2CO_3.

Raban[36] used ethanol–water mixtures to separate Congo Red (CI Direct Red 28; CI 22120; CSD I, 507), Trypan Blue (CI Direct Blue 14; CI 23850; CSD I, 514), Direct Blue BB (CI Direct Blue 6; CI 22610; CSD II, 1322), Direct Green B (CI Direct Green 6; CI 30295), and Direct Red F (CI Direct Red 1; CI 22310) into several zones on alumina plates. Gasparič and Cee[37] have investigated the diffusion coefficients of various substantive azo dyes, such as Dianil Blue G (CI Direct Blue 10; CI 24340; CSD II, 1280), Chicago Blue B (CI Direct Blue 4; CI 24380; CSD II, 1280), Sella Fast Brown DGR (CI Acid Brown 235), and Solophenyl Grey 4G, and have obtained separations into several zones with n-propanol–ammonia (60:30) and pyridine–n-amyl alcohol–ammonia (30:30:30) on silica gel G. Meckel et al.[27] separated Benzamin Green 3GS (CI Direct Green 38; CI 28280), Sirius Light Scarlet BN (CI Direct Red 95), Sirius Light Brown 6RL (CI Direct Brown 112; CI 29166), and other substantive dyes into several zones on alkalized layers of silica gel G or alumina, using n-butyl acetate–pyridine–water (30:45:25) as eluent. Similarly prepared alumina G layers were used by Ruiz and Laroche[39] in conjunction with ethylene glycol monoethyl ether–ammonia (2%)(80:20). Schlegelmilch and Khodadadian[40] separated a number of substantive dyes on silica gel–kieselguhr layers by using methyl ethyl ketone–diethylamine–ammonia (25%) (50:50:10). The hR_F values obtained here are shown in Table 2.5. The same authors also tried to differentiate substantive dyes from acid and metal complex dyes

Table 2.5 hR_F Values for Direct Dyes

Dye	CI	hR_F
Benzo Light Yellow G	—	80
Sirius Yellow GC Extra	29000; Direct Yellow 44	72
Sirius Green F4G	—	69
Sirius Bordeaux 5B	28110; Direct Red 77	65
Benzo Deep Black E	30235; Direct Black	63
Congo Red	22120; Direct Red 28	62
Sirius Light Orange GGL	40215; Direct Orange 39	56
Chlorantine Light Green BBL	34045; Direct Green 26	34
Sirius Light Scarlet BN	Direct Red 95	27
Sirius Light Red F4BL	Direct Red 212	22
Sirius Light Violet F2BLL	Direct Violet 95	6

layer: silica gel–kieselguhr.
eluent: methyl ethyl ketone–diethylamine–ammonia (25%) (50:10:10).[40]

by the R_F values. They exploited the different chromatographic behavior of the dyes when subjected to TLC under various pH conditions on cellulose acetate layers, and when subjected to reaction chromatography on cellulose powder; the substantive dyes remain on the starting line because of their affinity for cellulose.

5 REACTIVE DYES

Reactive dyes are attached to cellulose or wool by means of a covalent bond and cannot be removed unchanged from the fiber. Constitutionally, the reactive dyes include azo dyes and anthraquinone and phthalocyanine derivatives with sulfonic and reactive groups.

TLC work on reactive dyes has been concerned with the chromatographic separation of the dyes in their free, i.e., their uncombined, state. So far, insurmountable difficulties have stood in the way of isolating reactive dyes from textile fibers. In general, reactives can be separated more effectively by TLC than by PC because the interference and restraint on the migration of a number of reactive dyes owing to their substantivity for cellulose do not arise in TLC, and they are therefore not held back on the starting line.

The conditions for the TLC of reactive dyes on silica gel G are summarized in Table 2.6. Perkavec and Perpar[41] used Solvent 1 for resolving Procion dyes (ICI); Solvent 2 for Cibacron dyes (CGy); and Solvent 3 for Drimaren dyes (S), Reacton dyes (CGy), Remazol dyes (FH), Levafix dyes (FBy), and Primazin dyes (BASF).

Cee and Gasparič[42] made a detailed investigation of vinyl sulfone reactive dyes of the Remazol type and their behavior under chromatographic and electrophoretic separation conditions. Since the commercial dyes usually contain three products, the sulfates of 2-hydroxyethyl sulfone (dye–SO_2—CH_2CH_2—O—SO_3Na), the vinyl sulfone (dye–SO_2—CH=CH_2), and

Table 2.6 Solvents for TLC of Reactive Dyes on Silica Gel G

Solvent System	Ref.
1. Iso-butanol–n-propanol–ethyl acetate–water (20:40:10:30)	41
2. Dioxane–acetone (50:50)	41
3. n-Propanol–ethyl acetate–water (60:10:30)	41
4. n-Butyl acetate–pyridine–water (20:20:10)	42
5. n-Butyl acetate–acetic acid–water (20:20:10)	42

the 2-hydroxyethyl sulfone (dye–SO_2—CH_2CH_2OH), hydrolysis with 0.1 N potassium hydroxide is recommended before chromatography in order to obtain the stable 2-hydroxyethyl sulfone and thus make detection more reliable.

In almost all cases, three spots corresponding to these products are obtained when thin-layer chromatograms of Remazol dyes are prepared by means of either n-butyl acetate–pyridine–water or n-butyl acetate–acetic acid–water (Solvents 4 or 5).

6 METAL COMPLEX DYES

There are two types of metal (Cr or Co) complex dyes: (1) 1:1 metal–dye complexes, which always have sulfonic groups, and (2) 1:2 metal–dye complexes, which may or may not contain sulfonic groups.

6.1 Metal Complex Dyes with Sulfonic Groups

In my own experience, the conditions for the TLC of acid dyes are also suitable for the separation of metal complex dyes containing sulfonic groups. According to Meckel et al.,[27] such metal complex dyes can be separated on alkalized silica gel G or alumina G layers (see Table 2.2, Eluent 20).

6.2 Metal Complex Dyes without Sulfonic Groups

Brown[9] describes the separation of 1:2 metal–dye complexes not containing sulfonic groups, previously extracted from a wool dyeing, on a silica gel G layer by means of a chloroform–ethanol–morpholine (80:10:10) eluent. Both Schetty and Kuster[44] and Beffa et al.[45] have resolved various 1:2 Cr and Co complexes of azo, azomethine, and formazan dyes on alumina layers by using ethanol. Very good separations of 1:2 metal–dye complexes have been achieved by TLC on polyamide with the methanol–water–ammonia (conc.) (80:16:4) and methanol–ammonia (conc.) (95:5) solvent systems recommended by Schweppe[13] and by Pfitzner and Schweppe.[46] Even mixtures of several dyes and mixtures of complexes can be sorted in this way. The hR_F values obtained by the TLC of various 1:2 mixed complexes on polyamide with methanol–ammonia (95:5) are given in Table 2.7.

1:2 Metal–dye complexes without sulfonic, sulfonamide, or alkyl sulfone groups can be chromatographed on silica gel G layers with benzene–glacial acetic acid (80:20 or 70:30).[46] Since only this type of metal complex dye

Table 2.7 hR$_F$ Values of 1:2 Mixed Metal–Dye Complexes Without Sulfonic Groups[46]

1:2 Mixed Metal–Monoazo Dye Complexes	hR$_F$
Cr complex of 4-nitro-2-aminophenol → 1-phenyl-3-methyl-5-pyrazolone and anthranilic acid → 1-phenyl-3-methyl-5-pyrazolone	52, 59, 63
Co complex of 5-nitro-2-aminophenol → 2-naphthol and 5-nitro-2-aminophenol → 1-phenyl-3-methyl-5-pyrazolone	23, 37, 50
Cr complex of 2-aminophenol-4-sulfonamide → 2-naphthol and 2-aminophenol-4-sulfonamide → 1-phenyl-3-methyl-5-pyrazolone	17, 30, 43
Co complex of 4-nitro-2-aminophenol → 2-naphthol and 4-nitro-2-aminophenol → 1-phenyl-3-methyl-5-pyrazolone	25, 37, 50
A mixture of (1) Cr complex of 2-aminophenol-4-sulfonamide → 2-naphthol and 2-aminophenol-4-N-isopropylsulfonamide → 2-naphthol, and (2) Co complex of 2-aminophenol-4-sulfonamide → 1-phenyl-3-methyl-5-pyrazolone and 2-aminophenyl-4-N-isopropylsulfonamide → 1-phenyl-3-methyl-5-pyrazolone	17, 27, 39 41, 51, 62
Cr complex of 4-nitro-2-aminophenol → 2-naphthol and 4-nitro-2-aminophenol → 1-phenyl-3-methyl-5-pyrazolone	27, 39, 52
Cr complex of 4-nitro-2-aminophenol → 1-acetamido-7-naphthol and 2-aminophenol-4-sulfonamide → acetoacetanilide	31, 39, 47
Cr complex of 4-nitro-2-aminophenol → 1-(3′-sulfonamidophenyl)-3-methyl-5-pyrazolone and 2-aminophenol-4-ethylsulfone → 7-naphthol-1-N-methylsulfonamide	29, 41, 55

layer: Mikropolyamid F 1700 (Schleicher & Schüll).
eluent: methanol–ammonia (conc.) (95:5).
standard conditions: saturation of chamber.

can migrate on the plate under these conditions, the procedure offers a method of distinguishing such dyes from other types of metal complex dyes. Table 2.8 presents the hR$_F$ values obtained by this method.

6.3 Separation of Isomeric Metal Complexes

Two isomers are possible with the 1:1 metal–dye complexes of asymmetrically substituted *o,o′*-dihydroxyazobenzenes, and Pfitzner[47] has fractionated these on silica gel G with benzene–pyridine (90:10).

Three structural isomers are present in the 1:2 metal–dye complexes, obtained with *o,o′*-dihydroxyazobenzene, and these can be chromatographed with benzene–glacial acetic acid (80:20 or 70:30) on silica gel G plates.[46]

Table 2.8   hR$_F$ Values of 1:2 Metal–Monoazo Dye Complexes Without
Solubilizing Groups[46]

Monoazo Dyes	Metal	hR$_F$ (Eluent I)	hR$_F$ (Eluent II)	Color of Spots
2-Aminophenol → 2-naphthol	Cr	43	57	Violet
2-Aminophenol → 2-naphthol	Co	30	46	Violet-red
4-Nitro-2-aminophenol → 2-naphthol (CI 12197)	Cr	1	3	Violet
4-Nitro-2-aminophenol → 2-naphthol	Co	0.5	1	Red
5-Nitro-2-aminophenol → 2-naphthol (CI 12195)	Cr	24	34	Gray-blue
5-Nitro-2-aminophenol → 2-naphthol (CI 12196)	Co	11	22	Blue-violet
4-Chloro-2-aminophenol → 2-naphthol	Cr	40	53	Violet
Anthranilic acid → 1-phenyl-3-methyl-5-pyrazolone (CI 18690)	Cr	5	17	Yellow
4-Nitro-2-aminophenol → 1-phenyl-3-methyl-5-pyrazolone (CI 12714)	Cr	0	1	Orange
2-Aminophenol → 1-phenyl-3-methyl-5-pyrazolone	Cr	13	25	Scarlet
5-nitro-2-aminophenol → 1-phenyl-3-methyl-5-pyrazolone (CI 12715)	Cr	3	9	Red

layer: silica gel G (Merck).
eluent: benzene–acetic acid (80:20) (I); (70:30) (II).
standard conditions: saturated chamber.

Häfelinger and Baier[48] isolated various structural isomers of Co chelates
of 2-hydroxyazobenzene derivatives on silica gel G with benzene as the
solvent.

6.4   Mordant Dyes

The azo dye Alizarin Yellow R (CI Mordant Orange 1; CI 14030) can be
separated into three components on silica gel by using chloroform–acetic
acid (90:10).[32]

   Toul and Mouková[49] investigated the purity of various complex formers
of the 1-hydroxythiazolylazo type of dye by TLC on silica gel G. They

employed benzene–acetic acid (80:20), benzene–chloroform–acetic acid (25:5:6.2), carbon tetrachloride–acetic acid (30:8), carbon tetrachloride–ethyl acetate–acetic acid (30:3:2), and carbon tetrachloride–acetic acid (30:4) as developers to achieve separation of the impurities.

Pollard et al.[50] reported on the separation of some chromable dyes on a silica gel G containing starch instead of gypsum as the binding agent.

Masschelein–Kleiner[51] used thin layers composed of 10% acetylated cellulose powder, without binding agents, in conjunction with ethyl acetate–THF–water (6:35:47) for resolving mixtures of Alizarin (CI Mordant Red 11; CI 58000; CSD II, 819), Purpurin (CI 58205), and other hydroxyanthraquinones.

Voyatzakis et al.[52] separated hydroxyanthraquinones on silica gel G using benzene–carbon tetrachloride–acetic acid (50:75:0.8).

7 BASIC DYES

7.1 Basic Dyes for Dyeing

Solvent systems for the TLC of basic dyes on silica gel G are listed in Table 2.9. Solvents 1–3 are suitable for the separation of Bismarck Brown (CI 21000) and other basic azo dyes. The triphenylmethane dyes Malachite Green (CI Basic Green 4; CI 42000; CSD V, 147) and Methyl Violet (CI Basic Violet 1; CI 42535; CSD II, 719) can be chromatographed with Solvent 4. Astra Fuchsine B (CI Basic Violet 14; CI 42510; CSD V, 714), Rhodamine B (CI Basic Violet 10; CI 45170; CSD II, 751) and Rhodamine 6G (CI Basic Red; CI 45160; CSD IV, 107) respond to Solvent 5. Solvent 7 can be used for the separation of Rhodamine B, Malachite Green, Crystal Violet (CI Basic Violet 3; CI 42555; CSD IV, 141), Methylene Blue (CI Basic Blue 9; CI 52015; CSD II, 792), and Victoria Blue B on microscope slides. Solvents 8–10 have been used to distinguish basic dyes of the xanthene class, such as Acridine Red 3B (CI 45000; CSD II, 745), Pyronine G (CI 45005; CSD II, 745), Rhodamine S (CI Basic Red 11; CI 45050; CSD II, 745), Rhodamine G (CI Basic Red 8; CI 45150), and Rhodamine B. Several secondary components of basic dyes can be identified with Solvent 6. Numerous basic dyes suitable for dyeing acrylics can be separated under neutral conditions with solvent 11 on silica gel, and with ethanol–water (50:20) on alumina.[54] Arsov et al.[55] investigated the behavior of 23 basic dyes during TLC on silica gel G with Solvents 12–16. The chromatographic behavior of three xanthene, three phenazine, five triphenylmethane, two phenothiazine, one azo, and one phenoxazine dye

Table 2.9   Solvent Systems for TLC of Basic Dyes

Eluent	Ref.
1. Chloroform–methanol (90:10)	32
2. Benzene–methanol (90:10)	32
3. Chloroform–methanol (80:20)	10
4. n-Butanol–ethanol–water (90:10:10)	39
5. n-Butanol–acetic acid–water (40:10:50)	29
6. n-Butanol–acetic acid–water (20:10:50)	31
7. Methyl ethyl ketone–acetic acid–isopropanol (40:40:20)	33
8. n-Propanol–formic acid (80:20)	53
9. Chloroform–acetone–isopropanol–sulfurous acid (5–6% SO_2) (30:40:20:10)	53
10. 0.75% Sodium acetate–1% hydrochloric acid–methanol (40:10:40)	53
11. Pyridine–water (10:20)	54
12. Chloroform–methyl ethyl ketone–acetic acid–formic acid (8:6:1:1)	55
13. Chloroform–n-propanol–pyridine–acetic acid–water (8:6:1:1:2)	55
14. Chloroform–methyl ethyl ketone–formic acid (6:8:1)	55
15. Chloroform–isopropanol–pyridine–acetic acid–water (6:12:3:1:1)	55
16. Chloroform–isopropanol–pyridine–acetic acid–water (6:8:3:1:2)	55

Note: Our own checks showed that Eluents 5–8 and 14 produce the best effects.

on thin polyamide layers with numerous solvents were reported by Takeshita et al.,[56] the best separation effects being achieved with carbon tetrachloride–methanol (4:1).

For the TLC of basic dyes contained in ball-point pen inks, Van Dessel and Van Regenmortel[57] recommended separation on silica gel G plates impregnated with sodium p-toluenesulfonate (0.5%), the solvent system used being n-propanol–toluene (70:30). Reiners[58] distinguished dyes in ball-point pen inks by using acetone–toluene (90:10) on kieselguhr G plates; this method eliminates interference by the ink base.

7.2   Basic Dyes for Microscopy

Most dyes used in microscopy are basic; Table 2.10 gives the hR_F values determined by Waldi[59] for dyes frequently used in biology, bacteriology, and histology.

By using Solvents 8–10 in Table 2.9, it is possible to examine xanthene dyes used for the differential presentation of deoxyribonucleic acids in prepared histological sections.[53]

Table 2.10   Guiding hR_F Values of Staining Dyes for Microscopy[59]

Dye	CI	$hR_F{}^a$	Color^a
Acridine Orange	46005	41	Yellow
Alkali Blue	42765	16 (34)	Blue (blue)
Brilliant Green	42040	59 (0)	Green
Brilliant Cresyl Blue	51010	21 (52)	Green (green)
Eriochromazurol S	43825	39	Dark violet
Methyl Violet 2B	42535	43 (48)	Red (violet)
Crystal Violet	42555	43	Violet
Light Green, yellowish	42095	11 (0)	Green
Malachite Green	42000	35 (0)	Green
Metanil Yellow	13065	39	Yellow
Methylene Blue B	52015	9	Blue-green
Methylene Green	52020	18	Green
Victoria Blue B	44045	51	Blue

^{a} The hR_F values of the "side spots" and their colors are given in parentheses.
layer: silica gel G.
eluent: chloroform–acetone–isopropanol–sulfurous acid (5–6% SO_2) (30:40:20:10).

7.3   Basic Dyes in Lake Form used as Pigments

Basic dyes are frequently used as pigments in the form of lakes with phosphotungstic, phosphomolybdic, silicotungstic, or silicomolybdic acid, or a combination of these heteropolyacids. In my experience, it is advisable in such cases to separate the dyes from the heteropolyacids in the following manner before subjecting to TLC. The lake is boiled with 1 N sodium hydroxide, the dye base is extracted with ether after cooling, and the residue is taken up with ethanol after a few drops of dilute acetic acid are added. This solution can then be used for TLC with one of the eluents given in Table 2.9.

8   DISPERSE DYES

Little has been published on the TLC of disperse dyes, although it is more effective than other chromatographic methods. Wollenweber[60] described the separation of Celliton Red Violet RN (CI Disperse Violet 1; CI 61100; *CSD* II, 805), Celliton Pink B (CI Disperse Red 13; CI 60710; *CSD* II, 805), and Quinizarin (CI Pigment Violet 12; CI 58050) on acetyl cellulose layers using the solvent system THF–ethyl acetate–water (35:6:47). Many disperse dyes of the azo and anthraquinone class can be separated on the same adsorbent layer by using THF–water–4 N acetic acid (80:54:0.05) and similar compositions.[10] Chloroform–acetone (90:10) is suitable for separating a mixture of 1-amino-, 2-amino-, 1,2-diamino-, and 1,4-diaminoanthraquinone into the respective components on silica gel G.[10] Franc and Hájková[61] obtained excellent separations in the TLC of 1-amino-, 2-amino-, and 1,2-, 1,4-, 1,5-, 1,8-, 1,7-, 1,6-, and 2,6-diaminoanthraquinones on alumina (activity III, Brockmann), the solvent system being cyclohexane–ether (1:1). Brown[9] employed toluene–acetone (20:1) to obtain a distribution of disperse dyes on silica gel G. Sweeny[12] recommended benzene–acetone (90:10) and benzene–chloroform–acetone (50:20:10) for TLC on silica gel.

Excellent separations of disperse dyes, even complex mixtures, can be obtained with chloroform–methanol (95:5), toluene–acetic acid (90:10), and benzene–ethanol–ammonia (25%) (850:150:18) on silica gel G.[13, 62]

9 SOLVENT DYES

9.1 General TLC Separations

The first TLC separations of fat-soluble dyes were carried out by Stahl[1] on standardized silica gel G layers. He separated Sudan Yellow GG (CI Solvent Yellow 2; CI 11020; *CSD* I, 95), Sudan Red G (CI Solvent Red 1; CI 12150), and Indophenol (CI 49700; *CSD* II, 763) with benzene as the solvent. He also used silica gel G in conjunction with the solvent system benzene–carbon tetrachloride (50:50). Similar work was carried out by Ramamurthy and Bhalerao[63] on the detection of annatto and synthetic fat-soluble dyes by means of TLC. Hěrmánek et al.[64] separated various fat-soluble dyes of the azo class on alumina layers with carbon tetrachloride to determine the activity of the alumina in terms of the R_F values. Walker and Beroza[65] employed silica gel and the solvents chloroform, benzene, or their 9:1 mixtures with ether, ethyl acetate, acetone, methanol, or acetic acid to separate Sudan Yellow GG, Sudan Orange R (CI Solvent Yellow 14; CI 12055), Sudan III (Fat Red HRR) (CI Solvent Red 23; CI 26100), and Sudan Red BB (CI Solvent Red 24; CI 26105). Copius–Peereboom[66] investigated numerous fat-soluble dyes on silica gel G, alumina G, and kieselguhr G. The hR_F values obtained are found in Table 2.11.

Ruiz and Laroche[39] produced excellent separations of Yellow AB (CI Solvent Yellow 5; CI 11380; *CSD* I, 302) with benzene–carbon tetrachlo-

Table 2.11   hR$_F$ Values of Fat-Soluble Dyes[65]

Dye	CI	hR$_F$					
		S1, F1	S1, F2	S1, F3	S1, F4	S2, F5	S3, F6
Sudan Orange R	12055	68	60	77	70	56	63
Sudan Orange RR	12140	72	58	78	67	62	44
Sudan II	26100	56	52	68	61	41	15
Sudan Red BB	26105	56	53	68	61	38	15
Martius Yellow	10315	0	0	28	0	0	0
Sudan Yellow GG	11020	68	62	68	57	59	85
Sudan Red G	12150	18	46	30	36	19	16
Sudan Orange G	11920	14	24	36	37	0	0
Sudan Yellow 3G	12700	54	61	74	75	56	54
Sudan Yellow G	12740	60	64	81	80	68	40
Yellow OB	11390	27	82	50	49	27	87
Yellow AB	11380	25	80	46	41	22	88

Eluents: F1, hexane–ethyl acetate (90:10); F2, chloroform; F3, petroleum ether–ether–acetic acid (70:30:1); F4, petroleum ether–ether–ammonia (70:30:1); F5, hexane–ethyl acetate (98:2); F6, cyclohexane.
layers: S1, silica gel G; S2, alumina G; S3, kieselguhr G.

ride (50:50) and of Sudan III and Sudan Red BB with carbon tetrachloride, the alumina G layers having first been impregnated with 2% sodium carbonate solution. Chromatographs of the fat-soluble Waxoline Blue A (CI Solvent Blue 36), Waxoline Purple A (CI Solvent Violet 13; CI 60725), and Waxoline Green G (CI Solvent Green 3, CI 61565) dyes, all of which belong to the anthraquinone class, were obtained by Rettie and Haynes[10] on silica gel with toluene–cyclohexane (50:50). Fujii and Kamikura[67] described the separation of 15 fat-soluble dyes on silica gel using 12 different solvents. All the yellow and orange fat-soluble dyes of the mono- and disazo class have been separated in this way. Davidek et al.[68] employed alumina (activity III, Brockmann) for separating some fat-soluble dyes with petroleum ether–carbon tetrachloride (50:50). Dimethylaminoazobenzene and some of its metabolites were separated on silica gel G by Topham and Westrop[69] with chloroform–methanol (95:5). After the separation, the chromatogram was treated with hydrochloric acid vapor which turned the originally yellow spots orange to red. Davidek and Janicek[70] examined the separation of fat-soluble dyes on starch layers applied as suspensions in a 10% solution of paraffin oil in petroleum ether on glass plates. Solvents for this method include methanol–water–acetic acid (80:15:5) and (80:10:10). Copius–Peereboom and Beekes[71] separated pairs of fat-soluble dyes of very similar constitution, such as Yellow AB and Yellow OB, Oil Yellow XP (CI Solvent Yellow 18; CI 12740), and Ceres Yellow 3G (CI Solvent Yellow 16; CI 12700), on polyamide layers using the solvent systems chloroform–methanol–water (5:15:1), acetone–ethanol–water (6:3:1), and methanol–acetone–acetic acid (6:2:2). Hoodless et al.[72] employed a method of reverse-phase TLC with notable success for the separation of 10 frequently occurring fat-soluble dyes. After cellulose layers have been · dried, they are dipped in a 10% solution of paraffin oil in petroleum ether at 80–100°, and then allowed to dry in air in a horizontal position. The mixture Butter Yellow (CI Solvent Yellow 2; CI 11020; *CSD* I, 95), Yellow AB, Yellow OB, Ceres Orange GN (CI Solvent Orange 1; CI 11920), Oil Yellow XP, Sudan I (CI Solvent Yellow 14; CI 12055), Oil Orange SS (CI Solvent Orange 2; CI 12100), Sudan II (CI Solvent Orange 7; CI 12140; *CSD* I, 703), Sudan Red G (CI Solvent Red 1; CI 12150), and Citrus Red No. 2 (CI Solvent Red 80; CI 12156) can be satisfactorily separated with the solvent 2-methoxyethanol–methanol–water (55:15:30), the spot formation being very good.

Typical hR_F values for various fat-soluble dyes obtained on silica gel G with benzene[73] are listed in Table 2.12. Table 2.13 gives typical hR_F values for azobenzene derivatives on silica gel G using benzene.[74]

Table 2.12   Guiding hR_F values for Fat Soluble Dyes on Silica Gel G with benzene as eluent[73]

Dye	CI	hR_F Main Spot	Side Spot	Color of Main Spot
Sudan Orange G	11920	4	—	Yellow-orange
Sudan III	26100	12	30, 41[a]	Carmine red
Sudan Red G	12150	13	32	Carmine red
Sudan Blue G	61525	20	12, 35	Blue
Sudan Deep Black BB	26150	28	0.4, 16[a], 63[a]	Steel blue
Sudan Orange RR	12140	29	14	Pale red
Sudan Yellow GG	11020	40	—	Orange-yellow
Sudan Violet BR	61705	53	—	Violet-blue

[a] Slightly visible.

Table 2.13   Guiding hR$_F$ Values of Azobenzene Derivatives on Silica Gel G with Benzene as Eluent (Standard Conditions: Saturated Chamber)[74]

Dye	hR$_F$	Color after Spraying with Conc. HCl
p-Hydroxyazobenzene, *trans*	12	Orange-yellow
p-Aminoazobenzene, *trans*	19	Orange
1-Benzeneazo-2-naphthol, *trans*	44	Orange
p-Dimethylaminoazobenzene, *trans*	55	Red
p-Dimethylaminoazobenzene, *cis*	39	Red
4-Amino-4'-methoxyazobenzene, *trans*	64	Orange-yellow
p-Methoxyazobenzene, *cis*	12	Orange-yellow
Azobenzene, *trans*	72	Yellow
Azobenzene, *cis*	30	Yellow
Test dyes		
Guaiazulene	76	
Sudan Red G	22	
Indophenol	8	

9.2   Special Applications

9.2.1   Dyes in Natural Oils and Fats.   Davidek and Janicek[70] saponified colored fat with 50% alcoholic potassium hydroxide, and, after dilution, extracted with pentane to isolate the fat-soluble dyes. The dyes recovered from pentane were dissolved in ethanol and subjected to TLC.

9.2.2   Dyes in Carburetor Fuels.   Manufacturers of various brands of gasoline add dyes to characterize their products. According to both Häusser[75] and Machata,[76] these dyes can be compared and determined by TLC in the gasoline distillation residues. Häusser carries out an intermediate purification by evaporating a 5–10 ml gasoline sample to one-third its volume and chromatographing this solution in an Allihn tube charged with activated aluminum oxide, the solvent being petroleum ether. The column is pushed out of the tube, the dye zones are extracted with acetone, and the solutions are filtered and evaporated to dryness. The dyes enriched in this manner are dissolved in a few drops of acetone and then subjected to TLC on silica gel G, using benzene as the eluent. R$_F$ values are included in the paper.

With the exception of BP and Nordöl, it is possible to distinguish gasolines commercially available in Germany. This procedure is invaluable in dealing with fuel thefts. As a supplementary test, filtered UV light can be used to compare the less volatile components of gasoline.

9.2.3   Dyes in Polystyrene. Dyes in a transparent polystyrene sample can be isolated by the following method.[77] About 5 g of the colored polystyrene is dissolved in 25 ml benzene or chloroform at room temperature and the solution is shaken for several hours on a shaking machine or allowed to stand overnight. The resulting solution is then poured in a thin stream, with stirring, into double the amount of methanol. The polystyrene is precipitated and the dyes remain in solution. The polystyrene is filtered off and the filtrate is evaporated to dryness in a porcelain dish over a water bath. The residue is taken up with a few milliliters of acetone and the solution is subjected to the usual procedure for the TLC of fat-soluble dyes.

10   ORGANIC PIGMENTS

Many organic pigments are so sparingly soluble in water and organic solvents that chromatographic separations are difficult.

10.1   Pigments with Sulfonic Groups

These are azo or anthraquinone dyes with sulfonic groups converted into insoluble Ca, Sr, Ba, or Mn salts. In principle, these pigments can be chromatographed just as acid dyes, but it is necessary to bring them into solution before TLC. This is effected with DMF, aqueous pyridine, methanol plus a little hydrochloric acid, or ammonia plus little EDTA. McClure et al.[78] effected separation of CI Pigment Red 48, 49, 53, and 57 on cellulose layers by using a methanol–water–hydrochloric acid (75:75:1) solvent system. Gasparič[79] submitted some yellow and red pigments from this class to TLC on silica gel using the solvent systems n-butyl acetate–acetic acid–water (40:25:10) and n-propanol–ammonia (20:10). Schlegelmilch and Kuss[80] used acidic, neutral, and alkaline solvent systems for TLC on silica gel G, the best separation being obtained with methyl ethyl ketone–diethylamine–ammonia (5 N) (70:20:10). Baier[43] recommends ethyl acetate–pyridine–water (140:50:40) as the eluent.

10.2   Pigments without Sulfonic Groups

Fujii and Kamikura[81] separated a mixture of the following azo pigments on silica gel with dichloroethane: Hansa Yellow G (CI Pigment Yellow 1;

CI 11680; *CSD* V, 342), Hansa Orange (CI Pigment Orange 1; CI 11725; *CSD* V, 342), Permanent Orange GG (CI Pigment Orange 5; CI 12075; *CSD* V, 357), Flaming Red (CI Pigment Red 4; CI 12085; *CSD* V, 357), Brilliant Fast Scarlet (CI Pigment Red 22; CI 12315; *CSD* V, 366), and Deep Red (CI Pigment Red 18; CI 12350; *CSD* V, 366). Various azo pigments can be separated on silica gel G with a hexane–benzene–pyridine (65:20:15) system.[82]

The red azo pigments, arranged in order of increasing R_F values, CI Pigment Red 45, 5, 12, 3, 112, 10, 8, 7, and 11 can be separated by chloroform–xylol (30:10) on silica gel.[78] The solvent mixture chloroform–toluene–benzene (1:1:1) is suitable for the TLC of various yellow and orange azo pigments on silica gel.[78] The following pigments have useful R_F values under these TLC conditions: CI Pigment Yellow 1, 3, 4, 10, 12, and 17, and CI Pigment Orange 5 and 13. It is possible to distinguish chromatographically the azo derivatives of 1-phenyl-3-methyl-5-pyrazolone, such as CI 12700, 12705, 12710, 12720, 12730, and 21110, on silica gel with benzene.[79] It is also possible to distinguish a series of azo pigments with the solvent system benzene–chloroform–cyclohexane (10:20:10) on silica gel G, and the separations of the following pigments can be obtained in 40 minutes (the hR_F values are given in parentheses): Permanent Yellow FGL (CI Pigment Yellow 97; CI 11767; *CSD* V, 345) (4), Helio Fast Violet R (CI Pigment Violet 13) (10), Helio Brilliant Blue RR (CI Pigment Blue 23) (12), Helio Fast Red RN (CI Pigment Red 3; CI 12120; *CSD* V, 357) (25), Permanent Red FRR (CI Pigment Red 2; CI 12310; *CSD* V, 366) (30), Pigment Red B (CI Pigment Red 1; CI 12070; *CSD* V, 357) (43), Permanent Rubine FBH (CI Pigment Red 11; CI 12430; *CSD* I, 703 (50), Permanent Red R (CI Pigment Red 4; CI 12085; *CSD* V, 357) (60), and Hansa Yellow R (CI Pigment Yellow 10; CI 12710; *CSD* V, 354) (81).[80] Various azo pigments of the Hansa Yellow type can be distinguished on silica gel by using benzene[79] or ethylene chloride.[43] Disazo pigments of the acetoarylamide series (Benzidine Yellow pigments), such as Pigment Yellows 12, 13, 14, 17, and 106 (mixed coupling), can be resolved by TLC with ethylene chloride as eluent on silica gel.[43]

Naphthol AS combinations, when used with textile materials, must first be stripped from the fiber with DMF. After the solution is concentrated, thin-layer chromatograms can be prepared on, for instance, silica gel G with chloroform,[43] chloroform–xylene (30:10), or benzene–chloroform–cyclohexane (10:20:10). Sparingly soluble Naphthol AS pigments with carboxylamide groups in the diazonium component can be dissolved in hexamethylphosphotriamide for application to silica gel; pyridine–benzene (2:1) is used as the developing medium.[43]

11   VAT DYES

Though work on the separation of vat dyes in their reduced form is known
in PC, no substantial data have yet been published on the TLC of vat
dyes. Sweeny[12] has given toluene–pyridine (6:4), benzene–nitrobenzene–
acetone (8:1:1), butanol–butyl acetate–nitrobenzene–acetone (3:3:3:1),
butyl acetate–pyridine–water (5:4:2), and benzene–pyridine–dioxane–acetone (20:2:2:1) as solvent systems for the TLC of vat dyes. However, he
does not indicate which vat dyes can be separated with these solvents. In
my experience,[62] secondary products of the synthesis of indigo, such as
indirubine (2,3′-bis-indole-indigo), can be identified in the following manner: 200 mg indigo is boiled with 10 ml xylol and filtered hot; the filtrate
is evaporated to dryness, and the residue is taken up with 0.5 ml acetone;
2 mm³ is transferred to a silica gel G plate, and developed with chloroform–THF (90:10). Some pigments of the perylenetetracarboxylic imide
type (Pigment Reds 123, 149, 189, and 190) were separated by Baier on
silica gel with nitrobenzene as eluent.[43] He used o-dichlorobenzene for
resolving various other pigments of the vat dye class (e.g., Pigment Violets
23 and 36, and Pigment Red 168) on silica gel by TLC.

12   OXIDATION BASES

Commercially available oxidation bases may be in the form of organic or
inorganic salts. Kottemann[83] separated 30 oxidation bases (arylamines) by
two-dimensional TLC on silica gel. He used two types of eluent: (1) 20
ml conc. ammonia and 65 ml water (containing 2 ml 50% hypophosphorous
acid) shaken with 50 ml petroleum ether (30–60°), 250 ml chloroform, and
25 ml n-butanol in a separatory funnel (the lower phase can be used only
once); and (2) chloroform–ethyl acetate–ethanol–acetic acid (350:100:60:
20). Urquizo[84] obtained good separations of 15 aromatic amines and
aminophenols and four polyphenols on silica gel by eluting with (1) benzene–2-butanol–water (60:30:27), (2) n-butanol–acetic acid–water (40:100:
50), and the two Kottemann mixtures mentioned above. Takemura detected the bases in several commercial hair dyeing preparations by making
TLC comparisons on silica gel using n-butyl acetate–benzene (2:1) as the
solvent.[85]

   Since only a few oxidation bases are colored, they must be rendered
visible on the chromatogram by subjecting the separated substances to
color reactions. The following reagents can be used for identifying the
bases. (1) *Ehrlich's reagent:* 2 g p-dimethylaminobenzaldehyde, 100 ml
ethanol, and 10 ml conc. hydrochloric acid.[86] (2) *Ferric chloride:* 2%

aqueous solution.[9] (3) *Fast Red RC Salt:* 5-chloro-*o*-anisidine, diazonium salt, 10% aqueous solution.[9] (4) *Hydrogen peroxide–ferricyanide:* 3 parts 10% hydrogen peroxide solution and 1 part 1% potassium ferricyanide solution.[9] (5) *Sawicki's reagent:*[87] 0.35% aqueous solution of 3-methyl-2-benzothiazolone hydrazone hydrochloride, followed by 0.5% ferric chloride solution.

Other color reactions have been described by Brown.[9] Pearl and McCoy compared the utilizability of various stabilized diazonium salts for the detection of oxidation bases.[88]

13   DYE INTERMEDIATES

13.1   Aromatic Amines with Sulfonic Groups

Asmus and Schulze reported on the TLC of 12 naphthylamine monosulfonic acids on cellulose layers with *n*-butanol–*n*-propanol–water–ammonia (25%) (10:5:4:1).[89] In the following list the positions of the NH_2 and SO_3H groups, respectively, are indicated, followed by the hR_F value in parentheses and the UV fluorescence color: 1, 2 (53), violet; 1, 3 (43), violet; 1, 4 (36), blue-violet; 1, 5 (36), yellow-green; 1, 6 (42), blue; 1, 7 (47), pale blue; 1, 8 (56), yellow-green; 2, 1 (50), violet; 2, 5 (38), blue; 2, 6 (39), violet; 2, 7 (40), blue-violet; and 2, 8 (43), blue-violet.

13.2   Aromatic Amines without Sulfonic Groups

The TLC of aminoanthraquinones was discussed in Section 8.

Gillio-Tos et al.[90] chromatographed the isomeric toluidines, aminophenols, aminobenzoic acids, anisidines, nitroanilines, phenylenediamines, and bromo- and chloroanilines on silica gel G, e.g., with the eluents dibutyl ether–ethyl acetate–acetic acid (50:50:5, 75:25:5, and 25:75:5). Pastuska and Petrowitz[91] reported on the separation of nitrogen-containing aromatics by TLC, e.g., of aromatic monoamines, diamines, and nitro compounds on silica gel G with benzene, benzene–methanol (80:20), and benzene–dioxane–glacial acetic acid (90:25:4) as the solvents. The last of these solvents is suitable for strongly polar compounds. The authors also discussed the relationship between the constitution and chromatographic behavior of these compounds. Perkavec and Perpar[92] distinguished between Fast Bases on silica gel by using *n*-butanol–acetic acid–water (4:16:20) and *n*-butanol–pyridine–water (25:50:25). They obtained high hR_F values of between 82 and 96, and some slight scattering of these values, for seven Fast Bases. A large number of these amines were separated by

Gasparič[93] on layers of loose alumina by employing benzene. The possibility of using TLC on alumina (activity III) for the separation and identification of 80 primary aromatic amines was reported by Gemzová and Gasparič.[94] Benzene and chloroform were given as the solvents for monamines and diamines, respectively. Sharma and Ahuja[95] described a method by which aromatic amines were chromatographed as charge-transfer complexes on layers consisting of silica gel G and m-dinitrobenzene, using n-heptane, chloroform, or carbon tetrachloride as the eluent. Shrivastava et al.[96] separated the isomeric phenylenediamines and aminophenols on silica gel with n-propanol, the isomeric toluidines with chloroform, and the isomeric nitroanilines with benzene. Havličkova and Arient chromatographed various 1,5-diaminoanthraquinone derivatives on silica gel by using hexane–acetone (30:10).[97]

The following reagents for color reactions can be used for identifying aromatic amines on a chromatogram (see also Section 12): (1) 1% aqueous potassium persulfate[96]; (2) 1% p-dimethylaminobenzaldehyde in ethanol–conc. hydrochloric acid (95:5); (3) 5% sodium nitrite solution in 0.2 N hydrochloric acid sprayed on the plate, which is then dried at 50°, then sprayed with a 5% solution of 1-naphthol in methanol.[90]

13.3 Diazonium Salts

In TLC identification, Fast Salts were dissolved in 30% acetic acid and separated on silica gel by means of n-butanol–acetic acid–water (10:10:50).[92] Very clearly defined spots were obtained when a 0.1 N boric acid solution was used instead of water in the preparation of the silica gel plates. In this case, n-butanol–acetic acid–water (20:10:50) was the eluent.[92] Identification was effected by spraying with a solution of Naphthol AS-LR (0.15 g dissolved in 0.3 ml 28% sodium hydroxide, 2 ml ethanol added, and the solution made up to 50 ml with water). The hR_F values obtained are listed in Table 2.14.

Gritter separated a number of diazonium salts as chlorozincates and fluoroborates by TLC on silica gel G plates, using dimethyl sulfoxide–acetic acid–water (60:10:10) as the eluent system.[98]

13.4 Coupling Components

De Deyne[99] separated the isomeric 1-naphthol monosulfonic acids on silica gel with methylene chloride–ammonia (25%)–methanol (80:6:30) or acetonitrile–ammonia (25%) (80:6). Identification is achieved by spraying with diazotized sulfanilic acid. Pastuska and Petrowitz[100] described the TLC of a large number of phenolic products on silica gel by eluting with

Table 2.14   hR$_F$ Values of Fast Salts on Silica Gel G[92]

Fast Salt	CI	Color of Spot	hR$_F$ (1)	hR$_F$ (2)
Fast Orange Salt GGD	37045	Red-yellow	46	96
Fast Orange Salt GR	37025	Orange	23	17
Fast Red Salt ITR	37150	Red	18	32
Fast Red Salt RC	37120	Red	14	21
Fast Scarlet Salt GG	37010	Orange	17	20
Fast Brown Salt VA	37200	Yellow-brown	97	86
		Gray	86	
Fast Blue Salt B	37235	Violet-blue	64	2
Variamine Blue Salt FGC	37250	Reddish blue	33	43
Fast Black Salt K	37190	Violet	97	86
		Yellow	92	78

layer/eluent: 1, silica gel/*n*-butanol–acetic acid–water (10:10:50); 2, silica gel–boric acid/*n*-butanol–acetic acid–water (20:10:50).
color reaction: Naphthol AS-LR (see Section 15.3).

benzene, benzene–methanol (95:5), benzene–dioxane–acetic acid (90:25:4), and benzene–methanol–acetic acid (45:8:4). Phenol and the three isomeric cresols were chromatographed by Thielemann[101] on silica gel G with benzene–acetone (90:19) as eluent. Perkavec and Perpar employed methanol–methyl ethyl ketone (5:2) and ethanol–methyl ethyl ketone (5:2) as solvents for the TLC of Naphthols including the AS-G type on silica gel.[92]

14   OPTICAL BRIGHTENING AGENTS

In the TLC of optical brightening agents, difficulties arise that are not encountered in the chromatography of dyes. For instance, brightening agents of the stilbene and oxazolyl type are normally present in the *trans* form, but they undergo a partial conversion to the *cis* form on exposure to UV light. Since this conversion can also take place in sunlight (daylight?), such substances are chromatographed in the dark, or the spots of brightening agent applied to the plate are first irradiated with UV light to enable *cis–trans* equilibrium to be established before an attempt is made to separate the substances. When the latter method is used, two principal spots are produced on the chromatogram. Because of its greater substantivity for cellulose, the *trans* form has the smaller R$_F$ value on cellulose layers, whereas it migrates faster than the *cis* form on silica gel layers. Another difficulty in the TLC of optical brightening agents arises from the multiplicity of secondary components which contain mainly stilbene derivatives and which can vary considerably in amount. This may well make identification by TLC somewhat problematic.

Most of the optical brightening agents of the stilbene type are anionic products with substantivity for cellulose. They are used for the brightening of cellulosic and polyamide fibers and of paper, and they are also added to detergents. Various solvents have been proposed for liberating such brighteners from fibers or paper: Kurz and Schuierer[102] extracted with acetone; Theidel and Schmitz[103] with methoxyethanol–ammonia ($d = 0.91$) (70:30) or pyridine–water (50:50); Meckel[104] with dioxane–water (50:50); and Schlegelmilch et al.[105] with DMF–water (20:10). Pyridine–water extractions should be carried out at room temperature, since some brighteners change at the boil.[104] If dyed material has been extracted, it may be advisable to make a preliminary separation by column chromatography. The migration of the brightener zone can be followed by illuminating the column with a UV lamp. If acrylic fibers that have been optically brightened in the melt are being investigated, the fibers are first dissolved in DMF, the polymer then being precipitated by the addition of acetone.[102] Testing for optical brightening agents in detergents can proceed either by cold extraction with methanol, or by first "dyeing" on cotton or polyamide fabric, this material then being extracted in the indicated manner.[103]

Brown[9] recommended *n*-butanol–ethanol–pyridine–ammonia ($d = 0.88$) (40:10:30:20) and chloroform–methanol–ammonia ($d = 0.88$)–water (11:7:1:1) for the TLC of optical brightening agents on silica gel G. Löffel[106] used *n*-propanol–isopropanol–ethyl acetate–water–ammonia (conc.) (23:23:30:23:1) for separating cellulose brightening agents of the stilbene type on silica gel G layers, and he resorted to diethanolamine–water–benzene–acetone (1:9:20:70) for investigating the secondary products. Schlegelmilch et al.[105] described group-selective methods involving either a pH-dependent TLC on cellulose acetate or reaction chromatography on the starting line of cellulose plates to identify flavonic acid derivatives (4,4-diaminostilbene-2,2'-disulfonic acid). The identification of a substance thus recognized as being a flavonic acid derivative is then made by carrying out a TLC comparison on silica gel G plates with the aid of methyl ethyl ketone–diethylamine–ammonia (conc.) (30:10:10). Excellent separations of optical brightening agents can be achieved on polyamide layers with methanol–water–ammonia ($d = 0.91$) (10:1:4), methanol–6 N hydrochloric acid (10:2) or *n*-hexanol–pyridine–ethyl acetate–ammonia ($d = 0.91$)–methanol (5:5:5:5:3).[103] Benzene–chloroform (40:60) is suitable for resolving optical brightening agents that do not contain sulfonic groups on polyamide layers.[103] For the TLC of coumarin-type optical brightening agents, Copenhaver and Carver[107] recommend separation on silica gel G plates with acetone–2,2,4-trimethylpentane–water (100:40:1), acetone–ethyl acetate–petroleum ether (40–60°)–water (100:100:33:3.5), or 4-methyl-2-pentanone–acetone–petroleum ether (30/60°) (60:20:20).

Figge[108] reported comprehensively on the possibility of separating commercial optical brightening agents into ionic and nonionic groups by polar basic solvent systems on various sorption layer substances and mixtures of these. He suggested a total of 19 solvent systems and 19 sorption agents or mixtures for effecting TLC comparison within the two groups. Because of his very extensive coverage, the reader is referred to the original paper for further information.

15 PREPARATIVE TLC

It is possible to increase the amount of substance separated by TLC by applying it in the form of bands on layers of increased thickness. Honegger[109] and Stahl[110] examined the effect of layer thickness on separation efficiency. In general, the layers have a thickness of the order of 0.5–1 mm. To avoid cracking of thicker layers, it has been suggested that less water be incorporated in the swelling compositions and that special drying procedures be employed.[109,111] Special silica gels (the P series of Merck, Darmstadt) and 20 × 20-cm plates with a 2-mm-thick layer (Merck) have also been developed.

Besides the 20 × 20-cm plates, the still very easily manageable 20 × 40-cm plates are used as carriers for preparative layers. On the other hand, Halpaap prefers 1-m plates and has constructed a correspondingly large stainless-steel developing tank and other accessories.[112]

Some firms manufacture basic equipment for preparative TLC.[16–18] "Do-it-yourself" spreaders for preparative TLC have also been described.[111,113,114]

Special techniques are needed for producing a uniform application of relatively large volumes of samples as narrow starting bands on preparative TLC plates.

Making a series of dots with a pipette is time-consuming and usually produces irregular zones. A better starting band is obtained with a wide-band pipette,[16] a microspray pistol,[16] or automatic applicators.[16,17] Stahl gave a detailed description of preparative TLC.[2,3]

REFERENCES

1. E. Stahl, *Chem.-Ztg.*, **82**, 323 (1958).
2. E. Stahl, *Dünnschicht-Chromatographie, ein Laboratoriumshandbuch*, 2nd ed., Springer, Berlin, 1967.

3. E. Stahl, *Thin-Layer Chromatography, a Laboratory Handbook*, 2nd ed., Springer/ Academic Press, New York, 1969.

4. K. Randerath, *Dünnschicht-Chromatographie*, 2nd ed., Verlag Chemie, Weinheim, 1965.

5. K. Randerath, *Thin-Layer Chromatography*, Verlag Chemie/Academic Press, New York, 1966.

6. J. G. Kirchner, *Thin-Layer Chromatography*, Wiley-Interscience, New York, 1967.

7. G. B. Marini-Bettòlo, *Thin-Layer Chromatography*, Elsevier, Amsterdam, 1964.

8. K. Macek and I. M. Hais, *Stationary Phase in Paper and Thin-Layer Chromatography*, Elsevier, Amsterdam, 1965.

9. J. C. Brown, *J. Soc. Dyers Colour.*, **80**, 185 (1964); **85**, 137 (1969).

10. G. H. Rettie and C. G. Haynes, *J. Soc. Dyers Colour.*, **80**, 692 (1964).

11. J. F. Feeman, *Can. Text. J.*, 83 (February 1970).

12. C. D. Sweeny, *Am. Dyest. Rep.*, 70 (September 1972).

13. H. Schweppe, refs. 2, 3.

14. Suppliers of precoated TLC sheets: (*a*) E. Merck AG, 6100 Darmstadt, West Germany; (*b*) C. Schleicher & Schüll, 3354 Dassel, Kreis Einbeck, West Germany; (*c*) Macherey, Nagel & Co., 5160 Düren, West Germany; (*d*) Eastman Kodak Co., Rochester, New York; (*e*) Analtech., Inc., 100 S. Justinson St., Wilmington, Delaware; (*f*) Mann Research Laboratories, Inc., 136 Liberty St., New York; (*g*) Kodak-Pathé, Vincennes/ Paris, France; (*h*) Cheng Chin Trading Co. Ltd., Importers & Exporters, No. 75, Section 1, Hankow Street, Taipei, Taiwan (Formosa); (*i*) Kodak Ltd., Kirkby Industrial Estate, Kirkby, near Liverpool; (*j*) Gelman Instrument Co., 600 South Wagner Road, P.O. Box 1448, Ann Arbor, Michigan.

15. Filmolux UV Manufacturer: Hans Neschen, 4967 Bückeburg, P.O. Box 1340, West Germany.

16. Supplier: C. Desaga GmbH, 6900 Heidelberg, Maass-Str. 26-28, West Germany.

17. Supplier: Camag AG, Muttenz, B. L., Homburger Str. 24, Switzerland.

18. Supplier: Shandon Scientific Co., 65 Pound Lane, Willesden, London NW 10, England.

19. A. McClure, J. Thomson, and J. Tannahill, *J. Oil Colour Chem. Assoc.*, **51**, 580 (1968).

20. F. Schlegelmilch and W. Kuss, *Dtsch. Farben-Ztg.*, **27**, 484 (1973).

21. M. Dallas, *J. Chromatogr.*, **17**, 267 (1965).

22. W. Garner, *Textile Laboratory Manual*, 3rd ed., Vol. 4, *Dyestuffs*, Elsevier, Amsterdam, 1967, p. 128.

23. T. Vickerstaff, *The Physical Chemistry of Dyeing*, Interscience, New York, 1950, pp. 46–52.

24. U. Baumgarte, *Melliand Textilber.*, **53**, 790 (1972).

25. W. Trappe, *Biochem. Z.*, **305**, 150 (1940); **306**, 316 (1940).

26. H. H. Strain, *Chromatographic Adsorption Analysis*, Interscience, New York, 1942.

27. L. Meckel, H. Milster, and U. Krause, *Text. Prax.*, **16**, 1032 (1961).

28. E. Stahl, *Arch. Pharm.*, **292**, 411 (1959).

29. G. R. Jamieson in *Modern Aspects of Chromatography*, Institute of Chemistry, Dublin, Sept. 1963.

30. L. F. Druding, *J. Chem. Educ.*, **40**, 536 (1963).

31. S. Logar, J. Perkavec, and M. Perpar, *Mikrochim. Acta*, 712 (1964).
32. K. C. Walker and M. Beroza, *J. Assoc. Off. Agr. Chem.*, **46**, 250 (1963).
33. M. B. Naff and A. S. Naff, *J. Chem. Educ.*, **40**, 534 (1963).
34. D. Waldi, in ref. 2, p. 592.
35. G. Pastuska and H. Trinks, *Chem.-Ztg.*, **86**, 135 (1962).
36. P. Raban, *Nature (London)*, **199**, 596 (1963).
37. J. Gasparič and A. Cee, *J. Chromatogr.*, **14**, 484 (1964).
38. W. Voegelin, W. A. Vetterli, and S. Napier, *CIBA Rev.*, No. 3, 10 (1966).
39. S. L. Ruiz and C. Laroche, *Bull. Soc. Chim. France*, 1594 (1963).
40. F. Schlegelmilch and C. Khodadadian, *Melliand Textilber.*, **54**, 1098 (1973).
41. J. Perkavec and M. Perpar, *Z. Anal. Chem.*, **206**, 356 (1964).
42. A. Cee and J. Gasparič, *Collect. Czech. Chem. Commun.*, **33**, 1091 (1968).
43. E. Baier, *Farbe Lack*, **80**, 614 (1974).
44. G. Schetty and W. Kuster, *Helv. Chim. Acta*, **44**, 2193 (1961); **45**, 809, 1095 (1962); **46**, 1132 (1963).
45. F. Beffa, P. Lienhard, E. Steiner, and G. Schetty, *Helv. Chim. Acta*, **46**, 1369 (1963).
46. H. Pfitzner and H. Schweppe, *Z. Anal. Chem.*, **268**, 337 (1974).
47. H. Pfitzner, *Angew. Chem.*, **84**, 351 (1972); *Angew. Chem. Internat. Ed.*, **11**, 312 (1972).
48. G. Häfelinger and E. Baier, *Naturwissenschaften*, **51**, 136 (1964).
49. J. Toul and N. Mouková, *J. Chromatogr.*, **67**, 335 (1972).
50. F. H. Pollard, G. Nickless, T. J. Samuelson, and R. G. Anderson, *J. Chromatogr.*, **16**, 231 (1964).
51. L. Masschelein-Kleiner, *Mikrochim. Acta*, **6**, 1080 (1967).
52. E. Voyatzakis, G. Vasilikiotis, and H. Alexaki-Tzivanidou, *Anal. Lett.*, **5**, 445 (1972).
53. A. Stier and W. Specht, *Naturwissenschaften*, **50**, 549 (1963).
54. S. Logar, J. Perkavec, and M. Perpar, *Mikrochim. Acta*, **6**, 496 (1967).
55. A. M. Arsov, B. K. Mesrob, and A. B. Gateva, *J. Chromatogr.*, **81**, 181 (1973).
56. R. Takeshita, N. Itoh, and Y. Sakagami, *J. Chromatogr.*, **57**, 437 (1971).
57. L. Van Dessel and P. Van Regenmortel, *Z. Anal. Chem.*, **247**, 280 (1969).
58. W. Reiners, *Z. Anal. Chem.*, **219**, 272 (1966).
59. D. Waldi, in ref. 2, p. 590.
60. P. Wollenweber, *J. Chromatogr.*, **7**, 557 (1962).
61. J. Franc and M. Hájková, *J. Chromatogr.*, **16**, 345 (1964).
62. H. Schweppe, unpublished work.
63. M. K. Ramamurthy and V. R. Bhalerao, *Analyst*, **89**, 740 (1964).
64. S. Hěrmánek, V. Schwarz, and Z. Čekan, *Collect. Czech. Chem. Commun.*, **26**, 3170 (1961).
65. K. C. Walker and M. Beroza, *J. Assoc. Off. Agr. Chem.*, **46**, 250 (1963).
66. J. W. Copius-Peereboom, *Chem. Weekblad*, **57**, 625 (1961).
67. S. Fujii and M. Kamikura, *Shokuhin Eiseigaku Zasshi*, **4**, 96 (1963); *CA*, **59**, 11691 (1963).
68. J. Davidek, J. Pokorný, and G. Janiček, *Z. Lebensmitt.-Untersuch.*, **116**, 13 (1961).

69. J. C. Topham and J. W. Westrop, *J. Chromatogr.*, **16**, 233 (1964).

70. J. Davidek and G. Janiček, *J. Chromatogr.*, **15**, 543 (1964).

71. J. W. Copius-Peereboom and H. W. Beekes, *J. Chromatogr.*, **20**, 43 (1965).

72. R. A. Hoodless, J. Thomson, and J. E. Arnold, *J. Chromatogr.*, **56**, 332 (1971).

73. D. Waldi, in ref. 2, p. 585.

74. P. J. Schorn and E. Stahl, in ref. 2, p. 586.

75. H. Häusser, *Arch. Kriminol.*, **125**, 72 (1960).

76. G. Machata, *Arch. Toxikol.*, **127**, 1 (1961).

77. H. Schweppe, in ref. 2, p. 587.

78. A. McClure, J. Thomson, and J. Trannahill, *J. Oil Colour Chem. Assoc.*, **51**, 580 (1968).

79. J. Gasparič, *J. Chromatogr.*, **66**, 179 (1972).

80. F. Schlegelmilch and W. Kuss, *Dtsch. Farben-Ztg.*, **27**, 484 (1973).

81. S. Fujii and M. Kamikura, *Shokuhin Eiseigaku Zasshi*, **4**, 135 (1963); *CA*, **60**, 9883 (1964).

82. H. Schweppe, in ref. 2, p. 588.

83. C. M. Kottemann, *J. Assoc. Off. Anal. Chemists*, **49**, 954 (1966).

84. S. Urquizo, *Ann. Fals. Expert Chim.*, **62**, 27 (1969); *CA*, **71**, 77112 (1969).

85. I. Takemura, *Japan Analyst*, **19**, 899 (1970); *CA*, **74**, 23634 (1971).

86. G. W. Watts and J. D. Chrisp, *Anal. Chem.*, **26**, 452 (1954).

87. E. Sawicki, T. W. Stanley, T. R. Hauser, W. Elbert, and J. L. Noe, *Anal. Chem.*, **33**, 722 (1961).

88. I. A. Pearl and P. F. McCoy, *Anal. Chem.*, **32**, 1407 (1960).

89. E. Asmus and G. Schulze, *Z. Anal. Chem.*, **217**, 176 (1966).

90. M. Gillio-Tos, S. A. Pretivera, and A. Vimercati, *J. Chromatogr.*, **13**, 572 (1964).

91. G. Pastuska and J.-J. Petrowitz, *Chem.-Ztg.*, **88**, 311 (1964).

92. J. Perkavec and M. Perpar, *Mikrochim. Acta*, 1029 (1964).

93. J. Gasparič, *Z. Anal. Chem.*, **218**, 113 (1966).

94. I. Gemzová and J. Gasparič, *Collect. Czech. Chem. Commun.*, **31**, 2525 (1966).

95. J. P. Sharma and S. Ahuja, *Z. Anal. Chem.*, **267**, 368 (1973).

96. S. P. Shrivastava, R. C. Gupta, and A. Gupta, *Z. Anal. Chem.*, **262**, 31 (1973).

97. L. Havličkova and J. Arient, *Collect. Czech. Chem. Commun.*, **36**, 2074 (1971).

98. R. J. Gritter, *J. Chromatogr.*, **20**, 416 (1965).

99. V. J. R. De Deyne, *J. Chromatogr.*, **31**, 260 (1967).

100. G. Pastuska and H.-J. Petrowitz, *Chem.-Ztg.*, **86**, 311 (1962).

101. H. Thielemann, *Z. Anal. Chem.*, **269**, 127 (1974).

102. J. Kurz and M. Schuierer, *Fette, Seifen, Anstrichmittel*, **69**, 24 (1967).

103. H. Theidel and G. Schmitz, *J. Chromatogr.*, **27**, 413 (1967).

104. L. Meckel, *Text.-Prax*, **16**, 737 (1961).

105. F. Schlegelmilch, H. Abdelkader, and M. Eckelt, *Z. Ges. Text.-Ind.*, **73**, 274 (1971).

106. H. Löffel, *Textilveredlung*, **8**, 349 (1973).

107. J. H. Copenhaver and M. J. Carver, *J. Chromatogr.*, **16**, 229 (1964).

108. K. Figge, *Fette, Seifen, Anstrichmittel*, **70**, 680 (1968).

109. C. G. Honegger, *Helv. Chim. Acta*, **46**, 1772 (1963).
110. E. Stahl, *Lab. Practice*, **13**, 496 (1964).
111. P. Dauvillier, *J. Chromatogr.*, **11**, 405 (1963).
112. H. Halpaap, *Chem.-Ing.-Tech.*, **35**, 488 (1963).
113. C. E. Bell, *Chem. Ind. (London)*, 1025 (1965).
114. B. P. Korzun, L. Dorfman, and S. M. Brody, *Anal. Chem.*, **35**, 950 (1963).

CHAPTER THREE

Paper Chromatography and Paper Electrophoresis

JIŘÍ ŠRÁMEK

Paper chromatography and electrophoresis are used for rapid determination of the purity and identity of dyes. Both methods are valuable aids in the constitutional analysis of dyes and in the study of their coloristic properties.

1 PAPER CHROMATOGRAPHY[1]

1.1 Introduction

The main reason for the continuing popularity of paper chromatography (PC) is its simplicity. A paper chromatogram represents a lasting proof of the performed analysis, which can be kept on file. The chromatographed substances remain virtually unchanged and accessible for further analytical or other evaluation.

Dye purity determination and separation of mixtures of dyes are closely linked with the history of chromatography and the development of individual techniques. Paper chromatography was first used in connection with the food, pharmaceutical, and cosmetics industries to check if nontoxic and pure dyes were used. In forensic science chromatographic analysis has become an important tool for the identification of writing and rubber-stamp inks. Chromatographic methods have been elaborated for practically all groups of textile dyes to determine their purity and to identify dyes of various trade names as well as the composition of mixed dyes. There are also methods for the identification of dyes stripped from textile fibers. Equally, paper chromatography is used to study some properties of dyes (substantivity, leveling, reactivity of reactive dyes, etc.) and their degradation or changes during manufacture (hydrolysis, reductive cleavage, thermal destruction, stereoisomerism) or after application to the textile substrate (by textile finishing auxiliaries, light, fumes, etc.). In conjunction with spectroscopic and other physicochemical methods, chromatography is also used for the constitution analysis of dyes. New theoretically substantiated methods of paper chromatography of dyes have been evolved, enabling a systematic analysis of dyes.[2-4] Chromatographic behavior of dyes has also been correlated with chemical structure. It will be possible in the future to characterize the chemical structure of a dye, as well as its dyeing properties, in terms of its chromatographic behavior. Chromatographic data obtained by PC or TLC will become internationally recognized for the official evaluation of some properties of dyes.

1.2   Method and Theory of PC of Dyes

In the PC of dyes, generally valid principles of partition chromatography are applied.[1,5] The experimental requirements are a suitable chromatography paper, a solvent system, an apparatus for developing the chromatogram, a micropipette, and an atomizer for spraying with reagents to detect colorless compounds.

According to the direction the solvent system migrates through the paper, we recognize an ascending and a descending technique of development, as well as radial or centrifugal chromatography.[6,7]

For separating very complex dye mixtures two-dimensional chromatography is employed. To isolate larger quantities of dye from a complex commercial mixture, preparative PC is used.[1] The method of continuous PC is not used for dyes.

Water-soluble dyes can be chromatographed by a number of systems and techniques. Vat dyes and sulfur dyes dissolve in water by alkaline reduction. Dyes insoluble in water, but soluble in organic solvents, may be chromatographed by using suitable solvent systems. Chromatography of pigments, which are very sparingly soluble even in special solvents, depends on finding a suitable solvent.

The theoretical problems of the stationary and mobile phases in the chromatography of dyes have been elaborated by Šrámek.[8,9] For accurate and reproducible results a defined chromatography paper is essential. Chromatography paper cellulose differs considerably from the pure linters cellulose. It is a cellulose that has been mechanically, oxidatively, and hydrolytically degraded and that contains various functional groups which are able through their reactivity to take part in the chromatographic separation. Various types of chromatography paper differ in the DP value and in the content of amorphous cellulose. The average DP of cellulose ranges between 1400 and 500 (determined by the nitration method). The content of amorphous cellulose, calculated from the value of the iodine sorption, ranges for the different types of chromatography paper from 3.5 to 1.5%. On chromatography paper with a lower DP of cellulose and lower content of amorphous cellulose, the quality of separation is worse. The sorption of water by the paper decreases with an increase in R_F, and the rate of flow of the solvent system through the paper becomes higher.

By using chromatography paper suitably modified for dyes, the following observations have been made.[8] (1) The chromatographic behavior of dyes on ion-exchange papers is influenced by the affinity of the dye ions, anion exchangers being favorable for anionic dyes and cation exchangers for cationic dyes. (2) In chromatography on anionic papers, the R_F of anionic dyes is influenced by the number of groups in the dye capable of interaction, e.g., SO_3H, COOH, and by the character of aromatic nuclei, the chromatography paper acting in chemisorbing capacity. (3) Chromatographic separation of anionic dyes is more effective on strongly or moderately basic anion-exchange papers of the Whatman DE 20 and ET 20 type than on unmodified cellulose papers. (4) Anionic dyes give on cation exchangers an increased R_F which is in agreement with the chromatographic behavior of these dyes on papers containing oxycellulose. (5) For cationic dyes normal chromatography paper is sufficient, because it nearly always contains COOH groups. (6) Hydrophobic papers show a substantially lower sorption of the polar phase of the solvent system and therefore give higher R_F values for hydrophilic dyes. These papers are of interest for the chromatographic separation of hydrophobic dyes.

Šrámek's study[8] on the selection of solvent systems for the partition PC of water-soluble dyes yielded the following conclusions. (1) The solvent system must always contain water and a further component enabling the formation of hydrogen bonds, as well as a solubilizing agent possessing also the property of reducing adsorption, e.g., pyridine, DMF, formamide, dioxane, and some ketones and esters. The dyes must be insoluble or only partly soluble in the mobile phase. It is the hydrogen bond causing an organized agglomeration of molecules that is essential for the amorphous liquid system, which is the basis of the chromatographic partition. (2) Solvent systems containing as mobile phase aliphatic, aromatic, hydrogenated, nitrated, chlorinated, or terpene hydrocarbons are not suitable for the chromatography of dyes. In these systems conditions suitable for the partition phenomenon cannot be obtained. (3) Suitable conditions for the partition chromatography are obtained with solvent systems containing alcohols, glycols, and ethers (substances containing functional OH groups) as mobile phase. Especially suitable are primary alcohols, characterized by cohesion of hydrogen bonds. (4) In one-component aqueous solvent systems, it is the adsorption effect that is most important.

The individual components of the solvent system n-butanol–pyridine–water are effective in the chromatographic partition in the following manner. Water acts as both stationary phase and solvent in which the differential solubility of dyes gets utilized. Pyridine levels solubility differences of the dyes and is also preferentially linked to cellulose by hydrogen bonds, thereby inhibiting adsorption of dyes on cellulose; it restrains the formation of hydrogen bonds between cellulose and the separation system, thus enabling separation between the stationary and the mobile phases, whereby the stationary phase consists of a ternary complex, cellulose–water–part of the organic solvent. n-Butanol acts as mobile phase with limited water miscibility, rendering possible the separation on the basis of differential partition coefficients; moreover, it is effective in the interaction of hydrogen bonds. Hydrophilic dyes are practically insoluble in n-butanol, a condition for the separation between two immiscible liquids.

The same partition principle is the basis of the solvent systems listed in Table 3.1. When the polyzonal technique of developing chromatograms is used with these systems, the progress of the separated dyes is practically ideal, nearly a linear increment of R_F relative to the length of travel. With centrifugal chromatography and these solvent systems, separation results are equivalent to those obtained by the ascending or descending technique: the sequence of spots remains the same, and they are as distinct as with the ascending or descending technique; moreover, the development time is reduced from 12–14 hours to 5–45 minutes.

Under conditions of defined chromatography paper and a suitable solvent system, chromatographic separation is based on the formation of hydrogen bonds. Interaction takes place between the ternary complex, cellulose–water–organic solvent, the mobile phase composed of a mixture of "free water" and organic solvent, and the dye. The phenomenon of adsorption is greatly suppressed on account of the water contained on the surface of

Table 3.1   Solvent Systems for the PC of Water-Soluble Dyes

1. Methanol–pyridine–water
2. Ethanol–pyridine–water
3. n-Propanol–pyridine–water
4. Isopropanol–pyridine–water
5. n-Butanol–pyridine–water
6. 2-Butanol–pyridine–water
7. Isobutanol–pyridine–water
8. t-Butanol–pyridine–water
9. n-Amyl alcohol–pyridine–water[a]
10. t-Amyl alcohol–pyridine–water[a]
11. Isoamyl alcohol–pyridine–water[a]
12. Benzyl alcohol–pyridine–water[b]
13. Cyclohexanol–pyridine–water
14. Hexanol–pyridine–water[c]
15. Methylcyclohexanol–pyridine–water
16. Furfural–pyridine–water
17. Furfuryl alcohol–pyridine–water
18. Tetrahydrofurfuryl alcohol–pyridine–water
19. Isoamyl alcohol– pyridine–25% ammonia[d]
20. Isopropanol–pyridine–25% ammonia[e]
21. n-Butanol–DMF–water[f]
22. n-Butanol–dioxane–water
23. n-Butanol–2-methoxyethanol–water

[a] 0.8:1:1   [d] 1:1.3:1.
[b] 1:1:0.4.   [e] 8:0.2:1.8.
[c] 1.1:1:0.5.   [f] 1:0.5:1.
All the others are 1:1:1.

the cellulose exercising a strong solvating influence. Ion exchange on normal papers is improbable.

The following general rules were established for standard PC conditions regarding the influence of the chemical structure of dyes on their chromatographic behavior.[10] (1) Structurally simple dyes displaying an overall physicochemical activity possess a higher R_F than more complex dyes. With increasing complexity of the dye molecule its physical and chemical susceptibility to reaction between phases and phase carrier increases, being most pronounced with azo dyes and polycyclic vat dyes. (2) The greater the chain length of conjugated double bonds traversing the entire dye molecule, the greater its capacity to be polarized, its substantivity, and its adsorption affinity, the R_F decreasing in proportion. The R_F increases if the chain of conjugated double bonds is broken, although judging from the number of N=N bonds a decrease would be expected. (3) The greater the number of azo groups, the lower the R_F. Amide connecting bridges cause a decrease in R_F. (4) An increase of the number of keto groups causes a decrease in R_F. (5) With dyes of the same basic skeleton the R_F value is decreased by substituents (SO_3H, OCH_3, COOH, OH, NH_2, and NO_2). Their effect is additive. Halogens and heterocycles produce a similar effect, and so do alkylation, acylation, and arylation of the amino group of anthraquinone dyes. (6) Symmetric dyes show a lower R_F than unsymmetric dyes. Dyes with a smaller dipole moment have a higher R_F. (7) With stereoisomers, the R_F of *cis* isomers is higher. (8) The R_F value depends usually on the molecular weight of the dye, and its increase causes an increase in capillary adhesion and therefore a decrease in R_F. (9) With dyes of the same skeleton the adsorption affinity of dyes, relative to the R_F, is an additive function of individual adsorption affinities of the basic skeleton and functional groups, provided there is no possibility of tautomerism or solvation through the influence of the solvent system.

1.3   Evaluation of Chromatographic Analysis

In the evaluation of chromatographic analysis, the properties of the analyzed dye are compared with a standard (such as a CI equivalent dye with a different trade name), which is chromatographed simultaneously. On the chromatogram the number of spots, their intensity and coloration in normal light, their fluorescence in UV light, and their positions expressed by R_F values are evaluated. A pure or homogeneous dye produces only one spot on the chromatogram. More than one spot indicates the dye is an impure, shaded, or mixed dye. An impure dye may contain some colored or fluorescent impurities formed in the course of synthesis, e.g., through side reactions of isomers or impurities present in the intermediates. Shaded dyes contain small quantities of a dye added by the manufacturer for obtaining the desired shade. If several homogeneous dyes are mixed, blends (such as greens and blacks) are produced.

1.4   Water-Soluble Dyes

Reliable chromatographic separation methods are available. From the chromatographic analysis of individual groups relationships have been established between the chromatographic behavior of the dyes and their constitution.[2,10,11] Also certain rules have been derived regarding the relationships between the R_F of some groups of water-soluble dyes and their coloristic properties, especially the relation between R_F and substantivity.[12–17]

Šrámek[2,10,11,18] elaborated a systematic method for water-soluble dyes by which it is possible to analyze them with one fundamental solvent system: descending chromatography using Whatman No. 1 paper and a solvent system of pyridine–isoamyl alcohol–25% ammonia (1.3:1:1). This system also gives satisfactory results with a solvent ratio of 1:1:1 and maintains its effectiveness even if the pyridine ratio is increased to 1.9:1:1. An increase of the quantity of pyridine improves the sharpness of the spots, which is already optimal at a ratio of components of 1.3:1:1. This solvent system is sufficiently sensitive to detect differences in chemical composition and structure of dyes, thus permitting separation of very complex mixtures of dyes.

For purity determinations of highly substantive azo dyes n-butanol–pyridine–water (0.5:1:1) is used. In this method 0.1-μl samples of 1% aqueous solution of dye are applied as spots on the start of the chromatogram. The size of the chromatogram is 160 × 470 mm, the distance of the start from the edge being 70 mm. The dyes are spotted on the start at 20-mm intervals from each other. The development of the chromatogram takes place at a temperature of 20–22° for 12 hours, preferably overnight, and the length of the run is 400 mm.

With an isoamyl alcohol system water-soluble dyes of all chemical classes have been chromatographed. This system is compatible with the conditions of partition chromatography and particularly distinguishes differences in partition coefficients and solubility of dyes. The rate of flow of the solvent through the paper, which is usually incompatible with the conditions of partition chromatography and influences the reproducibility of results, fails here to exert any effect whatsoever. This is shown when this solvent is applied in chromatography in the centrifugal field, where the rate of flow of the solvent system through the paper increases many times.

Table 3.2 shows mean R_F values of individual groups of water-soluble dyes obtained by compilation of minimum and maximum R_F values of several hundred dyes of known chemical constitution. The R_F values refer to the isoamyl alcohol solvent system on Whatman No. 1 paper.

1.4.1 Direct Cotton Dyes. Although purity and identity investigations have been of foremost interest, chromatography has been widely used for the assessment of their dyeing properties, notably their substantivity.[10,12,13,19] Venkataraman was the first to correlate the PC behavior of direct dyes with their substantivity.[19] Changes in the dye taking place during fixation

Table 3.2   Mean R_F Values of Water-Soluble Dyes

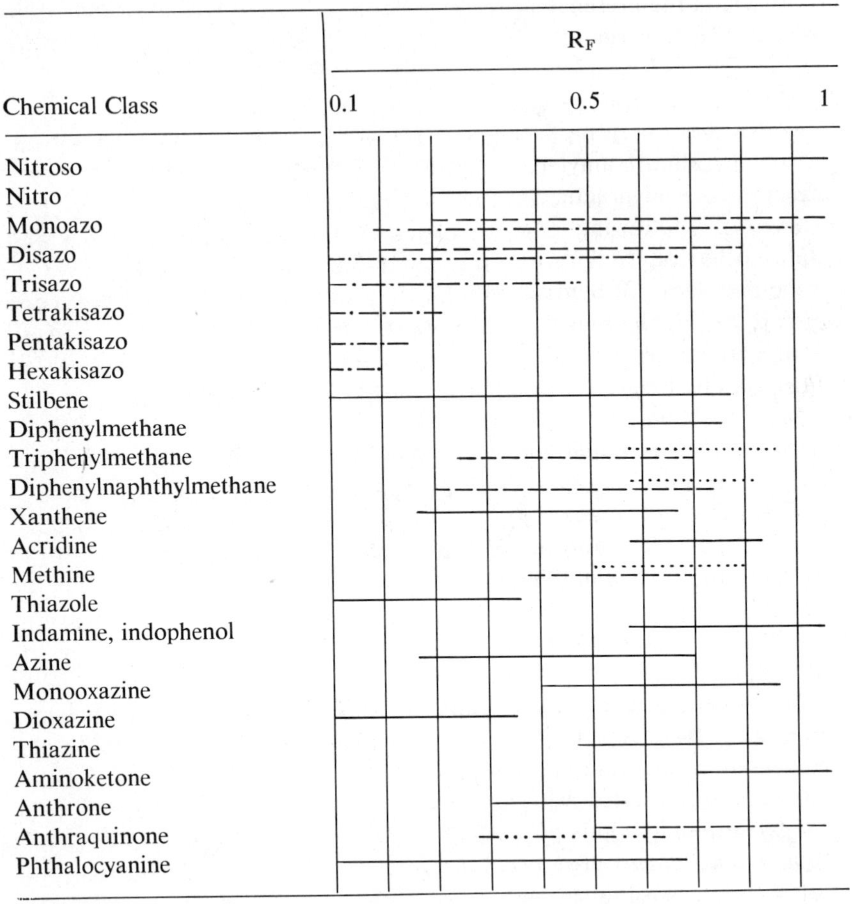

Chemical Class	R_F		
	0.1	0.5	1
Nitroso			
Nitro			
Monoazo			
Disazo			
Trisazo			
Tetrakisazo			
Pentakisazo			
Hexakisazo			
Stilbene			
Diphenylmethane			
Triphenylmethane			
Diphenylnaphthylmethane			
Xanthene			
Acridine			
Methine			
Thiazole			
Indamine, indophenol			
Azine			
Monooxazine			
Dioxazine			
Thiazine			
Aminoketone			
Anthrone			
Anthraquinone			
Phthalocyanine			

Acid dyes, – – – – – – –; basic dyes, · · · · · · · · · ·; mordant dyes,— · · ·—· · ·—;

substantive dyes, — · — · — · — ·

by various agents have been chromatographically investigated,[10] together with the progress of alkaline reduction of dyes in connection with their stripping from the fiber when faulty dyeings are rectified. Also the reduction of dyes occurring when dyeing improperly desulfurized rayon has been chromatographically investigated.[10]

Chromatography of direct dyes indicates their nonuniformity, the cause of which appears to be the multistage syntheses.[10,20,21] This fact must be considered when evaluating chromatographic analyses. For instance, the chromatogram of the direct black trisazo dye, CI Direct Black 38 (CI

30235), shows 11 spots that correspond with the total procedure of the synthesis and the presence of monoazo to tetrakisazo dyes, substantially a mixture of acid, direct, and basic dyes.[10] Brown[20] found that the red disazo dye, CI Direct Red 23 (CI 29160), also contains CI Direct Orange 26 (CI 29155) and another red dye. Many other examples of nonuniform direct dyes have been reported.[21-23]

Using pyridine–n-amyl (or isoamyl) alcohol–25% ammonia (1.3:1:1), Šrámek examined practically all direct azo dyes of known structure and observed the following relationships between structure and chromatographic behavior.[2,10,11,24] (1) Acid azo dyes always have higher R_F than substantive dyes. (2) Symmetric dyes usually have lower R_F than unsymmetric dyes. (3) The longer the chain of conjugated double bonds running through the entire molecule, the lower the R_F because of the greater substantivity. The longer molecules are more easily polarized and so there is greater possibility of mutual interaction with permanent dipoles of the hydroxyl groups of cellulose. (4) With dyes of the same basic structure with a larger number of azo groups, the R_F decreases owing to increasing substantivity, if a benzene nucleus is gradually replaced by naphthalene, anthracene, or other more condensed aromatic ring. This is again an effect of increasing polarizability of the dye molecule. (5) With dyes having an interrupted chain of conjugated double bonds, the R_F is large in comparison with the R_F expected from the number of N=N groups. (6) Substantivity of the dye becomes more pronounced and the R_F decreases as the dipole moment of the dye increases. (7) Dyes containing COOH, SO_3H, OH, and OCH_3 groups possess lower R_F. The R_F decreases in proportion to the number of these groups. (8) Dyes containing SO_3H, COOH, and NO_2 groups connected with auxochromic groups through a system of conjugated double bonds possess lower R_F. (9) If a SO_3H group is shifted further from the azo group in a position isomer, the R_F decreases as a result of an increase in substantivity. (10) Specific features of constitution, above all the presence of thiazole rings in the dye molecule, decrease the R_F owing to an increase in substantivity. (11) Dyes containing amide groups as connecting bridges in the chain have higher R_F than analogous dyes with an uninterrupted chain of N=N bonds. (12) The presence of a s-triazine ring increases the R_F. (13) Condensed stilbene and oxygenated azo dyes always possess higher substantivity and a lower R_F. (14) 1:1 metal complexes of o,o'-dihydroxyazo dyes have lower R_F than the 1:2 complexes, owing to replacement of sulfonic groups by sulfonamide groups in the latter.

1.4.2 Acid Dyes. Acid dyes have been chromatographed chiefly to determine their purity and identity,[2,11,18,20,23,25-31] but also to follow the extent of metallization in dyes,[32] and to identify the substituents in anthraquinone,[2,10,30] azo,[2,10,33] and arylmethane dyes.[2,10] Dyes with good leveling characteristics for covering tippiness of wool have been selected on the strength of their chromatographic behavior.[34] Chromatography assists in selecting acid dyes for dyeing polyamide.[24]

Gemzová and Gasparič[30] established relationships between the chromatographic behavior and chemical constitution of anthraquinone acid dyes, using the following solvent systems: (1) n-propanol–25% ammonia (2:1); (2) n-propanol–lauryl alcohol–25% ammonia (240 ml:137 g:120 ml) (chromatography paper impregnated with 5% lauryl alcohol in ethanol); (3) pyridine–n-amyl alcohol–25% ammonia (11:10:10); (4) n-propanol–25% acetic acid (2:1); (5) methanol–1 N hydrochloric acid/lauryl alcohol (1:1) (chromatography paper impregnated with 5% lauryl alcohol in ethanol); (6) ethanol–25% ammonia/lauryl alcohol (1:1) (chromatography paper impregnated with 50% lauryl alcohol in ethanol). Using pyridine–n-amyl (or isoamyl) alcohol–25% ammonia (13:10:10), Šrámek derived the following relationships.[2,10] (a) Acid anthraquinone dyes usually have higher R_F and behave similarly to acid monoazo dyes. (b) There are no marked differences in the R_F of individual derivatives. The R_F is highest with the arylaminoanthraquinone sulfonic acids having an alkyl chain, lower with arylaminoanthraquinones possessing a sulfonic group on the anthraquinone nucleus, and lowest with aminohydroxyanthraquinone sulfonic acids and heterocyclic derivatives. (c) With an increasing number of OH, SO_3H, and NO_2 groups on the anthraquinone nucleus or in substituent rings, the R_F decreases. (d) Dyes containing two aryl or alkyl groups or two arylamino or alkylamino groups have lower R_F than dyes containing one such substituent. Dyes containing o-aminothioglycol groups behave similarly. (e) In the group of amino- and arylaminoanthraquinone sulfonic acids, dyes having long alkyl and hydroaromatic groups have higher R_F than dyes without these substituents. (f) Heterocycles with a ring condensed to positions 1, 2 or 2, 3 on the anthraquinone ring possess lower R_F than anthrone derivatives with a heterocyclic ring linked to positions 1, 9. Generally, heterocyclic rings cause a decrease in R_F. (g) Hydroxyanthraquinone sulfonic acids (mordant dyes) have a medium to low R_F. The R_F decreases with an increasing number of OH groups.

1.4.3 Reactive Dyes. Chromatography is used for identifying and estimating the purity of reactive dyes,[2,10,24,29,35–42] determining constitution,[37,43] studying reactivity,[44–66] determining relative substantivity,[8,15,17] and identifying reactive dyes from stripped dyeings.[67]

Certain problems are encountered in connection with the stability of reactive dyes under the conditions of chromatographic separation. It is always necessary first to examine the way in which their reactivity and substantivity are affected in the chromatographic system. In nearly all cases a compromise between the stability of reactive dyes and the separating efficiency of the chosen solvent system must be made.[24,35-37] The problem of the kinetics of the hydrolysis and the reactivity of these dyes has been the subject of numerous theoretical studies,[35,36,44-49,51-63,66] and the published results confirm the complexity of the problem of the optimal conditions for the chromatography of reactive dyes.

Šrámek[24] found that alkaline as well as acidic and neutral systems effect a change of the reactive dyes (hydrolysis or reaction with cellulose), especially during the prolonged period required for developing chromatograms. With some systems the substantivity of the reactive dye is the more important factor. DMF forms an adduct with some dyes having a diazine reactive system. In all solvent systems containing primary and secondary alcohols, alcoholysis can occur. Equally detrimental are alkaline systems. Apart from the hydrolytic effect, the alkalinity causes interaction of highly reactive dyes with the paper. Alkaline hydrolysis is effective with dyes that react by nucleophilic addition; acidic systems hydrolyze dyes that react by nucleophilic substitution.

Solvent systems should be selected which produce reproducible changes in dyes. Alternatively, it is advantageous to chromatograph them after hydrolysis of the reactive groups, which renders possible an accurate appraisal of the dye chromophore.[37] The following solvent systems are suitable[24,37,41,47]: 25% ammonia; 25% ammonia–pyridine–water (1:1:4); n-butanol–ethanol–water (4:1:1); n-butanol–ethylene glycol–water (1:1:1); n-butanol–pyridine–water (1:1:1); n-butanol–DMF–water (1:0.5:1 or 11:3:11); pyridine–isoamyl alcohol–25% ammonia (1.3:1:1); ethylene glycol–water (4:1); n-propanol–acetic acid–water (5:2:1)[37]; n-propanol–water (2:1).

1.4.4 Fluorescent Brightening Agents. When chromatographing these products, we must prevent cis–trans changes taking place by the action of UV radiation. cis Isomers invariably possess a higher R_F than the trans, the reason being their difference in substantivity; trans isomers are planar and have high substantivity.[68-70] Fluorescent brightening agents must be chromatographed in the dark; the stock solution and the chromatogram must also be kept in the dark. When stilbene types are chromatographed under exposure to light, eight or possibly more spots appear on the chromatogram, displaying a mixture of trans and cis isomers. The actual optical brightener, which is prepared by a multistage synthesis, contains products of the individual stages of the synthesis which are subject to stereoisomeric changes.

For the chromatography of optical brightening agents several methods have been elaborated.[24, 67, 69, 71-74] Lanter[69] recommends the following systems for the individual types of brighteners: for coumarins 10% sodium carbonate and DMF (9:1); for oxazoles DMF and 1 N formic acid (8:2); and for stilbenes and imidazoles, n-butyl acetate–water–pyridine (4:1.5:1). Brown[67] chromatographs cellulose brighteners with benzyl alcohol–DMF–water (3:2:2). Latinák[71] recommends for stilbenes n-butanol–pyridine–water (1:1:1). Šrámek[24] uses for stilbenes and imidazoles pyridine–isoamyl alcohol–25% ammonia (1.3:1:1), and for the separation of *trans* from *cis* isomers 2% sodium monohydrogen phosphate in 5% ammonia, which is sensitive to differences in substantivity. Gasparič[72] elaborated a method for the disperse types of brightening agents, using paper impregnated with 50% DMF in ethanol. After impregnation the paper is dried 10 minutes at room temperature. For the descending development n-heptane or n-hexane is used.

For brightening agents with a low R_F, paper impregnated with 20% formamide in ethanol is used; development is with n-heptane or n-hexane. Similarly, brighteners having a high R_F in the above chromatographic system can be advantageously chromatographed on paper impregnated with 10% paraffin oil in hexane and developed in 80–95% methanol. The chromatograms are evaluated in UV light.

1.4.5 Solubilized Vat Dyes (Indigosols). Because oxidation by light can occur, chromatograms must be developed in the dark. Autoxidation proceeds continuously during the development of the chromatogram, numerous spots appearing when sensitive indigosols are chromatographed in daylight. When chromatographing without exposure to light, we usually find that the dye is pure.

PC has been used to identify the dispersing and stabilizing agents present in indigosols (4-dimethylaminobenzenesulfonic acid, glucose, molasses, urea).[75] PC of indigosols has been described by the ascending technique on SS 2043b paper with n-butanol–acetic acid–water (4:1:5) and n-butanol–pyridine–water (4:1:1).[76] Šrámek[77] chromatographed all indigosols in *CI* by the descending technique, using the following solvent systems: (1) 25% ammonia–methanol–water (1:2:3); (2) pyridine–isoamyl alcohol–25% ammonia (1.3:1:1); (3) methanol–acetic acid–water (4:1:1). With Solvent 1 the R_F is dependent on the chemical structure of the dyes, their functional groups and substituents. Solvent 2 gives excellent separation suitable for examining the purity and identity of the indigosols, but the relation between the R_F and dye structure is not as marked as Solvent 1. Solvent 3 is suitable only for some dyes, because in acidic solvent systems gradual hydrolysis of the leuco sulfuric ester takes place with formation of monoester, which is exceedingly susceptible to oxidation by atmospheric oxygen to semiquinone derivatives. Alkaline systems minimize the possibility of oxidation.

Centrifugal chromatography was carried out with the same solvent systems on a pressureless apparatus with central spot development.[6] The chromatograms were cut from Whatman No. 1 paper and separation was performed during 45 minutes at 600 rpm.

With a few exceptions, the color of the indigosols is very faint, thus making detection of the chromatogram necessary. This can be done by spraying with warm (40°) 2% sodium nitrite in 2% hydrochloric acid, when the color of the vat dye immediately appears. Alternatively, the dried chromatograms can be exposed to UV radiation.

With Solvent 1 the following relationships were established between chromatographic behavior and dye structure.[77] (a) In all instances it is obvious that the chromatographic behavior of the parent vat dyes is analogous, the size of the dye molecule being of decisive influence. Dyes with a simple structure possess the highest R_F, decreasing with increasing size of the molecule as a result of increasing dye adsorption. (b) Simpler indigoid, thioindigoid, and arylaminoquinone dyes have a higher R_F than the more complex anthraquinone dyes. (c) Thioindigoid dyes have a higher R_F than indole–thionaphthene dyes and "miscellaneous dyes" (CSD II, pp. 1041–1044). (d) Symmetric indigoid dyes usually have a higher R_F than unsymmetrical dyes. (e) Dibenzanthrones have higher R_F than iso-dibenzanthrones. (f) In dyes with the same carbon skeleton, an increase in the number of substituents, e.g., Cl, Br, Me, or OMe, decreases the R_F.

1.4.6 Solubilized Sulfur Dyes. Chromatography of these dyes is as complicated as that of the insoluble sulfur dyes on account of the size of the molecules. The method elaborated for the insoluble sulfur dyes (Section 1.5.4) or descending chromatography with the following solvent systems can be used: pyridine–n-butanol–water (2:1:1 or 3:1:1); pyridine–ethyl acetate (1:1 or 2:1); pyridine–benzene–ethyl acetate (2:2:1).

1.4.7 Cationic Dyes. Numerous authors have dealt with the chromatography of basic dyes.[2,10,24,25,29,78,79] Triphenylmethane dyes may be chromatographed as carbinol bases or as the dyes, in which the anion is oxalate, perchlorate, or chloride. In an acidic medium the amino groups on the triphenylmethane skeleton become protonated, with other changes (e.g., color) taking place. For this reason it is advantageous to chromatograph basic triphenylmethane dyes in an ammoniacal medium in which the dyes are converted to carbinol bases. Since these bases, as well as the dyes, are readily soluble in alcohol, lauryl alcohol is used as stationary phase

(2–5% solution in ethanol), with methanol–ammonia (1:1) as mobile phase.[78] The detection of carbinol bases takes place spontaneously when the chromatogram is allowed to dry freely, or it may be exposed to hydrochloric or acetic acid vapors. Gasparič and Matrka[78] also described the chromatography of nigrosine and quinoneimine dyes. The alcohol-soluble nigrosine dyes are suitably chromatographed using lauryl alcohol for the stationary phase and ethanol–ammonia or ethanol–1 N hydrochloric acid (1:1) for the mobile phase. The quinoneimine dyes, such as indophenols, are conveniently chromatographed on paper impregnated with 5% lauryl alcohol by employing ethanol–phosphate buffer pH 6.5 (3:7) as the mobile phase. Formamide/hexane–benzene is sometimes used instead.

Using the descending technique on Whatman No. 1 paper and pyridine–isoamyl alcohol–25% ammonia (1.3:1:1), Šrámek[2,10,24] made the following observations on the chromatographic behavior of basic dyes in comparison with related acid and mordant dyes.

Arylmethane and Related Dyes. (a) Acidic arylmethane dyes always have lower R_F than basic dyes. (b) With an increasing number of SO_3H and COOH groups, the R_F decreases proportionately, the effect of the COOH group being more pronounced. With triphenylmethane dyes the effect of the SO_3H group on the decrease of R_F may be partly explained by its formation of an inner anhydride with the carbinol. (c) The *p*-phenetidine, *p*-anisidine, and *p*-toluidine residues and substituents such as CH_3, Cl, and OCH_3 have no appreciable influence on R_F. The presence of pyrazole or indole derivatives in the triphenylmethane skeleton causes reduction of R_F (mordant and acid dyes). (d) Diphenylmethane dyes possess lower R_F than substituted diamino derivatives of triphenylmethane. (e) Triamino derivatives of triphenylmethane have generally lower R_F than diamino derivatives. (f) Aminohydroxy derivatives of triphenylmethane possess lower R_F than the di- and triamino derivatives. Mordant dyes containing COOH groups have lower R_F than other acid dyes. (g) Of the hydroxy derivatives of triphenylmethane, mordant dyes have lower R_F than acid dyes. (h) Among derivatives of diphenylnaphthylmethane, basic dyes behave similarly to di- and triamino derivatives of triphenylmethane. Acid and mordant dyes have lower R_F than basic dyes, but higher than mordant dyes or hydroxy derivatives of triphenylmethane. (i) Miscellaneous triarylmethane derivatives having a substituted indole residue or a pyrazole ring (e.g., 3-methyl-1-phenyl-5-pyrazolone) have low R_F. (j) Xanthene dyes have generally lower R_F than diphenyl- and triphenylmethane dyes. Hydroxyphthaleins and anthrahydroxyphthaleins with a concealed anthraquinone skeleton have the lowest R_F. (k) 9-Phenylacridine dyes have the same R_F as the corresponding triphenylmethane dyes.

Polymethine and Azamethine Dyes. The R_F of polymethine dyes is higher than that of azamethine dyes. The R_F is generally high, with the exception of Cr complexes and dyes having substituents in the side chain, such as heterocycles and condensed nuclei, which have lower R_F.

Thiazole Dyes. The R_F is low owing to the effect of the thiazole ring, depending on the number of such rings. Usually these dyes are mixtures.

Quinoneimines, Azines, Oxazines, Thiazines. (*a*) The R_F of indamines and indophenols is high, owing to the basic character and simple structure, (*b*) In the azine group of dyes the R_F of indulines and nigrosines is low. Safranines have a higher R_F than aposafranines. (*c*) In the oxazine group monooxazines have higher R_F than dioxazines. Basic dyes have a higher R_F, and mordant dyes have a lower R_F. Dioxazines are substantive dyes and the R_F depends chiefly on the number of SO_3H groups. (*d*) Thiazines have R_F of the same order as monooxazines.

Ciglar et al.[79] chromatographed basic dyes on paper impregnated with a 5% solution of cetyl alcohol in ethanol, using the solvent system ethanol–ammonia–water (2:2:1). Jungbeck[29] chromatographed basic dyes with two systems: methanol–water–glacial acetic acid (8:1:1) and methanol–5 N ammonia (8:1). Kacprzak and Olszewski[25] chromatographed basic dyes using ethanol–water–glacial acetic acid (7:2:1). For cationic dyes for polyacrylonitrile fiber, butyl acetate–pyridine–water (3:4:4) has been found efficient.

1.4.8 Azoic Components and Dyes. For azoic diazo and coupling components and for their ready mixtures (azoic compositions), several methods have been found suitable for the determination of their purity and identity.[10,80–84] PC has also been used for substantivity assessments of naphthols.[10,14,15,24]

Coupling Components. Pagani[80] chromatographed naphthols in ethanolic sodium hydroxide on Schleicher-Schull No. 2040a and No. 2043 papers, using pure methanol as eluent. The spots were detected by spraying with a 1% solution of a diazonium salt and then drying at 40–50°. In agreement with Kitahara and Hiyama[14] Pagani found that the R_F of naphthols decreases with increasing substantivity. Kitahara and Hiyama[14] chromatographed naphthols in ethanol–5% ammonia (1:3) on Whatman paper No. 4. Kiel and Kuypers[81] used acetylated Schleicher-Schull 80/100 paper and THF–water (80:54). Gasparič[82] used the ascending technique with paper impregnated with 10% 1-bromonaphthalene in chloroform, developing with 80% acetic acid. Plesník and Čepčiansky[15] used the descending technique on Whatman No. 1 paper and 25% ammonia–water–ethanol (2:1:2). From the R_F they calculated the substantivity of the naphthols. Perkavec and Perpar[83] employed n-butanol–glacial acetic acid–water (4:1:5).

Azoic Diazo Components. Kitahara and Hiyama[14] used 2 N hydrochloric acid or hydrochloric acid–n-butanol (4:1). Ethanol–pyridine–water (4:9:10) has been used.[83] With acetylated paper THF–water (80:54) is a suitable solvent system.[81]

Stabilized Diazonium Salts. Aqueous 1% solutions are spotted. Suitable solvent systems are n-butanol–glacial acetic acid–water (4:1:5)[83] and 1% hydrochloric acid.

Azoic Compositions. These are chromatographed in the same manner as the individual components. Use is made of the fact that naphthols possess a lower R_F owing to their substantivity, whereas the diazo components usually have a higher R_F. After complete separation the chromatogram is inspected in UV light or sprayed alternately with a naphthol (for the top part) and a diazonium salt (for the bottom part).

For developing the chromatogram pyridine–25% ammonia–water (6:1:1),[3] methanol–ethyl acetate (1:1), and methanol–methyl ethyl ketone (5:2)[83] are suitable.

1.5   Water-Insoluble Dyes

Disperse and solvent dyes can be chromatographed in organic solvents; the method does not differ fundamentally from the PC of water-soluble dyes. Vat and sulfur dyes are converted to water-soluble leuco compounds by alkaline reduction, and the procedure is complicated by the necessity to prevent oxidation during PC. Most complicated of all is the PC of organic pigments, which resolve with great difficulty, and it has to be adapted to the chemical composition of the pigment and its solubility.

1.5.1   Disperse Dyes. Because of the importance of these dyes for the coloration of synthetic fibers, their chromatographic analysis has interested many authors. The methods described may be divided into four groups.

(a) In the first group standard chromatography paper is the stationary phase and various mixtures of polar and nonpolar organic solvents are employed for the solvent system. These methods are not suitable for a systematic analysis of disperse dyes or for an accurate study of the relationship between chromatographic behavior of dyes and their structures.

Zahn,[85] in probably the first paper on the chromatography of disperse dyes, separated some Celliton dyes (BASF) by the ascending technique using ethylene glycol as eluent. Elliot and Telesz attempted such correlation, using light petroleum (b.p. 65–75°) saturated with methanol.[86] Jungbeck[29] used methanol–water–acetic acid (8:1:1), as well as 80% aqueous DMF. Brown[20] made an extensive study of the descending technique with two solvent systems, cyclohexane–glacial acetic acid–water (25:24:1) and cyclohexane–formic acid–water (4:3:1), and of the ascending technique with cyclohexane–dimethylaniline (3:1). Šrámek elaborated the saturation of hydrophobic eluents with water [light petroleum, benzene, or carbon tetrachloride–methanol–water (2:2:1)].

(b) In the second type of methods, paper of DP 500–600 determined by the nitration method is used for the stationary phase, with aqueous pyridine as eluent.[2,7,86–88] Very satisfactory separation of disperse dyes can thus be obtained. For a systematic analysis Šrámek used filter paper Schleicher-Schull 589[3] (blue ribbon) by the descending or ascending technique. The start-to-solvent front distance was 400 mm. The dyes (0.05 mg) were applied as 1% acetone solutions and the chromatograms were developed for 12 hours at 20–22°. For both azo and anthraquinone dyes pyridine–water was appropriate, but in the proportion 1:3 and 1:5, respectively. Practically all CI Disperse Dyes were analyzed by this method. The following relations were found between their chromatographic behavior and chemical constitution. (1) Disazo dyes possess lower R_F than monoazo dyes. (2) Increase in molarity of azo and anthraquinone derivatives tends to lower the R_F. (3) Anthraquinone dyes are adsorbed to a lesser degree, therefore possessing a higher R_F than azo dyes, nitro dyes, methine derivatives, and dyes of the arylaminoquinone and aminonaphthalimide groups. (4) Increase in the number of OMe and Me groups and halogens present reduces the R_F of azo dyes. (5) With the anthraquinone dyes, considerable decrease in R_F is due to alkylation and arylation of amino groups. With aminoanthraquinones the R_F decreases with increase in the number of amino groups. Ethanolamine derivatives have a higher R_F than amines. (6) Methine derivatives possess a lower R_F than nitro dyes and dyes of the arylaminoquinone and aminonaphthalimide groups. (7) The position and character of the substituents in the aromatic nuclei considerably influence the R_F. With compounds having the same basic skeleton but substituents of different character, dyes with smaller dipole moments show a higher R_F.

The mechanism of the chromatographic separation of disperse dyes in aqueous pyridine can be explained by adsorption, or by partition chromatography where separation into two aqueous phases occurs. There is an analogy in solvent systems of aqueous solutions of alcohols, as observed by Synge and Tiselius.[1a] Consden also explains the mechanism of the one-phase aqueous solvent system by the formation of two phases (cf. Martin, Moore, and Stein in ref. 5). The symmetrical shape of the separated spots of dyes on the chromatogram and the independence of R_F of the concentration of the dyes, where pyridine solvent systems are used, are in agreement with the principles of partition chromatography.

(c) Chromatography on acetylated paper is a suitable method for determining the purity of disperse dyes,[89,90] and for systematic analysis.[91]

(d) The last group of methods utilizes chromatography on impregnated paper. Johnson and Telesz[92] chromatographed disperse dyes on paper impregnated with petroleum, using ethanol–water–acetic acid (20:14:1) as solvent system. Harris and Lindley[93] impregnated paper with a 1% solution of sec-cellulose acetate in acetone, using as solvent system butyl acetate–pyridine–water (1:5:10). Brown[20] used reverse-phase partition chromatography on silicone-treated paper, using as solvent system chloroform–glacial

Table 3.3 Chromatographic Analysis of Disperse Dyes on Different Chromatography Papers

Commercial Name	CI	$S_1{}^a$ Color of band	R_F	$S_2{}^b$ Color of band	R_F
Celliton Fast Yellow RR	10345	Yellow	0.55	Yellow	0.29
Celliton Fast Orange GR	11005	Dull orange	0.00	Orange	0.11[c]
		Orange	0.51	Orange	0.50
		Orange	0.87[c]		
Dispersol Fast Scarlet B	11110	Pink	0.23	Red	0.49
		Pink	0.28[c]		
		Red	0.59		
		Pink	0.68		
Celliton Fast Rubine 3B	11215	Rubine	0.62	Orange	0.09[c]
				Red	0.41[c]
				Red	0.53
Celliton Yellow 5G	12790	Yellow	0.63		
		Yellow	0.87[c]	Yellow	0.45
Dispersol Fast Orange B	26080	Orange	0.00	Orange	0.19
		Orange	0.09		
Celliton Fast Green 3B	56060	Blue green	0.69	Blue	0.04
		Green	0.87	Green	0.48
		Yellow	0.90		
Duranol Brilliant Yellow 6G	58900	Yellow	0.25	Yellow	0.39
Duranol Red 2B	60710	Red	0.73	Red	0.48[c]
				Red	0.54

(Continued)

acetic acid–water (1:1:1). Dokunikhin and Kolokolov[94] separated chlorinated derivatives of anthraquinone on variously impregnated paper (paraffin oil, 1-bromonaphthalene, anisole). The solvents were 60 and 80% acetic acid for the first two, and n-hexane for the last.

Gasparič and Táborská[95] elaborated a theoretical treatment of the separation phenomena using the ascending or descending technique on paper impregnated with a 10% solution of 1-bromonaphthalene in chloroform. The solvent was 1-bromonaphthalene/pyridine–water (1:1 or 2:1). Gasparič et al.[95,96] used this method for analyzing most CI Disperse Dyes. They also synthesized 88 insoluble azo compounds and examined the relationships between their chromatographic behavior and structure, and found that the validity of the Martin relationship concerning the additivity of group constants in paper chromatography is limited to a narrow group of compounds defined by the same molecular interactions. Table 3.3 gives

Table 3.3 (Continued)

Commercial Name	CI	$S_1{}^a$ Color of band	R_F	$S_2{}^b$ Color of band	R_F
Cibacet Violet 2R	61100	Violet	0.00	Violet	0.39^c
		Violet	0.73	Violet	0.78
		Violet	0.81		
Celliton Fast Blue FW	61510	Blue	0.34	Violet	0.30^c
		Blue	0.54	Blue	0.71
		Blue	0.64	Blue	0.97
		Blue	0.80		
Celliton Fast Blue FFG	62050	Blue	0.08	Blue	0.08
		Blue	0.48	Blue	0.43
		Dull blue	0.58^c		
		Dull blue	0.65		
		Dull violet	0.82		
Celliton Blue ex.	64500	Grey	0.00	Blue	0.87
		Blue	0.29		
		Violet	0.58		
		Blue	0.83		

^{a} S_1 = N 60 paper, running length 45 cm. Eluent: pyridine–water (1:3 for azo dyes and 1:5 for anthraquinone dyes); descending method.
^{b} S_2 = Whatman No. 3 paper, running length 43 cm. Eluent: 1-bromonaphthalene/pyridine–water (2:1); descending method.
^{c} Spot very faint.

a comparison of the behavior of disperse dyes on two chromatography papers and two developing systems.[24]

1.5.2 Solvent Dyes. Because they are mostly mono- and disazo dyes and anthraquinone dyes of the same character as disperse dyes, methods for disperse dyes are applicable. Particularly suitable are methods using impregnated paper, since they allow good separation of arylmethane dyes. For systematic analysis the Gasparič method[78] is especially suitable. Very satisfactory results have also been obtained by the ascending method on paper impregnated with a 5–10% solution of paraffin oil in benzene, in conjunction with a solvent system of paraffin oil and methanol (1:4).[97]

1.5.3 Vat Dyes. Rao, Shah, and Venkataraman chromatographed vat dyes after reduction with aqueous sodium dithionite and tetraethylene-pentamine.[98] Klingsberg[99] carried out the separation in an atmosphere of nitrogen. For quantitative determination the dyes were extracted from the chromatograms with DMF and the solutions were evaluated spectrophotometrically. Tajiri[100] prepared vat dyes for chromatography as the esters with Leukotrope W (BASF). Some vat dyes are soluble enough in organic solvents for PC.[76]

The following method elaborated by Šrámek[88,101] gives consistent results. The dyes are used as 1% solutions of the vats prepared by normal technical methods. The eluting solvent, freshly prepared, consists of the following, added in the given order: distilled water (32 ml), Turkey Red oil or sodium alkylsulfonate (1% solution; 48 ml), 35% sodium hydroxide (4 ml), sodium dithionite (4 g), and pyridine (16 ml). Four to eight test tubes, each containing 10 ml solvent, are completely immersed in a thermostat at 80°. The chromatogram (1 × 16-cm strip) is suspended from a hook in a tightly fitting rubber stopper and kept taut by small glass weights. The vat (5–10 ml) is applied to the starting line, and the strip is placed immediately in a test tube, so that the reducing solvent starts to ascend the paper. Although some oxidation of the leuco compound occurs, the solvent regenerates it quickly. The separation is complete within 2 hours (4 hours for 25-cm strips). The chromatogram is then exposed to air and rinsed in water to remove residual solvent. All the important CI Vat Dyes of known constitution, as well as some mixtures, have been examined thus. The results are reproducible and the method is sufficiently sensitive to permit separation of structurally similar dyes. The R_F depends on the size of the molecule and its structure. Large molecules travel slowly owing to enhanced substantivity for the paper and decreased solubility in the mobile phase. The PC behavior of vat dyes can be divided into five groups, as in Table 3.4. The following general conclusions regarding chemical structures can be drawn. (1) Substitution by Me, OMe, or PhCONH groups

Table 3.4 PC Behavior of Vat Dyes (Šrámek)

		Examples	
Group	Approximate R_F	CI Vat	CI
1	0	Orange 16	69540
1, 2	0–0.1	Yellow 9	66510
		Red 10	67000
		Green 3; 5	69500; 69520
		Black 8; 25	71000; 69525
2, 3	0.1–0.5	Yellow 28	69000
		Orange 2; 15; 11	59705; 69025; 70805
		Red 14	71110
		Black 9	65230
3	0.5	Yellow 1	70600
		Red 18; 13	60705; 70320
		Blue 4; 11; 7; 29	69800; 69815; 70305; 74140
		Green 11	69850
3, 4	0.5–0.7	Yellow 20	68420
2, 3, 4		Yellow 12; 26	65405; 65410
		Red 23; 29	71130; 71140
		Blue 26	60015
1, 2, 3, 4		Green 1; 9	59825; 59850
		Brown 39; 45; 9	59270; 59500; 71025
		Black 16; 29	59855; 65225
4	0.6–0.7	Violet 19	52100
		Sulfur Blue 6	53460
4, 5	0.7–1	Red 41	73300
		Blue 1; 5	73000; 73065
		Brown 5	73410

reduces the R_F; substitution by halogens increases it. (2) Dyes containing a thiazole, oxazole, acridone, s-triazine, or N,N'-dihydropyrazine ring have lower R_F than dyes without such a ring, the thiazole ring being the most effective. (3) Increasing the number of keto groups progressively reduces the R_F. (4) Dibenzanthrones have higher R_F than isodibenzanthrones. (5) Thioindigoid dyes have higher R_F than indigoid dyes. (6) Among the naphthoylene imidazoles, the *cis* isomers have higher R_F than the *trans*. Using an aqueous cellosolve solution of sodium hydroxide and dithionite as the eluent, a correlation has been found between R_F and affinity for cellulose.[102]

1.5.4 Sulfur Dyes. These dyes have been subjected to radial chromatography in their leuco form, using sodium sulfide and dithionite in pyridine and methanol. To prevent oxidation, the chromatogram is positioned
between two glass plates.[103,104] Šrámek's vat dye method can also be
used.[88,101] Sulfur dyes are divided into two typical groups: (a) those that
elute only with difficulty from the starting point (30–60 minutes) and (b)
those that move a considerable distance (10–15 minutes). Group a includes
thiazole dyes (yellows, oranges, and browns), and thionated mono- and
binuclear-substituted amino and nitro compounds (CI 53005–53160), polycyclic compounds (CI 53320–53335), and acridine, azine, oxazone, and
thiazone derivatives (CI 53680–53830; browns, bordeaux, and violets).
Group b includes thiazine dyes (blues, greens, and blacks) and thionated
phenols and naphthalene derivatives (CI 53165–53300) and indophenols
(CI 53400–53640).

Because of the complex nature of sulfur dyes, the chromatograms
(especially of group b dyes) are usually composed of a series of bands.

1.5.5 Pigments. Success in separation by PC and TLC depends on
suitable solvents.[105] According to their solubility, it is possible to divide
pigments into three groups: (a) soluble in chloroform (e.g., CI Pigment
Yellow 1, 3, 5, 74, and 98; Orange 1; Red 7–12, 14, 48, 53, 54, and 68;
Violet 28; Blue 18, 56, and 61; Brown 1); (b) soluble in DMF, DMSO,
or pyridine (e.g., CI Pigment Yellow 12–14, 17, 106, 109, 117, and 120;
Orange 36, 38, and 43; Red 31, 122, 123, 146, 147, 149, 168, 170, 171, 183,
187–190, and 194; Violet 19, 23, 32, and 36; Brown 25); and (c) insoluble
and cannot be analyzed chromatographically.

For pigments soluble in pyridine, paper impregnated with a 10% solution of 1-bromonaphthalene in ethanol is used.[106] Chromatograms are
developed in pyridine–water (3:2).

Since R_F values of pigments are usually low, development by the descending method with overflow is recommended.

1.6 Special Combination Dyes for Mixtures
of Synthetic and Natural Fibers

Since the textile industry is producing textiles from fiber blends (e.g., wool
with cellulose, polyester with cellulose, polyester with wool) and these
materials are being dyed or printed, suitable dyes are required that can
dye both fibrous substrates the same shade. The selection of these dyes is
rather critical and special dyes have been prepared by the dye manufacturers for this purpose. These special dyes are really mixed dyes, and they
contain the dye for the native as well as the synthetic fiber.

1.6.1 Dyes for Wool–Cellulose Fiber Blends. The situation is complicated because the mixture is composed of acid dyes and direct dyes, both of which are readily soluble in water. The direct dyes are common direct dyes or lightfast dyes, and possibly metallized dyes. For dyeing wool, simple acid dyes or 1:1 and 1:2 metal–dye complexes or acid-mordant dyes are used. Chemically they are mostly mono- to polyazo dyes, anthraquinone derivatives, and arylmethane dyes.

The chromatographic separation can be effected by systems based on the differentiation of the dye molecule size (e.g., the solvent system pyridine–isoamyl alcohol–25% ammonia, 1.3:1:1); the overflow technique is used mostly. Thus a green dye was found to be a mixture of CI Direct Blue 78, Direct Yellow 29, Acid Green 25, and Acid Yellow 25.

The dyes can also be separated according to their substantivity for cellulose, using 2% sodium monohydrogen phosphate in 5% ammonia.

Because half-wool dyes are frequently very complex mixtures (often prepared from nonuniform dis- or polyazo dyes), it is necessary to use a high-capacity chromatogram paper that allows an intensive deposit of the analyzed dye. This improves the "legibility" of the chromatogram, rendering possible identification of even very small quantities of dyes contained in a mixture.

Two-dimensional chromatography can be used successfully, whereby in one direction a solvent system is used to separate dyes according to their substantivity for cellulose, and in the other direction a system to separate dyes according to the size and complexity of their molecules. Also radial chromatography is suitable in some cases because the individual zones of the separated dye are very distinct.

1.6.2 Dyes for Polyester–Cellulose Fiber Blends. These dyes usually contain a disperse dye for polyester and a reactive, vat, or solubilized vat dye for cellulose. For both fiber components dyes are chosen that dye the same shade.

Mixtures of Disperse and Vat Dyes. A dispersion of the dye in water is centrifugally separated for 15 minutes at 15,000 rpm. The water layer is decanted, and the sediment is repeatedly dispersed in water and centrifugally separated. After removing the dispersing agent, the disperse dye is extracted by methanol or acetone, and a solution in 90% aqueous pyridine is chromatographed by the ascending or descending technique on Whatman No. 3 paper impregnated with a 7.5% solution of 1-bromonaphthalene in ethanol, using pyridine–water (1:1) saturated with 1-bromonaphthalene for development.

For chromatographic analysis of the residual vat dye the ascending technique is used at 80°, as described in Section 1.5.3.

Mixtures of Disperse and Reactive Dyes.   A dispersion of the dye in water is centrifuged for 15 minutes at 15,000 rpm. The water layer contains the dissolved reactive dye and dispersing agents. The residual pigment of the disperse dye is dissolved in 90% pyridine and chromatographed.

The reactive dyes are chromatographed by the ascending technique using Whatman No. 1 paper and the following three solvent systems: pyridine–isoamyl alcohol–25% ammonia (1.3:1:1); DMF–n-butanol–water (3:11:11); 2% sodium monohydrogen phosphate in 5% ammonia. The third system serves to determine the relative substantivity of the reactive dyes which may frequently help to improve the accuracy of the identification.

The same procedure of separation by dissolving in water is used to identify mixtures of disperse dyes with solubilized vat dyes.

1.7   Assessment of Textile Application
Properties of Dyes

Although the chief objective of PC is the assessment of purity and identity of dyes, a closely related field where PC is used is in studying the application properties of dyes.[24]

The mere determination of the purity of a dye may be able to solve a number of problems appearing when dyeing with complex dye mixtures, such as those encountered in connection with the reproducibility of the shade. Dyes having markedly different R_F values differ in the characteristics of their dyeing isotherms and their rates of dyeing. This can be exemplified by vat dyes of the anthraquinonecarbazole group.

Artym and Moryganov[102] established a relationship between the R_F and the affinity of vat dyes. They were able to show that with vat dyes having a similar chemical constitution a correlation exists between the affinity value and the R_F, where increasing affinity of the leuco compound of the vat dye corresponds to a decrease of the R_F. They also derived from the chromatographic behavior of vat dyes their leveling properties.

With vat dyes it is further possible by means of chromatography to study all changes that take place owing to a departure from the optimal dyeing conditions (e.g., overreduction, overoxidation, oversaponification, dehalogenation, and enol–keto rearrangement).[24]

Numerous authors have found that under favorable chromatographic conditions a relationship exists between the R_F of a direct dye and its substantivity for cellulose.[12–17,19,24] From the R_F it is possible to calculate the relationship between substantivity and the R_M, and to apply the same for the calculation of substantivity.

Plesník and Čepčiansky[15] based their calculations of the substantivity of naphthols on the observation that those with a high substantivity have a low R_F, as well as on Kitahara's observation[107] that a linear relationship exists between the affinities of direct dyes (with equal numbers of sulfonic groups) for cellulosic fiber and their R_M. The affinity of a dye for a fiber is defined as the difference between the standard chemical potential of the dye in the fiber and in the solvent.

Practical chromatographic substantivity determinations of naphthols have been carried out by descending chromatography on Whatman No. 1 paper with a solvent system of 25% ammonia–water–ethanol (1:1:1).[15]

In Table 3.5 the values of chromatographically determined substantivity of some naphthols are given.

PC has proved useful for the assessment of the substantive properties of reactive dyes, as first shown by Capponi and Barthold.[16] Šrámek[17] undertook to classify the entire European commercial ranges of reactive dyes. Using 2% sodium monohydrogen phosphate in 5% ammonia, he established a relationship between the chemical structure of reactive dyes and their substantivity. The substantivity is influenced by the character of the chromophore system as well as the reactive system. With reactive dyes having the same chromophore, substantivity for cellulose decreases with various reactive systems in the following sequence: dichlorotriazine; dichloroquinoxaline; dichlorophthalazine; bis-monochlorotriazine; monochlorotriazine; chlorobenzothiazole; dichloropyridazone; β-sulfato- or β-chloroethylsulfamoyl; acryloylamino; modified chloropyrimidine; vinyl

Table 3.5   The Relative Substantivity of Naphthols

| Naphthol | R_F | $R_M \times 10^2$ | Substantivity (%) | |
			Established Coloristically	Established Chromatographically
AS-D	0.533	5.74	18	17
AS	0.525	4.35	22	18
AS-LT	0.496	−0.70	22	22
AS-BG	0.412	−15.45	24	31
AS-RL	0.419	−14.20	25	31
AS-OL	0.474	−4.52	26	24
AS-BO	0.387	−19.98	35	35
AS-E	0.379	−21.45	37	36
AS-BT	0.296	−37.63	47	46
AS-LC	0.285	−39.95	50	48
AS-SW	0.237	−50.78	58	55
AS-S	0.166	−70.11	67	68

sulfone. It is chiefly the heterocyclic systems that have the greatest effect on substantivity.

It is obvious that substantivity is also influenced by the size and complexity of the chromophore. The highest substantivity is possessed by the black and brown disazo dyes and the turquoise blue phthalocyanine dyes; then the yellow monoazo dyes obtained by coupling C-acid with m-toluidine and C-acid with acetyl-m-phenylenediamine; the orange dyes formed by coupling C-acid with 2,5-dimethoxyaniline, or sulfanilic acid and orthanilic acid with J-acid; the scarlet dyes formed from p-anisidine-3-sulfonic acid and J-acid; the blue dyes formed from p-aminodiphenylamine-2-sulfonic acid and H-acid; condensation products of 4-bromo-1-aminoanthraquinone-2-sulfonic acid (bromamine acid) with m-phenylenediamine-4-sulfonic acid; and further rubine red metal complex dyes synthesized from 2-aminophenol-4-sulfonic acid and J-acid.

Especially high substantivity is possessed by the green dyes, representing an intramolecular mixture of a blue dye derived from bromamine acid and a yellow stilbene dye. Substantivity is least influenced by the pyrazolone chromophore, which is used for lemon yellow dyes, the 3-Me derivatives possessing lower substantivity than the carboxylic acids.

Substantivity is further influenced by the number and position of solubilizing groups, but chiefly by substitution of one Cl in the triazine component in dichlorotriazine dyes by metanilic or sulfanilic acid, which strongly enhances substantivity.

Substantivity becomes reduced by substitution of the NH_2 group forming a link between the chromophore and reactive system. Substantivity decreases by changing the bridging group NH to NR (e.g., NMe).

Based on a vast number of statistically processed values of substantivity of reactive dyes determined both chromatographically and by direct measurement, Šrámek[17] divided reactive dyes into five groups according to their substantivity. The R_F of dyes, determined in a solvent system of 2% sodium monohydrogen phosphate in 5% ammonia, characterizes directly the relative substantivity (Table 3.6).

The validity of this classification of substantive properties of reactive dyes was proved on a large group of acid and substantive dyes, whose substantivity was checked by dyeing.[108]

The advantage of the chromatographic substantivity test consists in its speed and the possibility of directly comparing the substantive properties of a large number of dyes. The substantivity of direct dyes[12,19] and indigosols[24] has thus been determined. PC has also proved useful in the study of the reactivity of reactive dyes with amino acids, polysaccharides, and alcohols. The formation of the respective bond is proved chromatographically.[51–53,55–62,66] PC has also been employed for the study of hy-

Table 3.6   Chromatographic Classification of the Relative Substantivity of Reactive Dyes

Dye Substantivity	$R_F{}^a$	Substantively Adsorbed Dye on Cellulose (%)
I. Very high	0.00–0.20	85–95
II. High	0.21–0.40	65–84
III. Medium	0.41–0.60	45–64
IV. Low	0.61–0.80	30–44
V. Very low	0.81–1.00	0–29

a Determined by the ascending chromatography technique on Whatman No. 1 paper, start-to-front distance 400 mm, samples spotted in 0.1-μl quantities of 1% aqueous solution of dye, developed at 20–22°C in a system of 2% Na_2HPO_4 in 5% NH_4OH.

drolysis of reactive dyes.[35,36,44–49,54,63] Dawson in 1960 reported a chromatographic study of the hydrolysis of dichlorotriazine dyes, which explained the kinetics.[48]

Šrámek[109] investigated by PC the reaction of reactive dyes with thickeners, solubilizing agents, and wetting agents used in textile printing and continuous dyeing methods. He found that the dyes react with all substances possessing a functional group capable of nucleophilic substitution or addition, thus affecting adversely the yield of the dye in the dyeing process. Wetting agents may contain unreacted substances from their manufacture (e.g., diethanolamine, amino acids, polyglycols), which then react with the reactive dye.

Chromatography has also been used to investigate the effect of the chromophore system of reactive dyes on their lightfastness in the wet state; imperfectly coppered or chromed dyes catalyze oxidative destruction.[110]

PC has also been used in the study of the washfastness of hydrolyzed reactive dyes,[111] and of the possibilities of reaction between disperse and reactive dyes in one-bath dyeing by the thermosol method.[112] PC also helps to assess the compatibility of dyes for dyeing, where a mixture of two or more dyes is used in one dyebath[113]; chromatography using paper coated with polyacrylonitrile enabled the prediction of the compatibility of mixtures of dyes for acrylic fiber.[114]

Johnson and Telesz attempted to correlate R_F with the structures of some disperse dyes and related compounds.[115]

PC has proved useful in the study of stereoisomeric fluorescent brighteners.[24,68–72] *cis* Isomers are unsubstantive and produce a variable quality of whiteness of optically brightened textiles. Chromatographically it was also proved that colored ozonides and aldehydes accompany photodestruction of fluorescent brightening agents, causing their yellowing.[24]

PC can be a valuable aid for determining the lightfastness of dyes.[24] It is possible to observe the lightfastness directly on the chromatogram, which is advantageous when assessing the fastness properties of mixed dyes or an isolated dye identified from a dyeing. It is further possible to study on the chromatogram the progress of light degradation of the dye and determine the mechanism of the reaction.[116,117]

PC can be used to study changes in a dye in the course of hydrolysis, reduction, oxidation, and thermal destruction, as well as to observe the progress of dye fixation.[24] It is also possible to study on the chromatogram the interaction of disperse and reactive dyes, which may occur when applied together in dyeing blends of polyester with cellulose fibers.[24]

In connection with fastness to crocking of mixed dyes it is possible, on the strength of chromatographic identification of the rubbed-off dye, to determine which of the components is responsible for the poor fastness.[118]

1.8   Dye Identification

According to the outcome of the chromatographic analysis, it is sometimes possible to determine the particular dye immediately from the R_F and the color and shape of the spot; otherwise, the appropriate identification reactions can be effected on the chromatogram.[24,20,66,119] The accuracy of the analytical results may be increased by photometric measurement of the extract obtained from the spots on the chromatogram. It is also possible to redye these extracts on the textile substrate; this is essential for reproducing the shade of the analyzed dyeing. The success of the chromatographic dye identification from dyeings primarily depends on the effectiveness of the extraction system for the individual textile substrates and dyes. (See Chapters 15 and 19.)

1.9   Dye Constitution Analysis

PC is invaluable in determining the constitution of dyes. Its primary object is to identify degradation products (e.g., after reductive cleavage and hydrolysis by hydrochloric acid); further, results of the chromatographic analysis (additive ΔR_M values) can be used for determining the constitution of a dye. Jones identified cleavage products stripped from textile fibers by PC[120]; Kitahara and Hiyama[14] and Fujii et al.[121] also used PC to identify dye degradation products. Panchartek et al.[43] and Gasparič et al.[5] adapted these methods for azo dyes (metal complexes, reactive dyes, and azo pigments). They perfected the method for identifying degradation products to such a degree that all identification reactions can be carried out after separating the degradation products directly on the chromatogram, thus eliminating the complicated process of isolation, which is necessary with classical methods of constitution analysis.

Water-soluble azo dyes are subjected to reductive splitting by heating with a solution of stannous chloride and the degradation products are chromatographed in 2 N hydrochloric acid, n-butyl alcohol saturated with 2 N hydrochloric acid,[43,14,121] or n-propyl alcohol–ammonia (2:1).[50] Water-soluble azo dyes can be reduced with zinc and acetic acid; the resulting amines are chromatographed with ethyl acetate–acetic acid–water (12:4:1) or n-butanol–formic acid–water (4:1:5).[4]

Gasparič and Marhan[122] identified products of acid hydrolysis of vat dyes by PC.

Gasparič et al. have used the additive group constants ΔR_M in the systematic constitution analysis of acid anthraquinone dyes,[30] basic triphenylmethane dyes,[78] disperse dyes,[96] aromatic p,p'-diamines,[123] and vinyl sulfone reactive dyes.[50]

2 PAPER ELECTROPHORESIS

The theory and technique of paper electrophoresis are described in several monographs.[1b,124,125] Electrophoretic separation methods are based on the differential mobility of charged molecules or particles in an electric field. Of the various electrophoretic methods, paper electrophoresis appears to be the most useful for dye examination; only for analyzing very complex mixtures need chromatography be combined with electrophoresis. In comparison with PC, paper electrophoresis is used much less frequently for analyzing dyes, and no systematic method has been evolved. The first papers on the application of paper electrophoresis for determining the properties of dyes appeared around 1950.

The paper electrophoretic separation of dyes is based on their mobility in an electric field. The dyes are spotted on the chromatography paper which is saturated with a suitable buffer. The most frequently employed is the low-voltage method with a horizontally placed paper, a system represented, e.g., by the horizontal apparatus of Wiel and Fischer or Cremer and Tiselius.[1b,124,125] In these devices the paper is deposited horizontally with ends dipping into the cathode and anode chamber containing a suitable electrolyte. Low-tension DC is used, usually less than 10 V/cm.

In continuous electrophoresis apparatus the paper is usually placed the same way as in descending chromatography. For continuous electrophoresis, the equipments mostly used are those of Grassmann and Hannig, Durrum, and Strain and Sullivan.[1b,124,125]

2.1 Water-Soluble Dyes

Papers published on the electrophoresis of water-soluble dyes deal mostly with nontextile dyes, the chief interest being in dyes for bacteriological and indicator purposes. Paul and Durrum[126] used organic solvents to study the migration of Eosine, Methylene Blue, Oil Red O, and Alizarin Blue in absolute alcohol–glacial acetic acid. Evans and Walls[127] separated Eosine Y into three components on Whatman No. 1 paper, using 0.1 N ammonium hydroxide (pH 11.1) as the electrolyte, applying a potential gradient of 3.5 V/cm for 2–15 hours. They also studied the behavior of Wright's stain (Eosine + Methylene Blue), Crystal Violet, and Fuchsine, which they separated by continuous electrophoresis into a number of fractions. Strain and Sullivan[124] separated a mixture of Methyl Orange and phenolphthalein. Grassmann and Hannig used continuous electrophoresis for the separation of Bromophenol Blue and Cresol Red.[124] Grassmann and Hübner[128] described the chromatographic and electrophoretic separation of numerous similar substances, and also an interesting process for verifying addition compounds, illustrating it with pairs of dyes, such as Orange II–Methylene Blue and Amido Black–Fuchsine. Lederer[129] separated acridine dyes in 0.1 N hydrochloric acid using a potential gradient of 8 V/cm for 1–2 hours. Atabrine, 5-aminoacridine, actiflavine, and proflavine were easily separated.[129] Franglen studied sulfonphthalein dyes; for the electrophoretic analysis 5 μl of the solution was placed on Whatman No. 4 paper and runs were carried out in pH 8.6 veronal buffer at a potential gradient of 8V/cm for 3 hours.[130]

Schwartzkopff and Bartelheimer[131] studied the amount of dye in biological fluids using Evans Blue. Bermes and McDonald[132] used Bromophenol Blue for measurement of the electroosmotic effect on glass fiber paper. Peeters and Vuylsteke studied electrophoretic techniques using dyes as an experimental tool.[133]

Šrámek used low-voltage electrophoresis in the range 250–350 V for the study of textile dyes.[134] He found that with nitro, nitroso, azo, and arylmethane dyes, as well as anthraquinone dyes, their mobility along the path through the electrophoregram depends on the presence of polar groups in the dye molecule (e.g., SO_3H). Increase in the number of polar groups increases the mobility of the dye, whereas in PC the R_F decreases. It is possible by means of electrophoresis to characterize the electrophilic properties of dyes; also the effect of the size of the dye molecule becomes apparent in the same manner as in PC. The complexity and the size of the dye molecule reduce its mobility in the electric field. In various electrolytes the polarization or dissociation tendency of the dye becomes apparent in a varying degree.

Iijima and Sekido[135] studied paper electrophoresis of monohydroxyazo dyes ($ArNH_2 \rightarrow$ G-acid). The length of track of each dye (U) was compared with that of a nonsubstituted reference dye (U_0) and the relative mobility U/U_0 was calculated. The influence of electroosmotic effects on the mobility of these dyes was eliminated by the use of xylose, glucose, and cellobiose as neutral markers. Adsorption effects were established using the relationship derived by Edward[136] for the limiting mobility of organic ions in water at 25°. The calculated and determined values for relative mobility were shown to differ widely. These deviations were attributed to effects resulting from the adsorption of the acid dyes on cellulose, and they were approximately proportional to the difference between the standard affinities of the dye and the reference dye for the cellulosic fiber. This relation also held for a series of azo dyes based on $ArNH_2 \rightarrow$ R-acid. These adsorption effects indicated the existence of nonelectrostatic interaction in dyeing with acid dyes.

Androsov et al. used low-voltage paper electrophoresis to study conditions of sorption of acid monoazo dyes on polyamide and found a relationship between the mobility of dyes in electrophoresis and their sorption by the polyamide fiber.[137]

Gasparič employed low-voltage paper electrophoresis for the separation and identification of acid anthraquinone dyes, which were commercial products of known structure or pure model compounds.[138] They were applied as 0.5–1% solutions in aqueous pyridine. The apparatus used was of the type with a free-hanging paper strip in a moist chamber designed by the Czechoslovak Academy of Sciences. During the preliminary experiments carried out in both alkaline and acidic media, alkaline medium was found to be more suitable. Aqueous solutions of electrolytes led to the formation of elongated streaks. The addition of ethanol to the electrolyte solution caused a considerable decrease of the mobility of the dyes, but the spots became very sharp. The positive influence of the presence of an organic solvent in the electrolyte solution on the quality of electrophoregrams of acid dyes has been observed by several authors. Ethanol,[139] propylene glycol,[140] and formamide[141] have been used. Optimum results were obtained with phosphate buffer (pH 9) containing 50% ethanol. The mobility of the individual compounds within each group depends predominantly on the number of sulfonic and carboxyl groups, the presence of each of these groups causing a considerable increase in mobility. The substitution of the first member of each group by other functional groups is usually of only slight influence. If buffer solution pH 4 is used, the carboxyl groups of the dyes containing one sulfonic and one carboxyl group are no more dissociated, which results in a considerable decrease of the mobility of the dyes. Their mobility is close to that of the monosulfonic derivatives under these conditions. Thus the detection of the carboxyl group in a dye of known structure is possible by comparing its electrophoretic behavior at pH 5 and 9. The most successful result was obtained with isomeric derivatives of 2,6- and 2,7-disulfonic acids.[138] This fact is in accordance with the observation of Franc[142] on the resolution of isomeric anthraquinone 2,6- and 2,7-disulfonic acids in alkaline medium, the 2,7 isomer showing greater mobility.

2.2   Water-Insoluble Dyes

Tajiri has described a method suitable for sulfur and vat dyes.[143] Development and separation of leuco sulfur dyes were accomplished using aqueous ethylenediamine–ammonium hydroxide–ammonium chloride–thiourea dioxide as electrolyte solution, with the leuco dyes completely protected from atmospheric oxygen. The method is applicable also to sulfurized vat and vat dyes. Air is completely excluded by using the sandwich technique, with the moist paper strip placed between glass plates; the dye is allowed to migrate in the leuco form, and displays its color immediately on contact with air.

REFERENCES

1. G. Zweig and J. R. Whitaker, *Paper Chromatography and Electrophoresis*, (*a*) Vol. II. J. Sherma and G. Zweig, *Paper Chromatography*. (*b*) Vol I. J. R. Whitaker, *Electrophoresis in Stabilizing Media*, Academic Press, New York, 1971, 1967.

2. J. Šrámek, "Application of Paper Chromatography to Systematic Analysis of Synthetic Dyes," in I. M. Hais and K. Macek, Eds., *Some General Problems of Paper Chromatography*, Czechoslovak Academy of Sciences, Prague, 1962, p. 157.

3. F. Kacprzak, B. Klimek, and H. Kwapinska, Eds., *Chromatografia barwników.*, Wydawnictwa Naukowo-Techniczne, Warsaw, 1969.

4. J. Gasparič and I. Gemzová-Táborská, *Collect. Czech. Chem. Commun.*, **27**, 2996 (1962).

5. I. M. Hais and K. Macek, *Paper Chromatography*, Czechoslovak Academy of Sciences, Prague, 1963.

6. Z. Deyl and J. Rosmus, "Centrifugal Chromatography," in M. Lederer, Ed., *Chromatographic Reviews*, Vol. 6, Elsevier, Amsterdam, 1964, p. 19.

7. J. Šrámek, *Man-Made Text.*, **39**, No. 544, 51 (1961).

8. J. Šrámek, "Einfluss der chemischen Eigenschaften der Cellulose chromatographischer Papiere und des Charakters der stationären Phase auf das chromatographische Verhalten von Farbstoffen," in K. Macek and I. M. Hais, Eds., *Stationary Phase in Paper and Thin-Layer Chromatography*, Czechoslovak Academy of Sciences, Prague, 1965, p. 35.

9. See also G. H. Stewart, "The Stationary Phase in Paper Chromatography," in J. C. Giddings and R. A. Keller, Eds., *Advances in Chromatography*, Vol. I, Dekker, New York, 1965.

10. J. Šrámek: *Věda Lýzkum Prům. Textilním*, **5**, 85 (1962); **6**, 99 (1963).

11. J. Šrámek, *J. Chromatogr.*, **15**, 57 (1964).

12. A. Lörinz, O. K. Dobozy, and F. Péter, *Text. Res. J.*, **37**, 60 (1967).

13. F. Péter and A. Karle, *Kol. Ert.*, **10**, 255 (1968).

14. S. Kitahara and H. Hiyama, *J. Soc. Ind. Japan*, 1184 (1956); *CA*, **52**, 13265 (1958).

15. S. Plesník and I. Čepčiansky, *Sb. Věd. Prací, Vys. Škola Chem.-technol.*, Pardubice, Part 1, 89 (1961); *CA*, **58**, 5821 (1963).

16. M. Capponi and A. Barthold, *Text.-Prax.*, **17**, 255 (1962).

17. J. Šrámek, *Textil.* **17**, 390 (1962); **18**, 190, 392 (1963).

18. J. Šrámek, *Dtsch. Textiltech.*, **13**, 594 (1963).

19. O. A. Stamm, R. Wirz, and H. Zollinger, "Correlation between Paper Chromatographic Behaviour and Substantivity of Direct Dyes," in T. S. Gore et al., Eds., *Recent Progr. Chem. Nat. Synth. Colouring Matters and Related Fields*, Academic Press, New York, 1962.

20. J. C. Brown, *J. Soc. Dyers Colour.*, **76**, 536 (1960).

21. E. G. Kiel and H. Hout, *Tex*, **19**, 131 (1960); *CA*, **60**, 11354 (1964).

22. E. G. Kiel and G. H. A. Kuypers, *Tex*, **22**, 779 (1963); *CA*, **62**, 15401 (1965).

23. L. Meckel, *Text.-Rundsch.*, **15**, 353 (1960).

24. J. Šrámek, *Applications of Chromatography in Dyeing and Finishing*, Research Institute of Textile Finishing, Dvůr Králové n.L., 1969.

25. F. Kacprzak and Z. Olszewski, *Przem. Chem.*, **11**, 677 (1955).

26. E. G. Kiel and G. H. A. Kuypers, *Tex*, **22**, 607; 873 (1963).

27. C. McNeil, *J. Soc. Dyers Colour.*, **76**, 272 (1960).

28. W. F. Lindner, *Chem.-Ztg.*, **86**, 103 (1962).

29. J. Jungbeck: *SVF Fachorgan Textilveredlung*, **15**, 417 (1960).

30. I. Gemzová and J. Gasparič, *Collect. Czech. Chem. Commun.*, **34**, 3075 (1969).

31. H. E. Nurstein and K. E. Williams, *J. Soc. Dyers Colour.*, **89**, 49 (1973).

32. H. Tajiri, *J. Chem. Soc. Japan (Ind. Chem. Sec.)*, **63**, 122 (1960); *CA*, **56**, 1443 (1962).

33. F. Schlegelmilch and H. Schulz, *Text.-Ind.*, **71**, 334 (1969); F. Schlegelmilch and M. Fuchs, *Text.-Ind.*, **72**, 388 (1970).

34. J. Kryštůfek, *Textil*, **27**, 373 (1972).

35. E. G. Kiel, *Teintex*, **31**, 91 (1966).

36. G. H. A. Kuypers and E. G. Kiel, *Tex*, **21**, 691 (1962).

37. A. Cee, *Sb. Věd. Prací, Vys. Škola Chem.-technol.*, Pardubice, Part 2, 205 (1967).

38. J. Šrámek, *Textil*, **13**, 387 (1958).

39. J. B. Caldwell and B. Milligan: *Text. Res. J.*, **33**, 481 (1963).

40. J. Perkavec and M. Perpar, *Kem. Ind. (Zagreb)*, **13**, 404 (1964).

41. J. Reif, *Dtsch. Textiltech.*, **13**, 86 (1963).

42. J. Perkavec and M. Perpar, *Z. Anal. Chem.*, **206**, 356 (1964).

43. J. Panchartek, Z. J. Allan, and F. Mužík, *Collect. Czech. Chem. Commun.*, **25**, 2783 (1960).

44. F. J. Sadov and G. E. Kričevskij, *Text. Prom.*, **22**, 29 (1962).

45. Z. A. Kovžin and A. A. Charcharov, *Zavod. Lab.*, **29**, 542 (1963).

46. W. Beckmann, D. Hildebrand, and H. Pesenecker, *Melliand Textilber.*, **43**, 1304 (1962).

47. T. L. Dawson, A. S. Fern, and C. Preston: *J. Soc. Dyers Colour.*, **76**, 210 (1960).

48. T. L. Dawson, *J. Soc. Dyers Colour.*, **80**, 134 (1964).

49. G. E. Kričevskij, Marvi, and F. J. Sadov, *Izv. Vysšh Učheb. Zaveden., Tekhnol. Tekst. Prom.*, No. 1 (80), 79 (1971).

50. A. Cee and J. Gasparič., *Collect. Czech. Chem. Commun.*, **33**, 1091 (1967).

51. E. Bohnert, *Melliand Textilber.*, **42**, 1156 (1961).

52. M. A. Čekalin, *Text. Prom.*, **21**, 40 (1961); **23**, 67 (1963).

53. O. A. Stamm, *Helv. Chim. Acta*, **44**, 1123 (1961); **46**, 3008; 3019 (1963); **49**, 2279 (1966).

54. S. R. Sivarajan and N. G. Parikh, *Curr. Sci.*, **28**, 322 (1959).

55. G. Hornuff and G. D. Gollnisch, *Wiss. Z., Tech. Univ. Dresden*, **11**, 677 (1962).

56. V. Einsele, *Melliand Textilber.*, **42**, 427 (1961).

57. E. Elöd and V. Einsele, *Melliand Textilber.*, **42**, 1377 (1961).

58. J. Všianský, *Textil*, **14**, 430 (1949).

59. F. Osterloh, *Melliand Textilber.*, **41**, 1533 (1960); **44**, 57 (1963); **49**, 1444 (1968).

60. U. Baumgarte, *Melliand Textilber.*, **43**, 1297 (1962); **46**, 851 (1965); **49**, 1432 (1968).

61. U. Baumgarte and F. Feichtmayr, *Melliand Textilber.*, **44**, 163, 267, 600, 716 (1963); **45**, 775 (1964).

62. O. A. Stamm, *Text.-Rundsch.*, **17**, 245 (1962).

63. D. Hildebrand, *Melliand Textilber.*, **49**, 67 (1968).

64. H. Tajiri, *Kogyo Kagaku Zasshi*, **65**, 178 (1962); *CA*, **57**, 8695 (1962).

65. N. A. Pačeva and L. M. Golomb, *Legk. Prom.* (*Kiev*), No. 2 (1965).

66. T. J. Abbott, R. S. Asquith, D. K. Chan, and M. S. Otterbrun, *J. Soc. Dyers Colour.*, **91**, 133 (1975).

67. J. C. Brown, *J. Soc. Dyers Colour.*, **80**, 185 (1964).

68. H. Theidel, *Melliand Textilber.*, **45**, 514 (1964).

69. J. Lanter, *J. Soc. Dyers Colour.*, **82**, 125 (1966).

70. E. H. Daruwalla and R. T. Shet, *Text. Res. J.*, **32**, 165 (1962).

71. J. Latinák, *J. Chromatogr.*, **14**, 482 (1964).

72. J. Gasparič, *Chem. Listy*, **93**, 1363 (1969).

73. J. Kiger and R. Bon, *Ann. Pharm. Franc.*, **18**, 853 (1960); *CA*, **55**, 26451 (1961).

74. L. Meckel, *Text.-Prax.*, **16**, 737 (1961).

75. M. Matrka, F. Navrátil, and J. Filipi, *Chem. Prům.*, **7**, 343 (1957).

76. J. Kolsek, F. Mlakar, and M. Perpar, *Z. Anal. Chem.*, **188**, 345 (1962).

77. J. Šrámek, *J. Chromatogr.*, **12**, 453 (1963).

78. J. Gasparič and M. Matrka, *Collect. Czech. Chem. Commun.*, **24**, 1943 (1959).

79. J. Ciglar, J. Kolšek, and M. Perpar, *Chem. Ztg.*, **86**, 41 (1962).

80. F. Pagani, *Tinctoria*, **58**, 107 (1961); *CA*, **55**, 20438 (1961).

81. E. G. Kiel and H. G. R. Maas, *Tex*, **22**, 377; 468 (1963); E. G. Kiel and G. H. A. Kuypers, *Tex*, **23**, 229 (1964).

82. J. Gasparič, *Collect. Czech. Chem. Commun.*, **29**, 1723 (1964).

83. J. Perkavec and M. Perpar, *Mikrochim. Acta*, 1029 (1964).

84. G. H. A. Kuypers and E. G. Kiel, *Tex*, **23**, 143 (1964).

85. H. Zahn, *Text.-Prax.*, **6**, 126 (1951).

86. K. Elliot and L. A. Telesz, *J. Soc. Dyers Colour.*, **73**, 8 (1957).

87. J. Šrámek, *J. Chromatogr.*, **9**, 476 (1962).

88. J. Šrámek, *J. Soc. Dyers Colour.*, **78**, 326 (1962).

89. F. Micheel, *Eröffnungs- und Vortragstagung, Leipzig, 21–23, Oct., 1953*, Dtsch. Verlag der Wissenschaften, Berlin, 1954.

90. J. Janoušek, *J. Soc. Dyers Colour.*, **73**, 328 (1957).

91. E. G. Kiel and G. H. A. Kuypers, *Tex*, **21**, 403 (1962).

92. C. D. Johnson and L. A. Telesz, *J. Soc. Dyers Colour.*, **74**, 858 (1958).

93. P. Harris and F. W. Lindley, *Chem. Ind. (London)*, 922 (1956).

94. N. I. Dokunikhin and B. I. Kolokolov, *Z. Anal. Chim.*, **20**, 398 (1965).

95. J. Gasparič and I. Táborská, *J. Soc. Dyers Colour.*, **77**, 160 (1961).

96. J. Gasparič, I. Gemzova, and D. Snobl, *Collect. Czech. Chem. Commun.*, **31**, 1712 (1966).

97. H. Kwapińská and B. Glebko, *Biul. Inf. Inst. Przem. Org., Warsaw*, 87 (1963).

98. N. R. Rao, K. H. Shah, and K. Venkataraman, *Curr. Sci.*, **19**, 149 (1950); **20**, 66 (1951).

99. E. Klingsberg, *J. Soc. Dyers Colour.*, **70**, 563 (1954).

100. H. Tajiri, *Kogyo Kagaku Zasshi*, **61**, 164 (1958).

101. J. Šrámek, *J. Chromatogr.*, **11**, 524 (1963).

102. M. I. Artym and P. V. Moryganov, *Tekhnol. Tekst., Prom. Jz. V.U.Z.*, No. 3, 102 (1965).

103. N. Kolev and R. Kurteva, *Khim. Ind. (Sofia)*, **34**, 89 (1962); *CA*, **58**, 4667 (1963).

104. H. Kwapińská, *Biul. Inf. Inst. Przem. Org., Warsaw*, 31 (1964).

105. E. Baier, *Farbe Lack*, **80**, 614 (1974).

106. J. Gasparič, *J. Chromatogr.*, **66**, 179 (1972).

107. S. Kitahara, *J. Chem. Soc. Japan, Ind. Chem. Sect.*, **60**, 746 (1957).

108. H. Schaeffer, *Chemieder Farbstoffe und deren Anwendung*, Verlag Theodor Steinkopff, Dresden-Leipzig, 1963, p. 76–83; *Melliand Textilber.*, **39**, 68, 182, 289 (1958); **41**, 988 (1960).

109. J. Šrámek, *Textil*, **22**, 141 (1967).

110. J. Šrámek, *Textil*, **27**, 328 (1972).

111. W. J. Marshall, *J. Soc. Dyers Colour.*, **82**, 169 (1966).

112. M. Duschewa, L. Jankov, and K. Dimov, *Melliand Textilber.*, **56**, 147 (1975)

113. H. H. Sumner, *J. Soc. Dyers Colour.*, **81**, 193 (1965).

114. E. V. Burnthall, *Am. Dyest. Rep.*, **52**, 684 (1963).

115. C. D. Johnson and L. A. Telesz, *J. Soc. Dyers Colour.*, **78**, 496 (1962).

116. H. C. A. van Beck, Thesis, Delft, 1960; *J. Soc. Dyers Colour.*, **79**, 661 (1963).

117. R. S. Asquith and B. Campbell, *J. Soc. Dyers Colour.*, **79**, 678 (1963).

118. J. Šrámek and O. Týfa, *Textil*, **23**, 390 (1968).

119. G. H. A. Kuypers and E. G. Kiel, *Tex*, **23**, 365 (1964).

120. J. H. Jones, *J. Assoc. Off. Agr. Chem.*, **36**, 914 (1953).

121. S. Fujii, M. Kamikura, and Y. Hosogai, *Eisei Skikenjo Hôkoku*, **75**, 29 (1957); *CA*, **52**, 12685 (1958).

122. J. Gasparič and J. Marhan, *Collect. Czech. Chem. Commun.*, **27**, 46 (1962).

123. J. Gasparič and D. Šnobl, *Sb. Věd. Prací, Vys. Škola Chem.-technol.*, Pardubice 25, 33 (1971).

124. M. Lederer, *Introduction to Paper Electrophoresis and Related Methods*, Elsevier, Amsterdam, 1957.

125. L. P. Ribeiro, E. Mitidieri, and O. R. Affonso, *Paper Electrophoresis*, Elsevier, Amsterdam, 1961.

126. M. H. Paul and E. L. Durrum, *J. Am. Chem. Soc.*, **75**, 4721 (1952).

127. E. E. Evans and K. W. Walls, *J. Bacteriol.*, **63**, 422 (1952).

128. W. Grassmann and L. Hübner, *Naturwissenschaften*, **40**, 272 (1953); *Leder*, **5**, 49 (1954).

129. M. Lederer, *Anal. Chim. Acta*, **6**, 267 (1952). See also I. Mori and M. Kimura, *J. Pharm. Soc. Japan*, **74**, 179 (1954); F. Patti, *J. Chim. Phys.*, **52**, 77 (1955).

130. G. T. Fraglen, *Nature*, **175**, 134 (1955).

131. W. Schwartzkopff and H. Bartelheimer, *Z. Ges. Expt. Med.*, **125**, 409 (1955).

132. E. W. Bermes, Jr., and H. J. McDonald, *Biochim. Biophys. Acta*, **20**, 416 (1956).

133. H. Peeters and P. Vuylsteke, *Clin. Chim. Acta*, **4**, 58 (1959).

134. J. Šrámek, *Applications of Paper Electrophoresis in Dyeing and Finishing*, Research Institute of Textile Finishing, Dvůr Králové n. L., (1962).

135. T. Iijima and M. Sekido, *J. Soc. Dyers Colour.*, **78**, 619 (1962).

136. J. T. Edward, *Chem. Ind. (London)*, 929 (1956); *Sci. Proc. Royal Dublin Soc.*, **27**, 273 (1956).

137. V. F. Androsov, L. I. Zaktreger, E. N. Golovanov, and K. I. Andreeva, *Izv. Vysšh. Učhebn. Zaved., Tekhnol. Tekst. Prom.*, No. 6. (73), 86 (1969).

138. J. Gasparič, *J. Chromatogr.*, **54**, 436 (1971).

139. G. Pastuska and H. Trinks, *Chem. Ztg.*, **86**, 135 (1962).

140. T. Terashima, *Shokuhin Eiseigaku Zasshi*, **2**, No. 2, 44 (1961); *CA*, **57**, 16789 (1962).

141. L. N. Werum, H. T. Gordon, and W. Thornburg, *J. Chromatogr.*, **3**, 125 (1960).

142. J. Franc, *Collect. Czech. Chem. Commun.*, **25**, 657 (1960).

143. H. Tajiri, *J. Soc. Dyers Colour.*, **74**, 860 (1958).

CHAPTER FOUR

High-Pressure Liquid Chromatography

LOUIS J. PAPA

---

1 INTRODUCTION

1.1 Historical Development of the Technique

Column chromatography[1] of dyes gradually gave way to PC in the 1940s and 1950s and to TLC in the late 1950s because these techniques were much faster and gave better resolution. The chromatographic literature for dyes separations and analyses of the last 20 years is almost exclusively PC and TLC.

According to Kirkland and Snyder,[2] modern liquid chromatography or, as it is called in this chapter, High-pressure liquid chromatography (HPLC) had its beginnings in the late 1950s when the automated amino acid analyzer was introduced and the pioneering work of Giddings[3] and Hamilton[4] on the fundamental theory of high-performance LC columns opened the door to active research by a number of workers, which led to a breakthrough in 1969, reviewed in ref. 5. This was the result of the combined developments of new pellicular packings, small-diameter porous packings, pumps capable of attaining high pressures (up to 5000 psi), and detectors with sufficient sensitivity to sense the small amounts of materials injected. The end result has been an increase from 0.02 effective plates per second for classical LC to more than 50 plates per second for modern HPLC. Since that time research activity and literature of HPLC have grown rapidly, and improvements in column packings and other equipment are continually being made. Reference 6 gives a comprehensive review of all the books through 1969 and refs. 2 and 7–11 list books published since that time. Two review articles[12,13] cover the technique, equipment, and applications of HPLC, and recent reviews of the current literature are given by Zweig and Sherma.[14]

Despite these recent developments in HPLC that make it quite apparent that the technique is ideally suited for the separation and analysis of dyes, very little has been published in this area. The general field of HPLC is too immense to be adequately covered in this chapter, but a rudimentary understanding of the principles of the technique is necessary to gain an appreciation for dye applications. Therefore, the purpose of this chapter is to review very briefly the basic theory, the basic equipment available for HPLC, the various modes of HPLC and where each is most useful, quantitative aspects of the technique, and applications of the technique to dyes and related compounds (both published and unpublished).

1.2 Basic Theory

A detailed description of the basic theory and derivations of equations is covered elsewhere, including refs. 2, 7, and 8. The more important terms and equations are given here as a condensed presentation to aid in subsequent discussions. The capacity factor, k', is defined as the total number of molecules in the stationary phase divided by the total number of molecules in the moving phase. From this can be derived a fundamental equation of LC:

$$k' = \frac{t_R - t_0}{t_0} \tag{1}$$

where t_R is the time required for the solute molecules to pass through the column and t_0 is the time for solvent or unretained species to pass through the column. The optimum values of k' for solutes lie between 1 and 10 although useful separation often can be made outside this range. It is often necessary to determine k' values of the components to be separated for better planning of experiments to improve inadequate separations.

The theoretical plate number, N, is also an important fundamental chromatographic term and is expressed by the equation

$$N = 16 \left(\frac{t_R}{t_w}\right)^2 \tag{2}$$

where t_w is the bandwidth of the solute peak at the base. This quantity N is a measure of the column efficiency and generally is constant for each peak in the chromatogram. If N is constant the peak widths, t_w, should vary in proportion to t_R. Thus N is one of the best criteria to test whether a column is correctly packed and is still performing properly after use.

The height equivalent to a theoretical plate (HETP), or H, is defined as

$$H = \frac{L}{N} \qquad (3)$$

where L is the column length. The smaller the value of H, the more efficient the column. Chromatographers have long struggled to maximize N and hence minimize H.

Achievement of resolution, R_s, of two adjacent peaks is the heart of chromatographic problems. It is defined as

$$R_s = \frac{2(t_R{}^2 - t_R{}^1)}{t_w{}^1 + t_w{}^2} \qquad (4)$$

where the superscripts 1 and 2 refer to compounds 1 and 2. Equation 4 by substitution, rearrangement, etc., can be shown to become

$$R_s = \frac{1}{4}\sqrt{N}\,(\alpha - 1)\left(\frac{k'}{k' + 1}\right) \qquad (5)$$

where α is defined as the separation factor k'_2/k'_1. This equation is another fundamental LC term and is composed of three terms. The separation efficiency term, $\sqrt{N}$, is normally varied by changing the column length, packing particle size, or carrier (mobile phase) velocity. The selectivity term $(\alpha - 1)$ is varied by changing the composition(s) of mobile and/or stationary phase. The capacity factor term $k'/(k' + 1)$ normally is varied by changing the solvent strength. These three terms are essentially independent, and each can be adjusted or optimized separately to improve a separation.

Snyder and Kirkland[2] have an excellent chapter on control of separation, in which they discuss estimating R_s and controlling its magnitude and resolution versus k', N, and α. The knowledge of the proper use of these variables is very valuable in developing an LC method. The manner in which to use these variables is discussed briefly below.

2 EQUIPMENT

The equipment for HPLC can vary from simple to rather sophisticated, depending on the complexity of the mixtures to be separated. A schematic diagram of the general system is shown in Figure 4.1. Excluded from this is a solvent programmer, which is discussed below. Each section of the hardware is now considered. A more complete and detailed description of this equipment including commercial availability can be found in ref. 2.

2.1 Reservoirs

The nature of reservoirs varies rather widely among instruments. Some common reservoirs are coiled stainless-steel (SS) tubing, glass flasks or bottles, SS beakers, high-pressure cylinders, and 35-l oxygen cylinders of the type used in jet aircraft. Each should be constructed of material inert to the solvent. In some cases degassing is necessary to eliminate dissolved oxygen which may react with the column or solute. Degassing may also be necessary to eliminate bubble formation in the detector and/or column. This occurs most often when programming two solvents together, especially water and alcohol. Degassing can be carried out by heating the solvents in situ with stirring at a temperature above that to be used in the analysis. In unusual cases where more stringent degassing is necessary, the reservoir should be equipped to hold vacuum and slightly positive nitrogen pressure. The degassing is then carried out by alternately applying vacuum and nitrogen while heating and stirring.

2.2 Pumps

The types of pumps used in HPLC also vary widely. They can be broadly classified into two groups, pneumatic and mechanical. Each is considered here, along with their inherent advantages and disadvantages.

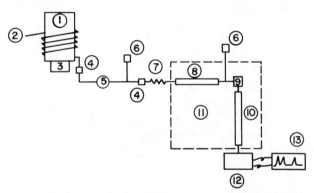

Figure 4.1 Schematic diagram of general LC system.   1, Reservoir; 2, heater; 3, stirrer; 4, filters; 5, pump; 6, pressure sensors and/or overpressure device; 7, pulse dampener (optional); 8, precolumn; 9, sample inlet; 10, analytical columns; 11, column oven (optional); 12, detector; 13, recorder.

2.2.1 Pneumatic Pumps. At least two types of *pneumatic pumps* run directly off compressed gas cylinders with appropriate regulators. One type uses a direct hookup to SS tubing containing the carrier solvent. The compressed gas displaces the liquid into the chromatographic column. The other allows the compressed gas to enter a metal tank which can withstand the pressure. The incoming pressurized gas displaces the carrier at the same pressure.

The pneumatic amplifier pump also is gas driven. The gas pushes on a piston of large area which drives a piston of small area (liquid side). These pumps are engineered to give 30–45:1 amplification in pressure. When the piston reaches the end of the stroke it automatically and rapidly returns ($\sim$1 second) to refill. The volume of the liquid stroke varies from 2 to 75 ml in different pump models.

The advantages of pneumatic pumps are that they give rapid pressure buildup and low noise backgrounds (as seen by the detector) and are well suited for high-sensitivity or quantitative work. Pneumatic pumps are among the lowest in cost and are the most convenient to use with stop-flow injection. The disadvantages are that the pumps operate at constant pressure and the flow rate depends on the back pressure of the system. The reservoir capacities are limited; however, pneumatic amplifier pumps refill rapidly. They are not as well suited as others for solvent programming and some (simple pneumatics) are practically limited in pressure to $\sim$1500 psi.

2.2.2 Mechanical Pumps. The *reciprocating pump* is a constant volume positive displacement pump which utilizes a plunger pushing a small volume of liquid with each stroke. The pump refills on each return stroke by use of a check valve system. Diaphragm pumps operate by essentially the same system. The flow rate is easily adjusted by changing the stroke length and/or the motor speed. The reservoirs on these pumps are limitless. Many mechanical pumps deliver solvents at up to 5000 psi pressure. These pumps are also particularly well suited for recycle chromatography (a technique used to increase resolution by multiple passes through the column of the eluting compounds).

The biggest problem with these pumps is the pulsations transmitted to the detection system. Pulse dampeners can be connected, but these add volume to the system, making solvent changeover more difficult, and can adversely affect the formation of accurate gradients. The pulsation problem is largely compensated for by use of a more expensive variety of multihead pumps which produce sinusoidal output, easier to dampen. These multihead pumps have the same properties as the other reciprocating pumps except that the pulsation problem is reduced. All reciprocating pump systems must be watched carefully since leaks in the check valves cause flow rates to vary considerably.

The *syringe type* or displacement pump is powered by a screw-feed gear box with a stepping motor assembly. Flow is electrically controlled by the voltage applied to the motor. This pump delivers a pulsefree carrier flow at pressures up to 8500 psi for some models, and is well suited for high-sensitivity or quantitative work. It is very versatile for flow or solvent programming because the flow is electrically controlled. The disadvantages of this pump are its high cost, limited reservoir capacity (250–500 ml), and inconvenience in refilling. Also, some minor flow changes can result from variations in compressibility of the solvents.

2.3   Detectors

Snyder and Kirkland[2] and other authors dedicate entire chapters to the discussion of detectors, including photometers, spectrophotometers, differential refractometers, and devices that measure transport, radioactivity, polarographic current, infrared absorption, fluorescence, conductivity, and others. Only two of these detectors, photometers and spectrophotometers, are important in dye analysis and are discussed here, although others may be potentially applicable.

2.3.1   UV and Visible Photometers.   The *UV absorption photometers* have been widely used in HPLC. Some of these devices have sensitivities as high as 0.002 absorbance units full scale with noise levels of $\pm 1\%$. The most common types use UV radiation at 254 nm from a low-pressure Hg lamp. In a typical system this radiation passes via a beam splitter through a reference cell (generally air) and a sample cell, containing the carrier, to matched photocells. The current output from the photocells are log-amplified to produce an absorbance response. Photometers are available to operate at other wavelengths via appropriate filters, e.g., 220, 280, 292, 313, 334, and 365 nm. Typical path lengths, diameters, and volumes of these cells are 10 mm, 1 mm, and 8 μl, respectively. *Visible absorption photometers* have rarely been used in HPLC except when post-column color-forming reactions are used, because most of the HPLC work reported thus far has been with nonvisible compounds. However, in dye analysis, the visible photometer should be very useful. This photometer is identical with the UV photometer except that the source is different, e.g., a quartz–iodine lamp.

2.3.2   Spectrophotometers.   For dye analysis these commercially available detectors should be the most useful. These devices have two sources to cover most of the UV–visible spectrum. Unlike photometers, these detectors allow one to work at any wavelength for maximum absorbance. Therefore, they are more convenient, more versatile, more selective, and in a sense, more sensitive. In dye analysis, the ability to select wavelength adds another dimension of selectivity for some compounds that are difficult to resolve chromatographically but absorb light at different wavelengths. A spectrophotometer is the detector of choice for dye analysis, as well as for general HPLC analysis.

2.4 Solvent Gradient Formation Equipment

Gradient elution is often used in lieu of multiseparation systems to solve the problem of separating complex mixtures with widely varying k' values. This technique is extremely useful in scouting work to arrive at the proper mobile phase mixture as quickly as possible. This is helpful in quality-control work when several analyses are performed on a single column, but with different mixtures of two solvents. The operator can change mobile phase mixtures (hence methods) by dialing rather than changing over the entire carrier solvent.

There are many devices available, depending on the nature of the pump(s) used. The syringe type pump system requires that two pumps be used to form a high-pressure gradient and is therefore a very expensive system. However, because these pumps are actuated by stepping motors which are electrically controlled, it is possible to generate almost any shape and direction of gradient. The pneumatic pumps can be used only with gradients that are mixed at high pressure. Generally the gradient programmer controls two high-pressure solenoid valves to make exponential or linear gradients. One pump may be used, as in Figure 4.2, or alternatively two pumps may be used. The system used in Figure 4.2 has the inconvenience of requiring that the holding coil be filled with solvent B periodically. Also the entire system is somewhat harder to change to two new solvents.

Gradient systems that mix the solvent on the low-pressure side of the pump are generally simpler, more versatile, and cheaper; also they permit wider changes of k' values to be made during a single run. (This means that compounds of greater polarity difference or greater retention time difference can be more easily eluted.) Programmed gradients may be made with two or three solvents or incrementally.[15–18] A convenient two- or three-solvent programming system used in my laboratory is shown in Figure 4.3. In this system a two-headed reciprocating pump was used with a low-pressure gradient formation and an LKB Ultragrad 11300 Gradient Mixer. This LKB unit is an optical-electrical device that can be used to

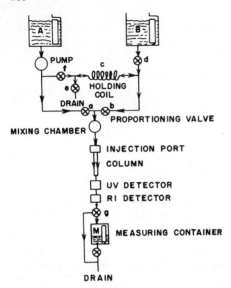

Figure 4.2 One-pump high-pressure gradient system (reprinted with permission of Du Pont Instrument Products Division).

form any gradient representable by a paper template. The unit has also been used to control three high-pressure solenoid valves from pneumatic amplifier pumps to form high-pressure gradients. In this case the system in Figure 4.3 would have a pump between each solvent reservoir and solenoid valve rather than a single pump downstream of the solenoids.

Wide-range incremental gradients[16] probably provide the best method of covering a very large k' value range ($\sim 10^4$) for analyzing certain mixtures. The system starts with heptane and ends with water. A flame ionization transport detector is used. This system has not been used much by other workers with UV detectors because several of the intermediate solvents are UV absorbing. To avoid this problem it is possible to use an abbreviated series of solvents which do not absorb UV radiation.[18] The limitation of using UV-absorbing solvents should not affect dye analysis with a visible detector, and the incremental gradient scheme or some modification thereof might be useful.

2.5   Sample Injection Apparatus

As in GLC, two types of sample injection are widely used in HPLC. On-column syringe injection gives the sharpest injection profile, hence the greatest efficiency of separation. The injection can be made directly through a septum using a high-pressure syringe at pressures up to about 1500 psi. A stop-flow procedure can be used at pressures above (or below) 1500 psi. The septum may be eliminated by using septumless injectors (available

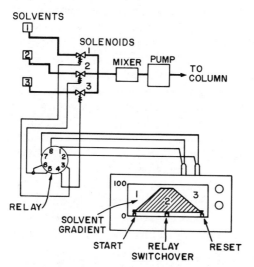

Figure 4.3 Two- or three-solvent program systems—high or low pressure.

from Varian Associates and Hewlett-Packard). Pneumatic pumps are particularly useful for stop-flow injection because the pressure is restored almost instantaneously, whereas mechanical pumps are slower to build up the pressure.

The second general sampling technique is via the use of sampling valves. Valves are now commercially available that allow from 1 μl to several milliliters to be injected at pressures up to 7000 psi. The advantages of valve sampling are high-pressure operation, minor flow disturbance, high precision, and accommodation of larger sample sizes. Disadvantages compared to syringe injection are high cost and difficulty in changing sample size.

2.6 Other Equipment

The remaining HPLC equipment such a filters, pressure monitoring devices, ovens, column materials, fittings, plugs, and flow monitoring devices are all significant,[2] though not as important as those discussed above.

3 MODES AND MANIPULATIONS

3.1 Packings

The column is the most important part of a HPLC system. The development of modern column packings led the way to the recent breakthrough in the LC technique. The modern packings minimize band broadening because of rapid equilibrium between mobile and stationary phase. Packings are either small-diameter porous particles (5 or 10 μm most common) of a narrow size range or are pellicular (superficially porous) materials. Pellicular packings are made up of solid spherical core particles $\sim$30 μm in diameter which have porous outer layers $\sim$1-2 μm thick. This type of packing is also of a narrow size range. These packings yield homogeneously packed columns with minimum channels between particles and shallow pools of stagnant liquid phase, leading to vastly improved separation efficiency.

Packings are generally made of silica, and most of the available commercial packings are adsorbents that are active to some degree. A notable exception is Zipax (Du Pont) controlled porosity support which is virtually inactive. Active adsorbents (except Zipax) can be used for liquid–solid chromatography and some can be used for partition chromatography if properly coated with stationary liquid. Factors to be considered in choosing the packing are the following. The smaller the particle size, the more efficient the column. Spherical particles generally produce better, more reproducible columns of higher efficiency. Pellicular packings are not as efficient as totally porous packings of <10 μm diameter, but are easier to pack, yield more reproducible columns, and have larger dead volume requirements. Pellicular packings are more expensive than totally porous packings, but scouting of separations is quicker and lower pressures can be used. Pellicular packings have much less sample capacity than totally porous packings.

In short, the separation needed and/or cost dictate the packing selected. One must balance the cost, convenience of packing time, and the efficiency needed to do the job. Reference 2 lists commercially available packings; more are undoubtedly forthcoming.

3.2   Liquid–Liquid (LLC)

LLC or partition chromatography utilizes a moving liquid phase and an immobile, immiscible liquid stationary phase either coated or chemically bonded on the support. The solute molecules, passing through the column, partition between these phases. It is normal practice for the moving phase to be less polar than the stationary phase, but when the reverse is true the technique is called *reverse-phase* LLC. In "normal"-phase LLC the retention times of the eluting components generally increase with polarity. The opposite is true in reverse-phase LLC.

The stationary phase in LLC may be either physically coated on the support or chemically bonded to it. In the case of *physical coatings* the solvent–liquid phase pair used must be of very different polarity and immiscible. A presaturator column is generally necessary to ensure that the liquid phase is not stripped from the analytical column with mobile phase flow. The saturator column is often a high surface area support containing a high concentration ($\sim 30\%$) of the same liquid phase used in the analytical column. Analytical columns can last for at least 2 years with no performance decay, if a saturator column is used and changed monthly. Because of the necessity of immiscible pairs of phases, solvents in LLC are generally solvents of low polarity, such as n-hexane, for normal LLC or high polarity, such as alcohol–water mixtures, for reverse-phase LLC. In the former case, the low-polarity solvent can be modified with small amounts ($\leq 10\%$) of more polar solvents, such as chloroform or acetonitrile, to control sample retention. The amount of polar modifier that can be added before stripping occurs depends on the liquid phase used.

The chemically bonded LLC packings are made by binding organic groups to siliceous supports with Si—O—C or Si—O—Si—C bonds. Materials of the former type are usually termed "brushes"; an example is Durapak (Waters Associates). These can be used with many solvents, but are reactive with water and lower alcohols. Bonded phases of the latter type are not removed by organic solvents and are hydrolytically stable. Examples of these are Bondapak (Waters Associates) and Vydac (Sep/a/ra/tion Group), which are essentially a monolayer thick, and Permaphase (Du Pont), which is polymolecular.

LLC is applicable to a wide range of sample types owing to the many partitioning pairs that can be used. This versatility can provide separation selectivity not available by other techniques. LLC is generally useful for separating compounds by difference in functionality or members of a homologous series. It is generally less suited for separating isomers. Other important aspects of LLC when compared with the other modes of LC are that columns can be reproducibly prepared, column performance generally is long lasting and less affected by sample variations, and the results usually are more reproducible and better suited for high-precision work.

3.3 Liquid–Solid (LSC)

LSC or absorption chromatography is still one of the most important separation techniques available. The principles and experimental techniques have been reviewed by Snyder.[19] In the last 7–8 years LSC has developed into a rapid, high-efficiency technique, owing to the combined efforts of many workers, but only a brief description can be given here.

Separation occurs because compounds are *adsorbed* on the polar surface to varying extents in competition with the mobile phase. In general, the more polar the compound, the more strongly it is adsorbed, and the more polar the carrier must be to elute it. The technique is especially good for separating isomers. It is generally less effective for homologues, but should be useful for compounds of different functionality (hence polarity) or of differing numbers of the same function group on a given backbone molecule. After some experience is obtained, LSC separations are relatively easy to predict and in some cases close predictions of k' values can be made.[19,20] Small-particle ($<$10 μm) LSC generally gives very high column efficiencies and can be used with a complete range of solvent polarity for proper adjustment of k' values. Eluotropic series of solvent strengths are available in many publications, including ref. 2. Saunders has reported a system for selecting a binary solvent mixture for various functionalities.[21]

One of the greatest advantages of LSC is the ability to handle complex mixtures with widely different k' values (or retention times). Multicolumn, multisolvent, or flow programming methods can be used to solve this problem, but generally the most effective technique is solvent programming or gradient elution. Two- and three-solvent programs can handle wide k' ranges. However, reequilibration of the adsorbent with the initial mobile phase may be a problem. If the starting and finishing solvents are not widely different in polarity, a simple reverse program is effective. If the polarities are widely different, one or more intermediate solvents may be necessary. Scott and Kucera describe the use of five intermediate solvents to reproducibly attain starting conditions after programming incrementally from heptane to water.[16]

LSC is not without operational disadvantages. Water and other very polar compounds have a drastic effect on k' values and resolution. Therefore, the concentration of highly polar solvents, especially water, must be rigidly controlled for reproducible separations. Alternatively, the concentration of these polar modifiers may be deliberately varied (controlled variation) to obtain the desired separation(s). When the sample itself contains varying amounts of compounds capable of modifying the stationary phase, problems result that can make the method useless. In some cases a guard column, changed frequently, can protect the analytical column and in other cases the column can be regenerated by a series of solvents as described by Scott and Kucera.[16] The activity of the analytical column must be monitored carefully, especially in control work or when the same column is used for more than one method.

When the liquid phases are chemically bonded as monolayers to active silica (many commercially available today) the resultant column is often considered as operating in an LLC mode. We have found that these columns generally behave more similarly to LSC columns. These packings generally are affected by water and polar modifiers, though not to the same extent as unmodified silica adsorbents. Furthermore, the bonded phase

packings do not usually exhibit the same selectivity as might be antici-
pated if the same type of functional group were in physically coated liquid
phases. In short, monomolecular bonded phases behave somewhat like
deactivated silica packings. Only in a few cases do these monomolecular
bonded materials exhibit selectivity somewhat different from silica. The
bonded reverse-phase columns do behave somewhat like LLC columns in
some aqueous mobile phases with organic modifiers. Permaphase packings, which have organic coatings many layers thick bonded to an inactive
support, Zipax, also exhibit true LLC behavior in many instances.

3.3.1 Comparison of LSC with TLC. TLC is widely used in many fields
including dye analysis. TLC is similar in principle to modern LSC and,
in many cases, similar separations can be obtained by each method.
Stewart et al. found that LSC was faster and more efficient than TLC,
although the separations were generally comparable.[22] Others have found
similar results. To illustrate this point, Figure 4.4 shows the similarity of
separation obtained by TLC and LSC under similar conditions on azobenzene (1) and its derivatives: (2) 4-NEt$_2$-3'-Br; (3) 4-NEt$_2$; (4) 4-NEt$_2$-
3'-NO$_2$; (5) 4-NEt$_2$-4'-NO$_2$; and (6) 4-NH$_2$. The TLC experiment required
50 minutes, compared with 6 minutes for LSC. Moreover, compounds (4)
and (5) were not separated by TLC. If the mobile phase composition used
in TLC is not altered during development of the plate by solvent demixing,
it would be generally expected that TLC and LSC should give similar
separations and that only slight carrier modifications should be required

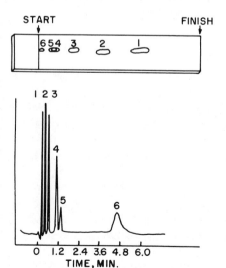

Figure 4.4 Comparison of TLC and
LSC of azobenzene (1) and its derivatives
(2)–(6). 15-cm × 2.1-mm i.d. Micropak
Si-10 column with carrier of 10% CH$_2$Cl$_2$
in hexane at flow of 132 ml/hour (reprinted
with permission of Varian Associates).

for equivalence. Aside from solvent demixing problems, equal separations of nonpolar compounds using nonpolar carriers are often difficult to match for the two methods, for in these cases the water content of the carrier and the silica are difficult to maintain comparable in the two systems.

TLC and LSC are very valuable companion methods. Separations can be scouted much more quickly and easily with TLC. All the compounds present in the sample are on the plate (assuming no volatile compounds) for viewing, and compounds that may not elute from an LSC column usually can be visualized in TLC. Another value of TLC is that a spectrodensitometer and/or a variety of visualizing reagents makes all components visible, and this provides a valuable start toward developing an LSC method with the proper detector(s). On the other hand, LSC provides better and faster routine control analysis, better precision, and better resolution; is more adaptable to preparative work; and has no exposure to air or light in the case of sensitive compounds. The wealth of separations of dyes reported in the literature and reviewed in this book make an excellent starting point for converting TLC separations into column separations.

3.4 Developing the Separation

It is convenient to discuss the effects of the important chromatographic variables on the separation now that the basic theory, the equipment, and the two most important modes—LLC and LSC—have been covered. Recall from Equation 5 that $k'/(1 + k')$, $(\alpha - 1)$, and $\sqrt{N}$ are all proportional to resolution, R_s, and can be independently varied to change R_s. If we first examine the effect of k' on R_s, it is readily seen from

$$R_s \propto \frac{k'}{1 + k'} \tag{6}$$

that if k' is small (0–1) and is slowly increased, then R_s increases rather rapidly at first, then more slowly as k' approaches 10. With k' values larger than 10, R_s changes more slowly, separation times get longer, bands get broader, and detection becomes difficult. Thus the optimum range of k' is $1 \leq k' \leq 10$. If a separation is marginal and k' is small, the best approach is to increase k' into the optimum range. If, however, k' is already in the optimum range, then an increase in N is generally the more convenient step to obtain the desired separation. This increase in N can be readily calculated. In those cases where k' is close to 10 and the separation is poor, then the only practical approach is to attempt to change α or selectivity because of the inordinate length of time that would be necessary to effect such a separation by changing N. Reference 2 reviews methods for predicting these changes. The need for such a method must dictate if the time expenditure is worthwhile. In LSC α changes are easier to predict, but are not as dramatic as in LLC.

The second type of problem encountered is a complex chromatogram with many unseparated or partially separated components at low k' values and other components at intermediate and high k' values. If the solvent strength is decreased to raise k' and effect a separation of the early eluting components, the latter components elute at impractically long times and bands are so diffuse that they would be difficult to detect. The most common and probably the most practical solution to this problem is to use gradient elution. A weaker solvent is used to increase k' values and obtain the desired separations of the early eluting components. The solvent polarity is then increased in some programmed fashion to continually adjust the k' values for optimum separations.

The nature of the gradient program depends on the nature of the solutes present in the mixture. For complex mixtures, a flexible gradient system is advisable. Figure 4.5a shows a moderately complex chromatogram such as that just described. The use of linear or curved gradients can greatly improve the separation, often showing peaks that were not previously visible, e.g., e_1 and e_2, and can decrease the analysis time (as seen in Figure 4.5b) by continually adjusting k' to more optimum values. In some cases two or more components can still not be separated as depicted by e_1 and e_2. In this particular case the program can be modified to include a hold in solvent composition (isocratic) between 7.5 and 12 minutes to allow separation of e_1 and e_2 before continuing with the program. This technique increases the time of analysis somewhat, but gives complete separation (in the case shown) of the mixture with sharp, well defined peaks.

3.5 Ion Exchange (IEC)

The principles of IEC are well established and can be reviewed in recent books.[1,2,23] The classical technique is typically very slow and has long elution times. Horvath and his co-workers vastly improved the speed and efficiency of IEC when they introduced their development of a small-particle (~ 50 μm) pellicular ion-exchange support.[24,25] As in the case of the other chromatographic modes, the new high-performance IEC packings greatly increased speed and efficiency to make them comparable to GLC. The technique has shown great promise for ionic species in numerous biomedical samples and has application in the area of ionic dyes, as is shown below.

Reference 26 lists tables of porous and pellicular packings for HPLC that are now commercially available. New materials seem to be continually forthcoming so that the literature should be watched carefully.

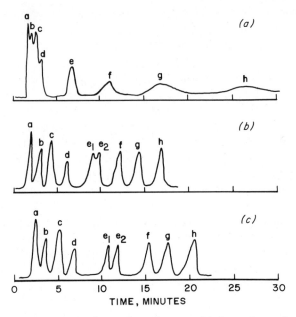

Figure 4.5 Chromatograms of complex mixtures. (*a*) Isocratic carrier; (*b*) linear or exponential solvent gradient; (*c*) linear program with a hold at 7.5–12 minutes.

3.6   Exclusion Chromatography E_xC

E_xC is a technique that separates molecules by their size in solution and thus is probably the least applicable chromatographic method for the analysis of dyes. The packings can be gels, rigid gels, or porous glass beads. The method is unique in that all molecules elute at or before t_0 (time required for the smallest molecules to completely permeate the pores of the packing) and at or after t_e (time required for molecules too large to enter the pores to permeate the interstitial column volume). All molecules small enough to completely permeate the packing elute at t_0 and all molecules excluded from the packing elute at t_e. Thus the range of pore size of the packing must be chosen to match the components to be separated. In E_xC the separation times are predictable, single solvents are used, and values of t_R are predictable if the molecular size is known.

The disadvantages of E_xC are that the imposed boundaries t_0 and t_e limit each column to only a few separable components and compounds of similar size may not be separated. Thus the technique is not suited for isomer or functionality separations. Aside from the normal use of E_xC in determining polymeric molecular weight distribution, the technique is well suited to a quick look at unknown samples to determine the size(s) of molecule(s) to be studied. Reference 2 gives a more detailed discussion of the technique, including lists of available packings.

3.7 Preparative-Scale Separations

Although any of the separation modes discussed above can be scaled up to a preparative level, the cost of the packings usually limits the technique to totally porous particles such as silica or the exclusion packings. These packings can be used in short, wide columns and recycle techniques sometimes can be attempted for more difficult separations in lieu of expenditures for more packing to make the column longer. Other practical aspects are that volatile, low-viscosity carriers should be used, insensitive detectors are permitted, and valve injection is preferable. It is possible to obtain component throughputs of 1 g per run for samples when the R_s value is 1.25.[27]

When planning a preparative-scale run, one should remember that speed, resolution, and capacity are interrelated. Any one of these separation goals can be improved at the expense of the other two. It is expedient to first develop the desired separation on the analytical scale (this also saves sample). Next the column diameter and carrier flow rate are increased to maintain the same separations as with the analytical column, but with larger samples. The flow rate or the carrier polarity can then be decreased somewhat for increased resolution so that the sample load can be increased to the limit—beginning of serious peak overlap. Figure 4.6 shows chromatograms of analytical and preparative separations obtained for three dyes. The first is a proprietary blue dye; the other two are azobenzene derivatives: (5) 4-NEt$_2$-4'-NO$_2$ and (7) 4-N(Et)(CH$_2$CH$_2$OH)-4'-NO$_2$. The separation was scouted on an analytical system (Figure 4.6a) and scaled to a preparative column. Time was sacrificed in the interest of sample capacity. In Figure 4.6b the injected quantities of the compounds were 0.05, 0.06, and 0.10 mg, respectively, in the elution order. In Figure 4.6c these quantities were 15, 15, and 25 mg.

When the peak(s) to be isolated are major in comparison to surrounding impurities, it is often quickest to greatly overload the column and take a heart cut of the peak(s) of interest. Minor components in the tail of the major peak are best isolated by collecting the fraction from one or more overloaded runs, concentrating, and then rerunning the fraction. Both these approaches save more time than trying to further improve the separation by reducing the load or changing the chromatographic conditions.

In cases where the bands for two components of similar size overlap greatly, it is usually most expedient to collect the leading portion of the

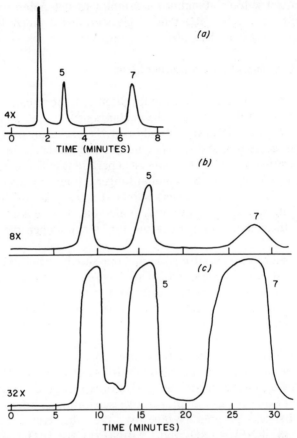

Figure 4.6   Scale-up to preparative HPLC.   (*a*) Analytical separation: 50-cm × 2.2-mm i.d.   Si-60 silica column, 10-μm particle size with chloroform carrier at 1 ml/minute; (*b*, *c*) 4-ft × ½-in o.d.   Si-60 silica column, 40-μm particle size, with chloroform carrier at 8 ml/minute.

early eluting peak and the latter portion of the later eluting component. The middle overlapped portion may be concentrated and recycled to repeat the process until enough sample has been collected. A more complete discussion of preparative techniques is found in ref. 27.

3.8   Quantitative Aspects

HPLC can usually be used with good precision if good technique is employed. In our laboratory we have obtained precisions of 3–4% relative standard deviation (RSD) with syringe injection and 1–1.5% RSD with sampling valves in LLC. Internal standard methods are generally intermediate, $\sim$2–2.5% RSD with either syringe or valves. We have further found that LSC with valves gives somewhat poorer precision than LLC, e.g., 2–3% RSD as compared with 1–1.5% RSD. Leitch has reported a 2σ deviation of 1% for 28 analyses over a 6-month period using an internal standard.[28] Thus it is seen that HPLC is quite applicable to quantitative analysis, and precision equal to or better than that of GC can be obtained. In the case of dye analysis, HPLC is far superior in precision to GC, TLC, and PC.

4 APPLICATIONS

There have been very few publications on the applications of HPLC to dye analysis. This section reviews the published work on dyes and related compounds and includes unpublished work in our laboratory. The application of HPLC to all classes of dyes has not been investigated to my knowledge. Therefore this section is organized by the mode of HPLC rather than by dye class.

4.1 Applications of LLC

4.1.1 Homologues. As mentioned earlier, LLC is usually a choice method for the separation of homologues. This is illustrated in Figure 4.7 by the separation of 2,4-dinitrophenylhydrazones (DNPH) of six aldehydes.[29] Although these compounds are not dyes, they have structural similarities and nicely illustrate the point.

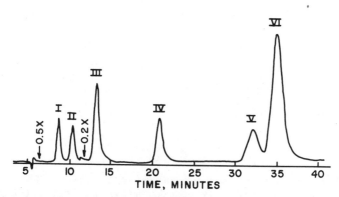

Figure 4.7 Separation of 2,4-dinitrophenylhydrazones of (I) *n*-pentanal; (II) *n*-butanal; (III) propanal; (IV) acetaldehyde; (V) benzaldehyde; (VI) formaldehyde . Column: 3-m $\times$ 2.1-mm i.d. of 1% tris-(2-cyanoethoxy)propane on Zipax; Carrier and flow rate: *n*-hexane at 1 ml/minute (reprinted with permission of *Journal of Chromatographic Science*).[29]

Although the bulk of the molecule is the polar DNPH moiety, small changes in the carbonyl R group are sufficient to allow separation in this LLC system. The mobile phase, hexane, is not polar enough to elute bis-DNPH derivatives of dicarbonyl compounds, and a significant increase in polarity of the carrier would strip this physically coated packing of the liquid stationary phase. A bonded column of somewhat lower polarity and different selectivity gave similar but inferior separations of the mono-DNPH derivatives. This bonded packing was used with solvent programming to elute and separate the bis-DNPH derivatives. This separation is shown in Figure 4.8.[29]

Another separation of a series of homologues involved alkyl-substituted anthraquinones. Again, these compounds are not dyes, but are closely related structurally and illustrate the point. Figure 4.9 is a chromatogram of five of these homologues separated in the reverse-phase mode.[30]

4.1.2 Anthraquinone Dyes. Many anthraquinone dyes can be separated by LLC in both the normal and reverse-phase modes. One case of a separation of a dye from impurities is shown in Figure 4.10 for 1-amino-5-benzoylaminoanthraquinone.[31] Such a chromatogram can, of course, be used to determine the concentrations of the active ingredient of the dye and important impurities; such an approach can be used to monitor reactions for optimization or control.

Another interesting separation[32] of the following anthraquinones, carried out in the reverse-phase mode, is shown in Figure 4.11: **(8)** 1,4-$(NH_2)_2$-2-

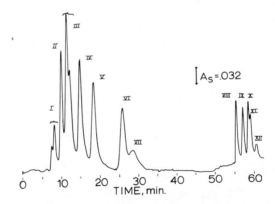

Figure 4.8 Separation of dinitrophenylhydrazones of (I) hexanals; (II) n-pentanal; (III) butanals; (IV) crotonaldehyde; (V) acetaldehyde; (VI) formaldehyde; (VII) benzaldehyde; (VIII) salicyladehyde; (IX) ½-glyoxal; (X) glutaraldehyde; (XI) glyoxal; (XII) unknown. Column: 3-m × 2.1-mm i.d. of Permaphase–ETH. Carrier and gradient: n-hexane to chloroform at 4%/minute and initial flow rate of 2 ml/minute (reprinted with permission of *Journal of Chromatographic Science*).[29]

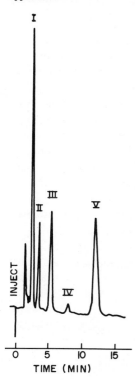

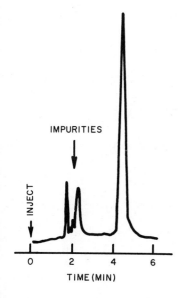

Figure 4.9 Separation of alkyl-substituted anthraquinones: (I) unsubstituted; (II) 2-methyl; (III) 2-ethyl; (IV) 1,4-dimethyl; (V) 2-t-butyl. Column: 1-m × 2.1-mm i.d. of Permaphase ODS. Carrier and flow rate: water–methanol (4:6 (v/v) at 2.2 ml/minute. Tempertaure 40° (reprinted with permission of Du Pont Instrument Products Division).

Figure 4.10 Separation of anthraquinone dye from impurities. 1-m × 2.1-mm i.d. of β,β'-oxydipropionitrile (ODPN) on Zipax. Carrier, hexane (reprinted with permission of Du Pont Instrument Products Division).

OMe; (9) 1-NHMe-4-(NH-*p*-tolyl); (10) 1-OH-4-NHPh; (11) 1-OH-4-(NH-*p*-tolyl); and (12) 1,8-(NH-*p*-tolyl)$_2$. It is interesting to compare the retention of the individual dyes with the structures to get a feel for the functionality and structural differences that can be separated. In particular note that compounds (10) and (11) are almost completely separated, yet differ by only a methyl group. Other modern small-particle reverse-phase columns probably would separate this mixture, and solvent programming would greatly reduce the time of separation by reducing k' for dye (12).

The reverse-phase systems described above seem to provide a powerful technique for separating anthraquinone dyes. Another separation variable worth discussing at this point is temperature. Figure 4.12 taken from ref. 32 illustrates the dramatic effect temperature can have, especially in the reverse-phase mode. Dye (11) is separated from impurities and the increase in temperature of 28° reduces the analysis time threefold by increasing the solubility and reducing the mobile phase viscosity, thus increasing the speed of the equilibration of the sample between the mobile and stationary phases.

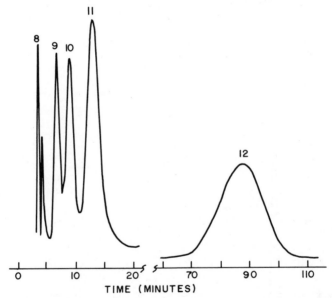

TIME (MINUTES)

Figure 4.11 Separation of anthraquinone dyes. Column: 1-m $\times$ 2.1-mm i.d. of hydrocarbon polymer on Zipax. Carrier and flow rate: water–ethanol (1:1 v/v) at 0.46 ml/minute. Temperature 50° (reprinted with permission of *Journal of Chromatographic Science*).[32]

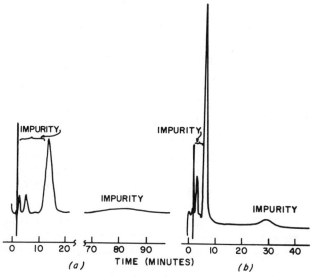

Figure 4.12 Effect of temperature on reverse-phase separation. Same column and carrier as in Figure 4.11; flow rate 1.0 ml/minute; (*a*) 22°, (*b*) 50° (reprinted with permission of *Journal of Chromatographic Science*).[32]

4.1.3 Azo Dyes. Several azo dyes and dye systems have been separated by LLC. Passarelli and Jacobs compared two column types and two carriers for one particular system.[32] Figure 4.13 is a chromatogram of four azo dyes **(5)**, **(13)**, **(14)**, and **(15)**, illustrating how unknown dye mixtures may be separated and isolated for subsequent identification.

(13)

(14)

$$CH_3$$

$$-N=N-\langle\quad\rangle-NHCCH_3$$

OH

(15)

Two commercial packings were used in Figure 4.14*a* and *b* to separate the components in the coupling reaction of diazotized *p*-nitroaniline to 1-naphthylamine to form the *o*- and *p*-coupled dyes. It should be noted that the packing in Figure 4.14*a* is more polar and less efficient than that in 4.14*b*. The results obtained by doubling the liquid load of the packing in 4.14*b* and using a less polar carrier to increase k' are shown in Figure 4.15. This approach gives the best separation, but at a sacrifice in time. *p*-Nitroaniline is not detected in the separation shown in Figure 4.14*a* (owing to band spreading), and the 4.14*b* separation is incomplete. The

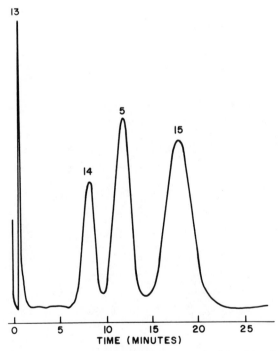

Figure 4.13 Separation of azo dyes. Column: 1-m × 2.1-mm i.d. of 1% ODPN on Zipax. Carrier and flow rate: *n*-hexane at 1.5 ml/minute (reprinted with permission of *Journal of Chromatographic Science*).[32]

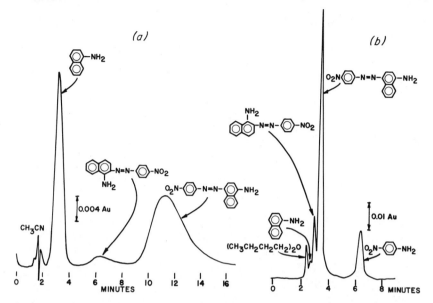

Figure 4.14 Comparison of separation on two LLC systems. (*a*) Column: 1-m × 2.1-mm i.d. of Durapak/OPN. Carrier and flow rate: di-*n*-butyl ether at 0.63 ml/minute. (*b*) Column: 1-m × 2.1-mm i.d. of 0.5% ODPN on Zipax. Carrier and flow rate: di-*n*-butyl ether at 2.2 ml/minute (reprinted with permission of *Journal of Chromatographic Science*).[32]

best solution to this problem is probably a mixture of the mobile phases used in these two figures.

Final examples of LLC separations are shown in Figure 4.16, which is a normal phase separation of an azo dye and its precursor, and in Figure 4.17 for a reverse-phase separation of an anthraquinone dye (**8**), an azo dye (**16**), and the dye dispersant. Figure 4.17 illustrates the symmetry of the peak for compound (**16**), a disazo dye, in this LLC system. This type of compound often tails in LSC, and LLC may be the preferred mode.

$$\langle\!\langle\ \rangle\!\rangle - N\!\!=\!\!N - \langle\!\langle\ \rangle\!\rangle - N\!\!=\!\!N - \langle\!\langle\ \rangle\!\rangle - OH$$

(16)

4.1.4 Ionic Dyes. Conventional LLC is generally not suitable for separating ionic dyes. It would be expected that ion pair LLC would be a good method to evaluate for separating these types of dyes. However, two cationic dyes (**17**) and (**18**) were separated on a Pellidon column (pellicular silica, coated with a polyamide) as shown in Figure 4.18. The initial carrier

(17)

(18)

eluted (17), but not (18), and an increase in carrier polarity was made at 5.5 minutes to elute (18). Two triphenylmethane dyes, Crystal Violet and Malachite Green, were almost completely separated on the same column using a weaker solvent mixture (Figure 4.19). Other separations of ionic dyes are shown in subsequent sections.

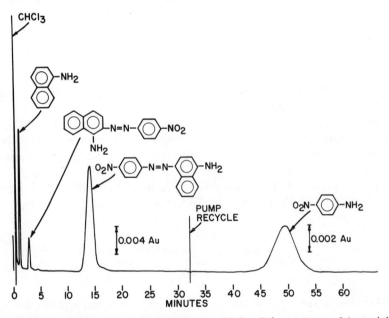

Figure 4.15 Separation of typical dye mixture by LLC. Column: 1-m × 2.1-mm i.d. of 1% ODPN on Zipax. Carrier and flow rate: n-hexane at 3.8 ml/minute (reprinted with permission of *Journal of Chromatographic Science*).[32]

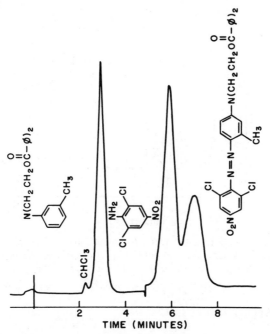

Figure 4.16 Separation of typical dye mixture. Column: 1-m × 2.1-mm i.d. of 1 % ODPN on Zipax. Carrier and flow rate: *n*-hexane at 0.8 ml/minute.

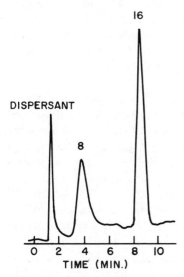

Figure 4.17 Reverse-phase separation of dispersed dyes. Column: 1-m × 2.1-mm i.d. of Permaphase ODS. Carrier and flow rate: methanol–water (1:1 v/v) at 1.0 ml/minute.

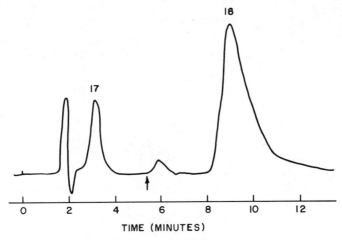

TIME (MINUTES)

Figure 4.18 Separation of cationic dyes. Column: 1-m × 2.1-mm i.d. of Pellidon. Carrier: chloroform–methanol (4:1 v/v) plus 0.1% formic acid, and change at 5.5 minutes to chloroform–methanol (3:1 v/v) plus 0.1% formic acid. Flow rate: 1.0 ml/minute.

4.2 Applications of LSC

LSC is a powerful mode of HPLC for separation of some dyes, especially azo dyes. The high efficiency of the modern packings, the high polarity of the packings (usually silica), and the ability to adjust k' values over very wide ranges by simple adjustment of the solvent polarity are reasons for the versatility and usefulness of LSC for dyes as well as other molecules. The many separations reported by TLC can probably be readily adapted to HPLC. This section also covers some published and unpublished separations and compares some of these to TLC separations.

4.2.1 Azo Dyes. The separation of some azo dyes and intermediates by LSC and a comparison with TLC separations was discussed and illustrated in Figure 4.4. Majors[33] separated the azo dyes (19)–(27) on 10-μm silica and "cyano"-bonded silica using varied solvent programs, as illustrated in Figure 4.20: (19) aniline → 1-dimethylaminonaphthalene; (20) 1-naphthyl-amine → dimethylaniline; and the azobenzene derivatives (21) 4-NMe$_2$; (22) 4-NMe$_2$-3'-OEt; (23) 4-NHMe; (24) 4-NH$_2$-3,5-Me$_2$; (25) 4-NMe$_2$-4'-OAc; (26) 4-NMe$_2$-3'-Ac; and (27) 4-NMe$_2$-4'-NH$_2$. The separation of the following azo compounds on 5-μm alumina[34] is shown in Figure 4.21: (1) azobenzene; (6) 4-NH$_2$; (28) 4-NH$_2$-4'-NEt$_2$; and (29) 4-NH$_2$-4'-NHEt.

The effect of polar moderators in the mobile phase in LSC separations has been mentioned earlier. This effect is shown in the chromatograms of

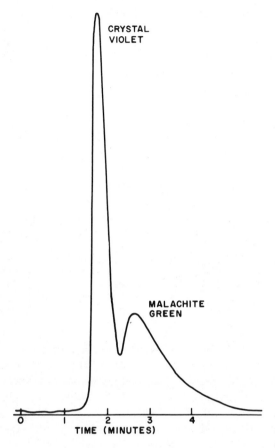

CRYSTAL
VIOLET

MALACHITE
GREEN

TIME (MINUTES)

Figure 4.19 Separation of triphenylmethane dyes. Column: 1-m × 2.1-mm i.d. of Pellidon. Carrier and flow rate: chloroform–methanol (10:1) at 1.0 ml /minute.

Figures 4.22–4.24 taken from ref. 32. Figure 4.22 illustrates the effect of the moderator polarity on the separation, showing that the more polar ethanol (Figure 4.22*b*) gives sharper peaks and more rapid elution than butanol (Figure 4.22*a*). In Figure 4.23 the effect of the moderator concentration is shown on the separation of the same two dyes. Figure 4.24 also shows the effect of the moderator concentration on the azo coupling system described earlier for LLC separations (Figures 4.14 and 4.15). Note that with the conditions of Figure 4.24, LSC gives faster elution, but much less separation and selectivity, than the LLC systems of Figures 4.14 and 4.15. In fact, the 4-substituted coupling product (not shown) does not separate from the 2-substituted product with the conditions of Figure 4.24.

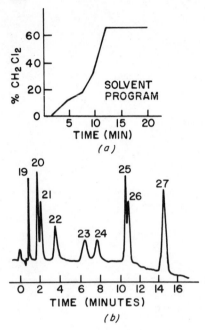

Figure 4.20 LSC Separation of azo dyes.[33] Column: 15-cm × 2-mm i.d. of Micropak C-N. Carrier: 0.2% isopropanol in hexane, programmed to 0.2% isopropanol in 35% hexane, 65% methylene chloride; flow rate: 1 ml/minute (a) solvent program (b) chromatogram (reprinted with permission from R. E. Majors, *Anal. Chem.*, **45**, 755 (1973). Copyright American Chemical Society.

These two isomers (the 4- and 2-substituted coupling products) are easily separated using the LSC conditions shown in Figure 4.25a. For comparison the TLC–spectrodensitometric scan obtained with the same carrier is shown in Figure 4.25b. This is another case of the similarity of separations obtained by modern LSC and TLC. The HPLC separation in Figure 4.25a is apparently less efficient than the corresponding TLC run because the silica particles used in the former case were 20–44 μm compared with 5–10 μm in TLC.

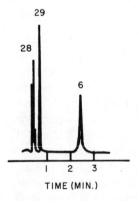

Figure 4.21 Separation of azo dyes on alumina. Column: 15-cm × 2-mm i.d. of Micropak Al-5. Carrier and flow rate: 1% methylene chloride in hexane at 2 ml/minute (reprinted with permission of Varian Associates).

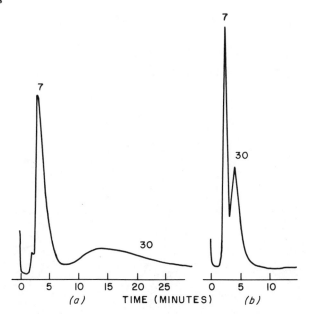

Figure 4.22 Effect of moderator type on separation. Column: 1-m × 2.1-mm i.d. of Adsorbosil-CAB, 200/250-mesh. Carrier: (*a*) 10% butanol, (*b*) 10% ethanol in chloroform. Flow rate: 0.95 ml/minute (reprinted with permission of *Journal of Chromatographic Science*).[32]

A more efficient separation of seven azo and two anthraquinone dyes on a 5-μm silica column is shown in Figure 4.26. Note the tailing peaks for compounds **(15)** and **(16)**, both hydroxyazo dyes. This asymmetry was not seen in LLC separations (Figures 4.13 and 4.17). Compound **(30)**, a dihydroxy dye, does not elute in a convenient time with the initial carrier; therefore the methanol content of the carrier was significantly increased after 31.4 minutes to elute this dye.

$$O_2N-\langle\bigcirc\rangle-N{=}N-\langle\bigcirc\rangle-N(CH_2CH_2OH)_2$$

(30)

A separation of three pairs of 1,5- and 1,8-dinitroanthraquinones substituted by R_1, R_2, or R_3 in the 4 position, **(31)**–**(36)**, on 10-μm silica is shown in Figure 4.27. It illustrates the utility of LSC for separating isomers and compounds with different functional groups.

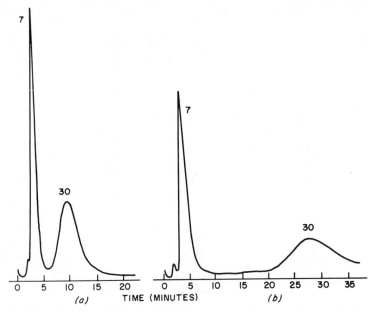

Figure 4.23 Effect of moderator concentration on separation. Column and flow rate: same as Figure 4.22.   Carrier: (*a*) 5% ethanol, (*b*) 2.5% ethanol in chloroform (reprinted with permission of *Journal of Chromatographic Science*).[32]

4.1.4 Ionic Dyes.   Ionic dyes are among the most difficult to analyze and separate. In some cases they can be separated by LSC using polar mobile phases. An example of such a separation (Perkin-Elmer applications bulletin) is shown in Figure 4.28. Here FD&C Yellow 5 (CI 19140) is separated from its precursors, 1-(*p*-sulfophenyl)-3-carboxypyrazolone and sulfanilic acid, using LSC and a gradient elution technique.

A quaternary amine with structural similarity to dyes was chromatographed by LSC using a rather complex mobile phase, as shown in Figure 4.29.[35] The scouting work for this quaternary amine was performed by TLC using the same solvent composition, except that dichloroethane was used instead of methylene chloride. A mobile phase of the same four components as used in Figure 4.29, but in a different ratio, was used to separate C.I. Basic Blue 21, (**37**), and some impurities, as illustrated in Figure 4.30. Three other dyes, CI Basic Red 18, (**17**), and (**18**), were chromatographed using the same conditions. Basic Red 18 and (**17**) eluted between the two dyes shown in Figure 4.30, and (**18**) eluted with Basic Blue 21. Thus this system can be used to separate these cationic dyes from their impurities,

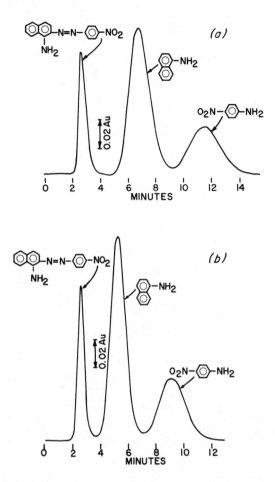

Figure 4.24 Separation of typical dye mixture by LSC. Column: same as Figure 4.22. Carrier and flow rate: (*a*) 1% isopropanol, (*b*) 2% isopropanol in chloroform at 0.83 ml/minute (reprinted with permission of *Journal of Chromatographic Science*).[32]

but does not provide good separation of many cationic dyes from each other.

4.3 Applications of IEC

Ionic dyes are generally difficult to separate by LC. However, sulfonic acids and sulfonic acid dyes have been separated by IEC and by LSC as described earlier. The separation of the three isomeric sulfanilic acids by weak anion-

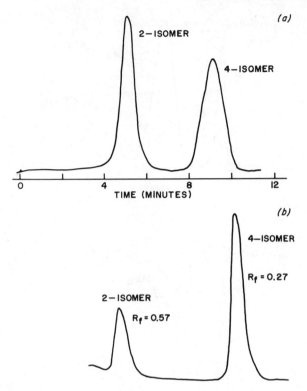

Figure 4.25 Isomer separation by LSC and TLC. (*a*) Column: 1-m × 2.1-mm of Biosil A, 40 μm. Carrier and flow rate: chloroform at 1 ml/minute. (*b*) Silica G-HR Plate, 250-μ thickness with chloroform developer.

exchange chromatography is shown in Figure 4.31.[32] Such separations suggested that typical dye intermediate sulfonic acids might be resolved on strong anion exchangers. Subsequent studies showed that para acid (4-nitrotoluene-2-sulfonic acid), J-acid, H-acid, and dinitrostilbene disulfonate could be separated in this manner, as shown in Figure 4.32. This chromatogram required only 20 minutes whereas similar separations on Sephadex G25 required hours.[36] Conditions similar to those used in Figure 4.32 will separate gamma-acid, amino-J-acid, *N*-benzoyl-J-acid, Rhoduline acid, and J-acid urea, but not gamma- and J-acids.

The separation of Schaeffer salt, FD&C Green 3, FD&C Yellow 6, and FD&C Blue 2 from their respective impurities has been reported.[37] Chromatograms of two of these are shown in Figures 4.33 and 4.34. The separation of an anthraquinone dye intermediate and its precursor is shown in Figure 4.35.

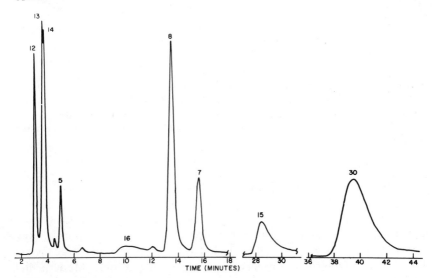

Figure 4.26 LSC separation of anthraquinone and azo dyes. Column: 15-cm × 4.6-mm of Partisil, 5 µm. Carrier and flow rate: chloroform at 1 ml/minute.

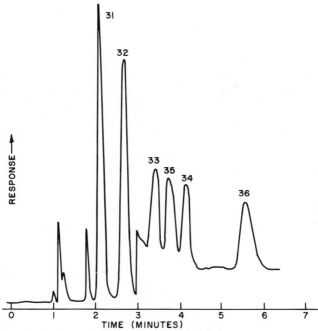

Figure 4.27 LSC separation of substituted anthraquinones. Column: 25 cm/2mm of Micropak-Si-10. Carrier and flow rate: n-hexane–methylene chloride–methanol (77.5:15: 7.5) at 1 ml/minute.

Figure 4.28   Separation of dye and precursors: (I) pyrazolone; (II) sulfanilic acid; (III) FD&C Yellow No. 5.   Column: 50-cm × 3-mm of Sil-X, 13 μm.   Carrier: gradient of 1:6 to 1:2, methanol–tetrahydrofuran with 1% acetic acid.   Flow rate: 1.6 ml/minute (reprinted with permission of The Perkin-Elmer Corporation).

4.4   Application of E_xC

E_xC is not very useful for dye analysis when compared with other modes of HPLC. Figure 4.36 shows a separation of two dyes on a porous cross-linked polystyrene gel, Poragel 60 Å, and indicates that rather large molecular weight differences are needed for complete separation. Modern high-speed exclusion packings such as spherical silica and μ-Styragel would be expected to give much better resolution, but do not compare with LLC or LSC in versatility.

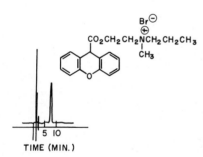

Figure 4.29   Chromatogram of cationic compound.   Column: 25-cm × 2:1 mm i.d. of Zorbax-Sil.   Carrier and flow rate: methylene chloride–methanol–water–formic acid (72.4:25:2.5:0.1 v/v) at 0.7 ml/minute (reprinted with permission of Du Pont Instrument Products Division).

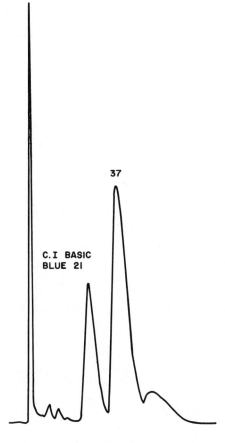

37

C.I BASIC
BLUE 21

Figure 4.30 Separation of cationic dyes. Column: 15-cm × 2.1-mm of LiChrosorb Si-60, 5 μm. Carrier and flow rate: methanol–methylene chloride–water–formic acid (50:44.8:5:0.2 v/v) at 1 ml/minute.

(37)

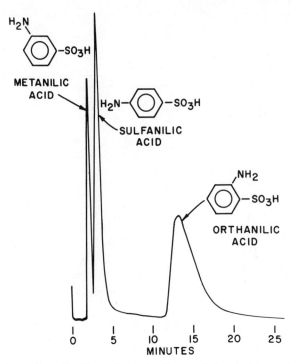

Figure 4.31 Separation of sulfonated intermediates. Column: 1-m × 2.1-mm i.d. of Zipax/WAX. Carrier and flow rate: 0.01M aqueous citric acid (pH 2.8) at 1.02 ml/ minute (reprinted with permission of *Journal of Chromatographic Science*).[32]

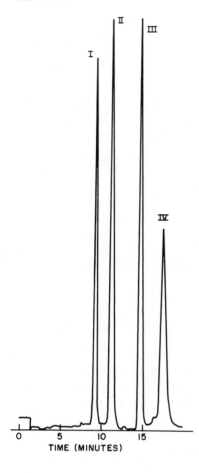

II

III

I

IV

0   5   10   15
TIME (MINUTES)

Figure 4.32 Separation of sulfonated intermediates: (I) para acid; (II) J-Acid; (III) H-
Acid; (IV) dinitrostilbene disulfonate. Column: 1-m × 2.1-mm i.d. of Zipax/SAX.
Carrier: 0.01 M sodium borate (pH 9.2)
programmed to 0.01 M sodium borate (pH 9.2)
and 0.1 M sodium perchlorate with exponential
convex gradient at 7%/minute. Flow rate:
1 ml/minute. Temperature 50°.

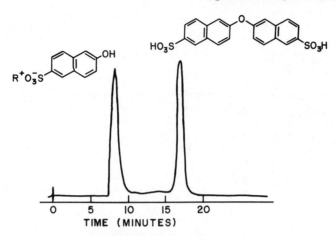

Figure 4.33 Separation of Schaeffer salt and impurity. Column: SAX. Carrier: same as Figure 4.32 except 0.4 M sodium perchlorate and 10%/minute gradient. Flow rate: 1 ml/minute. Temperature 40° (reprinted with permission of Du Pont Instrument Products Division).

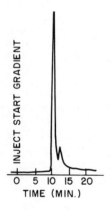

Figure 4.34 Separation of FD&C Blue 2 from major impurity. Column: SAX. Carrier: same as Figure 4.32 except 0.05 M sodium perchlorate and 4%/minute linear gradient. Flow rate: 1.2 ml/minute (reprinted with permission of Du Pont Instrument Products Division).

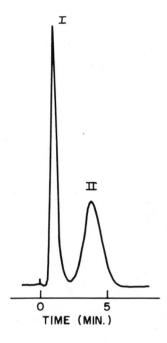

Figure 4.35 Separation of anthraquinone intermediates: (I) 1,4-diaminoanthraquinone 2,3-dicarboximide; (II) 1,4-diaminoanthraquinone 2,3-disulfonic acid. Column: 1–m × 2.1 mm i.d. of SAX. Carrier and flow rate: 0.01 M Na$_3$PO$_4$ at 2.5 ml/minute.

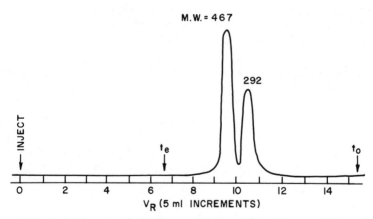

Figure 4.36 Exclusion separation of dyes. Column: 8-ft × $\frac{3}{8}$-in. o.d. of Parogel 60 Å. Carrier and flow rate: chloroform at 1.5 ml/minute.

REFERENCES

1. E. Heftman, Ed., *Chromatography*, Reinhold, New York, 1967.
2. L. R. Snyder and J. J. Kirkland, *Introduction to Modern Liquid Chromatography*, Wiley-Interscience, New York, 1974.
3. J. C. Giddings, *Dynamics of Chromatography*, Dekker, New York, 1965.
4. P. B. Hamilton, *Advan. Chromatogr.*, **2**, 3 (1966).
5. A. Zlatkis, Ed., *Advances in Chromatography*, Preston Technical Abstract Co., Niles, Ill. 1969.
6. *J. Chromatogr. Sci.*, **8**, D2 (July 1970).
7. N. Hadden et al., *Basic Liquid Chromatography*, Varian Aerograph, Walnut Creek, Calif., 1972.
8. J. J. Kirkland, Ed., *Modern Practices in Liquid Chromatography*, Wiley-Interscience, New York, 1971.
9. J. Q. Walker, M. T. Jackson, and J. B. Maynard, *Chromatography Systems. Maintenance and Trouble Shooting*, Academic Press, New York, 1972.
10. S. G. Perry, R. Amos, and P. I. Brewer, *Practical Liquid Chromatography*, Plenum Press, New York, 1972.
11. P. R. Brown, *High Pressure Liquid Chromatography: Biochemical and Biomedical Applications*, Academic Press, New York, 1973.
12. A. F. Michaelis, D. W. Cornish, and R. Vivelecchia, *J. Pharm. Sci.*, **62**, 1399 (1973).
13. P. M. Rajcsanyi and L. Ötvös, *Sep. Purif. Methods*, **2**, 361 (1973).
14. G. Zweig and J. Sherma, *Anal. Chem.*, **44**, 47 (1972); **46**, 73 (1974).
15. R. P. W. Scott and P. Kucera, *J. Chromatogr. Sci.*, **11**, 83 (1973).
16. R. P. W. Scott and P. Kucera, *Anal. Chem.*, **45**, 749 (1973).
17. L. R. Snyder and D. L. Saunders, *J. Chromatogr. Sci.*, **7**, 195 (1969).
18. *Technical Bulletin 10M*, Reeve Angel Co., Clifton, N. J., October 1973.
19. L. R. Snyder, *Principles of Adsorption Chromatography*, Dekker, New York, 1968.
20. L. R. Snyder, *J. Chromatogr.*, **63**, 15 (1971); *Advan. Chromatogr.*, **4**, 3 (1967).
21. D. L. Saunders, *Anal. Chem.*, **46**, 470 (1974).
22. H. N. M. Stewart, R. Amos, and S. G. Peery, *J. Chromatogr.*, **38**, 209 (1968).
23. F. Helfferich, *Ion Exchange*, McGraw-Hill, New York, 1972.
24. C. G. Horvath B. A. Preiss, and S. R. Lipsky, *Anal. Chem.*, **39**, 1422 (1967).
25. C. G. Horvath and S. R. Lipsky, *Anal. Chem.*, **41**, 1227 (1969).
26. Ref. 2, pp. 294–296.
27. J. J. DeStefano in ref. 2, pp. 399–429.
28. R. E. Leitch, Jr., *J. Chromatogr. Sci.*, **9**, 531 (1971).
29. L. J. Papa and L. P. Turner, *J. Chromatogr. Sci.*, **10**, 747 (1972).
30. *Technical Bulletin 820PB4*, Du Pont Instruments, Wilmington, Del., August 1971.
31. *Technical Bulletin 820M6*, Du Pont Instruments, Wilmington, Del., March 1970.
32. R. J. Passarelli and E. S. Jacobs, *J. Chromatogr. Sci.*, **13**, 153 (1975).
33. R. E. Majors, *Anal. Chem.*, **45**, 755 (1973).

34. *Technical Bulletin SEP-1842A*, Varian Instrument Division, Walnut Creek, Calif., July 1973.

35. *Liquid Chromatography Methods Bulletin—A-87414*, Du Pont Instruments, Wilmington Del., November 1973.

36. H. Steuerle, *Z. Anal. Chem.*, **220,** 412 (1966).

37. *Liquid Chromatography Application Report—A-85314*, Du Pont Instruments, Wilmington, Del., February 1973.

CHAPTER FIVE

Gas–Liquid Chromatography

LOUIS J. PAPA

1 INTRODUCTION

GLC has long been recognized as an important analytical technique for many classes of organic compounds. Methods based on GLC are generally rapid and convenient for obtaining qualitative and/or quantitative analysis of one or more components in a mixture. Important criteria that organic molecules must meet to be amenable to GLC analysis are that they must be sufficiently volatile to elute through the GLC column and they must be thermally and chemically stable at the temperature necessary for elution. Furthermore, they must not interact in any way with the column packing or any materials of construction in the GLC system.

Apparently very few dyes or related compounds meet these criteria, as evidenced by the lack of literature on the application of GLC to dye analysis. This fact and the success that the various forms of liquid chromatography have had in separating virtually every type of dye in existence have made GLC a very unpopular way of doing dye separations and analyses.

Three reviews[1-3] published in the late 1960s either make no mention of GLC methods or state that the technique offers little opportunity, owing to the very low volatility of the majority of the compounds. The latter statement is probably true, but Terrill and Jacobs[4] later published a paper showing the application of GLC methods to some anthraquinone dyes and intermediates, and this is the only current paper known to me showing GLC application to dyes.

Owing to the sparsity of published information and probable lack of applicability of GLC to most dyes, the purpose of this chapter is not to promote GLC for dye analysis, but rather to show previous applications, published and unpublished, the apparatus that offers the best chance of success, previously published techniques for other compounds that are difficult to analyze by GLC that may be applicable to dyes, and conversion methods that may make dyes more amenable to GLC analysis.

2 SPECIAL APPARATUS

2.1 Column Packings

2.1.1 Liquid Phases. The lack of volatility of most dyes immediately limits the choice of liquid phases to a few that are stable at high temperatures. The use of OV-1 (a methyl silicone), OV-101 (a liquid methyl silicone), UC-W98 (a methyl vinyl silicone), and OV-17 (a methyl phenyl silicone) was reported previously.[4] Other liquid phases that are stable to 300°+ and may be applicable are Apiezon L (a hydrocarbon) and the newer liquid phases such as Poly S-179 [a poly(phenyl ether sulfone)] and the Dexsils 300, 400, and 410 (all carborane silicones). The newest highly polar phases are APOLAR 10C and OV-275 (both cyanosilicones), but these are limited to ~275° and therefore have less applicability. All these liquid phases are available from chromatography supply houses.

2.1.2 Solid Supports. The solid supports that have been reportedly used thus far are the less active variety such as Chromosorb W, HP (80/100-mesh), Chromosorb G, HP (80/100-mesh), and Diatoport S (80/100-mesh).[4] Micro glass beads and textured glass that are lightly loaded should offer a good chance for success since the elution temperature should be lower. Also the newer bonded phase columns such as those reported by DeStefano and Kirkland[5] and others sold by Waters Associates, Milford, Mass., under the trade name Durapak, might have application to dyes analyses. However, the use of the glass beads and bonded columns for dyes has not yet been reported.

The low vapor pressure of most dyes generally necessitates the use of light liquid loads. Recommended loads are generally 1–4% for the deactivated diatomaceous supports, although as high as 8% has been reported,[4] and 0.1–1.0% for the glass and textured glass beads. Most of these supports are available from chromatography supply houses, but those reported in ref. 5 are not yet available in sizes for GLC.

2.2   The GLC System

If possible, the entire system should be constructed of glass. Individual parts of the system are described below.

2.2.1   Sample Inlet. There seems little doubt that the best chance of success in the GLC of dyes is to use direct on-column injection. Dyes[4] and 2,4-dinitrophenylhydrazones (DNPHs)[6] were successfully separated with this approach. Although the latter compounds are not dyes, they are rather nonvolatile, do not have good thermal stability, and have structural similarities to dyes. In this work the investigators resorted to stop-flow, room-temperature injection using a volatile solvent and observed no efficiency loss. In some cases an injection port may be used, but it should have a glass liner, which should be changed at least daily. This prevents small amounts of nonvolatile compounds and decomposition products from accumulating and promoting the decomposition of dyes.

2.2.2   Column Materials. The only column material successfully used thus far is glass.[4] The DNPH work[6] was performed on both glass and stainless-steel columns. The glass columns were much superior; the metal columns worked only at very short lengths, 18 in., and high carrier flow rates to minimize contact time and area. Zlatkis[7] has successfully used nickel columns for steroid analysis, and this approach may be useful for separating dyes. It is also noteworthy that silanized stainless-steel columns are sometimes an adequate substitute for glass. However, in many cases this leads to problems (e.g., tailing, decomposition) and is generally not recommended.

2.2.3   Detectors. The only detector successfully used for dyes is the flame ionization type.[4] Experiments using thermal conductivity and electron capture were unsuccessful owing to the high elution and detector temperatures, which caused the dyes to coat the detectors and decompose.[8] Mass spectrometers of the type used by Horning et al.[9] for steroid analysis would probably be applicable, but these of course are very expensive.

2.2.4   Other Hardware. Since the GLC separation of dyes should be done with glass columns, the problem of connecting the columns in the chromatograph is real. In this respect the choice of ferrules is very important.

In early work Teflon (Du Pont) TFE fluorocarbon resin ferrules were used, but these are temperature limited ($\sim$225°) and exhibit plastic flow, which can result in leaks. Recently available Vespel (Du Pont) polyimide resin SP-1 ferrules are superior. However, they tend to get brittle and crack after prolonged usage at elevated temperatures. The best ferrules (and the most expensive) are the Graphlok graphite type. All these materials are now commercially available.

2.2.5 Use of Capillary Columns. The use of capillary columns has not yet been reported for dyes. Zlatkis et al.[7] and German and Horning[10] have successfully applied nickel and glass capillary columns, respectively, to steroid analysis. It appears that glass capillaries offer a very good opportunity for dye analysis by GLC because they allow work at lower temperature and offer higher column efficiency. However, preparation of efficient, stable glass capillary columns is somewhat difficult. Perkin-Elmer Corporation of Norwalk, Connecticut, is now marketing these columns, and this convenience may result in more widespread use.

3   METHODS TO MAKE COMPOUNDS MORE SUITABLE FOR GLC

3.1   Esterification

Esterification reactions to make compounds more amenable to GLC have long been used. Various silylation reagents such as N,O-bis(trimethylsilyl)-acetamide (BSA) and anhydrides such as acetic, trifluoroacetic (TFAA), and perfluorobutyric are generally common. T. Furuya et al.[11] used trimethylsilyl derivatives to chromatograph hydroxyanthraquinones, and Terrill and Jacobs[4] used BSA and TFAA derivatives in their study of anthraquinone dyes. When dyes contain hydroxy or amino functions, the use of these derivatizing agents can be very helpful.

3.2   Other Reactions

3.2.1 Caustic Fusions. Siggia, Whitlock, and Tao[12] used caustic fusion reactions in a preinjection pyrolysis unit to convert nonvolatile sulfonic acids to phenolic analogues, which are much more amenable to GLC. The reactions reported were quantitative (97–102% recovery); however, the compounds tested were rather simple sulfonic acids. Application of this technique to sulfonated dyes may yield quantitative reactions, but the successful chromatography of the resultant phenols may prove difficult.

Useful qualitative information might be obtained with this approach, but the technique has yet to be reported for dyes.

3.2.2 Carbohydrazide Reductions. Rahn and Siggia[13] reported a carbohydrazide reduction–GLC method for determining azo, nitro, and sulfonate compounds. The reactions are carried out in a preinjection pyrolysis unit and are not all quantitative (70–99 % recoveries). However, the precision is satisfactory and the techniques can be calibrated for quantitative work. Included among the compounds tested by these authors are Para Red, Sudan Yellow, and Methyl Orange. This reduction procedure appears to be feasible to apply to dye analysis, particularly to azo dyes that are difficult to elute without modification.

3.2.3 Functionality Methods. Siggia et al. reported several other reaction GLC methods for quantitatively determining carboxylic esters,[14] diazonium salts,[15] primary amines[16] and amides, urea, and nitrile compounds.[17] These reactions are also carried out in a preinjection pyrolysis unit and might be useful in piecing together dye structures, especially when a mass spectrometer is not available or the dyes are too nonvolatile for MS. Alternatively, all these reactions in Section 3.2 might be used in conjunction with MS or GLC–MS.

4 APPLICATIONS

4.1 2,4-Dinitrophenylhydrazones

The DNPHs of many carbonyl compounds were studied rather extensively in both metal and glass columns.[6] Under identical conditions of residence time and temperature the glass columns were much better. They yielded sharper peaks, better resolution, greater and more linear response, and better precision. Figure 5.1 shows a standard mixture, obtained with a flame ionization detector, of (1) anthracene and the DNPHs of (2) formaldehyde, (3) acetaldehyde, (4) propanal, (5) n-butanal, (6) n-pentanal, (7) benzaldehyde, and (8) p-tolualdehyde. This chromatogram readily demonstrates the usefulness of this technique for separating very closely related higher boiling compounds.

4.2 Anthraquinone Dyes and Intermediates

Terrill and Jacobs[4] in their study of some anthraquinone dyes and intermediates showed that mono-, di-, and trihydroxyanthraquinones tailed

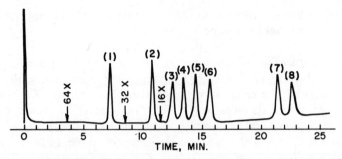

Figure 5.1   Chromatogram of anthracene (1) and 7 DPNHs (2)–(8)×.Column: 4-ft ×
$\frac{1}{12}$-in. i.d. glass column of 4% OV-17 on 80/100 Chromosorb G-AW-HMDS. Temperature:
150–300° at 7.5°/minute.   Carrier and flow rate: helium at 60 ml/minute.   Detector
temperature: 300° (reprinted with permission of *Journal of Chromatographic Science*).[6]

badly on nonpolar columns, but gave symmetrical peaks at longer retention
times on polar packings. Following the lead of Furuya and co-workers,[11]
they found that if the hydroxy functions are deactivated or masked by
conversion to the trimethylsilyl or trifluoracetic esters, the compounds can
be better chromatographed, and further that better results are obtained on
nonpolar than on polar columns. These results strongly indicate that hydrogen bonding by the anthraquinones caused the original tailing problems. This phenomenon is general for compounds other than anthraquinones, and this derivative technique is often used to make compounds with
amino groups more amenable to GLC.

Figure 5.2 shows the separation[4] of the following anthraquinone derivatives: (9) 1,4-$(NH_2)_2$-2-OMe; (10) 1-OH-4-NHPh; (11) 1-OH-4-NH-*p*-tolyl;
(12) 1-NHMe-4-(NH-*p*-tolyl); and (13) 1-NH_2-2-Br-4-(NH-*p*-tolyl). This
chromatogram illustrates the degree of separation that can be obtained
for compounds of similar structure, e.g., compounds (10) and (11), which
are different by only a side methyl group; the variety of functionality that
can be chromatographed, e.g., (9)–(13); and the magnitude of molecular
weight of compounds that can be eluted from the column, e.g., M 406 of
(13).

The separations shown in Figures 5.3 and 5.4 illustrate how GLC may
be used to monitor and/or optimize reactions involving dye intermediates.
The reaction of 1,5-dichloroanthraquinone (14) to form a mono- and di-
substituted derivative can be monitored by GLC. The chromatogram
(Figure 5.3) shows the separations of (14), (15) (1-Cl-5-R), and (16) (1,5-R_2)
with an internal standard for quantitative analysis.

Isomeric structures can often be readily separated and analyzed by
GLC. In Figure 5.4 two isomers of a trisubstituted anthraquinone, (17)

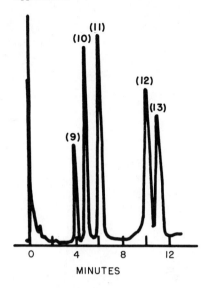

Figure 5.2 Chromatogram of mixture of five anthraquinone derivatives. Column: 4-ft $\times$ $\frac{1}{12}$-in. i.d. glass column of 7% UC-W98 on Chromosorb G, HP. Temperature 280–330° at 2°/minute (reprinted with permission of *Journal of Chromatographic Science*).[4]

(1-A-4,8-B₂) and (18) (1-A-4,5-B₂), are separated for analysis. The most important aspect to emphasize for the separation is that the substituted anthraquinone isomers have molecular weights well over 500. This represents the highest underivatized molecular weight dye successfully analyzed by GLC in our laboratory.

4.3   Other Dyes and Intermediates

Although the literature on the GLC of dyes is sparse, there are probably separations that have not been reported, and others that could be made. Ionic dyes cannot be handled by GLC unless some conversion reaction is performed to make the dye (or some fragment) chromatographable, such as the previously described reactions used by Siggia et al. Vat dyes and many other very nonvolatile dyes also fall into this category. Many non-ionic azo dyes can be directly chromatographed, but they are usually thermally unstable and give unreliable results. The chromatograms may be useful for qualitative information, but spurious peaks caused by compound degradation can provide misleading results.

GLC has also been used to monitor the production of a high molecular weight ($\sim$400) dye intermediate, namely, substituted phenyldiethanolamine dibenzoate. Figure 5.5 shows the separation of five compounds (19)–(23), in which Ar is phenyl with a *meta* substituent R: (19) ArNHCH₂CH₂OH; (20) ArN(CH₂CH₂OH)₂; (21) monobenzoate of (20); (22) dibenzoate of

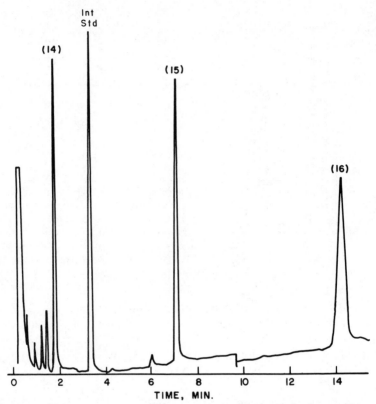

Figure 5.3   Utilization of GLC to follow an anthraquinone substitution reaction.   Column: 4-ft × $\frac{1}{12}$-in. i.d. glass column of 5% UC-W98 on 80/100 Chromosorb G, HP.   Temperature 240–345° at 15°/minute.

(20); and (23) dibenzoate of $ArN(CH_2CH_2OH)(CH_2CH_2OCH_2CH_2OH)$. Structures (21) and (23) were not conclusively proved. The utility of the GLC method for controlling or optimizing the production of this compound is evident.

4.4   Quantitative Aspects

GLC can be effectively used to quantitatively analyze certain dye systems. The study of DNPHs showed relative standard deviations of 3–5% for major components.[6] At much lower concentrations (tenfold), nonlinear response with somewhat higher standard deviations was obtained. These results are typical of many dye systems. However, some systems provide

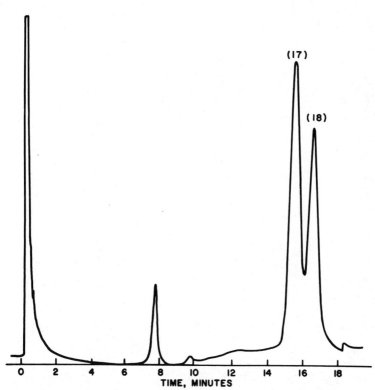

Figure 5.4   Utilization of GLC to separate high molecular weight dye isomers.   Column:
4-ft $\times$ $\frac{1}{12}$-in. i.d. glass column of 5% OV-101 on 60/80 Diatoport S.   Temperature 270–
360° at 13°/minute.

better results with linear response over a tenfold concentration range and
1–3% standard deviations. Unfortunately, however, many systems give
poor precision. Thermal instability at the elution and/or injection temperature is generally the cause. Whether or not this effect is limiting can
often be determined with thermal gravimetric or differential thermal
methods. In some cases, the dye can react with the solvent (e.g., methylene
chloride or DMF) at the high injection port temperatures. Using a non-
reactive solvent can sometimes remedy this problem. If not, alternatively,
the method of Papa and Turner may be useful.[6] This method involves
disconnecting the column at room temperature and injecting the dye in a
rather volatile solvent directly on the column. The column is then recon-
nected and the temperature is brought up to a modest level (e.g., 100–150°)
depending on the dye to be chromatographed and the solvent employed.

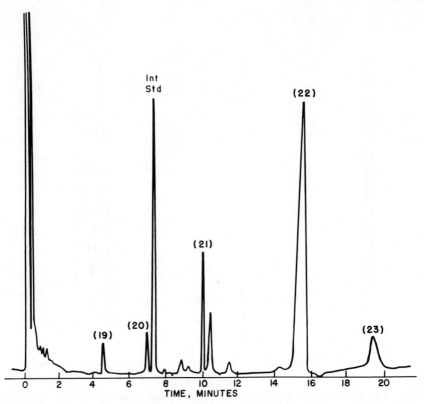

Figure 5.5 Chromatogram of reaction products for process optimization. Column: 6-ft × $\frac{1}{12}$-in. i.d. glass column of 3% OV-17 on Chromosorb W, HP. Temperature 180–335° at 16°/minute.

The conditions of flow, temperature, etc., are allowed to stabilize and the remainder of the solvent is eluted. Finally the temperature is increased to elute the sample.

REFERENCES

1. R. S. Williams, *J. Soc. Dyers Colour.*, **85**, 150 (1969).
2. J. C. Brown, *J. Soc. Dyers Colour.*, 137 (1969).
3. W. Titterington, *Chem. Ind. (London)*, 746 (1966).
4. J. B. Terrill and E. S. Jacobs, *J. Chromatogr. Sci.*, **8**, 604 (1970).
5. J. J. DeStefano and J. J. Kirkland, *J. Chromatogr. Sci.*, **12**, 337 (1974).
6. L. J. Papa and L. P. Turner, *J. Chromatogr. Sci.*, **10**, 744 (1972).

7. A. Zlatkis et al., *Anal. Chem.*, **45**, 763 (1973).
8. J. B. Terrill, E. I. du Pont de Nemours and Co., Inc., Haskell Laboratory, private communication.
9. E. C. Horning et al., *Anal. Chem.*, **46**, 706 (1974).
10. A. L. German and E. C. Horning, *J. Chromatogr. Sci.*, **11**, 76 (1963).
11. T. Furuya, S. Shibata, and H. Iizuku, *J. Chromatogr.*, **21**, 116 (1966).
12. S. Siggia, L. R. Whitlock, and J. C. Tao, *Anal. Chem.*, **41**, 1387 (1969).
13. P. C. Rahn and S. Siggia, *Anal. Chem.*, **45**, 2336 (1973).
14. S. P. Frankoski and S. Siggia, *Anal. Chem.*, **44**, 507 (1972).
15. A. Savitsky and S. Siggia, *Anal. Chem.*, **46**, 149 (1975).
16. *Ibid.*, 153 (1974).
17. S. P. Frankoski and S. Siggia, *Anal. Chem.*, **44**, 2078 (1972).

CHAPTER SIX

Solution
Coloristics

CHARLES E. GARLAND

---

1 INTRODUCTION

Coloristics combines spectrophotometric and colorimetric measurements to define and interpret color. The spectrophotometer measures color as energy distribution by wavelength, whereas colorimetric measurements determine color composition in terms of three artificial primaries. Although spectrophotometric techniques are not limited to the visible spectrum, most dye analyses are made in the visible region to simulate end use characteristics for assessment of dye quality. UV and/or IR spectra are useful in characterizing the chemical structure of a dye, but they contribute little to measurement of the subtle shade and strength differences that are important in quality control. Colorimetry is a valuable means of extending spectrophotometry, because it provides dimensions for color specification and the detection of small shade differences between samples. Computers make it possible to benefit from both measurement techniques, for colorimetric data can be computed from spectrophotometric data. More detailed discussions of spectrophotometry and colorimetry are available in textbooks and should be referred to for additional information.[1-8]

This chapter is devoted to the application of coloristics for the determination of intrinsic spectral and colorimetric properties of colorants (dyes, dye intermediates, by-products, or impurities). The measured properties are compared with those of either other colorants or a standard of the same species. The basis for comparison may be visual correlation, composition, spectrophotometric, colorimetric, or any combination of these properties. Practical uses of these comparative data are discussed here, together with some analytical pitfalls associated with solution coloristics.

2 COLOR MEASURING INSTRUMENTS

There are many diverse reasons for measuring color, and instrument require-ments vary widely with each application. Relative measurements at a single location are obviously less stringent than absolute measurements that must provide comparable data when measured at different locations. Spectro-photometers, colorimeters, and instruments that combine various features of both are available to meet most of these requirements. Although simple, low-cost colorimeters and spectrophotometers are usually adequate for relative color measurements on specific problems, the more complex and costly double-beam recording spectrophotometer, interfaced to a computer, is the preferred instrument system for the general analysis of synthetic dyes. Spectrophotometric data are massaged by the computer to provide colorimetric data. A comparison of available instruments and their various methods of operation are beyond the scope of this chapter. General dis-cussions of spectrophotometers are available,[1, 9–11] as well as vendors' speci-fications and operating manuals.

2.1 Instrument Calibration

Calibration requirements vary with the needs of the user. Simple calibration procedures are included in the operating manuals that accompany most spectrophotometers and more elaborate techniques are described in the literature.[12–15] The instrument should be calibrated in the wavelength and photometric range that will be used most frequently.

The minimum essential calibration for most work involves adjustment of the base line to $100\% \ T$, or zero absorbance, and checking wavelength and photometric accuracy with glass filters. Filters having a number of strong and narrow absorption bands, such as didymium and holmium oxide glass, are suggested for wavelength calibration. Filters having broader absorption bands are more desirable for checking photometric accuracy. Glass standards are available commercially, or they may be obtained with certified transmittance data from the National Bureau of Standards.[12,14] Solution transmittance standards for UV and visible spectrophotometry are also available.[14] Glass filters are superior to liquid solutions as inter-laboratory standards; however, they change with time owing to light exposure, wear, and the accumulation of surface films.[16,17] Although there are more problems with stability and handling when liquid solution standards are used, they may be more desirable for intralaboratory precision studies because the sample handling is identical to that used for the analysis.

Since in this discussion colorimetric data are computed from spectrophotometric data, uncertainties are to be expected in the colorimetric data that are attributable to spectrophotometric errors. Wavelength and photometric deviations are not descriptions of colorimetric deviations, and different colors may vary considerably in colorimetric response to the same error in spectrophotometric measurement. Therefore if colorimetry is to be used routinely, colorimetric data should be obtained as part of the calibration procedure. Tristimulus values and chromaticity coordinates can be obtained for the filters used in calibration, and chromaticity plots provide a convenient way of illustrating day-to-day fluctuations (See Section 5.1). The effects of spectrophotometric errors on colorimetric data have been investigated by the National Bureau of Standards.[12,18—21]

2.2   Computation Facilities

Computation requirements vary from one laboratory to another, depending upon the type of problems involved. Although many coloristics problems can be handled with a simple calculator, there are also problems that would be extremely difficult or impossible without a computer. Manual conversion from spectrophotometric to colorimetric data is tedious and time consuming. Spectrophotometer accessories are commercially available that automatically compute tristimulus values from a spectral scan.[22—25] Early work with large digital computers involved manual transfer of data from spectrophotometer to computer, and programs were written to compute colorimetric data,[26—31] and convert the data from one color system to another.[32] The current trend is toward automatic digitization of spectral data with simultaneous treatment by a computer, which may vary in size from a dedicated minicomputer to a large multipurpose computer.[29,30] Computers are also used to control spectrophotometers during measurement.[33—35]

Ernst distinguishes four steps in the spectroscopic data gathering process: (a) the spectroscopic experiment, (b) data transformation and filtering procedure, (c) the data reduction process, and (d) data interpretation.[29] It is shown that computers may enhance performance and efficiency at all four steps. Measured spectrophotometric data are improved by this approach via applications such as base-line correction, curve smoothing, differentiation, peak finding, and resolution of complex spectra into component peaks.[34-36] Improvements in the accuracy and precision of the measured data of course ameliorate the derived colorimetric data. Once reliable coloristics data are obtained they can be massaged further by the computer to derive additional information such as excitation purity, dominant wavelength,[37,38] color differences,[39] formulations for color matching,[40,41] and standard depth.[42] Although the computation possibilities are virtually unlimited, there are few applications reported in the literature, even though complex mathematics in the reports infers that computers were used.

3 FUNDAMENTAL CALCULATIONS AND TERMINOLOGY

When a beam of radiant energy is passed through a colorant solution photons are absorbed by the colorant, causing an electron transition from one energy level to another. Because colorants vary in molecular structure the energy contents of the absorbed photons also vary, producing absorption spectra that characterize the molecular species of colorant. Visible spectra are considered from two viewpoints: the radiant power transmitted and the radiant power absorbed by a solution of colorant. Transmittance determined by a double-beam spectrophotometer is defined by

$$T = \frac{P_{soln}/P_0}{P_{solv}/P_0} = \frac{P_{soln}}{P_{solv}} \tag{1}$$

where P_{soln} is the radiant power transmitted by the sample solution and P_{solv} is the radiant power transmitted by the reference solvent (blank). The incident power, P_0, in the sample beam is equal to that in the reference beam and the term cancels from the equation. By using careful technique and matched cells, errors attributed to reflectance and scattering are essentially eliminated, for they have an equal influence on numerator and denominator of Equation 1. A recording spectrophotometer usually plots transmittance spectra with percent transmittance ($\% T$) as the ordinate and wavelength (λ) as the abscissa. Percent transmittance is defined as

$$\% T = 100T \tag{2}$$

Transmittance is converted to absorbance by the following relationship:

$$A = \log\left(\frac{1}{T}\right) \tag{3}$$

Many recording spectrophotometers are capable of operating in the absorbance mode and provide plots in which absorbance is the ordinate and wavelength the abscissa.

The fundamental absorption law that relates radiant power absorbed to concentration of absorbent and the distance radiant power must travel through the absorbing medium is stated by the following equation:

$$A = \alpha bc \qquad (4)$$

where A is absorbance as defined in Equation 3; α is a constant, known as absorptivity, which is characteristic of the particular combination of colorant and solvent at a specified wavelength; b is the sample path length, or the internal breadth of the cell; and c is the concentration of colorant in the sample solution. Though it is recognized that the above law had several contributors, special significance is ascribed to Beer's investigation of concentration effects, and the law is commonly referred to as Beer's law.

A third mode of operating a recording spectrophotometer produces a plot in which the logarithm of absorbance is the ordinate and wavelength is the abscissa. The main advantage of this technique is that the curve shape does not change with concentration. An extensive discussion of the log A technique is offered by Stearns.[5]

Figures 6.1 and 6.2 illustrate the effect of concentration on spectral curves of Disperse Red 17 obtained by the two common methods of spectral scanning. Points on Curves A, B, and C vary linearly with concentra-

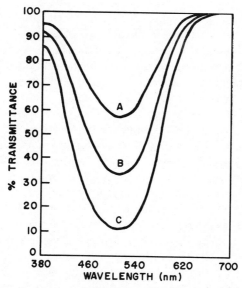

Figure 6.1 Transmittance curves of Disperse Red 17 at three levels of concentration. Concentrations of dye are in the ratio $1:2:4$, respectively, for curves A, B, and C.

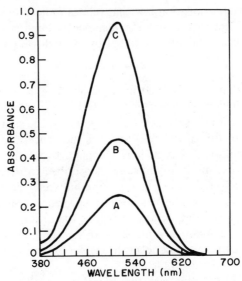

Figure 6.2 Absorbance curves of Disperse Red 17 at three levels of concentration. Concentrations of dye are in the ratio 1:2:4, respectively, for curves *A*, *B*, and *C*.

tion at all wavelengths in Figure 6.2, whereas in Figure 6.1 they are non-linear.

Many spectral analyses require data to be taken from a single point on a curve. The wavelength at which the data are taken is called the analytical wavelength. Stearns[5] lists six factors that influence the selection of an analytical wavelength: (*a*) wavelength errors, (*b*) transmittance errors, (*c*) solution effects, (*d*) magnitude of absorptivity, (*e*) resolution, and (*f*) effect of impurities. These factors should be considered for each new product that is to be analyzed before selecting an analytical wavelength. Errors associated with factors *a*, *d*, and *e* are minimized by using the absorbance maximum as the analytical wavelength and avoiding points along slopes of curves. Transmittance errors are minimized by selecting an analytical wavelength at a transmittance level that is within the optimum operating range of the instrument (See Section 4.2). Transmittance is adjusted to this optimum range by changing the concentration and/or the sample path length. Solution effects (See Section 4.1) that prevent accurate measurement in one solvent system are frequently avoided by changing solvents. In systems where there is an isosbestic point, it can be safely used as the analytical wavelength. If impurities are present, the analytical wavelength must be chosen at a point where their effect is minimum. In general, if there are no adverse solution or impurity effects, the analytical wavelength is chosen at the point of maximum absorbance (minimum transmittance) and is designated λ_{max}. In addition to its desirability as the analytical wavelength, λ_{max} is an intrinsic property of the colorant being analyzed. A second property commonly used in characterizing colorants is the absorptivity calculated at λ_{max} and designated α_{max}. It is a special adaptation of Equation 4, which may be rewritten as

$$\alpha_{max} = \frac{A_{max}}{bc} \tag{5}$$

where A_{max} is the absorbance taken at λ_{max}. The α_{max} values calculated for Curves A, B, and C of Figure 6.2 are all equal to 39.0, illustrating the conformance of Disperse Red 17 to Beer's law in the selected solvent system.

Ever since Isaac Newton found that a prism would separate sunlight into the spectral colors, experimenters have sought to analyze, or formulate, color in terms of its component parts. To date the culmination of this search was a component analysis based on artificial primary colors that was established in 1931 by the Commission International de l'Eclairage (CIE). The 1931 CIE system[43,44] is defined by the following equations

$$X = \sum_{380}^{770} E_s T \bar{x} \, \Delta\lambda$$

$$Y = \sum_{380}^{770} E_s T \bar{y} \, \Delta\lambda \tag{6}$$

$$Z = \sum_{380}^{770} E_s T \bar{z} \, \Delta\lambda$$

where the relative amount of artificial primaries (commonly referred to as tristimulus values) X, Y, and Z is equal to the sum of the products of spectral energy distribution of the illumination source (E_s); the transmittance of the sample (T); and the color-matching functions of the average observer ($\bar{x}$, $\bar{y}$, and $\bar{z}$) over the visible spectrum (from 380 to 770 nm) at some preestablished wavelength interval ($\Delta\lambda$). The three illumination sources defined by the CIE are: Source A, incandescent light (E_A); Source B, simulated noon sunlight (E_B); and Source C, simulated overcast sky daylight (E_C). Two sets of color-matching functions are currently being used: (a) those developed in 1931 using a 2° visual field, and (b) those developed in 1963 using a 10° visual field. The 10° observer functions supplement the earlier functions in situations requiring improved correlation with visual color matching of large samples. The 2° observer functions are normally used in transmittance measurements. Tables of spectral energy distribution for the three sources and color-matching functions for 2° and 10° observers are available in several texts at wavelength intervals of 1, 5,

10, and 20 nm.[1-3] Tables showing the products of spectral energy distri-
bution and color-matching functions (e.g., $E_c\bar{x}$, $E_c\bar{y}$, $E_c\bar{z}$) at incremental
wavelengths are also provided. These products are normalized by setting
the sum of $E\bar{y}$ values to equal 100 with a corresponding proportion adjustment to the sums of $E\bar{x}$ and $E\bar{z}$. Therefore the 100% T line ($T = 1.00$) has
a Y equal to 100 regardless of the illuminant used. Systems for the manual
calculation of tristimulus values are available, although since the advent
of computers they are seldom used.

The Y tristimulus value has special significance, for it was established
as a direct measure of luminance or lightness. The measured Y value is
equal to the luminous transmittance of the sample and is used as one of
three dimensions for specifying color. The other two dimensions define
shade, or chromaticity, and are calculated as the ratios of the tristimulus
values X and Y to the total stimulus:

$$x = \frac{X}{X + Y + Z} \quad \text{and} \quad y = \frac{Y}{X + Y + Z} \tag{7}$$

where x and y are known as chromaticity coordinates. A z coordinate can
be calculated in the same manner, although it is not needed for color
specification since $x + y + z = 1$. Therefore, the three dimensions used
for specifying color in the CIE system are x, y, and Y. A plot of chromaticity coordinates for the spectrum colors forms a horseshoe-shaped spectrum locus known as a chromaticity diagram. Figure 6.3 illustrates the
x, y, and Y space within which all real colors must lie. The point N, called

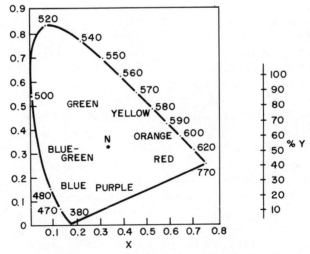

Figure 6.3 CIE chromaticity diagram and luminance axis (% Y). The spectrum colors
are shown by wavelength around the horseshoe-shaped spectrum locus.

the neutral point, indicates the position of the illuminant, which is source C in most transmittance work. The third dimension, Y axis, is perpendicular to the $x-y$ plane at the neutral point (N) and has a scale of 0–100%.

Variability of CIE tristimulus values and chromaticity coordinates with changes in colorant concentration are shown in Table 6.1. Tristimulus values decrease nonlinearly with increasing concentration, and if the chromaticity coordinates are plotted on a chromaticity diagram, they are found to move with dilution in an arc that reaches the neutral point at infinite dilution. Since x, y, and Y vary with concentration, any color specification using the CIE system must include the colorant concentration at which the measurement was made, and sample comparisons must be made at identical concentrations.

The nonlinear relationship between tristimulus values and colorant concentration decreases the utility of conventional colorimetry. This impediment is traceable to the transmittance component in Equations 6. Complementary tristimulus colorimetry provides a method of numerically characterizing colorants in solution by computing their tristimulus values in the absorbance mode.[45–49] By substituting absorbance for transmittance in Equations 6 the desired linearity is obtained. The equations are rewritten as

$$X' = \sum_{380}^{770} E_s A \bar{x} \, \Delta\lambda$$

$$Y' = \sum_{380}^{770} E_s A \bar{y} \, \Delta\lambda \qquad (8)$$

$$Z' = \sum_{380}^{770} E_s A \bar{z} \, \Delta\lambda$$

Table 6.1 Effect of Colorant Concentration on CIE Tristimulus Values and Chromaticity Coordinates[a]

Variable	Concentration (g/l)		
	0.00248	0.00496	0.00992
X	82.83	71.00	55.66
Y	73.80	56.12	36.52
Z	86.48	63.73	36.45
Σ	243.11	190.85	128.63
x	0.3407	0.3720	0.4327
y	0.3036	0.2940	0.2839

[a] Data obtained from the transmittance curves for Disperse Red 17 shown in Figure 6.1.

where only the photometric function (A for T) is affected, and all the other terms are as previously defined. The prime designation is used to indicate the different origin, and the name is changed to complementary tristimulus values. The Y' value is based on normalization of the $E_s\bar{y}$ sum to 1.000 instead of 100.0. Instruments that operate in the absorbance mode can be used for direct computation of complementary tristimulus values, provided that appropriate adjustment is made for the different Y' value.

Each of the three complementary stimuli is linear with respect to concentration (see below). Therefore, the total stimulus ($X' + Y' + Z'$), a function of the area under the absorbance curve, is linearly related to concentration and can be used to calculate a pseudoabsorptivity. Analogous to Equation 5, this absorptivity is calculated as

$$\alpha_{vis} = \frac{X' + Y' + Z'}{bc} \tag{9}$$

where α_{vis} is the absorptivity across the visible spectrum and the other terms are as previously defined. Similar to α_{max}, the α_{vis} is an intrinsic property of the dye.

Complementary chromaticity coordinates can also be calculated:

$$x' = \frac{X'}{X' + Y' + Z'} \quad \text{and} \quad y' = \frac{Y'}{X' + Y' + Z'} \tag{10}$$

Table 6.2   Effect of Colorant Concentration on Complementary Tristimulus Values and Chromaticity Coordinates[a]

	Concentration (g/l)		
Variable	0.00248	0.00496	0.00992
X'	0.0758	0.1512	0.3036
Y'	0.1377	0.2756	0.5514
Z'	0.1619	0.3227	0.6472
Σ	0.3749	0.7495	1.5022
α_{vis}	151.2	151.1	151.4
x'	0.2022	0.2017	0.2021
y'	0.3673	0.3677	0.3671

[a] Data obtained from the absorbance curves for Disperse Red 17 shown in Figure 6.2.

where the prime differentiates these coordinates from those of Equation 7. The x' and y' coordinates have two unique features that are described below.

1. Since X', Y', and Z' are individually proportional to concentration, the complementary chromaticity coordinates are invariant with concentration. Table 6.2 illustrates these properties of complementary tristimulus colorimetry by using data from the absorbance curves for Disperse Red 17 shown in Figure 6.2.

2. The use of absorbance to compute tristimulus values results in chromaticity coordinates that plot on the opposite side of the neutral point from coordinates derived from transmittance measurement. This behavior, which results from absorbance being a function of the reciprocal of transmittance (Equation 3), is the reason that the system is called complementary. The principle is illustrated by comparing the complementary chromaticity diagram of Figure 6.4 with the conventional CIE diagram in Figure 6.3. The wavelengths indicated are complementary with respect to dominant wavelength. Complementary wavelength approximates the wavelength at maximum absorption (λ_{max}) for bright colors.

The dimensions used for specifying color in complementary color space are x' and y' for shade definition and α_{max} or α_{vis} for strength definition. These terms may be used (1) as absolute values for identity or (2) in a relative way to compare one dye with another, or a sample to its standard.

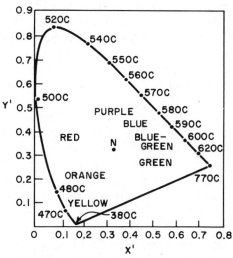

Figure 6.4 Complementary chromaticity diagram showing the positions of colors. The colors are 180° away from their positions in the CIE diagram (Figure 6.3).

4 VARIABLES IN THE ANALYTICAL METHOD

Specific details concerning sampling, solvents, weights, volumes, and special techniques to cope with solution and measurement idiosyncrasies must be established individually for each species of colorant.[50,51] Although several of these problems are minimized simply by good analytical technique, some problems are unique to the spectrophotometric measurement of colorants in solution. A few of the pitfalls encountered in solution coloristics are discussed below.

4.1 Solution Variables

Solution variables may have a pronounced effect on color measurement. Stearns[5] succinctly described their importance as follows. "Each effect should be considered from its dual aspect; by measuring the material the effect may be studied, and by controlling the effect the material may be determined."

In developing an analytical method each new colorant should be screened to determine its behavior toward each of the solution variables. If a solution variable is found to have a significant effect on the coloristics, conditions must be changed to maximize analytical precision. Individual solution variables that affect spectrophotometric data are widely discussed in the literature, and more generalized treatments are provided by Stearns,[5] White,[52] and Commerford.[53] Colorimetry is omitted from most discussions of solution variables, yet it adds additional dimensions necessary for total color specification. Shade and strength parameters may both vary with solution conditions; however, in some instances (see below) one parameter may change without any significant effect upon the other. In the following discussion a few examples are provided to illustrate solution effects on coloristic data and the use of coloristics to measure solution effects.

4.1.1 Solvent Effect.

Coloristic specifications for most colorants change quite markedly with changes in the solvent, and the effects are not predictable in any general way. Therefore, color specifications should include the solvent system in which the measurement was made, and coloristic data for different samples should not be compared unless measurements are made in the same solvent system. By selecting one solvent system for a class of dyes, and monitoring the quality of the solvent(s) used, one can minimize solvent effects.

If a mixed solvent is specified, care should be taken to ensure that the mixture contains the proper ratio of solvents. A mixture of water and dimethylacetamide (20:80 v/v) is an excellent solvent for several classes of dyes; however, the coloristic properties may vary if the solvent ratio is incorrect. Figure 6.5 illustrates a change in spectral characteristics of Acid Red 266 with the ratio of water to dimethylacetamide. Increasing the water content produces a hypsochromic effect with little change in absorptivity. A plot of the complementary chromaticity coordinates indicates the degree of shade change with solvent ratio. With this type of plot, with small incremental changes in solvent ratio, Acid Red 266 can be used as an indicator for controlling the desired 20:80 solvent ratio. The shade change is so gradual with small changes in solvent ratio that visual judgment of an end point near the desired 20:80 solvent ratio is impossible.

Theoretical explanations of the solvent influence on absorption spectra are discussed in the literature and should be referred to for a better understanding of both cause and effect.[5] It is important to recognize that although solution variables are discussed individually in this section, one variable may exert considerable influence upon one or more of the other variables. Changing solvents may alter the *cis–trans* equilibrium in an azo dye because

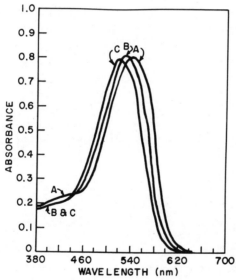

Figure 6.5 Curves showing the effect of water–dimethylacetamide ratio on the spectral characteristics of Acid Red 266.

Curve	Ratio Water:DMAC	λ_{max}	α_{max}	x'	y'
A	0:100	540	13.39	0.2560	0.4571
B	20:80	530	13.33	0.2167	0.4460
C	40:60	520	13.23	0.1929	0.4226

of differences in polarity of the solvents, because the isomeric balance is sensitive to irradiation or temperature effects in the different solvent, or both. Solvents affect aggregation of dyes and may result in solutions that do not conform to Beer's law. Therefore it is frequently possible to solve a problem with one of the effects listed below by changing solvents.

4.1.2 pH Effect. The color of many dyes varies quite drastically with pH, and in most instances this behavior is predictable from chemical structure. Spectrophotometry was used by W. R. Brode more than 50 years ago in pH studies where indicator dyes were used,[5] and more recently complementary tristimulus colorimetry was similarly applied.[45,46]

Changes in Acid Orange 132 with pH variations from neutral to strongly alkaline are shown in Figure 6.6. The wavelength (468 nm) where the four curves cross is known as an isosbestic point and is indicative of an equilibrium where the acid and basic forms of the dye have the same absorbance value. If pH cannot be controlled, the isosbestic point can be used to determine absorptivity values that are invariant with pH. Obviously colorimetric data also vary with pH. To provide reliable coloristic data for products that vary with pH, it is necessary to adjust the pH prior to measurement. Adjustment is made either by titration or by using a solvent buffered to a specific pH. For ease of operation the buffered solvent is preferred, provided its buffering capacity is capable of suppressing pH variations from one sample to another.

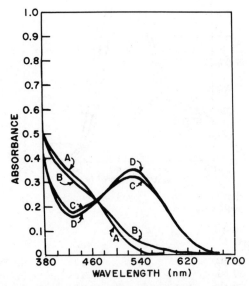

Figure 6.6 Curves showing the effect of pH on absorbance spectra of Acid Orange 132. Curve *A* is at pH 7.0, *B* at 8.2, *C* at 10.5, and *D* at 13.0.

4.1.3 Concentration Effect. Variation in absorptivity with concentration represents nonconformance to Beer's law rather than a failure of the law. Beer's law holds for single molecular or ionic species of the colorant being analyzed. If aggregate molecules and/or ions are present in equilibrium, the equilibrium may shift with changes in concentration, and the system does not conform to Beer's law. If the aggregate equilibrium is constant with changes in concentration, the system conforms. Even aqueous pigment dispersions conform to the law if particle size distribution is invariant with changes in concentration. The effects of association on Beer's law behavior of dye solutions was studied by Duff and Giles over an extended concentration range.[54] They found that dyes that did not conform to Beer's law because of aggregation phenomena in aqueous solution may exhibit ideal behavior over a thousandfold concentration range in organic solvents. Wide concentration ranges are usually not necessary in actual practice. Variations of $\pm 50\%$ relative to the dye concentration necessary to provide optimum absorbance are not too restrictive for most work.

Other studies of dye aggregation in various solvents have measured the effect on solution coloristics and then used the effect to determine the degree of aggregation.[55–58] A computer program was also used to separate overlapping monomer and dimer contributions to the spectra of azo dyes and determine the equilibrium constants of dimerization.[59]

Conformance to Beer's law is required to obtain reliable coloristic data (see Figure 6.2). Nonconformance is usually dealt with by narrowing the concentration range or by changing the solvent. Strength alone can be accurately determined in a nonconforming system by either measuring the absorbance at an isosbestic point or by making appropriate corrections from a predetermined plot of absorbance versus concentration.

4.1.4 Temperature Effect. At very low temperatures the molecular vibrations of a colorant may be so restricted that the solution becomes colorless. At room temperature and higher, color variation with temperature is usually attributed to isomerization, aggregation, or chemical reaction.[5,57] Temperature effects on coloristic properties are either reversible or irreversible. A reversible effect during heating to dissolve the dye is unimportant because the original form is obtained after cooling. If an irreversible change occurs during heating for dissolution, either the altered color can be measured per se or the dissolution conditions can be changed to avoid the temperature effect. If temperature affects the dilute solution, it should be thoroughly investigated to determine whether the change is reversible and at what temperature the change occurs. Jacketed cells are available for controlling temperature during a spectral scan. Once the behavior of the colorant solution with change in temperature is understood, a temperature for measurement is selected that will ensure reproducible results. A change in solvent may eliminate the temperature problem entirely.

4.1.5 Plating Effect. Some solutions have the property of depositing a monomolecular layer of solute on solid surfaces that touch them. Once this layer is formed it does not increase with further exposure. This phenomenon, known as plating, can be very troublesome in spectrophotometry if it is not recognized. Subsequent analyses in a plated cell show increased strength for the same species of dye, and chromaticity problems if the shade of the dye being analyzed is different from that of the plated dye. Figure 6.7 illustrates a plating effect with Basic Blue 82. The same solution was analyzed twice, originally with a clean dry cell and again after the cell was plated with the original solution. Plating increased the absorptivity of the second analysis by 1.7%, but the effect on chromaticity was negligible. If a yellow were analyzed in the same cell there would be a considerable effect on the chromaticity because of the blue plating. Although this effect is not limited to basic dyes, they are probably the worst offenders.

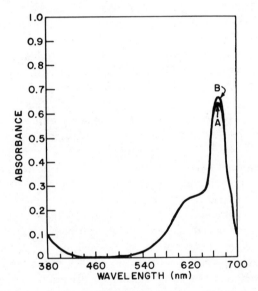

Figure 6.7 Curves showing plating of Basic Blue 82 in a 20:80 mixture (v/v) of water and dimethylacetamide. Curve A represents the initial measurement and curve B represents a repeat measurement after the cell was plated.

Curve	α_{max}	x'	y'
A	92.04	0.6019	0.3718
B	93.58	0.6013	0.3718

There are three techniques for coping with the plating problem: clean the cell thoroughly after each analysis, find a solvent that eliminates plating, or preplate both sample and reference cells prior to scanning. A dye solution that plates the cell also plates the glassware used in handling it, and care should be taken that contaminated flasks and pipettes are thoroughly cleaned.

4.1.6 Fluorescence Effect. Luminescence is the property of a material that absorbs radiant energy that allows the material to reemit radiant energy. If there is a measurable time delay between absorption and reemission, the phenomenon is called phosphorescence. If the reemission is immediate, without any measurable delay, the phenomenon is known as fluorescence. Under ordinary conditions fluorescence is much more common than phosphorescence. In most fluorescent materials a portion of the absorbed energy is converted to heat, resulting in emitted energy that has less energy per photon than the excitation energy, and hence a longer wavelength. Fluorescent radiation is emitted equally and randomly in all directions. This property introduces an error into absorption spectra obtained from a spectrophotometer with an integrating sphere because most of the fluorescent radiation is added to the transmitted energy, thus increasing the apparent transmittance. If the sample is moved back 8–10 cm from the entrance window of the integrating sphere, most of the fluorescent radiation is dissipated into the black sample compartment, and such a small fraction moves along the optical path that its contribution to the measured transmittance is negligible. Curve *B* in Figure 6.8 shows how fluorescence of a derivative of Basic Violet 10 changes its absorbance spectra from Curve *A*, where fluorescence was essentially eliminated. Absorptivity and chromaticity are both affected by the fluorescence.

Problems in measuring fluorescence,[60] combined with the many factors that influence it in solution as well as on the substrate,[61,62] lessen the probability of good correlation between solution coloristics and end use tests. An impurity may be more effective in quenching fluorescence in solution than it is on the substrate, or concentration differences may enhance (or inhibit) fluorescence of a dye in one system more than in another.

Fluorescent commercial dyes vary from those that absorb in the ultraviolet and fluoresce in the visible to those that absorb in the visible and fluoresce in the infrared.[63] Although this important property deserves more attention it can be discussed only briefly here as a potential source of error in solution coloristics.

4.1.7 Irradiation Effects. Color change with exposure to light may be either reversible or irreversible. The reversible property is known as photo-

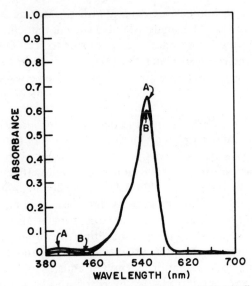

Figure 6.8   Curves of a derivative of Basic Violet 10 in a pH 10.5 buffer solution show the effect of fluorescence.   Curve *B* was obtained with the sample solution adjacent to the window of the integrating sphere, and curve *A* was obtained with the solution set back 8.0 cm from the sphere window.

Curve	α_{max}	x'	y'
A	44.77	0.2862	0.6170
B	43.00	0.2850	0.6240

chromism and the irreversible property is light fading.[64, 65] Solvent Yellow 2 is used as an example of photochromism in Figure 6.9. After 1 hour of exposure to ordinary laboratory fluorescent lighting the absorptivity decreased to about 56% of its original value and the complementary chromaticity changed quite drastically. After the irradiated solution was placed in the dark it gradually recovered, reaching its original coloristic value in about 48 hours (Curve *E* is superposed on Curve *A*).

Light fading is irreversible, and colorants that fade should not be exposed to light prior to measurement. Dye solutions that are sensitive to irradiation should be stored in the dark or low-actinic glassware. Very photochromic dyes should be allowed to stand in the dark cell compartment for about 15 minutes prior to scanning to ensure maximum color value. Conversely, the irradiated form of photochromic dyes can be studied by using a special illumination device during the scanning.[66] Sensitive dyes are not affected during spectrophotometric measurement if the light is monochromated prior to irradiation; however, they may be affected in instruments that irradiate the sample before the light is monochromated.

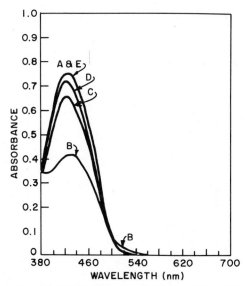

WAVELENGTH (nm)

Figure 6.9 Curves showing photochromism of Solvent Yellow 2 in dimethylacetamide. Curve A is the initial measurement, curve B after 1 hour exposure to laboratory lighting, and curves C, D, and E represent solution B after 1, 24, and 48 hours in the dark.

Curve	α_{max}	x'	y'
A	112.00	0.1518	0.0345
B	63.11	0.1495	0.0513
C	96.89	0.1512	0.0380
D	107.56	0.1517	0.0356
E	112.00	0.1519	0.0345

4.1.8 Surfactant Effect. Nonionic surfactants are frequently added in small amounts to the analytical solvent as a dissolution aid; this may be specified in the procedure. However, if a surfactant is inadvertently introduced as a contaminant it may affect the spectral properties of the dye being analyzed.

Many commercial dyes (especially the disperse class) contain surfactants to enhance their rheological and dyeing properties. These surfactants may affect coloristic measurement via the solvent effect discussed above, or they may impart additional color to the system. Figure 6.10 shows the effect of a surfactant on Disperse Yellow 54. It has also been reported that the presence of surfactants may enhance the sensitivity of a dye in solution to irradiation.[53]

There are two standard techniques for coping with samples containing problem surfactants: either use a standard that contains the same amount and type of surfactant as the sample, or separate the surfactant from the dye by extraction prior to analysis.

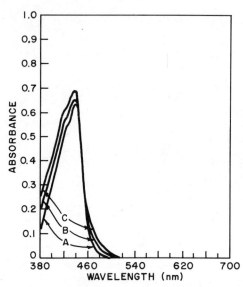

Figure 6.10 Curves showing the effect of a lignin sulfonate dispersant on a solution of Disperse Yellow 54 in a 20:80 mixture (v/v) of water in dimethylacetamide.

Curve	Parts dispersant/ part of 100% dye	α_{max}	x'	y'
A	0	136.38	0.1618	0.0170
B	2.3	140.85	0.1617	0.0243
C	4.6	146.38	0.1653	0.0381

4.1.9   Foreign Ion Effect.   Many dyes are good chelating agents as evidenced from their structures and the extensive commercial use of metallized dyes. Thus it should be no surprise that dyes scavenge metal ions from solution and that the metal ions change the coloristic properties. The effect of 10 ppm of metal ions on Direct Blue 15 is illustrated in Figure 6.11. The effect is a decrease in strength and a change in shade. Complementary chromaticity coordinates are also useful in monitoring intentional metallization reactions to determine when the reactions are complete. The stock solution for evaluating the effect of metal ions is prepared by dissolving each of the following in 250 ml distilled water in a volumetric flask: 3.480 g $Al(NO_3)_3 \cdot 9H_2O$; 0.476 g $Ba(NO_3)_2$; 1.470 g $Ca(NO_3)_2 \cdot 4H_2O$; 1.924 g $Cr(NO_3)_3 \cdot 9H_2O$; 0.951 g $Cu(NO_3)_2 \cdot 3H_2O$; 1.810 g $Fe(NO_3)_3 \cdot 9H_2O$; 1.240 g $Ni(NO_3)_2 \cdot 6H_2O$; 0.399 $Pb(NO_3)_2$; 0.538 g $SnCl_2 \cdot 2H_2O$ + 3 ml conc. nitric acid; and 0.522 $ZnCl_2$. The 10 solutions (2500 ml) are mixed, and the mixture is stored in an amber container. One milliliter of the metal ion solution is added to each 100 ml dilute dye solution. The

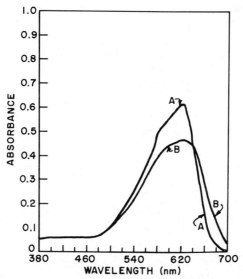

Figure 6.11 Curves showing the effect of metal ions on a solution of Direct Blue 15 in a 20:80 mixture (v/v) of water and dimethylacetamide. Curve A represents the initial solution and Curve B represents the same solution containing 1.0 ppm each of 10 different metal ions.

Curve	α_{max}	x'	y'
A	14.05	0.4685	0.4228
B	10.87	0.4597	0.4133

coloristic properties of some dyes are changed drastically by the addition of as little as 0.1 ppm metal ion.[5]

Some dyes are sensitive to electrolytes and the color changes with the concentration of ions in solution. A classic example of this is Direct Yellow 6, which has a different spectral curve in a buffered solution containing 1% sodium chloride than when the salt is omitted.[5,53]

Interfering ions present many problems in correlating solution coloristics with shade and strength determined in end use tests. The ion content is not the same for the two evaluations. Alum used in paper dyeing may change the shade and/or strength of a dye differently than can be obtained by simulating conditions for the same dye to be measured in solution. The effect of interfering ions can be minimized, and sometimes eliminated, by adding chelating agents, surfactants, or protective colloids to the colorant solution; however, it must be remembered that these measures are not being taken in the application tests.

4.1.10   Miscellaneous Effects.   Turbidity cannot be tolerated in the dilute dye solution because the amount of light scatter from particulate matter adds to the amount of light absorbed by the colorant. Turbid solutions frequently conform to Beer's law; nevertheless, they cannot be controlled from one sample to another and the measurements are not reproducible. Turbidity is usually not harmful in the stock solution provided it disappears with dilution.

Interaction of two or more dyes in admixture produce an absorbance curve that does not represent the sum of the individual component curves. Changing the solution conditions may reduce interaction to a negligible level; if not, compensation for the interaction may be made in the computation.[5]

Chemical reactions can occur inadvertently or intentionally depending on the colorants, solvents, reagents, and extraneous materials present in the solution. Indeed, many of the effects listed above are chemical rather than physical changes in the colorant. Many dyes are susceptible to hydrolysis, which is usually detectable by changes in the coloristic data with temperature and/or pH variations. Easily oxidizable colorants and leuco solutions of vat dyes may undergo color change because of oxygen dissolved in the solvent or overexposure to the surrounding air. Oxidation may be influenced by pH, temperature, irradiation, or a combination of these conditions. Since most chemical reactions affect coloristic properties, the solution conditions must be controlled to prevent unwanted reactions. If, on the other hand, the coloristic effect of a particular reaction is recognized and evaluated, it may be used to monitor the reaction under the same or different conditions.

In some instances reactive solvents such as sulfuric acid or alkaline sodium hydrosulfite solution are necessary to dissolve vat dyes and other colorants that have poor solubility in conventional solvents. Solutions containing reactive solvents require greater care in their handling to obtain the same analytical precision as solutions prepared with conventional solvents. The color difference between dye and dye solution also increases the difficulty in correlating colorimetric data with end use tests.

It is usually desirable to include aging at ambient temperature in the screening of solution variables. Dilute solutions are usually aged for 2 hours and stock solutions for 24 hours. Stability of the dilute solution over longer periods may be of technical interest; however, from a practical standpoint, the dilute solution is usually analyzed within 2 hours, and if longer times are necessary a fresh aliquot can be taken. The stock solution requires more work to prepare and is checked for longer aging periods in anticipation of interruptions in the work schedule.

4.2   Measurement Variables

Familiarity with the instrument and the manufacturer's instruction manual is the first step toward minimizing measurement variables. During this indoctrination the effect of slit widths and scanning speeds on resolution and measurement error should be determined.[67,68,69] Maximum resolution is required when measuring dyes having sharp absorption maxima. A preventive maintenance program should be adopted to ensure peak instrument performance. A record of routine calibration data will detect drift from normal operation.

The optimum range for measuring transmittance or absorbance should be determined for the instrument. A range of 10–50% T (A = 0.3–1.0) is usually recommended,[5] although in complementary tristimulus colorimetry a range of A = 1.0 ± 0.5 is more desirable.[49] Slight distortions in curves having absorbance maxima less than 0.5 may represent an appreciable percentage of one or more of the tristimulus values and appear as errors in chromaticity.

Optical cells should be kept scrupulously clean and free from scratches. Modern cells are manufactured with light paths accurate to ±0.005 mm and parallelism of faces within 5 minutes of arc. Therefore, cells of the same type should match unless they are scratched or dirty. A cell comparison can be made by filling the cells with distilled water and scanning, then reversing the cells from one compartment to another and scanning again. Positioning in the cell compartments is important and should be the same for all measurements.

4.3   Precision of the Method

The propagated error from weighing of sample through instrumental measurement varies depending upon technique and the equipment available.[50] Allowable limits also depend on the precision and accuracy required of the analysis. Most strength measurements (absorptivity) are satisfactory if the precision is ±1.0% relative. Complementary chromaticity coordinates (x' and y') encompass both photometric and wavelength accuracy of the instrument. The equipment should be calibrated to provide a maximum standard deviation in either chromaticity coordinate of ±0.0005, regardless of the color being measured. Within this limit 95% of the chromaticity coordinates determined on replicate analyses of a sample (or filter) should plot within a circle having a radius of 0.0014 chromaticity units.[49] Since x' and y' do not depend on concentration they are unaffected by weight and volume errors.

5 APPLICATIONS

The two most important parameters in characterizing a colorant for controlling its quality can be expressed in practical terms as shade and strength. The purpose of this section is to show how solution coloristics is used for measuring shade and strength as well as providing other information important to research, process development, and manufacture of dyes.

5.1 Shade Specification and Interpretation

Color order systems have evolved during the past 300 years from Isaac Newton's color wheel to the modern concepts involving tristimulus colorimetry. The Munsell system is unique because it is based on physical samples that are arranged at equal intervals of visual perception of color difference between adjacent samples. In 1943, CIE tristimulus specifications of the Munsell system were published, thereby providing a means of transformation between the two systems.[2] Two commonly used chromaticity coordinates derived from the CIE system are dominant wavelength and purity[2]; however, they have a disadvantage in that their spacing is nonuniform.

Regardless of the choice of coordinates the CIE system does not provide a satisfactory specification of color for two reasons: (a) the variability of chromaticity coordinates with colorant concentration; and (b) the nonuniformity of the color space with respect to visual perception. The latter problem has led investigators to search for the ideal color space.[70] Many new systems have been developed,[71-73] some of which are being used routinely to specify color in end use requirements; nevertheless the ideal system is yet to be discovered. Most of the color specification systems can be used with CIE tristimulus values determined from solution measurements, although they were originally intended for use with reflectance data.

Complementary tristimulus colorimetry is a better approach to color specification from solution measurement because the chromaticity coordinates are invariant with colorant concentration and the need for visual correlation is of secondary importance. Since these coordinates (x' and y') are intrinsic properties of the colorant, they identify the shade of the colorant in a particular solvent. If the magnitude of the coordinates varies from one sample to another, the shade also varies, in a predictable manner.

Shade orientation is established by plotting the coordinates of the standard dye on a complementary chromaticity diagram. The sample (S) plotted in Figure 6.12 represents a hypothetical reddish orange. Shade orientation is made with respect to the neutral point. Three-dimensional

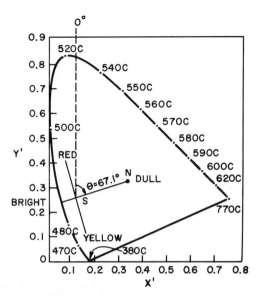

Figure 6.12   Complementary chromaticity diagram showing orientation of shade prediction axes for a hypothetical orange dye.   Chromaticity coordinates for the dye are $x' = 0.1102$ and $y' = 0.2318$ in Illuminant C.

complementary color space contains a line from top to bottom (white to black) which passes through the neutral point of the chromaticity planes forming a locus of grays, or for interpretive purposes, a dull direction. A sample that plots on the line connecting the standard point and the neutral point is duller than the standard. Conversely, if the sample plots on an extension of the line between the standard point and the spectrum locus, it is brighter than standard. Therefore, the line from the neutral point through the standard point to the complementary spectrum locus becomes the bright–dull axis. A line perpendicular to the bright–dull axis at the standard point becomes the shade axis. The shade axis may represent red–yellow, red–blue, blue–yellow, etc., depending on the location of the standard point in the diagram (see Figure 6.4). This provides the necessary orientation for interpreting the shade of sample versus standard, and for many dyes it is possible to predict accurately what the shade would be if the same samples were dyed on suitable substrates.[49]

A more versatile technique for using colorimetric data in dye quality control is obtained by converting chromaticity coordinates from rectangular to polar (Figure 6.13). Since the interest here is in the degree of variation in color composition from a standard, the equations below are based

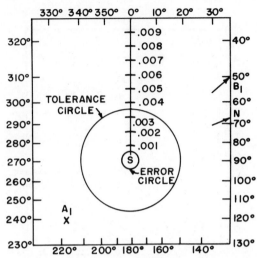

Figure 6.13   Polar chromaticity plot for an orange dye.   The center point (S) represents the practical standard having chromaticity coordinates of $x' = 0.1102$ and $y' = 0.2318$ in Illuminant C.   The point A_1 represents the pure standard and B_1 is an impurity which is outside the diagram at 50°.   The radial scale is in chromaticity units.

on chromaticity differences from the standard point at the center of the plot. The equations for converting rectangular to polar coordinates are

$$R = [(\Delta x')^2 + (\Delta y')^2]^{1/2} \qquad (11)$$

$$\theta = \arctan\left(\frac{\Delta y'}{\Delta x'}\right) \qquad (12)$$

where R is the radius or distance from the standard point to the sample point in chromaticity units, θ is the angle from the standard point to the sample point with 0° at the vertical, and $\Delta x'$ and $\Delta y'$ are the algebraic differences in chromaticity obtained by subtracting the standard point from the sample point and maintaining the signs. By substituting the chromaticity coordinates for the neutral point (for Illuminant C, $x' = 0.3101$ and $y' = 0.3162$) into Equation 12 as a sample, the angle to the neutral point is obtained for shade orientation. The orientation for this particular orange standard is dull at 67.1°, yellow at 157.1°, bright at 247.1°, and red at 337.1°. The standard deviations (95% CL) for x' and y' determined from a precision study can be used in Equation 11 to determine the radius of the error circle. Figure 6.13 illustrates a two-component system in which one component is pure dye A and the other is a reddish blue impurity B. In this system all samples plot along the line AB, with their position on the line being determined by the ratio of A to B in the sample. If the impurity B can be obtained in pure form, the sample composition can be determined (see Section 5.3); however, this is usually not necessary for color specification. The radius of the tolerance circle is determined empirically by dyeing samples and correlating the results with the polar chromaticity plot. Although the radius of the tolerance circle is the limit of acceptability, the angle θ can be useful in diagnosing the cause of unacceptability. A sample plotting outside the tolerance circle in the 50° direction has too much impurity present, whereas at 230° there is too little impurity.

Probably the most significant pitfall in colorimetry is the situation in which two dye solutions have the same chromaticity coordinates for one illuminant and different spectral curves. This phenomenon is known as metamerism, and the two samples are known as a metameric pair. A metameric pair may be visually matched in one illuminant but quite different in shade when viewed in another illuminant. If the spectral curves and the color coordinates are identical the two colors are nonmetameric, or a spectrophotometric match. Metamerism can appear when more than three colorants are present in mixture. If two mixtures are prepared, each containing the same four colorants in the same proportion, the two mixtures are nonmetameric. However, if the compositions of the two mixtures are independently varied the spectral curves vary with four degrees of freedom, whereas the human eye and the colorimetric data are limited to three. Therefore, not all the changes in the spectral curves resulting from variations in the mixtures are visually or colorimetrically detectable as different colors. Figure 6.14 shows an example of metamerism in which the shade of a black ink is a metameric match to a mixture of three bright basic dyes. The difference in chromaticity, expressed as the distance between samples in a chromaticity plot (Equation 11), is only 0.0009 chromaticity units. Commercial color matches are usually metameric and not spectrophotometric.[74-77] Although metamerism is not as much of a problem in investigating individual dyes, it must be recognized as a potential pitfall when more than three colorants are present.

Often in research it is desirable to have a quick and easy method of determining brightness in a series of dye samples. Since bright dyes have sharper absorption peaks than dull dyes, the ratio of the absorbance maximum to the area under the absorbance curve can be used as an index of brightness. This index, or brightness factor (Bf_1), can be calculated from either absorptivities or absorbance and complementary tristimulus values according to the following equation:

$$Bf_1 = \frac{\alpha_{max}}{\alpha_{vis}} = \frac{A_{max}}{X' + Y' + Z'} \tag{13}$$

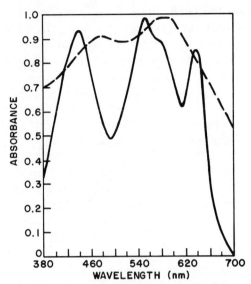

Figure 6.14 An example of metamerism where the broken line represents a sample of black ink and the solid line a black formulated form Basic Yellow 29, Basic Violet 16, and and Basic Blue 22. Measurements were made in Illuminant C.

	Black Ink	Dye Mixture
X'	0.8917	0.7752
Y'	0.8897	0.7724
Z'	1.0656	0.9305
x'	0.3132	0.3128
y'	0.3125	0.3117

In practice Bf_1 values range from about 0.33 for a neutral black to about 2.50 for a bright dye.

Another method of determining brightness in complementary color space is based on the concepts described in establishing a bright–dull axis for shade prediction and is analogous to purity in the CIE system. Figure 6.15 shows a complementary chromaticity diagram in which angles around the neutral point are substituted for wavelengths of the spectral colors. To coincide with wavelength the point on the spectrum locus representing a wavelength of 380 nm is set at 0° for Illuminant C. The angles of rotation clockwise from this point are called chromatic angles and are abbreviated as CA_c when determined in Illuminant C. The measured angle θ having 0° at the vertical is determined from

$$\theta = \arctan\left(\frac{y' - 0.3162}{x' - 0.3101}\right)$$

where x' and y' are the chromaticity coordinates for the sample. When $CA_c = 0°$ ($\lambda = 380$ nm), the measured angle θ is 203.6°. Therefore

$$CA_c = \theta - 203.6° \quad \text{when } \theta \text{ is } 203.6\text{–}360.0°$$

and   (14)

$$CA_c = \theta + 156.4° \quad \text{when } \theta \text{ is } 0\text{–}203.6°$$

At any chromatic angle the brightness factor Bf_2 is determined as the distance from neutral point to sample point divided by the distance from the neutral point through sample point to the spectrum locus. The latter distance (R') has been determined for the spectral colors and plotted orthogonally versus CA_c in Figure 6.16. Therefore Bf_2 can be easily calculated from

$$Bf_2 = \frac{R}{R'} \quad (15)$$

where R is determined from Equation 11 using chromaticity coordinates from sample and neutral point, and R' is taken from a plot similar to Figure 6.16. Bf_2 values vary from 0 for a neutral gray or black to 1.00 for maximum brightness.

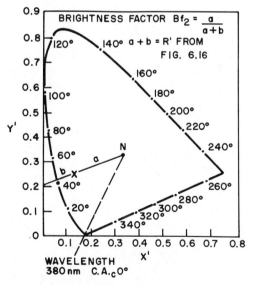

Figure 6.15 Complementary chromaticity diagram showing derivation of chromatic angle (CA_c) and brightness factor (Bf_2).

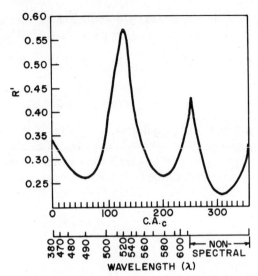

Figure 6.16   Plot of chromatic angle (CA_c) versus radius (R').   Data taken from spectrum ocus for 2° observer under Illuminant C.

5.2   Strength Determination

Absorptivity is used in all strength calculations whether they are to determine percentage of active ingredient ($\%\ AI$) in a dye sample or the strength relationship between sample and standard, or to relate the color value of a sample to some preestablished scale. The absorptivity can be either determined at a single point (a_{max}) or integrated over the visible spectrum (a_{vis}). The absorptivities are intrinsic properties that indicate the tinctorial value of a colorant; however, if strength is specified by absorptivity alone, the solvent used in the measurement should also be specified. Except for special situations (see below), a_{max} is the preferred absorptivity for strength calculations because a_{vis} is influenced by the brightness or dullness of the sample. The active ingredient content is calculated from

$$AI = \frac{a_{max}\ \text{sample}}{a_{max}\ \text{standard}} \qquad \text{or} \qquad \%\ AI = 100AI \qquad (16)$$

where the a_{max} of sample is divided by a_{max} of a pure standard.

Strength relative to a standard is usually expressed as a ratio of absorptivities (or $\%\ AI$ values) in one of two forms: (*a*) parts of sample equivalent to 100 parts of standard; and (*b*) a percentage of standard. Strength relationships determined from solution measurements usually agree with strength determined by visually or instrumentally evaluating the same samples and standard applied to the substrate. When strength differences occur between the two methods of measurement, they are usually caused by the presence of colorants in solution that have no affinity for the substrate.

Color value has different meaning depending on the type of work involved. To the researcher interested in inherent color value in the molecule, molar absorptivity may be important. In process development and manufacturing, color value may mean absorptivity per mill-cost dollar, whereas to sales personnel and dye consumers the selling price per 100 absorptivity units is important.

The influence of Illuminant C and 2° observer weighting functions on α_{vis} at different wavelengths is shown in Figure 6.17. It can be seen from the plot that colors having absorption peaks at extremes of the visible spectrum (380–400 and 660–780 nm) have little color value visually or by α_{vis}. A high α_{max} in these areas may be misleading if it is used as an indication of practical color value. Since α_{vis} is related to the standard observer and the integrated area under the spectral curve, it can be used for strength comparisons of dyes having different chemical structures and shades. Dyeings made on an equal α_{vis} basis are frequently found to be

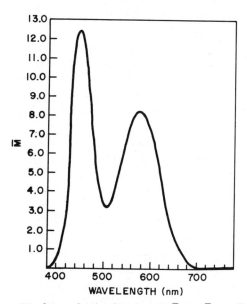

Figure 6.17 The sum (Σ) of the weighting functions ($E_c\bar{x} + E_c\bar{y} + E_c\bar{z}$) versus wavelength. The plot illustrates the effect of weighting functions on α_{vis} at different wavelengths.

visually equal in depth even though there may be small shade differences.[49] Thus α_{vis} can be used as a guide for determining dye concentrations for an initial set of dyeings when the properties of the dyes involved are not yet known. A cursory examination of a few samples differing in brightness suggests that an even closer agreement to visual strength can be obtained if the α_{vis} values are normalized for brightness. The equation used for brightness correction is

$$\alpha_{\text{vis}(BC)} = \frac{\alpha_{\text{vis}}}{Bf_2} \tag{17}$$

where $\alpha_{\text{vis}(BC)}$ is the brightness-corrected α_{vis} and Bf_2 is the brightness factor from Equation 15. This technique should provide a means of relating solution coloristics to the standard depth scales used in fastness testing and strength studies.[78–80]

5.3   Determining the Composition of Colorant Mixtures

The most important property in determining the composition of colorant mixtures is Beer's law behavior. If the component colorants follow Beer's law alone and in admixture, the composition of the mixture can be easily calculated provided the spectral profiles of the components are sufficiently different from each other to be individually discernible when mixed. If one or more of the components does not follow Beer's law, or if their absorbances are not additive in combination, corrections can usually be applied that fit most composition calculations.[5]

Four procedures are offered below for calculating the composition of mixtures. The first two are based on the additive property of absorptivity and the second two are based on the linear and additive nature of both absorptivity and chromaticity as determined in the absorbance mode.

5.3.1   Composition Analysis Based on Absorptivities at the Analytical Wavelengths of Components.   Simultaneous equations for two components are

$$P_a \alpha_a{}^{\lambda_a} + P_b \alpha_b{}^{\lambda_a} = \alpha_m{}^{\lambda_a}$$
$$P_a \alpha_a{}^{\lambda_b} + P_b \alpha_b{}^{\lambda_b} = \alpha_m{}^{\lambda_b} \tag{18}$$

where P_a and P_b are the proportionate amounts (parts/part of mix) of components a and b in the mixture m; $\alpha_a{}^{\lambda_a}$ is the absorptivity of component a at its analytical wavelength (λ_{max}); $\alpha_b{}^{\lambda_a}$ is the absorptivity of component b at the λ_{max} of component a; $\alpha_a{}^{\lambda_b}$ is the absorptivity of component a at λ_{max} of component b; $\alpha_b{}^{\lambda_b}$ is the absorptivity of component b at its λ_{max}; and $\alpha_m{}^{\lambda_a}$, $\alpha_m{}^{\lambda_b}$ are the absorptivities of the mixtures at λ_{max}

for components a and b, respectively. By the substitution of absorptivities of pure component standards the $\% \, AI$ of each ingredient in the mixture can be determined as well as the total $\% \, AI$ of the mix ($\% \, AI_m = \% \, AI_a + \% \, AI_b$). Similar equations can be written for additional components provided the spectral curves of the components are sufficiently separated to be distinguishable.

5.3.2 Composition Based on Multiple Linear Regression Analysis (MLRA).

In the preceding approach, composition was determined by fitting the spectral curves of the components to the curve of the mixture at the analytical wavelengths of the components. For two components the curves are fitted at two wavelengths, for three components at three wavelengths, etc. In MLRA the curve fitting is done by computer using the least squares method at selected wavelength intervals across the visible spectrum (e.g., 79 points at 5-nm intervals from 380 to 770 nm). An equation similar to Equation 18 is solved for each of the selected wavelength intervals and appropriate statistics for multivariable analysis can be applied to determine associated errors, a multiple correlation coefficient, and the intercept of the line of regression. The mathematics is too complex for inclusion here; however, a computer program for spectral analysis can be readily adapted from existing general-purpose MLRA programs.[81]

When used for color-matching problems,[41] MLRA has limited value because the colorants available are frequently not the same as those in the standard. The desired matches are metameric and require colorimetric data. On the other hand, MLRA with characterized components available provides a spectrophotometric match and avoids the problems of metamerism. Therefore, MLRA is more beneficial to quality-control problems and to formulating known mixtures than it is to color-matching problems.

5.3.3 Composition Analysis Based on Strength-Weighted Chromaticities.

For a two-component mixture the principle is illustrated by the following simultaneous equations:

$$P_a \alpha_{\mathrm{vis}_a} x'_a + P_b \alpha_{\mathrm{vis}_b} x'_b = \alpha_{\mathrm{vis}_m} x'_m$$
$$P_a \alpha_{\mathrm{vis}_a} y'_a + P_b \alpha_{\mathrm{vis}_b} y'_b = \alpha_{\mathrm{vis}_m} y'_m \tag{19}$$

where P_a and P_b represent the proportionate parts of components a and b per part of mix m; the α_{vis} values and complementary chromaticity coordinates (x' and y') are for the components and mix (a, b, and m). Three simultaneous equations can be used equally well for three components using the third chromaticity value z' ($z' = 1 - x' + y'$). Mixtures with four components cannot be solved with chromaticity coordinates from one illuminant because there are only three measured values. One set of chromaticity coordinates could have many metameric matches from four components in one illuminant. If two illuminants are used in the measurement, mixtures containing up to six components can be analyzed. By substituting α_{vis} values for the pure component standards into Equations 19 the composition is determined on a % AI basis. Most mixtures contain colorants of different strength requiring the chromaticities to be weighted by a strength function (α_{vis}); however, if the components of a mixture have the same α_{vis} value, this term may be deleted from the equations.

5.3.4 Composition Analysis Based on Distance-Weighted Strength. In a two-component mixture the α_{vis} of the mix (α_{vis_m}) is equal to the sum of the component parts as follows:

$$P_a\alpha_{vis_a} + P_b\alpha_{vis_b} = \alpha_{vis_m} \tag{20}$$

where P_a and P_b are the proportionate amounts of components a and b in the mix m. If the complementary chromaticity coordinates are determined for a and b and plotted, the chromaticity coordinates for any mixture (m) of a and b lie on the line ab. Any mix divides the line into two segments, am and bm, whose lengths are inversely proportional to the color intensity of the components such that

$$\frac{P_a\alpha_{vis_a}}{P_b\alpha_{vis_b}} = \frac{bm}{am} \tag{21}$$

Equation 21 is supported by Grassman's laws of additive color mixing. Note that where $\alpha_{vis_a} = \alpha_{vis_b}$ the values of P_a and P_b are inversely proportional to the lengths of am and bm. By combining elements of Equations 20 and 21 and simplifying algebraically, the following equations are derived for determining composition:

$$P_a = \frac{bm\alpha_{vis_m}}{ab\alpha_{vis_a}} \quad \text{and} \quad P_b = \frac{am\alpha_{vis_m}}{ab\alpha_{vis_b}} \tag{22}$$

The length measurements may be made with a ruler (millimeter scale) on a chromaticity diagram; however, with computation facilities it is much more precise and convenient to use color difference radii in chromaticity units. Pertinent radii for Equation 22 are determined as follows:

$$am = R_{am} = [(x'_a - x'_m)^2 + (y'_a - y'_m)^2]^{1/2}$$

$$bm = R_{bm} = [(x'_b - x'_m)^2 + (y'_b - y'_m)^2]^{1/2} \tag{23}$$

$$ab = R_{ab} = [(x'_b - x'_a)^2 + (y'_b - y'_a)^2]^{1/2}$$

where x' and y' are the complementary chromaticity coordinates for the components (a and b) and the mix (m). Equation 22 can be rewritten substituting the above radii for lengths, and using the α_{vis} values for pure standards to determine composition as $\% \, AI$.

$$\% \, AI_a = 100 \, \frac{R_{bm}\alpha_{vis\,m}}{R_{ab}\alpha_{vis \text{ pure } a}}$$

$$\% \, AI_b = 100 \, \frac{R_{am}\alpha_{vis\,m}}{R_{ab}\alpha_{vis \text{ pure } b}}$$

$$(24)$$

These versatile equations can be rearranged and manipulated to perform many uses in colorimetry.

Composition analysis is not limited to the four techniques described above. Stearns[5] discusses the use of log absorbance in composition analysis, and Rounds has developed a three-point integration technique.[82]

5.4 Impurity Analysis

Impurity is defined here as any undesirable colorant, or combination of colorants, that adversely affects the end use properties of a dye. If the impurity is identified as a single species and significant amounts of it are present, it can be quantitatively determined by one of the techniques in the preceding section. Unidentified impurities are usually indicated in MLRA when the multiple correlation coefficient is too low or the intercept value is too high. Stearns[5] offers an impurity index formula that is useful in measuring unknown colored impurities.

The above methods of impurity measurement apply only when the level of impurity is significantly large so that it can be seen to influence the profile of a spectral curve. It is also possible to have impurities present at such low concentrations that they are not detectable by conventional analysis yet create problems in dyeing. If these impurities absorb in an area of low absorbance for the dye being measured their absorbance can be exaggerated by measuring a more concentrated solution (the stock solution is frequently used) in this particular area of the spectrum. Figure 6.18 shows sample and standard curves produced by scanning the stock solution of a red dye. At this concentration level the curve for the red dye is off scale. The sample contains a blue impurity which can be measured in one of three ways.

1. The most convenient way with simple instrumentation is to determine the absorbance of sample and standard at wavelength a (Figure 6.18)

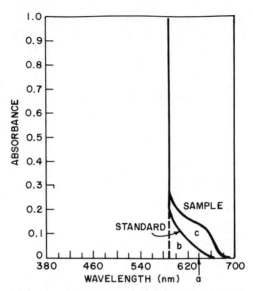

Figure 6.18 Impurity index measurement of blue impurity in a hypothetical red dye. The impurity index calculation is based on the absorbances at wavelength a, the area under the curves, b, or area c, which is the difference in areas under the sample and standard curves.

and normalize for concentration, path length, and AI according to the following equation:

$$\text{I.I.} = \frac{A^{\lambda_a}}{bcAI} \tag{25}$$

where I.I. is the impurity index; A^{λ_a} is the absorbance at wavelength a; b is the sample path length in centimeters; c is the dye concentration in grams per liter of the solution being measured; and AI is the active ingredient content (as decimal fraction) of the sample being measured.

2.   Pseudo-areas under the curves are obtained with a truncated scan starting at the wavelength at which the absorbance curve comes on scale and determining the complementary tristimulus values from there to the end of the visible spectrum. In Figure 6.18 the scan is truncated from 590 to 700 nm. The impurity index is calculated from the following equation:

$$\text{I.I.} = fA_t = \frac{X_t' + Y_t' + Z_t'}{bcAI} \tag{26}$$

where fA_t is a function of the truncated area; X_t', Y_t', and Z_t' are the complementary tristimulus values for the truncated scan; and b, c, and AI are as defined in Equation 25.

3. An impurity index based on area c in Figure 6.18 is determined as

$$\text{I.I.} = fA_t(\text{sample}) - fA_t(\text{standard}) \qquad (27)$$

where $fA_t(\text{sample})$ and $fA_t(\text{standard})$ are functions of the truncated areas under the curves, which are determined from Equation 26.

Selection of one of the above impurity indices depends on the character of the impurity being measured and the equipment available. In general, Equation 25 is used when the effect of the impurity is localized in a small portion of the spectrum, and Equations 26 and 27 are preferred when the magnitude of the impurity effect is less at one wavelength but covers a wider portion of the spectrum.

5.5 Coloristics in Dye Synthesis

Coloristics can be used to follow the course of any reaction that involves a color change. Changes from colorless to colored and from colored to colorless are followed with simple absorbance measurements at an analytical wavelength, whereas shade changes are followed with chromaticity plots or the radial distance from the initial color (Equation 11). These techniques are used to determine reaction rates and/or to provide a means of process control.

Figure 6.19 illustrates how the colorants and impurities of the indicated reactions can be plotted from their complementary chromaticity coordinates. The indicated reactions are fictitious although the associated problems are typical of those experienced in dye synthesis. The first reaction involves two colorless intermediates (A and B) which react under slightly acidic conditions to form the colored intermediate, C. By analyzing samples of the reaction mass at time intervals the course of the reaction can be followed. The reaction is complete when the a_{max} for C shows no further change with time. Dilute reactions are sometimes more conveniently studied when they are actually carried out in the spectrophotometer cell, or the reaction is run externally and pumped through the cell. If reaction 1 is a first-order reaction, a plot of the logarithm of the concentration of intermediate C versus reaction time is a straight line whose slope is proportional to the velocity constant.[5] Reaction 2 in Figure 6.19 indicates that impurity D can be formed if the pH is not properly controlled in reaction 1. Figure 6.20 is a polar plot (using Equations 11 and 12) having the practical standard for intermediate C as its center. The pure standard appears on the plot at the point X, which is at an angle complementary to impurity D, indicating that there is a small amount of impurity D in the practical standard. The impurity content in the practical standard can be easily calculated using Equation 19. If the radius of the tolerance circle is

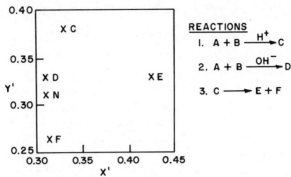

Figure 6.19   Chromaticity plot showing positions of colorants formed by reactions 1–3. Colorisitc data for the standard colorants is tabulated below.   *N* is the neutral point for Illuminant *C*.

Sample	Pure Standard			Practical Standard	
	α_{vis}	x'	y'	x'	y'
C	140.2	0.3301	0.3824	0.3284	0.3782
D	138.6	0.3102	0.3330	—	—
E	161.7	0.4239	0.3321	0.4199	0.3321
F	58.4	0.3150	0.2671	—	—

empirically determined to be 0.0030 chromaticity units, Equation 24 can be used to determine the concentration limits of *D* in *C*.

The third reaction of Figure 6.19 represents the conversion of the colored intermediate *C* to the dye *E*. Excessive temperature or too long a reaction time causes the degradation of *E* to the impurity *F*. If complementary chro-

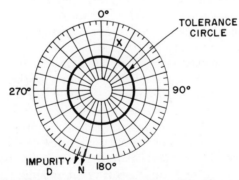

Figure 6.20   Polar chromaticity plot for intermediate *C* in Figure 6.19.   The practical standard is at the center, with impurity *D* off scale ($R = 0.0487$) at 201.9° and the pure standard for intermediate *C* at the point marked *X* ($R = 0.0045$, $\theta = 22.0°$).   The neutral point (*N*) for Illuminant *C* is off scale ($R = 0.0647$) at 196.5°.

maticity coordinates are determined for samples taken at intervals during the reaction they plot along the line connecting the practical standards for C and E in the chromaticity diagram. Equation 24 can be used to determine the completeness of the reaction from the coloristics data obtained in the sample analysis. The reaction is complete when the sample chromaticity coordinates plot within the tolerance circle for the dye E in Figure 6.21. It can be seen from Figure 6.21 that the practical standard for E is actually a three-component mixture, containing small amounts of intermediate C and impurity F. The composition of the practical standard can be calculated if desired (see Section 5.3).

It is often beneficial to analyze the filtrate during product isolation, e.g., to indicate yield losses, when an impurity is shed completely, or ecological information on the amount of colorants going to the sewer.

5.6 Applications to Dyeing Problems

Solution coloristics can be as important to dye application as it is to dye synthesis. It was recognized during early instrumental measurement of dyed fabrics that the accuracy of color specification was limited more by the dyeing process than by the method of measuring. As a result, solution coloristics in one form or another has been used to study all aspects of the dyeing process.

Solution spectra are usually obtained when the dye is received. Although most solution measurements are made to determine strength,[50] other coloristic criteria may also be used to determine acceptability. Before solution coloristics can be used in this way it must be established that solution data correlate with application testing. Dyes that exhaust differently or exhibit

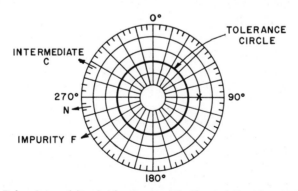

Figure 6.21 Polar chromaticity plot for the dye E in Figure 6.19. The practical standard is at the center with intermediate C off scale ($R = 0.1025$) at 296.7°, pure dye is at the point marked X ($R = 0.0040$, $\theta = 90.0°$), and impurity F is off scale ($R = 0.1234$) at 238.2°. The neutral point (N) for Illuminant C is off scale ($R = 0.1110$) at 261.7°.

fiber selectivity produce different results on the substrate than can be predicted from their behavior in solution.

Solution coloristics is also used in controlling the dyebath.[82] For proper control it is often necessary for the solubility of the dye to be known, because poor solubility causes weak dyeings and/or specking. Dye solubility is determined, with and without dissolution aids, by analyzing saturated solutions of the dye spectrophotometrically. The stability of a dye under various application conditions should also be known, especially if the dyeing process involves extraordinary conditions. Some information concerning dye stability may be learned from a screening to determine the effect of solution variables (see Section 4.1). A better approach is to analyze the dye before and after exposure to the intended conditions in a laboratory-scale experiment.[83]

Analysis of color remaining in the exhaust bath following dyeing may provide information on dyeing efficiency or component selectivity. Dyeing rates are measured by determining the color in the bath at time intervals throughout the dyeing cycle. If a flow-through cell is used, the dyebath can be continuously monitored throughout the dyeing cycle.[84]

If the dye is extracted from the fiber (see Chapter 19) and analyzed, the coloristics data can be combined with similar data from the pad bath and the exhaust bath to provide an overall material balance. This approach provides much information on dyeing efficiency and may provide a clue that will lead to improved efficiency.

Formulations for color matching can be made with solution coloristics by using the x'_m, y'_m, and a_{vism} values for the color to be matched in Equations 19 or 24. Components are selected from the same dye class and must meet the required application and fastness requirements without interacting. The unpredictability of substantivity and selectivity problems decreases the effectiveness of this approach; however, formulations from solution coloristics are frequently close first approximations that can be adjusted to a satisfactory match by the colorist or dyer. Once a satisfactory formulation is obtained, the techniques of Section 5.3 can be used to ensure that it is maintained.

Solution coloristics is often used in the maintenance of dye standards. Dye standards may change with time owing to the hygroscopicity of powders, evaporation of liquids, or the general degradation of quality with time. Periodic color analysis of dye standards and comparison with data obtained from earlier analyses will indicate quality changes. Standard drift is not easily detected from routine analyses where samples are compared to standard in a relative sense.

5.7   Color Scales for One-Dimensional Specification

Brightness factors and impurity indices are one-dimensional specifications that have been discussed because of their utility in defining the quality of a specific product. Color temperature is an important one-dimensional scale in specifying illuminants. Indeed, most one-dimensional scales are designated for a specific use and may be misleading, because of the three-dimensional nature of color, if applied indiscriminately. Single-dimension specifications are used extensively in defining lightness–darkness (achromatic scale), and in measuring small color differences from pure white or colorless (chromatic scale). Both types of scales can be specified either by visual comparison of samples with physical standards or by instrumental measurement.

An achromatic scale for measuring the lightness or darkness of a sample is often called a gray scale. Physical gray scale standards are available for the visual assessment of dyed substrates and stains.[85] The Munsell value scale is widely used for both visual comparisons and instrumental comparisons since the measured coloristics data can be mathematically transformed to the visually uniform Munsell value scale. Other lightness scales are derived from instrumental measurements by mathematically massaging the CIE tristimulus Y value.

Whiteness scales are designed primarily for measuring opaque samples and have little, if any, application to solution analysis. Since most organic matter degrades to a shade of yellow or amber, yellowness scales are the most common in solution measurement. Johnston lists 25 physical standards for yellowness scales and includes their location on a CIE chromaticity diagram.[86] Coloristics data can sometimes be manipulated to correlate with a given set of physical standards. The ASTM has adopted a yellowness index (Y.I.) which does not involve physical standards and is calculated from

$$Y.I. = \frac{128X - 106Z}{Y} \tag{28}$$

where X, Y, and Z are the CIE tristimulus values.[87] The yellowness index correlates with visual judgment for samples that appear yellow (positive index) or blue (negative index), and should never be used on samples whose shade description does not include either yellowness or blueness.

Recent interest in ecology has focused attention on color measurement of waste streams and natural bodies of water that are subject to contamination from industrial effluents (see Chapter 20).

provides a unique one-dimensional scale because of its weighting standard observer functions (see Section 3). With appropriate con-....... factors α_{vis} can be satisfactorily substituted for many of the existing scales.

5.8 Dye Identification

Most dye structures are too complex for complete characterization from spectral analysis, even if the spectrum includes ultraviolet and infrared. A single-instrument method is seldom able to supply all the information necessary for complete identification of a dye molecule. However, in modern, well-equipped laboratories it is possible to combine data obtained from solution coloristics, chromatography, IR, NMR, and MS with observations from dye tests and chemical wet tests to establish the identity of a complex dye within a few hours.

Although it is impossible to establish the structure of a hitherto unknown dye from coloristics data alone, it is frequently possible to identify a dye, or at least its major chromogen, by comparing its coloristics data with that previously obtained for similar dyes or chromogens. The effectiveness of comparative identification increases with the number of entries in a coloristics data file. Files are usually based on analytical data obtained in one's own laboratory because variations in solution preparation and instrument performance reduce the value of published data. Nevertheless, published spectra[88-92] often provide clues for further investigation. Probably the most common method of filing coloristics data is by analytical wavelength (λ_{max}). This approach is complicated by ill-defined absorption maxima, nonspectral colors, peaks outside the visible spectrum, and multiple peaks of about equal absorbance. Schurcliff copes with some of these problems with a curve shape index.[93] Filing by either dominant wavelength (CIE system) or chromatic angle (Equation 14) also circumvents the problems cited. If absorptivities filed for ionic species are calculated on the basis of the color-containing ion, the counterion need not be considered in data comparison.

5.8.1 Preparing the Sample for Identification. Most commercial dyes are impure because they are intentionally adulterated during standardization to meet specified limits of shade, strength, and application properties. Even prior to standardization they may contain substances, other than the desired dyes, that are formed during manufacture. Additives used in standardization may be loosely classified into five types: (1) diluents added to adjust tinctorial strength; (2) agents added to improve the physical form of dye powders and pastes; (3) agents added for pH control; (4) solvents added to achieve the desired solution strength and stability of liquid dyes; and (5) other dyes added to achieve the desired shade. Although it is frequently important to analyze the adjuncts as well as the dye, only the colorant analysis is considered here.

Before the identification analysis it is important that the dye be obtained in the purest form possible (see Chapters 1–4, 12). Fortunately with modern instrumental methods of analysis, it is rarely necessary to have more than a few milligrams of the unknown, and coloristics data are obtainable without sample destruction.

5.8.2 The Identification Process. Once a pure sample of the unknown is available, it is dissolved in the solvent system used for the dyeing class and scanned. For identification analysis and problems involving the analysis of dye mixtures it is important that a single solvent system be used to determine coloristics data for all dyes within a dyeing class. With chromatic angle (Equation 14) as a criterion of identity, the unknown is compared to file data, and those dyes having chromatic angles close to the unknown are selected for further comparison. Intrinsic coloristics data are used in a process of elimination to narrow the number of candidates that are similar to the unknown. If the analysis is qualitative, because of insufficient sample for weighing, absorptivities cannot be compared; however, the analytical wavelength, brightness factors, and chromaticity coordinates can be used in the comparison. Spectral curves of the best candidates must be compared with the unknown to avoid metameric matches that can occur if the comparison is limited to analytical wavelength and chromaticity. Small amounts of impurities in areas of low absorbance are often neglected in the interest of identifying the dominant species; however, the significance of their influence upon the coloristics data must be considered. Unfortunately, identical curve shapes are not proof of identity, although they are usually indicative of similar chromogens. One can be misled if the sample contains substituents on the chromogen that do not significantly influence coloristic properties; similarly, if the sample contains insulating linkages (e.g., CH_2) between molecules (or chromogens) it would be indistinguishable from an unlinked molecule.

The probability of correct identification increases with the number of analytical similarities that can be established between known and unknown samples. Coloristics data (λ_{max}, α_{max}, α_{vis}, Bf_1, Bf_2, x', and y') as points of comparison can be increased at will, depending on the number of variations made in the conditions of measurement. The following variations are suggested for known and unknown samples. (1) Compute chromaticity

Table 6.3   Comparative Identification of a Basic Blue: Solution Coloristics Data[a]

Variable	Equation in Text	Unknown	Blue 54	Blue 77	Blue 87	Blue 35
Solvent 1[b]						
$CA_c(°)$	14	225.4	214.0	225.6	229.5	230.0
λ_{max}	—	615.5	614.8	615.7	641.8	672.4
α_{max}	5	169.2	92.5	168.4	139.0	24.2
$\alpha_{vis}(A)^c$	9	159.4	133.7	157.7	122.7	21.8
$\alpha_{vis}(C)^c$	9	119.6	109.4	117.7	92.3	16.2
$Bf_1(C)$	13	1.41	0.85	1.43	1.50	1.49
$Bf_2(C)$	15	0.94	0.87	0.95	0.86	0.85
$x'(A)$	10	0.6006	0.5618	0.6020	0.6091	0.6126
$y'(A)$	10	0.3936	0.4230	0.3929	0.3789	0.3741
$x'(C)$	10	0.5659	0.5077	0.5687	0.5580	0.5557
$y'(C)$	10	0.4144	0.4414	0.4146	0.3914	0.3884
Solvent 2[b]						
CA_c	14	206.0	203.0	206.3	227.0	223.0
λ_{max}	—	600.0	599.9	600.1	641.0	660.2
α_{max}	5	120.8	84.5	120.4	127.9	15.7
$\alpha_{vis}(A)$	9	132.9	131.7	132.5	126.9	18.5
$\alpha_{vis}(C)$	9	114.5	115.0	114.0	97.1	14.8
$Bf_1(C)$	13	1.06	0.73	1.06	1.32	1.07
$Bf_2(C)$	15	0.85	0.83	0.86	0.84	0.78
$x'(A)$	10	0.5332	0.5281	0.5341	0.6007	0.5852
$y'(A)$	10	0.4483	0.4511	0.4476	0.3865	0.3926
$x'(C)$	10	0.4816	0.4688	0.4824	0.5480	0.5126
$y'(C)$	10	0.4622	0.4664	0.4615	0.3999	0.4038
Chemical class		—	Monoazo	Triaryl-methane	Oxazine	Anthra-quinone

[a] Anions in commercial dyes are replaced with the 4-nitrotoluene-2-sulfonate ion.[94]
[b] Solvent 1 is a 25:75 mixture (v/v) of acetic acid in dimethylacetamide; Solvent 2 is 5% aqueous acetic acid.
[c] A and C refer to the illuminant sources used in measurement.

192

in more than one illuminant. (2) Scan in more than one reactive solvent. (3) Change solution conditions to coincide with the variables discussed in Section 4.1. (4) Chemically react the known and unknown under identical conditions using a reagent that will cause a predictable shift in chromaticity, or split the molecule into identifiable fragments. Similarity of the coloristics data obtained with these variations for known and unknown is strong evidence that the two compounds contain the same chromogen.

Chemical classification is sometimes possible from coloristics data even though data corresponding to the unknown are not found on file. For example, absorptivity usually varies according to chemical class with low values for nitro, anthraquinone, and phthalocyanine dyes; medium values for azo, azine, quinoline, diphenylmethane, and xanthene dyes; and high values for methine, thiazine, triphenylmethane, and oxazine dyes. There is considerable overlapping, as well as some unique dyes that do not adhere to the pattern. Overall, the a_{max} values for pure dyes vary from 15 to 350 for most commercial products. Brightness also correlates with chemical class in a similar, but less distinct, pattern. Standard chemical tests are available for determining chemical class, and can be used to supplement coloristics data.

Positive identification from coloristics data is usually attainable where the number of possibilities is limited. For example, it should not be difficult to identify a dye in an unlabeled container from a production unit that manufactures only 20 dyes. The Association of Public Analysts uses a combination of chromatography, absorption spectra, and chemical tests to identify food colors where the number of colorants permitted is limited by law (see Chapter 17).

Table 6.3 illustrates how solution coloristics can be used for the comparative identification of a Basic Blue dye. A sample of the unknown dye was precipitated from aqueous solution with 4-nitrotoluene-2-sulfonic acid,[94] filtered, washed with a copious amount of deionized water, dried, and analyzed in two different solvent systems. Coloristics data were computed for two different illuminants and compared with those on file for basic dyes having CA_c values close to the unknown. The data indicate that the unknown is a triarylmethane closely related to, if not identical with Basic Blue 77. The spectral curves of the unknown and Basic Blue 77 are identical, but significantly different from those of the other Basic Blues. Additional evidence can be gathered by establishing a similarity of behavior of the known and unknown to solution variables (Section 4.1), chemical reactions and different reactive solvents. It is also desirable to compare coloristics data for other dyes that are chemically similar to Basic Blue 77.

REFERENCES

1. W. D. Wright, *The Measurement of Color*, 4th ed., Van Nostrand-Reinhold, New York, 1969.

2. F. W. Billmeyer, Jr., and M. Saltzman, *Principles of Color Technology*, Interscience, New York, 1966.

3. G. Wyszecki and W. S. Stiles, *Color Science Concepts and Methods, Quantitative Data and Formulas*, Wiley, New York, 1967.

4. I. Nimeroff, *Colorimetry*, NBS Monograph 104, U.S. Government Printing Office, Washington, D.C., 1968.

5. E. I. Stearns, *The Practice of Absorption Spectrophotometry*, Wiley-Interscience, New York, 1969.

6. G. W. Ewing, *Instrumental Methods of Chemical Analysis*, 3rd ed., McGraw-Hill, New York, 1969.

7. R. F. Gould, Ed., *Industrial Color Technology*, Advances in Chemistry Series 107, American Chemical Society, Washington, D.C., 1971.

8. J. J. Vos, L. F. C. Friele, and P. L. Walraven, Eds., *Color Metrics*, 1st ed., AIC/Holland, Svesterburg, 1972.

9. R. M. Johnston, *J. Color Appearance*, **1**, 27 (1971).

10. R. P. Bauman, *Absorption Spectroscopy*, Wiley, New York, 1962.

11. J. R. Edisbury, *Practical Hints on Absorption Spectrometry*, 2nd ed., Plenum Press, New York, 1968.

12. H. J. Keegan, J. C. Schleter, and D. B. Judd, *J. Res. Nat. Bur. Stand.*, **66A**, 203 (1962).

13. H. J. Keegan, J. C. Schleter, and M. A. Belknap, *J. Res. Nat. Bur. Stand.*, **67A**, 577 (1963).

14. J. C. Schleter, *Nat. Bur. Stand. Lett. Circ.* LC-1017, 1 (1967).

15. H. Hemmendinger and H. R. Davidson, Proceedings of A Colour Group (Great Britain) Symposium on *Colour Measurement in Industry*, London, 1967.

16. R. Mavrodineanu, J. I. Schultz, and O. Menis, Eds., *Nat. Bur. Stand., Spec. Publ.*, **378**, 1 (1973).

17. R. C. Hawes, *Appl. Opt.*, **10**, 1246 (1971).

18. I. Nimeroff, *J. Opt. Soc. Am.*, **47**, 699 (1957).

19. I. Nimeroff, R. R. Rosenblatt, and M. C. Dannermiller, *J. Res. Nat. Bur. Stand.*, **67A**, 475 (1961).

20. I. Nimeroff, *J. Opt. Soc. Am.*, **56**, 230 (1966).

21. I. Nimeroff, *Color Engineering*, **5**, No. 2, 25 (1967).

22. H. R. Davidson and L. W. Imm, *J. Opt. Soc. Am.*, **39**, 942 (1949).

23. S. G. Franklin, *J. Opt. Soc. Am.*, **52**, 604 (1962).

24. H. D. Einhorn and H. Nieuwmeyer, *J. Opt. Soc. Am.*, **54**, 1238 (1964).

25. A. C. Little, *J. Opt. Soc. Am.*, **54**, 1396 (1964).

26. H. J. Keegan et al., *J. Opt. Soc. Am.*, **48**, 863 (1958).

27. F. W. Billmeyer, Jr., and R. T. Marcus, *Color Engineering*, **6**, No. 5, 61 (1968).

28. F. M. Clydesdale and C. H. Podlesny, Jr., *Color Engineering*, **6**, 55 (1968).

29. R. R. Ernst, *Chimia*, **26**, 53 (1972).

30. H. Longerich and L. Ramsley, *Anal. Chem.*, **46**, 2067 (1974).

31. R. B. Timmer and H. V. Malmstadt, *American Laboratory*, **4**, No. 9, 43 (1972).

32. V. B. Ranalder, H. Känzig, and U. P. Wild, *Appl. Spectrosc.*, **28**, 45 (1974).

33. H. Känzig, R. Lorenz, and U. P. Wild, *Appl. Spectrosc.*, **28**, 52 (1974).

34. A. Savitsky and M. J. E. Golay, *Anal. Chem.*, **36**, 1627 (1964).

35. J. C. Schleter and J. D. Kuder, *J. Opt. Soc. Am.*, **56**, 1424 (1966).

36. L. M. Schwartz, *Anal. Chem.*, **43**, 1336 (1971).

37. J. E. McCarley et al., *J. Opt. Soc. Am.*, **55**, 355 (1965).

38. C. G. Leete and J. R. Lytle, *Color Engineering*, **4**, No. 1, 27 (1966).

39. F. W. Billmeyer, Jr., and R. Smith, *Color Engineering*, **5**, No. 6 ,28 (1967).

40. E. Allen, *Color Engineering*, **3**, No. 6, 15 (1965).

41. P. H. McGinnis, Jr., *Color Engineering*, **5**, No. 6, 22 (1967).

42. R. Kuehni, *J. Color Appearance*, **1**, No. 4, 35 (1972).

43. International Commission on Illumination, Proceedings of the Eighth Session, Cambridge, England, 1931.

44. D. B. Judd, *J. Opt. Soc. Am.*, **23**, 359 (1933).

45. C. N. Reilly, et al., *Anal. Chem.*, **32**, 1218 (1960).

46. C. N. Reilly and E. M. Smith, *Anal. Chem.*, **32**, 1233 (1960).

47. I. F. Trotter, *J. Soc. Dyers Colour.*, **78**, 76 (1962).

48. R. L. Rounds, *Text. Chem. Col.*, **1**, 297 (1969).

49. C. E. Garland, *Text. Chem. Col.*, **5**, 277 (1973).

50. R. Kuehni, *Text. Chem. Col.*, **4**, 133 (1972).

51. Inter-Society Color Council Report of Problems Subcommittee 25D, *Text. Chem. Col.*, **4**, 181 (1972).

52. R. G. White, *Dyestuffs*, **45**, No. 1, 1 (1964).

53. T. R. Commerford, *Text. Chem. Col.*, **6**, 39 (1974).

54. D. G. Duff and C. H. Giles, *J. Soc. Dyers Colour.*, **88**, 181 (1972).

55. W. West and S. Pearce, *J. Phys. Chem.*, **69**, 1894 (1965).

56. J. F. Padday, *J. Phys. Chem.*, **71**, 3488 (1967).

57. E. Coates, *J. Soc. Dyers Colour.*, **85**, 355 (1969).

58. A. R. Monahan, N. J. Germano, and D. F. Blossey, *J. Phys. Chem.*, **75**, 1227 (1971).

59. A. R. Monahan and D. F. Blossey, *J. Phys. Chem.*, **74**, 4014 (1970).

60. L. Costa, F. Grum, and D. J. Paine, *Appl. Opt.*, **8**, 1149 (1969).

61. H. E. Millson and E. I. Stearns, *Am. Dyest. Rep.*, **37**, 423 (1948).

62. A. Camerman and L. H. Jensen, *J. Am. Chem. Soc.*, **92**, 4200 (1970).

63. A. O. Ramsley, *Am. Dyest. Rep.*, **57**, 611 (1968).

64. G. H. Brown, *Photochromism*, Wiley-Interscience, New York, 1971.

65. H. Meier, *Photochemistry of Dyes, CSD IV*.

66. J. H. Gould and W. R. Brode, *J. Opt. Soc. Am.*, **42**, 380 (1952).

67. G. L. Buc and E. I. Stearns, *J. Opt. Soc. Am.*, **35**, 458 (1945).

68. A. C. Hardy and F. M. Young, *J. Opt. Soc. Am.*, **39**, 265 (1949).

69. J. R. Morrey, *Anal. Chem.*, **41**, 719 (1969).

70. D. B. Judd, *Color Engineering*, **8**, No. 2, 37 (1970).

71. K. D. Chickering, *J. Opt. Soc. Am.*, **57**, 537 (1967).

72. K. McLaren, *J. Soc. Dyers Colour.*, **86**, 354 (1970).

73. D. L. MacAdam, *J. Opt. Soc. Am.*, **64**, 1691 (1974).

74. A. Brockes, *Color Engineering*, **6**, No. 3, 48 (1968).

75. I. Nimeroff, *Color Engineering*, **6**, No. 6, 44 (1968).

76. E. Allen, *Color Engineering*, **7**, No. 1, 35 (1969).

77. G. Wyszecki, *Text. Chem. Col.*, **1**, 46 (1969).

78. L. Gall, *The Color Sicence of Pigments*, BASF Publication S399e, Ludwigshafen, Rhein, 1972.

79. R. Kuehni, *J. Color Appearance*, **1**, No. 4, 35 (1972).

80. D. A. Plant, *J. Paint Technol.*, **45**, 57 (1973).

81. IBM 1130 Scientific Subroutine Package, Sample Program REGRE (p. 145).

82. R. L. Rounds, *Am. Dyest. Rep.*, **57**, 297 (1968).

83. G. L. Royer et al., *Text. Res. J.*, **18**, 598 (1948).

84. G. L. Royer, H. R. McCleary, and J. M. A. de Bruyne, *Text. Res. J.*, **17**, 438 (1947).

85. *AATCC Technical Manual No. 50*, American Association of Textile Chemists and Colorists, Research Triangle Park, North Carolina, 1974.

86. R. M. Johnston, *J. Paint Technol.*, **43**, 42 (1971).

87. ASTM Designation D1925-70, American Society for Testing and Materials, Philadelphia, Pa.

88. H. M. Hershenson, *Ultraviolet and Visible Absorption Spectra* (Indices), Academic Press, New York, 1956, 1961, 1966.

89. L. Long, Ed., *Absorption Spectra in the Ultraviolet and Visible Region*, Vols. I and II, Academic Press, New York, 1961.

90. ASTM, *Molecular Formula List of Compound Names and References to Published Ultraviolet and Visible Spectra*, Technical Publication No. 357.

91. I. B. Berlman, *Handbook of Fluorescence Spectra of Aromatic Molecules*, Academic Press, New York, 1965.

92. Organic Electronic Spectral Data, Inc., *Organic Electronic Spectral Data*, Vols. I–X, Wiley, New York, 1960–1974.

93. W. A. Schurcliff, *J. Opt. Soc. Am.*, **32**, 160 (1942).

94. R. A. Clarke, E. Kissa, and H. I. Stryker, *USP* 3,765,835.

CHAPTER SEVEN

Infrared Spectroscopy

R. K. MILLER

1 INTRODUCTION

As is well known, an infrared spectrum can in theory be rigorously analyzed on the basis of fundamental principles. It can also be interpreted empirically, using so-called "functional group frequencies." An interesting discussion of the relationship of these approaches is given by Jones and Sandorfy,[1] who point out that the theroetical approach is not useful in the routine analysis of complex molecules. This must be especially true of dyes, which often have 50 or more atoms per molecule. Those authors also point out that the resulting spectral complexity is the basis for the fact that the IR spectrum is probably the most characteristic physical property of a compound, serving as a "fingerprint."

To the chemist used to dealing with simpler molecules, the interpretation of the IR spectrum of a dye is likely to be a surprisingly recalcitrant problem. In the first place, the chemical history of the sample is usually almost totally unknown. The structural complexity of the dye usually results in a fairly crowded spectrum. Overlapping may conceal bands otherwise readily recognizable, blot out weak but ordinarily usable confirmatory bands, or upset familiar intensity relationships. Finally, the customary functional group correlations are not always readily applied to structures in which the chromophore interacts strongly with substituent groups. The systems are often spatially compact, with functional groups so oriented that bonding or tautomerism seems inevitable.

But in spite of these difficulties, IR spectroscopy can be enormously useful in the analysis of dyes. (1) Pendant groups, of course, can be detected via the usual correlations, due consideration being given to intensities and the possibilities of overlapping. (2) Groups involved in the chromophore can often be detected, although the usual correlations must be applied with caution and frequency shifts must be expected. (3) Pattern recognition remains a most valuable tool, since the dye may thereby be identified exactly; or a similar spectrum, which may establish at least a partial structure, may be found.

2 HISTORY

2.1 Scope

A search of *Chemical Abstracts*, combining only the terms "IR" and "synthetic dyes," yields very few references. However, a number of important contributions are thereby omitted, since many titles use the terms "pigment" or "whitener," and a few recent titles stress the newer spectroscopic techniques. The original scope of this survey was therefore expanded to include the latter papers, and also to include some related work on naturally occurring pigments.

2.2 Fingerprint Identification

Many of the publications located were restricted to IR identification by the "fingerprint" technique,[2-16] most of the older references being in this class. One of the earliest was that of Harkins et al.[2]; although this work was primarily concerned with inorganic pigments, a number of organic pigments were included. Suzuki and co-workers applied the method primarily to food dyes,[3-5] as did Dolinsky and Stein,[6] who described a novel method of solubilizing sulfonic acid dyes in carbon disulfide using an ion-exchange resin. Haigh[7] preferred to restrict IR methods to those few cases in which systematic chemical testing gave ambiguous results. The method was remarkably successful in identifying dyes on ancient textiles[8,10] and in ancient pigments and lacquers.[9,10] Dyes and pigments in paints[11] and inks[12,13] have been identified. In more recent articles IR fingerprinting combined with TLC has been recommended as a more modern tool to supplement the classical dye identification schemes.[12-14] This combination was also used for identifying fluorescent whiteners by Latini[15] and by Werthmann and Borowski,[16] who refined the identification procedure by using a punched card system.

2.3   Fingerprint Identification plus Structural Analysis

A somewhat more sophisticated application of IR spectroscopy is to use the fingerprint method in conjunction with functional group analysis and degradation procedures. In an excellent paper, McClure et al.[17] elaborated on this procedure as applied to organic pigments. They recommend TLC for purification of samples, give an example of a degradation procedure, and present a collection of 96 reference spectra. Hummel and Scholl[18] also recommend the procedure for organic pigments and include a collection of 181 spectra of pigments, the chemical classes of which are largely similar to those given by McClure and co-workers.[17] Hummel and Scholl also include a collection of seven brightener spectra. Brown recommends using the fingerprint method to study dyes purified by TLC, and discusses functional group analysis to some extent, but does not mention dye degradation.[19] Functional group analysis is also recommended by Dolinsky and Jones,[20] Tamura et al.,[21] and Reichert.[22]

2.4   Combined Spectroscopic Methods

Recent literature indicates that IR, NMR, and MS techniques are a particularly valuable combination. Excellent examples of the procedure as applied to synthetic dyes as well as naturally occurring pigments are published in papers by Rao, Venkataraman, and co-workers,[23–30] and three papers by Manukian and co-workers describe the application of the technique to a number of complex organic pigments.[31–33]

3   EXPERIMENTAL PROCEDURE

3.1   Instruments

The IR spectra used for the dye analyses reported in Chapter 12 were recorded on Perkin-Elmer Model 21, 221, or 621 double-beam recording spectrophotometers. Since dye spectra must generally be obtained in solid samples, high resolution is rarely needed, and probably any modern spectrophotometer, prism or grating, would be satisfactory.

3.2   Sample Mounting

Our spectra were generally obtained by the potassium bromide pellet technique, although occasionally the mull procedure was used. Our reason for this is largely pragmatic: the pellet procedure is standardized, whereas mulling is largely an art which some laboratory technicians have difficulty in mastering, especially for microscale samples. We use a simplified pellet procedure which works well for both macro- and microscale samples, and avoids the complications of maintaining evacuated dies and their associated equipment.[34,35] The procedure requires 1 mg of sample ordinarily; with a beam condenser and a smaller pellet size, the quantity of sample routinely required can be reduced to about 10 μg (50 μg is preferred).

We routinely prepare two spectra of every sample. One scans the full frequency range of the instrument and is run with a sample concentration adjusted to give virtually no transmission at the strong peaks in the spectrum. The second spectrum is needed only in those regions where the first shows less than 10% transmission, and is made with a pellet containing only one-tenth the sample concentration of the latter. This procedure ensures that important weak bands are not missed, and clearly shows the spectral details in the regions of strong absorption.

3.3 Sample Preparation

The importance of sample purity and general procedures for purification are discussed elsewhere (see Chapter 12). However, it is probably worthwhile emphasizing that commercial dyes almost invariably have a number of additives (standardizers, surfactants, antidusting agents, etc.), most of which interfere seriously in IR analysis. The temptation to work with raw samples must be resisted, since the spectra are often worthless.

Commercial dyes also often have dye impurities and may contain major amounts of shading components deliberately added. Separations are necessary in almost all such cases if structures are to be determined, and TLC is by far the most useful tool for this purpose.[14,17,19] The sensitivity of the IR microprocedure is such that one or two 2 $\times$ 8-in. plates (using a sample streak across the entire 2 in. width) usually give enough material to produce good spectra of all but minor components. To obtain the spectrum of a component, we scrape the zone of interest off the plate, extract with a small amount of a polar solvent, filter the extract, and evaporate the filtrate on a watch glass under a stream of nitrogen. The pure dye can then be picked up by rubbing with the appropriate quantity of potassium bromide, which is then ground in a micromortar and pressed into a pellet. The procedure, with practice, is quick and simple. Some new techniques for this purpose have been described in the literature,[36-38] but we prefer the procedure described above.

Care and attention to detail, especially with regard to cleanliness, is of paramount importance in TLC/IR work. We always prewash commercial TLC plates by a blank run in a polar solvent, usually acetone. All apparatus must be thoroughly cleaned with a high-quality solvent, paying special attention to avoid contamination by skin oils through handling during or after cleaning. The filtration must be very efficient, since contamination with adsorbent will spoil the spectrum in the 1000–1100 region. The minimum amount of solvent should be used in the extraction, since it will never be entirely free of impurities.

3.4   Polymorphism; Solid-State Effects

It is well known that polymorphs of a compound usually show remarkably different IR spectra; interestingly, the phenomenon in organic compounds was first documented with spectra that included phthalocyanine pigments[39,40] and an azo dye.[40] The amorphous form has yet another spectrum, and it has been shown that with long grinding times the pellet spectrum of a solid may look like a solution spectrum.[41] Other factors that can affect a solid phase spectrum are reviewed by Duyckaerts.[42] These effects are particularly important when comparing the spectra of unknown and reference dyes, and they can also interfere in applying functional group correlations.[43]

The presence of these effects can often be detected when spectra are scanned at two concentrations, as described in Section 3.2, and due allowance can then be made for them. If sample and reference dyes are handled in identical manner, solid-state anomalies should cause little difficulty. In doubtful cases, sample recrystallization, longer grinding times, or a switch to the mull technique (with only hand grinding) may be necessary to clarify the situation.

4   GROUP FREQUENCY CORRELATIONS

4.1   Scope

There are a number of fine texts devoted more or less exclusively to qualitative analysis by IR spectroscopy.[1,44–49] These books have been drawn on heavily in assembling what I hope will be a useful résumé of correlations that are pertinent to interpretations of dye spectra. Some of the original references are cited where I feel that it is instructive for the newcomer to dye analysis to review details regarding intensities, band shapes, and distributions within the correlation ranges. Those details can never be adequately expressed by tables and charts.

Several kinds of functions are not discussed, such as those generally recognized as being poorly handled by IR (e.g., sulfides, isolated halogens).

Groups that are likely to be uncommon in dyes (e.g., acid chloride, iso-cyanate, phosphorus-containing groups) are also omitted. The ubiquitous aromatic C=C bonds, largely uninformative in dye spectra, are not dis-cussed. Isolated C=C is omitted, more or less arbitrarily, because it is difficult to handle in dye spectra, often requiring special techniques for identification (see, for example, the experiments of Jose and co-workers on flavones).[50] It is assumed that the reader has experience in interpreting IR spectra, and is familiar with the texts mentioned above.

The correlations are divided into groups which, with a fair amount of overlapping, proceed from short to long wavelength in the spectrum. This is somewhat different from the way the subject is usually handled, the purpose being simplicity and brevity.

4.2   X-H Stretching

4.2.1   OH.   For routine identification work, the spectra of dyes are of the solid phase, and free OH groups are rarely seen. The OH stretch band is then generally recognizable because of the substantial breadth of the band, which also helps to distinguish it from NH, which is usually relatively narrow (the distinction is not readily made if very strongly bonded groups are involved).

In the absence of intramolecular bonding, aliphatic hydroxyls are in the "polymeric" form, yielding a strong, broad band at $\sim$3400–3200.[51] The group is only rarely the "free" OH when intermolecular bonding is impeded by branching, as in triphenylcarbinol.[52] The free OH gives a single, sharp band near 3500. This effect is seen in the spectra of the carbinol form of triphenylmethane dyes. We have found a quite sharp band near 3330 in the spectra of some dyes containing the 2-hydroxyethylamine group, $HOCH_2CH_2NR$. This is probably a case of intramolecular bonding.[53]

Dyes with phenolic OH groups often show intramolecular OH $\cdots$ O bonds so strong that the OH stretch becomes extremely broad and shifted to the 3200–2500 range (Nakanishi[49]). 3′-Hydroxyquinophthalone (**1**) is an example.[54] Such a band may be easily overlooked. Similar strong bonding occurs in o-hydroxyazobenzenes,[55] in which case the OH stretch band is so broad and weak that it is not diagnostically useful. (It has been established[56]

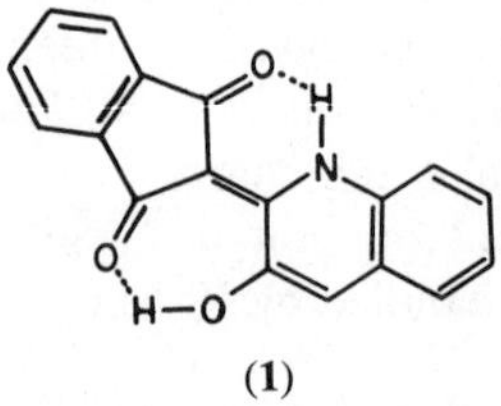

(1)

that many structures in this class are true *o*-azophenols, although some exist as *o*-quinonehydrazones.) Another diagnostically difficult case of importance in dyes is that of the OH in α-hydroxyanthraquinones.[57]

In a solid-state spectrum, phenolic OH that is not intramolecularly bonded generally shows a rather low frequency stretching, 3250–3200, which makes it fairly characteristic.[58] Substitution in the *ortho* position with bulky, nonbonding groups can shift the OH stretch to much higher frequency because of steric inhibition of intermolecular bonding.[52] 2,4,6-Tri-*t*-butylphenol absorbs at 3649 and the peak is very sharp.[52]

4.2.2 NH, NH₂. Except when involved in strong bonding, the NH stretch bands are usually fairly sharp even in condensed phases, which is a helpful feature but not an infallible test. In the case of primary amines, there are theoretically two bands corresponding to symmetric and asymmetric stretching. Often, in the condensed phases, there are more than two bands. The bands may be poorly resolved, but the obvious multiplicity still helps to distinguish them from OH bands.

For primary amines Bellamy[45] indicates that the bands (or pattern of unresolved bands) are usually found near the 3500–3300 range, shifting to lower frequency in the solid state. The intensities are somewhat lower than OH intensities, but they are usually detectable in mull or pellet spectra of high enough concentration. Difficulty may be encountered, however, because of scattering and absorption by moisture in potassium bromide pellets, and some effort may be required to get a satisfactory spectrum. Primary amino groups are found often in anthraquinone dyes, in which case the amine bands are readily recognized as sharp, well separated bands near 3425 and 3300.

Secondary aliphatic amines show NH stretch bands that are generally so weak that they have little utility,[59] especially with dye spectra, where scattering and moisture bands interfere. In the spectra of alkylaryl- and diarylamines, the band is substantially stronger[59] and, provided bonding does not take place, it is a readily recognized band. We have 21 examples of azo dyes with NHR or NHAr groups *para* to the azo group, and in every case a sharp band is outstanding in the 3460–3344 region. Although it does not rival the intensity of some of the other bands in those spectra, it is a very prominent band in the high concentration scan (see Section 3.2), and could not be overlooked. The situation is reversed again with intramolecular bonding, the NH stretch band often losing its diagnostic value. In our work we have examined several dyes with structure (2), and have been unable to find a band that would be reasonably diagnostic in the NH stretch region. This kind of problem has been discussed by Durie and Shannon[60] in connection with the spectra of indanthrone and related structures, in which they believe the bonded NH stretch band is a weak band near 2650. A similar case involves (3); in the spectra of four such compounds, only two were reported to absorb in the 3400 region, and the bands were weak.[61] PMR has demonstrated that these compounds exist in the quinone hydrazone form (3).[56]

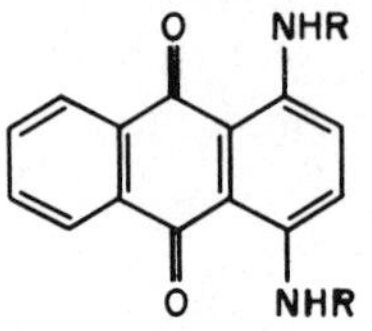

(2) 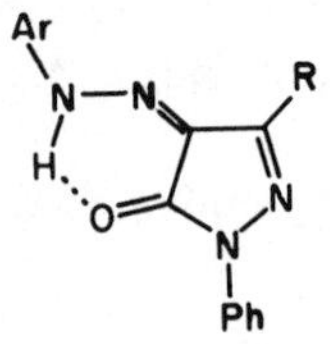   (3)

Amine salts, depending on the number of protons on the positively charged nitrogen, show complex patterns of bands in the 3000–2000 region; each type may have several groups of bands. These are tabulated by Nakanishi.[49] Care must be exercised in interpreting broad bands in the region around 2500, for these may be due to strongly bonded OH or NH bands as discussed earlier. We have been able to locate amine salt bands in several dyes [see Chapter 12, structure (53), for example]; an intense spectrum is required.

Primary and secondary amides show NH stretch bands near 3300 in the solid state.[62] Primary amides give doublets near 3350 and 3180, and secondary amides give a single band near 3270. These are also probably sensitive to intramolecular bonding in certain cases. In the spectra of 25 azo amides with structure (4) we have found that absorption at 3300 is either very weak or absent.

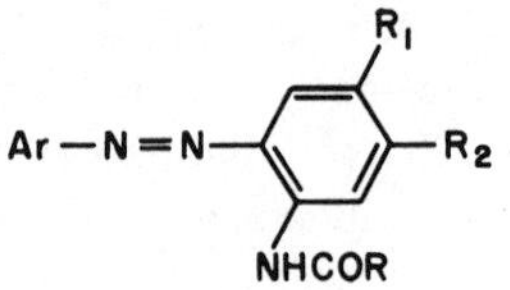

(4)

4.2.3 CH, CH$_2$, CH$_3$. The aromatic and aliphatic CH stretch bands in the 3100–2850 region require little comment. They are generally quite weak in dye spectra, owing to the low intrinsic intensity of the CH stretch bands[63,64] and the usually low concentration of aliphatic groups. Since scattering is usually a problem in this region of the spectrum, it is difficult to get much information from these bands, even using grating resolution.

Little effort in that direction is recommended, since the same kind of information is available from PMR, which is a much sharper tool for the purpose.

Strong absorption in the CH stretch region is often indicative of an impure sample (anti-dust agent, solvent residue, contamination, etc.), although dyes designed for oil solubility may have fairly high concentrations of hydrocarbon chains. Bands at frequencies lower than 2850 have occasionally been useful in identifying alkyl groups, particularly methyl, bonded to oxygen or nitrogen.[65,66]

4.3   C≡N Stretching

Although there are many functional groups in the class of triply bonded or allenic systems, only one appears with regularity in dyes—the nitrile group. It appears often, however, and one of the most useful aspects of IR spectroscopy in dye work is its ability to readily detect this group and to determine its environment. The nitrile correlations were systematized many years ago by Kitson and Griffith.[67] They showed that the frequency of the nitrile band increased with an increasing degree of saturation of the carbon to which the nitrile group was bonded. Thus the alkyl nitrile, often found in pendant side chains in dyes, absorbs in the 2260–2240 region. Conjugation with a double bond shifts the band to 2232–2218 and, according to Kitson and Griffith, conjugation with a system that is "more effective than a single double bond" may result in an even lower frequency. In our files, 11 methine dyes with the structure CH=C(CN)R (where R is C≡N or COOR) showed nitrile frequencies in the range 2217–2203.

Conjugation with an aromatic system, often the case in dyes, tends to give intermediate frequencies. Two bands are evident with compounds containing alkyl and aryl nitriles [see structure (**18**), Chapter 12], although with sodium chloride prisms they are usually poorly resolved.

These bands must be interpreted with care, with due attention to instrument frequency capability, since the regions are narrow and the shifts small. Splitting of the band must be handled cautiously also, since splitting does not always indicate two different kinds of nitrile groups. Thus a structure with what appears to be two equivalent aryl nitrile groups showed distinct splitting of the nitrile peak (crystal splitting? hindered rotation? hydrogen bonding?), and a dicyanoethylene derivative [structure (**32**), Chapter 12] showed splitting under grating resolution.

The intensity of the nitrile band is notoriously variable. Kitson and Griffith found examples in which the nitrile was totally undetectable, and Thompson and Steel[68] showed profound effects of ring substitution in benzonitriles. Felton and Orr[69] showed that the band of a nitrile conjugated with a nonaromatic double bond is substantially more intense than that of a saturated nitrile. Nitrile bands in the methine dyes mentioned above show outstanding intensities even under the low resolution of a sodium chloride prism instrument, but no precise quantitative data are available. We have found no case where the nitrile group in a dye could not be detected by IR methods, although some have been found with quite weak intensities. There is the risk that they might be overlooked if the overall spectrum is not very intense (see Section 3).

The nitrile peak is by far the sharpest peak that is encountered in the functional group region of dye spectra; this factor tends to make it readily recognized even at quite low intensities. Together with the relatively unique location of the peak in the spectrum, this correlation is probably the most reliable of all in dye analysis.

4.4 Double Bonds

4.4.1 C=O. A wide variety of carbonyl types is to be found in synthetic dyes. Although a few reactive groups (such as acid chloride or acid an-hydride) are very unlikely in dyes, most carbonyl types can be assumed to be possibilities. Many are located in pendant groups, and their IR behavior is usually in accord with the correlations that are thoroughly covered in texts, in particular by Jones and Sandorfy[1] and Bellamy.[45,46] They need no further comment here other than, perhaps, a reminder about intensities: if one is accustomed to the carbonyl being the strongest or nearly the strongest peak in the spectrum, the relatively low intensities sometimes seen in dye spectra are deceptive. This is especially true of pendant amide and urethane groups. The carbonyl intensities in several such dyes [(47) and (32), Chapter 12] are only about 10–20% of the strongest bands in their spectra.

Carbonyl groups in chromophores tend, in general, to be conjugated with double bonds or aromatic rings (often in both substituents on the carbonyl) with the result that the stretching frequencies appear toward the low-frequency end of the carbonyl range. Furthermore, those molecules that are the most practical dyes are often substituted with groups which by chelation or resonance tend to shift the carbonyl to lower frequencies. Since, in the region from 1620 to 1570, there are usually several aromatic C=C stretching bands,[45] it is not uncommon for chromophore C=O frequencies to be somewhat obscured. Thus the absence of an *easily recognizable* carbonyl band in a dye spectrum *does not prove the absence of a carbonyl group.*

This effect is prominent in anthraquinone dyes, a large and important synthetic dye class. Both hydroxyl and amino substituents are common, and both profoundly affect the carbonyl frequency. It was reported many years ago by Flett,[57] for example, that whereas unsubstituted anthraquinone absorbs at 1676, 1,4-dihydroxy- and 1,4-diaminoanthraquinones show their carbonyl absorptions at 1627 and 1610. More recently, data on a large number of hydroxysubstituted anthraquinones have been reported which show carbonyl shifts consistent with those previously reported.[70] Both publications suggest explanations for the shifts which help to explain why the OH group produces the effect when it is in the α, but not the β, position, whereas an amino group is effective in either position.

From a practical standpoint, these shifts interfere with IR identification of carbonyl groups. Many 1,4-diaminoanthraquinone derivatives show relatively weak bands in the region where the carbonyl bands would be expected according to Flett's work, some of them being barely detectable on the side of the stronger (aromatic C=C?) patterns in the 1600–1560 region. The OH group appears to cause less of a problem, judging from available spectra of 1-amino-4-hydroxyanthraquinone derivatives. The intensities apparently are not quite as weak as those in the diaminoanthraquinones and the shifts are somewhat smaller. Even in these cases, however, the highest frequency band is usually around 1613, and the intensity is not really outstanding. Bellamy[45] points out the possibility for "ambiguity" in the assignments of the bands in this region if one of the substituents is an NH_2 group, which should show a deformation vibration there. It is wise to be cautious in interpreting these spectra in detail (but see Section 4.9).

Spectra of a number of different carbonyl-containing chromophores can be found in the pigment collection published by McClure and co-workers.[17] It appears that the quinacridone derivatives might not be recognizable as carbonyl compounds, since a weak band at about 1610 is the highest frequency band in that region. Indigo has a slightly higher frequency band, the most intense in the spectrum, at ~1620. Thioindigo and several of its derivatives show sharp, strong carbonyl bands in the 1640–1660 region which are easily recognized. The perylene dicarboximides show two strong bands near 1660 and 1690, which also would be easily recognized.

Several available indoaniline derivatives showed strong bands near 1640, and several pyridone derivatives [see Chapter 12, (52) and (53)] showed two strong bands at 1681 and 1639 (C=N or C=C may be involved?).

Quinophthalone (1) and azopyrazolones (3) show bands readily assigned to carbonyls that are involved in strong bonding.[54,61] They are somewhat weak bands.

4.4.2   C=N.   Isolated C=N structural units are relatively uncommon in dyes. Bellamy[45] indicates that the highest frequency likely for the stretching vibration of such a group is about 1690, with the average around 1665.

With conjugation, especially when the C=N group is in a cyclic structure, the band is probably shifted to lower frequency, and with dyes is not likely to be diagnostically useful. An example of a dye containing the C=N group is given in Chapter 12, (10, X = NH). Its spectrum shows a strong band at 1653, which is presumably due to the C=N stretch vibration. Jones et al. assigned bands near 1600 to C=N vibrations in some pyrazolones, but admitted some uncertainty regarding the assignment.[61]

4.4.3 N=N. Azo dyes are a large and important class of dyes, and the idea of correlating an IR band with the N=N function is an attractive one. The substitution on the group in such dyes is likely to be fairly symmetrical, however, and the N=N stretch therefore is likely to be weak. Although the vibration has been reported[46,71] to be at 1450–1400, a search of our azo dye spectra showed no bands that would appear to be diagnostically useful in this area. Many of the spectra were virtually transparent in the region cited. No band was found consistently in the 927 region, where Tetlow reported a possible skeletal vibration.[72]

4.5 NO₂ Group

The NO_2 group is a common substituent in dyes, in which it is rarely found bonded to anything other than an aromatic nucleus. It can show asymmetric and symmetric stretch bands, and Bellamy[46] reports the overall ranges, with a few rare exceptions, of 1540–1510 and 1355–1338 for these vibrations. Our files contain a large number of mono- and dinitro azo dye spectra (other dye types with nitro groups are sparsely scattered), from which it appears that the azo substituent tends to shift the correlation to slightly lower frequency. Thus for 58 azobenzenes substituted with one NO_2 group and a variety of other groups not hydroxy or amino, we find that all show strong bands at 1517 ± 12 and 1333 ± 13. The 1517 band is generally distinctively sharp in those cases where the NO_2 group is alone on the ring or shares it with only one other substituent. The 1333 band is usually less well defined, in many cases giving the appearance of a poorly resolved group of bands. When the NO_2 group shares the ring with two substituents, many spectra show the 1517 band partially resolved into two sharp bands. The splitting appears to be sensitive to crystallinity since its appearance depends on the method of preparation. For 22 azo dyes in which there are two NO_2 groups and one other substituent on one ring, the correlation still appears to hold, but it is less certain because the bands in general seem less well defined.

As indicated by Bellamy,[45] when the NO_2 group is *para* to either a strongly electronegative or a strongly electron-donating group (e.g., NO_2 or NH_2), the NO_2 band in the 1500 region is strongly displaced, and may be difficult to find because of overlapping with the aromatic ring bands.

4.6 SO_2 Group

This grouping is found in sulfones, sulfonamides, and sulfonate esters, all of which are found occasionally in synthetic dyes. They give strong asymmetric and symmetric stretch bands which, unfortunately, occur in regions where dyes often have strong bands from other functions. Interpretation is therefore somewhat uncertain. Sulfur is readily detected by X-ray fluorescence or elemental analysis, and we generally do not look for these groups unless sulfur has been found in the unknown dye. In the spectra of dyes containing these groups, bands have been found consistent with the correlations given by Bellamy.[45]

4.7 SO_3^- Group

The sulfonate salt group is usually easily detected by IR spectroscopy. It shows a strong band centered near 1200, which almost always is conspicuously broad, and in dyes is often the strongest band in the spectrum. It is ordinarily accompanied by one or several sharper, somewhat weaker, but still often conspicuous bands in the 1080–1010 region.[45] It is rare that if a dye shows these features, it does not contain the sulfonate salt group, although we have occasionally found acid dyes that do not show distinct breadth of the $\sim$1200 band.

4.8 Other Correlations in the Fingerprint Region

Although they are not unique to dyes, a few functional group correlations involve bands in the long-wavelength region, say, 1400 and lower, which are so intense and so consistent in position that they are especially worth keeping in mind for dye analysis. They are well covered in the standard texts.

4.8.1 C—O and C—N Stretching. Ethers usually give C—O—C stretching bands of substantial intensity in the vicinity of 1100 or 1250, depending on whether the groups bonded to the oxygen are aliphatic or/and aromatic. The corresponding band in esters is usually in the 1290–1160 region; it is a very intense and characteristic band near 1270 for benzoates and phthalates, as in (34) and (33), Chapter 12. Nitrogen bonded to aromatic carbon usually gives a strong band in the 1360–1250 region. Bellamy[45] discusses the use of this band to distinguish primary, secondary, and tertiary amines.

4.8.2   Out-of-Plane Deformation of Ring Hydrogens. The use of these bands in establishing the position of substituents on aromatic nuclei is well known. Although the correlations can often be useful in dye analysis, their performance is variable. Dye spectra often show long-wavelength regions crowded with a large number of bands of similar intensities, and it is usually difficult to know which bands belong to this class. Furthermore, dyes often contain more than one aromatic nucleus and they are often substituted with strongly electronegative groups, such as nitro, carbonyl, or sulfonate, which tend to upset the correlations.[45] The technique should be used with caution.

Benzoates and phthalates show very strong bands near 710 and 746–725, respectively.

4.9   Special Correlations, Pattern Recognition

Szymanski[73] pointed out that a particular vibration may give a useful correlation in a series of closely related compounds even though the resulting correlation may not classify as a "good group frequency." It is not uncommon in dye analysis to find a band or pattern that is consistent enough within a series to become a useful identifying feature. McClure and co-workers made use of such bands in a dye identification example.[17] We have found that azo dyes made from 2-amino-5-nitrobenzothiazole show a weak-to-medium intensity band at 910, which is readily recognized because of its unusual sharpness. 2-Mercaptobenzothiazole derivatives all show a very strong band at about 1000, and the presence of such a band in a dye, **(35)**, in Chapter 12, was helpful in the identification. An outstanding example is the azo dye series **(5)** made by coupling to anilines with no ring substituents. The spectra of 70 such structures all show a band in the 1159–1129 region which is recognizable because of its very high intensity.

$$Ar-N\!\!=\!\!N-\!\!\left\langle\!\!\bigcirc\!\!\right\rangle\!\!-N\!\!\begin{array}{c}R_1\\ \\R_2\end{array}$$

(5)

1,4-Diaminoanthraquinones and 1-amino-4-hydroxyanthraquinones are much more recognizable by their overall pattern than by exact identification of their carbonyl bands, which are shifted into the aromatic C=C region and relatively weak in intensity (see Section 4.4.1). If the amino group is primary, they show an overall pattern which includes the following features: (1) two fairly strong, well resolved peaks near 3300–3500; (2) a multiple-band pattern in the 1640–1560 region with the intensity greatly increasing toward the low frequency end of that range; and (3) a very strong band in the 1230–1300 region. One of the latter two features usually includes the strongest band in the spectrum, and those two features usually persist even when the amino N is not primary (the split peak in the NH/OH region then is absent).

It is occasionally possible to virtually complete the identification of a dye by a combination of pattern matching and functional group analysis. For example, the spectrum of an unknown dye showed a distinct nitrile peak at 2245, but otherwise was very similar to a reference spectrum of (6). Since the frequency indicated that the CN group was probably bonded to aliphatic carbon, it was easy to speculate that the unknown dye might have a cyanoethyl group in place of one of the ethyl groups in (6). PMR and HRMS quickly confirmed this hypothesis.

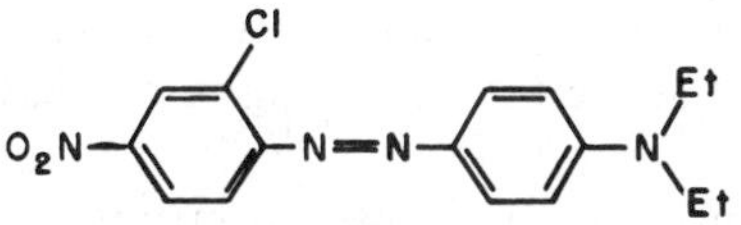

(6)

5 REFERENCE SPECTRA, SEARCH TECHNIQUES

5.1 Reference Collections

Of major importance to dye identification by IR is the availability of one or more good collections of reference spectra. As already discussed, they are needed as (1) exact references for "fingerprint" identification, and (2) sources of a well-rounded distribution of spectra of various dye types for pattern matching and general browsing. The requirements for application in these two capacities are not exactly the same, since the collection must be as large as possible for the former, but relatively small for the latter.

The Sadtler dye collection,[74] with 2400 spectra, fits in the first category. It is well indexed with regard to CI classification and manufacturer, and it has the added advantage that it is part of several search systems (non-manual; see Section 5.2). Its major disadvantage is that dye structures are not printed on the spectra. No other dye collection available to the public approaches the size of the Sadtler collection.

To serve in the second capacity a collection must be modest in size and fairly systematized. It is best assembled by the user, in the same way that most working spectroscopists collect general reference files. An in-house collection has the advantage that it can be organized to suit the user's needs. It has the disadvantage that it is not coded into a search system unless the user has his own system.

Generally available small collections are those of McClure et al.[17] and Hummel and Scholl.[18] They are well suited to manual searching, but rather limited in scope. Neither is coded into the Dow-ASTM SIRCH system (see Section 5.2).

The Sadtler Standard Spectra[75] have scattered through them a fairly large number of spectra of pure compounds which are dyes or dye-related structures. These are not suited at all to manual browsing, but many of them are coded into search systems and may be located thereby.

5.2   Search Techniques

Searching the files for a reference to match an unknown can be done manually or by some more or less mechanical or computerized method. The search is considered a success if it results in locating either an exactly matching reference or one so similar that the identification process is materially shortened. The methods to be discussed have all been successful in dye identifications.

Manual comparison of the unknown spectrum with each member of a reference collection is slow and laborious at best. In order for it to be at all feasible, some device must be used for narrowing the search to a small portion of the reference collection. This is fairly readily done since dyes fall into a number of distinct groups, and the unknown may already be classified accordingly (or the classification may be based on dye testing or on the IR spectrum itself). Subdivision of the major groups according to the presence or absence of readily detected elements or readily identified functional groups is usually necessary. Our in-house dye collection of about 350 spectra is fairly uniformly distributed among 19 folders, and a search usually takes about 15 minutes. The procedure is tedious, but it is fruitful often enough to make it worthwhile.

Sadtler's Specfinder system[76] is a manual/mechanical sorting procedure which narrows the search by comparing the location of the strongest band in each full micron segment of the spectrum of the unknown with the systematically tabulated strong band data of all the references. Once the unknown is coded, the procedure always narrows the search to a relatively small list of reference spectra, with which the original spectrum is then compared directly. This system has the advantage that it is always usable with the Sadtler file, since each addition to the file is coded into the Specfinder systems.

Computerized searching of IR reference collections is becoming increasingly popular. I have access to a commercially available program[77] originally developed by Erley.[78] The data collection for this system contains a large fraction of the Sadtler dye file, and part of my dye collection has been added to it. The yield of useful results from applications of this search system to dye unknowns is 30%. Unsuccessful searches, incidentally, should not be considered failures of the search program in view of the use of a finite reference collection.

REFERENCES

1. R. N. Jones and C. Sandorfy, "The Application of Infrared and Raman Spectrometry to the Elucidation of Molecular Structure," in W. West, Ed., *Chemical Applications of Spectroscopy*, Interscience, New York, 1956.

2. T. R. Harkins, J. T. Harris, and O. D. Shreve, *Anal. Chem.*, **31**, 541 (1959).

3. M. Suzuki, E. Nakamura, and Y. Nagase, *Yakugaku Zasshi*, **79**, 1116 (1959); *CA*, **54**, 1855c (1960).

4. M. Suzuki, E. Nakamura, and Y. Nagase, *Yakugaku Zasshi*, **79**, 1209 (1959); *CA*, **54**, 3957i (1960).

5. M. Suzuki, E. Nakamura, and Y. Nagase, *Yakugaku Zasshi*, **80**, 916 (1960); *CA*, **54**, 21764i (1960).

6. M. Dolinsky and C. Stein, *Anal. Chem.*, **34**, 127 (1962).

7. D. Haigh, *J. Soc. Dyers Colour.*, **79**, 242 (1963).

8. D. H. Abrahams and S. M. Edelstein, *Am. Dyest, Rep.*, **53**, 19 (1964).

9. R. Kleber, L. Masschelein-Kleiner, and J. Thissen, *Stud. Conserv.*, **12**, 41 (1967); *CA*, **68**, 22756g (1968).

10. L. Masschelein-Kleiner and J. B. Heylen, *Stud. Conserv.*, **13**, 87 (1968); *CA*, **70**, 16949x (1969).

11. T. R. McKay, *Aust. Paint. J.*, **16**, 9 (1970); *CA*, **74**, 43549f (1971).

12. R. L. Brunello and M. J. Pro, *J. Assoc. Off. Anal. Chem.*, **55**, 823 (1972); *CA*, **77**, 110174g (1972).

13. A. Quattrucci and P. Fiorucci, *Cellul. Carta*, **24**, 25 (1973); *CA*, **80**, 61128w (1974).

14. J. F. Feeman, *Can. Text. J.*, **83** (1970).

15. R. Latini, *Invest. Inf. Text. Tensioactivos*, **17**, 427 (1974); *CA*, **82**, 45606m (1975).

16. B. Werthman and R. Borowski, *Papier*, **28**, 235 (1974); *CA*, **81**, 107357w (1974).

17. A. McClure, J. Thomson, and J. Tannahill, *J. Oil Colour Chem. Assoc.*, **51**, 580 (1968).

18. D. O. Hummel and F. K. Scholl, *Infrared Analysis of Polymers, Resins and Additives—An Atlas*, Vol. II, Carl Hanser, Munich, 1973.

19. J. C. Brown, *J. Soc. Dyers Colour.*, **85**, 137 (1969).

20. M. Dolinsky and J. H. Jones, *J. Assoc. Off. Agr. Chem.*, **37**, 197 (1954); *CA*, **49**, 58f (1955).

21. T. Tamura, T. Totani, H. Harada, R. Yamazoe, T. Kan, and M. Taniguchi, *Tokyo-Toritsu Eisei Kenkyusho Kenkyu Hokoku*, **25**, 1 (1967); *CA*, **69**, 109748a (1968).

22. K. H. W. Reichert, *Farbe Lack*, **80**, 920 (1974); *CA*, **82**, 18664x (1975).

23. M. R. R. Bhagwanth, A. V. Rama Rao, and K. Venkataraman, *Indian J. Chem.*, **7**, 1065 (1969).

24. V. H. Deshpande, A. V. Rama Rao, R. Srinivasan, and K. Venkataraman, *Indian J. Chem.*, **10**, 681 (1972).

25. B. R. Dhruva, A. V. Rama Rao, R. Srinivasan, and K. Venkataraman, *Indian J. Chem.*, **10**, 683 (1972).

26. A. R. Mehendale, A. V. Rama Rao, and K. Venkataraman, *Indian J. Chem.*, **10,** 1041 (1972).

27. V. H. Deshpande, A. V. Rama Rao, M. Varadan, and K. Venkataraman, *Indian J. Chem.*, **11,** 518 (1973).

28. C. G. Karanjgoakar, A. V. Rama Rao, K. Venkataraman, and S. S. Yemul, *Tetrahedron Lett.*, **50,** 4977 (1973).

29. V. H. Deshpande, A. V. Rama Rao, K. Venkataraman, and P. V. Wakharkar, *Indian J. Chem.*, **12,** 431 (1974).

30. V. Parameswaran, A. V. Rama Rao, and K. Venkataraman, *Indian J. Chem.*, **12,** 785 (1974).

31. B. K. Manukian and H. Lichti, *Chimia*, **24,** 1 (1970).

32. B. K. Manukian and A. Mangini, *Helv. Chim. Acta*, **54,** 2093 (1971).

33. B. K. Manukian and A. Mangini, *Helv. Chim. Acta*, **54,** 2924 (1971).

34. R. H. Müller, *Anal. Chem.*, **28,** 37A (1956).

35. B. Weinstein, *Chem.-Anal.*, **49,** 29 (1960).

36. W. J. de Klein, *Anal. Chem.*, **41,** 667 (1969).

37. D. D. Rice, *Anal. Chem.*, **39,** 1906 (1967).

38. H. R. Garner and H. Packer, *Appl. Spectrosc.*, **22,** 122 (1968).

39. A. A. Ebert, Jr., and H. B. Gottlieb, *J. Am. Chem. Soc.*, **74,** 2806 (1952).

40. D. N. Kendall, *Anal. Chem.*, **25,** 382 (1953).

41. A. W. Baker, *J. Phys. Chem.*, **61,** 450 (1957).

42. G. Duyckaerts, *Chem. Anal.*, **84,** 201 (1959).

43. A. R. Monahan and J. E. Kuder, *J. Org. Chem.*, **37,** 4182 (1972).

44. N. L. Alpert, W. E. Keiser, and H. A. Szymanski, *Theory and Practice of Infrared Spectroscopy*, Plenum Press, New York, 1970.

45. L. J. Bellamy, *The Infrared Spectra of Complex Molecules*, 2nd ed., Wiley, New York, 1958.

46. L. J. Bellamy, *Advances in Infrared Group Frequencies*, Methuen, London, 1968.

47. N. B. Colthup, L. H. Daly, and S. E. Wiberley, *Introduction to Infrared and Raman Spectroscopy*, Academic Press, New York, 1964.

48. A. D. Cross, *An Introduction to Practical Infrared Spectroscopy*, Butterworths, London, 1960.

49. K. Nakanishi, *Infrared Absorption Spectroscopy—Practical*, Holden-Day, San Francisco, and Nankodo Company, Tokyo, 1962.

50. C. I. Jose, P. S. Phadke, and A. V. Rama Rao, *Spectrochim. Acta*, **30A,** 1199 (1974).

51. A. V. Stuart and G. B. B. M. Sutherland, *J. Chem. Phys.*, **24,** 559 (1956).

52. J. S. Cook and I. H. Reece, *Aust. J. Chem.*, **14,** 211 (1961).

53. M. St. C. Flett, *Spectrochim. Acta*, **10,** 21 (1957).

54. B. K. Manukian, P. Niklaus, and H. Ehrsam, *Helv. Chim. Acta*, **52,** 1259 (1969).

55. A. G. Catchpole, W. B. Foster, and R. S. Holden, *Spectrochim. Acta*, **18,** 1353 (1962).

56. B. L. Kaul, P. Madhavan Nair, A. V. Rama Rao, and K. Venkataraman, *Tetrahedron Lett.*, **32,** 3897 (1966).

57. M. St. C. Flett, *J. Chem. Soc.*, 1441 (1948).

58. T. A. Kletz, *Disc. Faraday Soc.*, **9,** 211 (1950).

59. R. A. Russell and H. W. Thompson, *J. Chem. Soc.*, 483 (1955).
60. R. A. Durie and J. S. Shannon, *Aust. J. Chem.*, **11**, 189 (1958).
61. R. Jones, A. J. Ryan, S. Sternhell, and S. E. Wright, *Tetrahedron*, **19**, 1497 (1963).
62. R. E. Richards and H. W. Thompson, *J. Chem. Soc.*, 1248 (1947).
63. H. L. McMurry and V. Thornton, *Anal. Chem.*, **24**, 318 (1952).
64. J. J. Fox and A. E. Martin, *J. Chem. Soc.*, 318 (1939).
65. H. B. Henbest, G. D. Meakins, B. Nicholls, and A. A. Wagland, *J. Chem. Soc.*, 1462 (1957).
66. R. D. Hill and G. D. Meakins, *J. Chem. Soc.*, 760 (1958).
67. R. E. Kitson and N. E. Griffith, *Anal. Chem.*, **24**, 334 (1952).
68. H. W. Thompson and G. Steel, *Trans. Faraday Soc.*, **52**, 1451 (1956).
69. D. G. I. Felton and S. F. D. Orr, *J. Chem. Soc.*, 2170 (1955).
70. H. Bloom, L. H. Briggs, and B. Cleverley, *J. Chem. Soc.*, 178 (1959).
71. R. J. W. LeFevre and R. L. Werner, *Aust. J. Chem.*, **10**, 26 (1957).
72. K. S. Tetlow, *Research*, **3**, 187 (1950).
73. H. A. Szymanski, *Interpreted Infrared Spectra*, Vol. 3, Plenum Press Data Division, New York, 1967, p. ix.
74. *Sadtler Commercial Spectra, Dyes, Pigments, and Stains*, Sadtler Research Laboratories, Inc., Philadelphia, Pa., 1973.
75. *Sadtler Standard Spectra*, Sadtler Research Laboratories, Inc., Philadelphia, Pa., 1975.
76. *Sadtler Spec-finder*, Sadtler Research Laboratories, Inc., Philadelphia, Pa., 1975.
77. *ASTM/Dow SIRCH—III, Infrared File Search System*, American Society for Testing and Materials, Philadelphia, Pa., 1969.
78. D. S. Erley, *Anal. Chem.*, **40**, 894 (1968).

CHAPTER EIGHT

NMR Spectroscopy of Synthetic Dyes

ANTHONY FORIS

1 INTRODUCTION

Nuclear magnetic resonance (NMR) spectroscopy[1,2,3] is of great value in the structural elucidation of synthetic dyes. The ability of proton NMR (PMR) to characterize aliphatic side chains and aromatic substitution patterns complements other spectrometric techniques such as IR and HRMS (see Chapter 12). In addition, ^{13}C NMR (CMR) allows the direct observation of carbon skeletons and of carbon-containing functional groups that have no attached protons (e.g., carbonyls, nitriles).

Analysis of dyes by NMR, however, presents some difficulties which, although not unique to this class of chemicals, are more pronounced than for many other types of materials. Many dyes have moderately or highly complex structures and are sparingly soluble in NMR-compatible solvents. Also, occasionally, only a limited amount of sample is available. Two relatively recent developments help the spectroscopist to cope with these problems: PMR at high magnetic fields,[3] and Fourier transform (FT) NMR.[4] The former provides greater chemical shift dispersion and higher sensitivity, and the latter not only facilitates the recording of PMR spectra of highly dilute solutions or of very small samples but also makes obtaining ^{13}C spectra a routine matter.[5]

2 BACKGROUND

2.1 Scope

There have been few publications dealing specifically with NMR of synthetic dyes. Significant contributions prior to 1970 have been reviewed by
Venkataraman.[6] Therefore, pre-1970 literature is not, in general, covered in
this chapter except when it is deemed necessary for reasons of continuity or
clarity. Also, coverage has to be selective because of space limitations, and
the interested reader is encouraged to consult the cited books and articles.

2.2 Structure Determination

The most widespread use of NMR in dye chemistry has been in structure
determination and confirmation. PMR was employed[7] to show that the
structure of Basic Blue 4 is 3,7-bis(diethylamino)phenazoxonium chloride
[(34), Table 8.15], rather than the 1-methoxy structure previously assumed.[8]
Reductive desulfonation of anthraquinones was used to render sulfonic
acid dyes more amenable to analysis by NMR and MS, and by analyzing
the desulfonated dyes it was shown that two β-arylanthraquinones had
structures which were the reverse of those assigned in relevant patents.[9]
Violanthrones were analyzed as the ethers of their leuco derivatives and the
structures of CI Vat Green 2, CI 59830, and of CI Vat Blue 16, CI 71200, were
determined.[10,11] The structures of Pigment Red 177, Pigment Red 149 and
178,[12] Pigment Yellow 109 and 110, and Pigment Violet 34 and 35[13] were
elucidated with the help of PMR. Reductive demethylation followed by
MS and NMR analysis permitted the identification of CI Basic Orange 27,
Basic Red 14, and Basic Yellow 28.[14]

2.3 Correlations

A series of papers describing various NMR studies of polymethine dyes
and dye intermediates has been published by Kleinpeter and co-workers.
PMR spectral data of 28 carbocyanine dyes were presented and the chemical
shifts of the methine protons were correlated with the π-electron densities
of the corresponding carbon atoms.[15] The influence of N-alkyl groups on
the PMR spectra of benzimidotrimethinecyanines was discussed, and it
was shown that the π-electron alteration in the polymethine chain is
influenced by the inductive effect of the N-alkyl groups. Calculations using
simple Hückel molecular-orbital (HMO) models confirmed these results.[16]
The reactivities of seven 2-methylcycloammonium salts were discussed

on the basis of chemical shift data and quantum mechanical calculations.[17] Carbon-13 spectra of these intermediates were determined.[18] PMR and visible spectral data for nine merocyanines were combined with HMO calculations to yield linear correlations.[19] The effect of a shift reagent on anils was discussed.[20] Chemical shifts and coupling constants of seven cyanine dye intermediates were compiled and their reactivities in the formation of unsymmetrical benzimidotrimethinecyanine and merocyanine dyes were investigated.[21]

Carbon-13 chemical shifts, [13]C-^{1}H coupling constants, and the effects of a shift reagent on the CMR spectra of simple polymethines were reported by Radeglia.[22] Ring size effects in saturated nitrogen heterocyclic polymethines on the ^{13}C chemical shifts of polymethine carbon atoms in simple cyanines were investigated.[22] Electron densities, bond orders, and atom–atom polarizabilities calculated for cyanines, merocyanines, and oxonols were correlated with the corresponding ^{13}C and ^{1}H parameters.[23]

2.4 Configurational Analysis

PMR has also been useful in configurational analysis of dyes. Evidence was presented to show that pyrazolone azomethine dyes exist with the p-phenylenediamine ring syn to the pyrazolone carbonyl group when there is a 4-Me substituent present.[24] In the absence of a 4-substituent, the dyes exist as a mixture of syn and anti forms with the latter predominating. It was shown that in dyes formed from 4-amino-N,N-diethylaniline, the p-phenylenediamine ring "flips" between two planar conformations.

Several pyrido- and azapyridocyanines were examined by PMR, and it was concluded that N,N'-diethyl-2,2'-pyridocyanine and its aza analogue exist in the all-trans form and that N,N'-(1,2-ethylene)-2,2'-pyridocyanine probably exists in a twisted rather than a planar form.[25]

2.5 Hydrogen Bonding and Tautomerism

It was shown by Manukian and co-workers[26] that the chemical shifts of the two exchangeable protons at positions 1 and 3' in 3'-hydroxyquinophthalone are essentially constant in solvents of different polarities; this indicates strong intramolecular hydrogen bridges. It was suggested that the good lightfastness of these dyes is related to the strong hydrogen bond between the OH in the 3' position and the C=O in the five-membered anhydride ring. Dale, Jones, and Peters confirmed, with the help of long-range coupling constants NH–5H, in the PMR spectra of some 4-substituted 2-nitrodiphenylamine disperse dyes, the presence of intramolecular

NH···ON hydrogen bonding.[27] Measurements in polar and nonpolar solvents indicated weakening of the bonding, which is related to lightfastness, when the 4-substituent is a strong electron acceptor. PMR spectra of azobenzenes substituted in the *para* and *para,para'* positions were examined by L. Skulski and co-workers.[28] Their results suggested that either the potentially tautomeric *p*-hydroxy-, *p*-amino-, and *p*-*N*-methylaminoazobenzenes possess a true azo structure or the postulated tautomeric equilibria in their solutions are strongly shifted toward the more stable azo forms, regardless of the solvent polarity. 1-Phenylazo-2-napthylamine and 4-phenylazo-*N*-methyl-1-naphthylamine exist only in the azo form.[28–30]

Azo–hydrazo equilibrium constants for 1-phenylazo-2-naphthol and 2-hydroxy-5-*t*-butylazobenzene substituted with ^{15}N alpha to the monosubstituted benzene ring have been estimated from the [15]N-^{1}H coupling constants.[31] The tautomeric equilibria of 1-phenyl-3-methyl-4-phenylazo-5-pyrazolone, 2-phenylazoresorcinol, 2,4-bis(phenylazo)-1-naphthol, anthraquinone phenylhydrazone, and 1-phenylazo-4-naphthol,[32] and of 10 *para*-substituted ethyl arylhydrazonocyanoacetylcarbamates and of arylhydrazono-2-cyanomethylbenzimidazole[33] were determined by PMR using ^{15}N-labeled compounds. Quantitative estimates of the amounts of hydroxyazo and hydrazone tautomers in 10 1-(substituted phenyl)azo-2-naphthols have been obtained from indirectly measured ^{14}N chemical shifts.[34]

The tautomerism of aromatic azo compounds has been reviewed by Bershtein and Ginzburg.[35]

2.6 Other Applications

PMR has been evaluated by Marmion as a tool for the study of certifiable food colors.[36] The technique was found useful as a means of identifying individual colorants, differentiating between mixtures and single colors, identifying and estimating the dyes in secondary mixtures, establishing the presence of excipients, and detecting the adulteration of a color additive with forbidden colorants. PMR was also said to show promise as a method for the determination of the purity of food colors and for studying process conditions.

3 EXPERIMENTAL DETAILS

Continuous wave (CW) PMR spectra were recorded on Varian A-56/60, T-60, XL-100, and HR-220, and on Bruker HX-60 spectrometers. FT PMR spectra were obtained on Varian HR-220/620i, and CMR spectra on Bruker HFX-90/Digilab NMR-3 and WH-90 spectrometer systems.

Procedures for the removal of standardizing materials, surface-active agents, etc., and for separating components in multicomponent or impure dyes by TLC are described in some detail in Chapter 12, Section 2.2.

3.1 Solvents and Preparation of Solutions

The low solubility of some dyes can be a serious problem in obtaining good-quality NMR spectra. Sulfonic acid dyes, some basic (cationic) dyes, and especially vat dyes may not always dissolve sufficiently in many of the usual NMR-compatible solvents to yield good CW spectra. Most of the dye samples encountered in my laboratory, however, were soluble enough in solvents such as $CDCl_3$, CD_2Cl_2, DMSO-D_6, DMF-D_7, or TFA to provide either CW or FT PMR spectra with reasonably good signal-to-noise ratios. Other investigators have used powerful solvents such as sulfuric acid, liquid SO_2, and arsenic trichloride. Tetramethylurea has been useful in dissolving some violanthrone derivatives.[10,11] The use of D_2SO_4 as an NMR solvent is fairly widespread. This solvent may cause partial deuteration of aromatic rings, resulting in nonsensical or confusing integrals. Arsenic trichloride is not only highly toxic, but is also a suspected carcinogen. DMSO, one of the most useful solvents for dyes, is readily absorbed through the skin along with the solute itself and should also be used with caution. In my laboratory all samples and solvents are treated as potentially hazardous materials, and technicians wear neoprene gloves and prepare solutions in well-ventilated hoods.

Whenever saturated solutions have to be prepared or the sample contains insoluble (and sometimes paramagnetic) particles, Swinnex filter units with Mitex (Teflon, Du Pont) filters (both available from Millipore Corporation, Bedford, Mass.) attached to a hypodermic syringe have been found very satisfactory for removing undissolved material.

3.2 Handling of Small Samples

Occasionally, as a result of TLC separations only a very small amount of sample is available. When preparing such samples for analysis, it is important to filter the extracts to remove residual silica *before* the final evaporation of the solvent which is best done in a small vial with a cone-shaped bottom such as the Reacti-vials available from Pierce Chemical Co., Rockford, Ill. In this manner the solid dye sample is concentrated in the conical bottom of the container and can be dissolved in a minimum amount of solvent under dry nitrogen to avoid the absorption of moisture. Removal of all traces of solvents used in extractions and scrupulously clean glassware are mandatory when handling small samples. Only the highest-grade deuterated (100 atom %) solvents should be used to keep residual solvent proton signals at manageable levels.

There are a number of commercially available "microcell" tubes in which the sample solution is confined to a small spherical or cylindrical cavity within the receiver coil. Especially when examining samples in a superconductive system, I prefer the type of coaxial tubes available from Wilmad Glass Co., Inc., Buena, N.J. These tubes, with a capacity of about 150–250 μl, depending on the diameter of the inner tube, have several advantages over many of the other types of sample tubes: easier loading and retrieval of samples for further spectrometric work, less severe spinning side-band problems at the high spinning rates required in such instruments, and relative ease of cleaning after use. In addition, centering of the tubes in the coil is not necessary.

Some manufacturers of NMR spectrometers now also offer micro inserts which accommodate capillary tubes as sample containers. These devices should be useful in the handling of small samples. Real gain in sensitivity is achieved, however, with FT spectrometers.

4 PMR SPECTRA OF SYNTHETIC DYES

There is relatively little published information concerning PMR spectrometry of synthetic colorants. Most of the examples described in this chapter are, therefore, taken from my own spectral collection, supplemented by some data gathered from the more recent literature. The quality of the data varies somewhat since the spectra have been recorded over a period during which NMR instrumentation has undergone some major changes. Some of the correlations are based on limited numbers of observations and should, therefore, be considered only as guidelines.

Although coupling constants can be as important as chemical shift data and relative proton counts in structural identifications, because of limitation of space they are not listed in every case. In general, in PMR spectra of dyes containing benzene rings, *ortho* coupling constants are approximately 7–10 Hz and *meta* coupling constants about 1–3 Hz; *para* coupling is usually less than 1 Hz and is, in most cases, not clearly observed. PMR spectra of dyes containing aromatic heterocyclic rings show a greater variation in *ortho* coupling constants (~5–10 Hz), a fact that can be of considerable value in recognizing the presence of such ring systems and their substitution patterns. In the case of simple aliphatic side chains, vicinal coupling constants are usually of the order of 6–7 Hz, whereas in more complicated aliphatic systems both vicinal and geminal couplings vary considerably with the geometry of the system and with the substituents on the bonded carbon atoms.

4.1   Water-Insoluble Azo Dyes

The simplest azo dyes include the p-monosubstituted and p,p'-disubstituted azobenzenes. The chemical shifts of the side-chain protons in a number of these derivatives which were studied by L. Skulski and co-workers[28,30] are summarized in Table 8.1. These authors also observed that the azo group deshielded the *ortho* positions more than the *para* or *meta* positions and that protons *ortho* to a nitro group were strongly shifted downfield beyond the signals derived from the protons *ortho* to the azo group. Aromatic protons *ortho* to electron-donating groups, however, appeared at higher fields than protons *meta* and *para* to the azo group in the other ring.

Some simple azo dyes contain hydroxyazobenzene or its derivatives. Kaul and co-workers studied a number of azophenols and observed strong paramagnetic shifts for the hydroxyl protons *ortho* to the azo linkage.[38] They found, for example, that the chelated hydroxyl protons of 2-phenylazo-p-cresol in carbon tetrachloride and of 4-phenylazoresorcinol in DMSO appeared at 12.25 and 12.77, respectively. I also observed such low-field shifts in both mono- and disazo dyes, and found them to be of diagnostic value in structural elucidation.

Azo dyes of the general structure (1) are most often encountered. Chemical shifts of the side-chain protons in a number of these dyes are summarized in Tables 8.2–8.4. Chemical shifts of aromatic protons are given in Tables 8.5 and 8.6. The diazo component, Ar in (1), may be a substituted phenyl group, as in (2), or a heterocyclic moiety; however, neither acid nor cationic dyes have been included in this tabulation. Most of the data in Tables 8.2 and 8.3 require no further explanation. Several generalizations, however, can be made which may be useful in structural elucidations of unknown dyes.

Usually, N-β-cyanoethyl groups [see, for example, (7) and (8) in Table 8.8] are easily identified from the triplets around 2.6–3.0 and 3.8–4.0 arising from the CH_2CN and NCH_2 protons, respectively. Occasionally, however,

(1)   (2)

Table 8.1 Chemical Shifts of Side-Chain Protons in p-Monosubstituted and p,p'-Disubstituted Azobenzenes[a]

Side Chains		Chemical Shifts		
R_1	R_2	R_1	R_2	Solvent
Me	H	2.38	—	CCl_4
SMe	H	2.47	—	CCl_4
NHMe	H	4.13, 2.48	—	$CDCl_3$
NMe_2	H	3.02	—	CCl_4
N(Me)COMe	H	3.17, 1.88	—	CCl_4
OMe	H	3.77	—	CCl_4
Me	Me	2.43	2.43	CCl_4[b]
OMe	NH_2	3.74	3.47	$CDCl_3$
OMe	N(Me)Ac	3.84	3.26, 1.90	$CDCl_3$
OMe	NHMe	3.80	—, 2.82	$CDCl_3$
OMe	NMe_2	3.80	2.99	$CDCl_3$
OMe	OH	3.80	8.90	$(CD_3)_2CO$
OMe	OCOMe	3.90	2.33	$(CD_3)_2CO$
OMe	OMe	3.96	3.96	$(CD_3)_2CO$
NMe_2	NH_2	3.06	~3.06	$(CD_3)_2CO$
NMe_2	NHAc	3.56	—, 2.51	TFA
NMe_2	N(Me)Ac	3.06	3.67, 1.92	$CDCl_3$
NMe_2	NHMe	2.98	—, 2.83	$CDCl_3$
NMe_2	NMe_2	3.60	3.60	TFA
NO_2	NH_2	—	5.84	$(CD_3)_2CO$
NO_2	NHAc	—	—, 2.50	TFA
NO_2	N(Me)Ac	—	3.30, 1.96	$CDCl_3$
NO_2	NHMe	—	—, 3.45	TFA
NO_2	NMe_2	—	3.69	TFA
NO_2	OH	—	9.65	$(CD_3)_2CO$
NO_2	OCOMe	—	2.35	$(CD_3)_2CO$
NO_2	OMe	—	3.96	$(CD_3)_2CO$
OH	OH	10.1	10.1	DMSO-D_6[c]

[a] From refs. 28 and 30.
[b] From ref. 37.
[c] Author's data.

Table 8.2 Chemical Shifts of Side-Chain Protons in Azo Dyes of Type (1) (Coupler Moiety)

R₁ and/or R₂	Chemical Shifts (Left to Right)	Solvent	No. of Observations
CH₂CH₃	3.3-3.7 1.1-1.3	CD₂Cl₂, CDCl₃, DMSO-D₆	24
(H)CH₂CH₃	6.95 3.33 1.24	DMSO-D₆	1[a]
CH₂CH₂Cl	~3.8 ~3.8	CDCl₃	1
CH₂CH₂OH	3.6-3.9 3.6-3.9	DMSO-D₆, DMF-D₇	12
CH₂CH₂CN	3.7-4.0 2.5-3.0 4.7-5.0	CD₂Cl₂, CDCl₃, DMSO-D₆	23[a]
CH₂Ph	4.7-4.9 7.3-7.7	CDCl₃, DMSO-D₆	4[a]
CH₂CH₂Ph	3.63 2.57 7.27	CD₂Cl₂	1
CHMe₂	4.2-4.3 1.3	CDCl₃	2
CH₂CH₂CONH₂	~3.8 2.53 6.96	DMSO-D₆	1
CH₂CH₂CH₂CH₃	3.56 1.61 1.37 0.95	DMSO-D₆	1[a]
CH₂CH₂OCOMe	3.6-3.9 4.2-4.4 2.0-2.1	CDCl₃, DMSO-D₆, DMF-D₇	20[a]
CH₂CH₂COOMe	3.89 2.73 3.73	CDCl₃	1
CH₂CH₂OCOOMe	3.9 4.42 3.78	CDCl₃	1
CH₂CH₂NHCOMe	~3.4 ~3.4 ~7.9 1.85	DMSO-D₆	1
CH₂CH₂OCOPh	4.0 4.6 b	CDCl₃, DMSO-D₆	2
(H)CH₂CH₂COOCH₂CH₃	6.3 3.7 2.8 4.2 1.3	CDCl₃	1[a]
CH₂CH₂COOCH₂CH₃	3.7-3.8 2.6-2.7 4.0-4.1 1.1-1.2	CDCl₃	2[a]
CH₂CH₂NCOCH₂CH₂CO	~3.7 ~3.7 2.6-2.7	CD₂Cl₂, CDCl₃	2
CH₂CH₂OCOCH₂CH₂CH₃	3.89 4.36 ~3.26 1.61 0.91	CDCl₃	1[a]
CH₂CH₂OCONHCH₂CH₂CH₃	~3.8 4.20 7.15 2.9 1.38	DMSO-D₆	1
(H)CH₂CH₂COOCH₂OMe	6.33 3.70 2.78 4.30 3.62 0.83 3.39	CDCl₃	1[a]

[a] Some or all of these data obtained at 220 MHz.

[b] Overlap with other aromatic proton resonances.

Table 8.3 Chemical Shifts of Side-Chain Protons in Azo Dyes of Type (1)

R_3	R_4	Chemical Shifts (Left to Right)				Solvent	No. of Observations
H	Me	—	2.4–2.8			$CDCl_3$, DMSO-D_6, DMF-D_7	11[a]
H	NHAc	—	9–13	2.1–2.3		CD_2Cl_2, $CDCl_3$, DMSO-D_6, DMF-D_7	19[a]
H	NHCOCH$_2$CH$_3$	—	9–11	2.4–2.6	1.1–1.3	$CDCl_3$, DMSO-D_6	4
H	NHCOCH$_2$CH$_2$Cl	—	~11–12	3.0–3.1	3.8–3.9	$CDCl_3$, DMSO-D_6	2
Me	NHAc	2.11	9.85	2.18		DMSO-D_6	1[a]
OMe	H	3.95				$CDCl_3$	1
OMe	NHAc	3.7–3.9	8.7–9.3	2.1–2.3		$CDCl_3$, DMSO-D_6	11[a]
OCH$_2$CH$_3$	NHAc	3.8–4.1	1.3–1.5	7.6–9.1	2.1–2.4	$CDCl_3$, DMSO-D_6	3[a]

[a] Some or all of these data were obtained at 220 MHz.

Table 8.4   Chemical Shifts of Side-Chain Protons in Azo Dyes of Type (2) (Diazo Moiety), Z = H

X	Y	Chemical Shifts	Solvent	No. of Observations
OMe	NO_2	4.1–4.2	$CDCl_3$, DMF-D_7	2
SO_2Me	NO_2	3.4–3.6	$CDCl_3$, DMSO-D_6	3
Cl	SO_2Me	3.1–3.3	$CDCl_3$, DMSO-D_6	2

overlaps with other types of protons may occur which may require high-field PMR or special techniques to resolve (see Section 6). The four protons of the N-β-chloroethyl group resonate at about 3.8, an interesting coincidence of shifts also observed by Parameswaran and co-workers[14] in CI Basic Violet 7; CI 48020. Similarly, all methylene protons of the N-bis(β-hydroxyethyl) group show a broad absorption at about 3.8 at 60 MHz in DMSO-D_6 or DMF-D_7. The four methylene protons in the N-mono-(β-hydroxyethyl) group are, at best, partially resolved at 60 MHz.

Amine protons in N-monoalkyl groups often show in their PMR spectra multiplets characteristic of the attached alkyl group, e.g., a doublet in the case of N-cyclohexyl, a triplet for N-ethyl, etc. (An exception is NHMe in p,p'-disubstituted azobenzenes, the room-temperature spectra of which were reported[30] to show no detectable NH resonance and only a singlet for the Me group.) Examples of such side chains are shown in Table 8.2 and Table 8.7, (4) and (6). Upon deuterium exchange, these NH multiplets disappear and the attached alkyl group resonance is simplified. Secondary amide protons also show this type of behavior, a fact that can be used to help distinguish between structures such as ArNHCOR and ArCONHR.

N-Benzyl groups in azo dyes are usually easily recognized; the 60-MHz spectra show a methylene singlet at $\sim$4.8 and a broad Ph singlet or near-singlet at $\sim$7.3. At 220 MHz, however, the Ph resonance is no longer a single peak [see (5), Table 8.7] and care must be exercised when comparing spectra obtained at different field strengths.

As the data in Table 8.3 show, Me groups *ortho* to the azo linkage normally appear around 2.4–2.8 unless influenced by electron-donating groups *para* to them. Methyl protons in acetamido groups *ortho* to the azo linkage appear in the 2.1–2.3 range, whereas the amide proton is usually found in the much wider range of 8–13 and is apparently more affected by structural differences, solvents, and moisture in the sample and the solvent. Nevertheless, the presence of the methyl singlet and the broadened NH resonance is usually a good indication for the probable existence of the acetamido group in an unknown dye. One must be careful, however, not to mistake ArMe and arylamide resonances for those of the acetamido group. The chemical shifts of the aromatic protons in azo dyes (1) are recorded in Table 8.5. Alkylamido groups in the 5 position result in paramagnetic shifts for H-6 in spite of the presence of the electron-donating NR_1R_2 group in the 1 position (see Table 8.5).

Aromatic proton shifts of some azo dyes of type (2), especially if X = Y = NO_2 and Z = Br or CN, are quite sensitive to solvents. Thus, for example, the H-3' and H-5' in the diazo component of dyes such as (4) (Table 8.7) in $CDCl_3$ are clearly observable even at 60 MHz as two distinct doublets with *meta* coupling constants. The same compounds, however, in DMSO-D$_6$ yield only a two-H singlet for H-3' and H-5'. This apparent singlet is barely resolved into a typical AB pattern at 220 MHz. Conversely, the 60-MHz spectrum of (5) in DMSO-D$_6$ shows two doublets, but yields in $CDCl_3$ a near-singlet for two H. Similarly, in the 60-MHz spectrum of (6) in $CDCl_3$, the outer peaks in the AB pattern are barely detectable, for the H-3' and H-5' resonances approach a broad singlet. On addition of a few few drops of TFA-D, the spectrum clearly shows doublets at 8.86 and 9.33 with typical *meta* coupling constants ($\sim$2.5 Hz).

The chemical shift ranges of the aromatic protons in variously substituted diazo moieties of dyes of the general structure (2) are summarized in Table 8.6. Some examples of azo dyes, together with proton chemical shift data, solvent, and instrument frequency, are shown in Tables 8.7 and 8.8.

The 60-MHz PMR spectra of disazo dyes in which the central benzene ring is substituted only in the *para* positions show a four-H singlet at about 8 [see, for example, (11); DMF-D$_7$, 60 MHz]. Disazo dyes in which the central ring is further substituted show more complex 60-MHz PMR spectra and may require analysis at a higher frequency [see (12); $CDCl_3$, 220 MHz]. *o*-Phenylazo-phenol [(13);DMF-D$_7$, 60 MHz] and naphthol [(14); $CDCl_3$, 60 MHz] derivatives yield PMR spectra that are indicative of strongly chelated protons.[35,38] In the hydroxyazo compounds of the naphthalene series, the hydrazone form is favored.

(11)

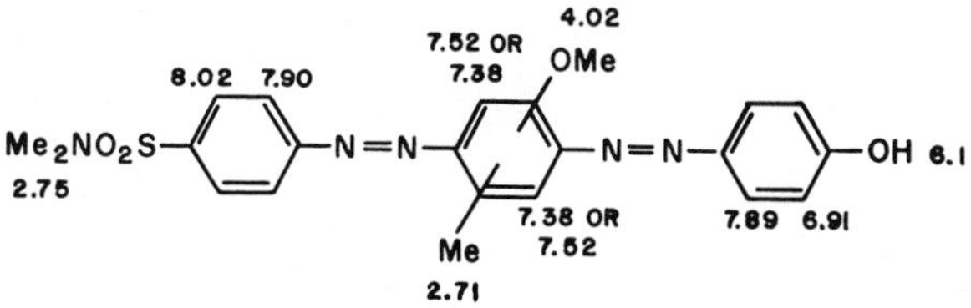

(12)

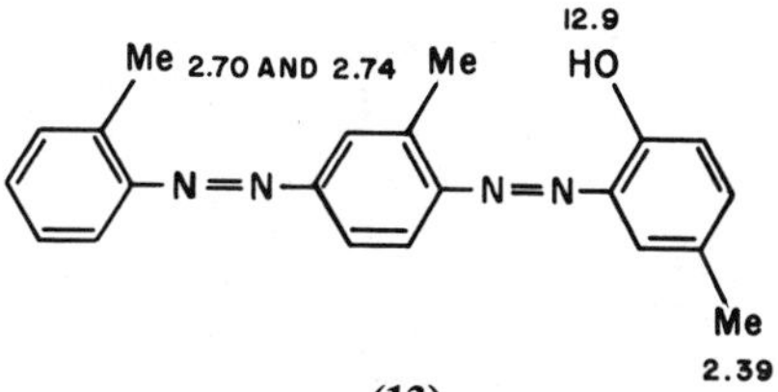

(13)

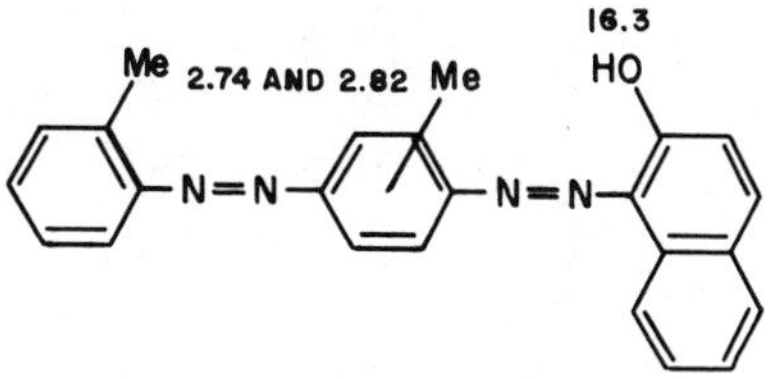

(14)

4.2 Disperse Anthraquinone Dyes

The characteristic carbonyl chromophore can be readily detected by CMR. If the A ring is unsubstituted, its proton patterns are characteristic enough so that, barring serious overlaps by other aromatic protons, the presence of the anthraquinone system can be inferred.

Aliphatic and aromatic side chains in the anthraquinone dyes vary from simple to fairly complex structures and their exact identification may require decoupling experiments, high-field PMR, or both. Chemical shift data for a number of anthraquinones of the types (15), (16), and (17) are summarized in Tables 8.9–8.11.

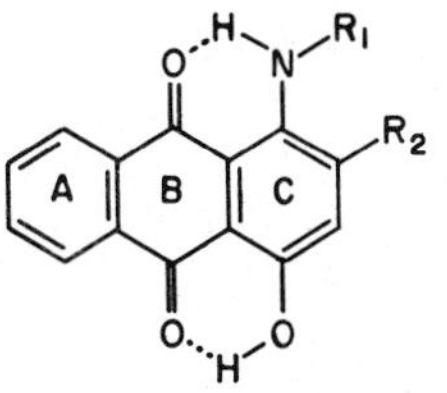

(15)

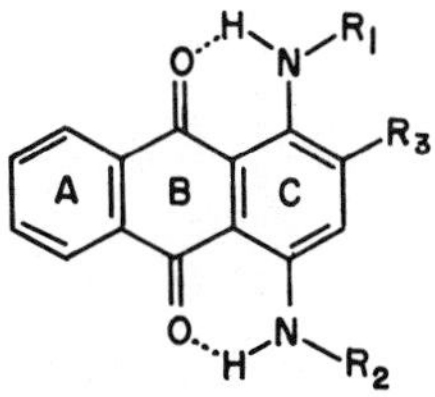

(16)

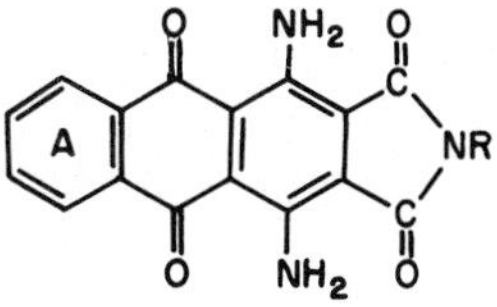

(17)

Table 8.5 Chemical Shifts of Aromatic Protons in Azo Dyes of Type (1) (Coupler Moiety)

R₃	R₄	2	3	5	6	Solvent	No. of Observations
H	H	6.67–7.30	7.79–8.02	7.79–8.00	6.67–7.30	CDCl₃, DMSO-D₆	18[a]
H	Me	6.58–7.08	7.60–8.02	—	6.6 –7.2	CDCl₃, DMSO-D₆, DMF-D₇	8[a]
H	Cl	6.72–6.88	7.62–7.94	—	6.83–7.01	CDCl₃, DMSO-D₆	7[a]
H	NHCOMe	6.47–6.88	7.62–7.98	—	7.80–8.30	CDCl₃, CD₂Cl₂, DMSO-D₆	18[a]
H	NHCOEt	6.41–6.71	7.65–7.79	—	7.95–8.23	CDCl₃, DMSO-D₆	4
H	NHCOCH₂CH₂Cl	6.67	7.72	—	7.93	DMSO-D₆	1
Me	NHCOMe	—	7.52	—	7.66	DMSO-D₆	1[a]
OMe	H	—	7.51	7.63	6.93	CDCl₃	1
OMe	NHCOMe	—	7.14–7.30	—	7.86–8.25	CDCl₃, DMSO-D₆	10[a]
OEt	NHCOMe	—	7.22–7.27	—	7.95–8.24	CDCl₃, DMSO-D₆	2[a]

[a] Some or all of these data were obtained from 220-MHz spectra.

Table 8.6 Chemical Shifts of Aromatic Protons in Azo Dyes of Type (2) (Diazo Moiety)

Substituents			Chemical Shifts				Solvent	No. of Observations
X	Y	Z	2'	3'	5'	6'		
H	NO_2	H	7.65–7.93	8.15–8.38	8.15–8.38	7.65–7.93	$CDCl_3$, DMSO-D_6, DMF-D_7	11
NO_2	NO_2	H	—	8.67	8.41	~7.9	$CDCl_3$	1[a]
SO_2Me	NO_2	H	—	8.94–8.95	8.42	7.90–7.93	$CDCl_3$	2
CN	NO_2	H	—	8.53–8.78	8.37–8.53	7.90–8.05	$CDCl_3$, DMSO-D_6	3
Cl	NO_2	H	—	8.25–8.42	8.07–8.23	7.67–7.92	$CDCl_3$, DMSO-D_6	11
Cl	SO_2Me	H	—	8.11–8.21	7.90–8.03	7.77–7.90	$CDCl_3$, DMSO-D_6	2
Cl	NO_2	Cl	—	8.18–8.40	8.18–8.40	—	$CDCl_3$, DMSO-D_6, DMF-D_7	7
Br	NO_2	Br	—	8.47–8.60	8.47–8.60	—	$CDCl_3$	3
Br	NO_2	Cl	—	8.43–8.51	8.32–8.38	—	DMSO-D_6	2
CN	NO_2	CN	—	8.52.	8.52	—	CD_2Cl_2	2
CN	NO_2	Br	—	8.26 or 8.46	8.26 or 8.46	—	$CDCl_3$	1
NO_2	NO_2	Br	—	8.51–8.70	8.16–8.48	—	$CDCl_3$	10[a]
CN	NO_2	NO_2	—	8.43–8.53	8.43–8.53	—	$CDCl_3$	4

[a] Some or all of these data have been obtained at 220 MHz.

Table 8.7 Proton Chemical Shifts of Azo Dyes

(3)

```
        Cl                    3.56 1.26
  8.38                7.93 6.78  CH2CH3
O2N—          —N=N—        —N                        1.80        CDCl3, 220 MHZ
                                 CH2CH2OCH(Me)OCH2CHMe2            (FT)
  8.15 7.78
                          CA. 3.6-3.9 4.70 1.30  3.15      0.88
                                                  3.29
```

(4)

```
                          3.90
          NO2             OMe
  8.56         7.19              O
O2N—    —N=N—        —    —NHCH2CH2COCH2CH2OMe          CDCl3, 220 MHZ
  8.22                      6.33 2.78    3.62
        Br       NHAc       3.70   4.30  3.39
                 7.89
        CA. 8.7 2.30
```

(5)

```
          CN                    3.68 1.25
  8.85         7.83 6.85  CH2CH3
O2N—    —N=N—        —N                        DMSO-D6, 220 MHZ
  9.01                   CH2Ph  CA. 7.4-7.7
        NO2     NHAc     4.84
                8.10
                9.5 2.17
```

(6)

```
          CN             OMe 3.88
  8.48         7.18
O2N—    —N=N—        —    —NH—    S    CA 1-2.4        CDCl3, 60 MHZ
  8.48                    6.18
        NO2     NHAc      H
                8.02      CA 3.62
                9.17 2.32
```

Primary amine protons in the 1 and 4 positions of anthraquinones usually result in very broad signals, often under the aromatic proton patterns, although occasionally distinct broad peaks have been observed (see Table 8.9). Their presence is normally quite evident from the integrals and can be further substantiated by adding a few drops of acid, such as TFA-D, to effect exchange. Reactions of this type may also be desirable to clarify the aromatic proton patterns, which may be partially obscured by the broad amine resonance.

Secondary amine protons in the 1 and 4 positions are bonded to the carbonyls in the B ring and, consequently, are shifted downfield to about 10–13 (see Tables 8.9 and 8.10). Similarly, hydroxyl protons alpha to the carbonyls are strongly bonded and appear in the neighborhood of 13–15 (see Table 8.9). The secondary amine signal is normally a multiplet if it is part of an aliphatic side chain. Decoupling experiments or simple deuterium exchange can often be used to help elucidate such structures.

Isolated C ring protons as in types (15; $R_2 \neq H$) and (16; $R_3 \neq H$) generally appear at about 6–7. These sharp singlets are normally quite

Table 8.8 Proton Chemical Shifts of Azo Dyes

(7)

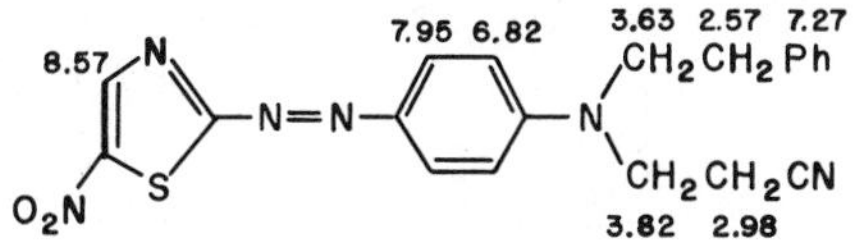

CD_2Cl_2, 60 MHZ

(8)

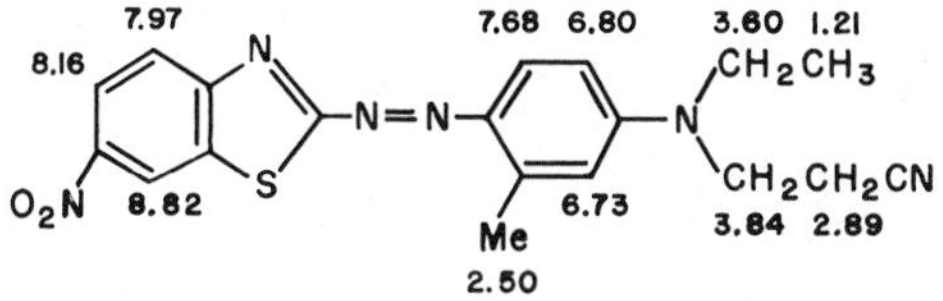

DMSO-D_6, 220 MHZ

(9)

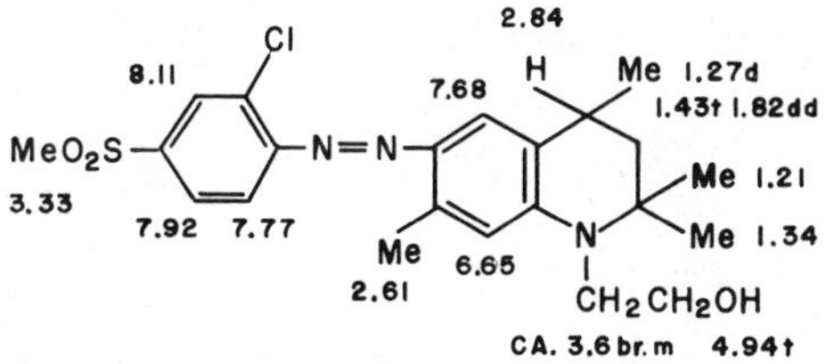

DMSO-D_6, 220 MHZ

(10)

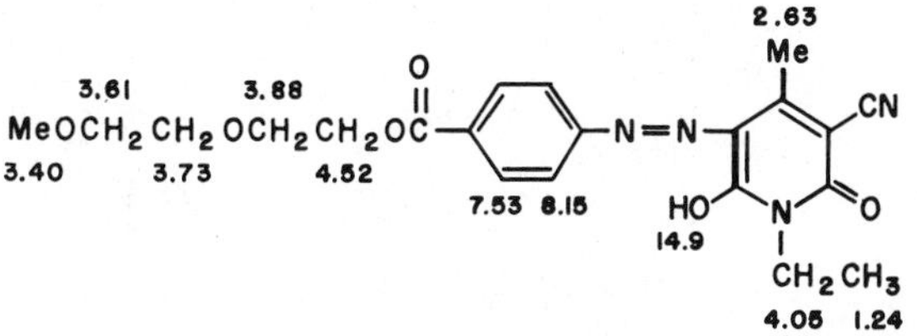

$CDCl_3$, 220 MHZ

readily recognized and can therefore be used to determine the substitution pattern of this ring in the anthraquinone system.

Anthraquinone dyes in which the *A* and *C* rings are substituted are also fairly common. An example is (18). The 220-MHz PMR spectrum of (18) in DMSO-D_6 is summarized in Table 12.6. The exact structure of the side chain was ascertained by irradiating the CH multiplet at 3.93; this resulted

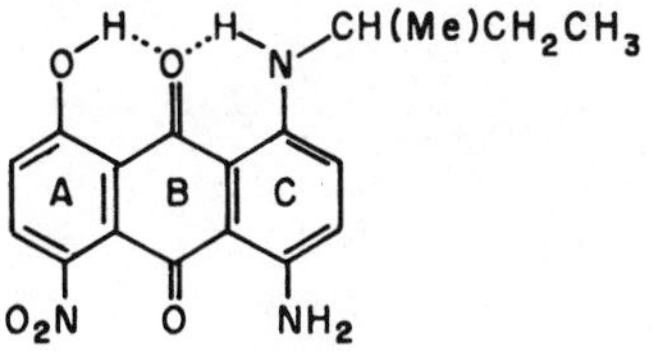

(18)

Table 8.9 Chemical Shifts of Protons in Anthraquinone Dyes of Type (15)

	Chemical Shifts					
Substituent	*A* ring	C ring	NH_2/ NH	OH (Bonded)	Side Chain	Solvent
R_2 (R_1 = H)						
OMe	7.73 *m*, 8.33 *m*	6.53 *s*	7.3 *v br*	14.3 *s*	3.98 *s*	$CDCl_3$
OCH_2CH_2OH	7.86 *m*, 8.27 *m*	6.77 *s*	*v br*[a]	14.6 *s*	4.33 *t*, 3.98 *t*	DMF-D_7
SCH_2CH_2OH	7.33 *m*, 8.0 *m*	7.02 *s*	8.0	13.6 *s*	3.20 *t*, 3.75 *m*, 5.15 *br*	DMSO-D_6
$OCH_2CH_2OCH_2CH_2CN$	7.8 *m*, 8.2 *m*	6.67 *s*	*v br*[a]	14.4 *s*	4.32 *m*, 3.98 *m*, 3.81 *t*, 2.87 *t*	DMSO-D_6
$OCH_2(CH_2)_4CH_2OH$	7.83 *m*, 8.20 *m*	6.67 *s*	*v br*[a]	14.5 *s*	4.17, ~1.2–2.1, 3.43 *m*, ~4.2 *m*	DMSO-D_6

p-OC$_6$H$_4$OH	7.80 m, 8.12 m	6.03 s	v br[a]	14.1 s	7.14, 6.95 (AA'BB'), 9.62 br s	DMSO-D$_6$[b]
p-OC$_6$H$_4$CH$_2$NCH$_2$(CH$_2$)$_3$CH$_2$CO	7.63 m, 8.17 m	6.25 s	v br[a]	13.9 s	~7.35 d, 7.08 d; 4.58 s, 3.32 br, ~1.7 br, 2.60 br	CDCl$_3$
p-OC$_6$H$_4$SO$_2$NHCH$_2$CH$_2$CH$_2$OCH$_2$CH$_3$	7.75 m, 8.27 m	6.45 s	7.3 br	13.8 s	~7.3, 7.96, 5.47 br t, 3.50 t, 1.78 qn, 3.46 t, 3.14 q, 1.12 t	CDCl$_3$[b]
OCH$_2$CH$_2$OC$_{10}$H$_7$[c]	7.87 m, 8.2 m	6.98 s	v br[a]	14.6 s	~4.7 br	DMSO-D$_6$
R$_1$(R$_2$ = H)						
p-C$_6$H$_4$Me	7.73 m, 8.32 m	7.1 d, 7.5 d	11.7 br	13.7 s	7.18 s	CDCl$_3$
p-C$_6$H$_4$NHAc	7.8 m, 8.2 m	7.09 d, 7.42 d	11.5	13.4 s	7.17 d, 7.66 dd; 9.85 br s, 2.09 s	DMSO-D$_6$

[a] Very broad bands under aromatic proton patterns.
[b] From 220-MHz spectra.
[c] Naphthyl.

235

Table 8.10 Chemical Shifts of Protons in Anthraquinone Dyes of Type (16)

R₁	R₂	R₃	Chemical Shifts					
			A ring	C ring	NH₂	NH	Side Chain (left to right)	Solvent
H	p-PhN(Me)COMe	H	7.62 m, 8.23 m	6.33 d, 7.40 d	v br[a]	11.98 s	7.20 s, 3.27 s, 1.93 s	CDCl₃
H	p-SO₂C₆H₄Me	OPh	7.68 m, 8.20 m	7.13 s	6.31 br s	12.7 s	7.08 d, 7.46 d, 2.33 s; 7.12 dd, 7.52 m, 7.38 m	CDCl₃[b]
CHMe₂	CHMe₂	H	7.67 m, 8.35 m	7.24 s	—	10.9 br d	3.96 m, 1.36 d	CDCl₃
Me	Me	H	7.67 m, 8.31 m	7.13 s	—	10.46	3.04 br	CDCl₃[c]

[a] Broad band under aromatic proton patterns.
[b] At 220 MHz.
[c] From ref. 48.

Table 8.11 Chemical Shifts of Protons in Anthraquinone Dyes of Type (17)

R	Chemical Shifts			
	A ring	NH$_2$	Side Chain (from left to right)	Solvent
CH$_2$CH$_2$CH$_2$OMe	7.88 m, 8.25 m	—	3.92 t, 2.18 qn, 3.80 t, 3.57 s	TFA
CH$_2$CH$_2$CH$_2$OMe	~7.7 m, 8.15 m	~7.7 br	3.71 t, 1.93 qn, 3.45 t, 3.32 s	CDCl$_3$
CH$_2$CH$_2$OCH$_2$CH$_2$CH$_2$CH$_3$	7.70 m, 8.20 m	v br[a]	3.82 t, 3.64 t, 3.44 t, 1.52 m, 1.30 m, 0.87 t	CDCl$_3$[b]
CH$_2$CH$_2$COOCH$_2$(CH$_2$)$_2$CH$_3$	7.63 m, 8.03 m	~7.5 br	3.90 t, 2.75 t, 4.12 t, 1.1–2 overl. m., 0.93 dist. t	CDCl$_3$[c]

[a] Very broad band under aromatic proton patterns.
[b] 220-MHz spectrum.
[c] Side chain identified with the help of double resonance experiments.

in the collapse of both the NH and the Me doublets and in simplification of the CH_2 multiplet.

4.3   Dyes Containing the Ar—CH= Group

Characteristic of this group of dyes is the presence in the molecule of the methine group =CH or a conjugate chain of such groups.[40] The chemical shifts of the methine protons vary over a fairly large range. Barring serious overlaps, however, they are generally recognizable as singlets or multiplets in or near the aromatic region. Thus in spectra of dyes containing the dicyanoethylene group [see Figure 8.1; also structures (32)–(35), Chapter 12, Section 3.2.3], the =CH signal has been observed in the range 7.6–8.5, depending on structural features and the solvent used. The methine proton peak in ArCH=N—R(Ar) has been seen between 8.1 and 8.7; in ArCH= N—N=CH—Ar' between 8.5 and 9.1; and in pyrazolone derivatives, such as rubazonic acids [see Structure (38), Chapter 12, Section 3.2.3], at about 7.

The =CH—CH= protons in Fischer's aldehyde derivatives appear $\sim$6 and 8.5 as doublets ($J = \sim$13 Hz); in 3-ethyl-2-(p-phenyliminoethylidene)-benzazolines at $\sim$5.0–5.6 and 8.1–8.5 ($J = $ 6.4–10.4 Hz), depending on the heteroatom in the benzazoline moiety[20]; in merocyanines at $\sim$4.4–6.1 and 6.5–7.8 ($J = \sim$12–14.4 Hz), depending on the heteroatom in the keto-methylene heterocyclic moiety.[19]

Because of wide variations in the structural features of the various groups attached to the =CH unit(s), generalizations of the PMR spectra of methine dyes are difficult to make. Nevertheless, features such as the singlets due to the geminal methyl groups and to the NMe group in Fischer's aldehyde derivatives, combined with the characteristic =CH—CH= doublets, can be excellent clues to the type of dye being analyzed. Similarly, the OH absorption at an unusually low field together with the =CH singlet [see Structure (38), Chapter 12, Table 12.14] may suggest a pyrazolone.

An example of a dye containing the dicyanoethylene group is (19). The 220-MHz CW PMR spectrum is reproduced in Figure 8.1. Although a 60-MHz PMR spectrum showed considerable overlap of some of the aliphatic proton patterns, the 220-MHz spectrum was completely resolved,

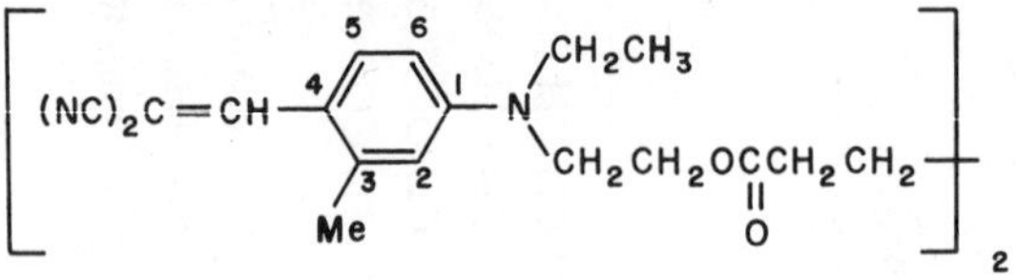

(19)

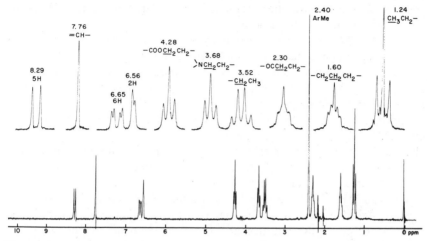

Figure 8.1   220-MHz PMR spectrum of (19).

permitting unambiguous assignments to be made. The aromatic substitution pattern was readily deduced from the doublet at 6.56 (J_m = 2.5 Hz), the doublet of doublets at 6.65 (J_0 = 9.5 Hz, J_m = 2.5 Hz), and the doublet at 8.29 (J_0 = 9.5 Hz).

A particularly interesting 220-MHz PMR spectrum was obtained for (20), indicating two methylene groups, each containing nonequivalent protons and thus giving rise to a fairly complex aliphatic proton pattern, which was not at all evident in a 60-MHz spectrum. The nonequivalence of the methylene protons in the hydroquinoline ring is due to the vicinal asymmetric center, and the nonequivalence of the NCH₂ protons in the side chain is attributed to the lack of rotational freedom around the N—C bond. Chemical shifts and coupling constants obtained from the high-field spectrum of this dye are listed in Table 12.11.

$$(NC)_2C{=}CH{-}$$

(20)

4.4   Cationic Dyes

Cationic dyes belong to a variety of chemical classes such as azo, anthraquinone, triarylmethane, cyanine, oxazine, and thiazole. Their PMR spectra, therefore, show characteristic features, but somewhat modified by the positively charged heteroatom.

Cationic dyes are usually isolated for NMR analysis as iodides or picrates, although occasionally methosulfates and tetrafluoroborates are encountered. The two equivalent picrate protons appear at ~8.5–8.6 as a sharp *s* and can often serve, except for overlaps or an excess of picrate, as a reference for counting protons.

The structures and chemical shifts of some heterocyclic, cationic azo dyes **(21)**–**(23)** are shown in Table 8.12. Alkyl groups attached to the charged heteroatom are shifted downfield, as are the aromatic protons in the heterocyclic ring. Otherwise, these dyes exhibit in their PMR spectra all the features common to neutral azo dyes.

The 220-MHz PMR spectrum of an unusual, almost entirely aromatic cationic azo dye, **(24)**, in DMSO-D_6 is shown in Figure 8.2. Although it contains 10 nonequivalent aromatic H, all assignments except two could be made by inspection (H-2: 9.46, *br s*, suggesting two *meta* neighbors. H-4: 8.85, *br d*, suggesting one *ortho* and two *meta* neighbors. H-5: 8.15,

Table 8.12 Proton Chemical Shifts of Cationic Dyes

(21)

DMSO-D6, 60 MHZ

(22)

DMSO-D6, 220 MHZ, FT

(23)

DMSO-D6, 60 MHZ

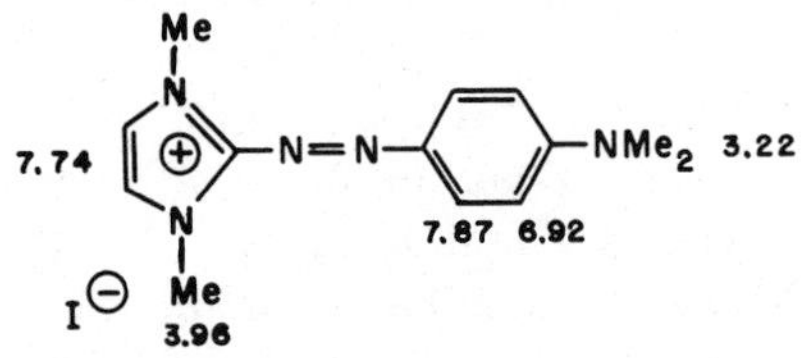

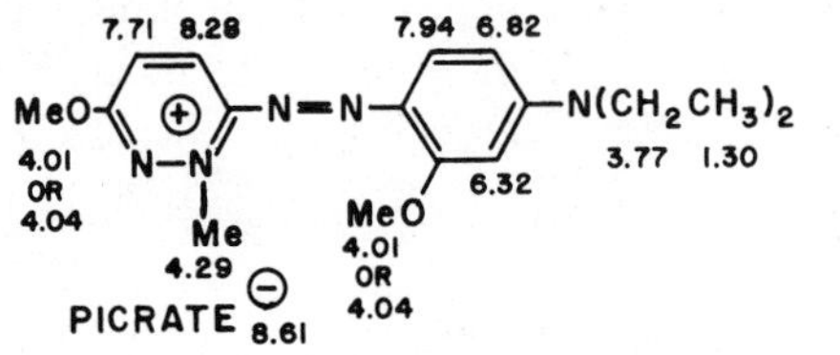

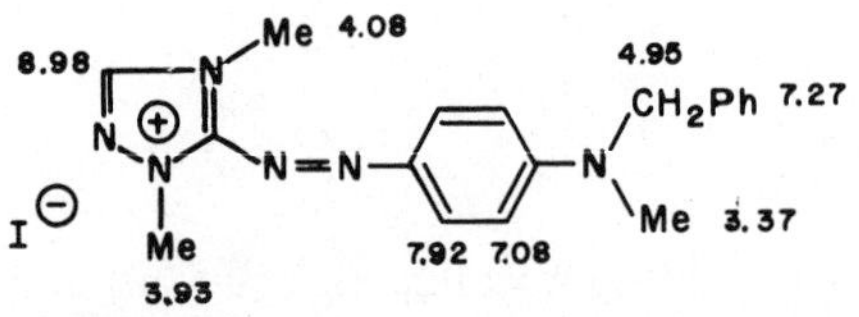

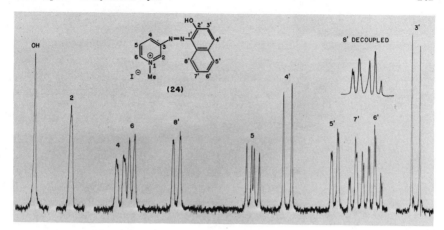

Figure 8.2   220-MHz PMR spectrum of (24).

dd, J$_0$ ~6 and 8.9 Hz. H-6: 8.79, *br d, J*$_0$ ~6 Hz. H-3′: 6.75, *d, J*$_0$ ~9.8 Hz. H-4′: 7.96, *d, J*$_0$ ~9.8 Hz. H-5′: 7.72, *dd, J*$_0$ ~7.3, *J*$_m$ ~2.0 Hz. H-8′: 8.55, *br d, J*$_0$ ~8.0 Hz). H-7′ (7.61) and H-6′ (7.51) were identified by double resonance in which H-8′ was irradiated; this resulted in the collapse of the H-7′ triplet of doublets to a doublet of doublets and of the H-6′ triplet of doublets to a triplet. The Me protons appeared at 4.46 and the bonded hydroxyl at 15.2.

Cyanines constitute a large portion of cationic dyes of interest to the fiber and film industries. The PMR spectral features are similar to those of the related neutral dyes, except that *N*-alkyl groups appear at lower fields when *N* is quaternized.

Table 8.13 shows some examples of cyanine dyes (25)–(28) and their proton chemical shifts. The Fischer's base or aldehyde derivatives are common and are easily recognized by their characteristic CMe$_2$, $\overset{+}{>}$NMe, and CH=N or CH=CH absorptions in the 1.6–1.9, 3.8–4.3, and 7.8–8.3 or 6.0–6.5 and 8.0–9.0 regions, respectively. Although the =CH signal in diazatrimethine dyes such as CI Basic Yellow 28 iodide [(25), Table 8.13] is a singlet, the CH=CH signals in dimethine dyes such as (26) are doublets (*J* = ~13 Hz); the nonequivalent methylene protons in the indoline moiety result in a doublet, *J* = 16.6 Hz, and a doublet of doublets, *J* = 16.6 and 8.6 Hz. The CH=CH—CH= groups in symmetrical trimethine dyes such as (27) and (28) result in a doublet and a triplet (*J* = ~13.0–13.5 Hz).[15,16] The magnitude of these coupling constants varies considerably depending on the ring heteroatom.[15] In unsymmetrical carbocyanines the R—CH=CH—CH=R′ absorptions become more complex.[15]

Table 8.13   Proton Chemical Shifts of Cationic Methine Dyes (Iodides)

(25)   CDCl$_3$, 60 MHZ

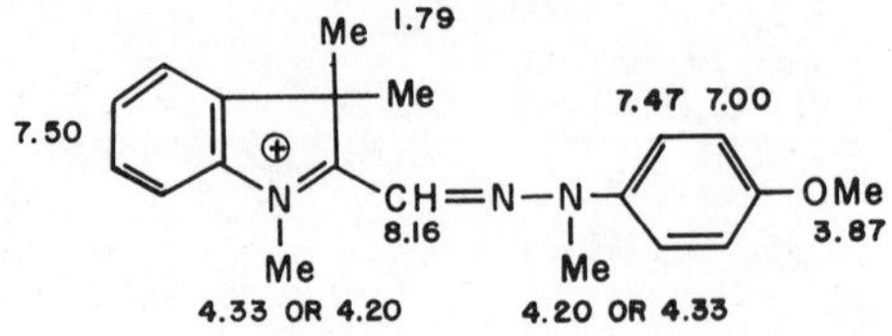

(26)   CDCl$_3$, 220 MHZ

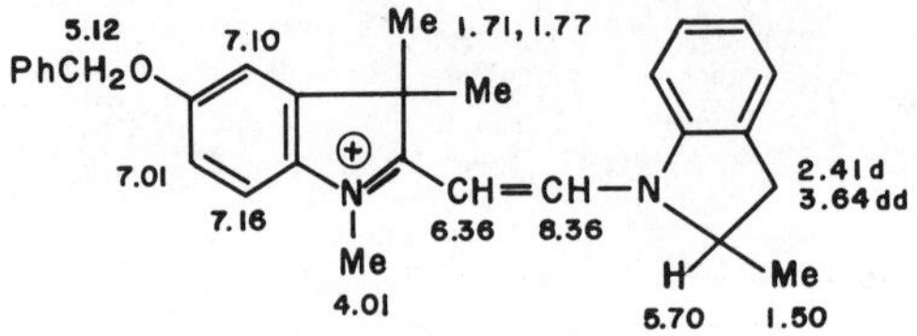

(27)   DMSO-D$_6$, 100 MHZ ^{a}

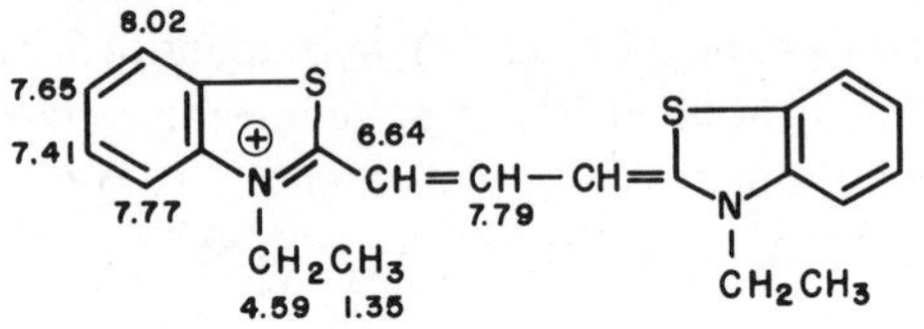

(28)   DMSO-D$_6$, 100 MHZ ^{b}

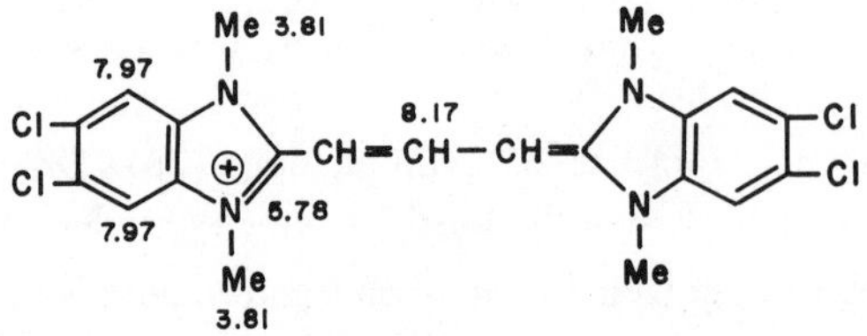

^{a} From ref. 15.
^{b} From ref. 16.

Pyrido- and azapyridocyanines[25] are of interest in the study of super-conductive polymers.[41] A few of these interesting structures and their proton chemical shifts and coupling constants are shown in Table 8.14. The two sterically different pairs of hydrogen atoms in N,N'-(1,2-ethylene)-2,2'-pyridocyanine, (30), are said to be due to a staggered configuration. N,N',N''-Trimethyl-4,4',4''-tripyridocyanine diiodide (31) is a heterocyclic analogue of triphenylmethane dyes, e.g., Crystal Violet.[25]

Table 8.14 Proton Chemical Shifts and Coupling Constants of Pyrido and Azapyri-Docyanines[a]

(29)	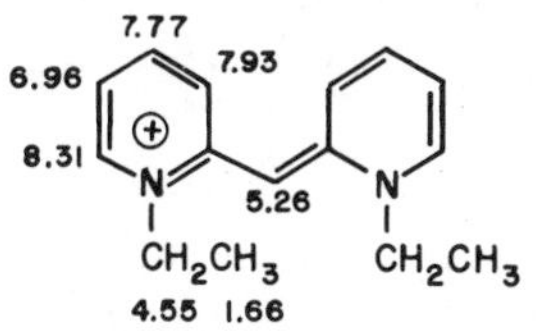	$J_{CH_2CH_3} = 7.0$ $J_{3,4} = 8.8$ $J_{3,5} = 1.5$ $J_{3,6} = 0.5$ $J_{4,5} = 6.5$ $J_{4,6} = 1.5$ $J_{5,6} = 6.5$
(30)	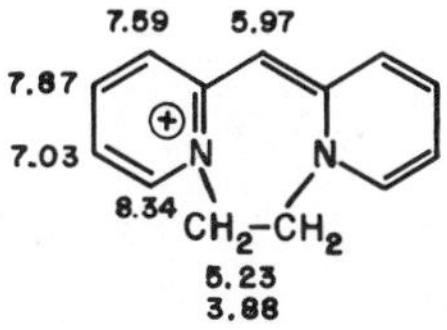	$J_{C_2H_4} = 14$ $J_{3,4} = 9.0$ $J_{3,5} = 1.8$ $J_{3,6} = 0.5$ $J_{4,5} = 6.7$ $J_{4,6} = 1.0$ $J_{5,6} = 6.7$
(31)	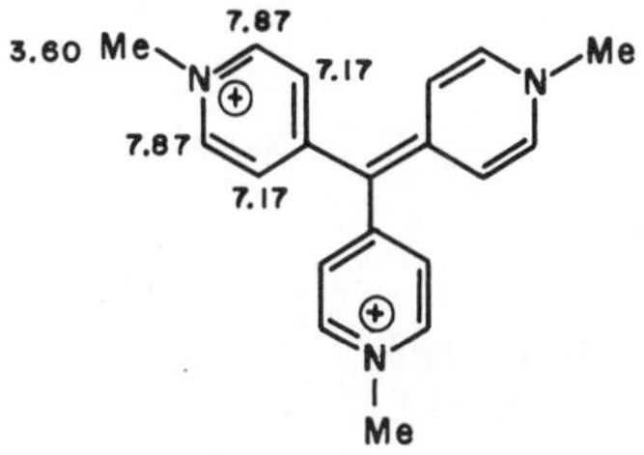	$J_{2,3} = 8.0$ $J_{5,6} = 8.0$
(32)	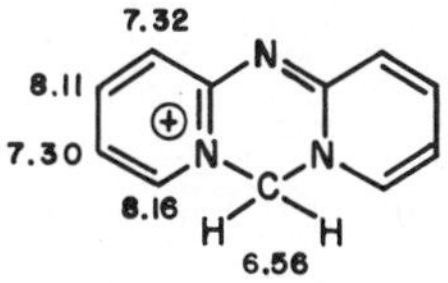	$J_{3,4} = 9.2$ $J_{3,5} = 1.5$ $J_{3,6} = 0.5$ $J_{4,5} = 7.0$ $J_{4,6} = 1.5$ $J_{5,6} = 7.0$

[a] From ref. 25. All compounds were examined as iodides in DMSO-D_6 at 60 MHz.

Because Crystal Violet (CI Basic Violet 3; CI 42555) has a center of symmetry, all the methyl groups are equivalent as are all the aromatic rings (see Table 8.15).

Structures (34) and (35) in Table 8.15 are examples of oxazine dyes.

Table 8.16 shows some typical azo and anthraquinone pendant cationic dyes. Their PMR spectra are very similar to those of the corresponding neutral species, but usually show a relatively large concentration of N-alkyl protons.

Table 8.15   Proton Chemical Shifts of Triphenylmethane and Oxazine Cationic Dyes

(33)   DMSO-D$_6$, 100 MHZ

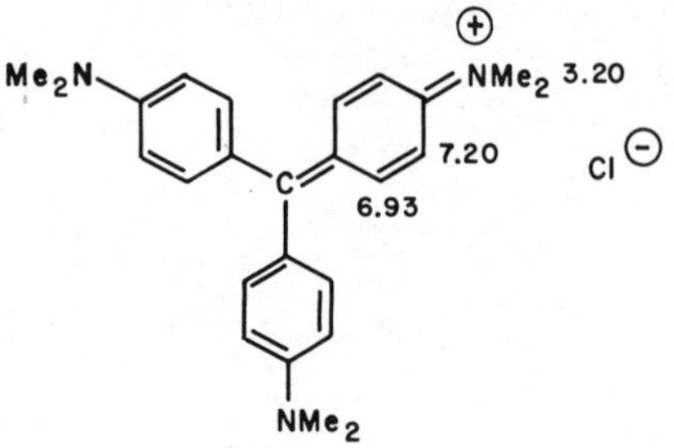

(34)   D$_2$O, 60 MHZ

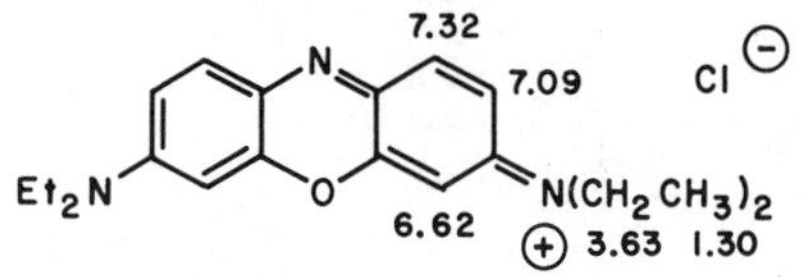

(35)   DMSO-D$_6$, 220 MHZ

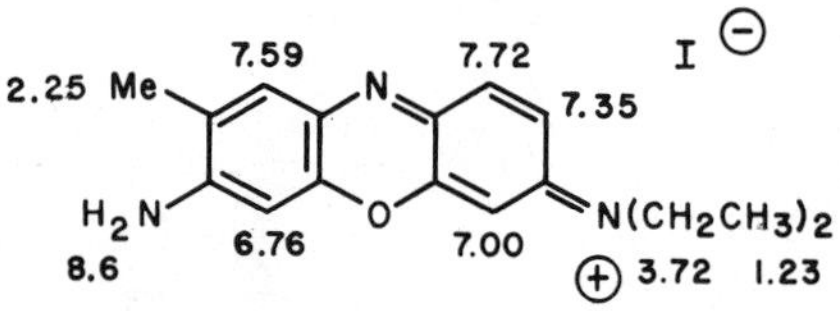

4.5   Acid Dyes

The characteristic SO$_3$H proton in sulfonic acid dyes is usually not observed in PMR spectra because of moisture. However, very careful repeated grinding and drying can produce samples in which, barring other intramolecular exchange reactions, the acid proton may be observed. An example is the sulfonic acid proton in (3), Section 3.1, Chapter 12, which appears at 10.5 in DMF-D$_7$. Moreover, acid dyes are usually isolated in the salt form.

PMR can, however, supply information about other structural features, such as the aliphatic side chains, aromatic substitution patterns, or bonded hydroxyl and amine protons. In general, PMR spectra of acid dyes strongly resemble those of the corresponding neutral compounds. The electron-withdrawing sulfonic acid or sulfonate group has, of course, an effect on the chemical shifts of neighboring protons. Thus, anthraquinone dyes (16), in

Table 8.16 Proton Chemical Shifts of Pendant Cationic Dyes

(36)		DMSO–D_6, 60 MHZ
(37)		DMF–D_7, 60 MHZ
(38)		DMSO–D_6, 60 MHZ

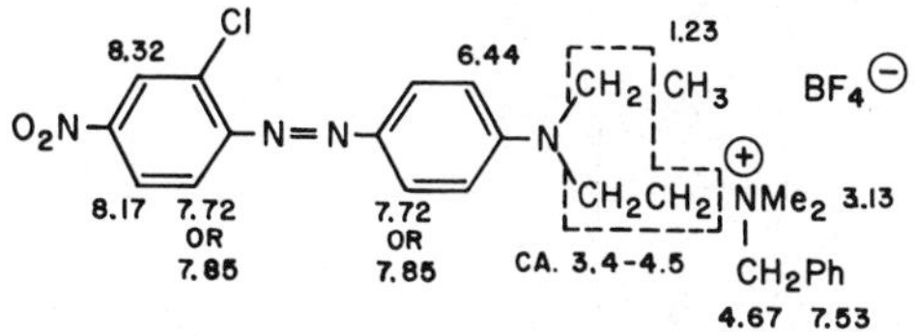

which R_1 = H, R_2 = substituted phenyl, and R_3 = SO_3Na, show *C*-ring protons in the 8.0–8.2 range (based on six observations) as compared with 6.9–7.3 for similar neutral anthraquinones (see Table 8.10). In azo dyes, a sulfonate group *para* to the azo linkage produces very nearly the same paramagnetic shifts on the two *ortho* protons as does the azo group on its two *ortho* proton neighbors. Sharp singlets may result from such *p*-disubstituted benzene rings, as observed, for example, by Marmion[36] in the 60-MHz PMR spectrum of FD&C Yellow No. 5 (7.93; D_2O/DMSO-D_6). Even at 220 MHz this type of substitution may result in a singlet or partially resolved pattern.

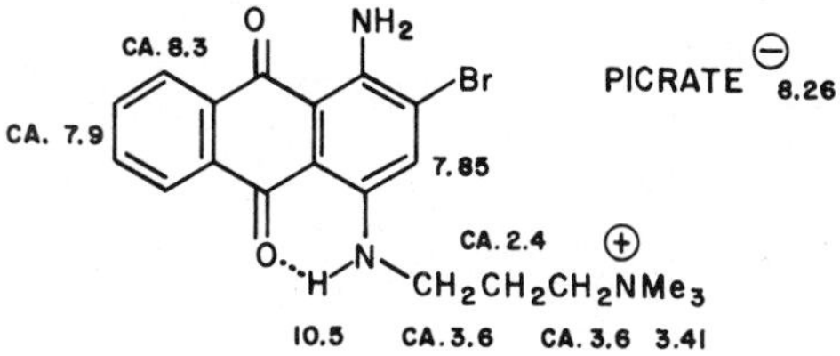

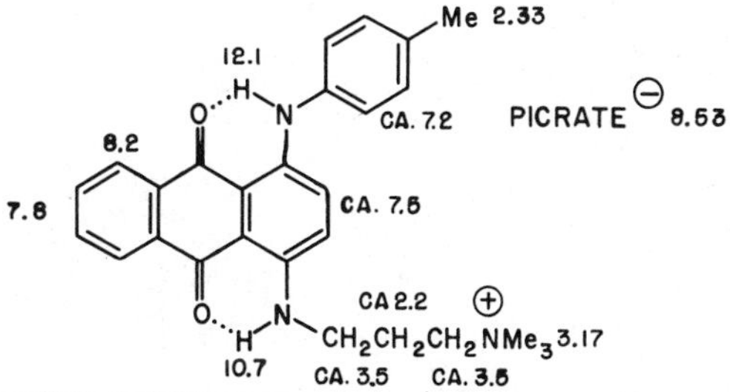

The sulfonate group(s) can be located on the aromatic rings, in the aliphatic side chains, or in both. Table 8.17 shows three sulfonic acid dyes **(39)**–**(41)** and their proton chemical shifts. More examples of acid dyes can be found in Chapter 12, Section 3.1. 60-MHz PMR spectra of a number

Table 8.17   Proton Chemical Shifts of Sulfonic Acid Dyes[a]

(39)

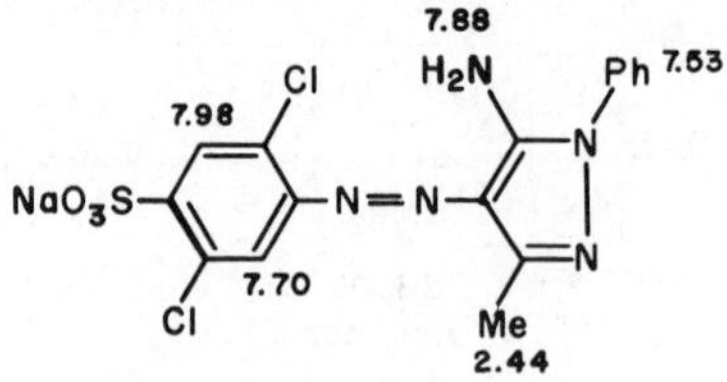

(40)

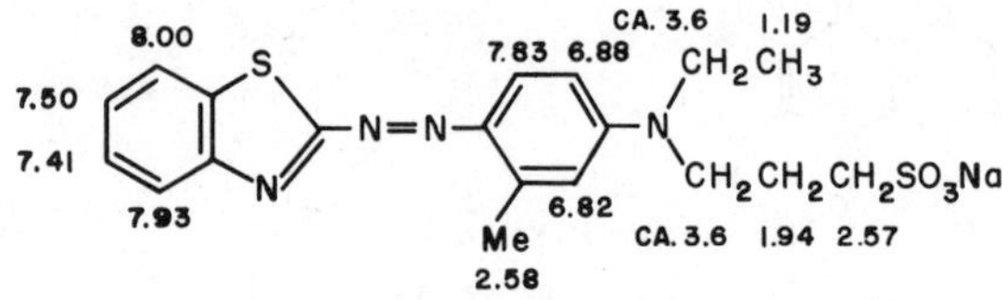

(41)

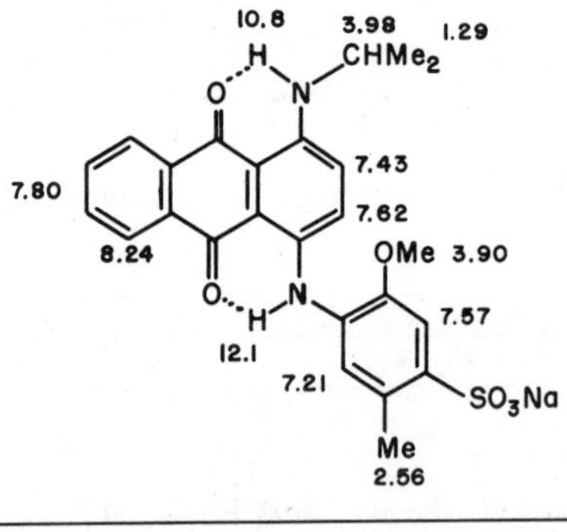

[a] DMSO-D$_6$ solutions. Dye (39) at 60 MHz; (40) and (41) at 220 MHz.

of certifiable food colors containing sulfonate and carboxylate groups have been recorded by Marmion.[36]

Sometimes it is advantageous to reductively desulfonate anthraquinone acid dyes to obtain products with higher solubility and volatility which can be more readily analyzed by PMR and MS.[9] An example of this approach is given in Chapter 12, Section 3.1.

5   NMR OF OTHER NUCLEI

Published information on NMR of nuclei other than protons in the analysis of synthetic eyes is scarce. Until recently, when FT spectrometry has become routine, obtaining ^{13}C or ^{15}N spectra was simply not practical in an industrial laboratory. It is a safe assumption that future work concerning the chemistry of synthetic colorants will increasingly include the use of FT NMR.

5.1 Fluorine-19 NMR Spectra

^{19}F chemical shifts are reported from CCl_3F, positive values indicating shifts to higher frequency. The presence of a CF_3 group in a suitable position of the molecule is said to improve the brightness, tinctorial value and lightfastness of dyes.[42] Thus occasionally a colorant may require analysis by ^{19}F NMR to confirm the presence of the trifluoromethyl group.

An example of a fluorinated azo dye is (42). The 56.4-MHz ^{19}F NMR spectrum in conc. sulfuric acid showed a singlet at about -62.2 from external CCl_3F. Trifluoromethyl resonances of similar molecules in which the CF_3 group is meta or ortho to the azo linkage have been observed in the -61 to -57 region (DMSO-D_6; internal CCl_3F).

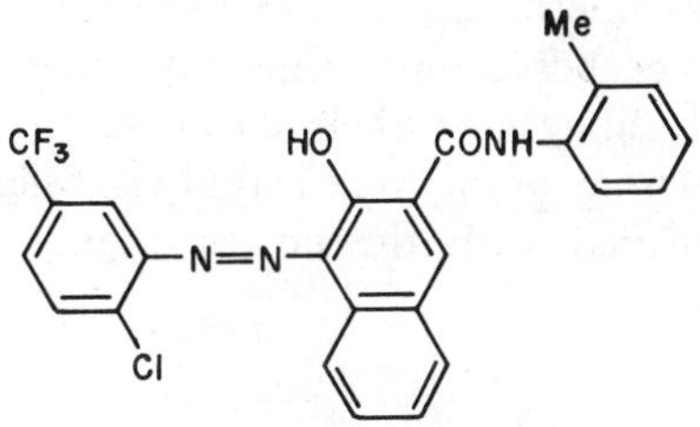

(42)

5.2 Nitrogen-14 NMR Spectra

Berrie and co-workers[34] determined the ^{14}N chemical shifts of nine 1-phenylazo-2-naphthols by observing the labile NH proton resonance of the hydrazo forms while sweeping the ^{14}N decoupling frequency. By comparing these indirectly obtained ^{14}N chemical shifts with known ^{14}N shifts for the nitrogen atom alpha to the phenyl ring in the pure azo and hydrazo forms of azobenzene and 10-(4-methoxyphenylazo)-9-phenanthrol, respectively, they have calculated the proportions of hydroxyazo and hydrazone forms.

5.3 Carbon-13 NMR Spectra

^{13}C chemical shifts are referred to tetramethylsilane via the solvent peak. The literature contains very few publications on the CMR of synthetic dyes and intermediates. CMR spectra of substituted and unsubstituted 2-methylcycloammonium salts, (43), important intermediates in the syn-

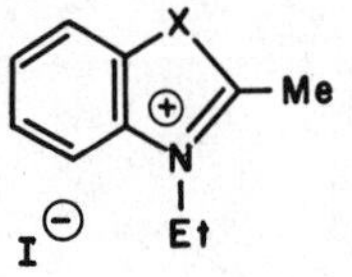

X = NR, HC=CH, O,
S, Se, CMe$_2$

(43)

thesis of symmetrical and unsymmetrical cyanine dyes, were obtained by Kleinpeter and Borsdorf.[18] The chemical shifts of the individual ring carbon atoms were compared with results from Extended Hückel and Hückel molecular orbital calculations, and a linear correlation between the chemical shifts and the electron densities was found. Furthermore, the ^{13}C chemical shifts of the C-2 atom proved to be an excellent indicator of the CH acidity of the compounds. The acidity was found to decrease in the following order: $CMe_2 > Se > S > O > CH=CH > NR$.[17]

^{13}C chemical shifts and ^{13}C-^{1}H coupling constants were determined for simple cyanines, (44), merocyanines, (45), and oxonols, (46), by Radeglia.[22] Assignments of the carbon atoms in merocyanines were supported by the Eu(DPM)$_3$-induced changes in their chemical shifts. Electron densities, bond orders, and atom–atom polarizabilities calculated for these compounds were correlated with the corresponding CMR and PMR parameters.[22,43]

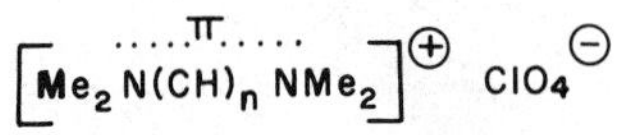

$$\left[Me_2 N(CH)_n NMe_2 \right]^{\oplus} ClO_4^{\ominus} \quad \text{(CYANINES)}$$

(44)

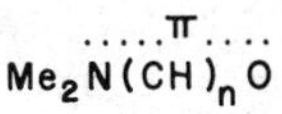

$$Me_2 N(CH)_n O \quad \text{(MEROCYANINES)}$$

(45)

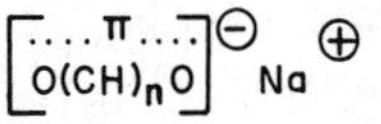

$$\left[O(CH)_n O \right]^{\ominus} Na^{\oplus} \quad \text{(OXONOLES)}$$

(46)

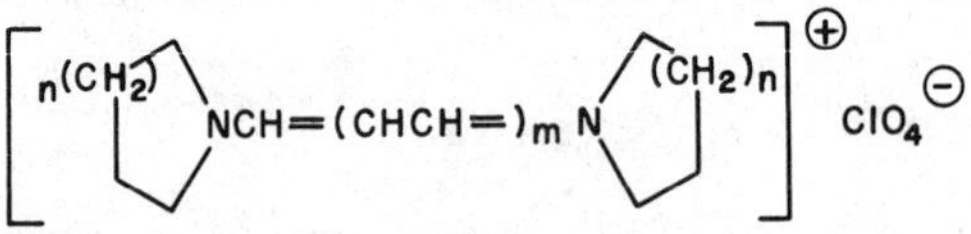

(47)

[13]C chemical shifts of the CH and CH_2 carbon atoms in simple cyanines of the type (47) were determined by Radeglia and were discussed in relation to ring size of the cyclic amino groups as well as electronic and steric effects.[23]

CMR spectrometry is also useful in structural elucidation. An example is the identification of a blue azo dye (48). The aromatic proton patterns and a broad NH triplet at 8.75 in the 220-MHz PMR spectrum of the dye in DMSO-D_6 were consistent with (48). Broad bands between 4.5 and 5.5 proved to be due to exchangeable protons, such as OH, upon addition of TFA-D. Broad aliphatic proton patterns at about 3.5, 3.7, and 3.9 corresponding to three, one, and one H, respectively, were also observed. When TFA-D was added, these bands became somewhat better defined (although still too complex for interpretation by inspection), suggesting that at least some of the aliphatic protons were coupled to the labile protons.

The identity of the side chain was unambiguously established by CMR spectrometry. Figure 8.3 shows broad band and gated proton-decoupled ^{13}C spectra of the dye. The chemical shifts and multiplicities (two triplets and a doublet) clearly indicated NCH_2, OCH_2, and OCH type carbons. The aromatic carbon region showed seven =CH peaks, one of them of double intensity, and eight =CX peaks, also in agreement with (48).

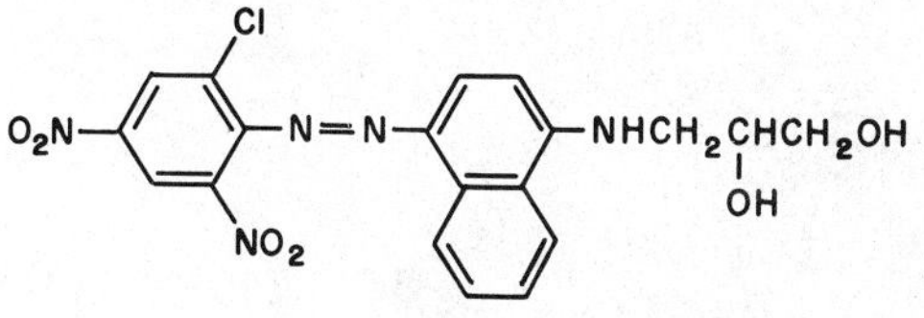

(48)

6 LANTHANIDE ION SHIFT REAGENTS[44]

The use of lanthanide-induced shift (LIS) reagents[45] for the simplification of the NMR spectra of various organic solutes has greatly increased during the last few years. However, very few applications to synthetic dyes have been reported.

Kleinpeter and Borsdorf[20] determined the $Eu(fod)_3$ [europium tris-(1,1,1,2,2,3,3-heptafluoro-7,7-dimethyl-4,6-octadionate)]-induced shifts of five cyanine dye intermediates of the general structure (49) and correlated them with calculated spectra, bond order, and π-electron density. They concluded that all the anils examined existed in the all-*trans* chain configuration and had the same steric arrangement about the chain N atom.

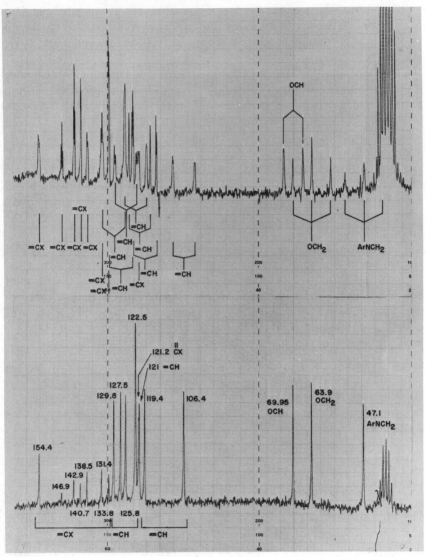

Figure 8.3 22.63-MHz ^{13}C spectra of **(48)**. **(48)** Top: gated (48,942 pulses). Bottom: broad band proton-decoupled (10,000 pulses).

Graves and Rose described the application of LIS reagents to organic cations by outer sphere complexation.[46] Because of the low dye concentration in CDCl$_3$, they employed FT PMR to observe spectra of the cationic dye, 1,1'-diethyl-2,2'-cyanine (psuedoisocyanine) chloride, **(50)**, in the absence and in the presence of Eu(fod)$_3$ and Pr(fod)$_3$ shift reagents. The

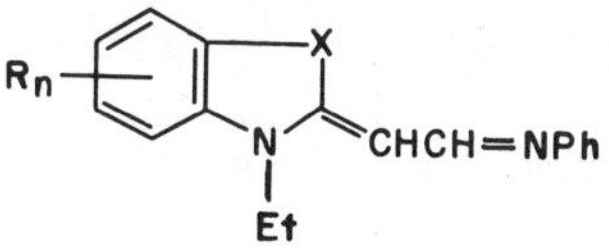

R = Me, OMe, CN

X = S, O, NR

(49)

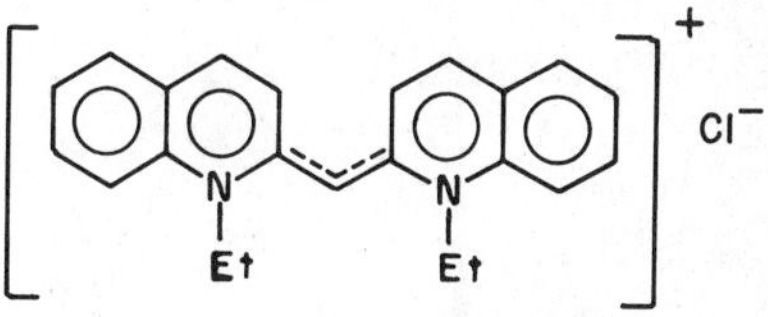

(50)

lanthanide-induced shifts were adequate for the analysis of the simplified aromatic proton spectrum of (50).

The effects of the shift reagent Eu(DPM)$_3$, tris(dipivaloylmethanato)-europium(III), on the ^{1}H and ^{13}C chemical shifts of merocyanines, (45), were investigated.[43,22] The results of both studies showed that complexation occurred at the oxygen atom. The induced proton shifts could be quantitatively explained on the basis of pseudocontact interactions. The changes in the ^{13}C chemical shifts, however, were attributed to both pseudocontact and contact interactions between the ^{13}C nuclei in the polymethine chain and the associated paramagnetic europium complex.

In my laboratory LIS reagents have been occasionally used to simplify spectra of azo and anthraquinone dyes. An interesting example is the identification of (51), discussed in detail in Chapter 12, Section 3.2.2,

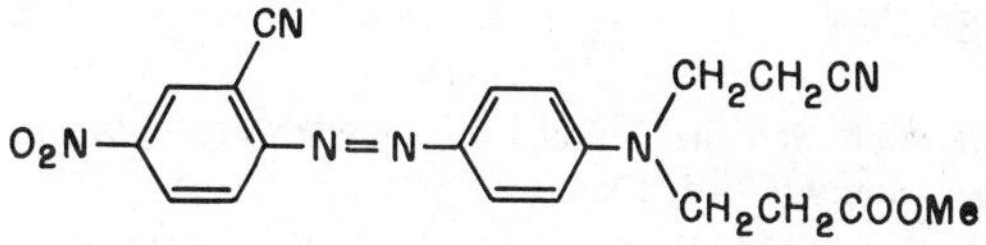

(51)

Example 1. As shown in Figure 8.4, the CH$_2$CN and the CH$_2$CO signals coincided in the normal spectrum; but on addition of Eu(fod)$_3$ to the CDCl$_3$ solution, the two triplets were adequately resolved to allow the proper assignments to be made with the help of double resonance experiments involving the various methylene groups.

ACKNOWLEDGMENTS

The author gratefully acknowledges the assistance of G. F. Eastlack, M. C. Heritage, and D. Lewandowski in the preparation of samples and R. L. Bujalski and R. A. Bell in obtaining much of the spectral data. Special appreciation is extended to F. W. Barney, R. C. Ferguson, and G. S. Reddy for providing high-field PMR spectra and to D. W. Ovenall for the CMR spectra.

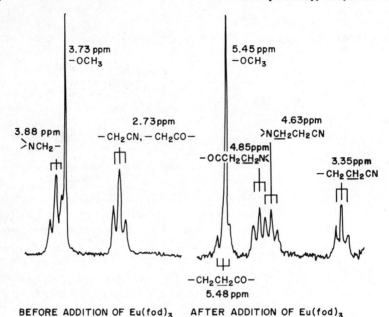

Figure 8.4   60-MHz PMR spectra of the aliphatic proton region of **(51)**.

REFERENCES

1. L. M. Jackman and S. Sternhell, *Nuclear Magnetic Resonance Spectroscopy in Organic Chemistry*, Pergamon, Oxford, 1969.

2. F. A. Bovey, *Nuclear Magnetic Resonance Spectroscopy*, Academic Press, New York, 1969.

3. F. C. Nachod and J. J. Zuckerman, Eds., *Determination of Organic Structures by Physical Methods*, Vol. 4, Academic Press, New York, 1971.

4. T. C. Farrar and E. D. Becker, *Pulse and Fourier Transform NMR*, Academic Press, New York, 1971.

5. G. C. Levy and G. L. Nelson, *Carbon-13 Nuclear Magnetic Resonance for Organic Chemists*, Wiley-Interscience, New York, 1972.

6. *CSD* III, pp. 53–58.

7. M. S. Moores, W. J. Balon, and C. W. Maynard, Jr., *J. Heterocyclic Chem.*, **6**, 755 (1969).

8. CI 51004; 51005; *CSD* IV, pp. 180–181.

9. E. D. Pandhare, V. B. Patil, A. V. Rama Rao, and K. Venkataraman, *Indian J. Chem.*, **9**, 1060 (1971).

10. P. Madhavan Nair, T. G. Manjrekar, A. V. Rama Rao, and K. Venkataraman, *Chem. Ind.* (*London*), 1524 (1967).

11. P. Madhavan Nair, T. G. Manjrekar, A. V. Rama Rao, and K. Venkataraman, *Indian J. Chem.*, **9**, 925 (1971).

12. B. K. Manukian and A. Mangini, *Helv. Chim. Acta*, **54**, 2093, 2924 (1971).

13. B. K. Manukian and H. Lichti, *Chimia*, **24**, 1 (1970).

14. V. Parameswaran, A. V. Rama Rao, and K. Venkataraman, *Indian J. Chem.*, **12**, 785 (1974).

15. E. Kleinpeter, R. Borsdorf, G. Bach, and J. v. Grossmann, *J. Prakt. Chem.*, **315**, 587 (1973).

16. E. Kleinpeter, R. Borsdorf, and J. v. Grossmann, *J. Signalaufzeichnungsmaterialien*, **1**, 293 (1973).

17. E. Kleinpeter, R. Borsdorf, and F. Dietz, *J. Prakt. Chem.*, **315**, 600 (1973).

18. E. Kleinpeter and R. Borsdorf, *J. Prakt. Chem.*, **315**, 765 (1973).

19. E. Kleinpeter and R. Borsdorf, *Z. Chem.*, **14**, 194 (1974).

20. E. Kleinpeter and R. Borsdorf, *Z. Chem.*, **13**, 183 (1973).

21. E. Kleinpeter, R. Borsdorf, G. Bach, and J. v. Grossmann, *J. Prakt. Chem.*, **316**, 761 (1974).

22. R. Radeglia, *J. Prakt. Chem.*, **315**, 1121 (1973); **316**, 766 (1974).

23. R. Radeglia, *J. Prakt. Chem.*, **316**, 344 (1974).

24. P. J. S. Pauwels, *J. Am. Chem. Soc.*, **89**, 580 (1967).

25. I. H. Leubner, *Org. Magn. Reson.*, **6**, 253 (1974).

26. B. K. Manukian, P. Niklaus, and H. Ehrsam, *Helv. Chim. Acta*, **52**, 1259 (1969).

27. B. J. Dale, D. W. Jones, and A. T. Peters, *J. Soc. Dyers Colour.*, **90**, 101 (1974).

28. L. Skulski, W. Waclawek, and A. Szurowska, *Bull. Acad. Pol. Sci., Ser. Sci. Chim.*, **20**, 463 (1972).

29. L. Skulski and W. Waclawek, *Inst. Nucl. Phys., Cracow, Rep., 1972*, INP No. 802/PL, 99–120; *CA*, **78**, 31394w (1973).

30. L. Skulski and J. Kleps, *Bull. Acad. Pol. Sci., Ser. Sci. Chim.*, **21**, 859 (1973); *CA*, **80**, 65304g (1974).

31. V. Bekarek, K. Rothschein, P. Vetesnik, and M. Vecera, *Tetrahedron Lett.*, 3711 (1968).

32. V. Bekarek, I. Dobas, J. Socha, P. Vetesnik, and M. Vecera, *Collect. Czech. Chem. Commun.*, **35**, 1406 (1970).

33. V. Bekarek and J. Slouka, *Collect. Czech. Chem. Commun.*, **35**, 2936 (1970).

34. A. H. Berrie, P. Hampson, S. W. Longworth, and A. Mathias, *J. Chem. Soc.*, 1308 (1968).

35. I. Ya. Bershtein and O. F. Ginzburg, *Russ. Chem. Rev., Engl. Trans.*, **41**, 97 (1972).

36. D. M. Marmion, *J. Assoc. Off. Anal. Chem.*, **57**, 495 (1974).

37. C. L. McGehee and C. H. Summers, *Dev. Appl. Spectrosc.*, **9**, 405 (1964); Publ. 1965.

38. B. L. Kaul, R. Srinivasan, and K. Venkataraman, *Chimia*, **19**, 213 (1965).

39. N. S. Bhacca, D. P. Hollis, L. F. Johnson, and E. A. Pier, *High Resolution NMR Spectra Catalog*, Vol. 2, No. 652, Varian Associates, Palo Alto, Calif., 1963.

40. Cf. *CSD* II, p. 1146; III, p. 449; IV, p. 212; V, pp. 427, 433–347, 450.

41. R. Liepins and C. Walker, *Ind. Eng. Chem., Prod. Res. Dev.*, **10**, 401 (1971).

42. *CSD* I and II, p. 916 and other refs. to the trifluoromethyl group.

43. R. Radeglia and A. Weber, *J. Prakt. Chem.*, **314,** 884 (1972).
44. R. E. Sievers, Ed., *Nuclear Magnetic Resonance Shift Reagents*, Academic Press, New York, 1973.
45. B. L. Shapiro, J. R. Hlubucek, G. R. Sullivan, and L. F. Johnson, *J. Am. Chem. Soc.*, **93,** 3281 (1971).
46. R. E. Graves and P. I. Rose, *J. Chem. Soc., Chem. Commun.* 630 (1973).

CHAPTER NINE

Mass Spectrometry

T. E. BEUKELMAN

1 INTRODUCTION

1.1 Methodology

There are two general methods by which MS may be used to identify unknown organic compounds. The first method treats the MS as a "fingerprint" or pattern, and identification is accomplished by pattern recognition methods or by matching against a reference library or file of MS patterns. The other method is to treat the MS analytically and to attempt to deduce from the mass-to-charge ratios the kind of compound that would produce such a pattern.

The "fingerprint" method suffers from several disadvantages. The most serious is that if the reference library does not contain a spectrum of the unknown, the method fails. In some limited cases a partial match may be found with a closely related material which may give clues to the identity of the unknown. However, this is much less likely in the case of MS than with methods such as IR.

Commercially available libraries of MS data contain very few references to synthetic dyes. Furthermore, for the "fingerprint" method to work well spectra must be quite reproducible. MS of low molecular weight compounds are adequately reproducible to make pattern recognition methods useful, but higher molecular weight compounds such as synthetic dyes are normally introduced directly into the source of a mass spectrometer as solids and vaporized by heating. In this case, the MS pattern observed is a function of temperature, the rate of heating, and other less tangible factors. The extent of pyrolysis depends on temperature and many other factors. As a consequence, the MS of synthetic dyes are much less reproducible than those of smaller molecules, and the fingerprint method is therefore less satisfactory. Even if difficulties did not exist, IR spectra are so much more characteristic as fingerprints and IR reference libraries are so much more complete that if "fingerprint" methods are to be used, IR spectroscopy is much preferred.

For synthetic dyes, the analytical method is much more productive. The methods of inferring structures of organic compounds from the analysis of their mass spectra are well described by many authors.[1-4]

Owing to the complexity of dye molecules it is seldom that a complete structure can be deduced from the MS alone; such structural features as positions of substitution in aromatic rings are very difficult to determine. Extensive MS studies on related compounds may sometimes answer this type of question. However, the same question can usually be answered much more easily and with more confidence by NMR. The use of complementary techniques such as NMR and IR spectroscopy is far preferable to more extensive MS studies, which often add to the problems. It is often a temptation for a spectroscopist to prove that his particular technique is the most powerful and can stand alone, but such a tour de force is often very expensive and loses sight of the main problem of identifying an unknown dye.

One of the very useful concepts in the interpretation of the MS of dyes is that of "rings plus double bonds" (RDB). If the molecular formula of a dye can be deduced either from the MS alone or in combination with other techniques, the RDB of the structure may be calculated. If the chemical formula is $C_xH_yN_zO_n$, the RDB $= 1 + x - \frac{1}{2}y + \frac{1}{2}z$. Halogen atoms may be treated as hydrogen atoms.

The RDB can often be very useful as a starting point in postulating a structure. For example, a formula that corresponds to nine RDB's might well be a simple derivative of azobenzene with four RDB's from each benzene ring and one from the azo linkage. It certainly cannot be an anthraquinone dye since unsubstituted anthraquinone has 11 RDB's. Sometimes the presence of a naphthyl group in the dye molecule may be inferred from a fragment having seven RDB's. It should be noted that a NO_2 group counts as one RDB, but a $C\equiv N$ group counts as two RDB's.

The RDB figure can also be used to help decide whether a given ion is the molecular ion. Molecular ions must have an RDB that is a whole number. An ion with an RDB of 10.5 cannot be a molecular ion.

1.2   High-Resolution MS

The most useful mass spectral technique for identification of dyes is high-resolution MS (HRMS). Modern high-resolution mass spectrometers are capable of measuring mass-to-charge ratios (m/e) with a practical accuracy of 10 ppm. Higher accuracies are theoretically possible, but in practice are difficult to attain.

The importance of such accurate mass measurement may be most clearly stated by pointing out that in the 400 m/e range there are about 300 chemically possible formulas composed of only C, H, N, and O that lie within a range of ±0.5 amu. At an accuracy of 10 ppm there are only about eight chemically possible formulas in the range ±0.004 amu. These numbers are only representative and were taken from a table prepared in this laboratory with the following restrictions. The RDB must not be less than −0.5 (to permit protonated species). The RDB is not greater than the number of C atoms when there are six or more C atoms. Finally, the numbers of N and O atoms must each not be greater than the number of C atoms plus two. Under these conditions some formulas are generated which are not really chemically reasonable and, in particular, some of the formulas clearly do not represent dyes (for example, hydrocarbons). Thus the number of formulas may often be reduced to three or four at the 10-ppm level of accuracy. Unfortunately the number is seldom reduced to only one.

2   EXPERIMENTAL DETAILS

2.1   Spectrometer and Data Handling

The mass spectrometer used in this laboratory is a Du Pont 21-110B high-resolution mass spectrometer. It is equipped with a direct insert probe for the introduction of solid samples. The magnet is scanned with a simple electronic device which gives a nearly linear scan of m/e with time. The output of the electron multiplier goes to a specially built amplifier with variable bandwidths to permit relatively rapid scanning. The output from the amplifier is fed to a Sigma 5 computer where it is digitized and thresholded.

Each sample is run with a bleed of perfluorokerosene (PFK) to provide a mass scale. The computer recognizes the PFK peaks based upon an empirical algorithm and calculates the precise mass of all sample peaks. The computer provides a report of sample peaks with their precise masses and areas and the possible chemical formulas corresponding to each peak. See Table 9.1.

Since resolution is obtained at the sacrifice of sensitivity, a compromise must be reached between the two. With the use of computer-acquired and computer-treated data, extremely high resolution is not so critical. We normally operate our spectrometer at a resolution of 7 or 8 K and a scan

Table 9-1.

WIDTH	AREA	AVE. MASS	ERROR	RDB	C	H	N	O
13	110	101.0397	.5	6.5	8	5	0	0
21	522	119.0366	..5	6.0	7	5	1	1
21	414	127.0544	..4	7.5	10	7	0	0
34	340	128.0521	2.1	7.5	9	6	1	0
18	193	139.0539	..8	8.5	11	7	0	0
13	106	153.0579	.0	9.0	11	7	1	0
21	528	154.0657	..0	8.5	11	8	1	0
23	207	164.0504	.3	10.5	12	6	1	0
29	895	181.0775	.9	9.5	12	9	2	0
22	432	182.0619	1.3	9.5	12	8	1	1
16	124	182.0851	.7	9.0	12	10	2	0
22	340	209.0714	..1	10.5	13	9	2	1
20	253	210.0797	.4	10.0	13	10	2	1
19	281	223.0640	.7	11.0	14	9	1	2
43	1544	237.0651	.1.3	11.5	14	9	2	2
56	14805	238.0731	.1.1	11.0	14	10	2	2
39	2892	239.0752	1.6	15.0	18	9	1	0
21	230	240.0787	.2.6	14.5	18	10	1	0

- 6 -

rate such that the mass range from 16 to 700 is covered in 5 minutes. Under these conditions mass measurement accuracies are well within 10 ppm at masses greater than 300 and within ±0.003 amu for lower masses. Faster scan rates such as would be required for GC–MS lead to much lower sensitivities. The sensitivities would be adequate for low-resolution work on low molecular weight materials, but not for high-resolution work on molecules with masses greater than 300.

The great advantage of computer collected data is that the precise masses of all the peaks are available, whereas in the peak matching technique, the time and work required to get comparable data are prohibitive. It is important to have a list of all the precise masses because often the difference between two masses is more instructive than the masses themselves.

2.2 Sample Preparation

One of the serious problems in the mass spectrometry of synthetic dyes involves the difficulty of preparing pure samples. This problem is more acute with mass spectrometry, which may be described as a trace analysis technique, than with something like NMR, which is not as sensitive to trace impurities (except for Fourier transform techniques).

As a result of the difficulty of preparing synthetic dye samples without trace impurities, care must be taken in the analytical interpretation of mass spectra since some peaks may well be caused by impurities. One of the serious pitfalls into which the mass spectroscopist can easily fall is the situation where a major component of a sample has a very low volatility and a minor or trace component has a high volatility. This can lead to completely erroneous results.

For this reason it is important to exhaust, as completely as possible, samples inserted into the source with a direct insert probe. Since some heating is usually necessary to vaporize samples, it is important not to stop heating after a mass spectrum has been obtained and the ion beam begins to wane since there may be another component that requires a higher temperature to volatilize.

Unfortunately, inspection of the sample after analysis to determine if the entire sample has been volatilized does not always lead to a clear answer. At temperatures necessary to volatilize synthetic dyes there is usually some thermal decomposition, and often there is a cinder or some tar left so that it is difficult to determine if all components have been observed.

One of the more powerful techniques for purification of synthetic dyes is TLC (see Chapter 2). Since mass spectrometry needs very little sample it is possible to prepare quite pure samples by this technique without undue work or expense. In most cases TLC is preferable to classical column chromatography since it is usually faster and separations are better. The techniques of high-pressure liquid chromatography (see Chapter 4) may sometimes be applicable. Fortunately, synthetic dyes give easily observable bands which need not be made visible in any of the usual ways which might alter the sample. To isolate a component, the area of the TLC plate containing the band desired is scraped clear of the adsorbent containing the sample.

It would be convenient if the adsorbent along with the adsorbed dye could be introduced directly into the mass spectrometer and the dye vaporized from the silica gel (or other adsorbent). Unfortunately, attempts to use this technique are usually unsuccessful for two reasons. First, the temperatures necessary to desorb the dye from the silica gel are higher than simple volatilization temperatures, leading to increased thermal degradation. There may be some catalysis involved. Secondly, the silica gel tends to "pop" or dehydrate in the heated probe, leading to extreme variations in the pressure and in the total ion beam intensity. As a consequence, it is usually necessary to extract the dye from the adsorbent with a suitable solvent. Unless unusual care is taken during the preparation of samples by TLC, the resulting spectrum will be a "greasy" spectrum. Of particular importance is the necessity to use carefully distilled solvents. Since large volumes of solvents are used and finally evaporated away from the sample, it is important that the solvents do not contain residual impurities. Even a carelessly placed fingerprint on the glassware used can result in a "greasy" mass spectrum.

A useful technique for handling small samples obtained by TLC purification involves a section of m.p. tube stuffed with clean glass wool. The sample is dissolved in a fractional drop of suitable solvent and the solution drawn into the tube by capillary action. The solvent should be volatile enough so that it will be removed in the vacuum lock of the spectrometer. The section of m.p. tube with the sample on the glass wool is then inserted directly into the source of the mass spectrometer.

The technique of gas chromatography can be used for purification in some cases, but relatively few synthetic dyes are amenable to this treatment. Mixtures of a few anthraquinone dyes have been separated by GLC. Components were trapped by simply condensing them in an open-end m.p. tube placed in the exit port of the chromatograph. The m.p. tube with the condensed sample can then be placed directly into the source of the mass spectrometer.

3 ANTHRAQUINONE DYES

Perhaps the easiest dyes to work on are the anthraquinones. They usually give strong molecular ions. The anthraquinone nucleus with simple substituents such as hydroxyl, amino and halogen is quite stable. The most prominent mode of fragmentation is the loss of one and two carbonyl groups. The spectra of a wide variety of anthraquinones have been reported by Beynon and Williams.[5]

When the substituents become more complex, such as anilino, toluidino, or alkylamino, fragmentation of the substituents occurs. In the case of monosubstituted amines, it is quite common to find the loss of the amine substituent and recombination with a proton to give a primary amine. Thus an anilinoanthraquinone gives, in addition to the molecular ion, a strong aminoanthraquinone peak. Hydrogen bonding substituents in the 2, 3, 6, and 7 positions are more easily lost than in the 1, 4, 5, and 8 positions. However, the positions of substitution are far more easily determined from NMR.

Sulfonate substituents, however, render the molecule involatile as is the case with other acid dyes. Desulfonation of the anthraquinone nucleus may be accomplished with ease. See Chapter 12, Section 2.4. The fragmentation of substituents follows ordinary rules of mass spectrometry.

4 AZO DYES

Comprehensive studies of substituted azobenzenes have been made by a number of workers.[6-8] Bowie, Lewis, and Cooks[6] pointed out that all the substituted azobenzenes studied by them showed skeletal rearrangement ions which arise from loss of N together with various substituents. Biphenyl is formed from loss of N_2 from azobenzene, and biphenylene is formed by the loss of two H from biphenyl. However, this type of fragmentation is not important in the overall spectra and not very useful for identification purposes. Molecular ions are usually present and often quite strong. The intensity of the molecular ion depends on the molecular weight and the lability of the substituents more than on the azo linkage itself. For example, azo dyes containing a diethylamino group show a relatively weak molecular ion because of the ease of fragmentation of the diethylamino group. In fact, the pattern of losses from the diethylamino group (CH_3, C_2H_4, C_2H_5, C_3H_8) is quite characteristic.

Cleavage at the azo group can occur in three ways. The most common appears to be at the NC bond on the coupler side of the azo linkage, the positive charge remaining with the coupler component. Cleavage at the other CN bond appears to be very weak. Mehta and Peters[9] made an interesting study relating the ratio of cleavage between the two azo CN bonds with lightfastness. Whether cleavage ever occurs between the two N of the azo linkage is not clear. However, it is not at all unusual to find an ion that appears to come from cleavage between the two azo N with the azo component recombining with two H to form the amine. In other words, if the azo dye had been made by coupling a diazotized nitroaniline, it is quite likely that nitroaniline would appear in the mass spectrum. This may come from cleavage between the two azo N or may be a secondary result, perhaps from a diazonium ion.

The fragmentation of the amine substituents can be quite instructive. When cleavage occurs alpha to the amine nitrogen, the positive charge remains with the amine substituent fragment. Thus the ion $^+$PhNHR would give the ion R$^+$ rather than $^+$PhNH. However, fragmentation beta to the amine nitrogen usually leaves the charge with the amine moiety. If the amine substituent is CH_2CH_2X where X is OH, OR, OCOR, or CN, beta fragmentation is very common.

The diazo components of azo dyes often contain one or more Cl or Br, which may be easily recognized by their isotope patterns. Nitriles are best characterized by their IR absorption and nitro groups give characteristic NO losses.

Kobayashi and Hirose[9a] have studied a large number of water-insoluble yellow monoazo pigments with the general structure $AC_6H_4N{=}NCH$-$(COCH_3)CONHC_6H_4B$, where A and B are various substituents on the phenyl rings. In all but one of the 27 cases discussed, the most intense peak was the amine component ion formed by the cleavage of the amide bond with hydrogen transfer. All showed molecular ions with relative intensities varying between 10 and 50%. They present an analytical method for the determination of the structure of this particular class of dye.

Disazo dyes seldom give good molecular ions because of the probability of cleavage of the two azo linkages. However, often a great deal can be inferred from the fragments present. For example, the HRMS of (25), Chapter 12, Section 3.2.2, showed, in addition to a weak molecular ion, prominent ions from all the fragments that might be formed from various cleavages of the azo groups. An aminophenol ion formed the strongest peak in the pattern. The second strongest peak had the formula C_7H_7NO and appears to be a fragment from the central ring system. Strong peaks due to the loss of one and two methyl groups from the parent molecule were observed. One of the most significant ions identified had the formula $C_8H_{10}NO$, which corresponds to a benzene ring with a methyl, a methoxy, and an amino group. This was important in establishing where the various substituents were placed on the disazo skeleton.

5 CATIONIC DYES

Because the dyes are salts they do not readily volatilize in a mass spectrometer. The main methods for dequaternization of quaternary ammonium salts have been reviewed by Venkataraman and associates.[10] Perhaps the easiest method is by pyrolysis in the source of the mass spectrometer. In isolating and purifying the cationic dyes, iodides or picrates are convenient to handle. Either the picrate or the iodide may be pyrolyzed at temperatures of the order of 200° within the source of a mass spectrometer, giving the volatile neutral species, which can be ionized in the normal manner. The spectrum also contains iodide ions or picrate ions. The presence of the picrate ions and their fragmentation products can sometimes confuse the interpretation of the MS of the neutral species. In this respect, the iodide is preferable since the iodide ion is easy to recognize, particularly in a HRMS. If the loss on dequaternization is a methyl group a methyl iodide peak is also present. These alkyl iodide peaks can sometimes be used to determine what alkyl group has been lost in the dequaternization. Great care should be taken in this type of interpretation since it is very possible for an iodide ion to recombine with an alkyl fragment from the neutral molecule. In particular, the presence of an HI ion cannot be interpreted as indicating the loss of only a proton since the HI ion is almost always present in the mass spectra of iodides of cationic dyes.

The MS of a cationic dye perhaps never shows an ion with the composition of the cation, but rather a pyrolysis product of the cation. In many cases this may be simply the loss of a methyl group if there is a methyl group on the quaternized amine. In some cases the loss may be more severe, such as in the case of (55), Chapter 12, Section 3.3, where a complete ethylpyridyl group was lost. In some cases only a proton is lost, as in (53) and (54), Chapter 12, Section 3.3. One interesting case is that of cationic dyes derived from Fischer's aldehyde. If the quaternized nitrogen in the indoline nucleus carries a methyl group, a mass spectral ion is observed whose composition is one H less than that of the original cation. This has been explained[10] by a rearrangement of the N-methyl-substituted indoline nucleus (1) to a dihydroquinoline nucleus (2).

(1) (2)

Another interesting case is that of the dye (47), Chapter 12, Section 3.3. Only relatively small fragments were observed in the MS; one was shown to have structure (50), Chapter 12, Section 3.3. It appears that pyrolysis in this case was quite different from that normally observed for cationic dyes.

Cleavage at the azo linkage with subsequent ring closure leads to structure (50).

6 ACID DYES

The most difficult dyes to study by mass spectrometry are the acid dyes. The salts of sulfonic acid-bearing dyes cannot be volatilized without thermal degradation. Even the free acids are extremely involatile. Some limited information may be gained from pyrolysis products. It is even possible that desulfonation may be accomplished thermally in the mass spectrometer (see Chapter 12, Section 3.1, Example 2). Chemical desulfonation can be accomplished in some cases (see Chapter 12, Section 2.4). The opposite approach from desulfonation is to form derivatives of the sulfonic acid groups which are more volatile. The methyl esters are commonly used. Heywood, Mathias, and Williams[11] describe two methods of preparing the methyl esters of sulfonic acids. Both methods have been tried in this laboratory with only limited success. As a test, the methyl ester of naphthalene-2-sulfonic acid was prepared by both methods. The ester prepared by the diazomethane route gave a moderately weak molecular ion, and the ester obtained from the tetramethylammonium salt gave a molecular ion only with great difficulty. As the tetramethylammonium salt begins to decompose in the spectrometer a strong trimethylamine peak is observed and the ester peak should also be seen. However, the decomposition is difficult to control, so that it is easy to miss the ester peak.

The problem with chemical modification of the sample, either desulfonation or formation of the ester, is that it is not always possible to know exactly what reactions have occurred. Even the methyl esters of acid dyes are not easy to handle. The volatility is still low and it is often difficult to get a molecular ion.

Reduction of azo dyes containing the SO_3Na group to a mixture of amines and subsequent conversion to SO_3Me has been tried with limited success. It is always very difficult to interpret the MS of a mixture, so it is very desirable to attempt isolation of the components of the mixture. This is usually a difficult procedure and there is always the danger of chemical modification. Reduction of the azo group is not always a clean process since other reductions may also take place. It is sometimes possible to learn the identity of part of the dye molecule by inserting the mixture of amines into the mass spectrometer without esterification. In this case the component containing the SO_3Na group does not vaporize and a spectrum of only one of the amines can be obtained.

A very promising technique for acid dyes as well as other nonvolatile materials is field desorption mass spectrometry (FDMS).[12,13] In a forthcoming paper entitled *High Resolution Field Desorption Mass Spectrometry III, Sulphonic Acids and Sulphonates*, to be published in *Z. Anal. Chem.*, H. R. Schulten and D. Kummler discuss the field desorption spectrum of a number of acid dyes as well as a large variety of other sulfonic acids and sulfonates. They point out that the FD spectra of free sulfonic acids all give high molecular ion intensities. Often elimination of SO_3 from the parent molecule is observed. Na and K ions are often observed, particularly in technical-grade materials, which may also come from contamination of the emitter or from the solvent. This can lead to cationization giving [M + Na] ions. In additon, the FDMS can give structurally significant fragments.

In the case of sulfonates a common feature of the FDMS spectra is the presence of cluster ions [nM + C], where C is a cation.[14] Often the first cluster [M + C] has a greater intensity than the molecular ion. However, this tendency is reversed as the molecular weight increases. Fortunately, most acid dyes have a high molecular weight. As with sulfonic acids the sulfonates often give structurally significant fragments. Ions due to the corresponding free acid of the sulfonates are of minor importance. As in the case of electron impact spectra, SO_2 ions are often observed.

Shulten and Kummler use integrating photoplate recording of their mass spectra. They point out that fluctuations in the ion current occur and question whether magnetic scanning and electrical detection are practical for FDMS. McEwen and Bolinski[15] have described the measurement of field desorbed ions by peak matching techniques.

FDMS is a new and fast developing technique that holds a great deal of promise for handling otherwise intractable molecules.

7 METHINE DYES

The characterization of methine dyes is best done by IR spectra; dyes containing the dicyanoethylene groups are particularly easily recognized. The methine dyes usually give good molecular ions so that an empirical formula can be found from a high-resolution mass spectrum. Fragmentations follow the general rules for organic compounds. The dicyanoethylene group appears quite stable, but sometimes a loss of HCN from the molecule indicates that it is fragmenting.

8 MISCELLANEOUS

Kadhim, Grayshan, and Peters[16] studied a series of benzo(k,1)thioxanthene-3,4-dicarboximides (3). They point out that, although *N*-alkylphthalimides often lose CO_2 to form M-CO_2 ions, the spectra of (3) are characterized by the absence of M-CO_2 ions. Several unusual rearrangements of the R groups are discussed. Similar results have been obtained for the dye (4).

Molecules with the structure (5), however, do show strong M-CO_2 ions and very weak or no hydroxyquinoline or phthalone ions. Cleavage

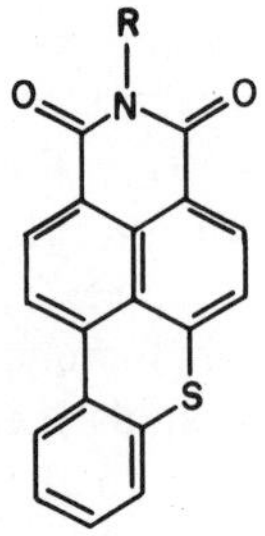

(3) 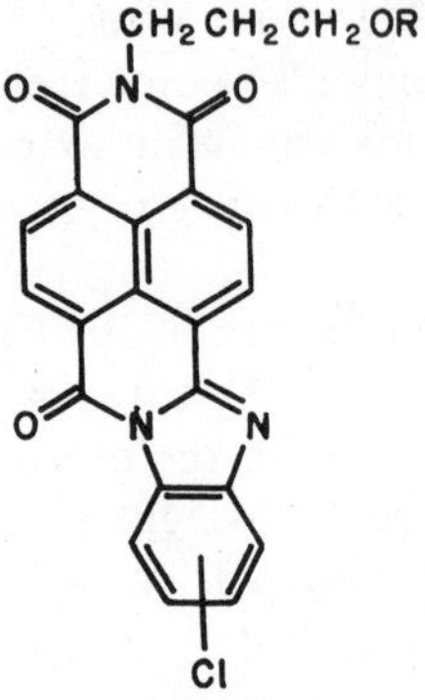   (4) 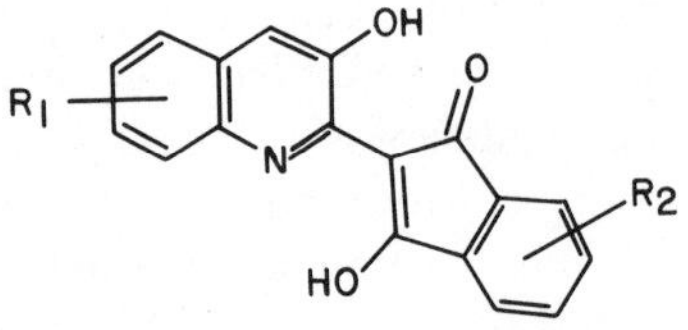   (5)

between the two ring systems is very uncommon. Instead, the molecular ion expels CO_2 and most likely undergoes a ring closure that stabilizes the daughter ion. The second step is loss of CO to leave an ion with no O. This makes it difficult to determine which substituents are on each ring system. The R groups obey normal rules of cleavage.

REFERENCES

1. K. Biemann, *Mass Spectrometry, Organic Chemical Applications*, McGraw-Hill, New York, 1962.
2. J. H. Beynon, R. A. Saunders, and A. E. Williams, *The Mass Spectra of Organic Molecules*, Elsevier, Amsterdam, 1968.
3. F. N. McLafferty, Ed., *Mass Spectrometry of Organic Ions*, Academic Press, New York, 1963.
4. H. Budzikiewicz, C. Djerassi, and D. H. Williams, *Mass Spectrometry of Organic Compounds*, Holden-Day, San Francisco, 1967.
5. J. H. Beynon and A. E. Williams, *Appl. Spectrosc.*, **14**, 327 (1960).
6. J. H. Bowie, G. E. Lewis, and R. E. Cooks, *J. Chem. Soc.*, (B), 621 (1967).
7. J. A. Völmin, P. Pachlatko, and W. Simon, *Helv. Chim. Acta*, **52**, 737 (1969).
8. J. C. Gilland, Jr., and J. S. Lewis, *Org. Mass Spectrom.*, **9**, 1148 (1974).
9. H. P. Mehta and A. T. Peters, *Appl. Spectrosc.*, **28**, 241 (1974).
9a. K. Kobayashi and K. Hirose, *Bull. Chem. Soc. Japan*, **45**, 1700 (1972).

10.—V. Parameswaran, A. V. Rama Rao, and K. Venkataraman, *Indian J. Chem.*, **12**, 785 (1974).

11. A. Heywood, A. Mathias, and A. E. Williams, *Anal. Chem.*, **42**, 1272 (1970).

12. H. D. Beckey and H. R. Schulten, *Z. Anal. Chem.*, **272**, 345 (1975).

13. H. D. Beckey and H. R. Schulten, *Angew. Chem.*, **87**, 425 (1975); *Angew. Chem. Internat. Ed.*, **14**, 403 (1975) and references cited therein.

14. H. R. Schulten and F. W. Röllgen, *Org. Mass Spectrom.*, **10**, 649 (1975).

15. C. N. McEwen and A. G. Bolinski, *Biomed. Mass Spectrom.*, 112 (1975).

16. A. M. Kadhim, P. H. Grayshan, and A. T. Peters, *J. Soc. Dyers Colour.*, **90**, 291 (1974).

CHAPTER TEN

X-Ray Powder Diffraction

A. WHITAKER

1 INTRODUCTION

Copper phthalocyanine and linear *trans*-quinacridone are well-known examples of pigments that crystallize in more than one form; the different crystal modifications vary in hue and other pigmentary properties. X-ray powder diffraction is a useful technique for characterizing crystal forms.

1.1 Diffraction of X-Rays from Crystals

It is not proposed to deal in great detail with the history, theory, and practice of X-ray powder diffraction, covered by several excellent books,[1-6] but rather to consider some of the misconceptions found in literature and to recommend a form of presenting results that will be the most useful to other investigators.

Very briefly, if an X-ray beam strikes a crystal, it may be diffracted; for this to occur the relationship between the glancing angle θ, the interplanar spacing d, and the wavelength λ is given by Bragg's law:

$$2d \sin \theta = \lambda$$

Before we proceed it is important to realize what is meant by a crystal; a crystal may be defined as a solid within which there is a three-dimensional atomic array. Thus in a crystal there are an infinite number of atomic planes and an X-ray beam may be diffracted from many of these in turn. If the crystal is then replaced by a polycrystalline (powder) specimen in which the crystals are oriented at random, the same diffraction peaks are produced, but owing to the random crystallographic orientation within the specimen the diffracted beams are now spread out so that they are cylindrically symmetrical about the incident X-ray beam. This gives rise to two effects, first, the disadvantage that diffracted beams with similar values of θ cannot be resolved owing to overlapping peaks, and second, the advantage that the apparatus is simpler in that one needs to record only an equatorial band around the specimen, provided this includes the direction of the incident beam. The record may be either photographic or diffracto-metric; both these techniques have their advantages and adherents.

It may not be realized that it is possible to get diffraction peaks from materials that are not crystalline within the definition used above, and this is probably best explained by an example. In several recent crystal structure determinations of azo pigments it appears that the molecules are planar or nearly so. Suppose these are stacked parallel in a column at equal intervals, with the column axes at random orientation with respect to each other; then this structure would give a diffraction peak corresponding to the distance between the molecules. However, this has only one-dimensional order and is not a crystal. There are examples of only one or two diffraction peaks being obtained from a compound and, in this chapter, these are referred to as disordered phases.

1.2   Advantages and Disadvantages of the Powder Technique

The main advantage of the technique is that the combination of interplanar spacings, d, and associated intensities, I, depends on the crystal structure. This means that the pattern is, to all intents and purposes, unique not only for the element or compound, but also for polymorphs of the same chemical composition and for solid solutions or mixed crystals (Section 1.3). There are added advantages of the method being nondestructive and requiring only small amounts of specimen (about 1 mg). It is for these reasons that the powder technique is excellent for phase analysis. Unfortunately there are also two disadvantages. First, the limit of detectability of a minor phase in a major phase is generally poor. It is impossible to put an absolute value on this because of its dependence on relative crystallinity, relative scattering power of the X-ray beam, and complexity of the patterns. But when these are similar the limit of detectability is probably of the order of

5%. The second disadvantage, when using the technique for analysis of unknown phases, is the large amount of background data required. In practice this is done by the publication of the X-ray Powder Data File (DF in this chapter), which at the moment contains patterns of some 8000 organic compounds. Unfortunately not all reported patterns are listed in DF and very few of the patterns are for dyes or pigments.

1.3 Solid Solutions and Mixed Crystals

In many references to quinacridone pigments the term "solid solution" is used incorrectly. A "solid solution" implies that it can exist over a range of chemical composition. Thus determining that one composition has a unique pattern is not in itself evidence for a solid solution. The pattern may only exist at that composition, in which case it is a mixed crystal.

Patterns of solid solutions may alter with variation of composition; the variation may be either or both of two types. If the atoms or molecules are not identical in size, then the unit cell size alters and there is an angular movement of the peaks. Secondly, if the replacing atom or molecule does not have the same X-ray scattering factor, the intensities alter. Both these are acceptable solid solution effects.

1.4 Peak Resolution, Choice of Radiation

The most commonly used radiation is copper; owing to the power loading of the X-ray tube, this requires the least X-ray exposure. However, the difficulty with complex organic compounds is the large number of diffraction peaks giving rise to overlapping lines,[7] and there is a case for using longer-wavelength radiation to increase the resolution. Because of this, I use copper radiation as a routine, but cobalt radiation for difficult patterns and for data that are to be reported.

1.5 Reliability of an X-ray Pattern

There is always the question whether an X-ray powder pattern is from a single phase or not, and this doubt still exists even if the specimen is chemically pure. One way of overcoming this is to examine the reproducibility of the pattern with different specimens, preferably made under different conditions. In this sense reports confirming an existing pattern are not wasted; the more confirming patterns there are, the greater the reliability.

There is an alternative way of checking a pattern if the unit cell dimensions are known: index the pattern, i.e., calculate the atomic planes that contribute to the diffraction peaks. If some lines cannot be indexed, then these at least are due to impurities and the pattern is suspect. If the pattern can be indexed in this way there is a good chance that it is reliable if one excludes the possibility of incorrect cell dimensions. An even more reliable way is where the intensities are compared with diffracted intensities from a single crystal, but this is unlikely to occur unless the crystal structure has been determined.

1.6   Presentation of X-ray Powder Data

There are several ways of presenting the results of an X-ray investigation. In Susich's classical paper[8] the powder films were printed; however, the loss of lines on the print, together with the fact that the magnification on reproduction is generally less than one, can cause considerable loss of information, although the method is excellent for comparative purposes. A common alternative is the reproduction of diffractometer traces, but again this is usually done on a small scale, leading to errors in measurement of diffraction angles and intensities. It is notable that published traces do not generally extend further than $2\theta = 30°$. Powder data from dyes and pigments do not usually extend much further than this, but for chemically simple compounds, e.g., sodium chloride and calcium carbonate, the reverse is true and there are few lines with the diffracting angle less than 30°. Because of this it is advisable to take much longer traces; had this been done, queries regarding the polymorphism of Lithol Red, Watchung Red, and the Calcium Lakes of the latter (Section 2.2.1) could have been answered.

A third way is to produce what might be called a line pattern, i.e., placing bars on a d, θ, or 2θ scale representing the peak positions; this is the least satisfactory because there are still errors in measurement, and furthermore one cannot reassess the data.

For the sake of accuracy it is preferable to report a list of interplanar spacings (d) and intensities (I) taken from the original photograph or trace; the ideal presentation is to report both the listing and a trace, a combination favored by Parrish,[9] which allows the reader to reassess the original trace in the light of subsequent developments and to make allowances for line broadening owing to different particle size.

Another alternative is to list the Bragg angle (θ) or diffracting angle (2θ); both these suffer from the disadvantage that they depend not only on the material under examination, but also on the wavelength of radiation used.

Thus for reporting powder data the recommendations are as follows: (a) list interplanar spacings, d, and intensities, I, measured above background; (b) assess the intensity as accurately as possible from original records and scale to a maximum of 100; (c) index the pattern on the cell dimensions (if known); (d) index using a knowledge of single crystal intensities (if known); (e) include a diffractometer trace (if available).

2 X-RAY POWDER DIFFRACTION DATA

As mentioned in Section 1.2, the major disadvantage of the X-ray technique is the amount of background knowledge of standard data required. The remainder of this chapter reviews the available powder data. Powder data from electron diffraction have been ignored, because of the unreliability of the intensity measurements. In cases where polymorphs have been X-rayed, the nomenclature used is that of the original reference. This has led to a variety of names for the polymorphs in this chapter, but avoids a change of nomenclature from the original articles.

2.1 Nitro Compounds

There appear to be data on only two nitro compounds, picric acid (CI 10305) (DF 9-789) and CI Disperse Yellow 42 (CI 10338).[10,11] The latter has two polymorphs, depending on whether it is recrystallized from acetone or from the melt; the latter form gives broad diffuse peaks. A mixture of the two is unsatisfactory for use as a disperse dye.[11]

2.2 Monoazo Pigments

Although there are very few X-ray powder data compared with the number of azo pigments, a reasonable proportion of those for which data can be found are polymorphic, and there have been several attempts to study polymorphism systematically.

2.2.1 Polymorphism in Lithol Red, Watchung Red, and Calcium Lakes of Watchung Red. Probably the most comprehensive attempt to investigate polymorphism has been that of Bansho and his co-workers,[12] who examined the formation of both Lithol Red (CI Pigment Red 49; CI 15630)[12a] and Watchung Red (CI Pigment Red 48; CI 15865)[12b] as a function of the pH of the coupling reaction and then investigated the calcium laking of the latter,[12c] again as a function of the pH of the reaction.

In the case of Lithol Red, depending on the pH and the presence of sodium carbonate, any one of four polymorphs, α, α', β, and γ, all monohydrates, could be obtained. If the coupling was carried out at 80°, the only phases obtained were α and α', depending on whether the pH was greater or less than 11. Another polymorph, δ, could be obtained by re-crystallizing any of the other four from methanol.

Reexamination of small-scale reproductions of the original diffrac-tometer traces indicates that α and α' are very similar; α contains three lines more than α', and two are very weak. Of these three lines, two (includ-ing the strongest) could be attributed to sodium chloride. In view of this it would be unwise to designate α and α' as two distinct phases.

Similar work was completed on Watchung Red[12b]; a Na_2 salt formed at pH >7; lower pH gave a Na salt. Three forms of the Na_2 salt, α, β', and β, and two of the Na salt, α and β, were described. For the Na_2 salt the patterns of β and β' are very similar; the pattern of β is sharper corre-sponding to better crystallinity, and because it is the higher-temperature form, this is to be expected.

In the case of the Na salt, the low temperature (lower than 50°) form, α, is characterized by only one line which is also the strongest line of sodium chloride, and thus the pattern could be interpreted as that from an amor-phous material containing a small amount of sodium chloride. In these circumstances it would be unwise to claim the α form as a polymorph. The β form occurs at the higher temperature (greater than 50°), and this tem-perature may not be a transition temperature between two phases, but simply the minimum temperature for crystallization.

The Ca lakes were produced by heating the Na salts with calcium chloride under various pH conditions.[12c] It was found that the lake was produced as the monohydrate (the anhydrous form is CI 15865.2). Three forms were produced, α, β, and γ, and the final product depended only on the pH of laking and not on the original salt. It was found that α occurred at pH 5, β from pH 7 to 9, and γ from pH 11 to 13. The traces of β and γ forms are almost identical, the latter giving an extra peak at $d = 3.04$ Å. This is the strongest line of calcium carbonate (calcite) and it is suggested that during the laking process at pH 11 calcium carbonate is coprecipitated with the lake. Thus only two Ca lake polymorphs may exist, one in acidic and the other in alkaline conditions.

2.2.2 Polymorphism in Other Azo Compounds. In general a polymorph may be obtained in one of several ways, such as varying the conditions of preparation, recrystallization from organic solvents, heating in water or organic liquid, or grinding. Evidence of a transformation may come from techniques other than the X-ray powder method (e.g., DTA); however, only examples proved with X-ray data are included.

In addition to Lithol Red and Watchung Red and its Ca lakes, several other dyes and pigments are known to exhibit polymorphism, depending on the conditions of coupling. It is claimed[13] that three polymorphs of the pigment (**1**) may be obtained, depending on the pH during synthesis. One gives only a single peak at 3.35 Å and is a partly ordered form, which may be a disordered version of one of the others. Thus only two forms are crystallographically acceptable. Coupling in the presence of a dispersing agent causes the production of a second polymorph of the pigment (**2**).[14]

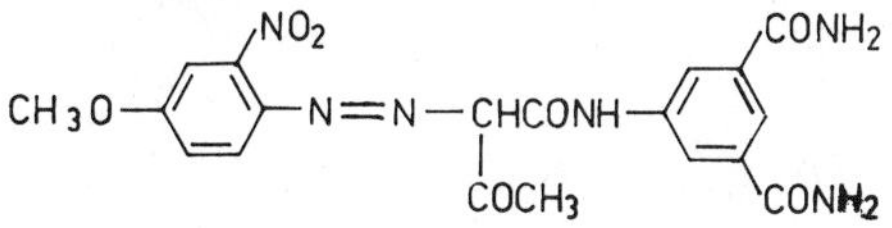

(**1**)

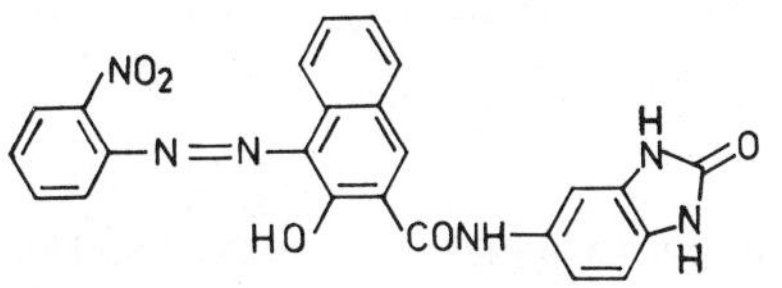

(**2**)

Of course not all transformations are due to coupling conditions. For pigment (**3**), three polymorphs have been reported[15]; either of two may be obtained on coupling, but the third is obtained by heating in water at 90–150°. Sometimes two different processes produce the same polymorph. The dye (**4**) has two forms[16]; one is produced at pH < 7, and the other may be obtained by either coupling at pH > 7 or heating the first in water at 80°.

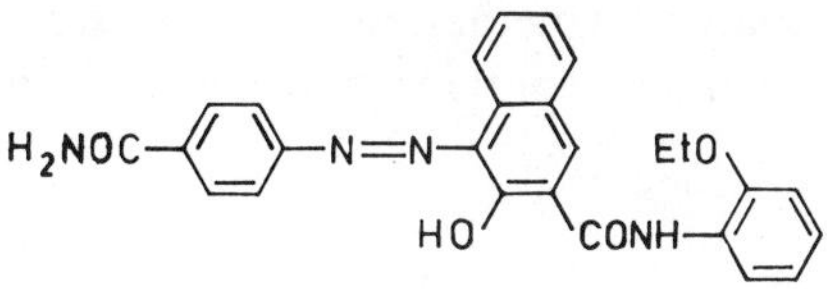

(**3**)

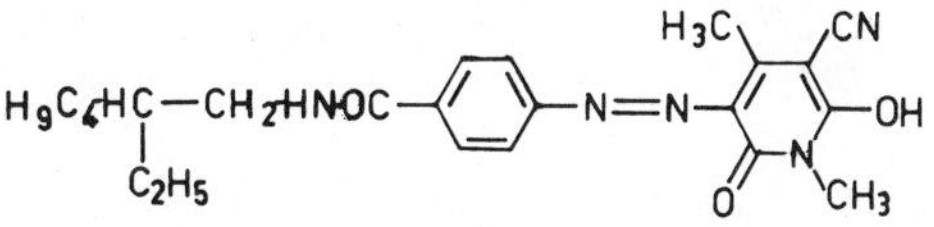

(**4**)

This example of two completely different processes causing the same transformation is not unique. The dye (**5**) has two forms,[17] α and β, and the α to β transformation is caused by either heating in water or hot milling with a dispersing agent. For CI Pigment Red 15 (CI 12465), the α to β

transformation may be obtained by refluxing in chloroform or recrystallization from tetrachloroethylene.[18]

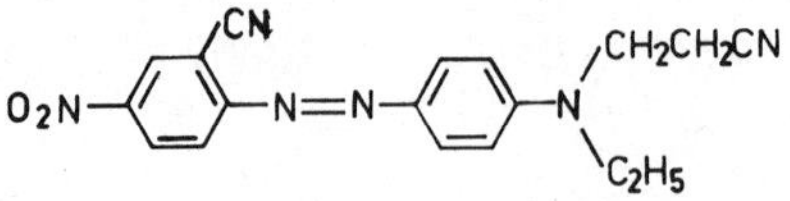

(5)

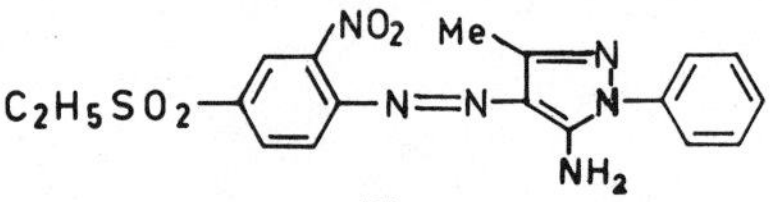

(6)

Aminopyrazole Yellow (6) exists in four crystalline polymorphs which are obtained by dissolving, heating, and recrystallizing from various organic solvents.[19] CI Disperse Yellow 3 (CI 11855) exhibits three polymorphs by the same general method.[10] Biedermann[19] has shown that crystal modifications are important in the disperse dyeing of cellulose acetate and polyester fiber because of their influence on color yield and the stability of the dispersion. Both CI Disperse Orange 61[20] and the dye (7)[21] have two polymorphs. The dye (8) has three,[22] and in all cases the conversion of the initial α form to the β or γ forms is accomplished by heating in water. On the other hand, the β form of (9) is obtained by heating a DMF solution with methanolic $(MeSO_2)_2Zn$ and cupric chloride.[23] Unfortunately this reference contains only the pattern of the β form and not of the α.

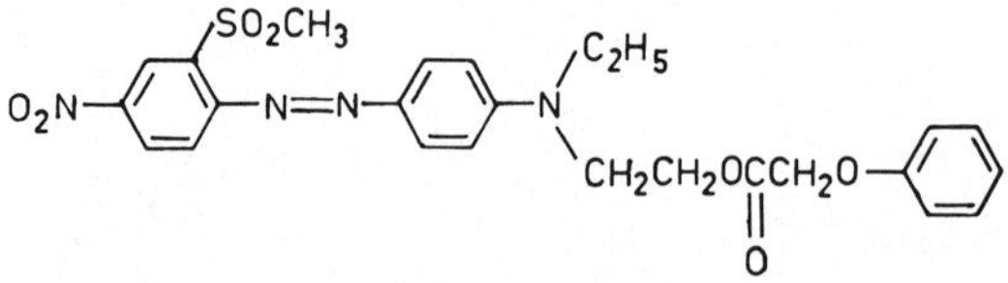

(7)

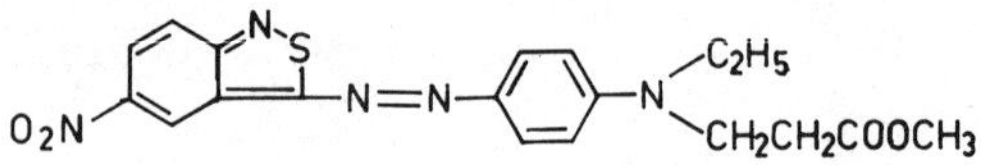

(8)

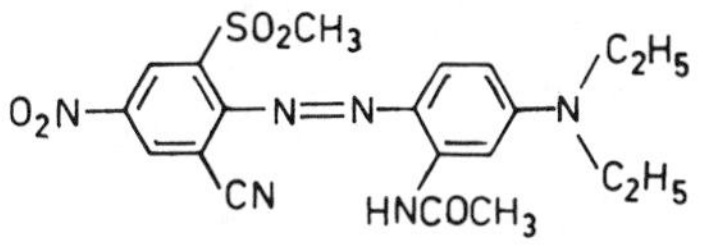

$$O_2N \overset{SO_2CH_3}{\underset{CN}{\diagdown}} N{=}N \overset{}{\underset{HNCOCH_3}{\diagdown}} N \overset{C_2H_5}{\underset{C_2H_5}{\diagup}}$$

(9)

Finally CI Pigment Red 12 (CI 12390) is dimorphic and the transformation is accomplished by grinding dry with barites.[24]

2.2.3 Nonpolymorphic Azo Compounds. X-ray data exist for several azo compounds for which only one form has been discovered. These include CI Pigment Yellow 3 (CI 11710) and its mono and dibromo derivatives, which are isomorphous.[25] The same source also includes data for CI Pigment Yellow 1 and 4 (CI 11680; 11665) and Red 2 (CI 12310). Two patterns of the last have been reported[25,26] and these are in very good agreement; the differences are mainly attributable to the better crystallinity of one specimen.[26] The same pattern has been indexed from single crystal intensities and thus the reliability is higher.

Data have also been reported for CI Pigment Red 3 and 6 (CI 12120; 12090).[27,28]

The patterns of a Mn azo lake (CI 15865.4) are in the form of two identical diffractometer traces, which are slightly offset along the 2θ axis with respect to each other, and there is no way of knowing which is correct.[29] There is no resemblance between these traces and any for the Ca lakes.

Finally, reproductions of Guinier powder photographs are available[30] for 16 pigments (of which five are polymorphic) of the Naphthol AS series. The reproductions are such that measurements cannot be obtained from them, but they may be useful for comparison.

2.3 Disazo Compounds

There are very few powder diffraction data on disazo compounds, and some are of poor quality. Particularly bad is that for 1,4-bis(4-hydroxy-phenylazo)benzene, for which only the three strongest lines for each of two forms are listed, without any indication of the relative intensities[31]; most of the information comes from another source that also ignores intensities.[32] In this reference the β form is that stabilized in gasoline. There are, however, good patterns of the α, β, and γ forms of the disazo compound from diazotized methyl anthranilate and bis(3-hydroxy-2-naphthoyl)-p-phenylenediamine.[33]

Patterns are available for pigments obtained by coupling tetrazotized 2,2′-dichlorobenzidine with various acetoacetic arylides. The diffractometer traces of the pigments from the m-xylidide, o-anisidide, and o-phenetidide are given, the last producing a pattern indicating very poorly crystalline material.[34] Two patterns are given for each of these, one as formed and the other after treatment with polyoxyethylene octylphenyl ether (OP-10). The effect of this treatment on the pigment from the m-xylidide is to produce crystal growth alone, but in the other two cases the patterns were sufficiently altered to suggest also a structural change.

Another source[35a] gives patterns of mixed crystals obtained by coupling tetrazotized 2,2′-dichlorobenzidine with a mixture of acetoacetanilide and a substituted acetoacetanilide, in which aniline is replaced by o-chloroaniline, o- or p-toluidine, or p-phenetidine. In all cases the patterns produced are different from either, or the sum, of those from the initial acetoacetic arylides, thus indicating the presence of a new phase. It is also notable that the patterns for the o-Cl or o-Me substituents are so similar as to indicate that these mixed crystals are isomorphs. The same researchers completed similar work,[35b] using a mixture of the o-toluidide and the o-anisidide, p-phenetidide, or o-chloroanilide. Again mixed crystals were obtained with unique patterns.

Similar work has also been done by coupling tetrazotized 3,3′-dichlorobenzidine with two substituted acetoacetanilides, where the substituent is H, o-Cl, o-Me, o-OMe, or 2,4-Me$_2$, in all possible combinations.[36] Diffractometer traces are given for all combinations, but they are too small for measurements. With the possible exception of the m-xylidide as the second acetoacetanilide, it is again notable that the mixed crystals involving either o-chloro- or o-methylacetoacetanilide are probably isomorphous.

2.4 Azoic Coupling Components

For 2-naphthol three patterns have been reported. In one (DF 3-0171) the low angle (i.e., high d) lines have been missed and so this pattern is best ignored. The other two patterns (DF 23-1785)[37] are in excellent agreement of line positions, but poor agreement of relative intensities. In addition to the room-temperature form of 2-naphthol there is a high-temperature polymorph with a reversible transition between the two at 118°.[38] Of course, the high-temperature polymorph should not exist at room temperature, but it is not unknown for high-temperature polymorphs to be stabilized at room temperature by the addition of other components. Unfortunately the powder pattern of the high temperature form has not been reported.

Practically all the X-ray patterns of azoic coupling components have been reported in one excellent paper, which includes not only the tables of interplanar spacings and intensities, but also relatively large-scale diffractometer traces.[39]

2.5 Stilbene Compounds

Although stilbene compounds may be divided into dyes (usually azo dyes of indeterminate composition) and fluorescent whiteners, the only X-ray data to hand concern the latter. These have the symmetrically substituted structure (10), in which R and R' are usually anilino or substituted anilino, and M is H or Na. Often it is found that there are two or more forms of the compound, one of which is usually yellow and causes discoloration of the washing agent, more pronounced in damp or humid conditions. The other forms are white. The yellow form is generally amorphous or poorly crystalline, and is usually termed the α form. The white forms are crystalline and are usually called β forms.

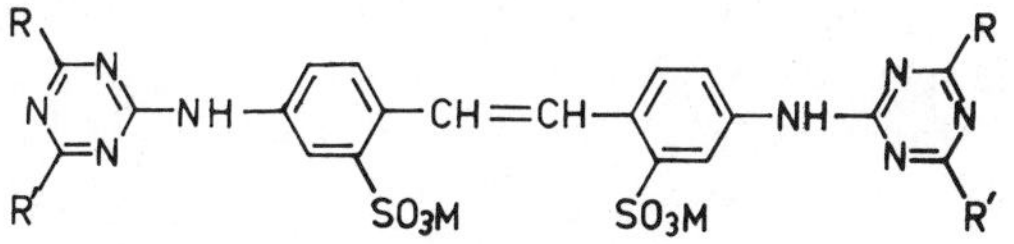

(10)

Probably the most comprehensive work has been done on (10; R = R' = PhNH; M = Na), for which there is some evidence of two α forms, α_1 and α_2, and four β forms, now termed β_1, β_2, β_3, and β_4 in order of their discovery.

Tscharner, Stahlbush, and Driver[40a] give a pattern of a β form, β_1, and state that certain lines are in common with the α form, α_1. Whether these lines are the only lines in the α_1 pattern or whether the pattern is incomplete is not clear. To some extent this reference is self-contradictory, for the same patent states earlier that the α form is an amorphous powder; thus to some extent this pattern for α must be suspect. However, the Japanese equivalent of this patent[40b] is extensively quoted in subsequent patents[41,42] in which there is a pattern of a second β form, β_2. A later reference[43] includes a diffractometer trace for a poorly crystalline α phase, α_2, and this pattern is not the same as that for α_1. It also includes a trace for a new β phase, β_3, as well as for β_1 and β_2. Subsequently a β_4 phase has also been reported.[44] In addition to these patterns of the Na_2 salt, patterns are also available for three β forms of the acid (10; R = R' = anilino, M = H).[45]

The second common group for which there are X-ray powder data is
(10; R = PhNH; R' = morpholino; M = H) and its salts. For the acid
itself one patent gives patterns for both the α (two lines) and β_1 (six lines)
forms,[46] and a second gives the patterns for three β forms, obtained under
different conditions of pH and temperature.[47] However, detailed examination indicates that for the second of these the six strongest lines coincide
with those given for the β_1 form in the earlier patent[46]; thus it would
appear that there are only three β forms for which X-ray data exist.

Both the α and β forms of the Na$_2$ salt have been characterized, the latter
twice independently.[48,49] Neither of the β patterns contains a list of the
intensities, but the spacings indicate that the patterns are probably the same.

Powder data (interplanar spacings only) also exist for the α and β forms
of (10; R = o-toluidino, R' = morpholino, M = Na),[50] the β form of the
K$_2$ salt (same pattern as the Na$_2$ salt, but no intensities are given),[51] and
the β forms of the K$_2$ salts of the m- and p-toluidine analogues.[50,51]

The terminology in a patent[52] for (10; R = NHPh, R' = N(CH$_3$)
CH$_2$CH$_2$OH, M = Na) is unusual; the patent contains powder data
for the yellow form and a white form. However, the white form is not a
polymorph of the yellow, but a monohydrate, not anhydrous; in addition
the white form is termed the "α modification."

In addition, X-ray powder diffraction data also exist for several other
variations of (10).[53]

2.6   Diphenylmethane and Triphenylmethane Dyes

Data are availabie for four CI Basic Dyes; Yellow 2 (CI 41000) (DF
18-1551), Green 4 (CI 42000) (DF 9-814), Green 1 (CI 42040) (DF 9-799),
and Violet 1 (CI 42535) (DF 9-811; 9-812). Commercial Methyl Violet is a
mixture and, of course, as the proportion of the constituents alters, so will
the pattern. However, the two patterns recorded have good agreement of
the strongest lines, but they are from the same investigators.

2.7   Quinacridones

In spite of the commercial importance and the amount of work carried out
on quinacridones, all are placed into two classes (cf. CSD V, p. 402).
The unsubstituted linear trans-quinacridone is CI Pigment Violet 19
(CI 46500), and a substituted product is CI Pigment Red 122.

2.7.1   Linear trans-Quinacridone.   There is some evidence for the ex-
istence of seven polymorphs, α, α', β, γ, γ', δ, and ϵ. Quinacridone is
surely one of the most X-rayed pigments, but not all the references make

it clear whether the pattern given is a redetermination or merely a quotation from another source. In these circumstances it has been decided to reexamine and tabulate the X-ray powder data for each polymorph (Table 10.1), but list the references which include a copy of the pattern, regardless of whether it is a redetermination. It is notable that references from the same company tend to reproduce the same pattern.

For α-quinacridone the numerous sources[24,54−69] are in very good agreement, but the pattern preferred is that due to Du Pont,[60−63] simply because the intensities may be measured from the given trace, and all other patterns agree with one exception[56,57] in which there are two extra weak lines. These could be due to better discrimination or a slight impurity. The various patterns of α'-quinacridone are identical.[56−59]

Although the number of lines with interplanar spacing greater than 3.3 Å in reported patterns of β-quinacridone varies from four to seven,[58−72] this is not important because the additional lines are invariably weak. The pattern given in Table 10.1 is a combination of two, the more intense lines being from one source[60−63] and the weaker ones from another.[71] The extra lines are less intense than the line at 4.06 Å. The pattern of γ-quinacridone[58−69,73−81] is well characterized; the only difference is the order of strength of the two most intense lines; both lists of intensities are included in the table.[60−63,81] The extra line in one is due to better resolution of the lines at 3.37 Å. It is the first column of intensities that should be compared with γ', because these are from the same source.[81] Unfortunately γ' is not characterized very well[81−84]; the only differences between the patterns of γ and γ' are an incompletely resolved doublet in γ at an interplanar spacing of approximately 6.5 A replaced by an incompletely resolved triplet in γ' and a small reversal of the intensities of the peaks at 3.56 and 3.74 Å. Both these differences could be attributed to γ' giving a better resolved pattern than γ, which may be because of either larger particle size or better crystallinity. The particle size of the γ'-quinacridone X-rayed was in the range 0.3–0.7 μ[101]; the particle size of the γ form is not mentioned, but commercially is often about 0.1 μ. However, it is claimed[81] that there are differences between the patterns "even when the particles are present in the same order of magnitude." Nevertheless there is the possibility of confusing the patterns of γ and γ', especially if the particle size or crystallinity is different.

The patterns for the δ form[58,59,68,69,85] are not identical, but there is agreement on the more intense peaks. The one recommended is that containing most peaks[85]; the others have some of the weaker ones missing. Whether the presence of more peaks is due to better discrimination or a slight impurity cannot be said. There are only two reports of the ϵ form, both by the same investigators.[69]

Table 10.1 Patterns of Unsubstituted Linear trans-Quinacridone[a]

α d	α I	α' d	α' I	β d	β I	γ d	γ I	γ I	γ' d	γ' I	δ[b] d	δ[b] I	ε d	ε I
14.24	90	14.3	s	15.23	64	13.60	100	80	13.60	100	15.1	w	14.03	s
7.13	33	7.14	w	7.55	22	6.71	39	34	6.76	39	13.6	m	6.97	m
6.32	67	6.37	s	6.4	w	6.42	56	66	6.66	49	6.63	m	6.46	s
5.30	10	6.15	w	5.47	28	5.25	8	6	6.46	58	6.41	s	5.31	w
4.27	10	5.54	w	4.06	17	4.33	8	6	5.21	10	5.23	w	4.37	w
3.70	w	3.72	w	3.8	w	3.74	25	25	4.33	8	4.36	w	3.74	m
3.56	w	3.54	m	3.31	100	3.56	30	—	3.74	32	4.11	w	3.37	s
3.46	100	3.44	ms			3.38	78	100	3.56	23	4.00	w		
3.20	88	3.37	ms						3.38	86	3.74	m		
		3.31	m								3.64	w		
		3.23	ms								3.55	m		
		3.16	m								3.37	m		
											3.34	s		
											3.28	w		
											3.247	w		
											3.184	wm		
											3.119	w		
											2.948	w		
											2.915	w		
											2.813	w		
											2.413	w		
											2.208	m		
											2.179	w		

[a] w = weak; m = medium; s = strong; ms = medium strong.

2.7.2   Linear cis-Quinacridone. Three forms, α, β, and γ, have been reported.[86]

2.7.3   Substituted Quinacridones. One paper reports 21 traces of substituted linear trans-quinacridones, unfortunately without including values of diffracting angle or interplanar spacing and using its own nomenclature for polymorphs regardless of whether they had been reported elsewhere.[86] In the following discussion, where these notations clash with other authors' nomenclature, the prefix T has been added, such as $T\alpha$. Where there is no clash, the T has been omitted. Forms not named in the original paper have simply been given the next letter in the Greek alphabet in order of discovery.

Chlorine-Substituted Quinacridones. X-ray powder data exist for four forms of 2,9-dichloroquinacridone,[87] termed α, β, γ, and "new." The first three of these are well characterized, but the last gives a poor pattern indicative of small crystallite size. The patterns of β ($\equiv T\alpha$) and γ ($\equiv T\beta$) have been independently confirmed.[86,88] Two forms of 3,10-dichloroquinacridone have been reported[86]; the data are in the form of diffractometer traces. Originally two forms of 4,11-dichloroquinacridone were reported, α and β[89]; the samples included quinacridone and so the patterns are unsatisfactory. These patterns have been reported subsequently,[90] and there appear to be data for five forms α, β, γ, δ, and ϵ. Two forms, α ($\equiv T\alpha$) and δ ($\equiv T\beta$), have been confirmed independently.[86]

Data also exist for 3,4,10,11-tetrachloroquinacridone, 2,3,9,10-tetrachloroquinacridone,[91] one form of each, and for three forms of 1,2,3,8,9,11-hexachloroquinacridone.[92] The latter data are in the form of traces. In addition, decachloroquinacridone has been X-rayed, but this has proved to be disordered, giving a single peak at 3.42 Å.

Methyl-Substituted Quinacridones. One of the earliest sources of X-ray data for 2,9-dimethylquinacridone included data for three polymorphs, termed Forms III, IV, and V.[93] It is claimed that Forms I and II had also been reported in previous patents, but these do not contain any X-ray data. The trace of Form V indicates that it is poorly crystalline and thus could be confused with a pattern from a poorly crystalline or small particle-size Form IV. Thus there must be some doubt as to whether Form V is a polymorph or merely a version of Form IV. The patterns for Forms IV and V have been reported several times, but these may not be independent.[91]

There are two other sources of X-ray data on this compound. In one,[95] the pattern is in good agreement with that for Form III, but with two differences. The specimen is of better crystallinity, and also this pattern lacks the lowest angle line (interplanar spacing 16.3 Å, relative intensity 60% of the maximum). This loss could be owing to the line being outside the range of the apparatus or possibly to an impurity in the earlier pattern. Other than this line, the agreement between these patterns is excellent.

The other source of data for 2,9-dimethylquinacridone[86] gives traces for two polymorphs, Tα and Tβ; that for Tα is in very good agreement with the previous pattern for Form III. However, the length of the trace is such as to indicate that the line at about 16.3 Å is very weak (about 5% of the maximum). Thus it would appear that the original specimen of Form III contained an impurity and its pattern should not be relied on. The most likely explanation of this impurity is that it is Form IV, for the other strong lines of Form IV are superimposed on the strong lines of Form III. The second polymorph, Tβ, is probably Form IV. Although the diffraction peaks are in identical positions, there are slight differences in relative intensities, but it is thought that this is not important in the present case.

In addition to 2,9-dimethylquinacridone, diffractometer traces are available for three polymorphs each of 3,10-dimethylquinacridone and 4,11-dimethylquinacridone.[86] It is worth noting that the pattern for the β form of 3,10-dimethylquinacridone is very similar to that of a 50:50 mixture of the α and γ forms; thus the data must be used with care because they may not represent a polymorph.

X-ray data also exist for four forms of 2,4,9,11-tetramethylquinacridone.[86]

Miscellaneous Substituted Quinacridones. In addition to the substituted quinacridones mentioned above, X-ray data exist for two forms, α and β, of 6,13-dihydroquinacridone[54,96–98]; three forms, α, β, and γ, of 2,9-dimethoxyquinacridone[99a]; two forms of 2,9-dicarboxyquinacridone[99b]; and two forms, α and β, of 2,9-difluoroquinacridone.[99c] In an earlier reference[89] this β form is called α. X-ray analysis has also been carried out on 2,9-bis-trifluoromethylquinacridone for which there are two forms, α and β,[99d] and 3,10-bis-trifluoromethylquinacridone.[99d] It would appear that the latter also exists in two forms, bluish violet and a scarlet; X-ray data are given for the former only.

The pattern for quinacridonequinone has been reported.[100]

In the cases of substitution for nitrogen or carbon atoms in the quinacridone rings, X-ray data have been reported[88] for 2,9-dichlorothiachromonoacridone and 2,9-dichlorobenzobisthiachromone (see *CSD* V, p. 417.). In addition, there are poor patterns available (no intensities given) for unsubstituted and substituted diquinolonopyridone (which may be considered to be a substituted linear *cis*-quinacridone).[101] The data given are for two forms each of diquinolonopyridone and 2,10-dimethoxydiquinolonopyridone and one form each of 2,10-dimethyldiquinolonopyridone and 2,10-dichlorodiquinolonopyridone. The data for diquinolonopyridone could cause confusion because one form gives spacings similar to β-quinacridone, whereas the other is similar to both α- and γ-quinacridone. The absence of intensity measurements adds to this confusion.

2.7.4   Quinacridone Solid Solution or Mixed Crystals. Solid solutions of two or more compounds sometimes give a pattern of one of the compounds or a different pattern. On occasions this different pattern appears to be isomorphous with a completely different compound, for example, 60% quinacridone and 40% 2,9-dichloroquinacridone form a compound whose pattern appears isomorphous with the β form of 2,9-difluoroquinacridone[89]; the original reference says α, but this is the β of a subsequent reference.[99c] On other occasions the pattern of the composition is unique; this section lists those for which distinctive patterns have been reported.

Quinacridone and 4,11-dichloroquinacridone give the same pattern over a composition range of 55–45% and 70–30%. At both these compositions the pattern obtained contains a weak pattern of one of the initial compounds. The same pattern is obtained from certain binary combinations of substituted 4,11-quinacridones with each other, or with quinacridone.[89] Both 60% 2,9-dichlorothiachromonoacridone–40% 2,9-dichloroquinacridone,[88] and 70% 2,9-dichlorothiachromonoacridone–30% 2,9-dichlorobenzobisthiachromone[88] give characteristic patterns.

In addition there is a pattern available for 80% 2-chlorothiachromonoacridone–20% quinacridone[88]; this is said to be nearly identical with that of 2-chlorothiachromonoacridone, but the pattern of the latter does not appear to have been reported.

2.8   Dioxazines

Some X-ray powder work[30,103] has been reported on members of the dioxazine group of dyes, but they are all in the form of powder photographs from which it is not possible to obtain reliable readings; they may be useful for comparison.

2.9   Anthraquinone Compounds

As in the case of monoazo pigments, we have relatively few X-ray data in comparison with the large number of anthraquinone dyes, and there is no logical order in those that have been analyzed. However, with the exception of perylene compounds, which have been treated as a separate group, almost all those for which there are data have been shown to be polymorphic.

Probably the anthraquinone dye that has been most thoroughly investigated is indanthrone (CI Vat Blue 4; CI 69800). According to Kunz[104] there are four forms of this dye, α, β, γ, and γ' (subsequently renamed α, β, γ, and δ by Susich[105]). However, Warwicker[106] could find only two of these, α and δ, and this has been confirmed by Honigmann,[107] who has reported patterns indicating that the β and γ forms are poorly crystalline versions of the α form. The patterns of these two investigators are in reasonable agreement except for the weakest lines. There is another pattern for indanthrone,[108] but in this case the low-angle lines are missing and it does not fit any of the other patterns for α or δ. Unfortunately this pattern is the one in DF 8-580.

Warwicker[106] studied the polymorphism of several other anthraquinone dyes, together with the methods of obtaining the polymorph. It is worth noting that there are only small differences in the X-ray data for the different samples of 4,10-dibromoanthanthrone (CI Vat Orange 3; CI 59300), flavanthrone (CI Vat Yellow 1; CI 70600), violanthrone (CI Vat Blue 20; CI 59800), and isoviolanthrone (CI Vat Violet 10; CI 60000), so that there may be some doubt as to whether these are dimorphic. It is not mentioned that chemical analyses were carried out and so it is possible that some of the samples may contain molecules of crystallization.

Other patterns (one of each) of violanthrone, isoviolanthrone, and pyranthrone (CI Vat Orange 9; CI 59700) have been reported.[109] Unfortunately, these patterns have the low-angle lines missing (the maximum interplanar spacing given is 7.6 Å), and because these are the most useful for diagnostic purposes, the usefulness of the patterns is reduced. Unfortunately these are the ones in DF 4-134, 4-133, and 4-473, respectively. The pattern for violanthrone agrees with Warwicker's, but the other two have substantial differences. It is impossible to say which is correct.

As in the case of azo pigments, one polymorph may be converted to another in one of several ways. One of the commonest is grinding; α_{II} of dichloroindanthrone (CI 69825) is thus obtained from α_{I}.[67] Second forms of 1-amino-4-hydroxy-2-(4'-methylmercapto)phenoxyanthraquinone,[110] CI Vat Red 15 (CI 71100),[111] and the bis-α-anthraquinonylamide of azobenzene-4,4'-dicarboxylic acid are produced by grinding with a mineral salt, in a liquid medium for the first two compounds, and dry at 150–180° for the last.[112] The reported patterns in ref. 110 are poor in that they consist of only three lines. The work on CI Vat Red 15 has been repeated subsequently[113]; the X-ray data are in agreement but are not as comprehensive.

On the other hand, the conversion of the pyrazolone from 1-aminoanthraquinone-2-carboxylic acid and 1-aminoanthraquinone is effected by heating with aluminum chloride in pyridine[114]; the patterns for both forms are given. γ-Phase tri-α-anthraquinonylmelamine is obtained by heating the crude compound either dry[115a] or in the presence of organic liquids.[115b] For 1-(methylamino)anthraquinone (CI Disperse Red 9; CI 60505) the two forms were obtained by recrystallization from n-butanol (Form I) and from the melt (Form II).[10]

An interesting practical example of the importance of polymorphism in anthraquinone dyes was demonstrated by Wegmann,[116] who showed that soaping produces crystallographic changes in three vat dyes: CI Vat Red 44 (*CSD* V, p. 148), its 4'-chloro derivative, and its bis-dimethylsulfamoyl analogue. Unfortunately his X-ray data are in the form of small-scale reproductions of the powder photographs from which it is difficult to obtain absolute data.

In contrast to all the other anthraquinone dyes that have been X-rayed, only one polymorph of 1,4-diaminoanthraquinone (CI Disperse Violet 1; CI 61100) has been reported.[10]

2.10 Perylene Compounds (cf. *CSD* V, 231)

Powder patterns exist for perylene-3,4,9,10-tetracarboxylic acid diimide (CI Pigment Brown 26, CI 71129) and several substitution products: CI Pigment Red 179, 190 and 123 (CI 71130; 71140; 71145).[117–119] In addition two reaction products with distinctive X-ray patterns have been prepared: 15–10% CI Pigment Brown 26—85–90% Pigment Red 179, and 50:50 Pigment Red 190 and 123.[117] The pattern of the latter has been confirmed independently.[118] There is good agreement between the two patterns, but one reference gives an extra weak line.[118]

The patterns for the two polymorphs of the diimide from 4-aminoazobenzene are given in the form of diffractometer traces.[120]

2.11 Indigoids

Indigo (CI Vat Blue 1; CI 73000) can be prepared in both the *cis* and *trans* forms, but the latter is the normal form (*CSD* II, p. 1010). Single-crystal X-ray studies[121,122] indicate the existence of two polymorphs of *trans*-indigo, Forms I and II, and from the unit cell dimensions given it is possible to calculate the permissible spacings in the powder pattern. Although this calculation gives similar lists, the differences suggest that both the powder patterns reported[10,123] are for Form II.[122] Comparison of the two observed patterns gives good agreement for the strong lines, but one[123] gives an extra weak line at an interplanar spacing of 6.69 Å. This line is forbidden in both forms and hence this specimen is not crystallographically pure. The color and pattern of this dye changes when heated to 340°.[10]

The only other member of this group for which data have been reported is 6,6′-diethoxythioindigo (CI Vat Orange 5; CI 73335), which exists in four polymorphs, each with its own characteristic pattern.[124] The pattern of one of these forms (β) has been confirmed by another investigation.[10]

2.12 Phthalocyanines

The phthalocyanines, an important class of pigments, have been extensively investigated by X-ray powder techniques. Metal-free, as well as many of the metal, phthalocyanines exhibit polymorphism, and these polymorphs are often isomorphs when the metal atom is removed or interchanged.

2.12.1 Metal-Free Phthalocyanine.   The first evidence of polymorphism was due to Susich,[105] who claimed that there were three polymorphs, α, β, and γ, but subsequently Honigmann[125] showed that the γ phase is a poorly crystalline form of the α, and later another polymorph, X phase, was produced.[126] Diffractometer traces for all three exist. The patterns for the α and β forms have subsequently been confirmed.[127] There is a pattern for an unstated form of metal-free phthalocyanine in DF 2-312 that suggests it is mainly the β form, but with a few extra lines that may be α.

Bansho, Sekiguchi, and Yamashita[127] also examined phthalocyanine sulfate, which is green; the positions of the lines in the pattern bear some relation to that of α-phthalocyanine, but the intensities are different, especially in the low-angle region.

2.12.2 Copper Phthalocyanine and its Derivatives.   Nine forms of copper phthalocyanine (CI Pigment Blue 15; CI 74160) have been claimed to exist at various times. Most processes initially yield a green shade, β form, but other forms may be prepared from this. The commonest modification, a red shade or α form, was first reported by Susich.[105] Sometimes the nomenclature of these two shades is reversed; and care must be taken to distinguish them. Seven more polymorphs have been claimed: a γ form, an R form which has subsequently been renamed ε-form,[128] two unrelated δ forms, a "new" form, an X form, and a π form.

As in the case of the linear *trans*-quinacridones, there have been many patterns reported; as a result it has been decided to reexamine and tabulate the best data for each (Table 10.2), but list the references that include data for that polymorph. In general, the various patterns for the same polymorph agree with each other after allowance for either variation in resolution and/or discrimination owing to different apparatus or crystallinity. In general the patterns chosen are those with better resolution or discrimination.

Table 10.2   X-Ray Powder Data for the Polymorphs of Copper Phthalocyanine

α		β		γ		δ_B	
d	I	d	I	d	I	d	I
13.0	100	12.7	100	13.5	100	15.3	6
12.1	71	9.64	67	12.0	99	11.5	36
8.85	17	8.46	10	9.12	22	7.85	6
6.55	vw	7.20	10	8.51	16	7.5	1
6.02	vw	5.76	3	6.55	vw	5.87	2
5.70	16	4.91	13	5.57	54	5.05	6
5.49	14	4.82	12	4.17	7	4.38	1
4.09	vw	4.17	7	3.85	vw	3.78	2
3.72	14	3.86	9	3.74	22	3.51	2
3.57	13	3.75	29	3.57	39	3.07	2
3.35	22	3.42	17	3.38	62		
3.24	24	3.19	7	3.22	26		
		2.94	12	2.95	16		

δ_K		R or ε		X		π	
d	I	d	I	d	I	d	I
12.0	100	11.6	100	11.6	61	17.4	26
9.55	82	9.67	93	9.20	39	13.2	13
7.78	2	6.24	7	6.19	5	9.93	44
6.24	6	5.27	9	4.98	6	9.76	25
5.18	7	5.07	15			8.90	21
5.07	10	4.35	6			8.14	5
4.31	4	4.17	8			5.14	11
4.17	7	4.05	14			3.83	3
4.08	7	3.77	14				
3.76	6	3.30	11				
3.43	4	3.14	18				
3.24	7	2.96	13				
3.11	9						
2.97	6						

The pattern suggested for the α form[24,129–145] is a combination of two sources[142,144] one[142] being used for the stronger lines and the other[144] for the weaker; that for the β form[24,135–143,146] is a reinterpretation of a trace due to Knudsen, Rolskov, and Lyng.[140] These two forms are the only ones in DF 22-1686 and 11-893; the pattern for α is one of those[144] used in Table 10.2, but the intensities are assessed on a coarse scale and thus the present pattern is preferred. On the other hand, the pattern for β has slightly better discrimination.

According to Honigmann, Lenné, and Schödel,[144] α and γ copper phthalocyanine are structurally similar, and therefore they prefer the nomenclature α_I and α_{II}; however, regardless of the similar structure the powder patterns are completely different and the original nomenclature is retained. There are several patterns for the γ form,[24,139–145,147–151] but that preferred is again a combination of two[144,147]; one[147] is used for the stronger lines and the other[144] for the weaker.

The two δ forms are unrelated and Booth[152] has suggested that they should be termed δ_B[24,139,153] and δ_K.[140,141,146] The pattern recommended for δ_B is that due to Honigmann,[139] because the original[153] does not include an estimate of the intensities. The figures for the pattern of δ_K are taken from the original.[140] The other reports are in agreement.

The pattern given for the R (or ϵ) form is from the original.[142] The other patterns[24,139,146,154,155] are in good agreement. Comparison of the figures in Table 10.2 indicates that the patterns of δ_K and R (or ϵ) are very similar; the differences of intensities can be accounted for by the latter having a larger particle size or better crystallinity. This view is reinforced by examining the original traces of δ_K[140] and R,[142] these show that the traces are virtually identical and the latter has better crystallinity. Thus it would appear that δ_K and R (or ϵ) forms are structurally identical and not independent polymorphs.

Both X and π forms have been reported only once[143]; the traces have been reinterpreted and included for completeness.

Examination of its original pattern indicates that the "new" form[144] is a poorly crystalline form of α. In fact, comparison with a series of traces of α of different particle size[139] indicates very good agreement. Because of this it would be unwise to accept this as an independent polymorph.

In addition to copper phthalocyanine itself, X-ray powder data exist for several derivatives, mainly halides, but also acid salts and an oxidation product. The main trouble with some of these compounds is that it is not always clear whether the chemical formula given corresponds to the pure compound or to a mixture of several isomers with an average composition given by the formula. This, of course, will have an effect on the reproducibility of the patterns.

Patterns have been reported[145] for two forms (α_I and α_{II}) of 4-monochloro copper phthalocyanine (CI Pigment Blue 15; CI 74250) and a diffractometer trace for a third, α_{III}.[139] In addition, the latter author has reported a pattern for 4-tetrachloro copper phthalocyanine[144] and a trace[125] for hexadecachloro copper phthalocyanine (CI Pigment Green 7; CI 74260). Shigemitsu[137] has reported traces for two forms each of 3-tetrachloro, 4-tetrachloro, 3,6-octachloro, and 4,5-octachloro copper phthalocyanine, and three forms of hexadecachloro copper phthalocyanine. Of these, one form only of 4-tetrachloro copper phthalocyanine is in common with the results of Honigmann.[144] Unfortunately the traces are not of sufficient quality to reinterpret, but the positions of the strongest peaks are indicated on the traces.

Traces exist for 4-monobromo, 4-tetrabromo copper phthalocyanine, a brominated compound containing 12 Br (eight in position 4, and four in position 5), and a hexadecabromo compound.[129] The color of these compounds varies from blue, when there are four Br per molecule, to a yellowish green when there are 16. Of these only the first and the last are sufficiently crystalline to give useful patterns; the tetrabromo compound gives only one peak (3.33 Å), whereas the dodecabromo gives two (3.46 and 2.81 Å).

Traces have been reported of 4-tetraiodo, 4,5-octaiodo, 3,6-octaiodo, 3,4-octaiodo, and a polyiodo copper phthalocyanine (13 I per molecule.)[156] The latter is almost certainly not a pure compound, for the attempt was to prepare an I_{16} derivative, but there was always a loss of iodine. Essentially only polyiodo copper phthalocyanine is crystalline, the others giving a single diffuse peak in the neighborhood of 3.4–3.5 Å.

The most extensively studied copper phthalocyanine acid salt is the monosulfate.[145,148,149,157] The pattern is similar to that for γ-copper phthalocyanine, but with a slight shift of the lines to the low-angle side of the pattern. This could be due to a slight expansion of the unit cell to accommodate the extra atoms, and it would appear that the sulfate group has stabilized the molecular configuration of the γ form. This close relationship of γ-copper phthalocyanine and the monosulfate is supported by the fact that either can be obtained from α-copper phthalocyanine using the same reaction; the γ form is formed up to 110° and the monosulfate at 120° and above.[158]

In addition, X-ray diffractometer traces have been obtained from copper phthalocyanine orthophosphate, pyrophosphate, chlorosulfonate, and perchlorate.[158] The traces of the first two are very similar.

The oxidation product of copper phthalocyanine with nitric acid at −5° has also been examined.[132] This is a red-purple powder, $C_{32}H_{16}N_8Cu \cdot (OH)_2$. A sandwich structure, H_2O-CuPc ← O_2 → CuPc-H_2O, has been proposed for this compound.

2.12.3 Nickel Phthalocyanine (CI 74160.1). X-ray data indicate the existence of three polymorphs, α,[136] $β^{136}$ (DF 11-744), and γ.[15] That for the α polymorph is in the form of a small-scale trace, which indicates that it is isomorphous with α-copper phthalocyanine.

2.12.4 Cobalt Phthalocyanine (CI 74160.2) **and Its Derivatives.** There would appear to be four polymorphs, α, β, X, and π. Patterns of the α and

β forms have been obtained several times independently,[136,159] but generally the α form is poorly crystalline; the traces of the X and π forms have been reported once.[143] There is general agreement between the various patterns for both the α and β forms (DF 22-1663; 14-948).

Several oxidation products of cobalt phthalocyanine have been studied by X-ray diffraction. With nitric acid one of two products may be obtained, depending on the reaction temperature.[159] At $-5°$ a purple powder, $C_{32}H_{18}O_2N_8Co$, is obtained. This is the cobalt analogue, Co-Pc-Ox(A), of the corresponding copper phthalocyanine oxide, presumably with a similar X-ray pattern although one is not given. However, at 20° a yellow-brown powder is obtained of empirical formula $C_{32}H_{24}O_6N_8Co \cdot NO_3$ [Co-Pc-Ox(B')].

When cobalt phthalocyanine is oxidized with a mixture of potassium manganate and sulfuric acid, a dark brown compound [Co-Pc-Ox(B)], $C_{32}H_{20}O_4N_8Co \cdot \frac{1}{2}SO_4$, is obtained.[160]

Another pigment has been prepared by combining cobalt phthalocyanine with a phthaloyl group to give a yellow-brown powder, $C_{40}H_{26}O_4N_{10}Co.NO_3$ or $C_{40}H_{26}O_4N_{10}Co \cdot Cl$. X-ray patterns[161] indicate that the former is amorphous, whereas the latter is crystalline.

2.12.5 Miscellaneous Phthalocyanines. Although it is not a pigment some interesting work has been carried out on zinc phthalocyanine.[162] The polymorphic transformation of the α form, when dispersed in various organic media, was studied. In many cases the resulting powder was the β form, but if the solvent had strong electron-donating properties, the precipitates were complexes of zinc phthalocyanine and the solvent. The report[162] contains the patterns of α- and β-zinc phthalocyanine and the complexes resulting from suspension in various bases and solvents. The report also includes small-scale traces of two further polymorphs of zinc phthalocyanine (designated X and θ), but neither was obtained in a pure form.

There are data available for α- and β-chromium(II) phthalocyanine and an oxidation product containing one atom of oxygen per phthalocyanine molecule (designated Cr-Pc-OH).[163] The same reference[163] contains a pattern of α-iron phthalocyanine; the pattern for β-iron phthalocyanine is available in DF 14-926. The only form of platinum phthalocyanine has been shown to be isomorphous with γ-copper phthalocyanine.[144]

X-ray data are also available for two forms of titanium phthalocyanine chloride, $C_{32}H_{16}N_8TiCl_3$.[164]

2.13 Coumarins

The pattern of coumarin (DF 11-704) and of three substituted coumarins[165] that are fluorescent brightening agents, have been reported. All three are polymorphic, but only the four strongest lines of each of these are given.

2.14 Indicators

Powder data are available for four indicators: Bromophenol Blue (DF 9-809), Bromothymol Blue (DF 9-824), Phenolphthalein (DF 4-307), and Thymol Blue (DF 11-844).

2.15 Miscellaneous Compounds

X-ray powder data are available for β-carotene (CI Food Orange 5; CI 40800) (DF 14-912); Fluorescein (CI Solvent Yellow 94; CI 45350) (DF 9-817); Acriflavine (CI 46000) (DF 10-806); Gallocyanine (CI Mordant Blue 10; CI 51030) (DF 4-0534); and Rhodamine B (CI Basic Violet 10; CI 45170) (DF 4-0211). Data are available for Methylene Blue as the chloride trihydrate (DF 9-803); CI Basic Blue 9 (CI 52015) is the salt with zinc chloride.

Data are available for 5,7,5',7'-tetrahalo-8,8'-dihydroxynaphthazine.[166] Patterns (five or six strongest lines) are given for one form of the tetrachloro and two forms of both the tetrabromo and the tetraiodo compounds. In addition the source reports patterns of the dichlorodibromo, trichloroiodo, and dibromodiiodo compounds. However, the last three are probably not single phases but a mixture of isomers.

The 1:2 Ni complex of 1-nitroso-2-naphthol has been prepared in a new crystal form; the powder patterns have been reported, but not the intensities.[167]

REFERENCES

1. H. P. Klug and L. E. Alexander, *X-ray Diffraction Procedures for Polycrystalline and Amorphous Materials*, Wiley, New York, 1954.
2. H. S. Peiser, H. P. Rooksby, and A. J. C. Wilson, Eds., *X-ray Diffraction by Polycrystalline Materials*, The Institute of Physics, London, 1956.
3. L. V. Azároff and M. J. Buerger, *The Powder Method in X-ray Crystallography*, McGraw-Hill, New York, 1958.
4. E. W. Nuffield, *X-ray Diffraction Methods*, Wiley, New York, 1966.

5. H. Lipson and H. Steeple, *Interpretation of X-ray Powder Diffraction Patterns*, Macmillan, London, 1970.

6. J. W. Jeffrey, *Methods in X-ray Crystallography*, Academic Press, New York, 1971.

7. V. Vand, in ref. 2, pp. 512–522.

8. G. Susich, *Anal. Chem.*, **22**, 425 (1950).

9. W. Parrish quoted in G. W. Brindley, *Norelco Reporter*, **4**, 71 (1957).

10. F. Jones and L. Flores, *J. Soc. Dyers Colour.*, **88**, 101 (1972).

11. H. Burkhard, C. Muller, and O. Senn (to S), *BP* 1,040,607.

12. Y. Bansho, et al., *Kogyo Kagaku Zasshi*, **67**, (a) 190, (b) 193 (1964); (c) **70**, 1711 (1967).

13. E. S. Lisitsyna, et al., *Zh. Prikl. Khim. Leningrad*, **47**, 1882 (1974); *CA*, **82**, 74543 (1975).

14. FH, *FP* 2,128,651 (1972).

15. FH, *FP* 2,105,194 (1972).

16. G. Lamm and H. Preugschas (to BASF), *DBP* 2,224,447.

17. L. von Rambach, E. Daubach, and B. Honigmann (to BASF), *DBP* 2,249,739.

18. A. R. Hanke (to DuP), *USP* 2,687,410.

19. W. Biedermann, *J. Soc. Dyers Colour.*, **87**, 105 (1971).

20. E. Daubach, B. Honigmann, and L. von Rambach (to BASF), *DBP* 2,336,717.

21. H. Preugschas, E. Daubach, B. Honigmann, and H. Weber (to BASF), *DBP* 2,323,759.

22. E. Daubach, B. Honigmann, H. Preugschas, and H. Weber (to BASF), *DBP* 2,251,706.

23. W. Groebke (to S), *SP* 559,767.

24. W. Herbst and K. Merkle, *Deutsche Farben-Zeitschrift*, **8**, 365 (1970).

25. S. J. Chapman and A. Whitaker, *J. Soc. Dyers Colour.*, **87**, 120 (1971).

26. A. Whitaker, *J. Appl. Cryst.*, **8**, 565 (1975).

27. F. H. Chung, *J. Appl. Cryst.*, **4**, 79 (1971).

28. A. Whitaker, *J. Appl. Cryst.*, **8**, 69 (1975).

29. W. Gerstner, *J.O.C.C.A.*, **49**, 954 (1966).

30. A. Pugin, *Chimia (Suppl.)*, 54 (1968).

31. R. Sommer, J. Schulze, and G. Wolfrum (to FBy), *DBP* 2,313,356.

32. R. D. Gano (to DuP), *USP* 3,004,821.

33. P. Müller and W. Müller (to CGY), *DBP* 2,344,313.

34. K. Tanaka, M. Haginoya, and E. Nakajima, *Shikizai Kyokaishi*, **41**, 116 (1968); *CA*, **69**, 78429 (1968).

35. K. Tanaka, K. Takagi, M. Haginoya, and E. Nakajima (to DIC), (a) *JP* 26371 (1973), *CA*, **80**, 134914 (1974); (b) *JP* 26372 (1973); *CA*, **80**, 134913 (1974).

36. K. Tanaka, K. Takagi, M. Haginoya, and E. Nakajima, *Shikizai Kyokaishi*, **36**, 392 (1963); *CA*, **66**, 86581 (1967).

37. L. J. E. Hofer and W. C. Peebles, *Anal. Chem.*, **27**, 1852 (1955).

38. N. B. Chanh, Y. Bouillaud, and P. Lencrerot, *J. Chim. Phys.*, **67**, 1198 (1970).

39. I. Schnopper, J. O. Broussard, and C. K. LaForgia, *Anal. Chem.*, **31**, 1542 (1959).

40. C. J. Tscharner, R. E. Stahlbush, and H. Driver (to Gy), (a) *FP* 1,361,065; (b) *JP* 28117 (1964).

41. K. Obayashi and K. Ishihara (to NSK), *JP* 9740 (1969), *CA*, **71**, 92664 (1969); *JP* 2661 (1970), *CA*, **72**, 122933 (1970); *JP* 2664 (1970), *CA*, **72**, 122932 (1970).

42. A. Yamane (to NSK), *JP* 38421 (1971); *CA*, **76**, 87179 (1972).

43. K. Okawa, A. Matsuo, and N. Obayashi (to NSK), *JP* 1894 (1970); *CA*, **73**, 4962 (1970).

44. H. Inoue and N. Tsuruta (to KYK), *JP* 27123 (1972); *CA*, **78**, 99061 (1973).

45. CGY, *BP* 1,355,219.

46. K. Obayashi and K. Ishihara (to NSK), *JP* 21859 (1969); *CA*, **72**, 112805 (1970).

47. Agripat, *BP* 1,301,429.

48. K. Okawa, et al (to NSK), *JP* 1897 (1970), *CA*, **73**, 4961 (1970); *BP* 1,254,252; NSK, *BP* 1,254,241.

49. J. W. Delaney, N. N. Crounce, J. C. Heath, and R. E. Werner (to Sterling Drug Co.), *BP* 1,093,507.

50. M. Matsuo and T. Sakaguchi (to NSK), *Japah Kokai* 28033 (1973); *CA*, **79**, 106151 (1973).

51. A. Yamane, K. Yamakawa, and M. Matsuo (to NSK), *Japan Kokai* 28030 (1973); *CA*, **79**, 67827 (1973).

52. Gy, *BP* 1,116,619.

53. CGY, *BP* 1,353,690; 1,355,218; 1,354,382.

54. W. S. Struve (to DuP), *USP* 3,009,916.

55. S. Ohira, M. Arai, and M. Sugimoto [to KKK(D)], *JP* 1709 (1969); *CA*, **70**, 97955 (1969).

56. Ciba, *BP* 986,737.

57. H. Streiff (to CIBA), *USP* 3,259,630.

58. A. P. Wagener (to SW), *USP* 3,547,925.

59. A. P. Wagener (to SW), *USP* 3,657,248.

60. A. D. Reidinger and W. S. Struve (to DuP), *USP* 2,844,484.

61. W. S. Struve (to DuP), *USP* 2,844,485.

62. C. W. Manger and W. S. Struve (to DuP), *USP* 2,844,581.

63. DuP, *BP* 828,052.

64. P. H. Griswold, F. F. Ehrich, and W. S. Struve (to DuP), *USP* 2,969,366.

65. W. S. Struve, C. W. Manger, and A. D. Reidinger (to DuP), *DBP* 1,137,156.

66. DuP, *BP* 911,881.

67. W. F. Spengeman, *Paint and Varnish Production*, **60**, 37 (1970).

68. H. R. Schweizer (to EKCo), *FP* 1,352,663; *CP* 695,729; *BP* 1,030,757; *USP* 3,272,821.

69. K. Hashizume, et al., [to KKK(T)], *JP* 20916 (1971); *CA*, **75**, 78140 (1971); *BP* 1,243,652.

70. FH, *BP* 943,597.

71. NAC, *BP* 948,307.

72. FH, *BP* 951,451.

73. DuP, *BP* 851,976.

74. FH, *FP* 1,254,049; *BP* 948,487; *BP* 976,553; *BP* 1,002,641.

75. A. Schuhmacher and A. Ekhardt (to BASF), *DBP* 1,177,268.

76. K. Yabe, et al. [to KKK(T)], *JP* 6098 (1965); *CA*, **63**, 15021 (1965).

77. Tekkosha, *BP* 1,110,997.

78. H. Tanaka, S. Ohira, and M. Arai [to KKK(D)], *JP* 1704 (1969); *CA*, **70**, 97954 (1969).

79. K. Adachi, et al., (to Tekkosha), *JP* 16343 (1970); *CA*, **73**, 57272 (1971).

80. K. Adachi, M. Kawai, and M. Hoshikawa (to Tekkosha), *JP* 9101 (1972); *CA*, **77**, 63341 (1973).

81. W. Deuschel, et al., (to BASF), *USP* 3,074,950; *BP* 945,675; *DBP* 1,183,884.

82. Acna, *BP* 1,069,753; *USP* 3,372,163 (1968).

83. M. Shigemitsu, et al., [to KKK(T)], *JP* 22420 (1969); *CA*, **71**, 125994 (1969).

84. H. R. Schweizer (to EKCo), *BP* 1,125,577.

85. G. Bock, B. Honigmann, and W. Deuschel (to BASF), *BeP* 625,666.

86. K. Takagi, K. Kurosu, and I. Fujii, *Shikizai Kyokaishi*, **41**, 437 (1968).

87. W. Deuschel, et al., (to BASF), *BP* 923,069.

88. D. G. Wilkinson (to ICI), *BP* 968,473.

89. F. F. Ehrich (to DuP), *USP* 3,160,510.

90. A. P. Wagner and G. J. Meisters (to SW), *USP* 3,524,856; 3,547,927-9.

91. S. Arikawa and K. Hashizume [to KKK(T)], *JP* 20072 (1964); *CA*, **62**, 10572 (1965).

92. R. I. Sweet (to DuP), *USP* 3,272,822.

93. J. J. Kelly and V. A. Giambalvo (to CCC), *USP* 3,264,300.

94. CCC, *BP* 1,030,216; 1,051,762; *USP* 3,264,298-9.

95. M. Shigemitsu, et al., [to KKK(T)], *JP* 11248 (1974); *CA*, **81**, 122787 (1974).

96. C. W. Manger and F. F. Ehrich (to DuP), *USP* 3,007,930.

97. Tekkosha, *BP* 1,093,692; 1,106,397.

98. K. Adachi, M. Kawai, M. Hoshikawa, and Tekkosha, *JP* 16340 (1970); *CA*, **73**, 77217 (1970).

99. E. E. Jaffe (to DuP), *USP* (*a*) 3,317,539; (*b*) 3,726,874; (*c*) 3,850,654; (*d*) *CP* 943,961.

100. F. F. Ehrich and W. S. Struve (to DuP), *BP* 1,146,362.

101. C. C. Chen (to DuP), *USP* 3,586,684.

102. D. G. Wilkinson (to ICI), *BP* 1,017,443.

103. A. Pugin, *Offic. Dig., J. Paint Technol., Eng.*, **37**, 782 (1965).

104. M. A. Kunz, *Angew. Chem.*, **52**, 269 (1939).

105. G. von Susich, *FIAT Final Report No. 1313*, **III**, 412 (1948).

106. J. O. Warwicker, *J. Text. Inst.*, **50**, T443 (1959).

107. B. Honigmann, *Farbe Lack*, **70**, 787 (1964).

108. H. Inokuchi, *Bull. Chem. Soc. Japan*, **25**, 28 (1952).

109. H. Akamatu and K. Nagamatsu, *J. Colloid Sci.*, **2**, 593 (1947).

110. W. Gohrbandt, et al., (to FBy), *BP* 1,292,247.

111. M. Nakano, S. Fujioka, and T. Akamatsu (to NSK), *JP* 3081 (1969); *CA*, **71**, 114, 263 (1969).

112. K. Ehrhardt, G. Geiger, and F. Kehrer (to S), *FP* 2,028,279.

113. FH, *FP* 2,104,116.

114. W. Braun and E. Anton (to BASF), *USP* 3,428,647.

115. S. Ooka and K. Sasaki [to KKK(D)], (*a*) JP 33232-3 (1971); *CA*, **76**, 60948 (1972); (*b*) *JP* 34518 (1971); *CA*, **76**, 73749 (1972).

116. J. Wegmann, *J. Soc. Dyers Colour.*, **76**, 282 (1960).

117. H. Gerson, W. E. Bachmann, and P. B. Woodlock (to NAC), *DBP* 1,810,817.

118. P. Ruby and J. J. Kelly (to CCC), *DBP* 2,009,073.

119. E. Anton (to BASF), *BP* 990,503.

120. A. Pugin (to CGY), *USP* 3,697,526.

121. H. von Eller, *Bull. Soc. Chim. France*, **22**, 1426 (1955).

122. H. von Eller-Pandraud, *Bull. Soc. Chim. France*, **25**, 316 (1958).

123. E. L. Prien and C. Frondell, *J. Urology*, **57**, 949 (1947).

124. G. Barlaro, *Jnl. Tinctoria*, **65**, 307 (1968).

125. B. Honigmann, *J. Paint Technol.*, **38**, 77 (1966).

126. J. F. Byrne and P. F. Kurz (to Xerox), *USP* 3,357,989.

127. Y. Bansho, T. Sekiguchi, and M. Yamashita, *Kogyo Kagaku Zasshi*, **65**, 2023 (1962); *CA*, **58**, 12705 (1963).

128. B. Honigmann and J. Kranz (to BASF), *DBP* 2,210,072.

129. Y. Bansho, et al., *Kogyo Kagaku Zasshi*, **65**, 2027 (1962); *CA*, **58**, 12705 (1963).

130. E. Suito and N. Uyeda, *Kolloid-Zeits Zeits. Polymere*, **193**, 97 (1963).

131. M. Ashida, N. Uyeda, and E. Suito, *Bull. Chem. Soc. Japan*, **39**, 2616 (1966).

132. T. Sekiguchi, E. Yamazaki, and Y. Bansho, *Kogyo Kagaku Zasshi*, **70**, 503 (1967); *CA*, **67**, 91666 (1967).

133. S. Suzuki, et al., *Nippon Kagaku Kaishi*, 362 (1975); *CA*, **82**, 157864 (1975).

134. T. Oohara, et al., (to Japan Catalytic Chemical Industry Co.), *Japan Kokai*, 1122-3 (1975); *CA*, **83**, 12209, 12210 (1975).

135. R. H. Wiswall, Jr. (to CCC), *USP* 2,486,351.

136. A. A. Ebert and H. B. Gottlieb, *J. Am. Chem. Soc.*, **74**, 2806 (1952).

137. M. Shigemitsu, *Bull. Chem. Soc. Japan*, **32**, 607 (1959).

138. S. Horiguchi, et al., [to KKK(D)], *DBP* 2,006,707.

139. B. Honigmann, *Ber. Bunsenges. Phys. Chem.*, **71**, 239 (1967).

140. B. I. Knudsen, H. S. Rolskov, and O. Lyng (to KVK), *USP* 3,160,635.

141. S. Horiguchi, et al., [to KKK(D)], *BP* 1,290,922; *JP* 6706 (1970); *CA*, **73**, 16300 (1970).

142. F. L. Pfeiffer (to CCC), *USP* 3,051,721.

143. P. J. Brach and H. A. Six (to Xerox), *DBP* 2,218,767; *USP* 3,708,292.

144. B. Honigmann, H.-U. Lenné, and R. Schödel, *Zeits. Kristallograph.*, **122**, 185 (1965).

145. S. Suzuki, Y. Bansho, and Y. Tanabe, *Kogyo Kogaku Zasshi*, **72**, 720 (1969); *CA*, **72**, 33224 (1970).

146. P. Kienzle, M. Huille, and L. Cabut (to Produits Chimiques Ugine Kuhlmann), *DBP* 2,424,531.

147. J. W. Eastes (to CCC), *USP* 2,770,629.

148. T. Sekiguchi, Y. Bansho, and O. Kaneko, *Kogyo Kagaku Zasshi*, **70**, 499 (1967); *CA*, **67**, 91665 (1967).

149. Y. Arai and T. Sekiguchi, *Tokyo Kogyo Shikensho Hokoku*, **62**, 195 (1967); *CA*, **68**, 31033 (1968).

150. Y. Arai and T. Sekiguchi (to BIT), *JP* 1708 (1969); *CA*, **70**, 97958 (1969).

151. H. Leister and K. Wolf (to FBy), *DBP* 2,104,200.

152. G. Booth, in *CSD* V, p. 247.

153. B. P. Brand (to ICI), *BP* 912,526; *USP* 3,150,150.

154. BASF, *FP* 2,174,089.

155. M. Miyatake, S. Tamura, and S. Ishizuka [to KKK(T)], *Japan Kokai* 76925 (1973); *CA*, **80**, 13496 (1974).

156. S. Suzuki and Y. Bansho, *Kogyo Kagaku Zasshi*, **72**, 712 (1969); *CA*, **72**, 33223 (1970).

157. Y. Bansho, T. Sekiguchi, and S. Suzuki, *Kogyo Kagaku Zasshi*, **65**, 2013 (1962); *CA*, **58**, 12705 (1963).

158. Y. Bansho, T. Sekiguchi, and S. Suzuki, *Kogyo Kagaku Zasshi*, **65**, 2018 (1962); *CA*, **58**, 12705 (1963).

159. T. Sekiguchi, M. Ariya, and Y. Bansho, *Kogyo Kagaku Zasshi*, **70**, 508 (1967); *CA*, **67**, 91667 (1967).

160. T. Sekiguchi, M. Murakami, and Y. Bansho, *Kogyo Kagaku Zasshi*, **70**, 514 (1967); *CA*, **67**, 91668 (1967).

161. T. Sekiguchi, Y. Bansho, and K. Seki, *Kogyo Kagaku Zasshi*, **70**, 519 (1967); *CA*, **67**, 91669 (1967).

162. T. Kobayashi, N. Uyeda, and E. Suito, *J. Phys. Chem.*, **72**, 2446 (1968).

163. C. Ercolani, C. Neri, and P. Porta, *Inorg. Chim. Acta*, **1**, 415 (1967).

164. J. C. Burbach (to UCC), *USP* 3,137,703.

165. U. Claussen (to FBy), *DBP* 2,313,030.

166. P. Mertens and H. Bien (to FBy), *BP* 1,270,173.

167. Hercules, *BP* 1,144,770.

CHAPTER ELEVEN

Chemical Degradation Methods

J. GASPARIČ

1 GENERAL CONSIDERATIONS

1.1 Fundamental Ideas

Chemical degradation methods are based on the degradation of the dye molecule under investigation, resulting in the formation of diagnostically valuable and simple fission products of known structure, the identification of which by means of proper analytical methods gives an idea of the structure of the original molecule. The azo group (N=N), the amide group (CONH), the ester group (COOR), and the olefinic bond are examples of such sites in the dye molecules which can easily be attacked by certain chemical reagents. Reduction, hydrolysis, oxidation, and thermal degradation are the most common reactions used for the cleavage of these bonds. When several bonds of the same type are present, complete degradation to simpler products is possible using one reaction. In other cases, e.g., (1), a systematic series of degradation reactions is required by which certain parts of the molecule are split off successively.

The efficiency of the procedures depends mainly on the methods available for the degradation and the identification of the products formed. Preparative work on a macro or semimicro scale, combined with the time-

$$\text{(A)}-NH \{ O_2S -\bigcirc- N \ddagger N -\bigcirc- CO \} HN -\text{(B)} \quad \begin{array}{l} \text{1. Reduction} \\ \text{2. Alkaline Hydrolysis} \\ \text{3. Acid Hydrolysis} \end{array}$$

3.   1.   2.

(1)

consuming isolation and purification of the degradation products, is used when identification is carried out by the determination of physical constants, spectral analysis, or conversion to derivatives of more suitable analytical properties, and also in cases when their physical and chemical properties have not been described in the literature and no authentic samples are available for analytical comparison. Then their chemical structure must be determined or their supposed identity confirmed by synthesis. Reactions must be used in which the characteristic products are formed in high yield. Usually no general procedure for this preparative work can be given, since both the conditions of the chemical reaction and the methods of isolation of the degradation products vary with individual dyes.

Chromatographic methods of both high separation efficiency and identification ability (PC, TLC, GLC, HPLC) have proved very successful, as in other fields of structural analysis, e.g., of proteins, polysaccharides, and lipids.[1] Chromatographic methods for the evaluation of the products of chemical degradation of dyes enable working on a micro or even ultramicro scale, and also simplify and speed up the whole experimental work. Success depends on the following factors.

1. Only those reactions are chosen in which products characteristic of the given dye structure are formed. In contrast with preparative work it is not necessary that the product of diagnostic value be obtained in good yield, since small amounts of characteristic products can be separated from the bulk of other reaction products and identified on the chromatograms.

2. It is necessary to verify the course of the reaction on a large series of carefully and systematically selected model dyes to prove that the compound found among the reaction products is of diagnostic value for the particular structure under consideration. Sometimes use can be made of a spot or a series of spots (peaks) on chromatograms that are characteristic for a certain structure without knowing to which compound they belong ("fingerprint"). In studying a degradation reaction attention must be directed also to all anomalies: the anomalous course of a reaction can also be characteristic for certain structures. Some examples can be found in

Section 2.1.4. Carefully controlled reaction conditions are always required. Therefore a large collection of authentic model dyes must be available and the procedures must be carried out simultaneously with both the compound investigated and the model compound.

3. For the analysis of the characteristic degradation products (e.g., amines, acids) chromatographic techniques must be found by means of which it is possible to reliably identify the products in the reaction mixture. All compounds that can result from the chemical reaction must be available for chromatographic comparison as authentic standards or in the form of model dyes (to suit point 2).

4. The simplicity of this work leads to many results in a short time. Therefore a faultless system of recording the results is required. Numerous primary aromatic amines can be expected as constituents of azo dyes after reductive cleavage. It is therefore necessary to have not only highly efficient chromatographic systems to differentiate them, but also reliable records of their chromatographic behavior (R_F values and colorations for detection). Tables, "maps," punched cards, or any other convenient systems can be used.

1.2 Experimental Techniques

Although the procedures used for the degradation of dyes are very simple and yield analytical results in a short time, high-quality micropreparative and analytical work is necessary because of the sensitivity of the chromatographic methods. The purity of the sample analyzed must first be verified, since reaction products of the impurities can be the source of false information. All necessary blanks should also be carried out.

Many of the reactions often used, such as the reduction of azo dyes with stannous chloride, zinc and acetic acid, or zinc and ammonia, which require the action of the reagent at normal or slightly elevated temperatures and which are sufficiently fast, can be carried out in small test tubes and the reaction mixture directly spotted on the chromatogram. Should the reaction require prolonged boiling, small flasks fitted with reflux condensers are suitable. When the reaction has to be carried out in a large volume (owing to the sparing solubility of the dye) or when the reaction mixture contains components that can cause complications on chromatograms, it is desirable to extract (after adjusting to the proper pH) the desired product into a small volume of a volatile solvent.

Reactions such as hydrolysis with dilute or conc. hydrochloric acid or with $2.5N$ or 50% potassium hydroxide or destructive reduction with the stannous chloride reagent are carried out at 100–180°. Sealed glass ampuls are suitable for this purpose and are heated in a graphite or aluminum block with bored holes heated electrically and the temperature controlled by a bimetallic element. Safety precautions must be taken (ampul explosion!). For smaller amounts of the reactants glass capillaries can be used from which the reaction mixture is directly spotted on the chromatogram.

Some reactions can be directly carried out on the starting point of the chromatogram. Hydrolysis of several types of dyes in the adsorbed state on silica gel or alumina can serve as an example.[2]

Reactions carried out by thermal treatment, e.g., the pyrohydrolytic procedure,[3,4] are carried out in the apparatus shown in Figure 11.1. The procedure is very simple. Several milligrams of the dye are placed in a glass tube (7 mm i.d., 15 cm long) and the tube is inserted into an electric furnace heated to 300–400°. In 1–2 minutes the reaction is finished and the volatile products distilled or sublimed off and condensed on the cold tube walls. Then the part of the glass tube with the condensate is cut off and the condensate rinsed with benzene (or other suitable solvent) into a micro test tube. This solution can be directly applied to the chromatogram. When less volatile products are formed, the operation can be carried out under reduced pressure. Some nonvolatile products can be obtained for chromatography by treating the residue in the glass tube with an appropriate solvent. In combination with the chromatographic identification of the products this simple procedure represents a valuable tool of structural analysis.

The same experimental technique is used for any other type of dry distillation, e.g., thermal hydrolysis in the adsorbed state of a part of the adsorbent from a chromatographic column, or distillation with soda lime or zinc dust.[5]

Gaseous compounds are sometimes among the degradation products of diagnostic value (CO_2, acetaldehyde). Generally the reaction is carried out in a small ground flask fitted with a capillary for the introduction of an inert carrier gas, a dropping funnel, and a reflux condenser from the top

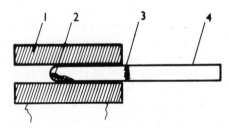

Figure 11.1 Apparatus for the pyrohydrolytic procedure. 1, Electric oven; 2, compound tested; 3, sublimate; 4, glass tube.

of which the gaseous products are transported by the carrier gas to an absorption system.

2 APPLICATION TO DIFFERENT DYE CLASSES

2.1 Azo Dyes

Azo dyes can be easily broken up into simpler constituents by fission of the azo bond by reduction, reaction with cold fuming nitric acid, or thermal degradation. A simple experimental procedure is usually required. The identification of the resulting products, however, has always represented a far more difficult problem, caused by the great variety and often poor stability of the products.[6,7] From the point of view of modern identification methods reductive cleavage and thermal degradation seem to be more advantageous than the nitration process, although nitrous fumes have been used recently.[8] Reactions for splitting off certain other parts of the azo dye molecule are also used.

2.1.1 Reduction. The suitability of a particular reduction procedure depends mostly on the solubility of the dye, the properties of the reduction products (solubility, stability, etc.), and the method of their isolation and/or identification.[9-12] Thus reductions with stannous chloride (90 g $SnCl_2 \cdot 2H_2O$ in 140 ml conc. HCl), zinc dust and dilute acetic acid, or aqueous alkaline hydrosulfite are suitable for acid, reactive, and direct dyes.[13,14,15] Zinc dust and glacial acetic acid[12] are used for disperse and solvent dyes; pigments[11] can be reduced with sodium dithionite and hydroxide in ethanol,[10] dioxane,[9] ethylene or diethylene glycol, or with zinc dust or stannous chloride and hydrochloric acid in the presence of glacial acetic acid and a high-boiling solvent (trichlorobenzene).[14,16]

Simultaneously with the reduction of the azo bond, reduction of other susceptible groups can take place, e.g., of nitro, nitroso, and azoxy groups. Hydrolysis of ester and amide groups must be avoided by the choice of proper experimental conditions. Another side reaction is the cyclization of o-nitroazo compounds to benzotriazoles when alkaline dithionite is used. When the reductive procedure is carried out for a prolonged period at high temperature, further bonds are cleaved. Boiling of pyrazolone azo dyes with conc. ammonia and zinc dust results in the fission of the N—N bond of the pyrazolone ring[17,18] and the formation of the corresponding primary amine which can be easily identified by PC. The pyrazolone derivative (2) can serve as an example.

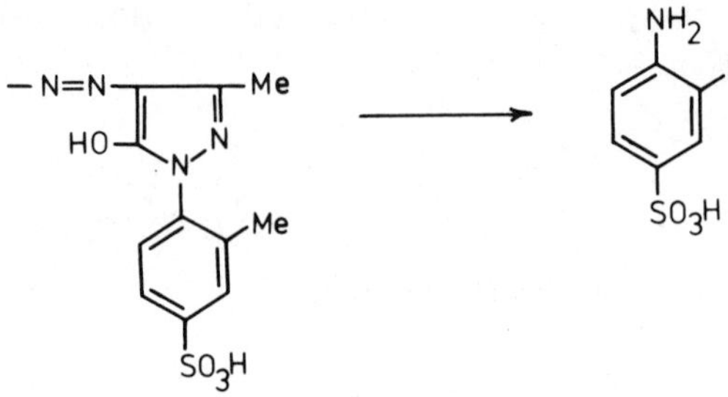

(2)

The next important step following the reductive cleavage is the identification of the reduction products. A variety of methods based on determination of physical constants has been used, but the isolation of the amine or its derivative from the complex reaction mixture was necessary, making the whole procedure laborious and time consuming. Examples of such preparative work with the physical constants and analytical properties of the cleavage products are available.[6,7] The first attempts with PC [14–17,19–25] and TLC[26] produced more promising results. PC has proved to be the most convenient method. It compares favorably with GLC and HPLC because it makes characteristic color reactions possible. Moreover, there are fewer difficulties caused by the high concentration of salts, acids, and alkalis in the solutions dropped on the chromatograms than in TLC.

For a systematic identification the reduction products can be classified into five groups.

Monoamines without Solubilizing Groups. These products present little difficulty. The most efficient PC separation and identification is achieved on paper impregnated with formamide using hexane, benzene, or chloroform as mobile phase.[27,28] For differentiating the more lipophilic compound the solvent system DMF/n-heptane (or n-hexane) can be used. The R_F and typical color reactions of a large number of such amines can be found in the literature.[27,28] All R_F values are in correlation and thus each compound can be taken as a standard for comparison with the unknown reduction product. The development of the chromatogram is carried out in an atmosphere of ammonia so that the mineral acid in the analyzed solution does not interfere and the amines migrate as free bases. Three main color reactions were chosen: (1) reaction with Ehrlich's reagent (*p*-dimethylaminobenzaldehyde); (2) diazotization and coupling; and (3) reaction with 2,4-dinitrobenzenediazonium salt. By means of the last reaction amines with a free and substituted *p*-position can be distinguished.

Mono- and Diamines Containing COOH and/or SO₃H Groups. These compounds are usually common and easily available dye intermediates.

They are water soluble, show no sharp m.p., and can be prepared in analytical-grade purity only with difficulty. PC with solvent systems n-propanol–ammonia (2:1) and n-butanol saturated with 2.5 N hydrochloric acid and the three color reactions described in the preceding paragraph can effect the separation of these amines according to the number of SO_3H and COOH groups (ammoniacal system) and amino groups (HCl system), and their differentiation and identification.[29] The amines of the preceding group do not interfere.

Aminophenols, Di- and Polyamines without Solubilizing Groups. Difficulties with these compounds are caused by their sensitivity to atmospheric oxygen. Only some of them can be chromatographed in the same way as the first-mentioned group of amines, but many disappear during chromatography in neutral or ammoniacal atmosphere or form colored streaks. Solvent systems containing strong hydrochloric acid, e.g., n-propanol–hydrochloric acid (2:1) are more convenient. Specific detection of o-diamines is based on the formation of fluorescent phenazines.[30]

For the tentative identification of a great variety of *N,N*-alkylated *p*-phenylenediamines and aminophenols, obtained, e.g., by the reductive cleavage of disperse dyes, the determination of their basic skeleton can be achieved in the following way: after reduction the diamines and aminophenols (3) are oxidized by ferric chloride to benzoquinones (4), which are converted to 2,4-dinitrophenylhydrazones or the tautomeric hydroxyazo dyes (5) by the action of 2,4-dinitrophenylhydrazine.[12] The procedure is quite simple and the colored products formed can be extracted and identified by PC or TLC.

Amines of the Naphthalene Series. The reduction of acid, direct, and reactive dyes prepared by coupling diazonium salts with naphthol-, naph-

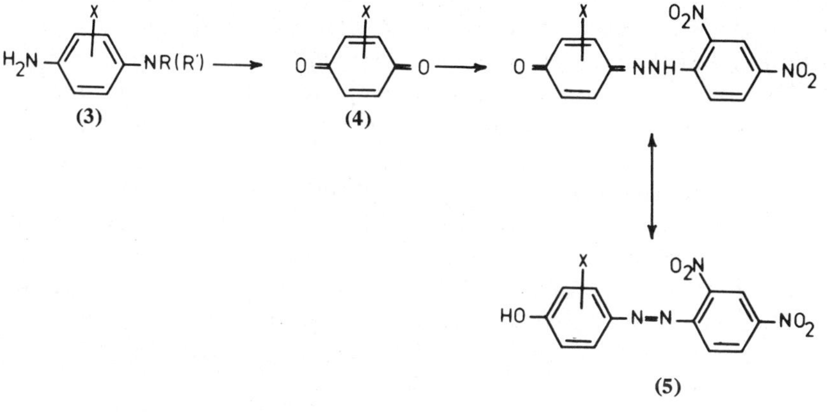

(3)   (4)

(5)

thylamine-, and aminonaphtholsulfonic acids results in the formation of naphthalene derivatives containing mainly different combinations of NH_2, OH, and SO_3H groups. The identification of these compounds is the most troublesome problem. Tin must be removed by electrolysis from the reaction mixture after reduction with stannous chloride when the amino-naphtholsulfonic acids are to be isolated, They have been characterized mostly by color reactions and preparation of derivatives.[6,7] Only a few members of this group can be identified by PC directly. For some dyes the formation of characteristic degradation products after the reaction with stannous chloride at 180–200° can be used.[31] For the identification of some 1,2-, 2,1-aminonaphthol-, and 1,2-diaminonaphthalenesulfonic acids a procedure similar to that described in the preceding paragraph can be used.[32] After reduction the naphthalene derivatives are oxidized with ferric chloride to the corresponding 1,2-naphthoquinonesulfonic acids and then treated with 2,4-dinitrophenylhydrazine.

The 1,2-diamino derivatives of this series are best characterized by condensation with phenanthraquinone to the corresponding quinoxaline derivatives.[6,7]

For the detection of 2,7,8-triamino-1-naphthol-3,6-disulfonic acid the dye is reduced with zinc dust and ammonia and the reaction mixture is immediately applied on a paper chromatogram. The spot turns blue in a few seconds. Overrun development is carried out with the mobile phase n-propanol–ammonia (2:1). The oxidation product of the acid migrates as a characteristic blue spot.

4-Aminopyrazolones. These are obtained by the reductive cleavage of azo dyes from pyrazolones as coupling components. After the reduction of the dye with zinc dust and ammonia, the solution is spotted on filter paper. Treatment with an ammoniacal solution of resorcinol[14] or 1-naphthol[11] produces a red or violet coloration in a few seconds or minutes by the formation of quinoneimine dyes. Pigments of low solubility are reduced with zinc dust at high temperature in DMF and a few drops of ammonia. The identification of the particular aminopyrazolone can be achieved by PC of the quinoneimine dye, using the mobile phase n-propanol–ammonia (2:1).[33]

When the reduction of disperse azo pyrazolone dyes is carried out with zinc dust and glacial acetic acid, and the reaction mixture is spotted on paper impregnated with formamide and developed with n-hexane, benzene, or chloroform in an atmosphere of ammonia, aminopyrazolones migrate as violet spots of the corresponding rubazonic acids with characteristic R_F.

2.1.2 Thermal Degradation.

Methods in which heat is used for partial degradation of the azo dye molecule are included here.

Dealkylation in the Adsorbed State.[2] Azo dyes containing the NRR' group can be dealkylated by a simple thermal treatment in the adsorbed state on silica gel or alumina. Temperatures in the range 110–160° and heating periods of 1–16 hours are used. All three possible dealkylated dyes are found among the reaction products:

$$Ar—N{=}N—Ar'NR(R') \rightarrow Ar—N{=}N—Ar'NH(R)$$
$$+ \; Ar—N{=}N—Ar'NH(R') \rightarrow Ar—N{=}N—Ar'—NH_2$$
$$(R,R' = H, Et, CH_2CH_2CN, CH_2CH_2OH, etc.)$$

It is the water in the substrate and surrounding atmosphere that seems to favor the shift of the equilibrium toward the right. The reaction

$$Ar—N{=}N—Ar'NR(R) + 2\;H_2O \rightleftarrows Ar—N{=}N—Ar'—NH_2 + 2\;ROH$$

can be carried out on a micro scale directly on the starting point of the TLC and the products identified by comparison with the authentic amino compounds, or on a preparative scale by using substrates from column chromatography when the dealkylation products are obtained in amounts sufficient for elemental, IR, and MS analyses.

Thermolytic Fission of the N{=}N Bond.[34] When azo compounds are heated to 300–400° for 1–2 minutes, the cleavage of the azo bond takes place and the corresponding amines are formed. The great advantage of this procedure is that nitro groups remain unchanged. Thus the often used diazo components of disperse dyes and pigments are obtained as the unaltered monoamines (e.g., 2-bromo-4-nitro-6-cyanoaniline, 2,4-dinitro-6-chloroaniline), whereas by reduction they are converted to the corresponding polyamines. Besides the azo bond, $CONR_2$, $COOR$, and SO_2NR_2 groups are cleaved. Secondary and tertiary amides give the corresponding carboxylic acid (or its decarboxylation product) and the amine. Primary amides are dehydrated to the corresponding nitriles.[35] Esters are split only partially if they are volatile enough and escape from the hot reaction zone quickly. Also alkylated sulfonamides are split partially. The results depend on the experimental conditions. Thus the thermolytic fission of the pigment (6) results in 4-cyanoaniline and 2,4-dimethoxy-5-chloroaniline. The same solvent systems are used for PC as described in Section 2.1.1; an atmosphere of ammonia is not required since the amines are present as

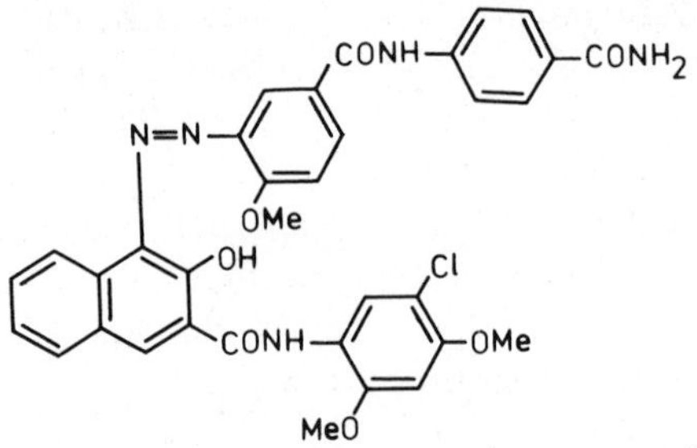

(6)

free bases. No changes in R_F are caused by this modification of the experimental conditions. When a crystalline sublimate is obtained, the procedure can be repeated with further portions of the dye and the product purified by sublimation or crystallization to obtain amounts sufficient for IR, NMR, and MS analyses.

Dry Distillation. Dry distillation with soda lime, anhydrous sodium dihydrogen phosphate,[36] or zinc dust[37] cleaves the azo bond to form amines. In the presence of zinc dust nitro groups were reduced and other changes were observed, but the authors did not work under controlled conditions. Blank experiments[34] have shown that the presence of any of the three agents not only is unnecessary, but rather causes complications.

Pyrolysis. Pyrolysis of simple azo compounds at 700°, followed by GLC coupled with MS, gives more valuable results in comparison with direct fragmentation by electron impact.[38] By the pyrolytic procedure the differentiation of isomeric dyes could be achieved. Thus the isomeric dyes (*m*- or *p*-chloroaniline → dimethylaniline) showed no significant differences in their MS; peaks of $m/e = 42, 77, 105, 111, 120, 148$, and 259 were found in both cases. Among the pyrolysis products the following were common to both dyes: benzene, chlorobenzene, dimethylaniline, and benzonitrile. *m*-Chlorobenzonitrile, however, was found in one case and *p*-chlorobenzonitrile in the other.

Fusion with Aldehydes. The cleavage of azo dyes by fusion with *p*-dimethylaminobenzaldehyde has been described.[39] The corresponding *p*-dimethylaminobenzylideneanilines were the reaction products. In the case of azo pyrazolones the corresponding *p*-dimethylaminobenzylidenepyrazolones (7) were found in the reaction mixture and identified by PC.

$$Me_2N-\!\!\left\langle\!\bigcirc\!\right\rangle\!\!-CH\!-\!\cdots\!-Me$$

(7)

2.1.3 Hydrolysis. Acidic or alkaline hydrolysis is often used for the fission of ester, amide, sulfonamide, and some other bonds in azo dye molecules. The reaction is carried out in aqueous or alcoholic media or in sealed ampuls at high temperature, depending on the dye solubility and the bond stability. Controlled reaction conditions must be used since further degradations can take place, e.g., the fission of the azo bond or heterocyclic rings, or other transformations. The action of mineral acids on azo compounds has been studied extensively.[40-42]

If an ester group is present in the dye molecule as CH_2—COOR, the carboxyl group remains after hydrolysis; but if the group is CH_2—O—COR, the carboxylic acid is split off from the OH group. To differentiate these two structure types[43] hydrolysis is carried out in aqueous or ethanolic media and the reaction mixture analyzed by PC or TLC using n-propanol–ammonia (2:1) as the mobile phase. In the first case the hydrolysis product has a considerably lower R_F than the original dye caused by the free carboxyl group. In the second case the original dye and its hydrolysis product do not differ in their chromatographic behavior under these conditions. The alcohol split off by hydrolysis can be identified by GLC or after conversion to the 3,5-dinitrobenzoate by PC or TLC.[44,45] The acyl group in CH_2—O—COR can be converted to the hydroxamic acid and identified by PC.[12]

For amide bonds, cleavage by alkaline hydrolysis is used. For azo pigments, sodium hydroxide in boiling diethylene glycol is used. Hydrolysis is complete in 30 minutes or less, but the azo bond is cleaved as well.[43] Thus both aniline and $ArNH_2$ are found by PC in the benzene extract of the reduction mixture from the dye ($ArNH_2 \rightarrow$ acetoacetanilide). To differentiate which amine is the diazo component reduction of the pigment with sodium dithionite and hydroxide in diethylene glycol at room temperature is carried out. Further degradation caused by boiling with sodium hydroxide in diethylene glycol can be observed if nitro groups are present. Characteristic spots of such products are found on chromatograms which can be used to identify the original nitroamine.

The detection of ureido groups (Ar—NH—CO—NH$_2$ or Ar—NH—CO—NH—Ar) can be achieved by hydrolysis with 63% sulfuric acid at

160° in a stream of nitrogen and detection of carbon dioxide evolved. The interference of sodium carbonate or bicarbonate, present sometimes in commercial dyes, is eliminated by pretreatment with acetic acid. To avoid the interference of hydrogen chloride evolved with carbon dioxide (sodium chloride or hydrolyzable chlorine in the dye) the gases are bubbled through a solution of silver sulfate.[46]

Hydrolytic procedures are useful also for azo dyes containing the s-triazine[47] or pyrimidine ring.[46] Hydrolytic cleavage of different bonds and the formation of diagnostically valuable products can be achieved under carefully controlled conditions. Hydrolysis of both mono- and dichloro-s-triazine dyes with 1 N hydrochloric acid at 150° in a sealed ampul results in the formation of cyanuric acid which is easily identified by PC and TLC,[48] using the solvent system n-propanol–ammonia (2:1) and by detection with mercuric acetate and diphenylcarbazone at 125°. In the case of metallized dyes demetallization takes place, and the metal ions give specific colorations with appropriate reagents on the chromatograms.

By treatment with 2.5 N potassium hydroxide at 200°, hydrolysis and also further destruction take place, so that only the $ArNH_2$ component bound to the heterocyclic ring can be identified by PC. When the same reagent is used at temperatures of 125–150° the azo dye bound to the triazine ring is split off and can be identified by PC.[46] Demetallization also takes place [cf. (8) → (9)].

(8)   (9)

The di- and tri-halogenopyrimidine reactive dyes give characteristic products of diagnostic value when treated with 1 N hydrochloric acid at 125° in sealed ampuls for 40 minutes. When the same solvent system and method of detection are used in PC and TLC, 3–4 spots can be found on chromatograms. Thus dichloropyrimidine dyes give barbituric acid as the product of complete hydrolysis, and trichloropyrimidine dyes give 5-chloro-barbituric acid and tetrahydroxypyrimidine on chromatograms.

The hydrolysis of sulfonamide bonds is achieved by heating with conc. hydrochloric acid in a sealed ampul at 180° for 1–2 hours. Identification of the aminosulfonic acid is carried out by PC; the aliphatic amine can be identified by PC and the solvent system n-butanol–conc. hydrochloric acid (4:1) and detection with ninhydrin.

The action of stannous chloride and hydrochloric acid on azo dyes in sealed ampuls at 180–200° for 1 hour results in complete destruction of the dye molecule.[17,46] Reduction of azo bonds, nitro groups etc., deacylation, dealkylation, decarboxylation, desulfonation, destruction of heterocyclic rings, splitting off of other groups like NH_2, OH, and halogen, and hydrolysis of ester, amide, and sulfonamide bonds as well as NH_2 groups are reactions involved in this drastic treatment. Halogenation of the reaction products has also been observed. When certain naphthol- or naphthylamine-sulfonic acids are coupling components, simple characteristic products of diagnostic value are found on chromatograms, 1-naphtholsulfonic acids with the azo group in the 2-position give a mixture of 1- and 2-naphthol and 2-naphthylamine; 2-naphtholsulfonic acids with the azo bond in the 1-position give only 2-naphthol; 6-amino-1-naphthol-3-sulfonic acid with the azo group in the 2-position gives a mixture of 2,6-diaminonaphthalene and 2-amino-6-naphthol; 7-amino-1-naphthol-3-sulfonic acid with the azo group in the 2-position gives 2,7-diaminonaphthalene and 2-amino-7-naphthol. Dyes from alkaline coupled H-acid (as well as K-, S-, and SS-acids) give characteristic spots on chromatograms, the identity of which has not yet been established. All these products can be characterized using PC and solvent systems formamide–benzene (NH_3), formamide–chloroform (NH_3), and n-butanol saturated with 2.5 N hydrochloric acid. Detection is carried out by spraying with 2,4-dinitrobenzenediazonium sulfate followed by 5% potassium hydroxide.

Under the same conditions the heterocyclic ring of aminobenzimidazolone present in a series of pigments is split. When the products are chromatographed in n-butanol saturated with 2.5 N hydrochloric acid and detected with Ehrlich's reagent, two characteristic spots (R_F = 0.10 and 0.15, yellow and brown) are found, but their identity has not yet been established.

2.2 Simple Anthraquinonoid Dyes

Hydrolytic or reductive–hydrolytic procedures are of great value for the degradation of anthraquinonoid derivatives containing hydroxyl and substituted amino groups in positions 1, 4, 1, 5, 1, 4, 5, and 1, 4, 5, 8, simple or sometimes more complex alkoxy substituents in position 2, and in acid dyes sulfonic groups. By hydrolysis[19] with hydrochloric acid at 180°, by reductive hydrolysis with stannous chloride and hydrochloric acid at high temperatures,[50] by heating in the adsorbed state on silica gel or alumina,[2] or by pyrohydrolysis,[51] acyl and alkyl groups attached to N or O are split off, and the amino groups converted subseqeuntly to hydroxyl groups. Simple amino-, aminohydroxy-, and hydroxyanthraquinones are formed, which are easily identified by PC or TLC. For the identification of hydroxyanthraquinones (quinizarin, purpurin) PC using 1-bromonaphthalene/80% acetic acid is the best method; for aminoanthraquinones 1-bromonaphthalene/pyridine–water (1:1) is suitable.[52] The liberated aromatic amines are identified by the method previously mentioned, and aliphatic amines by PC with n-butanol–conc. hydrochloric acid (4:1) and detection with ninhydrin.[53]

The behavior of alkyl- or arylaminoanthraquinones on heating with conc. hydrochloric acid or with the stannous chloride–hydrochloric acid reagent in sealed ampuls at 180° can be illustrated with the dyes (10) and (11). The former gives 1-amino-4-hydroxyanthraquinone and quinizarin,

(10)   (11)

and (11) gives purpurin. The reaction is carried out with a few milligrams of the dye and 1–2 ml conc. hydrochloric acid. After the ampul is cooled and opened, the mixture is diluted with a few drops of water and filtered in a microfunnel by suction. The filtrate is analyzed for amines; the usually crystalline precipitate is dissolved in acetone and analyzed for anthraquinone derivatives.

Alkylaminoanthraquinones can be easily dealkylated by heating in the adsorbed state.[2] 1,4-Dialkylamino derivatives undergo a much faster reaction than 1-alkylamino and 1,5-dialkylamino derivatives, which require 16 hours at 150°. The reaction products are analyzed by TLC.

The degradation of simple acylaminoanthraquinones can be achieved similarly by hydrolysis with hydrochloric acid in sealed ampuls at 180° for 1–2 hours[49] or by the pyrohydrolytic procedure.[51] For the determination of the aminoanthraquinone skeleton the hydrolytic procedure is suitable, whereas pyrohydrolysis is preferred for the identification of the acids split off from the acylamino groups. Halogenation of the simple aminoanthraquinones was observed as a side reaction in the hydrochloric acid procedure. When the acylaminoanthraquinones are submitted to pyrohydrolysis as described earlier (Section 1.2), the fission of the amide bond takes place and the volatile products sublime or distill off and condense on the cold walls of the glass tube. A good yield of the acid is usually obtained. Simple volatile anthraquinone derivatives are also present in the condensates in small amounts. Identification of the acids is carried out by PC, TLC, or GLC. If the procedure is repeated several times, amounts sufficient for further purification and elemental or spectral analyses can often be obtained.

Heating of acid anthraquinone dyes (e.g., CI Acid Blue 23, 52, 129) derived from bromaminic and sulfobromaminic acids with stannous chloride and hydrochloric acid to 60° for 30 seconds results in reduction to the corresponding anthrones, followed by splitting off of the sulfonic group in the 2 position and subsequent hydrolysis to the corresponding hydroxyaminoanthrone derivatives. When the reaction mixture is diluted with water, spotted on paper, and developed with n-propanol–ammonia (2:1), the yellow spots turn violet, owing to oxidation to the corresponding aminohydroxyanthraquinones, and migrate with different rates characteristic of compounds with or without a sulfonic group. When this reaction is carried out at 180–200° for 2 hours, quinizarin is formed, indicating the 1,4-diamine structure of the dye. Similarly, the action of boiling nitric acid on 1-amino-2-bromo-4-(p-toluidino)anthraquinone-2'-sulfonic acid results in the formation of 2-bromoquinizarin.[54]

2.3 Polycyclic Dyes

Vat dyes and some types of pigments are discussed here. The poor solubility is decisive for the selection of the proper analytical procedures. Only in some cases is it possible to split the original molecules into simple and readily identifiable compounds. Ozonization of indigoid dyes resulting in the formation of the corresponding isatins is an example[55]; thioindigoid dyes give the corresponding thionaphthenequinones. Many indigoid dyes, on heating with alkali, undergo hydrolytic fission into two components.[56]

For vat dyes containing acylamino groups the pyrohydrolytic procedure can be used to identify the acid part.[51] Hydrolysis with dilute hydrochloric acid at 150° or with conc. acid at 180° can be used for s-triazine derivatives of anthraquinone (e.g., CI 65705, 65710).

Reduction of the polycyclic quinonoid dyes to the parent hydrocarbons is one of the generally applicable methods. The resulting hydrocarbons or their heterocyclic analogues can be identified by PC, TLC, GLC, IR, MS, etc. Zinc dust distillation[5] (see also Section 1.2) and the so-called zinc dust fusion method[57] involving the treatment of the quinone in a melt of zinc dust, zinc chloride, and sodium chloride at 310° represent such versatile procedures. Other reagents are aluminum cyclohexoxide in cyclohexanol,[58] Raney nickel,[59] sodium borohydride and boron trifluoride etherate.[60]

In particular cases of different types of polycyclic dyes individual degradation reactions must be found by which the original dye molecule is degraded to less complex compounds; e.g., anthraquinone–acridone treated by caustic potash fusion gives benzoic acid and acridone-3-carboxylic acid.[54] Some of these products may be uncommon and their structures or identity must be proved by synthesis.

Chemical treatment is often necessary also to achieve transformation to compounds of more suitable physical properties than the original dye; e.g., the NMR and MS of violanthrones can be more conveniently determined after their conversion to the methyl ethers of the leuco derivatives.[61,62]

2.4 Azoic Coupling Components

Structure determination of acetoacetarylamides and arylamides of aromatic o-hydroxy acids used to be achieved mainly by hydrolysis and identification of the acid and the amine formed (*CSD* I, p. 656). Conc. hydrochloric acid at 180°,[63] 50% sodium hydroxide at 180–200° in glass ampuls,[63] distillation with solid sodium hydroxide,[64] and pyrohydrolysis[3,4] have been more recently employed. The pyrohydrolytic procedure with chromatographic evaluation of the degradation products seems to be the most versatile method. When no volatile decarboxylation products of the hydroxyacids are formed, hydrolysis with conc. hydrochloric acid at 180° can be used.

On the other hand, condensation of the arylamides of o-hydroxy-carboxylic acids with 2,4-dinitrochlorobenzene, resulting in the formation of the N-2,4-dinitrophenyl derivatives, followed by mild alkaline hydrolysis, is a useful procedure.[65]

3 CONCLUSIONS

Structure determination of synthetic dyes represents a complex problem because of the great variety of structures and different properties of the dyes investigated, involving their solubility, low volatility, difficulties in preparing samples of analytical purity, etc. Isolation and purification of the dye, the determination of its elementary composition, detection of the basic skeleton or type, and the detection and determination of functional groups or parts of the molecule by chemical and instrumental methods are the main steps. The combination of instrumental and chemical methods and the integrated application of each to a particular problem at a suitable stage of the analysis is the most efficient approach to solve the structural problems of synthetic dyes, completed by the reasonable and careful interpretation of the results and their confirmation by synthesis. Methods using chemical degradation have been used for years to convert the original molecule to more simple products, the identity or structure of which could be determined by available methods. The combination of different degradation methods with the chromatographic evaluation of the degradation products represents a modern, simple, inexpensive, and powerful approach by which reliable and important information about the structures of the dyes can be obtained within a short time. Several examples have been given in preceding sections to show the advantages and scope of this approach.

REFERENCES

1. J. Gasparič, *Adv. Chromatogr.*, **6**, 3 (1968).

2. C. Prandi, *J. Chromatogr.*, **48**, 214 (1970).

3. J. Skutil and J. Gasparič, Czech. Pat. 157934 (2.5.1974).

4. J. Skutil and J. Gasparič, *Mikrochim. Acta*, 828 (1972).

5. J. Gasparič, *Mikrochim. Acta*, 288 (1966).

6. A. Brunner, *Analyse der Azofarbstoffe*, Springer, Berlin, 1929, p. 15.

7. A. G. Green, *The Analysis of Dyestuffs*, 3rd ed., Charles Griffin, London, 1949, p. 117.

8. F. K. Sutcliffe and K. Watkin, *J. Soc. Dyers Colour.*, **84**, 422 (1968).

9. L. Koch and R. F. Milligan, *Anal. Chem.*, **19**, 312 (1947).

10. A. McClure, J. Thomson, and J. Tannahill, *J. Oil Colour Chem. Assoc.*, **51**, 580 (1968).

11. H. Schweppe, *Paint Technol.*, **27**, No. 8, 12 (1963).

12. I. Gemzová and J. Gasparič, *Collect. Czech. Chem. Commun.*, **32**, 2740 (1967).

13. J. Gasparič and A. Cee, *Collect. Czech. Chem. Commun.*, **40**, 371 (1975).

14. F. Mužík and Z. J. Allan, *Collect. Czech. Chem. Commun.*, **22**, 558 (1957).

15. J. Panchartek, Z. J. Allan, and J. Poskočil, *Collect. Czech. Chem. Commun.*, **26**, 268 (1961).

16. F. Mužík, J. Dobrovolný, and M. Veselý, *Chem. Prum.*, **15**, 151 (1965).

17. J. Panchartek, Z. J. Allan, and F. Mužík, *Collect. Czech. Chem. Commun.*, **25**, 2783 (1960).

18. A. Cee and J. Gasparič, *Mikrochim. Acta*, 268 (1966).

19. S. Kitahara and H. Hiyama, *J. Chem. Soc. Japan, Ind. Chem. Sect.*, **58**, 293, 620 (1955); *CA*, **49**, 14327d (1955), **50**, 7463f (1956); *Kogyo Kagaku Zasshi*, **59**, 1187 (1956); *CA*, **52**, 13265h (1958).

20. S. Kitahara, O. Manabe, and H. Hiyama, *Sci. Ind. Japan*, **30**, 13 (1956); *CA*, **50**, 6051a (1956).

21. S. Fujii, M. Kamikura, and Y. Hosogai, *Eisei Shikensho Hokoku*, **75**, 29 (1957); *CA*, **52**, 12685a (1958).

22. S. Kitahara, S. Miyazaki, and H. Hiyama, *Kogyo Kagaku Zasshi*, **61**, 189 (1958); *CA*, **53**, 20809c (1959).

23. L. Sassi, *Arch. Inst. Pasteur Tunis*, **33**, 429, 442 (1960); *J. Soc. Dyers Colour.*, **77**, 273 (1961).

24. R. R. Reed and D. M. Heinekey, *Analyst*, **87**, 391 (1962).

25. M. C. Dutt, *Analyst*, **89**, 142 (1964).

26. M. Kamikura, *Shokuhin Eiseigaku Zasshi*, **8**, 420 (1967).

27. I. Gemzová and J. Gasparič, *Mikrochim. Acta*, 310 (1966).

28. J. Gasparič and B. Horáková, *J. Chromatogr.*, in press.

29. A. Cee and J. Gasparič, *Mikrochim. Acta*, 295 (1966).

30. J. Gasparič and J. Skutil, *Mikrochim. Acta*, 395 (1975 I).

31. A. Cee and J. Gasparič, unpublished results.

32. J. Gasparič and A. Cee, *Collect. Czech. Chem. Commun.*, **40**, 371 (1975).

33. A. Cee and J. Gasparič, *Mikrochim. Acta*, 268 (1966).

34. J. Skutil and J. Gasparič, unpublished results.

35. J. Skutil and J. Gasparič, *Mikrochim. Acta*, 791 (1974).

36. K. G. Hargreaves, *J. Oil Colour Chem. Assoc.*, **35**, 139 (1952).

37. E. Gemza and I. Gemzová, *Chem. Prum.*, **19**, 313 (1969).

38. J. A. Völlmin, P. Pachlatko, and W. Simon, *Helv. Chim. Acta*, **52**, 737 (1969).

39. I. Gemzová and E. Gemza, *Chem. Prum.*, **22**, 621 (1972).

40. F. M. Rowe and W. G. Dangerfield, *J. Soc. Dyes Colour.*, **52**, 48 (1936).

41. H. H. Hodgson and C. K. Foster, *J. Chem. Soc.*, 755 (1941).

42. S. Kishimoto, O. Manabe, and H. Hiyama, *Kagaku To Kogyo*, **44**, 290 (1970); *CA*, **73**, 110844 (1970).

43. J. Gasparič, unpublished work.

44. J. Gasparič and J. Borecký, *J. Chromatogr.*, **5**, 466 (1961).

45. M. Večeřa and J. Gasparič, *Detection and Identification of Organic Compounds*, Plenum Press, New York and London, 1971, p. 154.

46. A. Cee and J. Gasparič, unpublished work.

47. A. Cee and J. Gasparič, *Mikrochim. Acta*, 823 (1972).

48. A. Cee and J. Gasparič, *J. Chromatogr.*, **56**, 342 (1971).

49. J. Gasparič and J. Marhan, *Collect. Czech. Chem. Commun.*, **27**, 46 (1962).

50. A. Cee, Czech. Pat. 128076 (15.6.1968); *CA*, **70**, 116227 (1969).

51. J. Skutil and J. Gasparič, *Mikrochim. Acta*, 81 (1976 II).

52. J. Gasparič, *J. Chromatogr.*, **4**, 75 (1960).

53. J. Borecký, *Mikrochim. Acta*, 279 (1966).

54. B. S. Joshi, N. Parkash, and K. Venkataraman, *J. Sci. Ind. Res.*, **14B**, 325 (1955).

55. J. van Alphen, *Rec. Trav. Chim.*, **57**, 911 (1938).

56. *CSD* II, p. 1044.

57. E. Clar, *Ber.*, **72**, 1645 (1939).

58. S. Coffey and V. Boyd, *J. Chem. Soc.*, 2468 (1954).

59. K. Venkataraman, *J. Ind. Chem. Soc.*, **37**, 247 (1960).

60. C. J. Sanchorawala, B. C. Subba Rao, M. K. Unni, and K. Venkataraman, *Indian. J. Chem.*, **1**, 19 (1963).

61. P. M. Nair, T. G. Manjrekar, and K. Venkataraman, *Indian J. Chem.*, **9**, 925 (1971).

62. K. G. Das, T. G. Manjrekar, and K. Venkataraman, *Indian J. Chem.*, **9**, 921 (1971).

63. J. Gasparič and B. Klouček, *Collect. Czech. Chem. Commun.*, **31**, 106 (1966).

64. W. S. Owen, *Mikrochim. Acta*, 19 (1963).

65. P. M. Nair, R. Srinivasan, and K. Venkataraman, *Tetrahedron*, **11**, 140 (1960).

CHAPTER TWELVE

Examples of Structure Determination—I

T. E. BEUKELMAN, ANTHONY FORIS, AND R. K. MILLER

1 INTRODUCTION

1.1 The Value of Combined Techniques

Structure determination of dyes is a relatively difficult undertaking because of the degree of complexity often encountered. When only optical spectroscopy and chemical tests could be brought to bear on the problem, the outcome with any particular dye was uncertain unless the analyst was prepared to apply a substantial amount of time and effort to the project. In order to obtain precise identification it was often necessary to carry out extensive degradation studies and to synthesize a number of standards. This picture has rapidly changed in recent years with the development of technology so that high-quality NMR and HRMS spectra of dyes can be obtained relatively quickly and easily. These highly precise methods complement so well the capabilities of the optical methods to identify functional groups and "fingerprint" molecules that dye analysis has become almost routine.

Although HRMS measures m/e ratios with such accuracy that there are generally few empirical formulas that fit a given peak, it is rare that the search is narrowed to only one formula by HRMS alone. PMR may give such a reliable proton count that it permits selection of the correct formula with virtual certainty. The presence of an ester carbonyl in the IR spectrum may allow the selection, if the number of oxygens is unique. PMR often shows resonances which are ambiguous until functional group information from IR is added. The presence or absence of chlorine or bromine is readily established by HRMS because of their characteristic isotope ratios; neither NMR nor IR can provide such strong, direct evidence. Close cooperation among spectroscopists can often produce a proposed structure with no inputs other than the HRMS, NMR, and IR spectra.

It should not be supposed, however, that it is always desirable, or even possible, to limit the tools used to these three. Elemental analysis, X-ray fluorescence, visible spectra, and chemical tests are all invaluable at times, especially in view of the fact that some dyes do not yield usable NMR or HRMS spectra. Furthermore, it should be pointed out that the patent literature and trade information are extremely useful sources of ideas that can save hours of time in the search for dye structures to fit the analytical data. Finally, the insight of an interested dye chemist is most helpful for dye identification.

It may be assumed that any of the above-mentioned aids that were available were used in the analyses described in this chapter.

1.2 Influence of Sample Purity

It would be hard to overemphasize the significance of sample purity for any analytical technique. Possibly because it appears to be such an obvious factor, purification is often given short shrift in the literature. It seems worthwhile to point out, however, that sample purity becomes a critical factor when combined spectroscopic methods are being employed, because of the differences in the way samples are treated. In HRMS the sample must be volatilized, and if more than one component is present the spectrum may vary with the time of observation. The NMR spectrum obtained from a mixture may be only that of the more soluble component. The IR spectrum of a mixture is, of course, representative of the mixture, but prominent features of the various components may dominate. It is entirely possible that the three spectra may not correspond to the same component in such a circumstance.

It has been our experience that samples which show evidence of low purity are the most difficult to analyze. Those samples that have resisted all efforts toward identification have generally either shown signs of instability or have been mixtures too complex to separate by routine procedures. Conversely, pure dyes, provided they are stable, soluble, and volatile enough to give a mass spectrum, are always readily analyzed by joint spectroscopy.

It should be pointed out that difficulties resulting from less than ideal sample purity are, fortunately, not always insurmountable. For various practical reasons, it is often necessary to work with samples that are obviously not pure, in which case one has to make the best of a bad situation.

1.3   Selection and Classification of Examples

The examples in this chapter represent actual unknowns which we identified for various practical reasons during the last 6–7 years. Therefore, they may not show a representative distribution of dye structures from the standpoint of the dye chemist. However, an attempt is made, within the limits of the data available, to present as wide a distribution as possible while also considering the objective of presenting useful examples of the application of combined techniques.

For practical reasons it is not always necessary to determine the exact structure of a dye being analyzed, particularly with regard to position of substituents. In those cases where chemical logic and published information seemed convincing, a precise structure was assigned even though the experimental evidence taken by itself would not warrant that conclusion. In some cases the data were inconclusive, and therefore provisional structures are presented.

2   EXPERIMENTAL DETAILS

2.1   Instruments

The instruments used in the examples that follow, together with the details of the spectral procedures, are described elsewhere (see Chapters 7–9). The examples presented were obtained during a period of rapid advances in NMR and HRMS, and the data therefore reflect varying levels of sophistication with regard to these methods. CMR was available largely on an experimental basis, and only one example of its application to dye identification is given. Also, 220-MHz PMR has become available to us only recently.

2.2   Purification of Samples for Spectrometric Analysis

The procedure employed to prepare a sample for analysis depended on whether it was a disperse, cationic, or acid dye. Since the examples to be discussed were practical cases, classification of each sample according to those groups was generally already established by its history. However, a totally unknown dye could be classified by its dyeing behavior toward various fabrics and its solubility characteristics, using modifications of the methods described by the AATCC Committee RA-72.[1]

Disperse dyes were extracted from their diluents with reagent-grade acetone in a Soxhlet extractor. The solvent was evaporated and the recovered dye was ground to a very fine particle size, slurried in water, filtered, and washed with water. The slurrying, filtering, and washing procedure was repeated using Freon 113 (Du Pont) fluorocarbon solvent. Finally, the purified dye was dried in a vacuum oven.

Cationic dyes were purified by preparing their iodides and/or picrates. The iodides were prepared by dissolving the standardized dye in water at 80°, clarifying the hot solution by filtration, adding sodium iodide to the solution, and stirring for 30 minutes at 80–90°. The mixture was cooled, and the precipitated iodide was filtered, washed with water, slurried in Freon 113, filtered, washed with Freon 113, and dried in a vacuum oven.

Picrates of cationic dyes were prepared by dissolving the standardized dye in water at room temperature, clarifying the solution by filtration, adding the dye solution to a mixture of picric acid, ethanol, and water, and stirring for 30 minutes at room temperature. The mixture was allowed to stand until the picrate precipitated. The precipitate was filtered and washed with water until all excess of picric acid was removed. The usual slurrying and washing with Freon 113 was carried out, followed by drying the salt in a vacuum oven.

Acid dyes were purified by one of two procedures. The degree of solubility of the free acid of the dye in butyl alcohol determined the procedure to be used.

If the free acid of the dye had good solubility in butyl alcohol, the standardized dye was dissolved in hot water, the solution was cooled, and hydrochloric acid was added to convert the dye to the free acid, which was then extracted with butyl alcohol. The butyl alcohol solution was washed several times with a dilute hydrochloric acid solution and it was then added dropwise to a stirred aqueous solution of sodium hydroxide. The mixture was allowed to stand until the sodium salt of the dye precipitated. The precipitate was filtered off, ground to a fine particle size, given the usual Freon 113 wash, and dried in a vacuum oven.

If the free acid of the dye had poor solubility in butyl alcohol, the standardized dye was dissolved in hot DMF and the hot solution was filtered and cooled. Acetone was then added to precipitate the dye. The crystals were ground, washed with Freon 113, and dried in a vacuum oven.

Individual components of multicomponent dyes were separated by TLC. The dyes were applied from solution to an 8 × 8-in. silica gel G thin-layer plate. After elution with an appropriate solvent system, the individual components were extracted from the silica gel with a solvent such as acetone or methanol and were recovered on evaporation of the solvent. Usually four to eight plates were necessary to obtain enough sample for analysis.

2.3   Cleavage of Azo Dyes

To facilitate the analysis of some azo dyes, the azo groups were cleaved to yield the corresponding amines which were isolated and identified.

The azo dye, along with some sodium carbonate, was dissolved in water or a methanol–water mixture at approximately 60°. Small amounts of sodium hydrosulfite and enough sodium carbonate to maintain alkalinity were added while stirring the mixture at about 60°. This addition was continued until the solution was decolorized. The solution was then cooled and the amine products were isolated by various separation techniques including filtration and extraction.

2.4   Desulfonation of Anthraquinone Dyes[2]

Dyes containing sulfonic acid groups attached to the anthraquinone nucleus were desulfonated by adding sodium hydrosulfite to a stirred solution of the dye and sodium hydroxide in water at 90°. This addition was continued at 90° along with enough sodium hydroxide to maintain a pH of 10 or higher, until a substantial precipitate had formed. The water-insoluble product was filtered off and washed as in the treatment of disperse dyes. If the desulfonated product was in the leuco form, it was readily oxidized at 125° in nitrobenzene containing a few drops of piperidine.

3   EXAMPLES

3.1   Acid Dyes

Acid dyes are usually more difficult to identify by spectrometric methods than dyes of other classes. Acid dyes seldom yield molecular ions in the mass spectrometer and often do not give useful MS at all. Their solubility in NMR-compatible solvents is often quite low. Although sulfonic acid or sulfonate groups generally show readily recognizable 1250–1000 patterns,

IR spectra of sulfonic acid dyes are often not very well defined. These dyes have a strong tendency to pick up moisture, which blocks out the NH/OH stretch region in the IR and may also cause some problems in PMR, especially if the molecule contains readily exchangeable protons. In addition, even if synthetic standards are available for comparison, exact matches of IR and PMR spectra are possible only if both the unknown and standard samples are completely in the acid or the salt form. Nevertheless, structural elucidation of sulfonic acid dyes by combined spectrometric techniques is possible.

Example 1. The structure of a blue anthraquinone dye was established as (1). The IR spectrum of the unknown showed moderate similarities to reference spectra of dyes of type (2), indicating that the basic structure was probably a similarly substituted anthraquinone. A 220-MHz PMR spectrum (Table 12.1) showed features in the aromatic proton region characteristic of an unsubstituted anthraquinone *A* ring. Patterns due to two *para*-disubstituted benzene rings and to a single isolated *C*-ring proton were also observed.

Table 12.1   220-MHz PMR Spectrum of (1)[a]

Chemical Shift	Multiplicity	Rel. No. Protons	Assignments
2.42	*s*	3	ArCH$_3$
2.56	*s*	3	$>$NCH$_3$
4.12	*s*	2	ArCH$_2$N$<$
7.32	*d* (*ortho*)	2	] *para*-disub. benzene
7.42	*d* (*ortho*)	2	
7.52	*d* (*ortho*)	2	] *para*-disub. benzene
7.79	*d* (*ortho*)	2	
7.87	*m*	2	H-6, H-7
8.08	*s*	1	H-3
8.29	*m*	2	H-5, H-8
10.1	*br*	1	$>$NH

[a] In DMSO-D$_6$ (100% D).

The presence of a sulfonic acid or sulfonate group was indicated by a strong 1250–1000 pattern in the IR spectrum and was confirmed by a strong SO_2 peak in the mass spectrum.

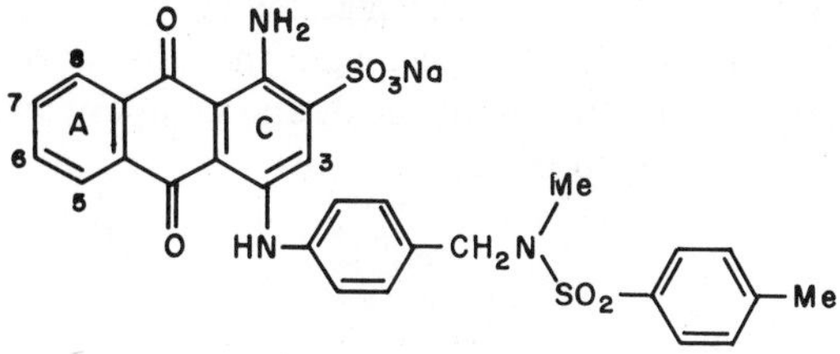

(1) 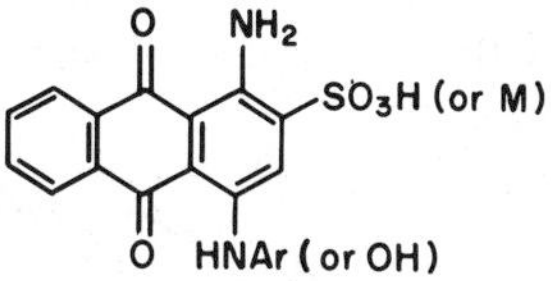   (2)

Based on PMR data, the side chain contained one methylene and two methyl groups in addition to the two *para*-disubstituted benzene rings. The IR spectrum showed moderate intensity bands at 1337 and 1160, suggesting the presence of a sulfonamide group. Although the HRMS did not yield a molecular ion, some characteristic fragments were noted. In particular, a very strong C_7H_7 ion was observed. Another fragment having the formula $C_8H_{11}NO_2S$ was attributable to $MeC_6H_4SO_2NHMe$.

The final step in the identification process involved desulfonation of the anthraquinone (see Section 2.4). The desulfonated sample did yield $M \cdot^+$ 511.1519; calc. for $C_{29}H_{25}N_3O_4S$; 511.1566.

Example 2. The structure of an azo acid dye was identified as (3) by spectrometric analysis of the dye and its degradation products.

The IR spectrum of the dye showed a strong pattern in the 1250–1000 region, suggesting the presence of the sulfonic acid group. Strong 1661 absorption was possibly due to amide carbonyl. Strong absorptions near 3300 could have been due to OH and NH, but could also have been partly due to moisture. The sharpness of the peak at 3279 suggested NH.

The highest mass found by HRMS was 431.1168, corresponding to $C_{23}H_{18}N_5O_2Cl$. The absence of sulfur indicated that this was not a molecular ion. The isotope pattern confirmed the presence of a chlorine atom. Peaks due to $C_6H_5 \cdot$ and $C_6H_5CO \cdot$ fragments were also observed.

The 60-MHz PMR spectrum of the dye in DMF-D_7 suggested a methyl group (*s* at 2.32), 12 aromatic H (complex patterns between ∼7.3 and 8.4), an amide H (*br s* at 8.52), one acid H (*br s* at 10.5), and a bonded NH or OH proton (*br s* at 14.2).

The dye was then reductively cleaved. One of the fragments contained sulfur and was therefore the sulfonic acid fragment. Its IR spectrum in the salt form showed, in addition to the expected very strong sulfonate salt pattern, strong, sharp bands at 3420 and 3340 (NH_2), a broader, strong band at 3279 (NH of secondary amide), and strong bands at 1654 (amide carbonyl) and 1528 (amide II?). These features, together with the strong indication of a benzoyl group in the dye (by HRMS), suggested the presence of benzamide. On the basis of these data it was speculated that the diazo component was an aminobenzamidobenzenesulfonic acid, and comparison with a reference IR spectrum indicated it to be structure (4).

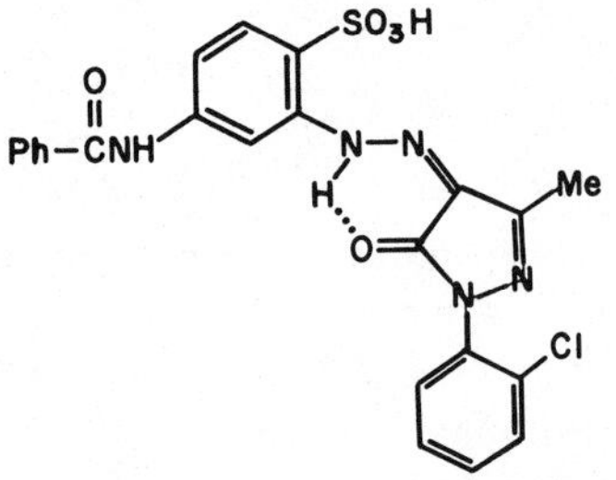

(3) 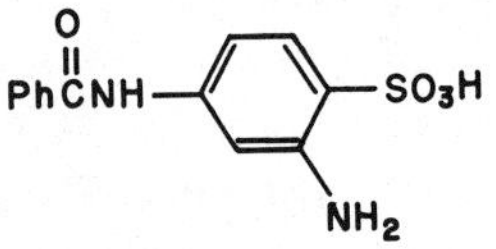   (4)

The second product from the cleavage reaction could not be immediately identified by IR. Surprisingly, it did not have the expected NH_2 group (it showed essentially no absorption in the NH/OH region). Its HRMS yielded M·+ 359.1368, corresponding to the formula $C_{20}H_{17}N_5O_2$. The sum of this formula and that of the sulfonic acid fragment greatly exceeds the highest mass observed for the dye. These data suggested that the coupler fragment had undergone further reaction, possibly dimerization via loss of NH_3. This was supported by the odd numbers of N and H.

Other data on the second cleavage product included HRMS fragments corresponding to C_6H_5· and C_6H_5N:. Both IR and PMR showed clear evidence for monosubstituted benzene rings, and PMR showed a singlet at 2.25 for =CMe. PMR also showed an unusual OH proton peak at exceptionally low field (17.3). The aromatic/Me/OH proton ratio was 10:6:1.

In view of the probable symmetry of the molecule and the proton ratio, it seemed likely that it contained two C_6H_5N groups, two =CMe groups, one OH, possibly a bonded C=O, and a central N. Subtracting the elements corresponding to these functions from the formula of the original fragment leaves C_4N_2 to be distributed symmetrically in the molecule. This could hardly be done without introducing some rings, and this suggested rubazonic acid (5) as a good possibility. The identification was confirmed by comparison of the IR and PMR spectra of the cleavage product with those of an authentic sample of (5).

Working backward from structure (5) it would appear that the initial cleavage product was the substituted pyrazolone (6). At this point an in-

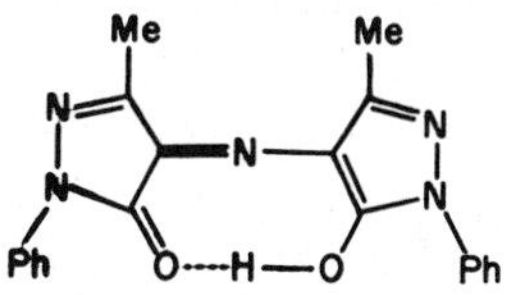

(5) 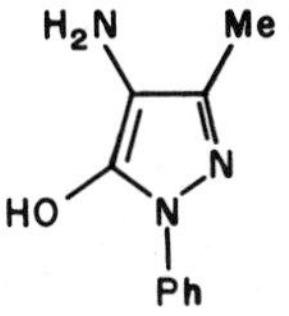   (6)

consistency was obvious, since chlorine was present in the dye, but not in either of the cleavage products. It appeared that the only way to explain this inconsistency was to assume that the chlorine was lost during the cleavage. On this basis structure (3) would fit all the data, and was confirmed by comparison with a synthetic sample. A "synthetic sample," here and in subsequent examples, is a sample synthesized by a method expected to produce the structure in question.

Example 3.   Another analytically challenging example was provided by the yellow dye (7). The IR spectrum suggested sulfonic acid or sulfonate group(s) (1250–1000) and a carbonyl function (broad band at 1672).

The two strongest peaks in the HRMS of the dye were at m/e 362.0911 and 235.0387. The isotope patterns indicated that both ions contained one Cl. Although several chemically possible formulas could be proposed for both ions, there was no clear way of choosing among them. The only strong clue was that the difference between the two observed masses corresponded to $C_{10}H_7$, suggesting a naphthyl group.

The 60-MHz PMR spectrum of the dye in DMF-D_7 solution indicated the presence of a Me group (s at 2.36), 10 aromatic H (complex patterns at ~7.2–8.4 and around 9.3), and a bonded NH or OH (*br s* at 15.3). The presence of moisture was also indicated both by PMR and IR.

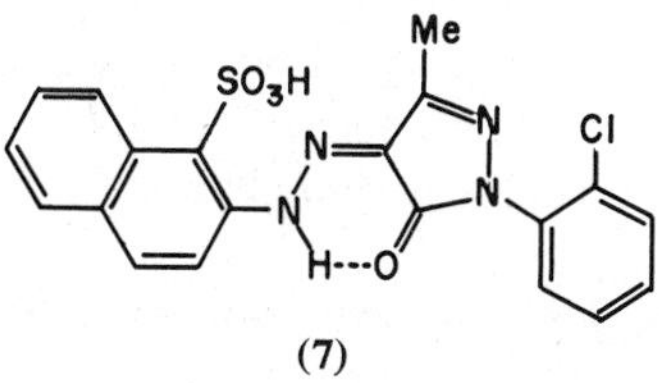

(7) 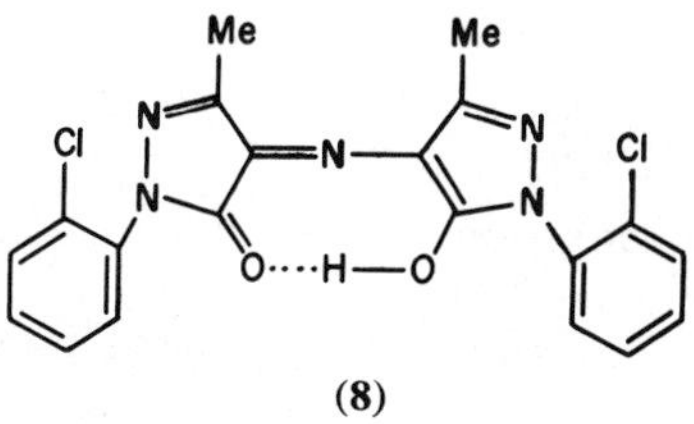   (8)

Since no likely structure could be postulated based on the foregoing data alone, the dye in water was cleaved by catalytic hydrogenation under milder conditions (10% Pd–C, 60°, 100 psi) than those used in the reduction of the preceding dye, (3), in order to avoid loss of chlorine. One of the reduction products was identified on the basis of reference spectra by both IR and PMR as 2-naphthylamine-1-sulfonic acid.

The IR spectrum of the second fraction was very similar to that of (5). It showed a strong band at 758 consistent with *ortho* disubstitution and, most significantly, no amine bands. The PMR spectrum (CDCl$_3$ solution) indicated the presence of two equivalent Me groups (s at 2.38), eight aromatic H ($\sim$7.2–7.7), and a bonded OH proton ($\sim$16.7). All the IR and PMR data were consistent with the substituted rubazonic acid (8).

Based on all the available spectrometric data, structure (7) was regarded as the most probable for the unknown dye. This compound was synthesized and both IR and PMR spectra of the synthetic and the unknown samples matched.

3.2   Disperse Dyes

3.2.1   Anthraquinones.   Spectroscopic features that help to classify anthraquinone dyes include (1) a generally recognizable proton pattern in the PMR spectra if one of the rings is unsubstituted, as is often the case; (2) multiple IR absorptions in the 1640–1560 region, at least one of which is among the strongest in the spectrum, and a strong band or bands in the 1300–1200 region; (3) a sharp IR multiplet at 3500–3300 if NH$_2$ groups are present; (4) strong mass spectra in which there almost always is a strong molecular ion and many fragments with masses not much greater than that of anthraquinone itself.

Example 1.   This is an example of the frequently encountered class of blue anthraquinone dyes with the general formula (9). Since this sample when first analyzed by PMR showed no simple proton ratios, it was examined by TLC, which showed it to be a two-component mixture. The components were separated by PLC and analyzed separately.

The first fraction gave an IR spectrum which showed sharp NH$_2$ bands at 3460 and 3330, a characteristic cyclic imide doublet at 1745 and 1696, a complex pattern in the 1634–1565 region, very strong 1294 absorption (Ar–N?), and a moderately strong 1111 band, probably due to an aliphatic ether group. The general appearance of the spectrum was very characteristic of dyes with structure (9).

The PMR spectrum (Table 12.2) showed only four aromatic protons, the pattern being typical of the unsubstituted anthraquinone *A* ring. It also

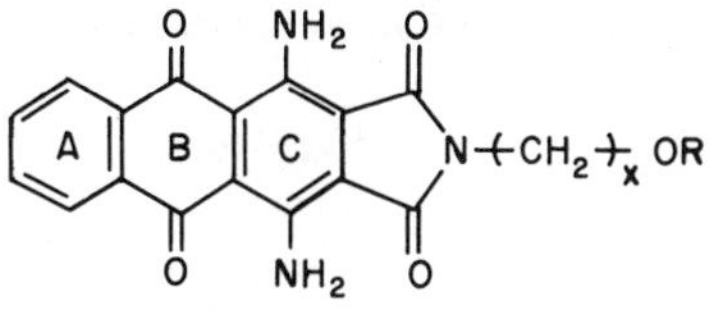

(9)

suggested a primary amino group. Since this confirmed the IR classification of the unknown, establishing the structure of the side chain was all that was necessary to complete the identification of this fraction. The PMR data showed that X = 3, R = Et.

HRMS confirmed the above identification. In particular, it showed the presence of three N, which was not directly established by either IR or PMR. It showed $M \cdot^{+}$ 393.1347 (m/e calc. for $C_{21}H_{19}N_3O_5$: 393.1325). Also consistent were fragments corresponding to loss of CH_2CH_2OEt with addition of H and loss of $(C\!\!=\!\!O)_2NCH_2CH_2CH_2OEt$.

The second TLC fraction showed the same general IR characteristics as the first fraction, although their spectra did not match exactly. Taken together with the IR evidence, PMR (see Table 12.3) clearly established that this fraction differed from the first fraction only in the composition of the side chain. The PMR data indicated that the only difference was that the second fraction had a Me instead of an Et group.

Table 12.2 220-MHz FT PMR Spectrum of Structure (9; X = 3, R = Et)[a]

Chemical Shift	Multiplicity	Rel. No. Protons	Assignments
1.05	t	3	CH_3CH_2—
1.89	qn	2	—$CH_2CH_2CH_2$—
3.37	q	4	—OCH_2CH_3
3.42	t		—OCH_2CH_2—
3.71	t	2	$(CO)_2NCH_2CH_2$—
7.71	m	2	Aromatic protons at positions 6, 7
8.21	m	2	Aromatic protons at positions 5, 8
Very broad band under "aromatic" region			—NH_2

[a] 6000 transients, $CDCl_3$.

Table 12.3   220-MHz FT PMR Spectrum of Structure $(9; X = 3, R = Me)^a$

Chemical Shift	Multiplicity	Rel. No. Protons	Assignments
1.89	qn	2	$—CH_2CH_2CH_2—$
3.26	s	3	$ROCH_3$
3.39	t	2	$—OCH_2CH_2—$
3.72	t	2	$(CO)_2NCH_2CH_2—$
7.72	m	2	Aromatic protons at positions 6, 7
8.23	m	2	Aromatic protons at positions 5, 8
Very broad band under "aromatic" region			$—NH_2$

^{a} 4000 transients, $CDCl_3$.

The quantity of this fraction was small, and only a weak, low-resolution MS could be obtained. However, the major peak at m/e 379 confirms the structure as $(9; X = 3, R = Me)$.

Example 2.   Another anthraquinone blue was shown by combined spectroscopic methods to be a mixture of dyes with structure $(10; X = O$ or NH$)$. The IR spectrum showed a very complex pattern in the 1670 region, suggesting a mixture. It was separated by PLC into two components which were identified as follows.

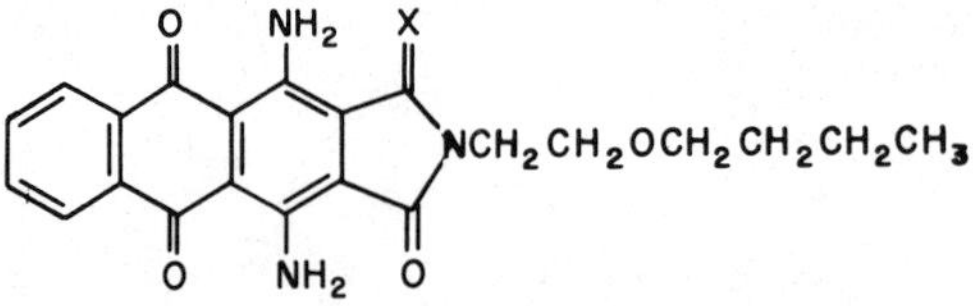

(10)

The first fraction gave an IR spectrum very similar to those of the components discussed in the previous example. Although it did not match either one exactly, there seemed to be little doubt that the dye had the general structure (9). The HRMS showed $M \cdot^+$ for $C_{22}H_{21}N_3O_5$ (m/e found, 407.1490; calc., 407.1481); subtracting the elements of the diaminoanthraquinone dicarboximide nucleus from this formula left $C_6H_{13}O$ for the side chain. Prominent peaks in the MS corresponded to fragments from losses of C_4H_9 and OC_4H_9 groups, clearly locating the O in the substituent. These data were consistent with structure (10; X = O), although branching of the butyl group could not be ruled out.

The PMR data (see Table 12.4) for this fraction were somewhat ambiguous because of the presence of interfering aliphatic impurities. However, it was clear that the data were consistent *only* with the *n*-butyl group as in structure (10). Except for the region overlapped by the aliphatic impurity bands, the PMR spectrum was entirely consistent with structure (10; X = O).

The second fraction showed strong IR bands at 1712 and 1653 instead of the 1748–1695 doublet in the first fraction. Since the IR spectra of the two fractions were otherwise very similar, it seemed reasonable to conclude that only the cyclic imide function was somehow changed.

The two fractions were not widely separated by TLC. To get enough material for NMR and HRMS analysis, it was necessary to overload the plate somewhat, with the result that the second fraction was rather badly contaminated with the major component of the first fraction. This was shown by the fact that the HRMS was obviously composed of two sets of unrelated peaks, one set corresponding exactly to the mass spectrum of structure (10; X = O). As is seen later, the presence of that impurity was also a significant factor in the PMR analysis.

Table 12.4   220-MHz FT PMR Spectrum of Structure (10; X = O)^a

Chemical Shift	Multiplicity	Rel. No. Protons	Assignments
0.87	*t*	3	$-CH_2CH_3$
1.25	*s*	4	Impurity
1.33	*m*		$-CH_2CH_2CH_3$
1.49	*m*	4	$-CH_2CH_2CH_2-$
1.55	*s*		Impurity
3.46	*t*	2	$-OCH_2CH_2-$
3.67	*t*	2	$>NCH_2CH_2O-$
3.86	*t*	2	$(CO)_2NCH_2CH_2-$
7.78	*m*	2	Aromatic protons at positions 6, 7
8.28	*m*	2	Aromatic protons at positions 5, 8
Very broad band under "aromatic" region		NH_2	

^{a} 2000 transients, CDCl$_3$.

In addition to the impurity peaks, the HRMS showed $M \cdot^+$ for $C_{22}H_{22}N_4O_4$ (m/e found, 406.1590; calc., 406.1641). This was one O less than the molecular formula of the first fraction, and one N and one H more. Substitution of NH for O *in the imide* structure of the first fraction gives (10; X = NH). The mass spectrum assignable to the latter structure was analogous to the spectrum of the former; of particular importance were peaks indicating losses of C_4H_9 and OC_4H_9.

The PMR spectrum of the second fraction (see Table 12.5) obviously was that of a mixture, but it was mostly consistent with structure (10; X = NH). The deficiency in the area assignable to the =NH proton gives an indication of the purity. As with the first fraction, the data were somewhat ambiguous because of the presence of interfering aliphatic impurities.

Example 3. A reddish dye was shown to have structure (11) by spectroscopic means.

The IR spectrum of this dye showed strong similarities to reference spectra of dyes with the general structure (12). There were sharp bands at

Table 12.5   220-MHz FT PMR Spectrum of Structure (10; X = NH)^a

Chemical Shift	Multiplicity	Rel. No. Protons	Assignments
0.88	*t*	} 3	CH_3CH_2—
0.92	*t*		CH_3CH_2—
~1.25	*s*	} 3	Impurity
~1.34	*m*		—$CH_2CH_2CH_3$
~1.55	*m*	4	—$CH_2CH_2CH_2$— + imp.
~3.43	Two *very* slightly different triplets	2	—OCH_2CH_2—
3.62	*t*	} 2	OCH_2
3.67	*t*		
~3.82	Two *very* slightly different triplets	2	$(CO)_2NCH_2CH_2$—
~7.8	*m*	2	Aromatic protons at positions 6, 7
~8.3	*m*	2	Aromatic protons at positions 5, 8
~9.2	*br s*	0.7	=NH
Very broad band under "aromatic" region			NH_2

^{a} 1000 transients, $CDCl_3$.

3472 and 3300 (probably NH or NH_2 + OH), a multiple band pattern in the 1645–1567 region, and a very strong 1272 band. The absorption at 1645 was unusually intense, suggesting a possible $C=N$ function or a $C=O$ other than the anthraquinone $C=O$. There was also a moderately strong 853 band, suggesting a *para*-disubstituted benzene ring in addition to the anthraquinone ring.

The "aromatic region" of the PMR spectrum $(CDCl_3)$ confirmed the IR classification. There was a singlet at 6.25 consistent with an isolated anthraquinone C-ring proton, and a complex partially overlapping pattern equivalent to 10 H which required an exchange experiment to clarify it. Upon exchange of two H (probably $Ar-NH_2$ type), the complex pattern was simplified to reveal (1) a four-H pattern centered around 7.20 consistent with the protons on a benzene ring substituted in the *para* positions with two unlike groups, and (2) two multiplets at 7.62 and 8.13, each corresponding to two H and typical of the unsubstituted anthraquinone A ring. A singlet at 13.9 for a hydrogen-bonded OH was also observed.

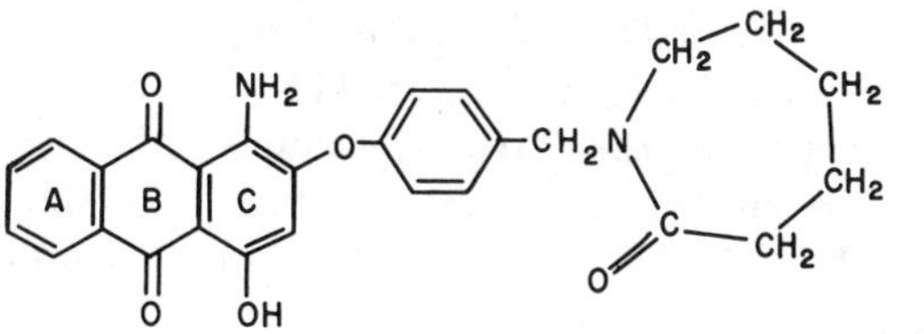

(11)

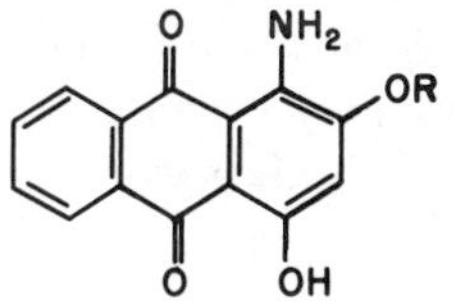

(12) 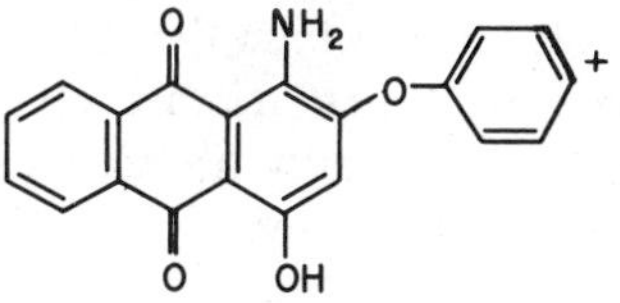   **(13)**

HRMS showed $M \cdot^+$ for $C_{27}H_{24}N_2O_5$ (*m/e* found, 456.1708; calc., 456.1685). A peak corresponding to structure **(13)** was also found. Subtracting the elements of **(13)** from the molecular formula left $C_7H_{12}NO$ still to be accounted for. Since this calls for $2\frac{1}{2}$ "rings plus double bonds," and since IR did not show a $C\equiv N$ band, there was likely to be at least one ring in the remaining segment. The IR band at 1645 and the presence of one O were taken as evidence for a carbonyl in this residue.

The aliphatic region of the PMR spectrum $(CDCl_3)$ gave the data necessary to complete the identification. It showed a broad band around 1.7 corresponding to six H of the $CH_2(CH_2)_3CH_2$ type; broad peaks at 2.6

and 3.3, each equivalent to about two H and consistent with CH_2CO and $\diagdown NCH_2$ types, respectively; and a two-H singlet at 4.58, probably due to $ArCH_2N(R)CO$. The data could fit no structure other than (11).

Example 4. In the same class as the preceding example was the pink dye (14). Both IR and PMR showed that its general structure was probably (12). A reference IR spectrum of (15), in fact, showed almost a band-for-band correspondence with the spectrum of the unknown, the difference being largely in the intensities.

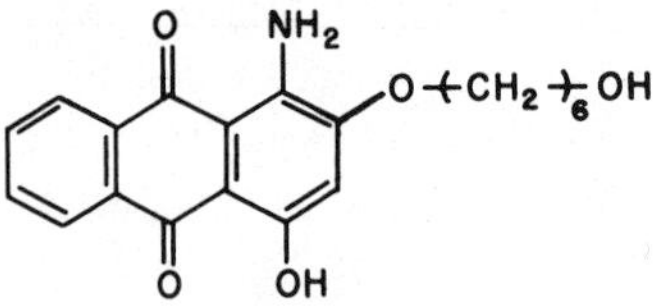

(14) 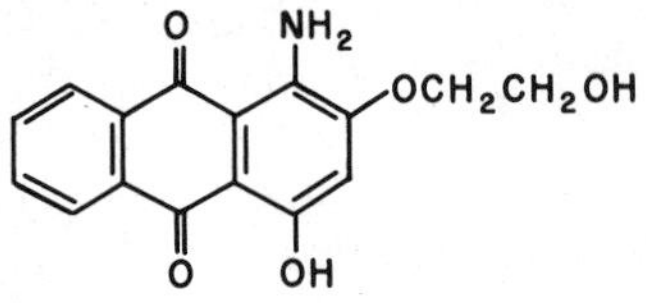   (15)

HRMS showed a formula of $C_{20}H_{21}NO_5$ (*m/e* found, 355.1414; calc., 355.1420). The formula for R in structure (12) was therefore $C_6H_{13}O$.

The aliphatic region of the PMR spectrum of the dye in DMSO-D_6 indicated protons of the types $ArOCH_2CH_2$ (4.17), $C(CH_2)_4C$ (about 1.5), and $-CH_2CH_2OH$ (3.43). No methyl protons were found. Only structure (14) fits these data.

Example 5. Anthraquinone dyes with alkylamine substituents may be encountered as in the blue dye (16). These present the difficulty that the NH stretch bands in the IR are very weak, possibly because of bonding, and are not diagnostically useful. Nevertheless, this class can be identified by combined spectroscopy.

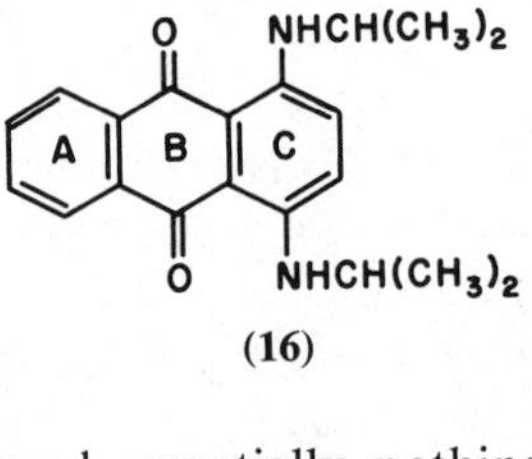

(16)

The IR spectrum showed essentially nothing in the OH/NH region. A pattern of bands at 1645–1563 and strong bands at 1258 and 723 strongly suggested an anthraquinone structure.

HRMS indicated the formula $C_{20}H_{22}N_2O_2$ (*m/e* found, 322.1682; calc., 322.1681), and also showed a strong peak at *m/e* 43 for C_3H_7 groups.

The presence of two N and only two O, together with the IR data, suggested that the unknown was a diaminoanthraquinone. In view of the lack of NH bands in the IR, the amino groups were probably alkylated.

PMR (CDCl$_3$) confirmed the locations and established the structures of the alkyl substituents: 1.36 (d) for 12 H and 3.96 (m) for two H, consistent with two equivalent N-isopropyl groups. The aromatic pattern was typical of unsubstituted A-ring anthraquinone protons (m at 7.67 and 8.35) and two equivalent C-ring protons in the 2 and 3 positions (s at 7.24). A broad doublet (at about 10.9) was consistent with two hydrogen-bonded NHCH protons.

All the data suggested structure (16) for the unknown, confirmed by synthesis.

Example 6. The turquoise dye (17) is an example of a more highly substituted anthraquinone. The IR spectrum showed strong, sharp bands at 3436 and 3279, indicating NH$_2$ and possibly also OH groups. Bands at 1527 and 1348 suggested a nitro group. The overall pattern was generally reminiscent of aminohydroxyanthraquinones.

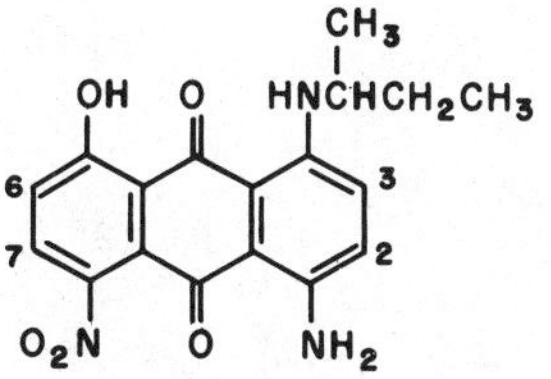

(17)

HRMS yielded M·+ for C$_{18}$H$_{17}$N$_3$O$_5$ (m/e found, 355.1152; calc., 355.1168) and fragments corresponding to loss of Me, Et, and NO. The latter fragment is particularly important since it is indicative of the presence of a nitro group. Subtracting the elements of an anthraquinone nucleus and a nitro substituent left C$_4$H$_{17}$N$_2$O to be accounted for. PMR data (Table 12.6) indicated four aromatic H and showed that the remaining elements were distributed among three groups: OH, NH$_2$, and CH$_3$CH$_2$CH(CH$_3$)NH. The *ortho* couplings for all the aromatic H, plus the evidence for bonded NH and OH, indicated that all the substituents were in α positions. Spectroscopically, the arrangement of the four groups could not be established unequivocally, but (17) is chemically likely. A double-resonance PMR experiment, in which the 3.93 multiplet was irradiated, resulted in the collapse of the 10.7 and 1.26 doublets into singlets and collapse of the 1.64 "quintet" into a quartet, clearly identifying the *sec*-butylamine substituent.

Table 12.6   220-MHz CW PMR Spectrum of Structure (17)^a

Chemical Shift	Multiplicity	Rel. No. Protons	Assignments
0.96	t	3	CH_3CH_2—
1.26	d	3	$CH_3CH\diagdown$
1.64	m	2	$CH_3CH_2CH\diagdown$
3.93	m	1	$—HNCH(CH_3)CH_2$—
7.15	d (ortho)	1	H-6
7.33	d (ortho)	1	H-2 or H-3
7.47	d (ortho)	1	H-2 or H-3
7.78	d (ortho)	1	H-7
6.4–10	v br	2^b	$ArNH_2$
10.7	d	1	ArNH (bonded)
14.4	s	1	ArOH (bonded)

^{a} 100% DMSO-D$_6$.
^{b} By difference after exchange with TFA-D.

3.2.2 Azo Dyes.   Spectroscopically, there is no generally applicable way to classify an unknown as an azo dye. There is the advantage that they usually give a molecular ion in the MS, and the presence of a high proportion of nitrogen tends to suggest the azo structure. Nonspectroscopic evidence, such as shade, fastness, and irreversible reduction to colorless products, is useful.

Example 1.   The IR spectrum of the red dye (18) showed a poorly resolved nitrile doublet, indicating two different nitrile groups. There was a carbonyl band characteristic of an ester group and indication of a nitro group. Although no exactly matching reference spectrum was found, the IR spectrum was very similar to the spectrum of the known red dye (19). The carbonyl band of the unknown was much weaker than in the reference spectrum, suggesting only one ester group. The absence of a fairly strong 1240 band argued against an acetate ester.

A 60-MHz PMR spectrum (CDCl$_3$) showed a triplet at 2.73 for four H and consistent with CH_2CH_2CN and/or CH_2CH_2COO protons. This meant that the CH_2CN and CH_2CO groups had the same chemical shift. This was clearly shown by the addition of Eu(fod)$_3$ shift reagent to the solution

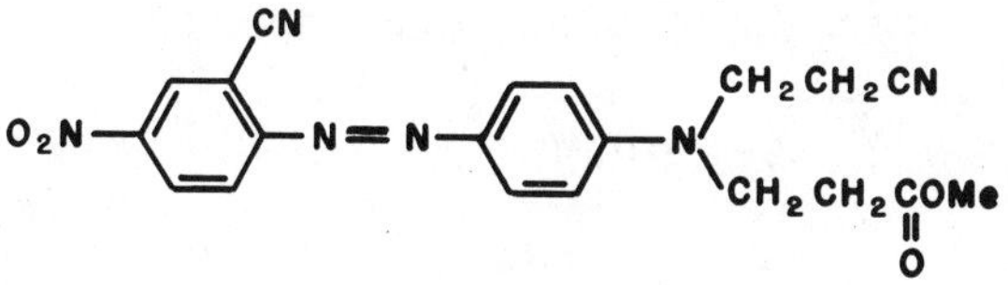

(18)

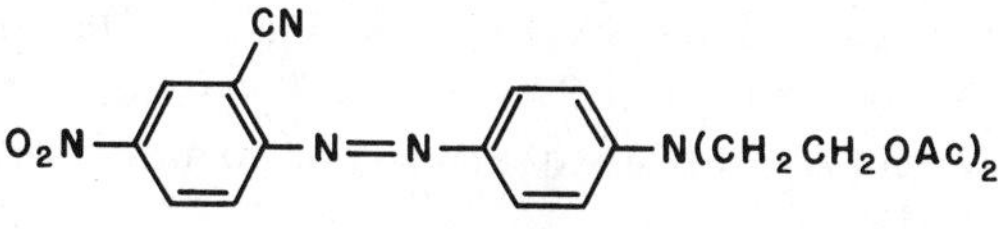

(19)

resulting in the separation of the two triplets (see Chapter 8). A singlet at 3.73 for OMe confirmed that the ester was not an acetate; it overlapped what appeared to be a triplet, the chemical shift of which was characteristic of NCH_2CH_2 protons. The total area of the complex pattern corresponded to about seven H, indicating one OMe and two NCH_2CH_2 groups. The aromatic proton pattern was typical of a *para*-disubstituted and a 1,2,4-trisubstituted benzene ring in azo dyes.

HRMS yielded $M \cdot^+$ for $C_{20}H_{18}N_6O_4$ (m/e calc., 406.1390; found, 406.1384), with peaks due to the loss of OMe, CH_2COOMe, and CH_2CN, and a strong peak corresponding to cyanonitroaniline.

Example 2. Another common type of azo dye is illustrated by the navy blue dye **(20)**. TLC showed three major components as well as several minor or trace components. Preliminary IR studies indicated that the major components had spectra similar to dyes having structure **(21)**. There were strong ester, amide, and nitro bands. There were NH bands of the ArNHR type and an OH (probably CH_2OH) band.

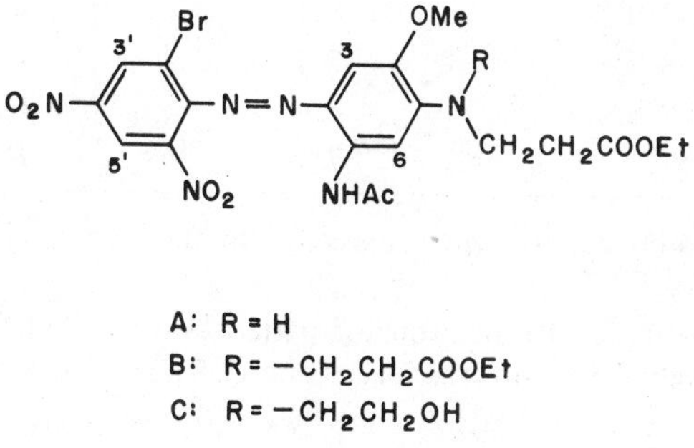

A: R = H
B: R = $-CH_2CH_2COOEt$
C: R = $-CH_2CH_2OH$

(20)

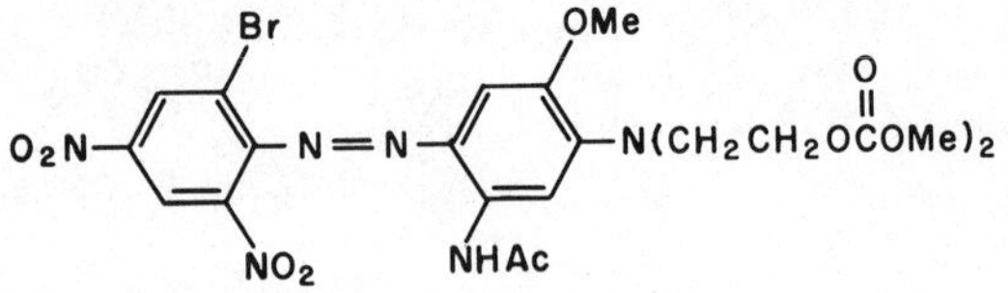

(21)

Three samples were isolated by PLC. Because of the limited amounts the PMR spectra were run on a 220-MHz FT system. A thousand scans were averaged to provide an adequate signal to noise ratio. Table 12.7 summarizes the PMR data.

HRMS of fraction A yielded $M \cdot^+$ 552.0606 for $C_{20}H_{21}N_6O_8Br$ (theory 552.0604). The other fractions also yielded molecular ions, but they were

Table 12.7   220-MHz FT PMR Spectra[a] of (20)

Chemical Shifts and Multiplicities			
Fraction A	Fraction B	Fraction C	Assignments
1.3 t	1.2 t	1.2 t	CH_3CH_2—
4.2 q	4.0 q	4.0 q	CH_3CH_2OCO
2.3 s	2.2 s	2.2 s	Ac—
2.8 t	2.6 t	2.6 t	—CH_2CH_2CO
3.7 m	~3.8 m ⎤ overlap	~3.8 t ⎤ overlap	$ArNCH_2CH_2$—
3.9 s	3.8 s ⎦	3.7 s ⎦	$ArOCH_3$
		3.58 t	—CH_2OH
6.3 br			ArNH
[b]	8.9 br	8.9 br	NHCO
		2.5 br	OH
[b]	8.0	8.1	H-6
[b]	8.2	8.2	H-3'
[b]	8.6	8.6	H-5'
[b]	[c]	7.2	H-3

[a] The relative proton counts, which agreed with the assignments given, are not tabulated.

[b] Fraction A was very small; the aromatic pattern was weak and not well defined, but was qualitatively similar to fractions B and C. The amide proton peak was not observed.

[c] This aromatic proton peak was lost under a chloroform solvent peak. The residual proton peak from 99.8 atom % $CDCl_3$ builds up very strongly after averaging 1000 scans.

both too weak for precise measurement either by computer or peak matching techniques. Fraction *B* gave $M \cdot^+$ 652 for $C_{25}H_{29}N_6O_{10}Br$. Fraction *C* gave $M \cdot^+$ 596 for $C_{22}H_{25}N_6O_9Br$. All fractions gave isotope patterns characteristic of a monobromo compound. In each fraction a strong peak corresponding to dinitrobromoaniline was observed, perhaps due to the cleavage of the azo bond with subsequent recombination with hydrogen to give the amine.

Example 3. A slight variation was observed in the navy blue dye (22). The IR spectrum showed two strong carbonyl bands at 1745 and 1695 (carbonate ester and anilide). HRMS gave $M \cdot^+$ 656.0715 for $C_{23}H_{25}N_6O_{12}Br$ (theory 656.0714). The pertinent feature was a fragment due to the loss of $C_3H_5O_3$, which can only be a $CH_2OC(=O)OCH_3$ group. The PMR spectrum was consistent in every way with (22).

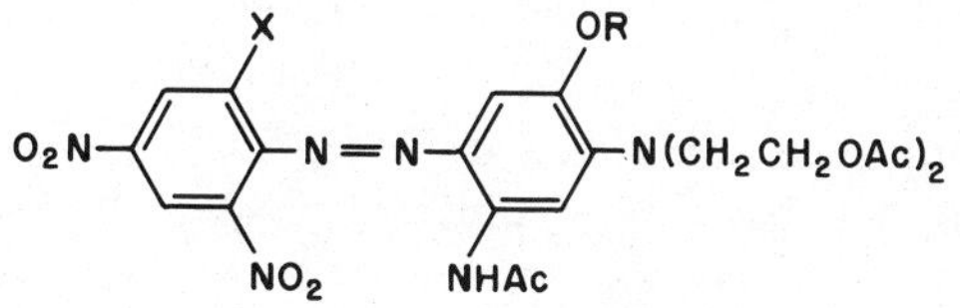

$$O_2N-\underset{NO_2}{\overset{X}{\bigcirc}}-N=N-\underset{NHAc}{\overset{OR}{\bigcirc}}-N(CH_2CH_2OAc)_2$$

(22)

Example 4. The IR spectrum of a red azo dye (23) showed a characteristic weak, short-wavelength carbonyl component that, together with a stronger, long-wavelength component, suggested the presence of a succinimide group. This was confirmed by an HRMS peak due to a loss of $C_5H_6NO_2$ from the molecular ion. This fragment is the succinimide group with one CH_2 group attached to the N. A singlet in the PMR spectrum at 2.67 for four H of the CH_2CO type confirmed the succinimide group.

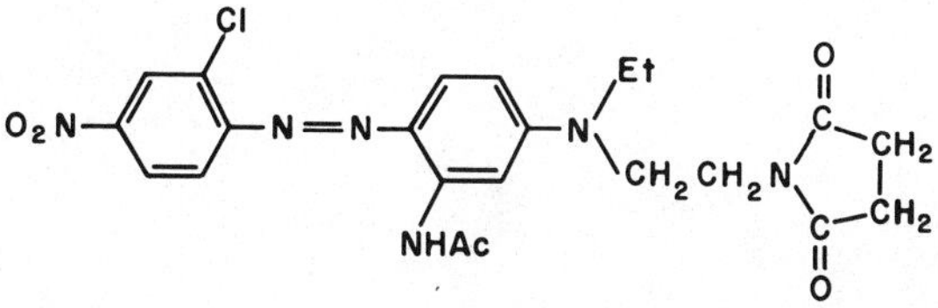

$$O_2N-\underset{}{\overset{Cl}{\bigcirc}}-N=N-\underset{NHAc}{\bigcirc}-N\underset{CH_2CH_2N}{\overset{Et}{<}}\overset{O}{\underset{O}{\overset{\|}{C}-CH_2}}\overset{}{\underset{C-CH_2}{}}$$

(23)

PMR also showed a characteristic NEt pattern and a pair of triplets due to the NCH_2CH_2N link. The long-wavelength carbonyl band in the IR spectrum showed a broad irregular pattern suggesting two unresolved peaks and, therefore, a carbonyl other than $C=O$ in the succinimide group. Ac-type methyl and ArNHCO PMR peaks suggested that the additional carbonyl was in an acetamido group.

HRMS gave M·+ 486.1420 for $C_{22}H_{23}N_6O_5Cl$ (theory 486.1419). The presence of Cl was very apparent from the isotope pattern. A strong peak from nitrochloroaniline established the structure of the diazo component. The aromatic region of the PMR spectrum was consistent with the substitution pattern of (23).

Example 5. Another variation is the rubine dye (24). The IR spectrum showed an acetate ester and strong similarities to other dyes having the methyl sulfone group in a similar environment.

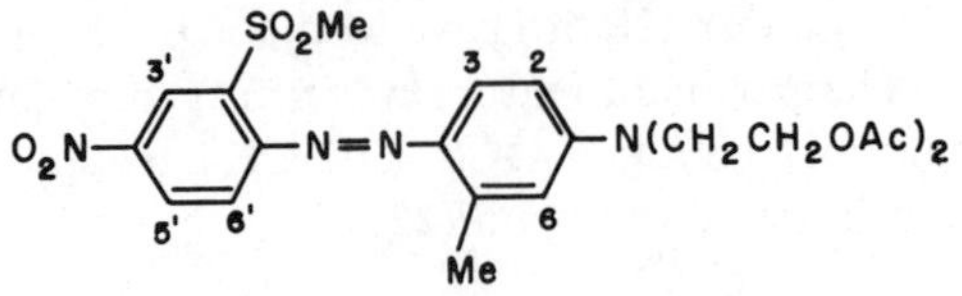

(24)

The PMR data are summarized in Table 12.8. The assignment of the sulfone Me group was based upon previous work with methyl sulfones in a similar environment. Sulfur was shown by X-ray fluorescence and by isotope patterns in the MS. M·+ 506.1475 for $C_{22}H_{26}N_4O_8S$ (theory 506.1471) and peaks for amines from the cleavage of the azo linkage were seen in the MS.

Table 12.8   60-MHz PMR Spectrum of (24)[a]

Chemical Shift	Multiplicity	Rel. No. Protons	Assignment
2.07	s	6	Ac—
2.72	s	3	ArMe (*o* to azo)
3.45	s	3	ArSO₂Me
3.75	t	4	ArN(R)CH₂CH₂—
4.30	t	4	—COOCH₂CH₂
6.7	Overl. *m*	2	H-2, H-6
7.75	d (*ortho*)	2	H-3
7.90	d (*ortho*)		H-6'
8.42	d of d (*ortho* and *meta*)	1	H-5'
8.97	d (*meta*)	1	H-3'

[a] $CDCl_3$.

Example 6. An example of a brown disazo dye is (25). HRMS yielded M·+ 453.1471 for $C_{22}H_{23}N_5O_4S$ (theory 453.1471). PMR indicated one Ar-Me, one OMe, and two N-Me groups. IR indicated a phenolic OH, not *ortho* to an azo group. HRMS gave two fragments from the cleavage of the second azo linkage, which established that the methyl groups were not on the phenolic ring. At this point the general features of the molecule were pretty well established; however, the substitution pattern was impossible to deduce from the 60-MHz PMR spectrum.

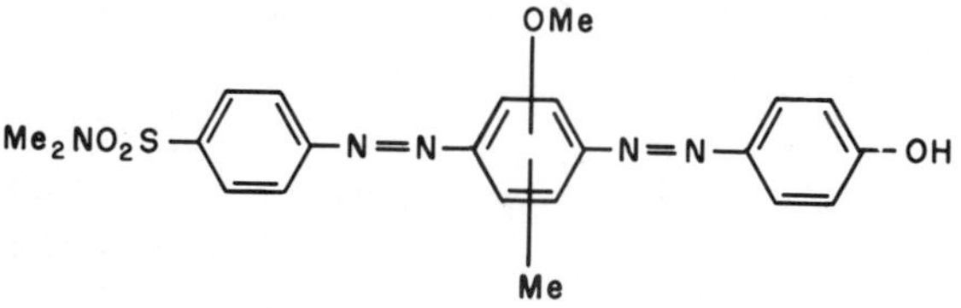

(25)

The 220-MHz PMR spectrum (see Chapter 8) showed four two-H doublets with *ortho* coupling and two singlets for two H.

Example 7. A rather unusual red azo dye is (26). HRMS yielded M·+ 364.1175. A peak at M+2 had an intensity of 10% of the molecular ion, strongly indicating two S. These data led to the formula $C_{15}H_{20}N_6OS_2$. The presence of sulfur was confirmed by X-ray fluorescence and the formula was in fair agreement with elemental C, H, and N analysis.

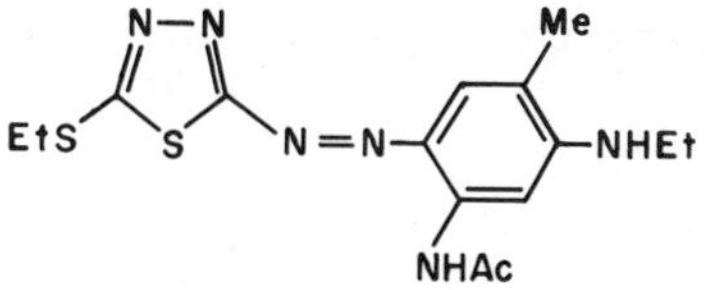

(26) 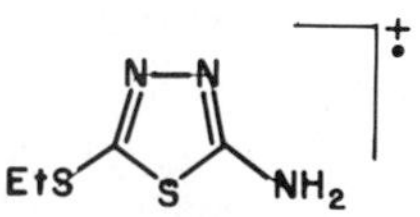   (27) 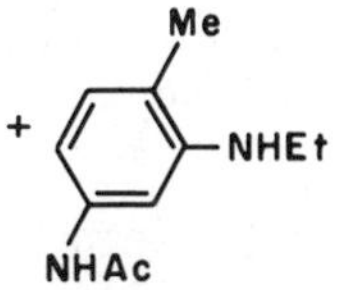   (28)

The PMR spectrum (Table 12.9) was unusual in that there were only two aromatic H. Lack of observable coupling constants suggested that they were probably *para* to each other. The PMR spectrum showed an ArMe peak. An Ac-type Me suggested an acetamide, confirmed by an IR band at 1689. Another unusual feature of the PMR spectrum was the presence of two Et groups in which the CH_2 groups had identical shifts, but the CH_3 groups were slightly different.

Table 12.9   220-MHz PMR Spectrum of (26)^a

Chemical Shift	Multiplicity	Rel. No. Protons	Assignment
1.24	t	3	CH_3CH_2—
1.41	t	3	CH_3CH_2—
2.11	s	3	=C(Me)—
2.18	s	3	Ac—
3.24 ⎤	br		H_2O
3.33 ⎦	q	4	—CH_2CH_3
6.95	t	1	—$NHCH_2$—
7.52	s	1	Aromatic
7.66	s	1	Aromatic
9.85	s	1	ArNHCO—

^{a} In DMSO-D$_6$.

The absence of an SO_2 peak in the MS indicated that the sulfur atoms were not in a sulfonate group. Strong peaks arising from fragments (27) and (28) were observed.

Example 8.   The IR spectrum of a yellow azo dye having the structure (29) showed a complex carbonyl region. The features suggested the possible presence of ester and secondary amide functions. A computer search of the IR reference file yielded no exact match, but did lead to a reference spectrum [structure (30)] which showed a number of strong similarities to the unknown.

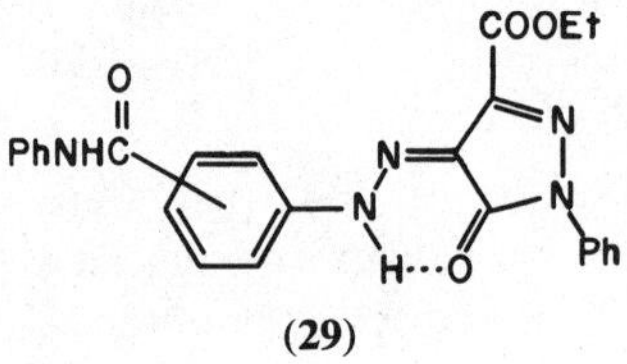

(29) 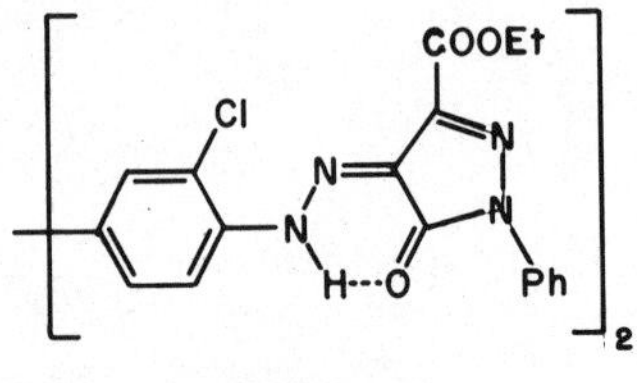   (30)

HRMS yielded M·+ 455.1635; calc. for $C_{25}H_{21}N_5O_4$ is 455.1594. Also suggestive of structure (29) were fragments due to the loss of PhNH and PhNHCOC$_6$H$_4$N and the fragment (31) formed by the indicated mechanism.

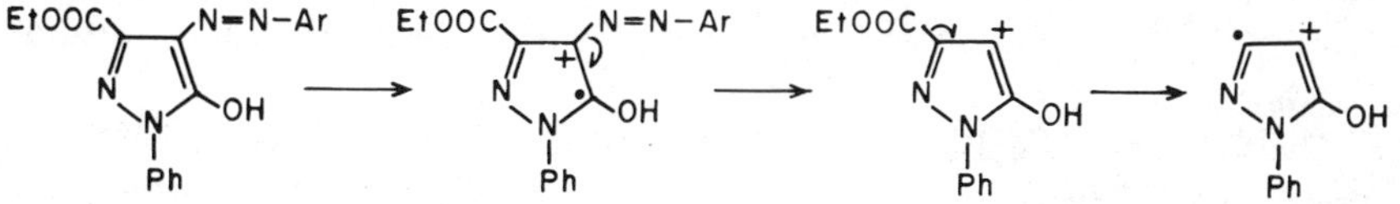

(31)

A 60-MHz PMR spectrum of the dye in DMSO-D_6 showed one CH_3-CH_2OCO-type Et group and about 14 H in the aromatic region which might include an NH proton. There was a singlet at 10.2 consistent with OH or NH. The aromatic pattern was second-order at 60 MHz, and therefore no substitution patterns could be determined.

3.2.3 Dyes Containing Ar—CH= and Related Groups. In general, identification of dyes of this type is not especially difficult; HRMS usually yields a molecular ion, the solubility in PMR-compatible solvents is normally favorable, and some of these dyes, especially those containing the dicyanoethylene group, show some strikingly unique features in the IR spectra.

Example 1. A good example that illustrates the complementary nature of IR, HRMS, and PMR is provided by the elucidation of structure (32).

The IR spectrum showed a rather high-intensity, complex C—H stretch pattern which was too poorly resolved to be readily interpreted. The most striking feature was the extremely intense, sharp nitrile band at 2212, consistent with the dicyanoethylene function. A sharp band at 3356 was undoubtedly an NH band.

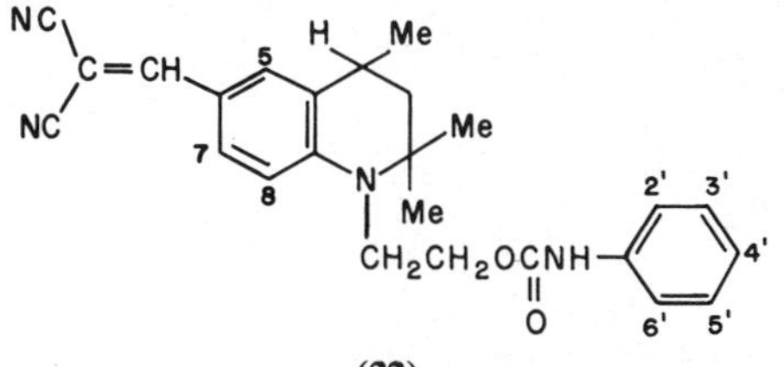

(32)

At lower frequencies the IR pattern was suggestive of an ester function, possibly acetate ester. There was a strong band near 1730 and a very strong band near 1235. The 1730 band was somewhat broad for an ester carbonyl. A strong HRMS peak corresponding to phenylisocyanate suggested the phenylurethane function as an alternative explanation. This was consistent with the 1730 and 1235 bands and with the previously noted strong NH band. The spectrum also showed the 756 and 692 "monosubstitution" bands expected for a phenylurethane.

Overall, both the IR and PMR spectra were very similar to reference spectra of a substituted hydroquinoline. The PMR spectral features, summarized in Table 12.10, showed CMe_2, CHMe, CH_2, $NCH_2CH_2OC(O)$, C(O)NHAr, and $=CH$ groups, as well as eight aromatic H in monosubstituted and 1,2,4-trisubstituted benzene rings. This spectrum is discussed in more detail in Chapter 8.

Based on the above data, structure (32) was proposed. HRMS confirmed this assignment by yielding $M \cdot^+$ 414.2091 compared to 414.2056 for $C_{25}H_{26}N_4O_2$. A fragment with m/e 264.1486 for $C_{17}H_{18}N_3$ (calc. 264.1501) was consistent with loss of $PhNHCOOCH_2$ from (32).

Table 12.10   220-MHz PMR Spectrum of (32)[a]

Chemical Shift	Multiplicity and Coupling Constants (Hz)	Rel. No. Protons	Assignments
1.26	s	3	—CMe
1.30	$d, J = 6.5$	3	CHMe
1.40	s	4	—CMe
1.50	$t, J = 13$		CH_2 (ring)
1.89	d of d, $J_g = 13, J_v = 4.5$	1	
2.88	m	1	CHMe
3.62	m	1	NCH_2
3.84	m	1	
4.27	m	2	—CO_2CH_2—
6.90	$d, J_o = 9$	1	H-8
7.01	t of d, $J_o = \sim 7, J_m = \sim 1$	1	H-4′
7.27	t, two ortho	2	H-3′, H-5′
7.46	d of d, $J_o = \sim 8, J_m = \sim 1$	2	H-2′, H-6′
7.71	d of d, $J_o = 9, J_m = 2.3$	1	H-7
7.86	$d, J_m = \sim 2.3$	1	H-5
7.94	s	1	$=CH$—
9.33	s	1	—CONHAr

[a] DMSO-D_6, 90°.

Example 2.   An intense low-frequency nitrile band in the IR spectrum of (**33**) strongly suggested that this dye was of the methine type containing the $=C(CN)_2$ group. Consistent with this was a singlet at 7.9 in the 60-MHz PMR spectrum (nitrobenzene-D_5) that could reasonably be assigned to the $CH=C(CN)_2$ proton. The aromatic pattern consisted of (*a*) one-H signals at 8.27 (*d*), 6.60 (*q*), and 6.67 (*d*) for a 1,2,4-trisubstituted benzene ring, and (*b*) a four-H singlet at 8.07 for a *p*-disubstituted benzene ring.

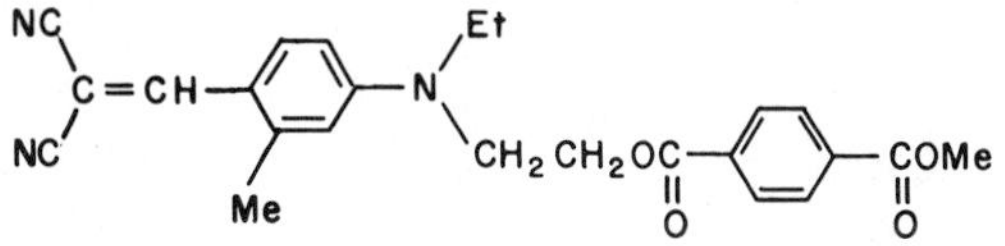

(**33**)

An empirical formula of $C_{24}H_{23}N_3O_4$ derived from the HRMS spectrum gave a "ring plus double bond" count of 15. Subtracting five for the $CH=C(CN)_2$ group and eight for the two benzene rings leaves only two double bonds for the rest of the molecule. The count of four O atoms from the HRMS and a strong ester carbonyl band in the IR spectrum suggested two ester groups. The low-field four-H singlet in the PMR spectrum and strong IR bands at 1271 and 729 indicated a terephthalate group. This hypothesis was further strengthened by a fragment in the HRMS corresponding to a loss of $CH_2OC(O)C_6H_4COOMe$ from the molecular ion.

PMR data showed an N-Et (1.32 *t* and 3.67 *q*), an Ar-Me (2.40), an OMe (3.92), and a $NCH_2CH_2OC(O)$ group (3.8 *t* and 4.6 *t*), completing the structure.

Finally, PMR and IR spectra matched those of a synthetic sample.

Example 3.   The IR spectrum of dye (**34**) showed some readily recognizable features. It was dominated by bands characteristic of the benzoate ester function: sharp 1706 carbonyl; very intense 1269 C-O stretch typical of esters of aromatic acids; a strong pattern in the 720–670 region; and a strong 2212 nitrile band, characteristic of methine dyes made from malono-nitrile.

The 220-MHz PMR spectrum (Table 12.11) clearly indicated two slightly different OMe groups, an $ArN(CH_2CH_2O—CO—Ph)_2$ moiety, as well as

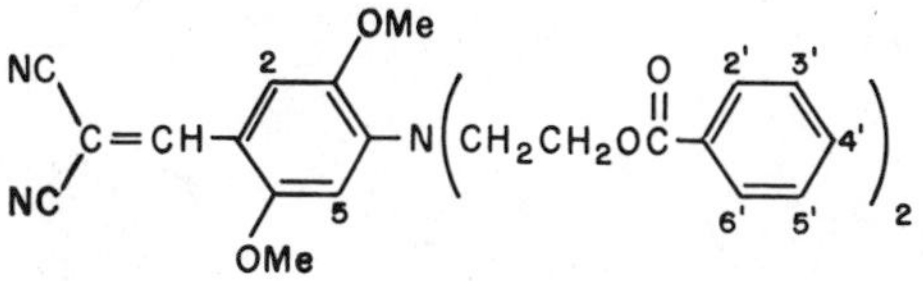

(**34**)

Table 12.11   220-MHz PMR Spectrum of (34)[a]

Chemical Shift	Multiplicity	Rel. No. Protons	Assignments
3.80	s	⎤ 6	—OMe
3.82	s	⎦	—OMe
3.93	t	4	—NCH₂CH₂—
4.54	t	4	—COOCH₂CH₂
6.55	s	1	H-5
7.39	t, fine structure	4	H-3', H-5'
7.55	t, fine structure	2	H-4'
7.72	s	1	H-2
7.92	d, fine structure	4	H-2', H-6'
7.99	s	1	=CH—

[a] $CDCl_3$.

a =CH and two additional aromatic H *para* to each other. Based on the IR and PMR data, structure (34) was proposed.

HRMS gave $M \cdot^+$ 525.1890 (calc. 525.1900). Peaks corresponding to losses of PhCOOH and $PhCOOCH_2 \cdot$ were also found.

Example 4. An interesting methine dye containing the benzothiazole nucleus was also identified by combining data from IR, HRMS, and PMR spectrometry.

The IR spectrum of (35) showed strong 2208 nitrile absorption. The pattern in the 1600–1500 region was very much like that found in the spectra of several other dyes containing the group (36). A strong pattern at 1000 suggested a 2-mercaptobenzothiazole derivative.

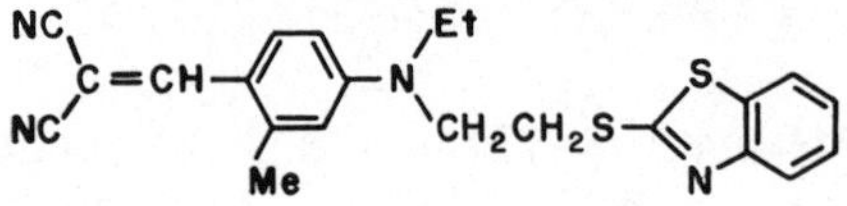

(35)

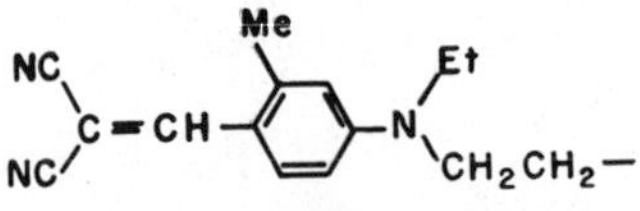

(36)

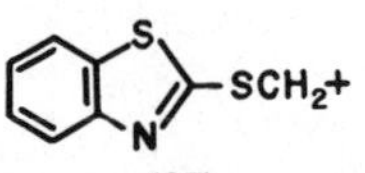

(37)

A HRMS showed an isotope pattern indicating two sulfur atoms and $M\cdot^+$ for $C_{22}H_{20}N_4S_2$ (found, 404.1134; calc., 404.1129). Peaks corresponding to losses of 2-mercaptobenzothiazole and fragment (37) were prominent.

The PMR spectrum (Table 12.12) indicated ArMe, NEt, and NCH_2CH_2X groups, where X could be O or S; HRMS data clearly showed that it was S.

Combining all the foregoing data readily led to structure (35).

Example 5. An unusual pyrazolone derivative was identified as (38).

The IR spectrum showed strong similarities to reference spectra of many azo dyes based on phenylmethylpyrazolone coupler, and was very similar to the spectrum of rubazonic acid (5). It showed a bonded $C{=}O$ at 1630 and strong bands at 754 and 686 consistent with monosubstituted benzene rings.

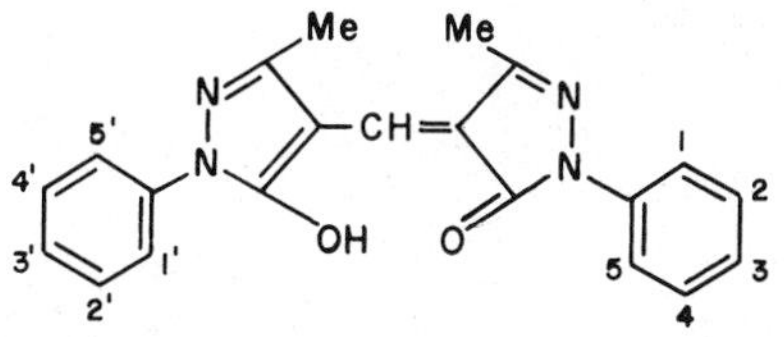

(38)

The types of protons found by PMR are summarized in Table 12.13. The proton count clearly showed that for an isolated $={=}CH$ proton there were two equivalent Me groups and two equivalent monosubstituted ben-

Table 12.12   60-MHz PMR Spectrum of (35)[a]

Chemical Shift	Multiplicity	Rel. No. Protons	Assignments
1.35	*t*	3	$CH_3CH_2{-}$
2.62	*s*	3	ArMe
~3.9	Overl. *m*	4	$\rangle NCH_2CH_3$, $\rangle NCH_2CH_2S$
4.35		2	$\rangle NCH_2CH_2S{-}$
~7.4–8.4	Complex	7	Aromatic
8.53	*s*	1	$={=}CH{-}$

[a] TFA.

Table 12.13   220-MHz PMR Spectrum of (38)[a]

Chemical Shift	Multiplicity	Rel. No. Protons	Assignments
2.13	s	6	=C—Me
6.94	s	1	=CH—
7.19	t, fine structure	2	H-3, H-3'
7.36	t, fine structure	4	H-2, H-4, H-2', H-4'
7.88	d, fine structure	4	H-1, H-5, H-1', H-5'
17.9	s	1	—OH

[a] $CDCl_3$.

zene rings, as well as an unusually strongly bonded proton reminiscent of the hydroxyl group in rubazonic acids. The resemblance to rubazonic acid suggested structure (38).

HRMS yielded M·+ 358.1473 (calc. for $C_{21}H_{18}N_4O_2$, 358.1430). Prominent peaks due to fragments resulting from loss of Me, OH, CO, and PhNH from the molecular ion were also observed, in agreement with the proposed structure.

Example 6.   The PMR spectrum of (39) (Table 12.14) suggested that this greenish yellow dye was a Fischer's aldehyde derivative. The two-H singlet at 5.27 and the five-H resonance at 7.37 suggested a benzyl group. The rest of the aromatic proton pattern was clearly consistent with a 1,2,4-trisubstituted benzene ring. The PMR spectrum also indicated an OMe, probably COOMe.

Absorption in the carbonyl region of the IR spectrum suggested two poorly resolved bands at about 1712 and 1695. A band at 2208 suggested a nitrile group probably conjugated with a double bond, as in a cyanoethylene group. HRMS yielded the molecular formula $C_{25}H_{24}N_2O_4$.

The presence of the Fischer's aldehyde moiety and the conjugated nitrile group suggested a methine dye. Since it could not be a dicyanoethylene (only two N in the molecule), some other group, such as an ester, should be conjugated with the cyanoethylene group. The evidence for 1,2,4-trisubstitution suggested a substituent on the Fischer's aldehyde part of the molecule. That group could be another ester, in view of the presence of four O and the possibility of two C=O groups.

Table 12.14 60-MHz PMR Spectrum of (39)^a

Chemical Shift	Multiplicity	Rel. No. Protons	Assignments
1.63	s	6	$>$CMe$_2$
3.37	s	3	$>$NMe
3.93	s	3	—COOMe
5.27	s	2	—COOCH$_2$Ph
5.90	d (J ≈ 13 Hz)	1	=CH—
6.75	d (ortho)	1	H-7
7.37	br s	5	—Ph
7.94	d (meta)	1	H-4
8.03	d (ortho and meta)	1	H-6
8.45	d (J ≈ 13 Hz)	1	=CH—

^{a} CDCl$_3$.

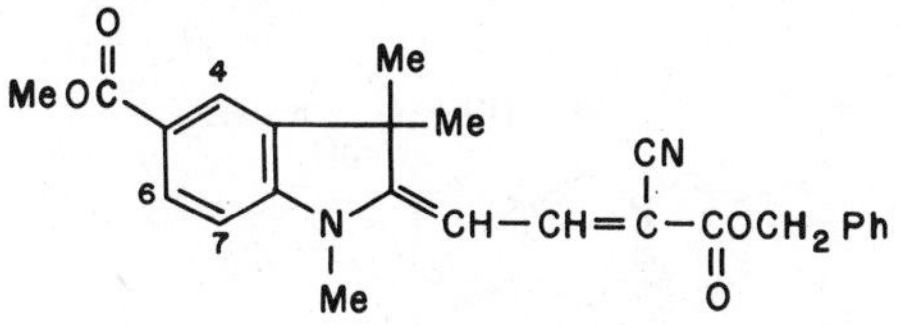

(39) 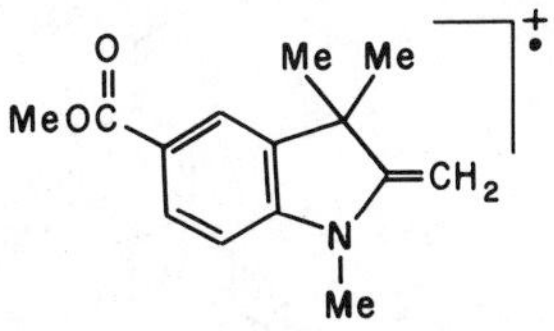　　　　　　　　　(40)

The structural elements identified could be assembled in a number of ways. A fragment in the MS with a nominal mass of 231 clearly eliminated structures other than (39) since it was consistent with fragment (40).

3.3 Cationic Dyes

Cationic dyes may have a wide variety of chromophores and substituents; thus they present varying analytical complexities. They are grouped together here because they are readily classified as cationic dyes, even before analysis has begun, by virtue of their recommended uses. They can usually be purified as the insoluble iodides and/or picrates (see Section 2.2). An interesting aspect which they have in common is that their HRMS never contain the molecular cation; rather, the molecule either expels a proton or an alkyl group, or undergoes more complex changes.

An advantage of the PMR analysis of the picrates is that the picrate protons often appear as a readily recognized two-H singlet, useful for calculating the proton count in other regions.

The anion is omitted from the structures in this section, but mentioned in the discussion where pertinent. The IR spectra were always obtained from the iodides.

Example 1. An olive green dye was identified as **(41)**. The IR spectrum of this cation was rather complex and showed no readily identifiable bands in the functional group region. A strong pattern in the 817–790 region suggested isolated pairs of adjacent ring hydrogens ("*para*-disubstitution"). HRMS showed an ion with m/e 400.1577 (calc. for $C_{28}H_{20}N_2O$, 400.1576). In view of the general behavior of cationic dyes, this would probably correspond to a related neutral amine rather than the original dye cation. Since the PMR data showed that the cation contained at least 22 H (in the solvent used, exchangeable protons would not be observed), it was concluded that a Me group was lost in the MS.

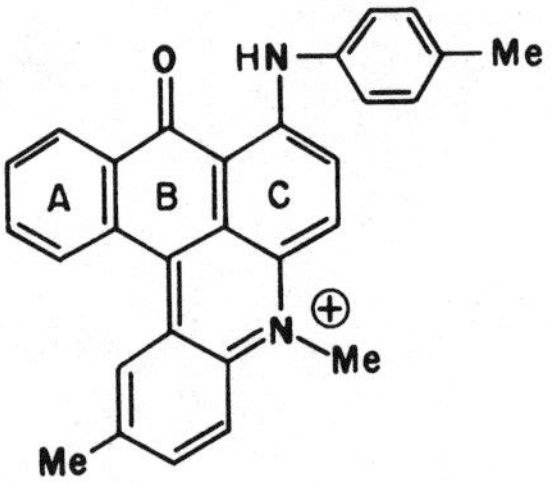

(41) 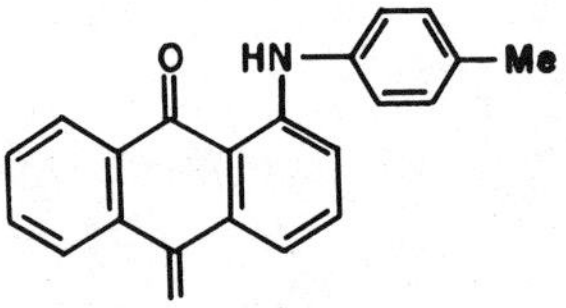   (42)

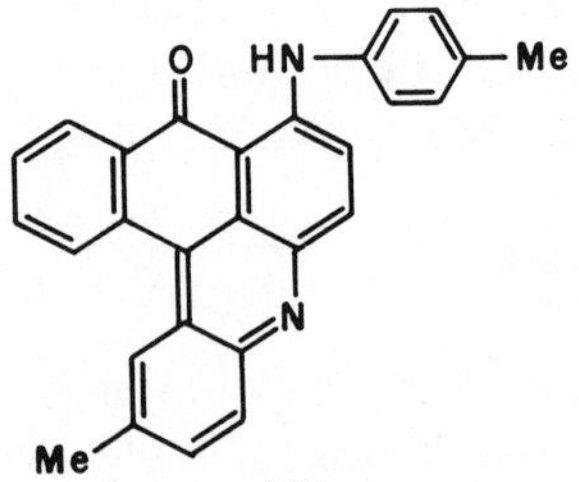

(43)

The picrate gave a PMR spectrum in TFA which showed, in addition to the picrate peak, the following features: (1) three singlets at about 2.5, 2.8, and 4.9, assignable respectively to two Me groups bonded to aromatic carbons and one $^+$NMe; (2) a four-H multiplet centered around 7.4 probably due to a *para*-disubstituted benzene ring; and (3) a complex pattern (nine H) between 7.8 and 9.0, part of which was typical of an unsubstituted anthraquinone A ring.

These data suggested a highly condensed ring system, possibly based on anthraquinone. Since PMR did not indicate a OMe group, it was logical to assume that the O was in a H-bonded C=O, not readily detected by IR. With the structural elements available, a *para*-disubstituted benzene ring with unlike substituents would most likely be a *p*-toluidino group, and the speculative partial structure (42) was drawn at this point.

Subtraction of the elements of (42) and *one* of the remaining methyl groups from the empirical formula of the neutral molecule, $C_{28}H_{20}N_2O$, left C_6H_2N. This fragment could be calculated to have 6.5 "rings plus double bonds" and could be accommodated only by expanding the condensed ring system. Speculation based partly on the spectral evidence and partly on chemical intuition suggested structure (43) for the neutral molecule. Since it lost Me rather than H in the MS, structure (41) was proposed for the cation. This was consistent with the IR spectrum which showed no evidence for $^+$NH.

The structure was confirmed by synthesis.

Example 2. The structure of a yellow dye was established to be (44).

The IR spectrum was very similar to a reference spectrum of Basic Yellow 21 (45), and the PMR spectrum clearly showed a pattern very characteristic of Fischer's aldehyde derivatives. Thus it seemed probable that the unknown was a cyanine dye with partial structure (46).

HRMS gave a strong peak at m/e 374.2346 (calc. for $C_{25}H_{30}N_2O$, 374.2358). Since the PMR data indicated 31 H in the dye, the 374 peak

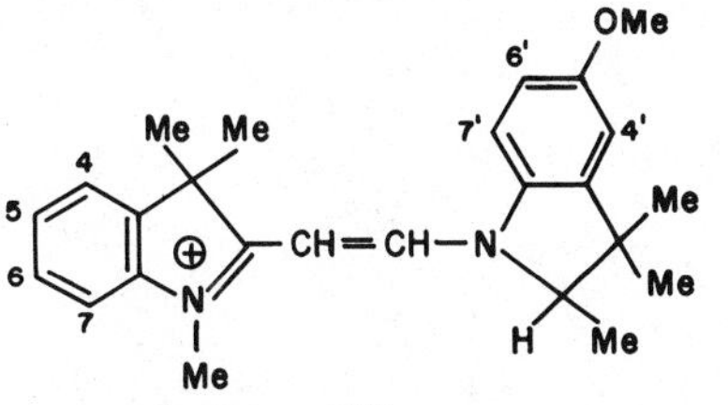

(44) 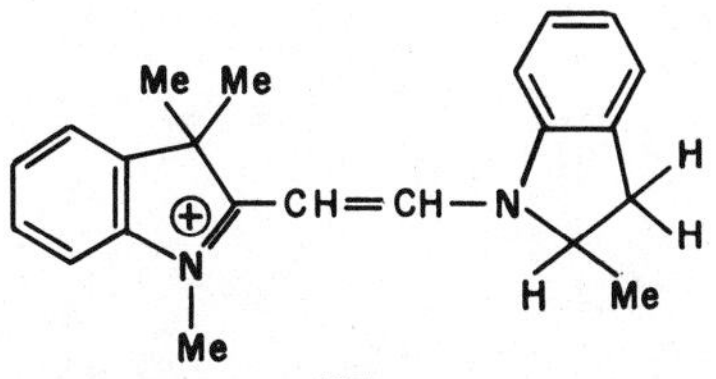   (45)

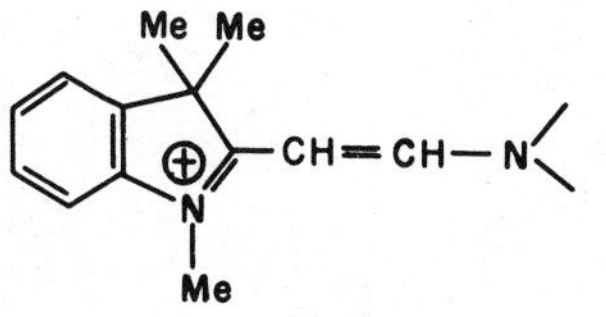

(46)

must have resulted from expulsion of a proton, and the cation must have the formula $C_{25}H_{31}N_2O$. Subtracting the elements of (46) left $C_{12}H_{16}O$ for the remainder of the cation. A MS peak with m/e for $C_{12}H_{17}NO$, which could be the amine containing that residue, was indeed found, tending to confirm the analysis to that point.

The structure of the remainder of the molecule was elucidated via 220-MHz PMR (Table 12.15). Part of the aromatic proton region was complex even at this frequency and some of the chemical shifts and assignments are tentative. A double-resonance experiment in which the 5.22 quartet was irradiated, resulting in the collapse of the 1.38 doublet, helped to elucidate the Me proton patterns, thus allowing the precise location of the remaining three Me groups and the one H on the hetero ring. PMR also indicated the O to be in a OMe group on the phenyl ring and established the 1,2,4 substitution on that ring.

Table 12.15 220_3MHz PMR Spectrum of (44)[a]

Chemical Shift	Multiplicity	Rel. No. Protons	Assignments
1.37	s		
1.45	s	9	—CH(Me)CMe₂
1.38	d		\CHMe
1.76	s	3	\N⁺=C—CMe₂
1.82	s	3	
3.87	s	3	\N⁺—Me and —OMe
3.96	s	3	
5.22	q	1	\NCH(Me)—
6.19	d	1	=CH—
8.42	d	1	=CH—
6.81	d (meta)	1	H-4′
6.96	d of d (ortho and meta)	1	H-6′
7.29	br d (ortho and meta?)	1	H-4 or H-7
7.30	t (two ortho)	1	H-5 or H-6
~7.40			H-4 or H-7
~7.42	Overl. m	3	H-5 or H-6
~7.46			H-7′

[a] $CDCl_3$.

Example 3.   A blue dye (**47**) was shown by elemental analysis to contain S. Its IR spectrum showed weak evidence for NH (overlapped probably by OH due to moisture), a medium-intensity 1684 band possibly due to an amide C=O, and a very strong 1160 band, suggesting an azo compound of general structure (**48**). A strong pattern in the 840 region was possibly due to adjacent pairs of benzene ring protons. Strong bands at 1263 and 1234 were probably due to Ar-N and/or Ar-O functions, and a band at 734 was possibly due to mono- or *ortho*-disubstituted benzene rings.

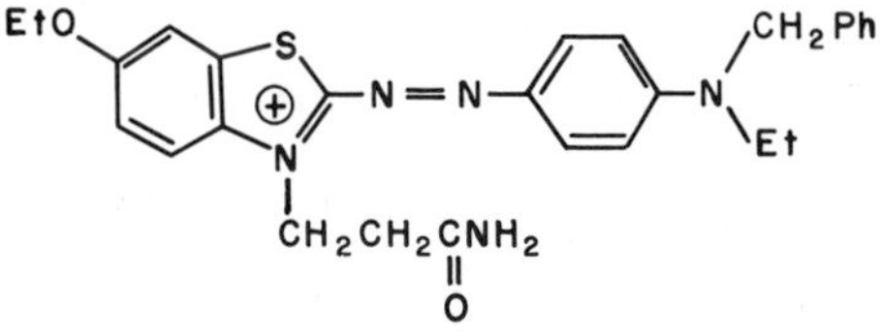

(47)

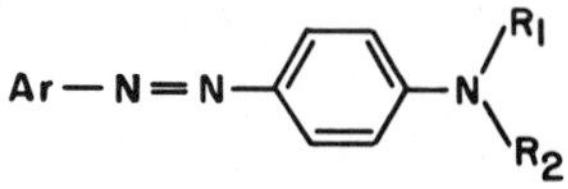

(48)

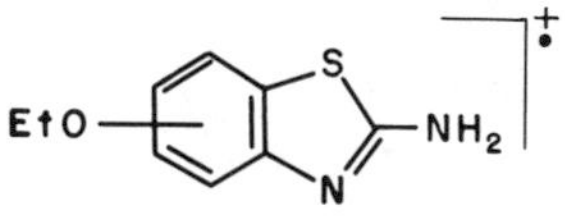

(49)

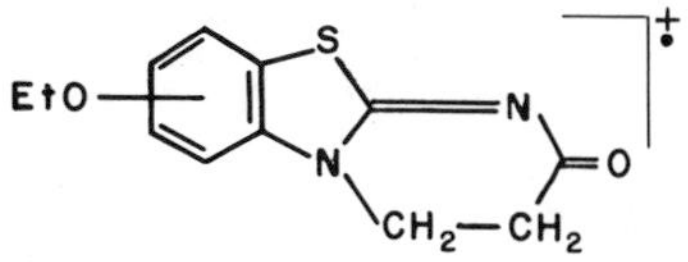

(50)

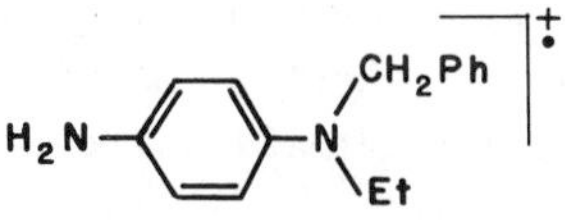

(51)

The PMR spectrum (Table 12.16) showed mostly broad resonance patterns suggesting overlapping multiplets. There was evidence for two non-equivalent ethyl groups (probably NEt and OEt) and an XCH_2CH_2Y group where X and Y could be quaternized N and C=O, respectively. Superposed on the largely complex, aromatic proton pattern was a peak at 7.38, which, together with the 5.13 resonance, suggested an *N*-benzyl group. The total "aromatic" area accounted for 14 H, two of which exchanged with TFA-D, suggesting NH_2.

HRMS gave no molecular ion, but did show fragments from which the dye molecule could be reconstructed. Thus a fragment was found with the probable formula $C_9H_{10}N_2OS$, as for (**49**). The presence of OEt was in agreement with the IR and PMR data. A second HRMS fragment, prob-

Table 12.16   60-MHz PMR Spectrum of (47)[a]

Chemical Shift	Multiplicity	Rel. No. Protons	Assignments
1.29 ⎤ ⎥ Overl. t 1.37 ⎦		⎤ 6 ⎦	$>$NCH$_2$CH$_3$ and —OCH$_2$CH$_3$
2.77	t	2	—CH$_2$CH$_2$CO—
~3.9 ⎤ ⎥ Overl. br q 4.12 ⎦		⎤ 4 ⎦	$>$NCH$_2$CH$_3$ —OCH$_2$CH$_3$
4.92 ⎤ ⎥ br, overl. 5.13 ⎦		⎤ 4 ⎦	$>\overset{+}{N}$CH$_2$CH$_2$— $>$NCH$_2$Ph
~7.8–8.4	Complex	14	Aromatic, NH$_2$

[a] DMSO-D$_6$.

ably $C_{12}H_{12}N_2O_2S$, appeared to be related to (49); in view of the PMR evidence for NCH$_2$CH$_2$CO, it was speculated that this fragment had structure (50).

A third HRMS fragment, $C_{15}H_{18}N_2$, was presumably (51) derived from the coupler portion of the dye.

Structure (47) was postulated for the dye, based on the MS fragments, amide carbonyl in the IR, and chemical likelihood of the orientation of the ethoxy group *para* to the nitrogen atom. The identification was confirmed by synthesis.

Example 4.   The IR spectrum of a yellow dye showed very strong similarity to a reference spectrum of (52). A sharp difference was that the former showed no nitrile band, but a broad absorption in the 2780–2500 region, indicative of $^+$NH.

HRMS gave an ion, m/e 399.1874 (calc. for $C_{20}H_{25}N_5O_4$, 399.1907). Subtracting $C_{14}H_{13}N_4O_4$ [(52) minus C≡N] left $C_6H_{12}N$. A striking peak

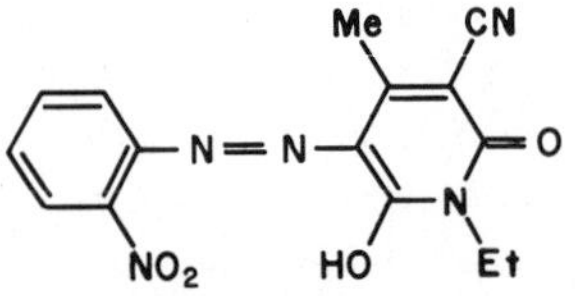

(52) 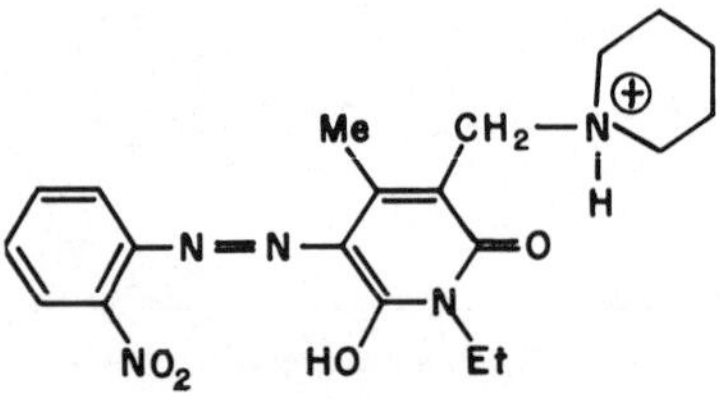   (53)

in the MS, m/e 84.0837, could hardly be anything other than the piperidyl group, $C_5H_{10}N$. This led to piperidylmethyl as the probable structure of the $C_6H_{12}N$ residue. Since the cation had ^+NH (from IR), structure (53) became the postulated dye cation. The 60-MHz PMR spectrum was consistent with (53), although it was weak and incompletely resolved. A proton broad band decoupled Fourier transform CMR spectrum was obtained to confirm the structure. The carbon chemical shifts are shown in Table 12.17. The assignments were made with the help of a gated decoupling experiment.

Table 12.17   22.63-MHz CMR Spectrum of (53)[a]

Chemical Shift	Assignments
12.82	—Me
14.91	—Me
21.05	—$CH_2CH_2CH_2$—
22.26	—$CH_2CH_2CH_2$—
34.61	NCH_2
52.35	NCH_2
52.69	—N(CH$_2$—)(CH$_2$—)
117.2	=CH
118.2	=CX[b]
124.5	=CH
125.9	=CH
127.8	=CX
134.9	=CX
136.7	=CH
137.7	=CX
151.5	=CX
160.1	=CX
162.9	C=O

[a] DMSO-D_6, 6000 pulses.
[b] X = substituent other than H.

Table 12.18   220-MHz PMR Spectrum of (54)[a]

Chemical Shift	Multiplicity	Rel. No. Protons	Assignments
1.23	t	6	CH_3CH_2—
2.25	s	3 ·	Me-Ar
3.72	q	4	CH_3CH_2
6.76	s	1	Ar-H (no o- or m-H neighbor)
7.00	d ($meta$)	1	Ar-H (no o-H neighbor)
7.35	d of d ($ortho$ and $meta$)	1	Ar-N (one o- and one m-H neighbor)
7.59	s	1	Ar-H (no o- or m-H neighbor)
7.72	d ($ortho$)	1	Ar-H (no m-H neighbor)
8.6	br	2	Exchangeable (NH_2)

[a] DMSO-D_6.

Example 5.   A blue dye was shown to have structure (54). The IR spectrum showed sharp bands at 3300 and 3125, suggesting NH or NH_2 (bonded), and a band at 1647, possibly due to C=O or C=N. The 220-MHz PMR spectrum showed the features listed in Table 12.18. HRMS yielded a peak at m/e 281.1540 (calc. for $C_{17}H_{19}N_3O$, 281.1528), probably the neutral molecule since PMR showed 20 H.

The PMR and IR evidence clearly identified Me, NEt_2, and NH_2 groups, leaving $C_{12}H_4NO$ to be accounted for. The formula of the neutral molecule indicated 10 "rings plus double bonds," all of which would be in that residue. Since there was no C≡N band in the IR spectrum, these data required a condensed ring system, and the chemical behavior of the dye favored the oxazine nucleus of (54). The exact positions of the substituents were not unequivocally established by spectrometry, but it was clear that one of the benzene rings was 1,2,4-tri- and the other 1,2,4,5-tetrasubstituted.

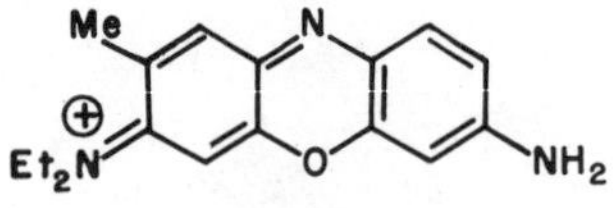

(54)

Example 6. Structure (**55**) was assigned to this bordeaux dye. The IR spectrum showed a strong band at 1149, consistent with the partial structure (**48**). It also showed a nitrile band at the frequency typical of substitution on an aromatic ring.

The PMR spectrum showed a triplet at 1.22 and a quartet at 3.69 for NEt. Two more triplets at 4.41 and 5.26 were probably due to $\overset{+}{N}CH_2CH_2X$. PMR also detected 12 aromatic H. A doublet centered around 9.57 ($J = 7$ Hz) suggested the H-2 and H-6 of a pyridinium ring, and a four-H pattern suggested a *p*-disubstituted benzene ring. The remainder of the aromatic proton pattern was too complex to be completely assigned.

The data thus far suggested structure (**56**). HRMS showed a prominent peak consistent with $C_{15}H_{13}N_5O_2$; since no C=O had been detected by IR, a NO_2 group was suspected, and a reasonable structure for the ion was (**57**).

Structure (**55**) was then proposed for the dye cation, and confirmed by synthesis.

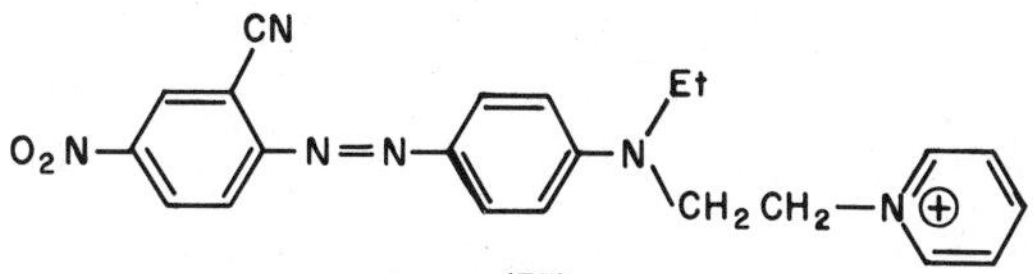

(55)

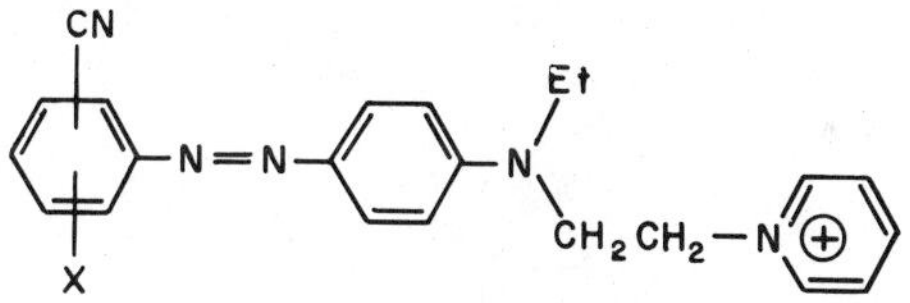

(56)

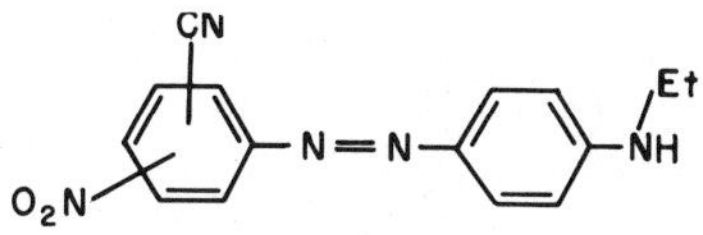

(57)

ACKNOWLEDGMENTS

The invaluable assistance of the following members of the Jackson Laboratory research staff in providing X-ray analyses, sample preparation, literature searches, and discussions is gratefully acknowledged: R. L. Bujalski, J. K. Buxbaum, G. F. Eastlack, A. A. Ebert, Jr., M. C. Heritage, D. Lewandowski, J. R. Martin, and J. S. Proctor. In addition we are indebted to D. W. Ovenall and F. W. Barney of the Central Research and Development Department of Du Pont for providing CMR and 220-MHz PMR spectra.

REFERENCES

1. V. S. Salvin et al., "Identification of Dye Classes on Fibers," in J. W. Weaver, Ed., *Analytical Methods for a Textile Laboratory*, 2nd ed., American Association of Textile Chemists and Colorists, Research Triangle Park, N.C., 1968, pp. 187–218.

2. F. B. Stilmar and M. A. Perkins, "Anthraquinone Intermediates," in H. A. Lubs, Ed., *The Chemistry of Synthetic Dyes and Pigments*, Waverly Press, Baltimore, 1955, p. 355.

CHAPTER THIRTEEN

Examples of Structure Determination—II

ROLAND M. LANZARONE

1 INTRODUCTION

1.1 Identification Techniques

The methods used in our laboratory for the analysis of dyes and pigments include the traditional chemical methods, such as reduction, hydrolysis, and pyrolysis, as well as more modern techniques such as electrophoresis, column chromatography, PC, TLC, GC, IR, NMR, UV, and visible absorption spectroscopy. The conditions used in each technique are those described in the literature[1,2] or elaborated in the laboratory for a particular identification or as a general method of analysis. For GC, for instance, the optimum conditions for identification of aromatic amines were determined. Some 300 such amines were then chromatographed against certain standards at definite temperatures in order to obtain their relative retention times. Tables of these results are now an important aid in the identification of such products. For IR spectroscopy, the different aminonaphtholsulfonic acids encountered after reduction of azo dyes were prepared and their IR spectra, as well as those of a great number of sulfonated or carboxylated aromatic amines, were obtained, thus forming a valuable library of spectra. We also have at our disposal a collection of pure compounds, many of them originally prepared in view of a specific identification. This collection of standards often permits the direct comparison of the substance isolated during the analysis or its known derivative with the pure authentic product.

The literature is scrutinized for new and interesting methods which may have been elaborated in other laboratories and which could be of direct or indirect help in our work. A method elaborated for biochemical or pharmaceutical identification may thus find its use in dye analysis. When a technique appears interesting, it is investigated, and if found of value, it may be adopted, developed, and passed on to other research or control laboratories of the company, either for general information or for use in a particular situation.

Another important aid in the identification of dyes is the patent literature. A good knowledge of the patent literature helps a great deal and sometimes, when other methods fail, it may be the only way of interpreting results.

Techniques such as punched cards are also in use for expediting information retrieval and reducing the time of analysis.

1.2   General Analytical Procedure

When a dye or pigment is received for analysis, it may be in its original container with its commercial name on the label. With the help of the *Colour Index* it is often possible to establish the type of dye: an acid, basic, or disperse dye, a pigment, etc., and sometimes its chemical class (e.g., azo, anthraquinone). If the commercial name is unknown, it is important to find out the fiber for which it is used, e.g., wool, acrylic, or polyester. If neither commercial name nor usage is known, it is possible to determine by electrophoresis, by dyeing on different fibers, or by solubility tests whether it is an anionic, cationic, or nonionic dye. The dye is then chromatographed, if possible, on paper or thin layers (silica gel or polyamide) with the appropriate solvents in order to ascertain its degree of purity. If a mixture is present, it often must be separated into the components prior to analysis.

A dye applicable to wool or cotton should be checked for a reactive group. Deactivation is then necessary to eliminate secondary reactions between the reactive group and the scission products, obtained, for example, after reduction of an azo dye. If the sample is a metal complex, as seen from the ash content, it is best to demetallize it and obtain the original dye or dyes.

Before starting an analysis, it may further be necessary to purify the dye by removing the diluent or dispersing agents. An acid or direct dye, for instance, can in most cases be washed with very dilute hydrochloric acid to eliminate the salts used as diluents. It is possible, on the other hand, to separate a disperse dye from dispersing agent by extraction with a solvent such as acetone or methylene chloride. The dye is then recrystallized and the pure compound submitted to elemental analysis or other quantitative determinations. If the purified dye is suspected, for example, by chromatography, to be a known product, it is compared by dyeing, chromatography, and IR spectroscopy with the standard to prove identity. On the other hand, if the purified dye is unknown, it is broken down by reduction, hydrolysis, or pyrolysis. The scission products are isolated by steam distillation, extraction, or fractional crystallization. They are then chromatographed in order to ascertain their degree of purity and to attempt an identification. Complete identification is then carried out by IR spectroscopy or m.p. or b.p. determination of the product and/or its derivative. After all scission products have been identified, the dye is synthesized and compared with the original compound by chromatography, IR spectroscopy, and dyeing.

2 EXAMPLES

2.1 Azo Pigments

2.1.1 CI Pigment Red 188. The pigment is classified in CI as monoazo. The red powder was washed with very dilute sodium hydroxide solution to eliminate any excess coupling component, then with distilled water, and finally with ethanol. Part of it was crystallized from nitrobenzene, m.p. 370°, $C_{33-34}H_{24}Cl_2N_4O_6$. Only one reducible group, the azo group, is present as determined by reduction with chromous chloride.[3] The molecule contains two methoxyls (Zeisel). Because the pigment was particularly difficult to reduce the reaction was carried out on 20 g in boiling DMF (400 ml) and glacial acetic acid (20 ml) with zinc dust (50 g). After complete decolorization, the zinc suspension was filtered and the filtrate was diluted with 1600 ml of water. The voluminous greenish precipitate was crystallized from acetic acid and found to be a primary aromatic amine (m.p. 212°), $C_{15}H_{12}Cl_2N_2O_3$, containing one OMe. Fusion with sodium hydroxide at 180° for 4 hours yielded 2,5-dichloroaniline, identified by GLC, and 2-amino-terephthalic acid, identified by its IR spectrum. The original amine must therefore have been (1) or the isomer with NH₂ *meta* to COOMe. Both were synthesized and the amine was identified as (1).

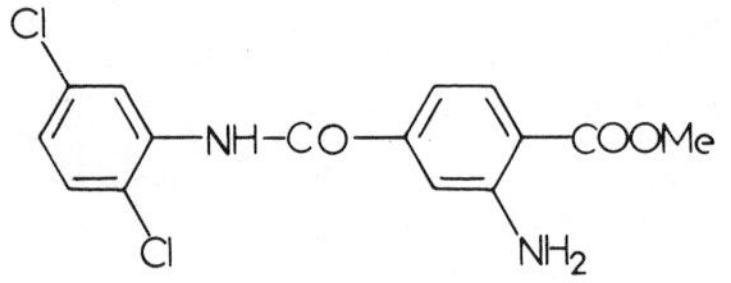

(1) 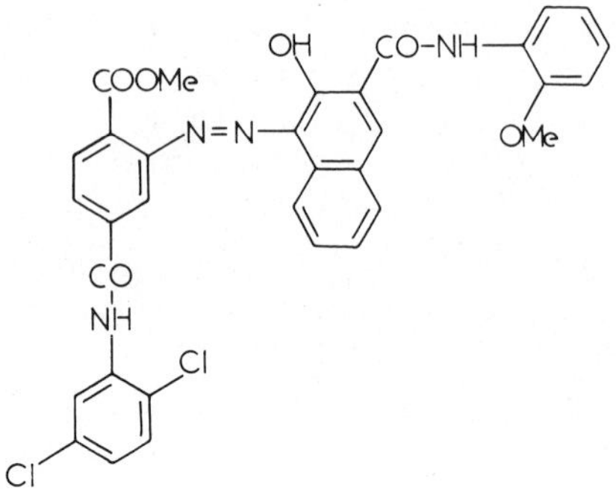   (2)

The formulas of the pigment and the diazo component led to $C_{18-19}H_{15}$-NO_3 for the coupling component. To obtain red azo pigments, three main types of coupling components are used: 2-naphthol, 2-hydroxy-3-naphthoic acid, and 2-hydroxy-3-naphtharylides. From the number of carbon atoms it was apparent that the coupling component is a 2-hydroxy-3-naphtharylide. Alkali fusion of the pigment yielded *o*-anisidine in addition to 2,5-dichloroaniline. The coupling component therefore is 2-hydroxy-3-naphth-*o*-anisidide and the pigment is (2), described in a patent.[4] Confirmation of (2) was obtained by synthesis and superposable IR spectra.

2.1.2 Pigment Light Yellow Z-410-112 (USSR). This pigment, m.p. 219°, is not registered in CI. It was easily reduced, giving rise to primary aromatic amines, and was therefore assumed to be an azo pigment. It contains neither halogen nor sulfur. The pigment was reduced in boiling ethanol and acetic acid with zinc dust. On complete decolorization, the zinc suspension was filtered and the filtrate treated with dilute hydrochloric acid. The yellowish precipitate (m.p. 217°) had the properties of a 2,5-dimethyl-1,4-dihydropyrazine-3,6-dicarboxyarylide.[1,5] Hydrolysis in boiling ethanolic potassium hydroxide liberated aniline. The coupling component therefore is acetoacetanilide. After the pyrazine derivative was filtered, alcohol was distilled off. The aqueous residue was made alkaline and extracted with ether. By PC,[6] two amines were detected. They were separated by PLC as follows. Whatman CC41 microgranular cellulose powder (120 g) was slurried in 20% formamide solution in ethanol (200 ml) and applied on glass plates in layers of 2 mm thickness. When the alcohol evaporated, the solution of amines was deposited and elution was carried out with benzene. The separated amines were then extracted and identified by their IR spectra as o-toluylenediamine and o-phenylenediamine. The diazo component is therefore a mixture of 2-nitro-p-toluidine and o-nitroaniline and the pigment a mixture of (3a) and (3b).

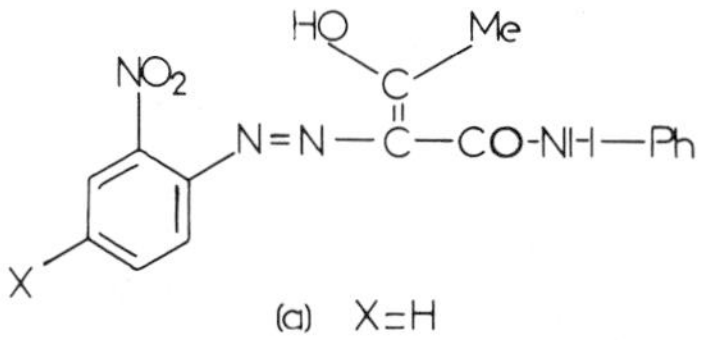

(a) X=H
(b) X=Me
(3)

These two pigments were prepared and the m.p. curve of their mixtures drawn; m.p. 219° corresponds to a mixture of 33% (3b) and 67% (3a). This mixture and Pigment Light Yellow Z-410-112 had identical IR spectra.

2.2   Acid Azo Dyes

2.2.1   CI Acid Red 301.   This dye is classified in CI as azo. By TLC it was found to be a mixture of a main dye (32%) with two other dyes (10%). Their solubility in ethanol enabled their separation from the diluent (58%). The main dye $C_{23}H_{20}ClN_3O_6S_2$ was separated by column chromatography of the aqueous solution on neutral alumina. Only one reducible group, the azo group, is present (chromous chloride).[3]

Treatment of the original dye (60 g) with a 12% NaCl solution (400 ml) at 50° dissolved the diluent, leaving the mixture of undissolved dyes. It was filtered, dissolved in water (400 ml) at 80°, and reduced with sodium dithionite (30 g). On cooling a precipitate was obtained. It was filtered and recrystallized from water, $C_{10}H_{10}N_2O_4S$. It reacted with phenanthraquinone, indicating an o-diamine. Solubility and spot tests[1] suggested 7,8-diamino-1-naphthol-3-sulfonic acid derived from γ-acid, the coupling component.

Another reduction was carried out on the original dye (40 g) in 1 N NaOH (330 ml) by heating the solution for 1 hour under reflux, the diluent being the reducing agent. On cooling an amine precipitated. It was soluble in benzene and was recrystallized from dilute methanol, m.p. 133°, $C_{13}H_{12}$-$ClNO_2S$. The acetyl derivative, m.p. 122–123°, was prepared. The literature[7] showed that (4) had similar properties and identity was confirmed by synthesis. The dye (5)[8] was prepared and found to be identical with the main dye present in the commercial dye.

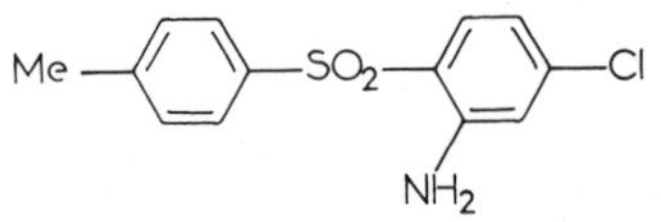

(4) 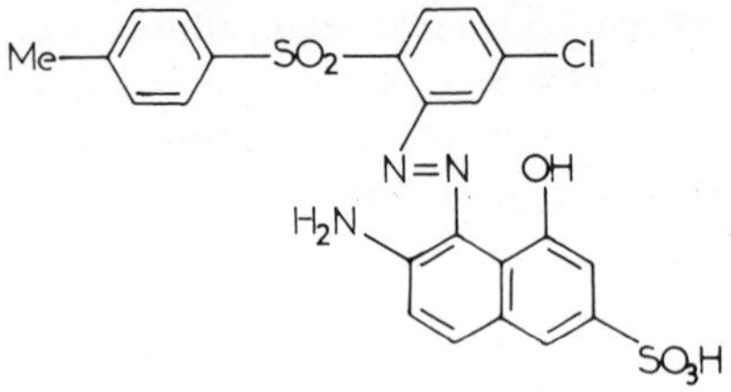   **(5)**

2.2.2   CI Acid Orange 127.   This dye is classified in CI as azo. The dye was treated with 1 N HCl at 65° in order to remove the diluent (68%). PC[6,9] of the solution obtained by reduction at 80° with sodium hydroxide and dithionite showed four amines. Steam distillation yielded p-phenetidine and 3-methyl-p-phenetidine in equal amount (GLC). In a second reduction the products were extracted with benzene. The two amines already identified and a diamine were thus obtained. Addition of acetic anhydride to the benzene layer resulted in acetylation; only the diamine derivative (m.p. 319°) precipitated, and was identified as the diacetyl derivative of 1,4-naphthalenediamine. The aqueous layer after benzene extraction was acidified and concentrated under vacuum. The crystalline product, after recrystallization from dilute hydrochloric acid, was identified (IR) as metanilic acid. A patent[10] describes a mixture of 5.2 parts dye **(6a)** and 5.8 parts dye **(6b)**.

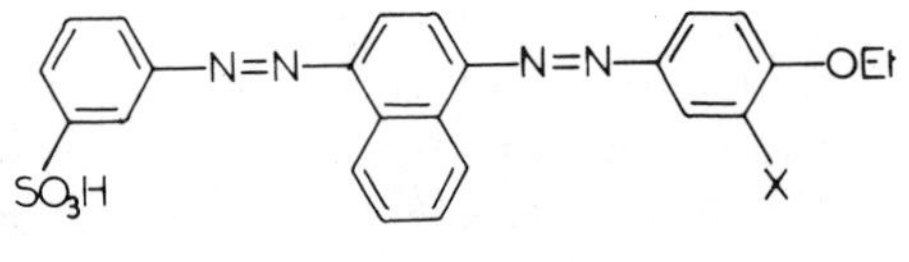

(a)   X=H
(b)   X=Me
(6)

The two dyes were synthesized and their mixture gave an IR spectrum superposable with that of the analyzed mixture of dyes.

2.2.3   CI Acid Orange 67.   The dye was treated with 1 N HCl in order to wash off the diluent (17%). For $C_{26-27}H_{21}N_4O_8S_2$ two reducible groups (an azo and a nitro) are present (chromous chloride).[3] PC[6,9] of the product obtained by alkaline reduction showed two amines, one of which was a sulfonic acid. The washed dye (45 g) was dissolved at 80° in 0.3 N NaOH (350 ml) and reduced with sodium dithionite (60 g). An amine precipitated. It was filtered and recrystallized from aqueous alcohol: $C_{14}H_{15}NO_3S$, m.p. 110°. PC[6] showed that it was not a sulfonic or carboxylic acid; and since it contained only one N, it could only be a sulfide, sulfone, or sulfo-ester. The chromatographic behavior suggested the last. On pyrolysis with zinc dust at 600° two compounds were obtained: toluene (identified by GLC) and 4-amino-*m*-cresol (m.p. 180°). The amine, m.p. 110°, was therefore (7).

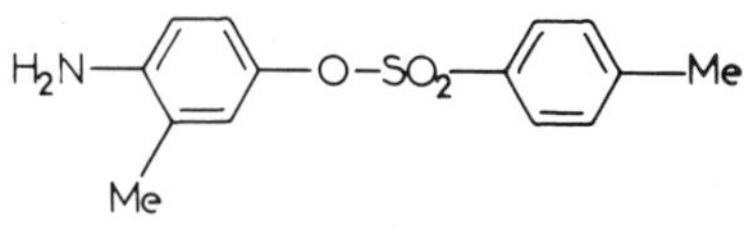

(7)

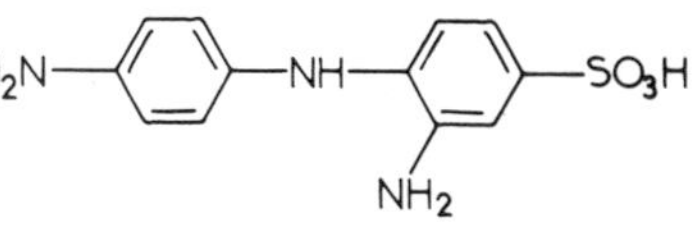

(8)

The filtrate from the reduction was extracted with ether and the aqueous layer acidified. Concentration under vacuum and recrystallization from 1 N HCl gave an aminosulfonic acid, $C_{12}H_{13}N_3O_3S$. On pyrolysis over zinc dust at 400–600° it liberated aniline and *p*-phenylenediamine, identified by PC[6] and GLC. Acetylation as shown by elemental analysis took place on two reacting sites. The amine was therefore thought to be a sulfonated diaminodiphenylamine. The IR spectrum was superposable with that of (8). Structure (9) for the dye was then proved by synthesis.

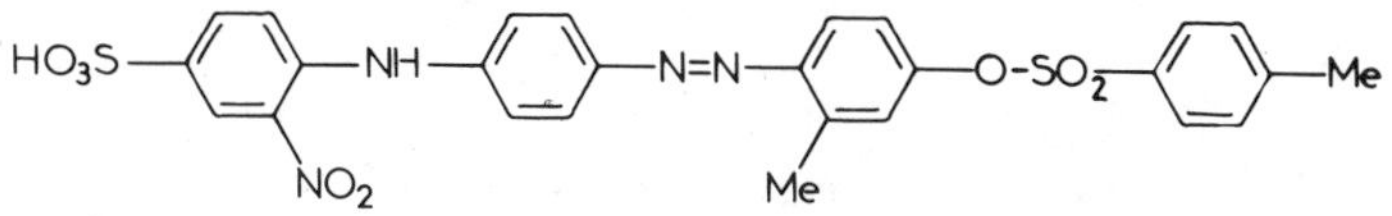

(9)

2.3 Reactive Azo Dye

2.3.1 CI Acid Yellow 127.

The dye is classified in CI as monoazo. A streak of dye solution was applied on a filter paper. It was cross streaked with sodium hydroxide solution and placed in an oven (80°). The paper was then washed in running water. Only the cross-streaked part of the dye was fixed in the paper, indicating a reactive dye. The dye (20 g) was treated with 20% sodium chloride solution (200 ml) and filtered. The original diluent was thus removed, leaving some sodium chloride. The dye, $C_{25-26}H_{19}Cl_2N_8O_6S$, was found to contain reactive chlorine. In order to hydrolyze the reactive group prior to reduction, the original dye (60 g) was heated under reflux in 1 N NaOH (400 ml). It was then precipitated by hydrochloric acid, filtered, and washed with water. The washed hydrolyzed dye was re-duced at 80° in 0.1 N NaOH (500 ml) with sodium dithionite (80 g). Because the reduced solution had a purple color, the coupling component was assumed to be a pyrazolone derivative. The corresponding rubazonic acid was obtained by bubbling air in presence of hydrogen peroxide. The orange precipitate was partly ether soluble. Pyrolysis of the ether-soluble derivative, m.p. 222°, over lime at 600° liberated 6-chloro-o-toluidine (GLC and m.p. 168° of the acetyl derivative). The coupling component was therefore assumed to be (10).

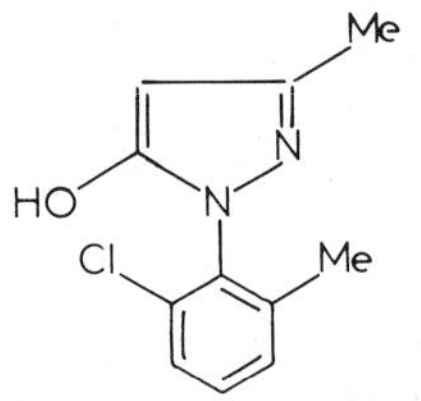

(10) 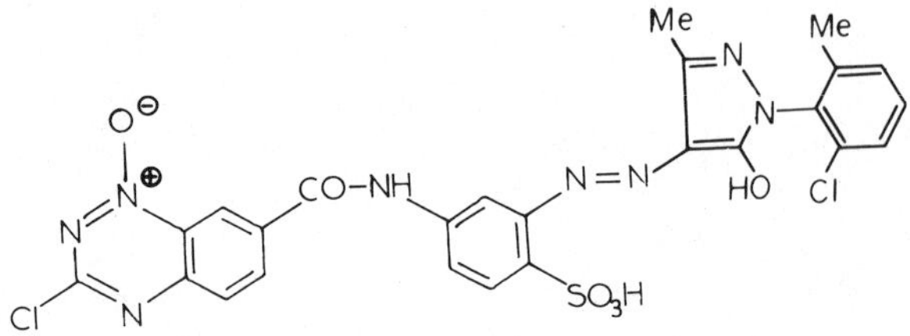   (11)

The identity of the rubazonic acid (m.p. 222°) was confirmed by synthesis.

The ether-insoluble product was found to behave on PC as an amino-sulfonic acid. It was purified by silica gel PLC using n-butanol–pyridine–25% ammonia (3:1:3). The empirical formula of the ammonium salt was $C_{14-15}H_{16}N_6O_6S$. Pyrolysis over lime liberated m-phenylenediamine. From a patent[11] the dye appeared to be (11), confirmed by synthesis and superposable IR spectra.

2.4   Metal Complex Acid Azo Dyes

2.4.1   Elbelan Bordeaux N-GL (LBH).   This acid dye is not registered in CI. Cobalt was found in the ash. After reduction two amines were detected by PC.[6,9] The dye was therefore assumed to be a cobalt complex azo dye. The diluent was removed by treating 100 g dye with 1 N HCl (200 ml) at 60°. The dye content was estimated to be 30%. Thirty grams of washed dye was dissolved in 0.2 N NaOH (300 ml) at 80° and reduced with sodium dithionite (70 g). With cooling a cobalt salt precipitated. The filtrate was extracted with ether. Addition of conc. hydrochloric acid to the ether layer precipitated an amine. It was recrystallized from glacial acetic acid and by PC identified as 1-amino-2-naphthol, confirmed by mixed m.p. 244° of the acetyl derivative. 2-Naphthol was therefore the coupling component. Conc. hydrochloric acid (75 ml) was added to the aqueous residue of the ether extraction. The suspension was filtered and the filtrate concentrated under vacuum. On standing an amine precipitated. It was filtered, redissolved in dilute sodium carbonate solution, and extracted with ether following addition of acetic acid. This behavior indicated the amine, m.p. 278°, to be a carboxylic acid, and a CO band at 1655 was found to be present in its IR spectrum, superposable with that of (12).

The 2:1 cobalt complex of dye (13) was then synthesized and, by IR spectroscopy as well as polyamide and wool dyeing, found to be identical with the analyzed dye. This type of dye is described in two patents.[12]

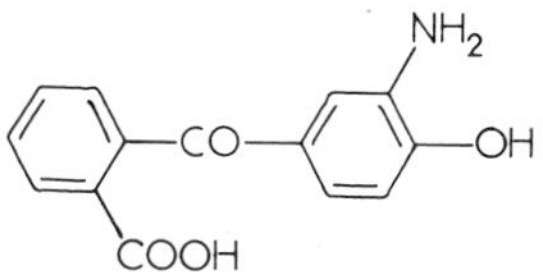

(12) 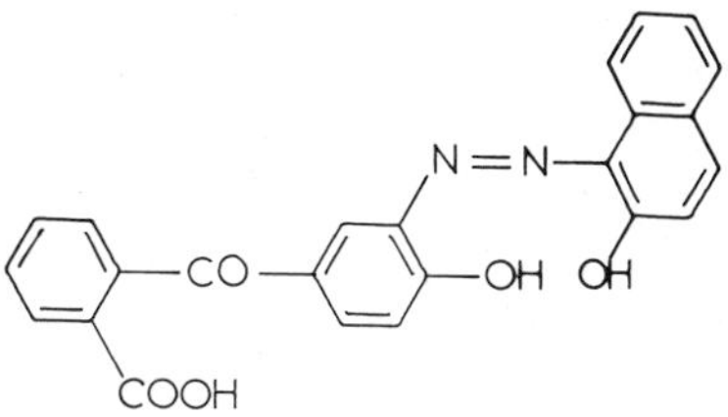   (13)

2.4.2   CI Acid Orange 148.   This dye was found to contain chromium. The dye was treated with 15% sodium chloride solution to wash off the diluent (45%).

Demetallization—Identification of the First Dye.   Twelve grams of washed dye was heated under reflux in 5% oxalic acid solution (300 ml). The dye was demetallized, liberating an oil which was steam distilled and identified as salicylaldehyde. An azomethine dye was therefore assumed to be present. Another 15 g of washed dye was hydrolyzed by heating under reflux in ethanol (200 ml) and 10 N NaOH (20 ml). From TLC[13] the solution was found to contain salicylaldehyde, an aromatic amine, and a second dye. When the solution was cooled, the amine precipitated. It was filtered (filtrate F), washed with alcohol, and recrystallized from dilute hydrochloric acid. PC of the amine and comparison of its IR spectrum proved its identity with 3-amino-2-hydroxy-5-nitrobenzenesulfonic acid. Structure (14) was therefore assigned to the azomethine dye.

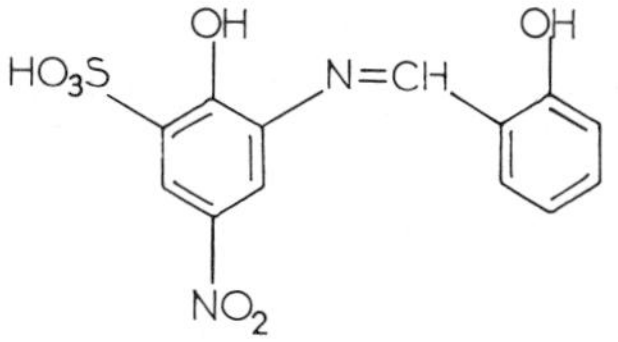

(14) 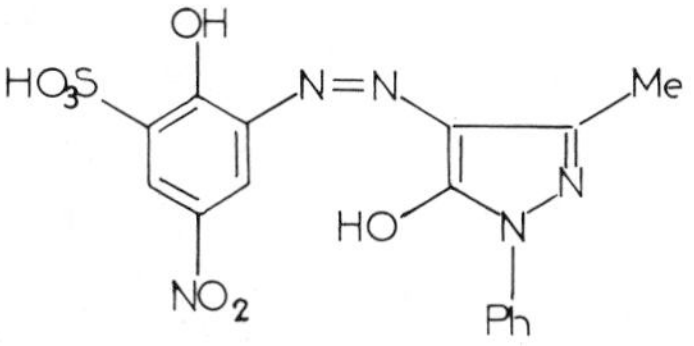   (15)

Identification of the Second Dye. The second dye was present in filtrate F, which was distilled to half volume. On addition of 10 N HCl (20 ml) an orange dye precipitated. It was filtered and redissolved in 0.25 N NaOH (200 ml) at 80°. Ethanol (100 ml) was added and reduction was carried out using sodium dithionite (30 g). The reduced solution was acidified by hydrochloric acid and distilled to remove the alcohol. Ammonia was added to the distillation residue, which was then filtered. Air was bubbled in the purple filtrate, whose color indicated an aminopyrazolone derivative.[5] On acidification the corresponding rubazonic acid derivative precipitated. It was filtered (filtrate L) and recrystallized from glacial acetic acid (m.p. 188°) and found to derive from 1-phenyl-3-methyl-5-pyrazolone, the coupling component. Filtrate L was concentrated and an amine precipitated. It was recrystallized from dilute sodium acetate solution. PC and the IR spectrum showed 3-amino-2-hydroxy-5-nitrobenzenesulfonic acid. Structure (15) was therefore assigned to the second dye and (16) to the original dye, confirmed by synthesis. This dye is described in a patent.[14]

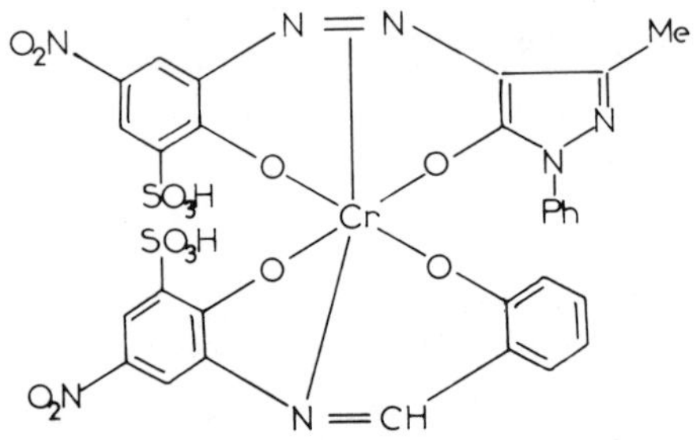

(16)

2.4.3 Lanacron Yellow S-2G (C-GY).

This dye is not registered in CI. Cobalt was detected in the ash. The diluent (35 %) was removed by treating the dye (50 g) with 1 N HCl (200 ml) at 60°. Preliminary tests showed an azo dye.

Twenty grams of washed dye was reduced in boiling ethanol (200 ml) and glacial acetic acid (25 ml) with zinc dust (60 g). The zinc suspension was then filtered and the filtrate diluted with water (700 ml). The voluminous white precipitate was not an amine and its properties were those of 2,5-dimethyl-1,4-dihydropyrazine-3,6-dicarboxyarylides.[1,5] Hydrolysis in boiling ethanolic sodium hydroxide liberated o-chloroaniline. The coupling component was therefore o-chloroacetoacetanilide. The filtrate, after collecting the pyrazine derivative, yielded on concentration a grayish precipitate, which was recrystallized from 5 N HCl. It was an aminophenol containing sulfur. PC[9] and the IR spectrum (band at 1670) showed a carboxyl group and its identity with (17).

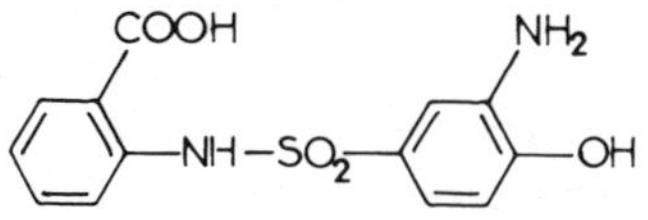

(17)

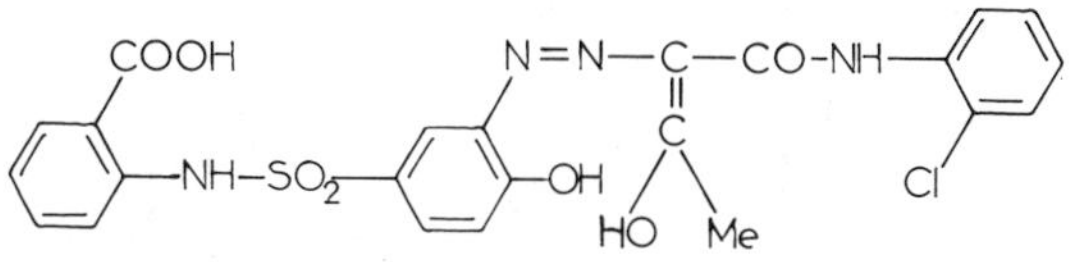

(18)

The 2:1 cobalt complex of the dye (18) was then synthesized[15] and found identical (IR, wool, and polyamide dyeing) with the analyzed dye.

2.5 Nitro Acid Dye

2.5.1 CI Acid Brown 248. This dye is classified in CI as nitro. It was washed with 1 N HCl to remove the diluent (70%). Some unwashed dye was treated with ether. An intermediate product, $C_6H_5ClN_2O_4S$, was extracted, which by mixed m.p. (178°) was identified as 4-chloro-3-nitrobenzenesulfonamide.

The NMR spectrum of the dye in heavy water shows the following: two H indicated by a doublet at 8.4 with a *meta* coupling constant and two H indicated by a doublet of doublet at 7.7 with *ortho* and *meta* coupling constants belonging to two sulfonamide molecules; eight H at 7, two of which also belong to the sulfonamide molecules; and one H indicated by a doublet at 7.6 with a *meta* coupling constant which indicated a central dissymmetry in the dye molecule $C_{24}H_{21}N_7O_{11}S_3$.

Dye (19) was synthesized and identity was confirmed by IR, spot tests, and chromatography.

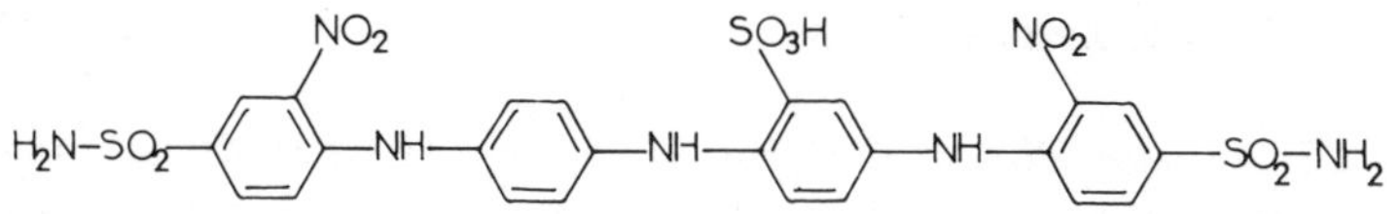

(19)

2.6 Direct Azo Dyes

2.6.1 CI Direct Green 85. This dye is classified in CI as trisazo. It was washed with dilute hydrochloric acid to eliminate the diluent (50%). Three reducible azo groups were present (chromous chloride).[3] Reduction with alkaline sodium dithionite and steam distillation yielded aniline, and ether extraction of the residue led to two other amines, which were separated by PLC on silica gel (benzene–methanol 80:20) and identified as o-tolidine and p-aminophenol. Reduction at 95° with 2 M $SnCl_2$ in 5 N HCl gave 1,2,7-triamino-8-hydroxy-3,6-naphthalenedisulfonic acid, identified by the IR spectrum. The dye is therefore (20), confirmed by synthesis.

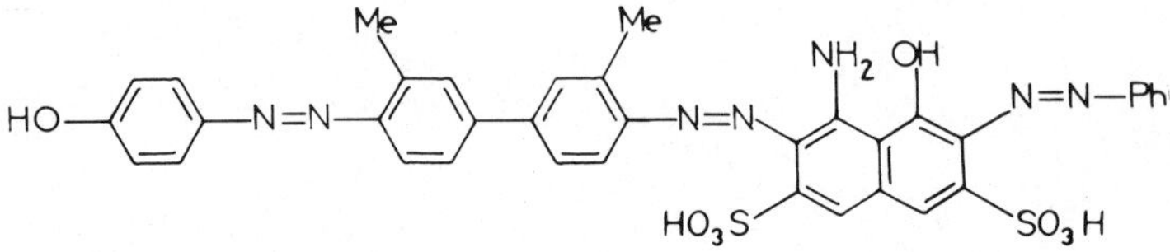

(20)

2.6.2   Direct Black ANB (ACNA).   This dye is not registered in CI. The dye was washed with dilute hydrochloric acid to remove the diluent (50%). Reduction with sodium dithionite and steam distillation yielded aniline. The residue contained a precipitate which crystallized from ethanol, m.p. 203°, and was identified as 4,4'-diaminobenzanilide. A second reduction was carried out with stannous chloride. A precipitate was obtained and identified by spot tests[1] and IR as 1,2,7-triamino-8-hydroxy-3,6-naphthalenedisulfonic acid. After electrolysis and vacuum concentration, 1,2,4-triaminobenzene was identified by its benzoyl derivative. Dye (21) is described in a patent.[16] It was synthesized, and its identity was confirmed by TLC, IR, and cotton dyeing.

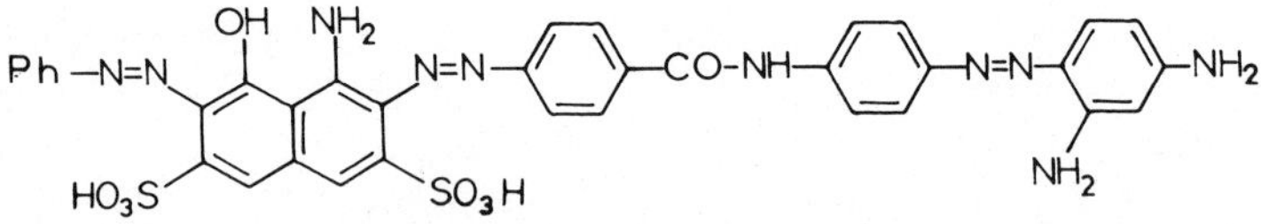

(21)

2.7   Azo Disperse Dyes

2.7.1   CI Disperse Blue 165.

This dye is registered in CI as monoazo. The dark powder was extracted with acetone to separate the dye from the dispersing agent and crystallized from glacial acetic acid; m.p. 257°; $C_{20-21}H_{21}N_7O_3$. An azo and a nitro groups were present as determined by reduction with chromous chloride.[3] The dye could be hydrolyzed, but not acetylated, as seen from TLC on silica gel (benzene–methanol 80:20). Its IR spectrum shows (1) two typical CN bands at 2210 and 2235; (2) a CO band at 1700, which because of a band at 3340 was interpreted as CO—NH;

and (3) two bands among others at 2935 and 2980 corresponding to alkyl groups. Reduction in boiling ethanol with aqueous sodium dithionite and distillation of alcohol gave an oily yellow residue. It was treated with ammonia and extracted with benzene. The precipitate in the aqueous layeɹ crystallized from aqueous ethanol. The chromatographically pure aromatic amine, m.p. 273°, $C_8H_6N_4$, ν 2210 (CN), was identified as 2,6-dicyano-p-phenylenediamine. The diazo component, therefore, was 2,6-dicyano-4-nitroaniline. The NMR spectrum of the dye shows (1) a peak at 8.75 corresponding to two equivalent aromatic H (3,5-H of the diazo component); (2) an AMX pattern of three aromatic H at 1, 2, 4 positions; (3) a quadruplet at 3.45 ($J = 6$ Hz) and a triplet at 1.18 ($J = 6$ Hz), for a diethylamino group often encountered in disperse dyes; (4) a singlet at 2.39 for N—Ac. The dye is therefore (22), confirmed by synthesis.[17]

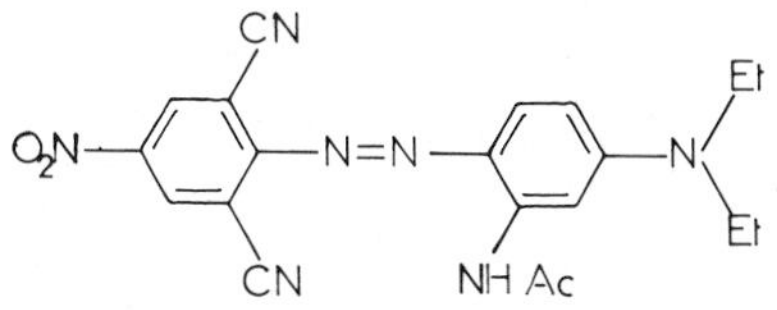

(22)

2.7.2 CI Disperse Red 220.

The dye flocculated from the fluid suspension on addition of ethanol. It crystallized from acetic acid, m.p. 232°, $C_{26}H_{22}ClN_3O_3$. IR shows an amide group (1650, 3230, and 1535). NMR shows 12 aromatic and 8 aliphatic H. The aliphatic protons give a quadruplet (two H) at 4.35 coupled with a triplet (three H) at 1.60 indicating OEt. A singlet (three H) at 2.55 indicates Ar—Me.

One gram of dye was reduced with zinc in ethanol and acetic acid. The suspension was filtered. Addition of dilute hydrochloric acid to the filtrate was followed by boiling to remove the alcohol. The residue was made alkaline and extracted with ether. 4-chloro-o-toluidine, the diazo component, was present in the ether layer. Pyrolysis of the dye over zinc dust liberated 4-chloro-o-toluidine and o-phenetidine. Dye (23) was synthesized, and by mixed m.p. and superposable IR spectra found to be identical with the dye under investigation.

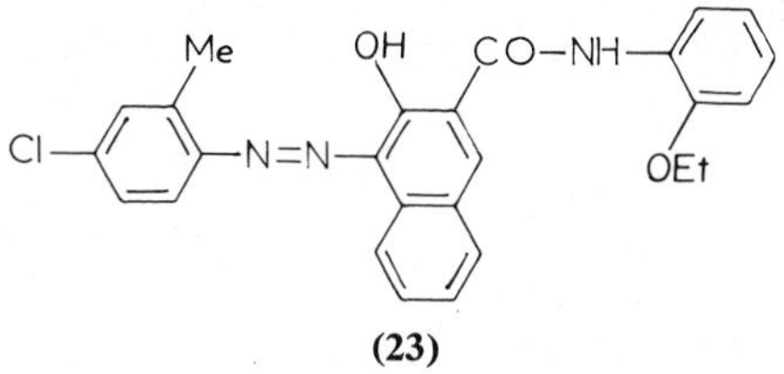

(23)

2.7.3   CI Disperse Orange 25.   This dye is classified in CI as monoazo. The brown powder was extracted with dichloromethane to separate the dye (40%) from dispersing agent. The dye crystallized from glacial acetic acid in reddish brown leaves, m.p. 175–176°; $C_{17}H_{17}N_5O_2$. An azo group and a nitro group are present (chromous chloride).[3] The IR spectrum shows a CN band at 2250. Zinc–acetic acid reduction gave two amines. PC[6] revealed one as *p*-phenylenediamine, derived from *p*-nitroaniline, the diazo component. The second amine was the amino coupling component. $C_{11}H_{14}N_2$ was deduced for the coupling component from the formulas of the dye and the diazo component. Coupling components of disperse dyes are often secondary or tertiary aromatic amines coupling *para* to the amino group. In such compounds *N*-cyanoethyl groups are often encountered. The coupling component could therefore be (24), verified by PC.[18] The dye, therefore, is (25), confirmed by synthesis.

Et
Ph — N
              CH₂–CH₂–CN
(24)

O_2N—⟨⟩—N=N—⟨⟩—N
                                          Et
                                          CH₂–CH₂–CN
(25)

2.7.4   Perliton Scarlet V-R (BASF).   This disperse dye is not registered in CI. Separation from dispersing agent (65%) was effected by dichloromethane. The dye was recrystallized from acetone, m.p. 188°; $C_{27}H_{20}ClN_5$. Two reducible azo groups are present (chromous chloride).[3] PC[6] of the reduced dye showed three components. The dye was reduced in boiling acetone and glacial acetic acid with zinc dust. The zinc suspension was filtered and the filtrate was diluted with water and hydrochloric acid. Acetone was distilled off, and after neutralization the residue was steam distilled. The volatile amine was *p*-chloroaniline. The second amine, extracted with ether from the steam distillation residue, was found to be *p*-toluylenediamine. The third component was altered in the preceding steps and it was obtained by the method described in a BASF patent.[19] The dye (10 g) in 100 ml methyl cellosolve at 90–93° was treated during 20 minutes with 2 N NaOH (125 ml) and sodium dithionite (13 g). The mixture was cooled and filtered, and the filtrate was diluted with water (400 ml). The orange precipitate, m.p. 180°, $C_{14}H_{12}N_2$, gave on pyrolysis over zinc dust a pyrrole derivative (violet coloration with Ehrlich reagent).[20] The orange precipitate was later identified as 3-amino-2-phenylindole.[21] The patent literature[22] showed that 2-phenylindole is used as a coupling component.

Dye **(26)** was synthesized and found to be identical with the analyzed dye.

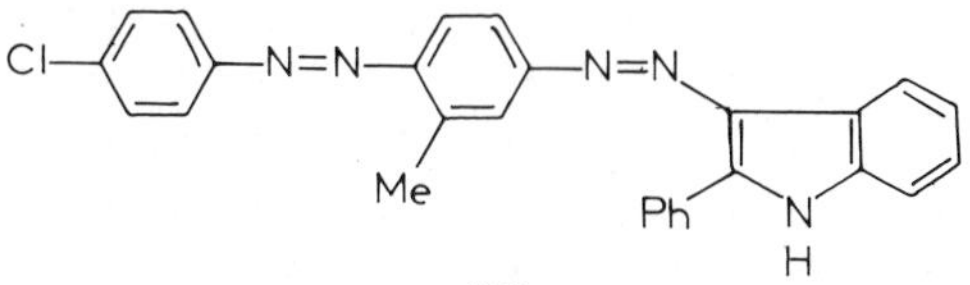

(26)

2.7.5   Perliton Gold Yellow V-G (BASF).   This disperse dye, not registered in CI, was separated from dispersing agent (70%) by acetone. It was recrystallized from tetrahydrofuran–water; m.p. 290°; $C_{24-25}H_{18}N_4O_3$. One reducible azo group is present (chromous chloride).[3] The dye can be acetylated and hydrolyzed (TLC, silica gel, benzene–methanol). A Zeisel determination excluded a lower alkoxy or ester group. Reduction in methyl cellosolve, as described earlier,[19] gave 3-amino-2-phenylindole, indicating 2-phenylindole as the coupling component. A patent[23] describes the orange dye **(27)**.

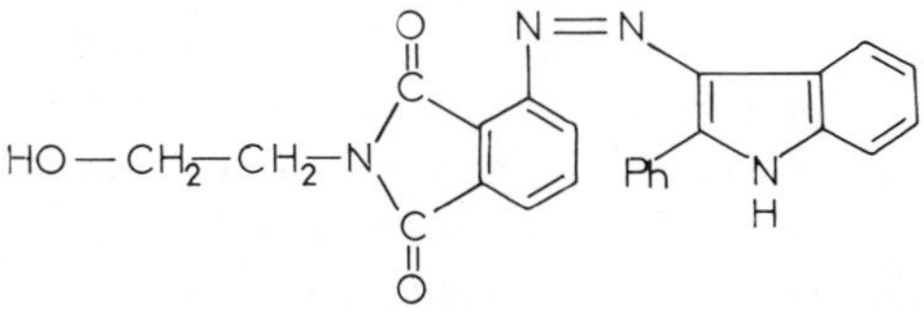

(27)

The IR spectrum of the dye under investigation has three C=O bands at 1770, 1700, and 1680, indicating a phthalimide.[24] Bands at 3510 for OH and at 3300 for NH are also visible. The NMR spectrum shows a ratio of one aliphatic to three aromatic H and a broad absorption centered at 3.7 ppm. If the empirical formula is taken into account, this can correspond to four aliphatic H, an overlap of two signals for CH_2N (2.5–3.5) and CH_2O (3.5–4.5). Confirmation of structure **(27)** was obtained by synthesis.

2.8   Anthraquinone Disperse Dye

2.8.1   Foron Brilliant Violet E-BL (S).   Extraction with dichloromethane gave the dye (37%), $C_{20}H_{13}NO_3$, m.p. 160°, after crystallization from acetic acid. Reduction with sodium dithionite and reoxidization showed that it is an anthraquinone derivative. Pyrolysis over zinc dust and salts[25] at 300° liberated anthracene, identified by TLC and GLC. The color of the dye in conc. sulfuric acid is green, turning blue on the addition of boric acid (α-hydroxyanthraquinone).[26] The dye can be acetylated as shown by PC.[27] Treatment of the dye (25 g) in DMF (250 ml) for 20 minutes at 100–110° with tin powder (6 g) and 10 N HCl (20 ml), and dilution with water (500 ml) yielded leucoquinizarin. From the filtrate aniline was recovered. The dye is therefore (28),[28] confirmed by synthesis.

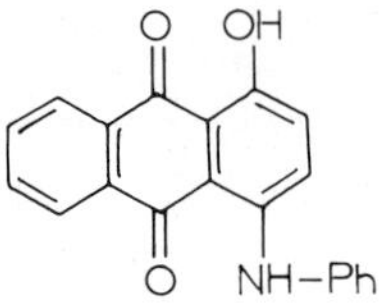

(28)

2.9 Basic Azo Dye

2.9.1 CI Basic Red 24. The dye is classified in CI as monoazo. It was extracted with methanol and sulfur was found to be present, but no halogen. The extracted dye was dissolved in water, salted out with sodium chloride, and reextracted with absolute ethanol. A second sodium fusion showed the absence of sulfur and the presence of halogen. The dye molecule is therefore marketed as a methosulfate, $C_{20}H_{25}N_6O_2Cl$ for the chloride. The extracted dye was dissolved in water and reduced with stannous chloride. The reduced solution was then electrolyzed,[1] made alkaline, and extracted with ether. A p-diamine crystallized from the ether layer on addition of petroleum ether. $C_7H_7N_3$, m.p. 90°, diacetyl derivative m.p. 211°. It was identified as 2-cyano-p-phenylenediamine deriving from 2-cyano-4-nitroaniline, the diazo component. This left $C_{13}H_{23}N_2$ for the coupling component. From the patent literature[29] the dye was assigned structure (29).

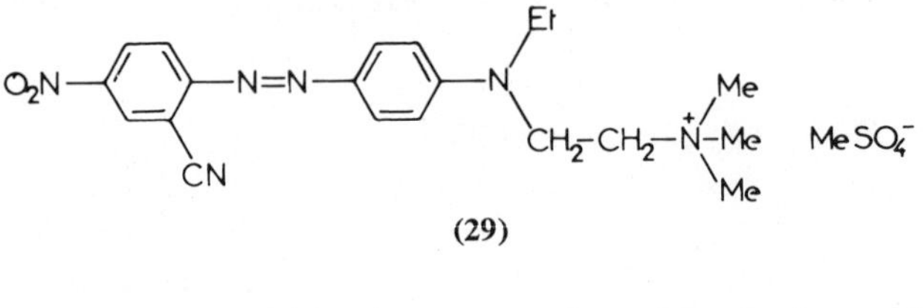

(29)

It was synthesized and identity was confirmed by dyeing and IR.

2.10   Vat Dye

2.10.1   CI Vat Blue 64. The chemical class is stated in CI as anthra-quinone. The dye (33 %) was separated from the diluent by treatment with boiling water and flocculation with monododecylpolyethyleneglycol. The color of the dye in conc. sulfuric acid is olive green, turning bluish green with paraformaldehyde (aminoanthraquinone). The dye was heated for 1 hour in 93 % H_2SO_4 at 100°. The brown solution on dilution gave a violet precipitate. The filtrate was neutralized with calcium carbonate, made alkaline with sodium carbonate, filtered, the filtrate concentrated, acidified, and ether extracted. Benzoic acid was thus obtained. The violet precipitate regenerated the parent dye when treated with benzoyl chloride in nitro-benzene at 130°, but it was further broken down by heating in 85 % H_2SO_4 for 2 hours at 150°. The purple-blue precipitate obtained on dilution was characterized by spot tests and spectroscopy as 1,4-diaminoanthraquinone-2-carboxylic acid.

A patent search revealed the dye (**30**),[30] which was synthesized and found to be identical with CI Vat Blue 64.

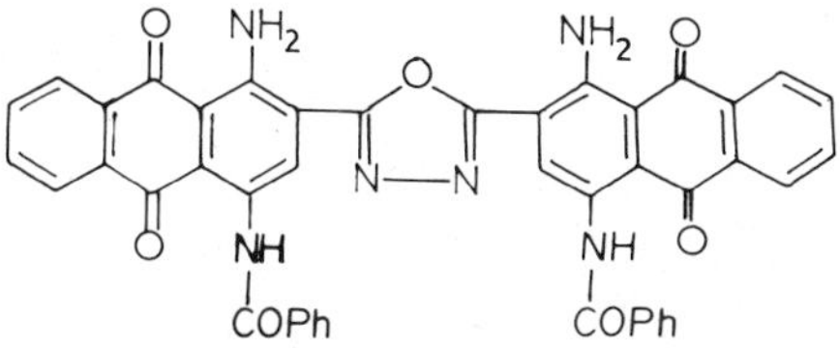

(30)

ACKNOWLEDGMENTS

The author wishes to thank Mr. P. Bourguignon, Ing. for the last analysis, Mr. G. Hazet for experimental assistance, Mr. C. Triquet, Ing. for the quantitative determinations, Messrs. L. Cabut, Ing. and C. Brouard, Ing. for a synthesis, Messrs. L. Sousselier, Ing. and G. Thirot, Ing. for the NMR spectra.

REFERENCES

1. A. Brunner, *Analyse der Azofarbstoffe*, Springer, Berlin, 1929.
2. J. Gasparič, *Adv. Chromatogr.*, **6**, 3 (1968).

3. (a) Y. A. Gawargious, *The Determination of Nitro and Related Functions*, Academic Press, London, 1973.
   (b) R. S. Bottei and N. H. Furman, *Anal. Chem.*, **27**, 1182 (1955).
4. FH, *FP* 1,306,941; Add. 82,848, p. 5.
5. *CSD* I, 696.
6. I. Gemzova and J. Gasparič, *Mikrochim. Acta*, **1–2**, 310 (1966).
7. (a) C. Buchanan and S. H. Graham, *J. Chem. Soc.*, 506 (1950).
   (b) J. D. London and T. D. Robson, *J. Chem. Soc.*, 245 (1937).
8. IG, *FP* 755,074.
9. A. Cee and J. Gasparič, *Mikrochim. Acta*, **1–2**, 295 (1966).
10. S, *FP* 1,571,783, 3rd example.
11. S, *FP* 1,462,672.
12. LBH, *BP* 864,093; 1,283,476.
13. J. Gasparič and A. Cee, in *Stationary Phase in Paper and Thin-Layer Chromatography*, K. Macek and I. M. Hais, Eds., Elsevier, Amsterdam, 1965, pp. 84–87
14. FBy, *F* Demande 2,174,926, example 2.
15. CIBA, *FP* 1,068,477, p. 4.
16. ACNA, *F* Demande 2,223,432.
17. FBy, *FP* 1,511,932; 1,511,933; 1,511,934.
18. I. Gemzova and J. Gasparič, *Collect. Czech. Chem. Commun.*, **32**, 2740 (1967).
19. BASF, *FP* 1,576,109.
20. F. Feigl and V. Anger, *Spot Tests in Organic Analysis*, Elsevier, Amsterdam, 1966, pp. 381–382.
21. *Beilstein*, **22**, pp. 463–464.
22. BASF, *DOS* 1,544,371; 1,544,405; 1,544,406; *FP* 1,532,004.
23. BASF, *FP* 1,440,473, example 8.
24. M. Avram and G. H. D. Mateescu, *Spectroscopie Infra-Rouge*, Dunod, Paris, 1970.
25. J. Gasparič, *Mikrochim. Acta*, **1–2**, 288 (1966).
26. H. E. Fierz-David, *Künstliche Organische Farbstoffe*, Springer, Berlin, 1926, p. 499.
27. J. Gasparič and I. Gemzova, *J. Chromatogr.*, **35**, 362 (1968).
28. FBy, *DRP* 93,223; 98,011.
29. FBy, *DAS*, 1,011,396.
30. FBy, *FP* 1,076,675; ICI, *FP* 1,019,976; see also *CSD* V, p. 174.

CHAPTER FOURTEEN

Examples of Disperse Dye Structures

M. SCHRIER

1 SAMPLE PREPARATION

The technique to be used in the identification usually determines the extent of the purification needed. A sample normally should be extremely pure for mass spectra; otherwise the spectra of the impurity instead of the desired dye may be obtained. An impurity of 5–10% can often be tolerated in an NMR spectrum and compensated for by a more careful interpretation with correlation of other data. In some cases valuable process data can be deduced by identification of intermediates found in the products. The purification normally used is intended to leave some impurities in the sample.

A convenient technique for separation of commercial disperse dyes from the large amounts of dispersing agents present is to use a Soxhlet extractor. Although many solvents are satisfactory, isopropanol has been found most useful for a large range of molecular weights and chemical types. For dyes of poor solubility such as Disperse Red 89 (dioxazine type), acetic acid can be used, and pyridine for almost all others.

Dyed polyester fiber can be extracted with hot pyridine. The pyridine is removed and the dye isolated by standard techniques.

After the isolated dye is dried, a TLC is run to visualize the components present and their relative strengths. The TLC's are usually run in chloroform with varying amounts of methanol to increase the polarity of the eluting system. The more polar dyes require a more polar eluent. The TLC plate is reserved for use during the interpretation of the data. TLC of dyes isolated from fabrics should be examined on a fluorescent plate under UV light to ensure the absence of textile auxiliaries. If the data obtained from the spectra are too complex because of impurities, the sample should be recrystallized.

In the case of blacks, which are usually mixtures, or the few dyes of other colors that are gross mixtures, the components are separated by TLC on 8 × 8-in. plates. The bands are scraped off and isolated by standard techniques.

2 PRELIMINARY TESTING

The sample is examined by observing the colors and state of solution respectively in water, in dilute alkali, on addition of sodium hydrosulfite (warm to 65–70° and allow time for complete reduction), and on oxidation with sodium perborate of the vatted solution. Interpretation of the data from the four test tubes indicates whether the dye is azo, anthraquinone, or a different class. Solubility or color change in the dilute alkali test should indicate presence of solubilizing groups. The color in conc. sulfuric acid is sometimes useful. Disazo phenols generally give a reddish blue to blue coloration. Diaminodihydroxy derivatives of anthraquinone with free amino groups usually give a yellow to brown solution.

If the above data in conjunction with the spectral data are insufficient, they can be supplemented by micro tests such as acetylation, benzoylation, or hydrolysis. TLC is used to confirm the reactions. Microsynthesis for azo dyes is especially useful in a research lab where many of the diazotizable amines and couplers are readily available.

Quantitative elemental analysis is sometimes useful for determining the number of each hetero atom present, but a further purification is usually necessary.

The data that yield the most information for structure elucidation are the various spectra, which are discussed individually.

3 IR SPECTRA

The IR spectrum is examined as a mineral oil mull. If the areas of mineral oil interference are desired free of the mineral oil peaks, halocarbon oil (fluorinated alkyl compound) is used. IR spectra can be used for identification of functional groups or a general structure type. Both are demonstrated below.

Primary amines show the typical doublet near 3300 and a strong band near 1600. Benzoylation with benzoyl chloride and an IR of the derivative will show confirmation by the amide carbonyl band. The single band for secondary amines does not always show for disperse dyes. The absence of this band should not be interpreted as the absence of a secondary amine. Tertiary amine bands are not reliable because the spectrums of dyes are usually rich in this area.

Care should be taken to examine the 2220–2280 region using a thicker layer of sample than for other areas of the spectrum; otherwise a cyano group can be missed. Alkyl cyano or ring cyano groups *ortho* to an azo are usually very weak. Strong cyano bands are found in the spectra of methine dyes that contain a cyanoacetate or malononitrile group. Examples are Resolin Brilliant Yellow P-8GL, CI Disperse Yellow 73, a cyanoacetate type,[1] and Foron Yellow 6GFL, CI Disperse Yellow 49, a malononitrile type methine dye.[2] A cyano group *para* to an azo also gives a strong cyano band (determined by synthesis in the laboratory).

Carbonyl groups give strong bands and generally can be easily interpreted, because the literature is well documented. The single carbonyl frequency at 1675 in anthraquinone is lowered by hydroxyl and amino substitution in α positions. It splits into 1665 and 1610 in 1-aminoanthraquinone and appears as a single absorption at 1610 in 1,4-diaminoanthraquinone. Because of such amide-resonance and hydrogen-bonding effects, the presence of quinones should be confirmed by the vatting and oxidation color tests.

Nitro groups show the usual strong band near 1520, but aromatic bands from heterocycles and condensed ring systems can interfere in this area.

3.1 Substitution Pattern

The use of this region can be demonstrated by the examination of structure (1). If R is a phenyl group the dye is CI Disperse Red 60, sold under many brand names. Substitution of the phenyl would give disperse dyes with substitution patterns in the IR showing differences in the 870–660 region

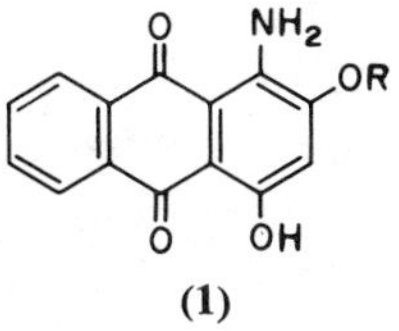

(1)

from Disperse Red 60. If R were alkyl, the bands in this region would be very similar for all R's, but different from R = Ar. If the spectrum of CI Disperse Red 4 (R = Me; CI 60755) is used as a model compound, it is immediately obvious that Foron Brilliant Red E-RLN,[3] Latyl Cerise B,[4] and Cibacete Brilliant Pink FG[5] have spectra that match Disperse Red 4 in the 870–660 region. Completion of the identification shows R to be different alkyl substituents.

Such structure elucidation can be extended to other dye types. In the case of azo dyes of structure (2), the substitution pattern will be similar

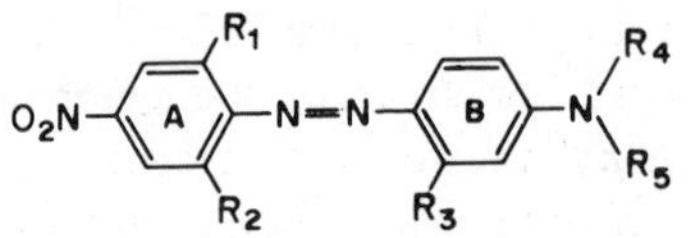

(2)

for dyes in which any given R_1 and R_2 are identical, and R_3, R_4, and R_5 are alkyl. In general, interchange of positive substituents does not affect the pattern to a large extent, and negative substituents such as nitro, halo, and cyano groups change the pattern radically.

The point to be emphasized is the necessity for a good library of spectra of dyes of known constitution.

4 VISIBLE SPECTRA

In conjunction with the molecular weight obtained from the mass spectra, the visible spectrum by calculation of molar absorptivity supplies valuable information on chemical type.

Table 14.1 illustrates some typical examples obtained only from commercial dyes. An example of the first group is CI Disperse Yellow 42 (3; R_1 = H, R_2 = Ph). The molar absorptivity is about 6000. Examination

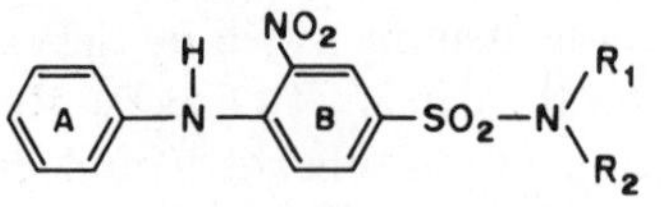

(3)

of CI Disperse Yellows 33 and 34 indicates the presence of sulfur by sodium fusion test, probable SO_2 group from IR, and molar absorptivities in the 5000–7000 range. Completion of the identification confirms that both match structure (3) in which ring A may be substituted and the proper R_1 and R_2 supplied.

Table 14.1   Molar Absorptivity of Commercial Dyes

Structure Type	Color	Range of Molar Absorptivity
Nitro	Yellow	5,000–15,000
Anthraquinone, 1-hydroxy-4-arylamino	Blue	10,000–12,000
Anthraquinone, 1 amino-4-hydroxy-2-OR	Red	10,000–14,000
Anthraquinone, 1-4-diamino-2,3-R,R_1	Blue-violet	10,000–15,000
Condensed ring systems (anthraquinone, xanthene, etc.)	Yellow-orange	10,000–16,000
Azo (4-nitro-2,6-dihaloaniline → $PhNR_2$)	Orange-brown	20,000–25,000
Anthraquinone-1,4,5,8- and 1,5,4,8-$(OH)_2$-$(NHR)_2$	Blue	20,000–25,000
Bisazophenols (A → M → phenol)	Yellow-orange	25,000–35,000
Azo (4-nitro-2-cyanoaniline → $PhNR_2$)	Red	30,000–40,000
Azo (2,4–dinitro-6-haloaniline → $PhNR_2$)	Blue	32,000–43,000
Azo (A → 6-Hydroxy-2-pyridone)	Yellow	34,000–45,000
Quinophthalones	Yellow	35,000–45,000
Azo (2-amino-6-R-benzothiazole → $PhNR_2$)	Red	35,000–50,000
Methine, one cyanoacetate or one malononitrile group	Yellow	35,000–70,000
Azo (2,4-dinitro-6-haloaniline → $PhNR_2$)	Blue	40,000–47,000
Azo (4-nitro-2,6-dicyanoaniline → $PhNR_2$)	Blue	80,000

Diphenylamines containing a phenolic OH and no sulfonamido group have molar absorptivities near 15,000. This type of classification is not absolute. Disperse Yellow 122 is a nitro (acridone) dye with a molar absorptivity in the 15,000 range. Testing for a phenolic group is negative. We must therefore conclude that condensed ring systems can give the same approximate molar absorptivity.

If the last two examples of Table 14.1 are compared, the data indicate that the substitution of two cyano groups on the A ring *ortho* to the azo has changed the chromophoric system to give one with much higher absorptivities. Adding an auxochrome to the molecule increases the molar absorptivity.[6] Halogens are weak auxochromes. Strong auxochromes are OH, NHR, and CN.

Literature is available demonstrating various chromophoric groups[6,7] and the effect of substituents on a phenyl ring.[7]

5 NMR SPECTRA

Using an empirical approach[8] gives good results. The *Band Handbook*[9] and a library of curves of similar compounds, using wherever possible the same solvent, are valuable assets.

The solvent effect can be illustrated by examining the spectrum of Resolin Brilliant Pink PBB (CI Disperse Red 107).[10] In structure (4) the two dif-

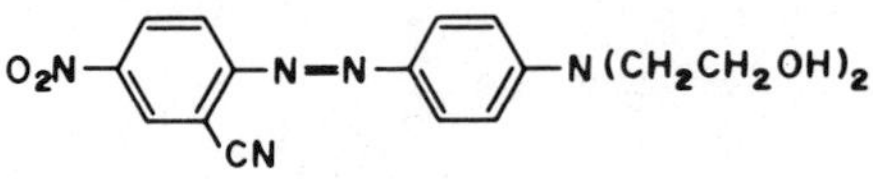

(4)

ferent types of CH_2 in deuterated pyridine appear as two overlapping triplets centered near 3.9, and in deuterated DMSO as a broad singlet near 3.7.

Deuterated pyridine is a good solvent because many dyes of different classes have sufficient solubility to yield useful data. In the cases where solvent cost or availability is a very important consideration, the alkyl area can be examined in pyridine.

Table 14.2 was developed from commercial dyes only. The structural portion of the dye relevant to the band location is indicated. All spectra are in deuterated pyridine except where indicated.

The aromatic area presents more difficult interpretation problems. An example of a proton that can be picked out easily is in Table 14.2, structure 12, H *ortho* to OH is at 6.6 (*s*).

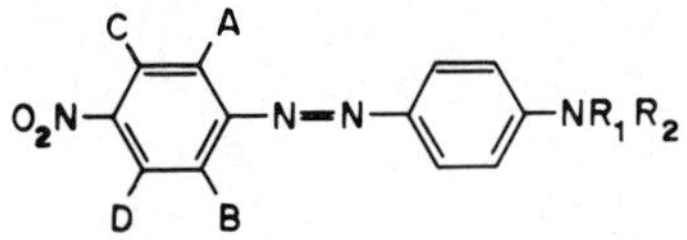

(5)

In structure (5), if *A* is nitro and *B* is halogen, H at *C* appears near 8.8 and H at *D* near 8.5. If the spectrum is well resolved, they appear as doublets, otherwise as unresolved singlets. If *A* is cyano and *B* is hydrogen, H at *C* appears as a doublet centered near 8.8, and H at *D* as a pair of doublets centered near 8.4.

Some dyes such as Samaron Brilliant Pink HPE (CI Disperse Red 89), listed as an oxazine, did not yield useful NMR spectra because of solubility problems. The knowledge of the types of dyes that yield poor NMR data is itself of some use.

Table 14.2 Typical Alkyl Groups in the NMR Spectra of Commercial Dyes

Structure Unit	Chemical Shift (ppm) (Multiplicity)
1. 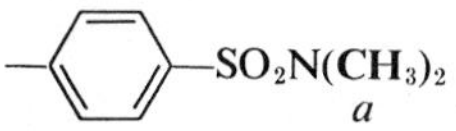 ![benzene]—$SO_2N(CH_3)_2$ _a_	_a._ 2.9 (_s_)
2. 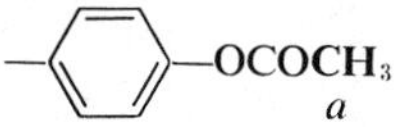 ![benzene]—$OCOCH_3$ _a_	_a._ 2.3 (_s_)
3. 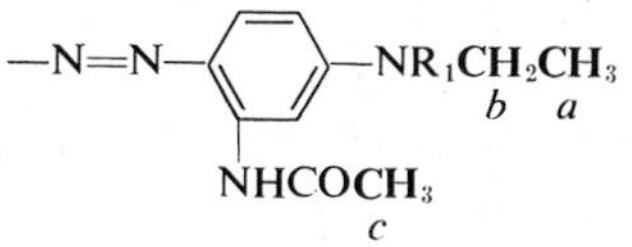 —N=N—![benzene]—$NR_1CH_2CH_3$ _b_ _a_ $NHCOCH_3$ _c_	_a._ 1.2 (_t_) _b._ 3.5 (_q_) _c._ 2.4 (_s_)
4. 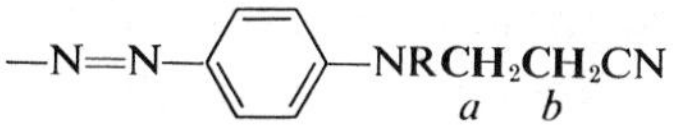 —N=N—![benzene]—$NRCH_2CH_2CN$ _a_ _b_	_a._ 3.9 (_t_) _b._ 3.0 (_t_)
5. 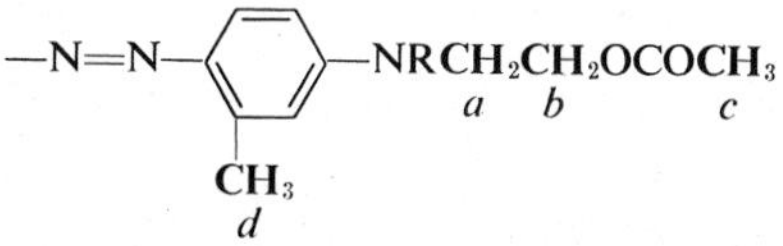 —N=N—![benzene]—$NRCH_2CH_2OCOCH_3$ _a_ _b_ _c_ CH_3 _d_	_a._ 3.9 (_t_) _b._ 4.5 (_t_) _c._ 2.1 (_s_) _d._ 2.8 (_s_)
6.  —N=N—![benzene]—$NRCH_2CH_2OCOCH_2O$—![benzene] _a_ _b_	_a._ 4.6 (_t_) _b._ 4.9 (_s_)
7. 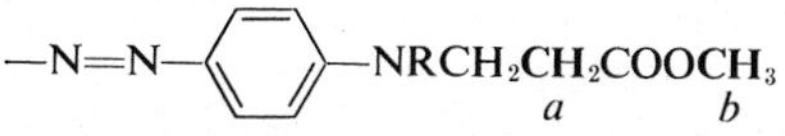 —N=N—![benzene]—$NRCH_2CH_2COOCH_3$ _a_ _b_	_a._ 2.9 (_t_) _b._ 3.7 (_s_)
8.  —N=N—![benzene]—$NRCH_2CH_2OCOCH_2CH_2CH_3$ _a_ _b_ _c_	_a._ 2.8 (_t_) _b._ 1.5 (_m_) _c._ 0.9 (_t_)
9. 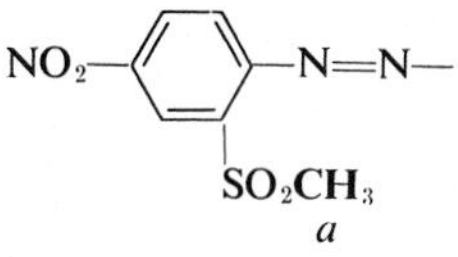 NO_2—![benzene]—N=N— SO_2CH_3 _a_	_a._ 3.4 (_s_) (CDCl$_3$)
10. 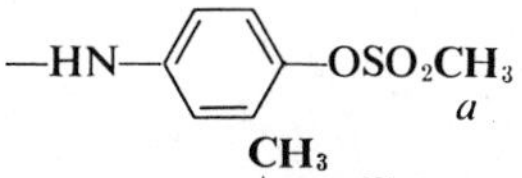 —HN—![benzene]—OSO_2CH_3 _a_	_a._ 3.5 (_s_)
11. 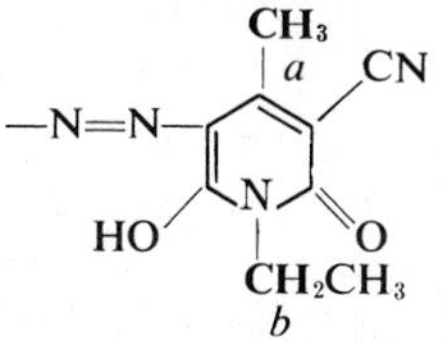 —N=N—![ring structure] CH_3 / _a_ CN / HO / N / O / CH_2CH_3 / _b_	_a._ 2.6 (_s_) _b._ 4.1 (_q_)
12. 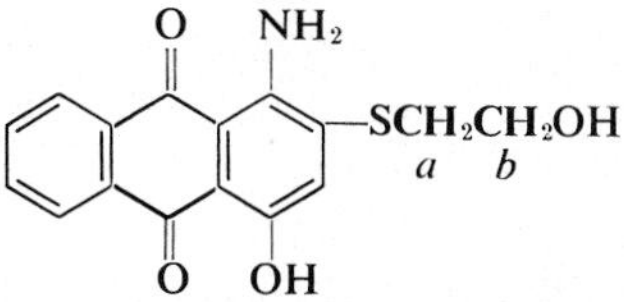 ![anthraquinone structure] O NH_2 / —SCH_2CH_2OH / _a_ _b_ / O OH	_a._ 3.4 (_t_) _b._ 4.2 (_t_)

6 MASS SPECTRA

The most important single piece of data in an identification is the molecular weight, usually obtained from the mass spectrum.

Carbamates give a molecular ion peak and peaks corresponding to loss of the isocyanate and the isocyanate itself. Genacron Rubine BLP, CI Disperse Red 216, for example, shows $M \cdot ^+$ 563, a strong 492 and weak 421 corresponding to loss of one and two isocyanates, and a strong 71 for ethyl isocyanate.

Knowledge of the chemical type makes the interpretation of the spectra easier. Besides giving a positive direction to the building of the molecule from the structural data, it prevents a loss in time and effort in trying to draw, for example, a proposed structure of a methine dye when it is an anthraquinone type.

Some of the fragments to look for in various types of dyes are the following.

6.1 Azo Dyes

The amine for diazotization usually shows, although the mechanism of its formation is not always clear. A loss of 28 corresponding to $N{=}N$ does not always show. A fragment corresponding to the coupler ion or M-coupler ion is usually found. Dyes with tertiary amines give fragments corresponding to predictable splitting of the side chains. For example, dyes with an N-cyanoethyl-N-ethylaniline coupler will show a comparatively strong M-40 (loss of CH_2CN) and a comparatively weak M-15 (loss of methyl).

6.2 Anthraquinones

Anthraquinones in general show little recognizable breakdown of the condensed ring system. A loss of 28 corresponding to a carbonyl loss can be found. Halogenated diaminodihydroxyanthraquinones show m/e 270 for the starting material and molecular ions corresponding to one, two, and sometimes three halogens, confirmed by the isotopic abundance.

2-Alkoxyanthraquinones derived from 1-amino-4-hydroxy-2-phenoxyanthraquinone usually show m/e 331 corresponding to the starting material. Substituents on the ring generally behave in an expected manner.

6.3 Nitrodiphenylamines

Sulfonamides lose SO_2, showing an M-64. They also fragment at the ring sulfur link, giving rise to an M-$SO_2NR_1R_2$. An M-30 shows loss of NO.

Loss of 46 corresponding to the nitro group will show, generally from one of the fragments (checked by the metastable ion).

6.4 Quinophthalones

This class is difficult to recognize from the mass spectra. Previous knowledge of the class from other data is very helpful. A large M-44 is usually found corresponding to a loss of CO_2. M-44 shows a small loss of 28 which is CO from a phenolic hydroxyl. A fragment at m/e 289 corresponds to 3'-hydroxyquinophthalone (CI Disperse Yellow 54), the starting material for the halogenated derivatives.

7 EXAMPLES

7.1 Methine Type

CI Disperse Yellow 99, Terasil Brilliant Yellow 6G,[11] is listed as a methine type. Absorptivity is 155.0. Using molecular weight from the mass spectrum, the molar absorptivity is 96,000. From Table 14.1, two methine groups would be expected.

Superficial examination of the IR indicates an ester and a strong cyano band.

NMR interpretation shows a triplet near 4.3 for OCH_2CH_2N. Overlapping triplet and quartet from 3.3 to 3.8 represent NCH_2CH_3 and NCH_2-CH_2O. Singlet near 2.4 is aromatic Me. Triplet near 2.3 partially overlapped by the methyl singlet is $OCOCH_2CH_2$; overlapping triplets near 1.6 show $CH_2CH_2CH_2CH_2$. Triplet near 1.2 is NCH_2CH_3.

Mass spectral data show $M\cdot^+$ 620; m/e 605 for M-CH_3; m/e 224 for M-396 (fragment split at α-carbon to the nitrogen in the ester side chain).

Using other fragments from the mass spectrum with the other data gives structure (6).

In a similar manner but with less detail in the description, other types are identified.

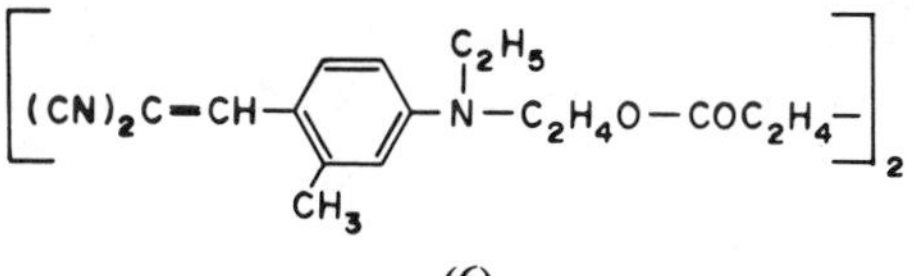

$$\left[(CN)_2C=CH-\underset{CH_3}{\underbrace{}}-\underset{C_2H_5}{\overset{|}{N}}-C_2H_4O-COC_2H_4- \right]_2$$

(6)

7.2 Nitro Dye

CI Disperse Yellow 2, Celanthrene Fast Yellow GL,[12] is listed as a nitro dye.

MS interpretation indicates M·+ 240 and typical nitro fragmentation. The NMR spectrum does not yield usable data due to poor solubility, showing a condensed ring system. The IR spectrum shows a carbonyl and nitro group. Sulfonamide is absent. Structure (7) is in agreement with physical data from a literature search.

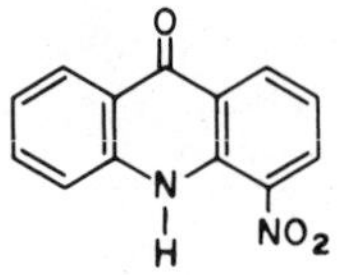

(7)

7.3   Anthraquinone Dye

CI Disperse Green 6, Polycron Green GP,[13] is listed as an anthraquinone type. The visible spectrum in pyridine has the general characteristics of a 1,4-diaminoanthraquinone. The NMR spectrum (CDCl$_3$) shows an aromatic Me and 15 aromatic H. The MS shows M·+ 404 with the presence of some ditolyl derivative (418) and diphenyl derivative (390). A weak m/e 240 is probably quinizarin, the starting material. The dye is (8), accompanied by the dianilino and ditoluidino analogues.

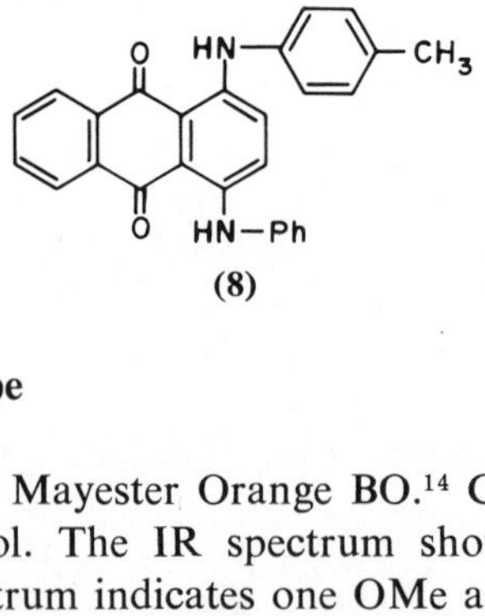

(8)

7.4   Disazo Type

CI Disperse Orange 29, Mayester Orange BO.[14] Color tests indicate azo, probably a bisazophenol. The IR spectrum shows nitro and hydroxyl groups. The NMR spectrum indicates one OMe and two H adjacent to a negative group in the aromatic region. The MS shows M·+ 377 and fragments in agreement with structure (9).

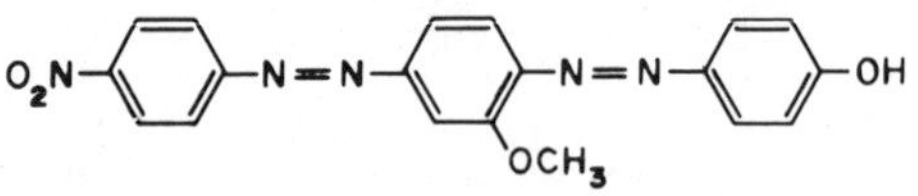

(9)

7.5   Aminonaphthoquinone Type

Artisil Brilliant Blue GFLN,[15] CI Disperse Blue 58, gives data in agreement with structure (10): $M \cdot^+$ 344 and the presence of compounds with three

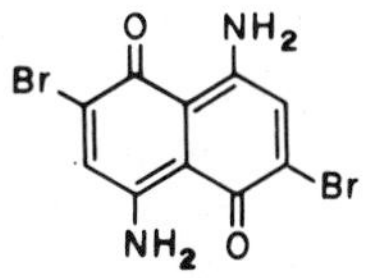

(10)

and four Br (appropriate isotope bands). The NMR spectrum shows no alkyl groups and only one species of aromatic H. The chemistry of this dye is discussed in detail by Straley[16]; structure (10) merely represents one form of a highly mobile tautomeric system.

7.6   Monoazo Type

Foron Red FL,[17] CI Disperse Red 72, is identified as (11). The MS shows M-40 for loss of CH_2CN, which is the predominant splitting in any side

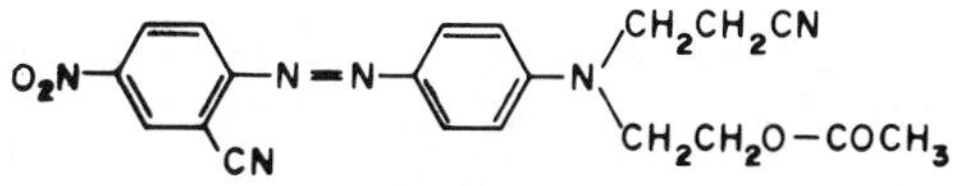

(11)

chain containing a cyanoethyl group, as well as M-60 (loss of AcOH). A small M-73 shows splitting at the α carbon in the ester side chain. Synthesis and comparison of IR and physical data were used for confirmation.

In a comparison of the MS of Samaron Red RL,[18] CI Disperse Red 90, and Red 72, it is apparent that both have $M \cdot^+$ 406. If care is not taken, they can be interpreted to give the same structure. The NMR spectrum of Red 90 clearly shows a singlet near 3.6 (OMe). Red 90 is identical with Red 72, except for the ester side chain, which is CH_2CH_2COOMe instead of CH_2CH_2OAc.

7.7   Benzothioxanthene Type

CI Disperse Yellow 105, Samaron Brilliant Yellow H6GL,[19] is listed as a xanthene type. NMR in $CDCl_3$ shows three triplets centered near 4.2, 3.5, and 2.0, corresponding respectively to OCH_2CH_2, NCH_2CH_2, and CH_2-

CH_2CH_2. A singlet near 3.4 is an aliphatic methoxyl, probably a methoxypropyl substituent.

IR shows two carbonyl bands that are typical of an imide.

MS data give $M \cdot ^+$ 375 and the first two fragments at M-15 and M-32 corresponding to loss of methyl and sulfur. Sulfur is confirmed by elemental test. Adding 73 mass units for the methoxypropyl, 70 for imide, and 32 for sulfur leaves 200 for the rest of the molecule. A naphthalene and benzene ring plus eight H fit this requirement. Assembling the components gives structure (12), a benzothioxanthene.

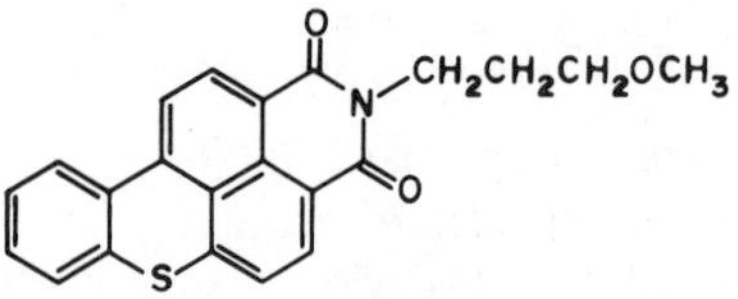

(12)

7.8   Derivative of Naphthalene-1,4,5,8-tetracarboxylic Acid

Samaron Brilliant Yellow HRL, CI Disperse Yellow 58, was examined by TLC after preliminary purification. Two yellow bands were found. N and Cl were present in the ratio 3:1. MS shows 487 and 445 with appropriate isotope peaks as the predominant peaks in the high end. Both show loss of 71. The low end shows 29, 43, and 57 (butyl group). The NMR spectrum in deuterated pyridine was unsatisfactory owing to poor solubility, but the butyl group expected from the MS could be identified. In addition bands were found which are consistent with a methoxypropyl group. A triplet centered near 4.5 is not accounted for.

A patent[20] describes "naphthoylene-arylimidazole-*peri*-dicarboxylic acid dyes." Specifically claimed are mixtures of two or more of the dyes because of the superior tinctorial strength. Structure (13; R = CH_3, C_4H_9) is consistent with M 445 and 487.

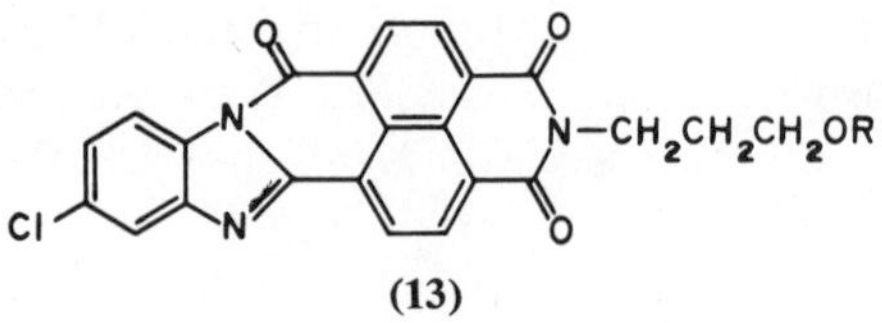

(13)

The triplet centered near 4.5 can be explained by a third compound with a CH_2CH_2 between two heteroatoms. The effort needed to identify the third component was not invested, since the identification of two components was sufficient to satisfy the purposes of the investigation. It is probable from the data and the relevant patent that the third component is **(13)** in which R is $CH_3OCH_2CH_2$ or $CH_3CH_2OCH_2CH_2$.

REFERENCES

1. FBy, *BP* 929,395.
2. S, *BP* 843,644.
3. S, *USP* 2,844,598.
4. DuP, *USP* 2,768,052.
5. MDW, JP 3296 (1963); *CA*, **60**, 12145 (1964).
6. *CSD* I, pp. 341–348.
7. J. G. Grasselli, *Atlas of Spectral Data and Physical Constants for Organic Compounds*, CRC Press, Cleveland, Ohio, 1973.
8. R. H. Bible, Jr., *Interpretation of NMR Spectra*, Plenum Press, New York, 1965.
9. H. A. Syzmanski and R. E. Yelin, *NMR Band Handbook*, IFI/Plenum, New York–Washington, 1968.
10. FBy, *BP* 760,618.
11. CIBA, *BP* 1,201,925.
12. DuP, *USP* 2,005,303.
13. LBH, *BeP* 746,475.
14. Koppers, *BeP* 604,935.
15. S, *USP* 2,553,048.
16. *CSD* III, p. 458.
17. S, *USP* 2,891,942.
18. FBy, *USP* 3,125,402.
19. FH, *USP* 3,367,937.
20. FH, *BP* 1,025,056.

CHAPTER FIFTEEN

Identification of Dyes on Textile Fibers

H. SCHWEPPE

1 INTRODUCTION

The determination of the class of dye in a dyeing or print is of great importance in matching, in the choice of finishing processes, and in the investigation of complaints. So often does the practical dyer ask "how to match the properties of the sample simply and with least expense."

Usually it is very difficult to determine the individual dyes on a fiber, and it is possible only in those laboratories where the analysts have considerable experience in dye analysis and an extensive collection of the dyes and dyeings for comparison purposes. For this reason, all practicable processes are concerned more with the recognition of the class of dye than with identification of the individual dye.

Green's tables provided the first systematic analytical procedure for determining the chemical and application classes of dyes on wool and cellulosic fibers.[1] Clayton[2] used improved reagents and brought the tables up to date. Bode[3] was the first to include dyeings on synthetic fibers in the scheme of analysis. The New York Section of the AATCC (American Association of Textile Chemists and Colorists) published a summary of American methods, and later issued them as a detailed committee report.[4] Giles et al.[5] produced a simple scheme for the rapid determination of the classes of dye on fibers. Subramanian and Taraporewala[6] suggested a simple method without prior determination of the fiber material with the exception of protein fibers. Dierkes and Brocher[7] described a systematic scheme which offers good reproducibility, and which is based on the experience of German dye analysts. Garner[8] reviewed methods of identifying dyes on fibers.

The identification of individual dyes or mixtures of dyes in dyeings is of great importance to the dye manufacturer. In cases of complaint, he might be able to establish whether or not he was indeed the supplier of a given dye. Furthermore, a method of checking must be available where, for instance, certain fastness properties have been guaranteed for dyeing by attaching the Indanthren label, and a limited number of suitable dyes then come into consideration. Derrett-Smith and Gray outlined tests for the identification of vat dyes on cellulosic fibers.[9] The identification of a dye requires a larger amount of material than is necessary for determining the class of dye. The principle of analysis by comparison is employed: the dye is subjected to chemical reactions, chromatographic investigation, and IR spectroscopy in comparison with known dyes.

2 GENERAL TESTS

2.1 Fiber Identification

Whenever possible, the investigation of a dyeing should commence with an analysis of the fiber. The number of dye classes that come into question can often be considerably reduced by carrying out a precise determination of the fiber or fiber blend. Cotton and other cellulosic fibers are readily identified by the burning test. They burn quickly and form no beads, the ash is soft, and the odor is of burning paper. Similarly, wool and silk can be identified by the odor of burnt horn, and are further distinguished by their solubility in boiling 5% sodium hydroxide. Man-made fibers can be identified by their solubility in various organic solvents. Table 15.1 shows the order in which the solvents should be applied; the procedure is based on the exclusion principle. The scheme is suitable for distinguishing between acetate, triacetate, polyamide, acrylic, and polyester fibers.

The $2\frac{1}{2}$ acetate of cellulose is soluble in benzyl alcohol at 50°, whereas the triacetate is insoluble.[4] A mixture of 80% acetone and 20% water can

Table 15.1   Solubility of Man-made Fibers in Various Solvents[4]

Fiber	Soluble	Insoluble
sec-Cellulose acetate	Acetone cold	
Cellulose triacetate	Methylene chloride cold	Acetone cold
Polyamide	85% Formic acid boiling	DMF boiling
		Acetone cold
		Methylene chloride cold
Acrylic	N-Methylpyrrolidone boiling	Acetone cold
	DMF boiling	Methylene chloride cold
Polyester	N-Methylpyrrolidone boiling	Acetone cold
		Methylene chloride cold
		DMF boiling

also be used to distinguish between sec-cellulose acetate and cellulose tri-acetate. The former dissolves very easily, whereas the latter merely swells and becomes transparent, the fibrous form persisting.[4] Acrylic fibers can be identified by their insolubility in 85% formic acid and their solubility in boiling DMF. They can be distinguished from polyester fibers by their insolubility in nitrobenzene and in o-cresol. Polyester fibers are completely saponified by boiling in 2 N potassium hydroxide in methanol to produce a white precipitate of potassium terephthalate. A clear solution is obtained on diluting with water, and a white precipitate of terephthalic acid is obtained on adding dilute sulfuric acid.

Polyamide types 6, 66, and 11 can be differentiated in the following way: cyclohexanone dissolves type 11, but not 6 and 66. A boiling mixture of 75% DMF and 25% formic acid (85%) dissolves type 6, but not type 66.[5]

With blend yarns, the results of the solubility tests are not always easy to assess. If one kind of fiber dissolves whereas a second remains unchanged, the identity of the dissolved fiber should be definitely established by evaporating the solvent to leave a film.

Microscopic examination of the fibers often gives important indications, and it is indeed indispensable when only a small amount of material is available. Water, or a mixture of water and glycerin, is used for embedding the fibers. The surface structure or the shape of the fibers, e.g., the scaly surface of wool and the spirally wound flat ribbon of cotton, provide a simple and nondestructive identification of these fibers. When warp and weft (filling) are made of different types of fiber, for instance, in colored woven fabrics, the yarns should first be separated mechanically, and the fiber and dye analysis should be carried out on the separated fibers.

The recognition of rarely occurring and synthetic fibers is dealt with in the AATCC Test Method 20-1973, "Fibers in Textiles: Identification."

2.2 Identification of Metals in Dyed Fibers

Identification of metals in dyeings or prints can show the presence of certain classes of dyes excluding inorganic pigments, special finishes (such as waterproofing, flameproofing, and weighting) and adventitious products.[2,4,7,10,11] In Table 15.2 the metals are arranged in decreasing order

Table 15.2 Metals in Dyeings and Prints in Relation to Dye Classes

Metal	Fiber	Class of Dye
Cr	Wool and nylon	Azo dye complexes (acid dyes and a few reactive dyes). Azo, triphenylmethane and other dyes on Cr mordant (mainly after-chromed)
Cu	Cotton	Azo dye complexes (direct dyes.) After-treated direct dyes. Reactive azo dye complexes. Aftertreated azoics (from Variogen bases). Copper phthalocyanine derivatives (direct dyes, reactive dyes, ingrain dyes, pigments)
Co	Wool	Azo dye complexes
Cu	Wool	Copper phthalocyanine derivatives (e.g., Wool Fast Turquoise Blue SW)
Cr	Cotton	Brown reactive azo dye complexes
Cr and Co	Cotton	Black reactive azo dye complexes
Co	Cotton	Co phthalocyanine derivatives (ingrain dyes; vat dye); aftertreated azoics (from Variogen bases)
Ni	Cotton	Ni phthalocyanine derivatives (ingrain dyes; azoic dyes from Naphthol AS-FGGR); azo pigments from pigment-printing methods
Sb	Cotton	Basic dyes on tannin
Fe	Wool and cotton	Nitrosonaphthols
Al	Wool, cotton	Alizarin and its derivatives
Ni, Al	Polypropylene	Mordant-dyes on metal-modified fiber
Ca, Ba, Sr, Mn	All fibers	Salts or lakes of acid dyes by pigment-dyeing or printing methods

of the frequency with which they are likely to be encountered on various fibers.

Ashing.   The dyeing or print (100–300 mg; about 2.5 × 2.5-cm woven or knitted material) is ashed. When subliming metal complexes such as copper phthalocyanine pigments are present, wet ashing is preferred; 100–300 mg of the dyed material is heated with 5 ml conc. sulfuric acid and a few drops of conc. nitric acid. A drop of perchloric acid (70%) is added, and the mixture boiled until no more yellow-green chlorine dioxide gas is generated; this procedure is repeated until the solution becomes almost colorless. The excess of sulfuric acid is then evaporated off.

Oxidizing Flux.   A portion of the residual ash is melted in four to five times the amount of a mixture of equal portions of anhydrous sodium and potassium nitrate. After cooling, the melt exhibits the following colorations: yellow (Cr), pale blue-green (Cu), royal blue (Co), blue-green (Mn), and brown (Ni).

Simplified Separation Process.   A portion of the ash is dissolved in boiling aqua regia. After dilution with double the amount of water, insolubles are allowed to settle out and the solution is decanted through a filter. The insolubles are boiled in a few milliliters of conc. sulfuric acid. Many silicates and intensively ignited oxides of Al, Fe, and Cr remain undissolved. After cooling, the sulfuric acid solution is diluted with water. Ba and Pb produce cloudiness. If a 5% hydrogen peroxide solution is added, an orange color reveals the presence of titanium.

The diluted and filtered aqua regia solution is treated with excess 25% ammonia. The precipitated hydroxides of Fe, Al, and Cr are filtered, their colors being brown, white, and gray-green, respectively. Aluminum is separated as soluble sodium aluminate. On the addition of hydrochloric acid, and then ammonia, to the filtrate, aluminum separates as the colorless hydroxide. If the filter residue is brown after the aluminum hydroxide is dissolved, Fe is present and is identified by the blue color with potassium ferrocyanide and sulfuric acid. If the precipitate is gray-green, Cr can be identified by an oxidizing flux.

The filtrate from the ammonia precipitate becomes blue if Cu or Ni is present. By adding a 5% sodium sulfide solution, sulfides of various colors are obtained: black (Pb, Cu, Ni, Co), yellow (Cd), or pink (Mn). After filtration, the filtrate is tested with ammonium oxalate for Ca and with dilute sulfuric acid for Ba.

Since normally only two or three cations are involved, and these usually belong to different analysis groups, it is possible to simplify the systematic inorganic separation procedure.[12]

2.2.1 Individual Tests for Metals. Emission spectroscopy provides a rapid and dependable method for the qualitative and quantitative analysis of metals.[13] The following are useful color reactions.

Copper and Nickel. The ash is dissolved in aqua regia, ammonia is added in excess, and the solution is filtered; a blue solution indicates Cu (or Ni, but much paler blue). The solution is now acidified with dilute acetic acid; potassium ferrocyanide solution gives a red-brown precipitate (Cu), and ethanolic dimethylglyoxime a fluffy pink precipitate (Ni). The sensitivity of the Ni test is reduced to a tenth by Co.

Antimony. The orange precipitate or cloudiness when formic acid and sodium sulfoxylate–formaldehyde are added to a solution of the ash indicates the presence of Sb.

Tin. A brown color or precipitate in the preceding test indicates Sn.

Aluminum. Traces are detected by the yellow-green solution and strong green fluorescence with methanolic morin.

Iron. The Prussian blue test detects Fe.

Chromium. A yellow oxidizing flux identifies Cr, confirmed by the yellow solution in water and precipitation of yellow lead chromate. Traces can be detected by diphenyl carbazide.

Titanium. The ash is dissolved in sulfuric acid, diluted, and treated with hydrogen peroxide. An intense yellow color is produced by Ti.

Manganese. The presence of Mn, shown by the blue-green oxidizing flux, is confirmed by the characteristic permanganate color when the aqueous solution is heated with conc. nitric acid, cooled, treated with a little sodium periodate, and again warmed.

Cobalt. The fiber is ashed with sulfuric acid–perchloric acid. After dilution with water, the product is neutralized and ammonium fluoride is added to prevent complex formation by the ever-present iron, followed by ammonium thiocyanate in acetone. A deep blue color is produced by Co. If Cu is present, black-brown cupric thiocyanate separates and is reduced to the yellow cuprous thiocyanate by prolonged heating, the blue Co color shifting somewhat toward green.

Chlorindazone DS is very suitable for detecting traces of Co on fibers.[14]

2.3   Microscopic Investigation

Examination of a dyed fabric with the microscope can provide not only information on the kind of fiber involved, but also on the presence of pigments. In pigment prints and dyeings, the pigments are fixed on the fiber by means of resin binders. They are nonuniformly distributed externally on the fiber, and they often form isolated clusters with dark shades. Spin-dyed and delustered fibers are usually recognized by inclusions that are fairly evenly distributed within the fiber. Since titanium dioxide is usually employed for delustering, the ash residue is tested for Ti. A few untwisted fibers are embedded in a drop of ethyl salicylate and covered with a cover glass for microscopic investigation of the fabric.

2.4   Detection of Organic Auxiliaries

Since finishes, waterproofing agents, and resin-finishing products can interfere with the detection of dyes, an attempt should be made to detect them before carrying out a dye analysis so that they can be removed with suitable agents. Starch finishes are detected quite simply by boiling and adding a drop of iodine/potassium iodide solution to the aqueous liquor after cooling. A violet or blue color indicates starch. Enzymatic desizing with 2% enzyme and 0.25% wetting agent can remove starch within 30 minutes at 70°.

When fats and waxes are present in considerable amounts, they can be recognized by the poor wettability of the fibrous sample. They can be removed by boiling with hexane or ether.

To identify resin-finishing products based on aminoplasts, 72% sulfuric acid is poured on a small sample of the dyed fabric in a porcelain dish, and a few crystals of chromotropic acid are strewn on the surface. If the dish is then heated on a water bath, a violet color soon develops if formaldehyde-yielding products are present. A blank test without the addition of chromotropic acid is necessary to avoid being misled by violet color emanating from the dye in the fabric. Formaldehyde can also be liberated by aftertreated substantive dyeings. Aminoplasts are removed by treating a portion of the fabric for 15–20 minutes at 70–80° with 1% hydrochloric acid, rinsing well with hot water, and then drying.

2.5   Solvent Stripping

The treatment of dyed fibers with solvents gives important information on the class of dye. Depending on the nature of the dye, the fiber, and the solvents, the dye may be removed entirely, partially, or not at all from the fiber. A. Seucker (BASF, unpublished work) developed a method based on solvent extraction, especially applicable to dyeings on cellulosic and protein fibers. The solvents used are (1) water, (2) ethanol, (3) glacial acetic acid, (4) 20% ammonia, and for cellulosic fibers, (5) a mixture of equal parts of ethanol and 20% ammonia. A small sample of the dyed material is boiled in a test tube successively with the solvents mentioned. The individual extracts are poured off and investigated separately. After the treatment with glacial acetic acid, the dyed fabric is rinsed thoroughly with water. The extracts obtained can be concentrated by evaporation and the residues taken up in water for reactions or dyeing tests in the same way as the dye in substance. In many cases, it is necessary to use liquids with better solvent power to bring the dye into solution. Table 2.1 gives a number of solvents suitable for the extraction of dyes. Azoic dyes can be dissolved by boiling with ethanol–1 N sodium hydroxide (20:1); if the solution is poured dropwise on filter paper, a scalloped fringe is produced.[15]

The Baumgarte Extractor. Baumgarte[16] developed an apparatus for the rational and protective stripping of dyes or other substances from fibers or films; it is possible to exclude oxygen if necessary. The sample to be extracted is secured tightly to a rod-shaped carrier, which is then introduced vertically into an atmosphere of vapor in which it warms as the vapor condenses. Water or an organic liquid, b.p. 80–130°, is preferred. When the sample attains the temperature of the vapor, a suitable eluting liquid is allowed to flow down on it. This solvent should readily dissolve the dye, loosen the bond between the dye and fiber, and if necessary swell the fiber without causing an irreversible change. It should form as continuous a phase as possible with the condensing vapor. There are practically no limits to the choice of solvents, which can consist of a single substance, mixture, or solution of convenient b.p. Systems can be chosen that permit the dye to be eluted with a minimum of liquid in the shortest time. The drops of eluate are collected below the carrier of the material and can be removed from the hot zone either immediately and continuously, or batchwise. After cooling, it can be made up to a definite volume for photometric examination, usually without first having to be concentrated by evaporation.

The equipment consists of a heating device, e.g., a dome heater, a 1-l round-bottomed flask with a standard ground socket and a second opening for inserting a glass tube through which an inert gas can be introduced when oxygen has to be excluded, an extractor at the top of the flask, and a reservoir for solvent fitted above the extractor.

The extractor (Figure 15.1) has a vapor zone (1) in which the temperature is that of the b.p. of the liquid in the flask. The cooling zone (2) causes the vapor to condense and flow down the walls of the vessel. Lower there

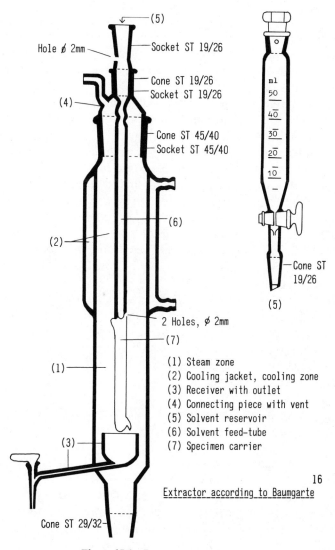

Hole ⌀ 2mm —
—Socket ST 19/26
(5)

—Cone ST 19/26
—Socket ST 19/26
(4)

—Cone ST 45/40
—Socket ST 45/40

(6)
(2)

2 Holes, ⌀ 2mm
(7)

(1)

(3)

Cone ST 29/32

ml
50
40
30
20
10

—Cone ST 19/26

(5)

(1) Steam zone
(2) Cooling jacket, cooling zone
(3) Receiver with outlet
(4) Connecting piece with vent
(5) Solvent reservoir
(6) Solvent feed-tube
(7) Specimen carrier

16
Extractor according to Baumgarte

Figure 15.1 Baumgarte extractor.[16]

is a receiver (3) which has an outlet tube with burette cock fitted with a Teflon stopper, i.d. 1.5 mm; this receiver collects the solution containing the eluted dye, which can be run off as required. At the upper end of the extractor there is a connecting piece (4) which has a vent through which nitrogen or unpleasantly smelling vapors can be led. The essential part of the apparatus is the insert with the specimen carrier (7), a mat-ground piece of glass rod with hooks for securing strips of cloth tapes. The carrier is fused on a glass tube, at the top end of which is a ground stopper that fits into the upper socket as indicated and which is used for adding solvent (6). Important features are an aperture at the top for establishing pressure equalization, and shortly above the specimen carrier two or three openings through which the eluting solvent can pass. Baffle devices at the upper end are useful for ensuring that the falling liquid always runs down the inner wall of the tube (6), thus preventing it from falling directly to the bottom of the tube and splashing out of the openings.

It is an advantage to wind yarn uniformly round the lower end of the carrier. A piece of fabric or film to be extracted is secured to the rod by winding a 1–2-cm-wide woven tape tightly round it, the tape being attached to the top hook of the carrier. Knitted strips have also proved very satisfactory since their elasticity holds them very tightly to the carrier. The lower end of the tape can either be slipped over the lower hook or fastened by means of a wire loop. The solvent reservoir preferably consists of a graduated dropping funnel (5) that can be fitted into the ground-glass socket of the solvent feed tube (6).

The liquid is heated to the boil until the vapor zone has attained the working temperature. The small amount of condensate in the receiver is removed. If oxygen has to be excluded, e.g., with vat and sulfur dyes, nitrogen is introduced rapidly during the heating phase, and a moderately rapid flow (2 bubbles/second) is maintained once the boiling temperature has been attained. The carrier, with an appropriate amount of material to be examined (about 0.2–0.5 g, depending on the dye content), is now inserted. During the warming stage, condensate again forms, and if still colorless it is drained off from the receiver. The amount of condensate depends on the heat of condensation of the vaporized liquid and on the specific heat of the carrier with the material being extracted. In the case of steam, about 1 ml condensate is formed.

The selected solvent is now allowed to flow from the reservoir, and an appropriate rate for the first 15 ml is about 1 drop/second; the remaining quantity (about 25 ml) is introduced more slowly (about 1 drop/2 seconds). The progress of the extraction can be followed quite well if the extract is removed from time to time from the receiver. The process should take about 20–25 minutes. A different rate of flow of droplets may be chosen. For instance, time can be saved with a more rapid flow if the material is readily extracted, but on the other hand, a lower rate can be employed with particularly slow extractions, 1 drop/2 seconds or even more slowly if this is found to be advantageous.

Examples of Extractions of Dyes with the Baumgarte Extractor. (1) Vat dyes and sulfur dyes on cellulosic fibers: 300 ml *N*-methylpyrrolidone, 60 ml sodium hydroxide (38°Bé), 30 g hydrosulfite, 640 ml water (steam and nitrogen atmosphere). (2) Azoic dyes on cellulosic fibers: pyridine (steam atmosphere). (3) Direct dyes on cellulosic fibers: 800 ml DMF, 200 ml ammonia (25%) (steam atmosphere). (4) Acid dyes, 1:1 and 1:2 metal complex dyes on wool: 900 ml pyridine, 100 ml formic acid (steam atmosphere). (5) Acid dyes, 1:1 and 1:2 metal complex dyes on polyamide: 800 ml pyridine, 200 ml ammonia (25%) (steam atmosphere). (6) Disperse dyes on polyamide: 900 ml DMF, 100 ml glacial acetic acid (steam atmosphere). (7) Disperse dyes on polyester fiber: pyridine (chlorobenzene as the vapor phase). (8) Basic dyes on acrylic fiber: 600 ml pyridine, 400 ml formic acid (85%) (steam atmosphere). (9) Disperse dyes on cellulose acetate: 800 ml benzene, 200 ml ethyl acetate (benzene in the vapor phase).

2.6 UV Fluorescence

Fluorescence phenomena can sometimes prove useful in the analysis of dyeings. For instance, the following dyes fluoresce on the fiber when exposed to UV light: CI Acid Yellow 7, CI Basic Violet 10, CI Basic Red 1, CI Acid Red 87, CI Acid Red 52, CI Acid Red 50, CI Basic Yellow 2, CI Basic Yellow 3, and CI Disperse Yellow 11.

Some dyes fluoresce under UV light in certain solvents, such as 98% sulfuric acid (e.g., yellow Acridines), benzene, pyridine (e.g., CI Vat Violets 15 and 17), ethylenediamine, DMF, and in the vatted state or when the vat is shaken with ether. Most of these reactions can be carried out on the fiber. Only purified solvents may be used, and these should be subjected to a blank test to ensure the absence of inherent fluorescence. A small sample of the dyeing is introduced into the solvent and briefly warmed. Conc. sulfuric acid is used only at room temperature. Cotton dyed with azo dyes derived from dehydrothiotoluidine fluoresce intensely after treatment with aqueous sodium hydroxide and dithionite, followed by rinsing and drying.

3 ANALYTICAL SCHEMES

3.1 The Green-Clayton Scheme

In 1893, A. G. Green developed a scheme that still survives, although modifications are necessary for incorporating new commercial dyes.[1] It is based on (a) solubility and dyeing behavior; and (b) the behavior of the dyes toward reducing agents (e.g., zinc dust and boiling 10% acetic acid) and reoxidation. Green kept his analytical scheme continually up to date, and finally summarized the reactions in 27 tables. The hue of a dye is an important clue to its identity, and Green therefore arranged his tables according to shade. In addition, dyeings on animal and vegetable fibers were dealt with in separate tables.

In 1937 Clayton described a scheme for the identification of dyes on the fiber, based on Green's tables, but using more effective reagents and including new commercial dyes; the scheme was revised in 1946 and 1963.[2] The following reagents are used: (1) dilute ammonia (1 ml ammonia, $d = 0.88$, in 100 ml water); (2) 5% sodium hydroxide solution; (3) 5% sodium carbonate solution; (4) 5% ammonium chloride solution; (5) 3% hydrogen peroxide; (6) vat dye developer (8 g ammonium chloride and 1 g ammonium persulfate in 100 ml water); (7) Formosul G (20 g sodium

Table 15.3   Action of Boiling Formosul G on Dyeings or Prints in Relation to Chemical Class of Dye

Color Reaction	Chemical Class	Example (CI)
Little or no change	Acridine	Basic Orange 14
	Xanthene (basic)	Basic Violet 10
	Anthraquinone	Disperse Blue 3
	(some disperse dyes)	
	Phthalocyanine	Direct Blue 86
	(except vattable Co	Pigment Blue 15
	compound)	
	Polymethine (basic)	Basic Red 12
	Quinophthalone	Acid Yellow 3
	(acid, pigment)	
	Thiazole (direct, basic)	Direct Yellow 59
Color change; solution	Anthraquinonoid vat dye	Vat Blue 6
dyes cotton		Solubilized Vat Green 1
Yellow to brown; color	Anthraquinonoid	Acid Violet 43
restored by H_2O_2 (or air)	acid or mordant dye	Mordant Red 11
	Indigoid	Vat Blue 1
	vat or acid dye	Acid Blue 74
Brown; color restored by	Azine	Pigment Black 1
air		
Decolorized; color re-	Triphenylmethane	Basic Violet 14
stored by weak H_2O_2 and	(basic, acid, mordant)	Acid Green 16
AcOH	Xanthene	Mordant Blue 1
	(some acid dyes)	Acid Violet 9

(Continued)

Table 15.3—(Continued)

Color Reaction	Chemical Class	Example (CI)
Decolorized; color restored by air	Azine (acid or basic) Oxazine (basic) Thiazine (basic)	Acid Blue 59 Basic Red 2 Basic Blue 3 Basic Blue 9
Decolorized permanently	Azo (acid, direct, mordant, disperse, basic). Some metal complexes may require prior boiling with acid. Some stilbenes become paler and duller. Thiazole-azo dyes become yellow. Azoic (some, especially yellows, with difficulty; reduction facilitated by organic solvent) Nitro Nitroso	Acid Yellow 1 Acid Green 4
Decolorized (with addition of NaOH); color restored by air	Dioxazine	Direct Blue 106

sulfoxylate–formaldehyde in 100 ml water and 50 g mono- or diethylene glycol); (8) ethylenediamine; and (9) Developer O (1 g ammonium persulfate and 0.5 g ammonium dihydrogen phosphate in 100 ml water).

The behavior of a dyeing or print when it is boiled with Formosul G and submitted to reoxidation gives an indication of the chemical class of a dye, as shown in Table 15.3 (see also *CSD* II, pp. 1375–1378).

The first tests in the Clayton scheme are (1) a simple stripping test (boiling for 2 minutes with dilute ammonia); (2) the behavior of the sample toward Formosul G (and dilute ammonia or sodium hydroxide solution) and subsequently toward air, 3% hydrogen peroxide, or Developer O. The stripping test may well give an immediate indication of a definite class of dye. Thus direct cotton dyes on wool and silk can be recognized at once when the dyed fiber is boiled together with undyed cotton for 1 minute in dilute ammonia; the white cotton is stained. The application and chemical class of a dye can usually be established by the color of the solution and the fiber, together with the behavior of both in the reoxidation test. A specific dye can also be identified occasionally.

The action of ethylenediamine on dyes offers good prospects of distinguishing them, because this organic base has an excellent dissolving action and, in addition to being strongly basic, it has reducing properties. Indigoid dyes are changed into their leuco compounds by ethylenediamine, often at 50–60°, or even at room temperature. Anthraquinonoid vat dyes are reduced only slightly on the fiber under these conditions. They are dissolved at the boil, however, either directly or as the leuco compound, especially when glucose is added.

Some Cr complexes of azo dyes can be reduced on the fiber only with difficulty by Formosul G, even after boiling with 16–30% hydrochloric acid. However, when heated with ethylenediamine the metal complex dissolves without change of shade; the solution is rapidly decolorized if a trace of hydrosulfite is included. Azoic dyes are extracted with ethylenediamine, and the solution is rapidly and irreversibly decolorized when hydrosulfite is added. When ethylenediamine is used on wool and silk samples, it should be remembered that this basic solvent has a degrading action on protein fibers, although the dyes dissolve much more rapidly than the fiber components. Although most substantive dyes on cotton and viscose bleed out within 1 minute on treatment with a boiling 5% sodium hydroxide solution, the lightfast Dioxazine Blue types (CI Direct Blue 108; CI 51320; *CSD* II, 787) are resistant to this treatment. On the other hand, these dyes are removed in a few minutes with cold ethylenediamine. Sulfur dyes on cotton are identified by boiling with zinc and 16% hydrochloric acid and testing for sulfide with lead acetate paper. Dyes of the Indocarbon type cannot be decolorized with sodium hypochlorite, but they are recognizable by the red solution they form in boiling ethylenediamine, reverting to black immediately on dilution with water. Sulfur Black dyeings give green solutions with ethylenediamine. ,

In seven tables each for dyes on (a) wool and silk and (b) cotton, arranged according to hue from yellow to black, Clayton has outlined tests for identifying the application and chemical classes. Reactive dyes figure only in a brief supplementary note, and the scheme does not cover dyes on synthetic fibers.

3.2   AATCC Scheme

This scheme[4] determines the class of dyes on natural and synthetic fibers. Where possible, only methods of test are used that can be carried out in any textile laboratory. The tests for the class of dye are preceded by a determination of the nature of the fibers, preference being given to simple methods of recognition (see Section 2.1). Subsequent procedure appropriately depends on the nature of the fiber. For each test 100–300 mg of the dyed sample is used.

3.2.1 Dyes on Cellulosic Fibers. The possible dyes include direct, acid, basic, cationic aftertreated direct dyes, sulfur, vat, oxidation blacks (aniline, diphenyl), azoics, developed dyes, direct dyes aftertreated with formaldehyde or metal salts, pigments, and reactive dyes. Dope-dyed viscose is usually identifiable by the cross-section of the fiber under the microscope (see Section 2.3).

Group I. This group covers direct, acid, basic, and cationic aftertreated direct dyes. The dyes are not classified merely by a single reaction, but by the degree of their bleeding in dilute ammonia or in dilute acetic acid, a series of treatments being prescribed.

Direct dyes. The sample is heated with 5–10 ml water and 0.5–1 ml conc. ammonia until sufficient dye has gone into solution for a piece of white cotton to be stained. The sample is removed, 10–30 mg white cotton fabric and 5–30 mg sodium chloride are introduced, and the mixture is boiled for 40–60 seconds, then cooled to room temperature. The cotton is removed, rinsed, and assessed. Redyeing of cotton from the ammoniacal solution after the addition of salt to the original shade and depth indicates direct dyes.

Acid dyes are hardly ever used for cellulosic material except acid-dyeable viscose. If the dye goes into solution during the test for direct dyes, but only slightly stains white cotton, the solution of the extracted dye is acidified with acetic acid, and 10–30 mg wool is boiled in it for about 30 seconds, then rinsed. Redyeing of wool from an acid bath proves the presence of acid dyes when direct and basic dyes have been eliminated.

Basic dyes are occasionally used for brightening shades. If the sample bleeds only slightly in the test for direct dyes, basic dyes are looked for. The sample is boiled with glacial acetic acid, water is added, and the sample is removed. Tannin-mordanted cotton is introduced and boiled for about 1 minute. Basic dyes are indicated if the cotton is stained, and can be confirmed by evaporating a portion of the acetic acid extract to dryness and redissolving in dilute sodium hydroxide solution. The dye base is transferred to ether, which is then shaken with dilute acetic acid. If the lower aqueous layer becomes colored, a basic dye is present.

Cationic-aftertreated direct dyes. If in the test for direct dyes there is only slight bleeding from the dyed sample, and if the test for basic dyes has proved negative, the possibility of a cationic-aftertreated direct dye is investigated. A sample is boiled with 1 % hydrochloric acid, the acid is discarded and fresh acid added, and the treatment is repeated; the sample is then rinsed. This removes the aftertreatment agent. If the sample now bleeds more readily in dilute ammonia and otherwise behaves like a direct dye, the original sample is a direct dyeing that has been cationically aftertreated.

Group II. Included in this group are those dyes whose shades change on treatment with an alkaline hydrosulfite solution, but are restored on re-oxidation in air: vat and sulfur dyes, aniline black, and diphenyl black. The sample is heated with 3–6 ml water and 1–2 ml 10% sodium hydroxide solution to the boil, 10–30 mg hydrosulfite is added, and boiling is continued for 2–5 seconds. All dyeings of this group, with the exception of the Indanthren Blues, undergo definite changes in shade. If the sample is removed from the reducing solution and exposed to air, the original shade is restored in 5–6 minutes.

Identification of Indanthren Blues. A few drops of conc. nitric acid are poured on the sample, which is then pressed between several layers of filter paper. If the pressed-out color is pure yellow and returns to the original blue shade on being spotted with an acidified tin(II) chloride solution, the dye is an Indanthren Blue.

Sulfur dyes. The sample is boiled with 2–3 ml water, 1–2 ml 10% sodium hydroxide, and 200–400 mg sodium sulfide for 1–2 minutes. The sample is then replaced by 25–50 mg white cotton material, 10–20 mg sodium chloride is added, and the solution is boiled for 1–2 minutes. The cotton is placed on filter paper and exposed to air. Only sulfur dyes color cotton in a shade that differs from the original merely in depth. Sulfur dyes can be confirmed by boiling the sample with 16% hydrochloric acid for a minute, then adding zinc, and testing for liberated hydrogen sulfide with lead acetate paper. Further, sulfur dyes are virtually destroyed in 5 minutes by treatment of the sample with hypochlorite (2% active Cl).

Vat dyes. Anthraquinone derivatives are only slightly affected by 10% sodium hypochlorite solution, but thioindigo and sulfurized vat dyes (such as Hydron Blue) are largely decolorized and bleached to a yellow. The dyed material is boiled for 1 minute with 2–3 ml water, 0.5–1 ml 10% sodium hydroxide, and 10–20 mg hydrosulfite. The sample is then replaced by 25–50 mg of white cotton fabric, 10–20 mg sodium chloride added, and the mixture is kept at the boil for 1 minute, then cooled to room temperature; the cotton is then laid on filter paper to oxidize. If a shade similar to the original, differing only in depth, is obtained, the presence of vat dyes is indicated. Sulfur dyes must have been eliminated in earlier tests.

Oxidation Blacks (*Aniline and Diphenyl*) are not taken up again by cotton, either from sulfide or hydrosulfite vats. The color changes to brown with boiling hypochlorite solution.

Group III. This group embraces dyes that are destroyed by alkaline hydrosulfite, and whose colored extracts do not stain white cotton. The group includes direct dyes aftertreated with metal salts or formaldehyde, azoic dyes, diazotized dyes, and developed dyes.

Direct dyes, aftertreated. Metal salts can be recognized by Cr or Cu in the ash. Aftertreatment with formaldehyde can be identified by the detection of formaldehyde (Section 2.4) in the absence of resin finishes: blue precipitate when an extract of the sample with boiling 5% sulfuric acid is added to 0.1% carbazole in conc. sulfuric acid.

Azoic dyes; diazotized and developed dyes. Although these two classes differ entirely in their properties, they are alike in that the dye is formed in situ on the fiber. Their identification comes at the end of the scheme after all other possibilities have been eliminated. Characteristically, azoic dyes bleed in pyridine. Because of their insolubility in water, they take longer to bleach with sodium hydroxide/hydrosulfite than azo dyes. The dyeing is boiled with 2 ml 10% sodium hydroxide solution and 5 ml ethanol, and then with 5 ml water and 40–50 mg sodium hydrosulfite until the sample has become colorless; after cooling, the liquor is filtered; 10–20 mg white cotton is placed in the filtrate and 20–30 mg sodium chloride added; after the mixture is boiled for 1–2 minutes, then cooled, the cotton is removed. A yellow stain that fluoresces in UV light proves that the original sample is an azoic dyeing or print.

Diazotized and developed dyeings do not bleed into pyridine and are readily reduced in a blank vat. However, some of these dyes do color pyridine somewhat, but if the pyridine treatment is repeated, bleeding soon ceases. By contrast, azoic dyeings bleed at a uniform rate.

Group IV. If the foregoing tests for other classes of dyes on cellulose have proved negative, pigments or reactive dyes should be looked for.

Pigments. Microscopic investigation, dissolving behavior, and chemical reactions provide information on the presence and nature of the pigment.

Extraction with DMF: a sample of the dyeing is boiled with 5 ml of (*a*) 1:1 DMF and water, and (*b*) 100% DMF. The intensity of solvent coloration distinguishes between pigments and reactive dyes. If reactive dyes have not been adequately washed out, DMF–water becomes somewhat colored. The dissolving behavior of various types of dye in DMF is summarized in Table 15.4.

Reactive dyes. There is no specific proof for reactive dyes, and it is therefore necessary to eliminate fully other types of dyes, such as azo, sulfur, and vat dyes. Pigments behave like reactive dyes in quite a number of reactions. Table 15.5 gives a series of indicative reactions for reactive and some other classes of dyes.

The reagents are as follows: 5% sodium hydroxide and 5% sodium hydrosulfite in water (reduction); 5% acetic acid in water (extraction); 5% hydrogen peroxide or 10% sodium perborate in water (oxidation); 100% DMF (extraction); sodium hypochlorite liquor containing 2% active chlorine (bleaching). The dyeing is placed in a blank vat at the boil and the progress of the reaction with time is observed. Substantive azo dyes and developed dyes are decolorized rapidly; vat and sulfur dyes and Aniline Black are quickly converted to their leuco form. Some red pigments become paler, but the reaction proceeds slowly and is easily distinguished from the rapid decolorations. Some reactive dyes with anthraquinone chromophores are reduced, but the original color is seldom restored on reoxidation; reactive dyes with azo chromophores are decolorized by the blank vat and by hypochlorite. If the sample has been converted to the leuco form in the blank vat, it is placed in dilute acetic acid. Vat, sulfur, and chrome dyes, as also Aniline Black, form leuco acids that have a different color from the original sample and the alkaline vat. After a

Table 15.4   DMF Extraction Test for Dyes[4]

DMF–Water (1:1)	100% DMF
Colored by:	**Colored by:**
All direct	Vat
Diazotized and developed	Azoic
Some basic	Sulfur
Some mordant	Pigment
	Some basic
	Some mordant
Not Colored by:	
Reactive	**Not Colored by:**
Azoic	Reactive
Pigment	
Some basic	
Some mordant	

Table 15.5 Procedures of AATCC[4]

| | Class Reactions | | | | | |
Dyes	Reduc-tion	Acetic Acid	Oxidation	DMF	Hypo-chlorite	Ash
Pigment	NC[a,b]	NC	NC	Bleeds	NC	—[c]
Azoic	Strips	NA[d]	NA	Bleeds	Strips	—
Vat	Reduces	Leuco	Original shade	Bleeds	NC	—
Sulfur	Reduces	Leuco	Original shade	Bleeds	Strips	—
Fiber reactive	Strips	NA	NA	No bleed	Strips	—
Direct	Strips	NA	NA	Bleeds[e]	Strips	—
Diazotized and developed	Strips	NA	NA	Bleeds[e]	Strips	—
Aniline Black	Reduces	Leuco	Original shade	Bleeds	Brown	—
Chrome	Reduces	Leuco	Original shade	Bleeds	Strips	+

[a] NC, no change.

[b] Inorganic pigments are affected by the reduction reagent. They are not completely restored by oxidation. Their presence should be confirmed by microscopic examination.

[c] Inorganic pigments and lakes of azoic reds are exceptions.

[d] NA, not applicable.

[e] Also bleed in 1:1 DMF–Water.

brief immersion in the blank vat, the dyeing is transferred to the oxidizing bath in which the original color is restored. In addition, the effect of hypochlorite is observed on a separate sample.

3.2.2 Dyes on Animal Fibers.

The following classes of dyes are normally employed for dyeing wool or silk: basic, direct, acid, soluble acid-dyeing 1:1 metal complex and chrome (only with wool), neutral-dyeing 1:2 metal complex, vat, solubilized vat, and azoic dyes.

Basic Dyes. The sample is boiled with 10 ml ethanol, and after the alcohol is evaporated, the dye is taken up in water. After adding sodium hydroxide solution, the dye base is transferred to ether and shaken with dilute acetic acid. The basic dye is now in the form of the salt and exhibits the original shade of the sample.

Direct Cotton Dyes.   The dyeing is boiled for 1–2 minutes with 5 ml water and 1 ml conc. ammonia. The sample is removed, 30 mg sodium chloride is added, and 10–30 mg undyed cotton is boiled in the solution for 1–2 minutes, then rinsed. If the dye is a direct color, the cotton becomes deeply stained.

Acid Dyes.   A portion of the ammoniacal extract of the dye is acidified with 10% sulfuric acid and 20–40 mg of wool is boiled in it for 1–2 minutes. Dyeing of wool from an acid bath indicates acid dyes.

Soluble, Acid-Dyeing 1:1 Metal Complex Dyes.   These are distinguished from acid dyes by the detection of Cr in the ash.

Chrome Dyes are formed in situ on wool by treating Cr-mordanted wool with a water-soluble dye. The resulting chrome dye is water-insoluble and is partially removed from the dyeing by treating with ammonia, but re-dyeing on wool is not possible.

Neutral-Dyeing 1:2 Metal Complex Dyes.   Unsulfonated metal complexes can be extracted from the fiber only in very small amounts. Nevertheless, in contrast to the chrome dyes, they can be redyed on wool, the shade being much paler than the original. Cr, Co, Ni, or Mn can be detected in the ash. A neutral-dyeing Cr complex contains less Cr than a chrome dye.

Vat Dyes.   The dyeing is boiled with 2.5 ml 10% sodium hydroxide until the wool has completely dissolved; 25–50 mg hydrosulfite, 10–15 mg white cotton, and 25–50 mg sodium chloride are then introduced and heated for 1–2 minutes almost to the boil. After the mixture is cooled to room temperature, the cotton is laid for 1–2 minutes on filter paper, then transferred to an oxidizing bath containing sodium nitrite and acetic acid. The development of color on the cotton proves the presence of vat dyes.

Azoic dyes.   Their presence is indicated after the possibility of all other dyes has been eliminated by the fact that they bleed strongly in pyridine. In addition, they are reduced to strong yellow shades in blank vats, and these are not susceptible to reoxidation. Furthermore, azoic dyeings give characteristic colorations in sulfuric acid.

3.2.3 Dyes on Cellulose Acetate or Triacetate.

The following classes of dyes are normally used for dyeing both fibers: disperse, acid, basic, vat, developed, and pigment dyes (by mass coloration or resin bonding). Notable quantities of acetate fibers are mass pigmented, but they are conventionally dyed with disperse dyes. Diazotized and developed dyes are mostly used for blacks and sometimes for navy blues.

The dye class can be identified by the following dye transfer test and extraction with solvents. The dyeing is treated with the same amount of undyed acetate material in 25 ml soap solution (5 g/l) for 10 minutes at 90°. The coloration of the liquor, change in shade of the original dyeing, and the degree of dye transfer to the undyed acetate are observed. Disperse dyes color the white acetate comparatively strongly. Pigment dyes are not transferred. Basic dyes migrate into the soap solution, but do not stain the white acetate. Developed dyes produce only a pale yellow shade on the undyed acetate, this being attributable to intermediate products.

The sample is treated with 5 ml of a 25% solution of N-methylpyrrolidone on a boiling water bath. The fabric is removed after 20–40 seconds, and the extract is well shaken with 3–5 ml toluene and 20 ml water; the colors of the aqueous and toluene layers are noted.

Disperse Dyes. If the toluene layer is deeply colored, a disperse dye is most probably present. The separated toluene portion is evaporated to dryness; the dispersion of the residue with lignin sulfonate in water stains white acetate fabric.

Acid Dyes. If the aqueous layer is deeply colored and the toluene layer remains colorless, acid dyes may be present. Coloration of wool from an acid bath indicates an acid dye.

Basic Dyes. Both the aqueous and toluene layers may be colored. A fresh sample is extracted for 10 minutes with 5% formic acid at 90°, and if anionic acrylic fibers can be stained with this extract, basic dyes are indicated.

Vat Dyes. The aqueous and toluene layers are colorless. Treatment of the sample with alkaline hydrosulfite and redyeing of cotton are used to identify a vat dye.

Developed Dyes. Their presence is indicated when the N-methylpyrrolidone extract is colorless or brown. Both the aqueous and toluene layers may be colored. When a sample is boiled with 10 ml 5% sodium hydroxide solution, 5 ml ethylene glycol, and 50 mg hydrosulfite, developed dyes change in shade and are irreversibly destroyed.

Pigments. When all other classes of dye have been ruled out, it can be assumed that pigments are present. There are no specific proofs, since pigments can belong to a wide variety of chemical classes. Inorganic pigments can be identified from the composition of the ash. Black mass dyeings made with carbon black do not change in shade on treatment with sodium hydroxide solution and hydrosulfite.

3.2.4 Dyes on Polyester Fibers. The following classes of dyes are commonly used: disperse, developed, basic, pigment (mass-dyed or resin-bonded), and vat dyes.

The sample is dissolved in 3–5 g molten caprolactam; 3 ml ethanol is then added to prevent setting of the caprolactam, and after the mixture is cooled to room temperature, it is diluted with 15 ml ether and filtered. If the ether extract is colored, it is shaken repeatedly with water containing sodium sulfate to remove the caprolactam. A layer of 10 ml water containing some dispersing agent is introduced under the separated ether layer which is then evaporated off; 100 mg white acetate fabric is then introduced into the dye dispersion and heated on a water bath for 10 minutes. If the acetate is strongly colored to the same hue as the original dyeing, the presence of disperse dyes is considered proved; if the coloration is weaker, developed or vat dyes are indicated. The acetate material is removed and sodium hydroxide solution and a few milligrams of hydrosulfite are added to the hot dye dispersion. If the color disappears on shaking, or if the shade is changed and is not restored on shaking in air, developed dyes are involved. Vat dyes are reoxidized under these conditions to the original shade.

Pigments and basic dyes strongly color the polyester precipitated by the ether from the caprolactam melt. In this case, a fresh sample of the dyeing is boiled for 1 minute with glacial acetic acid, and the solution is evaporated to dryness. The residue is dissolved in 5 ml water and boiled with tannin-mordanted cotton for 1 minute. Basic dyes color the cotton. Dope-dyeings are recognized under the microscope by the uniform distribution of pigment over the whole of the fiber cross-section.

3.2.5 Dyes on Acrylic Fibers. The following classes of dyes are used: disperse, metallized acid (neutral dyeing), basic, acid, and chrome dyes. The dyeing is heated with 2 ml 40% *N*-methylpyrrolidone on a boiling water bath until sufficient dye has gone into solution (10–20 minutes). A pyridine–water mixture (57:43) can also be used for extracting the dyes.

Toluene (10 ml) and water (1 ml) are added to the dye solution and the mixture is shaken well. After the phases have separated, the following distribution of the dyes between the two phases can be observed: disperse dyes color the toluene layer; basic, acid, and chrome dyes color the aqueous layer; some neutral-dyeing 1:2 metal complex dyes color both layers.

Disperse and 1:2 Metal Complex Dyes. Metal complex dyes can be recognized by the identification of Cr, Co, or Mn in the ash. For confirmation, the toluene layer is separated, washed with water, and evaporated to dryness. The residue is dispersed in water and the behavior toward wool and acetate fibers is investigated. Metal complex dyes stain only wool. Disperse dyes color acetate more deeply than wool.

Basic Dyes. The aqueous layer is made alkaline and the mixture is shaken with 10 ml toluene. A few drops of dilute acetic acid are added to the toluene layer and shaken. Basic dyes are present if the lower layer has the original color.

Acid Dyes. If basic dyes are excluded, and if no heavy metal can be found in the ash of the sample, an acid dye is present.

1:2 Metal Complex and Chrome Dyes. If Co or Mn is present in the ash of the sample, a 1:2 metal complex dye is most likely present. If Cr is present, a distinction between chrome and chromium complex dyes can only be made by a semiquantitative determination of the Cr.

3.2.6 Dyes on Polyamide Fibers. The following classes of dyes are used: disperse, direct, acid, basic, 1:1 and 1:2 metal complex, chromium, logwood, azoic, vat, and reactive dyes. The sample is submitted to the following tests.

Wash Test. The dyeing is warmed for 30 minutes with 10–15 ml of a solution of 0.5% neutral soap and 0.2% sodium carbonate on a boiling water bath and the sample is then withdrawn. The wash solution is divided into two halves. One is acidified with 1–2 ml glacial acetic acid, and a 12-mm wide strip of multifiber fabric No. 5* is introduced into both portions, which are then boiled for 3–5 minutes. The types of fibers that have been dyed or tinted under acidic or alkaline conditions are then ascertained.

---

* Multi Fiber Fabric No. 5 can be obtained from Testfabrics Inc., 55 Vandam St., New York, N.Y. 10013. It contains the following fibers: acetate, Acrilan 1656, Arnel, cotton, Creslan 61, Dracon 54, Dracon 64, nylon 66, Orlon 75, silk, Verel A, viscose, and wool.

Ash Test. The dyeing is ashed and melted with 200–300 mg of a mixture of equal parts of sodium carbonate and potassium nitrate. After cooling, the melt is colored yellow (Cr), Prussian blue (Co), weak blue-green (Cu), blue-green (Mn), or brown (Ni).

Solubility Test. The dyeing is heated for 15–30 minutes with 15 ml pyridine–water (57:43) on a boiling water bath. Dyes other than vat, chrome, and reactive disperse dyes bleed strongly. After cooling, the material is removed, and the solution is acidified with 1–2 ml conc. hydrochloric acid; 15 ml toluene is added and the mixture is shaken well. After phase separation, the dyes are distributed as follows: toluene layer—all disperse dyes and azoics, some vat, reactive disperse, and 1:2 metal complex dyes without sulfonic groups; aqueous layer—all direct, basic, acid, logwood and 1:1 and 1:2 metal complex dyes with sulfonic groups, some unsulfonated 1:2-metal complex. The dye classes can then be established by individual reactions.

Disperse dyes color acetate, triacetate, and nylon 66 from alkaline liquors. Nylon 66 and Verel A (modacrylic fiber) are dyed from an acid bath.

Direct dyes color cotton and viscose strongly from an alkaline solution, but nylon 66 and silk are only weakly stained. Redyeing from an acid bath produces deep dyeings on Acrilan 1656, nylon 66, silk, viscose, and wool.

Acid dyes color Acrilan 1656, nylon 66, silk, and wool strongly from an acid bath. They have only a slight affinity for any fiber from an alkaline solution and are thus in marked contrast to the direct dyes, which dye cellulosic fibers from an alkaline solution.

Basic dyes bleed strongly in the wash test and dye acrylic, cationic-dyeable polyester, and Verel A fibers deeply from acid liquors. All these fibers remain unstained in alkaline solutions. Dyeings with basic dyes bleed strongly with the pyridine–water treatment. If the solution is rendered alkaline and shaken with toluene, the dye bases go into the toluene phase and the dyes can be transferred to dilute acetic acid.

1:2 Metal complex dyes bleed considerably in the wash test. On redyeing from an alkaline solution, nylon 66 is strongly colored, but Acrilan 1656, wool, silk, and Verel A are more weakly dyed. Acrilan 1656, nylon 66, silk, and wool are markedly stained from acid liquors. If the ash contains Cr, Co, or Mn and if only the toluene layer is colored in the solution test, it is quite definite that unsulfonated 1:2 metal complex dyes are present.

1:1 Metal complex dyes also bleed very much in the wash test. In the dyeing test from an alkaline solution, none of the fibers in the test fabric is dyed. Acrilan 1656, nylon 66, silk, and wool are tinted in an acid solution. The metal is always Cr.

Chrome dyes contain Cr in comparatively large amount. In the wash test, afterchrome dyes bleed only slightly; the extract may differ in color from the original. They bleed slightly in pyridine–water.

Logwood is used on nylon exclusively with Cr as the mordant. In the wash test, logwood dyeings bleed slightly and usually have a red color. None of the fibers in the test fabric is dyed from either an alkaline or acid solution. On extraction with pyridine–water, logwood dyeings bleed profusely, and the solution assumes a dark wine red coloration, changing with hydrochloric acid to yellow brown. On shaking with toluene, the yellow-brown color remains in the water layer. For confirmation, logwood dyeings are boiled with 5% hydrochloric acid, into which they bleed red and themselves become red.

Azoic dyes bleed very little in the wash test, probably owing to unfixed dye or to uncoupled naphthol or base. Multifiber cloth is only slightly stained in redyeing tests. The dyes bleed readily into pyridine–water, and go into the toluene layer on being shaken with this solvent. For confirmation, the dye in the toluene layer is destroyed by alkaline hydrosulfite; the products stain white cotton yellow with a characteristic yellow UV fluorescence.

Vat dyes bleed only in traces in the wash test if the dyeing has not been sufficiently soaped. Vat dyes do not bleed, or bleed only very little, in boiling pyridine–water. If, however, some dye should have been extracted, it goes into toluene, or forms an intermediate layer as a precipitated pigment.

Vat dyes on nylon can be reduced with zinc formaldehyde sulfoxylate and acetic acid to form the leuco acids. If the sample is removed from the solution and treated with sodium bichromate and acetic acid, the original dye is restored.

Reactive disperse dyes do not bleed in the wash test, or bleed only very little. On boiling with pyridine–water, they undergo slight to moderate bleeding. To confirm a reactive dye, the whole of the material is dissolved in *o*-chlorophenol and the solution is poured into propanol when the nylon separates out. If the fiber has been dyed with disperse dyes, the dye remains in solution, whereas dyes of the Procinyl type remain on the precipitated nylon, showing that they have reacted with the fiber.

3.3   Dierkes and Brocher Scheme

The Dierkes and Brocher scheme[7] is an attempt to apply the inorganic analysis system in that, with each kind of fiber, the class of dye is determined by a specific classification procedure. The nature of the substrate is first investigated. Tables 15.6–15.8 respectively outline the schemes for dyes on cellulosic, animal, and synthetic fibers. The following abbreviations are used in the tables: GAA (glacial acetic acid); PAN (polyacrylonitrile), PE (polyester), and PA (polyamide) fibers, and MC (metal complex).

A sufficiently large amount of the dyed material is boiled with distilled water to remove any superficially held dyes and finishes. If a large proportion of the dye dissolves, the solution can be evaporated to dryness and the dye investigated directly. Unless otherwise indicated, a fresh sample of the dyed or printed material is used in each of the sequentially applied tests. If a dye is extracted by boiling with ammonia, GAA, ether, or other solvent, it is advisable to repeat this extraction several times, combine the extracts, and then proceed. It is recommended that comparisons should be made as described under (4) below.

The numbers in the tables refer to the following procedures and identification reactions: (1) Pigments (pigment/binder combinations, dope dyeings, and delusterings) can be recognized microscopically (see Section 2.3). (2) The dry sample is shaken in a test tube for 1 minute with cold pyridine. The sample must have been previously washed or at least rinsed. The pyridine test is conclusive only if the sample has been well dried. (3) The sample is treated with zinc chloride and boiling 20% hydrochloric acid and the liberated hydrogen sulfide is detected by lead acetate paper. (4) For easier assessment of the result of a reaction, appropriate "blank experiments" are carried out: e.g., a known sulfur dye in (3); water only in (5); reoxidation of only a part of the solution of the vat in (6). (5) The blank vat contains 15 g/l sodium hydroxide and 20 g/l dithionite. The sample dyeing is heated with a few milliliters of blank vat on a water bath at about 60°. If vat dyes are present, the shade of the sample usually changes. Azoic dyeings impart a more or less strong yellow color to the blank vat at 80°, and there may be a change in the shade of the sample, even to the extent of the dye being completely destroyed. In either case, the original shade is not restored by reoxidation. (6) For reoxidation, the sample is rinsed with water and then treated with very dilute hydrogen peroxide. If the original shade is restored, the dye is a vat dye; otherwise, it is an azoic dye. Frequently, the original shade returns simply on rinsing. With blue shades, a change in hue is often difficult to detect, and in this case an equivalent amount of acetic acid is added to the vatted dye (the vat-acid method) and the change in color is observed. If more alkaline dithionite solution is added, the blue shade is restored. (7) The ash is tested for Cr.

(8) The ash is tested for Fe. (9) The sample is stripped with GAA, and the extract is evaporated to dryness, then taken up in water. If basic-dyeing acrylic fibers are colored on boiling in the solution, basic dyes are present. (10) To confirm (9), a portion of the solution is made alkaline with sodium hydroxide before the redyeing test, and the dye base that is formed with a change in color is extracted by shaking with ether. The ethereal solution is separated and dilute acetic acid is introduced as a layer beneath it. If this is colored to the initial shade, a basic dye is present. (11) A tannin-mordanted substrate can be recognized in the case of pale shades by spotting with ferric chloride solution, which produces a dark spot. With deeper shades, the dyeing is boiled with 5% sodium hydroxide solution, which is then cooled rapidly. A coloration is produced immediately in the case of tannin, but not with Katanol mordants. (12) If a mordant of the Katanol type is present, the extract obtained by boiling with sodium hydroxide solution, as in (11), contains sodium Katanolate. On treatment with nitric acid and silver nitrate, a brown precipitate of silver Katanolate is obtained; this is converted to black silver sulfide on boiling. (13) Extracts of the dyed sample obtained with ammonia, or with GAA, are evaporated to dryness and taken up in water. One half (a) of the dye solution is treated with acetic acid, and the other (b) is used as a neutral liquor containing Glauber's salt. A wool thread and a cotton thread are boiled simultaneously for 1 minute in the two solutions. In (a), acid dyes stain wool deeper than cotton. If direct dyes are present, then the cotton dyes deeper than wool in (b). (14) The ash is tested for Al. (15) The ash is tested for Cu. (16) The dyeing is tested for products that split off formaldehyde (4). (17) The sample is boiled for 5 minutes with 10% phosphoric acid, and then removed from the solution. A few drops of a 1:500 solution of Sirius Light Scarlet BN (CI Direct Red 95) are added and the solution is again boiled. If the dyeing has had a cationic aftertreatment, the dye precipitates after some time. (18) The sample is boiled for 1 minute with distilled water. A dye diazotized and developed on the fiber does not stain the water very much, whereas a strong coloration is obtained with dyeings that have not been aftertreated. (19) The sample is treated for 5 minutes at 60–80° in a blank vat (5). With a reactive dye, the shade changes or completely disappears. The sample is rinsed and diazotized for 20 minutes with a cold 0.1% solution of sodium nitrite that contains 3 ml/l conc. hydrochloric acid. The sample is now rinsed and placed in a Developer ONL solution (2-hydroxy-3-naphthoic acid, sodium salt). In the event of a new dyeing, which may differ in shade from the original, a reactive dyeing is indicated. Confirmation is possible only when, after a reductive cleavage, the amine attached to the fiber can be diazotized. (20) The ash is tested for Ni. (21) The staining of hot GAA by some yellow azoic dyeings is hardly noticeable, but their shade distinguishes them from the blue and green phthalo-

Table 15.6 Identification of Dyes on Cellulosic Fibers[a]

Microscopic examination for pigments, dope dyeings, delustered materials (1)

Pyridine, cold, 1 minute (2)

Pyridine colored: sulfur, oxidation, mordant, acid, direct and basic dyes. Followed by sulfur test (3), (4)	Negative: oxidation, mordant, acid, direct, and basic dyes. Followed by blank vat test (5), (4)
Positive: sulfur dyes. Confirmation: reduction and reoxidation (4), (5), (6). Blue dyeings turn violet on spotting with cold conc. nitric acid	Black dyeings change to brown and on air oxidation to black: oxidation dyes. Followed by treatment with cold conc. sulfuric acid, then diluted with water

Black dyeings branch:

- Solution green: Aniline Black. Cr positive (7); with ferrocyanide vapor black, Fe positive (8)
- Solution unchanged: Diphenyl Black

If no black dyeing or if negative reaction: acid, mordant, direct, and basic dyes. Followed by stripping with GAA and staining test with white PAN (9)

- PAN stained: basic dyes. Confirmation (10) (a) tannic acid with tartar emetic mordant (11); (b) Katanol mordant (12)
- PAN not stained: acid, mordant, and direct dyes. Followed by stripping with conc. ammonia or GAA, and staining tests (13)

PAN not stained branch:

- Wool stained darker: acid and mordant dyes. Followed by tests for Cr (7), Fe (8), Al (14)
  - Positive: mordant dyes
  - Negative: acid dyes
- Cotton stained darker: direct dyes. Followed by tests for Cu (15), Cr (7), formaldehyde (16). cationic substances formaldehyde (17)
  - Positive: direct dyes aftertreated with Cu or Cr salts, formaldehyde, or cationic products
  - Negative: direct, diazotized, and developed dyes. Differentiation by comparative fastness tests (18)

TABLE 15.6 (Continued)

Microscopic examination for pigments, dope dyeings, delustered materials (1)

Pyridine, cold, 1 minute (2)

Pyridine not colored: sulfur, reactive, phthalocyanine, vat, and azoic dyes. Followed by sulfur test (3), (4)

Positive: sulfur dyes. Confirmation: blank vat and reoxidation (5), (6), (4)

Negative: reactive, phthalocyanine, vat, and azoic dyes. Followed by DMF (boiling)

Solution not stained: reactive dyes. Confirmation and differentiation (19)

Solution stained: phthalocyanine, vat, and azoic dyes. Followed by GAA (boiling, 1 minute)

Solution not stained: phthalocyanines. Confirmation: with cold conc. nitric acid violet, Cu or Ni detection (15), (20), (21)

Solution stained: vat and azoic dyes. Followed by blank vat and reoxidation (5), (6), (4)

Positive: vat dyes. Differentiation of indigo and other blue vat dyes with nitric acid and stannous chloride (22)

Negative: azoic dyes. Confirmation: fluorescence test (23). For green azoics, (24)

[a] Dierkes and Brocher scheme.

417

Table 15.7 Identification of Dyes on Animal Fibers[a]

Paraffin test (25)			
Paraffin colored: vat and azoic dyes. Followed by blank vat and reoxidation (5), (6), (4)			
Color changes, but is restored: vat dyes	Test solution changes to yellow, shade of the pattern does not change; but if changed, does not revert to original shade: azoic dyes		
Paraffin not colored: basic, 1:1 MC, 1:2 MC, mordant, acid, direct, and reactive dyes. Followed by test for metals (7), (26)			
Cr or Co positive: 1:1 MC, 1:2 MC, and chrome mordant dyes. Followed by stripping with ammonia, acidifying solution with HCl and shaking with ether (27)		Cr and Co negative: basic, acid, direct, and reactive dyes. Followed by GAA (cold) (9)	
Ether heavily stained: 1:2 MC dyes	Ether not or only slightly stained: 1:1 MC dyes and chrome mordant dyes	GAA stained: basic dyes Confirmation (10)	GAA not stained: acid, direct, and reactive dyes. Followed by pyridine (cold) (28)
			Pyridine stained: acid, direct, and direct dyes. Followed by staining tests (13)
			Pyridine not reactive dyes
			Wool more stained: acid dyes Cotton more stained: direct dyes

[a] Dierkes and Brocher Scheme.

Table 15.8   Identification of Dyes on Synthetic Fibers[a]

Add ether to A and B[b]

Ether stained: disperse, developed disperse, Procinyl, azoic, and vat dyes.
Followed by fluorescence test (23)

Positive: azoic and developed disperse dyes. Followed by pyridine–water (1:1), boiling (31)		Negative: PA: disperse, Procinyl dyes. PE: disperse dyes. Followed by GAA (boiling) + ether + water (32)	
Dye precipitates and solution is intensely stained: developed disperse dyes	Dye does not precipitate or solution is hardly stained: azoic dyes	Precipitate white: disperse dyes	Precipitate colored: Procinyl dyes

---

Add ether to A and B[b]

Ether stained: disperse, MC, and chrome mordant dyes. Followed by test for metals (7), (26)

Negative: disperse dyes	Positive: MC and chrome mordant dyes. Followed by pyridine–ether (27)	
	Ether stained: 1:2 MC dyes without sulfonic groups	Ether not stained: 1:1 and 1:2 MC dyes with sulfonic groups, chrome mordant dyes.

Add ether to A and B[b]

Ether not stained: MC, chrome, mordant, basic, acid and vat dyes. Followed by test for metals (7), (26)

Negative: basic and acid dyes[c]

With PA: acid dyes	With PAN: GAA, boiling, staining test (9)	
	PAN stained: basic dyes	PAN not stained: acid dyes

---

[a] Dierkes and Brocher Scheme.
[b] A = PE and PA treated with molten caprolactam (29). B = PAN stripped with GAA (30).
Identification of vat colors: To the residue of the ether extract of the dye in molten caprolactam (29), a blank vat solution is added, followed by reoxidation (5), (6), (4). Color changes indicate vat dyes.
[c] Positive: see second part of this Table.

cyanines. (22) To distinguish between Indanthren Blues and indigo dyeings, they are spotted with nitric acid ($d = 1.4$) and pressed between filter papers. Both become yellow, green, and finally colorless. If the spot pressed on the filter paper is treated with a hydrochloric acid solution of ferrous chloride, the blue color is restored with Indanthren Blues, but not with indigo dyeings. (23) A dyed sample is boiled for 5 minutes with 2 N sodium hydroxide–ethanol (1:2), some hydrosulfite is added, and the hot solution is again brought to the boil. With Naphthol AS dyes, the solution fluoresces yellowish green in UV light. The dyed sample itself is not treated as above, but the caprolactam melt is extracted with ether (30). The ether is evaporated off, and the dye taken up with sodium hydroxide solution and alcohol, the solution then being treated as above. (24) Dyeings that have been made with Naphthol AS-FGGR (CI Azoic Coupling Component 108) can easily be confused with vat dyes, because the shade changes in a blank vat and the original shade is restored on reoxidation. However, these dyeings fluoresce (23), though the fluorescence is weaker than with other azoic dyeings. (25) A thread is dropped into molten paraffin in a porcelain crucible. If the dye dissolves, the color is noted against the white porcelain background. (26) The ash is tested for Co. (27) An ammoniacal extract of the sample is evaporated to dryness and the residue is taken up in water. After dilute hydrochloric acid is added, the solution is shaken with ether. If most of the dye remains in the aqueous phase, a sulfonated metal complex dye or a chrome dye is present. If most of the dye is transferred to the ethereal layer, an unsulfonated 1:2 metal complex dye is present. (28) A few threads taken from the sample are shaken for 5 minutes with cold pyridine. If the pyridine is colored, an acid or direct dye is involved, but a reactive dye is indicated if it remains colorless. (29) A sample is heated with about 3 g caprolactam in a porcelain crucible while being stirred with a glass rod until the fiber has also melted. The melt is allowed to cool with constant stirring, and some ether is added shortly before the melt sets; a crumbly mass is produced. More ether is added and stirred, and the mixture is filtered. The residue is needed for testing for vat dyes. (30) The dye is not readily dissolved out of acrylic fibers by a caprolactam melt; it is usually extracted with GAA. The sample is removed after boiling for 5 minutes, and water is added to the cool solution, which is then shaken vigorously with ether. Two layers are formed after standing for a little time. (31) For distinguishing between azoic dyes and disperse dyes diazotized and developed on the fiber, the dyed sample is treated with pyridine–water (1:1). The solution becomes cloudy when heated gently, and the solution is heated further until it becomes clear. Unlike azoic dyes, developed disperse dyes color the solution. (32) To distinguish between disperse dyes and reactive dyes on nylon fibers (Procinyl type), the sample is dissolved by boiling in GAA. After cooling, ether is added, and then water in the ratio 1:1:1. The mixture is shaken well and, if necessary, a little more ether may be added. A white precipitate is produced in the presence of disperse dyes, and the ether becomes colored. With reactive dyes, the ethereal layer can also be somewhat tinted, but the precipitate exhibits a deeper shade because the dye is chemically bonded with the precipitated fiber substance.

4 SPECIAL METHODS

Systematic schemes of analysis (Section 3) lead to the identification of the application class of a dye and, in part, the chemical class. Methods for the closer differentiation of dyes on cellulose acetate, acrylic fibers, vat dyes, reactive dyes, and pigments are now considered.

4.1 Dyes on Cellulose Acetate

Haigh[18] has described methods for determining the application and chemical classes of dyes on sec-cellulose acetate and for identifying individual disperse dyes. Differentiation between the dyes within a range of hue (yellow, orange, etc.) is effected by UV fluorescence, attempts to diazotize and couple the dye (aromatic amines), reduction, oxidation, and various spot tests, and the coloration in conc. sulfuric acid. Many dyes can definitely be identified in this way, but dyes with identical reactions are further distinguished by chromatography or IR spectroscopy. The scheme must constantly be brought up to date for including new commercial dyes.

4.2 Dyes on Acrylic Fibers

Blackburn and Meldrum[19] have indicated that the solvent mixtures nitromethane–2-pentanone (50:50) and nitromethane–2-pentanone–acetic acid (50:50:10) are very useful for extracting basic and disperse dyes from acrylic fibers at 90–100°. Wagner and Pflug[20] strip acrylic fiber dyeings in turn with pyridine, DMF–water (1:1), and formic acid–acetic acid (1:1) for 5 minutes on a boiling water bath. The extracts are more or less strongly colored, depending on the class of dye present. The application class of the dye is then established by evaporating the extract to dryness and redyeing. However, the use of DMF and acetic acid is more effective and more generally used for stripping acrylic fiber dyeings as a kind of "precipitation method."[20] Compared with other stripping methods, a small amount of liquid is needed, so that the evaporation time is considerably shortened. In the precipitation method, the dyeing is dissolved in hot DMF, and an equal volume of glacial acetic acid is added and the mixture is brought to the boil. The polyacrylonitrile separates out as a coarse flocculate. This is filtered hot and the filter is rinsed once with a boiling DMF–glacial acetic acid solution. The filtrate is evaporated to dryness and the residue is used to identify the dye by redyeing tests, reactions, or chromatographic comparison.

With blends of acrylic fibers and wool or cellulosic fibers, the precipitation method can often effect a fiber and dye separation in one operation. In this case, the wool or cellulosic fiber can be removed from the solution after the acrylic fibers have been dissolved by DMF, and before the polyacrylonitrile has been precipitated with glacial acetic acid. The test then proceeds as described above. If the cellulosic component has been azoic dyed, the dye is also found in the DMF–glacial acetic acid filtrate.

The following reactions give important information for identifying dyes on acrylic fibers:[20] (1) acetic acid 6°Bé + sodium chlorite; boil for 30 seconds; (2) 2 parts glacial acetic acid + 1 part stannous chloride solution (100 g $SnCl_2 \cdot 2H_2O$ + 100 g conc. HCl + 100 ml water); boil for 30 seconds, rinse with hydrochloric acid, and oxidize with 3% hydrogen peroxide; and (3) 2 parts caustic soda solution 20°Bé + 1 part hydrazine hydrate pure; boil for 30 seconds, rinse, and oxidize with 3% hydrogen peroxide. With mixtures of basic dyes, these reactions sometimes achieve separation of dyes by destroying one or more of the component dyes.

4.3   Vat Dyes

Vat dyes are investigated almost without exception as dyeings on cotton hanks, even when the dye itself is available and it has been established by a vatting test that it is in fact a vat dye. If the vat-dyed fiber is other than cellulose, it is best to transfer the dye to cotton. Various reactions are carried out with the dyeing and, with the assistance of extensive reaction tables, a vat dye is sought which has reactions like those of the dye being investigated. Reactions with dyeings made from the known and unknown dye are then carried out in parallel to confirm the agreement of their characteristics. Naturally, this method of analysis requires the availability of a comprehensive collection of authentic vat dyes or dyeings.

Based on the earlier work of Herzog and others, Derrett-Smith and Gray[9] used the following reagents and produced tables covering 345 vat dyes: (1) alkaline hydrosulfite; (2) acid hydrosulfite (Rongalite C and acetic acid); (3) conc. nitric acid; (4) conc. sulfuric acid; (5) acid potassium permanganate, followed by acidic hydrogen peroxide. The dyeing is treated with each of these reagents and the color changes noted.

4.4   Reactive Dyes

The identification of reactive dyes on cellulosic fibers is based on work by Bode[21] that has been admirably adapted by Jordinson and Lockwood[22] to a wide range of more recently developed dyes. Before carrying out the identification reactions the dyed sample is boiled for 15 minutes with a nonionic surfactant to remove unfixed dye. The dyeing is then boiled for 4 minutes with the following solvents in sequence, the material being rinsed in between with cold water: (a) glacial acetic acid–ethanol (1:1); (b) 1% ammonia solution; (c) DMF–water (1:1); and (d) DMF. A reactive dye is most probably present if the dyeing does not bleed under these conditions. Reactive dyes derived from phthalocyanine are partially removed.

The ashed sample can be tested for Cu, Cr, Co, and Ni (see Section 2.2) for further identification of various reactive dyes. Rubine, bordeaux, violet, blue, and navy blue reactive dyes are frequently copper complexes of o,o'-dihydroxyazo dyes, and turquoise dyes are usually copper phthalocyanine derivatives. Cr and Co 1:2 complexes as reactive dyes are encountered in blacks, grays, navy blues, and browns; Levafix Turquoise IGG (FBy) contains Ni and is an exception.[23] Jordinson and Lockwood found the Burdett procedure[11] most suitable for detecting metals in reactive dyeings on cotton.

The azo groups can be split off by reduction where reactive azo dyes have been used, and two (or more) cleavage products with primary amino groups on the aromatic nucleus are produced. The component bound by its reactive group to cellulose remains attached to the fiber after reduction, whereas the other amine can be washed out. In many cases, the primary amines bound to the cellulose can be diazotized after a reduction, and then coupled with 2-naphthol to form a new dye (for procedure see Section 3.3). If this procedure gives a positive reaction, a reactive dyeing is definitely proved.[7, 24, 25]

However, the usual complications in this reduction test have to be remembered. An o-aminonaphthol derivative is oxidized by nitrous acid to a quinone and diazotization must be carried out in presence of copper sulfate. An aminopyrazolone yields a rubazonic acid (CSD I, p. 696).

Reactive dyes whose reactive groups are attached to the diazonium components of the dyes can generally be identified by the reduction cleavage method, even when they are in the form of metal complexes.[23] The amine left on the fiber after reduction can be diazotized and coupled with the appropriate coupling component, followed by metallization if necessary, to reproduce the original dye. On the other hand, when the reactive group is attached to the coupling component, the original dye cannot be reconstructed.[24]

Phthalocyanine derivatives may be identified by the following reactions: (1) The dyeing is spotted with conc. nitric acid, and then with stannous chloride and hydrochloric acid solution. Phthalocyanine derivatives become violet with nitric acid, and the original color is restored with stannous chloride solution.[22] (2) The dyeing is treated with a solution containing 20 g/l dithionite and 2.5 g/l sodium hydroxide. After reduction, the sample is rinsed successively for 2 minutes each with cold, hot, and again with cold water. To rule out any reversible change in shade due to alkali, a blank test is made with a 0.25 % sodium hydroxide solution containing no reducing agent. Phthalocyanine derivatives become blue, whereas anthraquinone dyes become brown.[23] Wagner and Pflug[26] distinguish reactive dyes of the phthalocyanine class from phthalocyanine pigments produced on the fiber by the violet color of the former in a blank vat; the pigments remain blue.

Identification of the Reactive System.   There are two distinct problems in identifying reactive dyes on the fiber: identification of (*a*) the chromophore and (*b*) the reactive system. The methods so far discussed relate to the former which, briefly, can be identified by the general methods for any class of dye. The identification of the reactive group, after it has reacted with the fiber, is a far more difficult and often intractable problem. The procedures suggested by Bode and others, including Jordinson and Lockwood, depend on relative stability of the dye–fiber bond to acidic and alkaline hydrolysis.

A sample of the dyeing is boiled together with white wool (about half the size of that of the dyed sample) for 15 minutes in a solution containing 1 ml/l conc. sulfuric acid and 2 g/l sodium sulfate. Bode found that only reactive dyes of the Remazol type (except Black B) do not bleed in this acid cross-dyeing test, but Jordinson and Lockwood found that four Levafix dyes examined by them were also resistant.

Conversely, the Remazols (except Brilliant Blue R and Red Violet R) lost much color by treatment at the boil for 2 minutes with dilute ammonia or sodium hydroxide (Clayton's test for distinguishing direct dyes from vat, sulfur, mordant, and azoic dyes on cotton), but the Procions, Cibacrons, Drimarens, Reactons, and Levafixes examined by Jordinson and Lockwood withstood the alkaline treatment. There were variations in stability among the members of each commercial range, and identification ultimately depended on empirical tests, not directly related to the reactive system, but dependent on a close study of the behavior of a large number of dyes. Thus black and gray dyeings of, e.g., a Procion, Cibacron, or Remazol, could be distinguished by characteristic colors with conc. nitric and sulfuric acids and of the extracts after dilution. Except for the phthalocyanine derivatives and a few blues derived from "bromamine acid," reactive dyes built from an identical chromophore and differing only in the reactive system are not encountered, making identification possible by a classification according to hue following Clayton's tables, differential behavior in the solvent stripping and acid cross-dyeing tests, and specific color reactions. A scheme for identifying 30 different reactive blacks on cotton has been presented by Jordinson and Lockwood. They have also reported the behavior in these tests of dyeings on cotton of a series of dyes belonging to nearly all the commercial types.

4.5 Pigments on and in Textile Fibers

4.5.1 Microscopic Examination. The presence of pigments on textile fibers is most simply confirmed by the microscope (Section 2.3). Resin-bonded pigments applied by printing or dyeing are nonuniformly distributed on the fiber surface, whereas mass pigmentation can be recognized by the uniform distribution of the pigment particles.

Burdett[27] has described the details of microscopic investigation. Table 15.9 lists the "optical solvents" useful for embedding fibers to prepare them for examination under a polarizing microscope. It is important to use solvents with a refractive index as near as possible to that of the fiber; the boundary of the fiber becomes invisible and does not interfere when the pigmented fiber is observed under polarized light, either longitudinally or transversely.

Table 15.9 "Optical" Solvents for Textile Fibers (Burdett[27])

Optical Solvents	Refractive Index	Fiber	Refractive Indices[a]	
			$n_{\downarrow\downarrow}$	$n_\perp$
Liquid paraffin A	1.468	sec-Cellulose acetate	1.479	1.477
		Cellulose triacetate		
Ethyl salicylate	1.522	Viscose rayon	1.544	1.520
		Acrilan	1.524	1.520
Ethyl salicylate or	1.522	Mercerized cotton	1.566	1.522
benzyl benzoate	1.569	Durafil	1.559	1.515
		Nylon	1.580	1.520
		Perlon	1.568	1.515
Methyl salicylate	1.536	Cotton	1.580	1.533
		Terylene[b]	1.725	1.537
		Dynel	1.536	1.531
o-Nitrotoluene	1.546	May be used for viscose rayon		

[a] $n_{\downarrow\downarrow}$ = refractive index for light vibrating parallel to the fiber axis.
  $n_\perp$ = refractive index for light vibrating perpendicular to the fiber axis.

[b] For Terylene a mixture of 1 part monobromonaphthalene (1.655) and 3 parts methylene iodide (1.742) ($n = 1.720$) may be used.

In mass-pigmented fibers and in pigment prints and dyeings, pigment particles have a diameter of $\sim$0.1–0.5 μ, with a maximum of 1.0 μ. Such particles are recognizable under the microscope at magnifications of 400–500. In many cases, they have about the same refractive index as the fiber, but the contrast in color between the pigments and the fiber is adequate for identification. The microscope must have a minimal chromatic aberration; nevertheless difficulties occur with yellow or pale pigments, even though these can be minimized to some extent with a blue filter. Similarly, identification presents great difficulties if the pigment concentration is low, e.g., with pastel shades.

Under microscopic examination, dyed fibers appear to be uniform without the individual colored particles being detectable. In mass-pigmented fibers, the distribution of the pigment particles is regular, but particulate, whereas solvent-spun synthetic fibers dyed in the mass with soluble dyes, e.g., spun-dyed secondary cellulose acetate, appear under the microscope to be as uniform as dyeings from a liquor. A difference between liquor dyeings and spin dyeings can be detected by viewing the fiber cross-section. With liquor dyeing the concentration of dye decreases toward the center of the fiber, whereas the whole of the cross-section is uniformly colored in spin dyeing.

When fibers have been superficially printed or dyed with resin-bonded pigments, unevenly distributed pigments embedded in the resin can be observed.

Difficulties can arise with synthetic fibers that contain large amounts of titanium dioxide as a delustering agent. When it is difficult to identify colored pigments, it is advisable to employ very thin fiber cross-sections under the microscope. The higher refractive index of the delustering agent causes its outlines to appear sharper than those of the colored pigments. Vat dyes can also cause confusion, but their particle size when used as pigments for mass pigmentation can distinguish them from dyes applied from a vat.

4.5.2 Isolation of Pigments. When resin-bonded pigments are present in prints, and now also in dyeings, it is necessary first to separate the pigment from the binder before the former can be identified. With inorganic pigments, it is simply a matter of identifying the pigment by ashing. In all other cases, the sample is boiled for 30 minutes with 0.1 N hydrochloric acid to destroy any formaldehyde-yielding groups that might be present as reactive or cross-linking components in the binder. The fabric is then rinsed thoroughly with water and dried, after which it is extracted in a Soxhlet apparatus successively with toluene, methyl ethyl ketone, and THF for 20 minutes in each case to bring the polymer binder into solution. If the extracts are colored with simultaneously liberated pigments, an attempt is made to separate pigment and binder on a heated alumina column. The boiling extract is poured on the column and is washed down with the same solvent. In many cases, the binder is washed through the column, whereas the pigments are retained. The pigment can be eluted by subsequently using a suitable solvent such as DMF or DMSO. Pigments that remain attached to the surface of the fiber after removal of the binder may be identifiable on the fiber, e.g., the copper phthalocyanines.

With spin-pigmented synthetic fibers, inorganic pigments and inorganic components of organic pigments may be identified from the ash. The method of separation of organic pigment from the fiber is governed by the nature of the substrate. After the type of fiber is determined, it is usually dissolved in an appropriate solvent (Table 15.1) and the pigment centrifuged if it has not also been dissolved. When both fiber and pigment have dissolved, it may be possible by using a second solvent to keep the pigment in solution while precipitating the fiber substance. Polyamide fibers can be hydrolytically degraded by boiling with 20% hydrochloric acid, the decomposition products being soluble in water. Many organic pigments are not destroyed by this treatment.

Polyester fibers can often be separated from the pigment by saponifying with alcoholic potassium hydroxide without the pigment being affected.

Cellulosic rayons can be dissolved in cold conc. sulfuric acid. On diluting with water, most pigments precipitate together with any cellulose that has not been converted to glucose. If the sample is boiled for some time, the remainder of the cellulose goes into solution and the flocculated precipitate can be filtered off.

Mass-pigmented polyethylene and polypropylene fibers are dissolved in boiling xylene or decalin. On cooling, the fiber substance separates out as a gel, whereas many azoic pigments remain in solution and can be separated by filtration from the precipitated fiber. To keep lakes of sulfonated pigments in solution, an equal volume of glacial acetic acid and 1 or 2 drops of conc. hydrochloric acid are added to the boiling xylene solution. The solution is then diluted to double its volume with water and shaken. The sulfonated pigments remain in the lower aqueous phase. Vat dyes and other organic pigments sparingly soluble in xylene, such as the phthalocyanines and quinacridones, can be separated by centrifuging the xylene solution at 100–110°.

4.5.3 Identification of the Pigments. When a sufficient amount of pigments has been isolated, identification proceeds by methods used in dye analysis, e.g., IR spectra and TLC for identifying organic pigments (see Chapter 16). Schweppe[15] has described color reactions for identifying certain classes of pigment or individual pigments. Thus phthalocyanines become violet when they are boiled in *N*-methylpyrrolidone in the presence of 1 *N* sodium hydroxide and hydrosulfite. Phthalocyanine greens also undergo this color change when DMF is the solvent. The blue pigments turn violet when spotted on filter paper with conc. nitric acid; if stannous chloride solution is added, the original greenish blue shade returns. On boiling with conc. nitric acid, the blue pigments are decolorized and destroyed, and the greens are stable.

4.6   Azoic Dyes

There are more than 3000 possible azoic combinations from the CI coupling and diazo components, but present commercial usage is restricted to about one-hundredth of this number. The hue (yellow, orange to red, violet to blue, green, brown, and black) readily provides a preliminary identification of the coupling and/or the diazonium component. Because the dyes are readily stripped in a very pure form from the fiber by DMF, preference is given to IR spectroscopy when an extensive collection of spectra with a suitable filing system is available, but other methods are also useful.[17]

Rowe and Levin[28] described the use of the crystal shape, hue, and m.p. of the dyes extracted with glacial acetic acid or toluene from the fiber and recrystallized, and the color of their solutions in conc. sulfuric acid.

When a solution obtained by reduction with alkaline dithionite is dropped on filter paper and dried, a characteristic yellow-green UV fluorescence is obtained with all azoic combinations from the arylides of 2-hydroxy-3-naphthoic acid. Naphthol AS-G dyeings give a weakly violet fluorescence; AS-LG and AS-L3G a bluish green fluorescence; AS-SG and AS-SR a yellow-green similar to the fluorescence of dyeings from 2-hydroxy-3-naphthoic arylamides; and AS-BT a greenish blue.

Dyes from diazonium components containing nitro groups react differently with aqueous sodium sulfide, depending on the position of the nitro group relative to the azo group. If it is *ortho*, the dyeing is practically decolorized (triazole formation), e.g., CI Azoic Diazo Components 8 and 1. If it is *meta*, there is a slight shift toward blue, e.g., CI Azoic Diazo Components 12 and 13. If it is *para*, there is a very strong shift toward violet or blue, e.g., CI Azoic Diazo Components 34 and 5.

4.7   Some Special Reactions

Several reactions for identifying the chemical class of a dye or an individual dye have been mentioned in earlier sections. Raab[17] has outlined a series of fundamental identification reactions for water-soluble and water-insoluble dyes. The following are some additional tests.

If a dye is sublimed at atmospheric or reduced pressure, the color of the vapor and the sublimate condensed on a cold surface can give useful information.[29] Thus indigo sublimes red and gives a blue deposit. Phthalocyanine pigments, some azoics, and some anthraquinones also sublime.

If a dyeing is reduced with alkaline hydrosulfite, thoroughly rinsed, diazotized, rinsed again, developed with alkaline 2-naphthol solution, rinsed again, and acidified with dilute acetic acid, a permanent red color of the dyeing indicates a Primuline dye or reactive dye. The former is confirmed by the yellow color and UV fluorescence of the reduced dyeing. A few sulfur dyes give a red color after development with 2-naphthol, but they can be eliminated by the hydrogen sulfide test.[29]

When a water-soluble azo dye is reduced with zinc dust and ammonia, and the solution is filtered and dropped on filter paper, the outer fringe of the spot is colored as follows if certain coupling components have been used; the color in parentheses appears on treatment with 10% sulfuric acid: chromotropic acid red-orange (yellow); γ-acid brown-red (gray-blue → brown-yellow); NW-acid blue-green (red); J-acid yellow-orange (olive green).[30]

If a basic yellow dye is present, an Auramine can be detected by boiling an ethanolic solution with zinc dust and ammonia until it becomes colorless. It is then filtered into hot glacial acetic acid. If the acid becomes blue, the dye is CI Basic Yellow 2 or 37; if the acid turns violet the dye is Basic Yellow 3.[30]

REFERENCES

1. A. G. Green, *The Analysis of Dyestuffs*, 3rd ed., Griffin, London, 1920; reprinted with "Key to Trade Designations," 1949.
2. E. Clayton, *Identification of Dyes on Textile Fibres*, 2nd ed., Society of Dyers and Colourists, Bradford, Yorkshire, 1963.
3. A. Bode, *Melliand Textilber.*, **38**, 289 (1957).
4. *Am. Dyest. Rep.*, **57**, 817 (1968); in German: L. Ostermeier, *Melliand Textilber.*, **50**, 961 (1969).
5. C. H. Giles, M. Bashir Ahmad, S. D. Dandekar, and R. B. McKay, *J. Soc. Dyers Colour.*, **78**, 125 (1962).
6. R. V. R. Subramanian and K. S. Taraporewala, *J. Soc. Dyers Colour.*, **88**, 394 (1972).
7. G. Dierkes and H. Brocher, *Melliand Textilber.*, **44**, 387 (1963). English translation by K. G. Roessler, *Canad. Text. J.*, 37 (Dec. 20, 1963).
8. W. Garner, *Textile Laboratory Manual*, American Elsevier, New York, 3rd ed., 1967.
9. D. A. Derrett-Smith and J. Gray, *The Identification of Vat Dyes on Cellulosic Materials*, Pergamon Press, Oxford, 1967.

10. A. Schaeffer, *Manual of Dyeing* (in German), Vol. IV, Analytical Part, Konradin Verlag R. Kohlhammer, Stuttgart, 1950.

11. B. C. Burdett, *J. Soc. Dyers Colour.*, **80**, 370 (1964).

12. For comprehensive nonspectroscopic methods of detection of metals, see F. J. Welcher, *Standard Methods of Chemical Analysis*, 6th ed., Vol. II, Part A, Van Nostrand, New York, 1963, pp. 64–83.

13. L. H. Ahrens and S. R. Taylor, *Spectrochemical Analysis*, 2nd ed., Addison-Wesley, Reading, Mass, 1961.

14. H. Schweppe, *Z. Anal. Chem.*, **244**, 310, 312 (1969).

15. H. Schweppe, *Qualitative Analysis of Organic Pigments*. VI. FATIPED-Kongress, Wiesbaden, 1962, Kongressbuch, pp. 162–168, Verlag Chemie Weinheim, 1962.

16. U. Baumgarte, *Melliand Textilber.*, **53**, 790 (1972). This apparatus is available from Otto Fritz GmbH, 6238 Hofheim am Taunus, Feldstrasse 1, Postfach 1269, West Germany, under the name "Gerät zum Extrahieren von Farbstoffen aus Fasern und Folien nach Dr. Baumgarte."

17. H. Raab in Ullmann, 3rd ed., Vol. 7, pp. 188–210.

18. D. Haigh, *J. Soc. Dyers Colour.*, **79**, 242 (1963); **80**, 479 (1964).

19. D. Blackburn and K. Meldrum, *J. Soc. Dyers Colour.*, **77**, 22 (1961).

20. H. Wagner and J. Pflug, *Bayer Farben Revue Nr. 5* (1963), p. 62.

21. A. Bode, *Melliand Textilber.*, **40**, 1304 (1959).

22. F. Jordinson and R. Lockwood, *J. Soc. Dyers Colour.*, **78**, 122 (1962); **84**, 205 (1968); **86**, 524 (1970); **88**, 117 (1972); **90**, 55 (1974).

23. O. Thumm and J. Benz, *Am. Dyest. Rep.*, **55**, 15 (1966).

24. J. Wegmann, *Melliand Textilber*, **39**, 1006 (1958); *J. Soc. Dyers Colour.*, **76**, 205 (1960).

25. B. J. Reuben and D. M. Hall, *Am. Dyest. Rep.*, **51**, 580 (1968).

26. H. Wagner and J. Pflug, *Melliand Textilber.*, **44**, 281 (1963).

27. B. C. Burdett, *J. Soc. Dyers Colour.*, **80**, 83 (1964).

28. F. M. Rowe and C. Levin, *J. Soc. Dyers Colour.*, **40**, 218 (1924). See also L. Löchner, *Melliand Textilber.*, **6**, 914 (1925).

29. P. Heerman and H. Agster, *Färberei- und textilchemische Untersuchungen*, Springer, Berlin-Göttingen-Heidelberg, 8th ed., 1951.

30. H. Schweppe, unpublished experiments.

CHAPTER SIXTEEN

Identification of Organic Pigments on Substrates Other than Textile Fibers

J. THOMSON

1 INTRODUCTION

This chapter is intended to be a practical guide to the analysis and identification of organic pigments. The basic criterion for defining the difference between a pigment and dye is that a pigment is insoluble in the medium in which it is used, whereas a dye is soluble in, or reacts with, the medium. Some pigments can, however, exhibit slight solubility in media, as in the case of Toluidine Red in plastics, or Arylamide Yellow in toluene-based ink. This definition permits the inclusion of many colors which started their industrial life as vat dyes and now play a very important role among organic pigments since they are employed in conditions where they are insoluble. Examples of this are some anthraquinones, quinacridones, and basic dyes like the triarylmethanes laked with complex inorganic acids.

The range of applications of pigments is so vast that no area is excluded from their coloring influence; they appear in many guises in most media ranging from paint, as liquid, dried, or stoved film, through paper, to films of every type including rubber, polyvinyl chloride, polyolefins, and polystyrene. They even have an important use in textiles since the advent of man-made fibers allows the pigment to be incorporated into the medium while it is a viscous liquid before extrusion. This produces a fiber that has greater light- and washfastness, greater stability, and more homogeneous color than can be achieved by dyeing. Extensive use is made of this property in the production of viscose rayon textiles and colored nylon sutures.

A comprehensive account of pigments and their properties, uses, and methods of application has been given by Lenoir.[1] However, in the analysis or identification of any group of chemicals, it is necessary to have a basic understanding of the compounds being examined, to be aware of the types, classes, or subgroups involved, and to be able to anticipate the physical and chemical reactions exhibited by the members of the group. To this end, it is essential to examine the chemical classification of organic pigments, and the system detailed by Lenoir based on that of Spencer[2] gives a suitable separation into groups that can be characterized by their structure, solubility, and general behavior. In the following section they are examined according to this classification, but if some of the classes in Lenoir's scheme appear to be omitted, it is because they have very little or no commercial significance and can be ignored by the analytical chemist attempting to identify organic pigments used in commercial products.

The majority of organic pigments, and by far the most common class, are azo pigments, which can be subdivided into the following groups: (1) acetoacetarylamide pigments; (2) pyrazolone pigments; (3) 2-naphthol pigments; (4) 2-hydroxy-3-naphthoic acid pigments; and (5) 2-hydroxy-3-naphtharylide pigments. The nonazo pigments can be grouped as follows: (6) triphenylmethane pigments and related pigments; (7) phthalocyanine pigments; (8) "vat pigments," i.e., indigo and thioindigo pigments, perylene pigments, and anthraquinone pigments; (9) quinacridone pigments; (10) dioxazine pigments; (11) azamethine pigments; and (12) miscellaneous pigments.

The identification of any pigment is a relatively simple matter, given 10 mg of a clean uncontaminated sample, an IR spectrophotometer, and a comprehensive library of IR spectra. The last is difficult to find, although commercial lists like those of Sadtler[3] in conjunction with the spectra of McClure et al.[4] give reasonable coverage of the most common organic pigments in commercial use. However, the 10 mg of clean uncontaminated sample is usually the most elusive link in the chain, and Section 3 discusses the main problems involved in achieving this separation and explains the techniques employed.

As a first step, it is essential to examine the classes of pigments in more detail. In each class specific information relating to its chemistry is given, along with a typical IR spectrum of one member and an outline of the important features of the spectrum. It is often possible to obtain a spectrum and find that it is not in one's library of spectra, but on many occasions closer examination of its characteristics in conjunction with the behavior of the pigment can give a strong indication of its chemical class. This information can be very valuable when a positive identification is not possible.

2 CLASSIFICATION OF PIGMENTS

2.1 Acetoacetarylamide Pigments

These are invariably yellow or orange and can be monoazo or disazo, depending upon whether an amine based on aniline or one based on a bisarylamine was used. The monoazo members are more solvent soluble than the disazo members, permitting them to be separated from each other on a qualitative basis by solvent extraction. It is essential to check the extract by TLC to ensure that only one pigment is being considered, and one successful solvent system is chloroform–toluene–benzene (1:1:1) on silica gel G plates, as shown in Table 16.1.

When only the slightest yellow bleed is obtained from a sample because of restricted sample size or insolubility of the medium, or because the yellow is present as a trace shading ingredient, it is advisable to apply the

Table 16.1 TLC of Mono- and Disazo Yellow Pigments

CI Pigment	CI	R_F	Relative R_F
Yellow 1	11680	0.34	1.10
Yellow 3	11710	0.56	1.81
Yellow 4	11665	0.36	1.12
Yellow 12	21090	0.31	1.00
Yellow 17	21105	0.15	0.48

small sample to a TLC plate and make a comparison with other members of the class.

A useful test at this point is to spray the TLC plate with conc. sulfuric acid and note the color of the spot. If it remains pale yellow, a monoazo is present, but if the spot turns orange, a disazo is present. This information in conjunction with the relative R_F of the spot should give the analyst a strong indication of the constitution of the unknown pigment.

The monoazo acetoactarylamides can be typified by CI Pigment Yellow 1 (CI 11680; 3-nitro-4-aminotoluene → acetoacetanilide). The IR spectrum of this pigment (Figure 16.1) is typical of the monoazo yellows. They have very "busy" spectra with many very sharp, well-defined peaks including two peaks at ～1600 and 1660. They all have a broad peak in the region of 1500 or a collection of closely packed peaks in that area, as found in the spectrum of CI Pigment Yellow 3 (CI 11710).

The disazo acetoacetarylamides can be typified by CI Pigment Yellow 12 (CI 21090), the simplest of this type (3,3'-dichlorobenzidine ⇉ acetoacetanilide, 2 mols). The IR spectrum of this compound (Figure 16.2) illustrates the salient features of this class of pigment. The same pair of peaks at 1600 and 1660 as were found in the monoazo pigments is also found in this type, but since they are derived from the amide linkage in the coupling component there should be no surprise to find them repeated here. The broadness at 1500 is also found, but in the area between 1180 and 1310 there is a pattern of five peaks, with the two at 1180 and 1250 generally

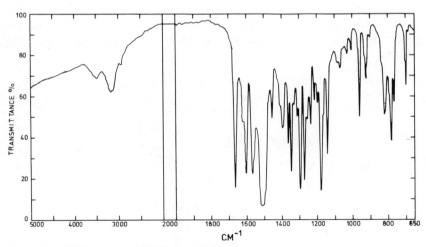

Figure 16.1   IR Spectrum of CI Pigment Yellow 1.

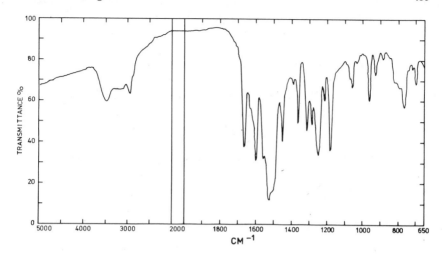

Figure 16.2   IR spectrum of CI Pigment Yellow 12.

being more intense than the other three. Most of the disazos have three peaks at 960, 920, and 880, with a decrease in intensity from 960 to 880.

There are exceptions to these rules, however, most notably CI Pigment Yellow 81, which is based on tetrachlorobenzidine and breaks most of the above rules. However, since the majority of disazo yellows are based on dichlorobenzidine it could be claimed that the features highlighted above are characteristic.

2.2   Pyrazolone Pigments

The color range of this group is from yellow-orange to red. The monoazo members constitute the yellow end of the spectrum, but there are very few of them; most of the pyrazolones are disazo, with the main amine being 3,3′-dichlorobenzidine which we found in the preceding class. They tend to be less solvent-soluble than the preceding group, but their limited solubility in solvents like chloroform and DMF is usually sufficient to allow enough sample to be extracted from media to permit identification. They are seldom used in conjunction with each other, but are often mixed with other pigments to achieve a particular effect.

Table 16.2 illustrates the TLC separation on a silica gel G plate with a developing solvent of chloroform–isobutyl methyl ketone (30:0.1).

The most common pyrazolone pigment is CI Pigment Orange 13 (CI 21110; 3,3′-dichlorobenzidine $\rightrightarrows$ 1-phenyl-3-methyl-5-pyrazolone); it exhibits the main features of the class in the IR spectrum (Figure 16.3).

Table 16.2   TLC of Pyrazolone Pigments

CI Pigment	CI	R_F	Relative R_F
Yellow 10	12710	0.84	1.56
Orange 13	21110	0.54	1.00
Orange 34	21115	0.58	1.07
Red 38	21120	0.19	0.35
Red 41	21200	0.30	0.56

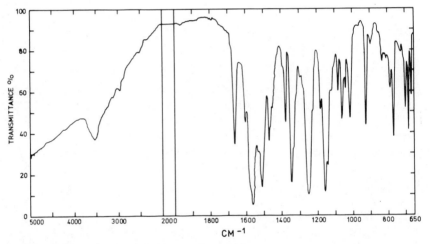

Figure 16.3   IR spectrum of CI Pigment Orange 13.

A number of significant features are shown in this spectrum, namely, the short band in the region of 1650 and long broad band at 1550 with a slightly shorter band between 1510 and 1530. These are found in all members of this class along with three, roughly equal-intensity, strong, broad "finger" bands at 1150, 1250, and 1350, which are much sharper in the monoazo pyrazolones. Other distinguishing features are that pyrazolones prepared from phenyl carbethoxy pyrazolone have an extra band of medium intensity at 1730, which is derived from the ester group of the carbethoxy, and that pyrazolones prepared from phenyl methyl pyrazolone have three short, sharp, needlelike peaks at 660, 680, and 700. With the aid of this guide, the solvent solubility, a TLC plate, and an IR scan, it should be relatively easy to recognize a member of this class and even to be more specific about its constitution.

2.3 2-Naphthol Pigments

This is a very simple class with some of the earliest known azo pigments among its members. The color range is orange to red, and they are easily prepared by coupling a diazotized amine to 2-naphthol. Most of the amines involved are mono, and in almost every instance a nitroamine is used. Their simple structure normally imparts poor solvent fastness, which means that the analyst can remove them from media and from pigment mixtures by solvent extraction using chloroform. It is often necessary to have tests that detect very low levels (100–200 ppm) of this class in higher-quality pigments since their presence would cause disastrous migration and bleeding effects when incorporated into media like plastics. Their high solubility in simple low-boiling solvents and ease of separation by TLC makes this task relatively simple. Table 16.3 illustrates the TLC of 2-naphthols.

An example of this class is one of the most common members, CI Pigment Red 4 (CI 12085; 2-chloro-4-nitroaniline → 2-naphthol). The absence in its spectrum (Figure 16.4) of peaks over 1620 is explained by the lack of amide groups which absorb around 1670. The nitro groups are usually evident by characteristic absorbances at 1350 and 1530, but there is little else to commend the spectra of this class other than their general "busy" appearance between 700 and 900. They are seldom found mixed with each other, but can be separated by TLC using a solvent of chloroform–toluene–petroleum ether (3:1:1) on silica gel G.

There are also a number of metal salts produced from 2-naphthol by coupling with diazotized amine sulfonic acids, but since, from the analytical viewpoint, the properties of this type of 2-naphthol pigment are closer to the next group they are considered in conjunction with them.

Table 16.3   TLC OF 2-Naphthol Pigments

CI Pigment	CI	R_F	Relative R_F
Orange 5	12075	0.16	0.67
Red 1	12070	0.24	1.00
Red 3	12120	0.14	0.58
Red 4	12085	0.41	1.70
Red 6	12090	0.22	0.92

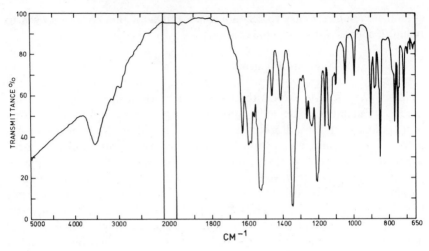

Figure 16.4   IR spectrum of CI Pigment Red 4.

2.4   2-Hydroxy-3-Naphthoic Acid Pigments

This is a very popular class for use in circumstances where bleeding and migration in solvents are undesirable, but not where alkali fastness is essential, e.g., soap powder packets. They are often used mixed with other organic pigments and, in many instances, with inorganic reds and yellows. The red component of three-color printing ink processes is often a member of this class, and it is not uncommon to give them a brighter appearance by shading with a trace of basic dye. Most members of the class are reds, but variations from reddish orange to deep maroon are possible. Sulfonic acid amines are almost always used in their preparation and the resulting dye requires the addition of a metal ion to precipitate a water-insoluble pigment: thus the reason for the poor alkali fastness. The metals used are Ca, Ba, Mn, and to a much lesser degree, Sr, with substantial color dependence on the metal used. For instance, starting from an organic nucleus like CI Pigment Red 48 (CI 15865), a change from yellowish red of the Sr salt to the deep blush red of the Mn salt can be produced. From the 2B acid amine used in the preparation, this group is called 2B metal salts or, more commonly, 2B Toners. The name "toner" is sometimes popularly used to describe this class of pigments, but is now preferred to describe any organic pigment containing only a few percent of diluent or extraneous additive.

With this information at hand, the analyst can investigate means of using these properties to help in the identification of the color. The pigments can be solubilized by adding a little ethanol acidified with hydrochloric acid; this procedure breaks the pigment back to the free acid, leaving the laking metal in solution as the chloride. It is then an easy matter to use inorganic spot tests, more sophisticated flame photometry, or better still, atomic absorption spectrophotometry to identify this laking metal. The main disadvantage is that pigments are often reduced and extended with such compounds as calcium carbonate and barium sulfate, making this metal identification a task to be approached with some caution. However, this technique provides the best solution for TLC applications using cellulose plates and a developing solvent of methanol–water–hydrochloric acid (75:75:1) (see Table 16.4).

Care should be taken to dissolve the sample with cold alcoholic acid, since heating effects some breakdown and causes "ghost" spots that can confuse the separation.

Fortunately for the analyst, this class of pigments is not completely insoluble in solvents. DMF dissolves them without breakdown and can be used to remove these pigments from substrates and inorganic ingredients. Evaporation of the solvent leaves the pigment, which can then be washed with one or two weaker solvents like ether or ethanol to remove organic impurities, which may also be extracted.

The resultant pigment can then be examined using IR to effect an identification. When the quantity of pigment is very low, however, the faint color can decompose during evaporation, and in such cases it is advisable to remove the DMF by steam distillation, which keeps the temperature low and prevents the breakdown effect described. This general technique is extremely valuable and is used often with other classes of pigments with a high success rate.

A common member of the class is CI Pigment Red 48 (CI 15865; 6-chloro-4-aminotoluene-3-sulfonic acid → 2-hydroxy-3-naphthoic acid),

Table 16.4   TLC of 2-Hydroxy-3-Naphthoic Acid Pigments

CI Pigment	CI	R_F	Relative R_F
Red 48	15865	0.16	0.84
Red 49	15630	0.12	0.63
Red 53	15585	0.27	1.42
Red 57	15850	0.19	1.00

mentioned earlier, which is found commercially as four different metal lakes.

Noteworthy features of its spectrum (Figure 16.5) are the complete lack of absorption peaks over 1620 similar to the 2-naphthol pigments, because neither class contains amide groups. However, most members of this class have a broad band or collection of bands around 1200 attributed to the sulfonic acid groups and quite indicative of their presence.

Most of the commercially popular toners have five equal intensity peaks between 1400 and 1620, but there are a few exceptions. Another feature of the 2B Toners is the appearance of two peaks at 1020 and 1040, but this is also found in the less common CI Pigment Red 52 (CI 15860), an isomer of Red 48.

2.5   2-Hydroxy-3-Napththarylide Pigments

These are all various shades of red. They have no free acid groups, unlike the previous type of pigments; thus they are water-insoluble and need not be precipitated with metals. There are hundreds of permutations possible, but only a few dozen members are produced and sold on a commercial scale. The solvent solubility of the simpler members of this group allows the analyst to extract them into solvents like chloroform and effect a separation by TLC on silica gel using a developing solvent of chloroform–xylene (3:1) (see Table 16.5). One such pigment is CI Pigment Red 2 (CI 12310; 2,5-dichloroaniline → Naphthol AS), and the IR spectrum

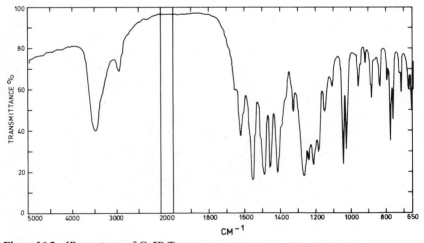

Figure 16.5   IR spectrum of Ca2B Toner.

Table 16.5 TLC of 2-Hydroxy-3-Naphtharylide Pigments

CI Pigment	CI	R_F	Relative R_F
Red 5	12490	0.02	0.10
Red 7	12420	0.40	1.48
Red 8	12335	0.34	1.26
Red 11	12430	0.47	1.74
Red 12	12385	0.19	0.70
Red 45 (23)	12355	0.15	0.56
Red 112	12370	0.27	1.00

(Figure 16.6) is in many ways typical of this class. They all have very "busy" spectra with a predictable pattern in the region 1450–1680. The pair of peaks around 1600 and 1680 are again indicative of the amide linkage, but the three peaks of roughly equal intensity at 1450, 1500, and 1550 appear with minor variations in most of their spectra. Another characteristic peak is the 1020 absorption, which is always present to some degree.

A number of variations to this basic formula have been produced in recent years, but the common aim has been to increase the molecular size,

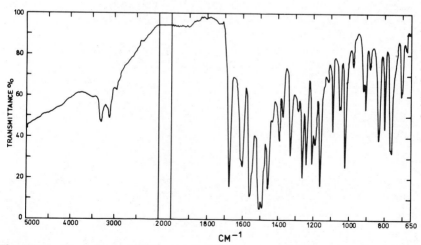

Figure 16.6 IR spectrum of CI Pigment Red 2.

either by doubling up the molecule as in CI Pigment Red 139 (1) or by modifying the coupling component in some way as in (2).

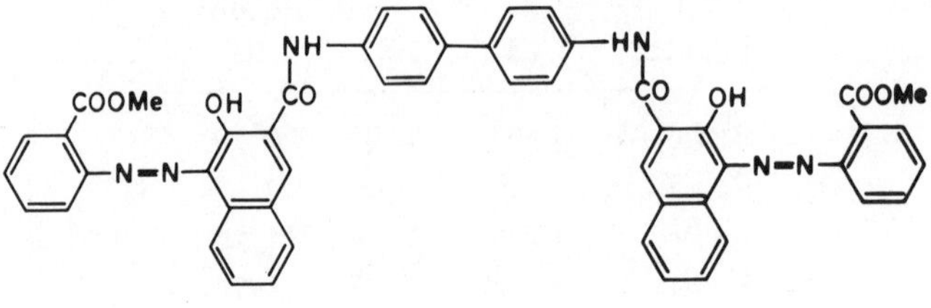

(1)

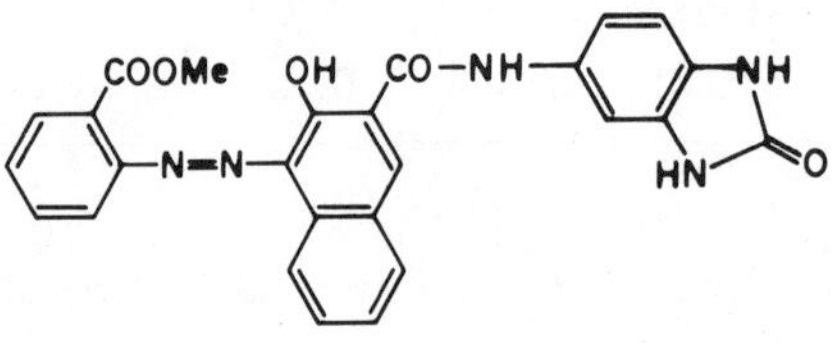

(2)

The pigments produced by either method have lower solvent solubility and DMF has very little effect on these pigments. This gives the analyst a problem that can be extremely difficult to solve and often depends on removal of the medium, leaving the pigment in the insoluble portion. If sufficient sample is available, the color can be dissolved in cold, conc. sulfuric acid and drowned in water, but this is not always acceptable since decomposition of some pigments can take place and this must be borne in mind when the sulfuric acid treatment has been employed.

2.6 Triphenylmethane Pigments and Related Compounds

The three subgroups worthy of consideration in this class are (*a*) pigments derived from basic dyes; (*b*) pigments derived from acid dyes; and (*c*) alkali blues. They must be discussed separately since the behavior of each subgroup is different from the others.

2.6.1 Basic Dye Derivatives. They are used almost exclusively in printing inks and can be exemplified by the three main types of dye used (*a*) Rhodamines, e.g., Rhodamine B (CI Basic Violet 10; CI 45170); (*b*) Methyl Violets, e.g., Methyl Violet 10B (CI Basic Violet 3; CI 42555); and (*c*) Victoria Blues, e.g., Victoria Blue B (CI Basic Blue 26; CI 44045). The laking compounds most commonly used to convert these water-soluble dyes into water-insoluble pigments are phosphomolybdic acid, phosphomolybdotungstic acid, copper ferrocyanide, and, to a much lesser extent, silicomolybdic acid.

The IR spectra of the Rhodamines are very similar to each other, but differ from those of the violets and the blues. However, it is possible to get a certain amount of information from the IR spectra since they confirm the dye type and give good indications as to which laking system is used. This is shown in the three scans of pigments (Figures 16.7–16.9) based on

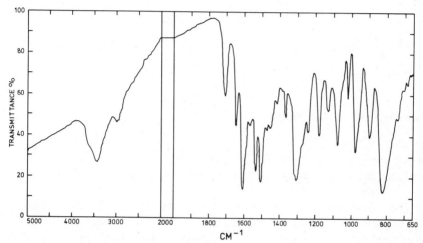

Figure 16.7 IR spectrum of phosphomolybdate complex.

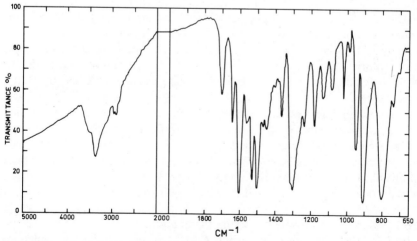

Figure 16.8 IR spectrum of silicomolybdate complex.

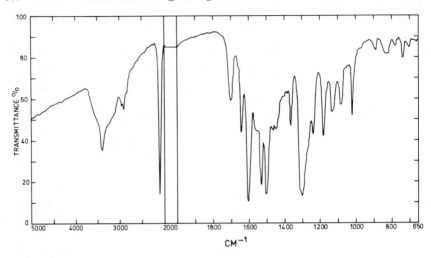

Figure 16.9   IR spectrum of ferrocyanide complex.

Rhodamine 6G (CI Basic Red 1; CI 45160): CI Pigment Red 81, 81:1 and 169, laked with phosphomolybdate, silicomolybdate, and ferrocyanide, respectively.

The ferrocyanide lake is obvious by the strong absorbance at 2300 of the triple bonds in the C≡N linkage. The differences between the phosphomolybdate and silicomolybdate appear at the lower end of the spectrum where the heavy inorganic ions absorb, mainly between 900 and 1000. Inorganic analysis of the ash is equally effective in this respect, but the test is destructive and more time consuming than the IR technique.

The dye portion of these pigments is very seldom present as a pure compound, but the constituent dyes can be separated and identified by TLC after breaking the pigment with warm ethanol containing a few drops of hydrochloric acid. The developing solvent used is n-butanol–water–ethanol (9:1:3) acidified with 1% glacial acetic acid, as recommended by Rettie and Haynes.[5]

The identification is best effected by running known dyes in parallel and making comparison of R_F, hue, and UV fluorescence.

The strong fluorescence of the solution in ethanol makes these pigments very easy to recognize, even when present as a minor shading component of an ink, which is a common use of this class of pigments. Confirmation of the exact dye is best effected by TLC (see Table 16.6).

2.6.2 Acid Dye Derivatives.   From the analyst's viewpoint, these are less important than the preceding group since very few members are encoun-

Table 16.6   TLC of Basic Dyes

CI Basic	CI	R_F	Color	Color under UV
Violet 1	42535	0.28	Violet	None
		0.38	↓	
		0.46		
		0.56		
		0.65	Mauve	
Violet 3	42555	0.29	Violet	None
Blue 7	42595	0.64	Ultramarine	None
Blue 11	44040	0.45	Ultramarine	None
Blue 26	44045	0.39	Ultramarine	None
Green 1	42040	0.39	Peacock green	None
Yellow 1	49005	0.19	Sulfur yellow	Greenish yellow
Violet 10	45170	0.34	Magenta	Pink
Violet 11	45175	0.41	Magenta	Pink
Red 1	45160	0.52	Coral pink	Yellow
		0.62	Coral pink	Yellow

tered regularly. The most common is Peacock Blue, which is the Ba lake of CI Acid Blue 9 (CI 42090) precipitated on alumina, but even this is only occasionally met with, and then it is usually mixed with Phthalocyanine Blue.

There are other members of the series, all very similar to the above, and mixtures are often found. They can be separated by TLC using an identical developing solvent to that used for the basic dyes, but replacing 1% acetic acid with 1% conc. ammonia. The pigments can be dissolved by breaking the lake with acidified ethanol to give blue solutions.

Another pigment in this group is Eosine (CI Acid Red 87; CI 45380), almost invariably found as the lead salt, wrongly but popularly known as Phloxine Toner, CI Pigment Red 90. The purity of the main dye, Eosine, is the main factor in determining the eventual shade of the pigment. This can be determined by TLC[5] on silica gel with benzene–dioxane–acetic acid (90:25:4).

2.6.3   Alkali Blues.   The only pigments worthy of mention here are the "Reflex Blues" used in a specific type of printing and usually found in black inks for toning the carbon black to remove the natural brown shade. They are sulfonated derivatives of phenylated rosaniline and can be extracted with alcohol. The colors are rarely met with by the analyst, except during the analysis of colors on printed paper, but it is worth remembering that they can complicate this task. These toning shades in the black ink are extracted from the paper along with the colors being examined and make a further separation necessary, usually by TLC.

2.7   Phthalocyanine Pigments

This class of pigments is one of the most important groups of organic pigments in commercial use today. Copper phthalocyanine (CI Pigment Blue 15; CI 74160) is the most common organic blue pigment found in paints, plastics and color printing.

Although many other metal complexes can be formed with this organic matrix, they are very rarely found in practice since few are produced in any commercial quantity. The only other simple Phthalocyanine Blue found by the analyst is the metal-free compound (CI Pigment Blue 16; CI 74100), where the Cu is replaced by two H. This is a turquoise shade occasionally found in automotive finishes because it exhibits the stability and fastness of the other members of the group.

Copper phthalocyanine can exist in four crystal forms, but the α and β forms are by far the most important. They can easily be identified by IR spectrophotometry and the quality control of the pigment can be effected by this technique. The two spectra are shown in Figures 16.10 and 16.11 to illustrate the differences.

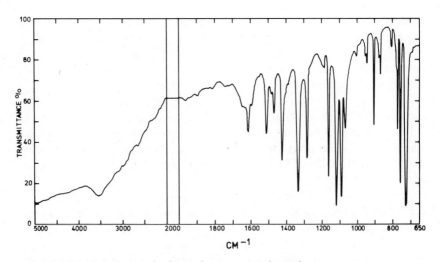

Figure 16.10   IR spectrum of α form of copper phthalocyanine.

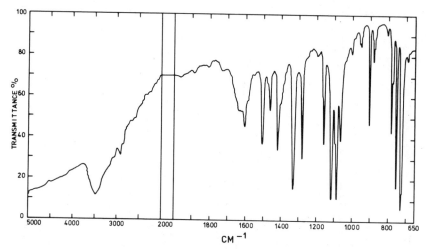

Figure 16.11 IR spectrum of β form of copper phthalocyanine.

Note the differences at 720–740, 770–790, and to a lesser extent, at 870–890. A calibration graph can be prepared from the peaks at 770–790 recorded on a higher-resolution instrument with expanded frequency scale (Figure 16.12); the α and β ratio can then be calculated from this graph. The spectrum must be run in Nujol since the high pressures involved in the potassium bromide disk technique effect changes in the crystal form, and hence in the peak ratio. The film is pressed out carefully until a constant transmittance value of 28–32% is obtained for the 755 band, which is common to both forms.

The α form can be stabilized by the addition of 2–6% chlorine to the molecule, and this is indicated by a peak around 840, which can be calibrated to give a quantitative measurement of the chlorine content.

Phthalocyanine Green (CI Pigment Green 7; CI 74260) is a very common pigment used in most applications. It is prepared by replacing 14 or 15 of the ring hydrogens by halogens, almost invariably chlorine, but sometimes chlorine and bromine mixtures. The more bromine used, the more yellow the shade, but the most common version is chlorinated only.

The insolubility of Phthalocyanine Blue and Green facilitates their separation from resins and polymers and from other pigments. Their use with other pigments is very common to achieve shades in the green range by mixing with yellows and in the maroon and violet range by shading reds with Phthalocyanine Blue. Occasionally, the blue and green are used together to prepare very stable greenish blue shades. When phthalocyanines

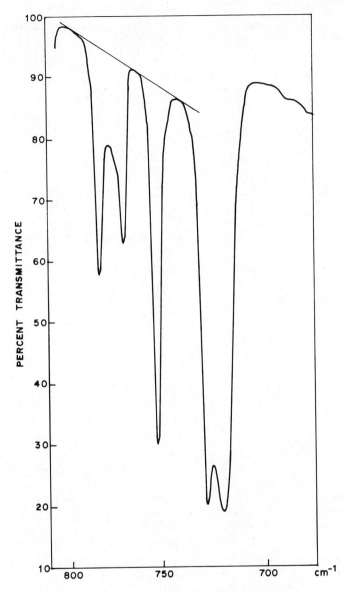

Figure 16.12   IR spectrum of mixture of α and β forms of copper phthalocyanine.

are present in very small quantities, they can readily be identified by dissolving in conc. sulfuric acid and recording an absorption curve over the range 400–1000 nm and comparing with the curves in Figure 16.13.[6]

This method can be adapted to detect traces of Phthalocyanine Green in Phthalocyanine Blue by placing a solution of the blue in sulfuric acid in the compensating beam to balance the absorbances from the blue and leave a curve of the green. Another method of separating small amounts of the blue from large quantities of green or from other insoluble pigments like Dioxazine Violet is to dissolve the blue in 1-methylnaphthalene. However, it should be emphasized that the solubility is very low even in this solvent, and therefore the technique should be used only as a last resort.

There are a few other phthalocyanine pigments, notably a sulfonated derivative of the blue, where the presence of sulfonic acid groups converts the pigment to a water-soluble dye which can be laked with metals on textiles.

Further treatment to convert the sulfonic acids to sulfonamides produces a solvent-soluble dye which is used as a lacquer dye. A number of non-flocculating varieties have been patented, but they should be ignored by the analyst since they are seldom encountered alone and are normally employed as additives on unsubstituted phthalocyanine. In this case they can be so well adsorbed that they are extremely difficult to remove or detect, being very similar in many ways to the basic pigment.

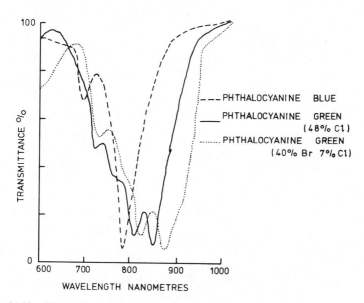

Figure 16.13   Absorption curves for phthalocyanine pigments in sulfuric acid.

Another analytical aid often used to quantify small amounts of phthalocyanines found combined with substrates is measurement of Cu content. The sample can be decomposed by dry ashing under controlled conditions, wet ashing with strong acids, or simply boiling with dilute nitric acid, which is a strong enough oxidizing agent to break the phthalocyanine molecule and free the Cu as copper nitrate. It is then relatively simple to determine the Cu content by atomic absorption or colorimetric methods, and from this figure calculate the original phthalocyanine content by taking the copper content of Phthalocyanine Blue as 10.9% (theory 11.02%) and of Phthalocyanine Green as 5.3% (theory 5.5%).

2.8 "Vat Pigments"

This group includes a number of pigments that began their lives as vat dyes, but found a place in other fields of application normally occupied by pigments; thus the name "vat pigments" rather than vat dyes. However, there are other pigments, e.g., some perylenes, which were developed purely as pigments and were never intended to be used as dyes.

2.8.1 Indigo and Thioindigo Pigments. Indigo, used for generations as a vat dye, has found some application as a deep blue pigment for coloring rayon. The pigment has some solubility in chloroform or acetone, with which it can be extracted from media. Substituted indigos are not used as pigments.

The substituted thioindigos form a series of pigments ranging in shade from pink to violet. The most popular of this group and the most lightfast is CI Pigment Red 88, 4,4',7,7'-tetrachlorothioindigo (CI 73312).

These pigments can sometimes be isolated from their environment by sublimation under controlled heating conditions on a cold-finger condenser. The IR scan of the condensed sublimate can be identified by comparison with standard spectra. Typical of this class is the spectrum of CI Pigment Red 88 (Figure 16.14). The thioindigo pigments all have three peaks at around 1450, 1550, and 1650, but the ratios of intensities can vary considerably, particularly for the 1550 peak. It is also usual to find a small peak around 850–870 and a longer peak at 900–920. They generally tend to be open spectra with long sharp peaks evenly spread from 750–1650.

2.8.2 Perylene Pigments. Some members of this class are less than 20 years old, in fact one (CI Pigment Red 123: CI 71145) was listed in CI in 1969. As a group they are very heatfast and migration resistant, which recommends their use in plastics or in high-quality applications. They are based on diimides of perylene-3,4,9,10-tetracarboxylic acid (cf. CI Pigment

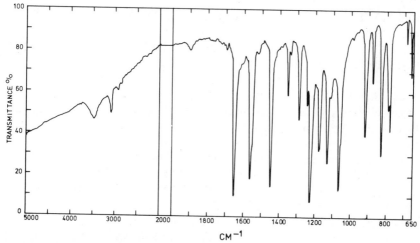

Figure 16.14   IR spectrum of Pigment Red 88.

Red 179, 189, 190 and 149; CI 71130, 71135, 71140, and 71137). They can be characterized by their spectra in conc. sulfuric acid (Figure 16.15); when very little sample is available, this test can give an indication that a perylene is present.

When more sample can be isolated, the IR spectrum can be most useful since they all have a similar form, as shown in the spectrum of CI Pigment

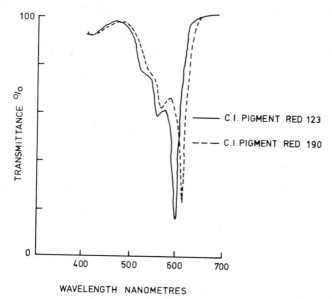

Figure 16.15   Absorption curves of perylene pigments in sulfuric acid.

Red 123 (Figure 16.16). Note the three peaks at 1590, 1650, and 1690, as well as the very sharp peaks at 740 and 810. There is usually another at 790–800, which is very short in Pigment Red 179, but longer in Pigment Red 190 and in Pigment Red 123.

2.8.3 Anthraquinone Pigments. This group has the broadest color range of any class of pigments, varying from yellow through orange to violet and blue. Almost every pigment in this class is based on a vat dye, as shown by the usual vatting and reoxidation color reactions.

The anthraquinone pigments vary in color from Anthrapyrimidine Yellow (CI Vat Yellow 20; CI Pigment Yellow 108; CI 68420) through the color spectrum to Indanthrone Blue (CI Vat Blue 4; CI Pigment Blue 60; CI 69800). These have been well documented by Vesce,[7,8] but since there are only about a dozen or so in common use, it is worthwhile obtaining samples of them for comparison purposes. This also applies to the IR spectra because there are few significant features as a class. IR spectra of the more common anthraquinones are given by McClure et al.[4]

They are expensive pigments to produce and are found in high-quality finishes, from which they can usually be extracted by warming a small sample with chloroform or DMF and recovering the pigment from this solvent as described in Section 2.4.

TLC is of little use with high-quality pigments of this class because of their low solubility in solvents—or good solvent resistance, from the point of view of a user rather than an analyst—but some members, like Anthra-

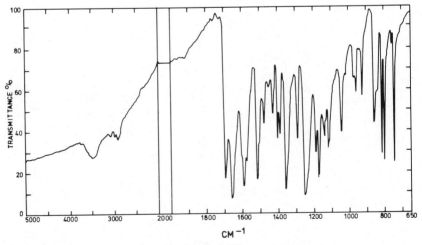

Figure 16.16 IR spectrum of CI Pigment Red 123.

pyrimidine Yellow, have sufficient chloroform solubility to permit their extraction.

2.9 Quinacridone Pigments

This is an important group of pigments, gold and red to violet, which have been on the market for less than 20 years. Although a number of quinacridones have been patented, there are only two or three commercially available, and of these by far the most commonly encountered is the simplest member, linear *trans*-quinacridone (CI Pigment Violet 19; CI 46500). For such a simple structure, it exhibits great insolubility, attributed to hydrogen bonding between adjacent molecules, and it is a perfect example of crystal modifications accompanied by color change. The γ form is red and the β form is violet, but mixtures of the two forms are possible, and by altering the particle size another shade variation can be introduced. The difference in shade of the two forms is so obvious that it is seldom necessary to resort to IR spectrophotometry to decide which is present. In cases of doubt, however, the IR spectrum of a Nujol mull of the sample can differentiate it with ease.[4]

The second most popular pigment of this class is the 2,9-dimethyl-quinacridone (3) (CI Pigment Red 122), which is magenta red and has high-quality applications.

A less common quinacridone is the brownish yellow quinacridone quinone (4), but this is rarely encountered on its own, although it is showing increasing importance in solid solutions with other quinacridone pigments.

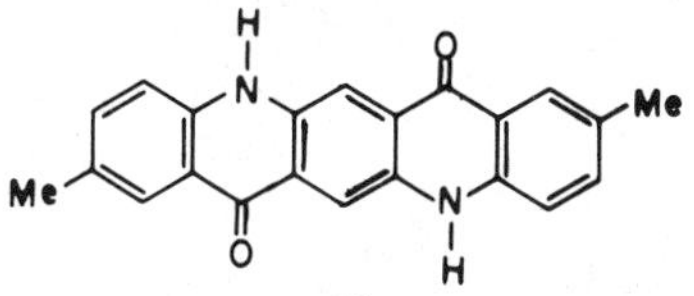

(3) 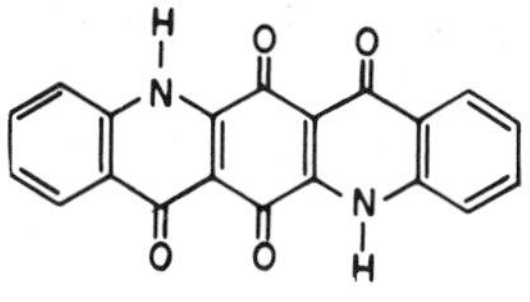   (4)

The insolubility of the class is such that hot DMF is necessary to extract the pigment from substrates like plastics or stoved paint films that are particularly insoluble. The hot solvent dissolves a limited quantity of quinacridones, giving a yellowish fluorescent solution, which can be treated again as in Section 2.4 to give an IR scan. Occasionally there is so little pigment, or the extract is so contaminated by substrate or other pigments, that the spectrum is unrecognizable; with such samples the visible absorption spectrum in conc. sulfuric acid is quite characteristic, as shown in Figure 16.17.

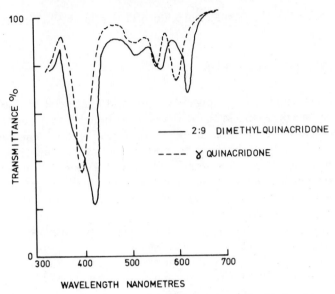

WAVELENGTH NANOMETRES

Figure 16.17   Absorption curves of quinacridone pigments in sulfuric acid.

The IR spectra of the class are easily identified from the characteristic pattern shown in the curve of linear *trans*-quinacridone, γ form (Figure 16.18).

The notable feature of the four closely situated peaks between 1550 and 1620 with two others at around 1330 and 1460 make this class easy to

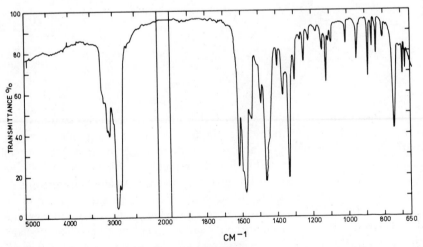

Figure 16.18   IR spectrum of γ form of quinacridone.

identify. In the substituted compounds there can be slight shifts in these positions, but the peaks in these areas are the strongest features of quinacridone IR spectra.

2.10 Dioxazine Pigments

This is a class of pigments that are almost exclusively violet; although dioxazines of other colors have been prepared and patented they have not yet found a commercial outlet. Foremost among these is Carbazole Dioxazine Violet (CI Pigment Violet 23; CI 51319; Pigment Fast Violet R Base, *CSD* II, 787). It is used only in high-quality applications or as a minor shading in pigments, like Phthalocyanine Blue, whose color range can be extended in the red direction by adding a low percentage of dioxazine. In such cases it is possible to blank out the IR spectrum of the Phthalocyanine Blue by placing a Nujol mull of phthalocyanine in the compensating beam, leaving the easily recognizable spectrum of the dioxazine (Figure 16.19).

Although only a few of these pigments are commercially available, it is not possible to select typical characteristics from the spectra because, apart from the dioxazine nucleus, the structures vary considerably. Once more the spectra in sulfuric acid are characteristic and at least permit the analyst to classify the pigment into this group of compounds. Two of the more recent additions to this group are Irgazin Violets BLT and 6RLT.

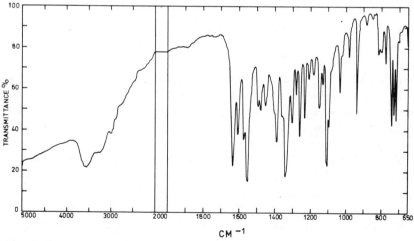

Figure 16.19   IR spectrum of CI Pigment Violet 23.

2.11   Azamethine Pigments

This class of pigments, which all have the chromophore C=N, is best considered in two distinct groups, (1) pure organics and (2) metal complexes, since their properties vary considerably. Most of the azamethines are yellow to greenish yellow, but there are a few reds.

2.11.1   Pure Organic Azamethines.   The group is fairly new, having been first marketed in quantity 30 years ago; at least one of the early arrivals is still encountered under the name Lumogen L Light Yellow (CI Pigment Yellow 101; CI 48052; azine from 2-hydroxy-1-naphthaldehyde). This is a very greenish yellow pigment which fluoresces in UV light and can easily be located on a TLC plate under UV radiation. It is slightly soluble in xylene, and a dilute solution sufficient for TLC can be prepared.

Another important type of azamethine is the isoindoline derivatives, but those most commonly met with by the analyst are the tetrachloroisoindolinone pigments which are less than 20 years old and have the general formula (5).

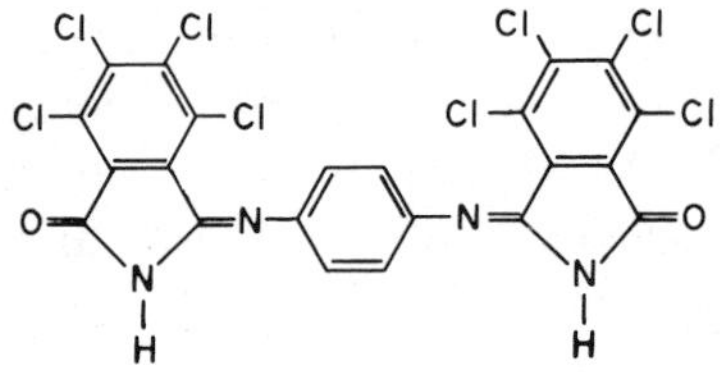

(5)

The *p*-phenylenediamine can be replaced by many diamines, giving the range of colors from red to yellow.[9] Soda lime distillation of the pigment breaks the azamethine linkage and yields this central diamine, which can be identified by any of the conventional techniques, e.g., m.p., TLC, GLC, or IR spectroscopy, but this approach assumes that there is a large sample available. In most instances where a small sample is available or when a few milligrams have been retrieved from a matrix, it is much more suitable to identify the presence of this pigment by IR spectrophotometry.

Note in Figure 16.20 the pair of strong peaks at 1710 and 1650 which, in conjunction with the three peaks at 1380, 1310, and 1270, are typical of this group of pigments. The color can vary through orange to red when *o*-dianisidine is used as the central amine. They are sparingly soluble in DMF and can be extracted from insoluble matrices with this solvent.

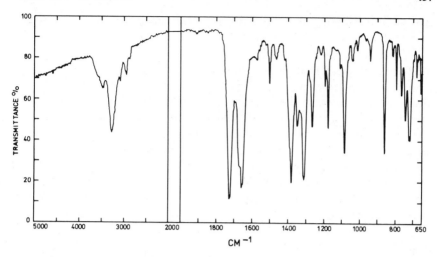

Figure 16.20   IR spectrum of pigment (5).

2.11.2   Metal Complex Azamethines.   The metal complexes tend to be unstable to acids, liberating the metal which can easily be identified, thus giving an indication of this class of pigments. Again there is only a small number to consider and the IR spectra are easily recognized, but cannot be classified by characteristic peaks since the organic ligands can vary considerably. They are all slightly soluble in solvents but most, like Paliotol Yellow 4G (BASF) and Irgazin Yellow 5GT (CGY), require hot DMF to extract them from media. There are still too few commercially available to effect a meaningful classification, and at this stage they must receive individual treatment by the analyst.

2.12   Miscellaneous

In this group we have a few pigments which, like the preceding group, must be considered individually. However, it is also a small group and its few members are slowly being superseded. The most common is the ferrous complex of 1-nitroso-2-naphthol, CI Pigment Green 8 (CI 10006) or, as it is commonly known, Pigment Green B. It is extremely unstable to acid and gives a deep brown solution with dilute hydrochloric acid which gives a strong test for Fe. The only other important pigment in this group could easily have been included in the azo yellows since it is the 1:2 Ni complex of the azo dye (p-chloroaniline → 2,4-dihydroxyquinoline). This CI Pigment

Green 10 (CI 12775), commonly called Green Gold, still has an outlet in automotive finishes. One particular property of this pigment is that when heated at low concentration in DMF, it quickly fades owing to decomposition. The pigment is usually indicated by its pale yellowish green color and by the presence of Ni after acid treatment when the pigment breaks down. Chloroform extraction of this fragmented sample removes the yellow organic ligand, which can be identified by IR spectroscopy.

Carbon Black is an organic pigment, but it is often ignored. From the analyst's point of view, it can be a very elusive and trying pigment to identify because it cannot be easily categorized. With a large sample there is no problem since it gives no ash, nor IR scan, is very black, and if it were necessary, could be positively identified by elemental analysis. Usually, however, there is not a large sample, but only a few dried flakes of dark paint film, and all the above tests become meaningless because of the overwhelming excess of organic resin. It must also be borne in mind that Carbon Black is often used in conjunction with other pigments to produce deeper shades or to prepare a brown by adding to an orange or red. So if a dark shade of finish yields only pale colors after analysis, then it is well worth looking for Carbon Black as a constituent.

3 ISOLATION OF PIGMENTS

As stated earlier in this chapter, it is usually more difficult to isolate the pigment from its surroundings than it is to identify it. Knowing how each class of pigment is likely to behave is a very strong weapon, but it is equally important to know how the matrix is likely to behave because different isolation techniques are employed with different matrices.

3.1 Aqueous Dispersions of Pigments

Aqueous dispersions of pigments are used to color compounds like emulsion paints and are composed of pigments suspended in a water or water-miscible solvent medium by means of surface-active agents. The pigment can be isolated and quantitatively determined by breaking this dispersion with a boiling mixture of water and acetone. To 5–10 g paste in a 100-ml centrifuge tube is added about 80 ml of the hot solvent mixture, and the resulting suspension is centrifuged to deposit the flocculated pigment. Further similar treatments completely remove the surfactants, and the tube containing the pigment is dried to constant weight. An added bonus of this technique is that the solvent can be evaporated to dryness when the surfactants are quantitatively recovered. Some pigments are resistant to flocculation, or the disperser is unaffected by the acetone treatment, so that a more severe approach is required in the form of a few drops of hydrochloric acid. Of course, this can cause difficulties with some pigments, like Pigment Green B, which are decomposed by the acid, and the acid treatment should be used only as a last resort.

Carbon Black dispersions are very resistant to flocculation and normally must be evaporated to dryness, when the surfactants can usually be removed by ethanol.

3.2 Liquid Printing Inks and Paints

Liquid printing inks and paints are basically blends of pigments, resins, and solvents prepared in a wide range of formulations. The pigments may be isolated by adding a solvent such as ether to dilute the medium and disturb the solvent balance. This is centrifuged to bring down the pigment and some, if not all, of the resin system. It is normally a very simple task to remove these resins by further extraction with a boiling mixture of ethanol and toluene in equal parts. Other solvents can be used; the choice of flocculating solvent depends upon the resin system employed, as demonstrated by Hanson,[10] who flocculated pigments with benzene.

3.3 Dried Films and Plastics

With dried films and plastics the problems are more acute since the pigments are sealed in the film. Two basic approaches can be adopted. One removes the pigments and leaves the binder; the other dissolves the resins and leaves the pigment. The system used depends on the components of the mixture and can usually be determined only by trial and error.

The pigments, if organic, can usually be extracted from the binder and since IR identification requires less than a milligram of sample, the solubility is normally sufficient to release this small quantity. Chloroform is a most useful solvent for the simple azo pigments, but the more complex azo pigments, the metal salts, and many of the "vat pigments" require stronger solvents like DMF to dissolve even the very small quantities required for identification.

When the alternative approach is used, it is desirable to have some idea as to which resin system is involved so that the correct solvent may be employed. One scheme is to make use of IR-attenuated total reflectance. In this technique, a beam of IR radiation is reflected from the surface of a film and a normal IR spectrum is recorded. Several collections of the IR spectra of resins and polymers[11–13] are available to simplify this task. The value of this technique should not be overemphasized since most samples are not suitable in form or dimensions. Recent advances in internal reflectance spectroscopy with reference to paint films are discussed by Frazee.[14] There are other systems, however, and even some of the most difficult polymers can be dissolved in a strong solvent and a film cast on a small pool of mercury on a watch glass. By heating the watch glass on a steam bath, the solvent is removed, leaving a resin film on the surface of the mercury which can be lifted with forceps and transferred to an IR plate and a spectrum obtained.

This second approach to pigment isolation creates problems since the severe treatments necessary to dissolve paint films and plastics are such that many pigments either decompose or alter during these treatments. Few resins are as easily treated as nitrocellulose, which dissolves in acetone, or polystyrene, which dissolves in 1,2-dichloroethylene. According to Schweppe[15] alkyd and polyurethane paint films can be destroyed by boiling for several minutes with 20% sodium hydroxide. Acrylic and urea formaldehyde films dissolve in boiling glacial acetic acid. Epoxy paint films dissolve in nothing less than conc. sulfuric acid, which can then be poured into water; the organic pigment can then be extracted with water-immiscible solvents like chloroform. These severe treatments adversely affect any metal salts or metal-ligand pigments; thus after such processes, the pigments are not present in their original form.

Suitable solvents for effecting the solution of plastics are given by Haslam and Willis,[13] but once more the treatments can be severe as in the case of formic acid to dissolve nylon or THF to dissolve polyethylene or polypropylene. Polymers of the polyvinyl chloride type require THF or DMF, but since these solvents are also given as suitable solvents for pigments, complications can occur. One system dilutes the solution with a less potent solvent like ethanol or chloroform and follows this with filtration or centrifugation to remove some of the polymer and, it is hoped, leave enough of the pigment in suspension or solution. This can be concentrated by steam distillation of the solvent and almost invariably requires further purification by TLC.

In a few cases, e g., Phthalocyanine Blue, the pigment is insoluble in the dissolving solvent and can be centrifuged away from the polymer; after a few washes it is in a form suitable for IR identification.

3.4   Additional Techniques

There are other uses that can be made of IR based on its general insensitivity to impurities; in many cases up to 20% of diluent can be present without adversely affecting the identification. If there is any suspicion of a second pigment it is usually possible to prepare a thick film of the sample and balance the peaks of the known pigment by adding a mull of this to the compensating beam. The spectrum of the minor component should then be recognizable.

It is not uncommon to have an effect known as "chalking" on the surface of paint films or plastics, usually resulting from a fault in the original preparation. The "chalking" or "bloom" can normally be identified by lightly rubbing the surface with clean cotton wool moistened with a solvent such as chloroform. The color can be removed from the cotton by solvent extraction, but this often results in a spectrum of resin or plasticizer. An alternative and often more successful procedure is to lightly rub the surface with potassium bromide and press this into a disk, which can give a perfectly clean spectrum of the offending pigment.

When a trace of pigment is present in a fluid, this gas or liquid can be drawn through a Millipore filter, allowing sufficient concentration of color to be produced at the center of the filter for it to be mounted in the beam of the IR spectrophotometer. Other filter absorbances can be compensated by mounting a clean filter in the reference beam[16]; a recognizable spectrum should be obtained.

Considerable work was done in the early days using paper chromatography, and some of this has been reported by Rubbi.[17] In most laboratories TLC has replaced this technique, but paper chromatography should not be forgotten as an analytical aid.

Physical properties, like solubility, must be exploited to the full. For instance, the simple azo reds like Toluidine Red are extremely chloroform-soluble, whereas the more complex azo reds are not; thus a separation can be effected. Another solubility difference is often applied in the analysis of paint films like automotive finishes where a common mixture of yellow pigments is Vat Yellow 20 and some of the azamethines. The film is first extracted with chloroform to remove the Vat Yellow 20 and when this treatment has been exhausted, an extraction with DMF separates the azamethine.

Thioindigo pigments can be purified by sublimation, a separation procedure that can also be applied to some of the simpler pigments. An example is CI Pigment Yellow 1 (CI 11680), a monoazo yellow which can be sublimed from CI Pigment Yellow 13 (CI 21100), a disazo yellow.[18]

An extremely valuable technique is TLC,[19] cited earlier as a possible system for categorizing the members of a particular class of pigments. It is equally effective when a mixture of classes is involved and can be used in the following manner to purify components in sufficient quantity for IR identification.

The colored solution is applied as a streak on a 20 × 20-cm TLC plate and developed in an appropriate solvent. The colored bands are scraped from the plate; if the bands are very weak, more than one plate may be necessary. The colored section for each band is extracted with a suitable solvent and filtered through very fine filter paper or a fine glass sinter to ensure complete removal of the silica. The color in solvent is then evaporated on a little potassium bromide and an IR scan is run. This technique is equally effective if the interfering matter is another pigment or a resin or plasticizer present to a small extent. Obviously the system fails if the resin or plasticizer is present as a major fraction since the pigment becomes sealed in the band at the bottom of the plate and cannot be moved. With low concentrations of these substances, it is possible to develop the plate first with a solvent like ether or petroleum ether which removes the compounds to the solvent front. The plate is then developed normally to effect a separation of the pigment.

This work has been documented by Brown[20] in connection with dyes, but the principles are equally applicable to pigment identification.

4   IDENTIFICATION PROCEDURES

Most commercial organic pigments can be identified by the procedures described in the preceding sections. In the classification of pigments in Section 2, considerable effort was devoted to the identification of each class with particular reference to IR spectrophotometry and TLC as desirable techniques. Many other methods of identification were used before such techniques were discovered, but most of these procedures have inherent disadvantages. Some require a very pure sample of pigment to effect an identification by its crystal form[21] or by determination of its m.p.[22] Alternatively, a study of the pigment's behavior toward acids and alkalis[23] can result in a successful classification; if the color is one of the more common "bread and butter" types, it can be identified precisely, but up to 1 g of sample is required to carry out the recommended range of tests.

Another scheme proposed that the visible absorption spectra[24] be examined, an approach that was recommended in Section 2 as a means of identifying the "vat pigments" and other nonazo classes. The spectra in sulfuric acid are valuable for classifying these pigment groups; the difference between a quinacridone and a perylene is obvious, but it would be more difficult to identify a specific constitution using this technique alone.

More attention has been devoted to the analysis and identification of the azo pigments than to any other single class of pigments. The simple explanation could be that they are presented to the analyst for identification more often than any other group since the azo pigments are the main class and contain most of the commonly used colors. However, it is more likely that they receive this attention because they are more amenable to systematic group separation and can easily be broken down to simple organic compounds. This is extremely useful when an azo pigment is encountered and the analyst finds that he can classify it, but cannot specify the exact constitution. Then he may select a fragmentation procedure from those available; his choice depends on the sample size and available facilities. Each system relies on the ease with which the azo and amide linkages can be cleaved, followed by identification of the amines and other fragmentation products. The azo linkage is normally broken with a reducing agent. Hargreaves[23] favored sodium hydrosulfite, whereas Muzik et al.[25] preferred acetic acid, hydrochloric acid, and tin. The amines can be isolated and identified by preparing derivatives[23] or by using IR spectrophotometry on the fragments themselves.[4] The amide linkages are normally broken by soda lime distillation, but Bassl et al.[26] preferred boiling hydrogen bromide and proceeded to identify the amines by TLC.

None of the ideas described above is original. Harkins et al.[27] recommended IR spectrophotometry for identifying pigments in paint in 1959, but at that time the technique was available to very few laboratories. Rybicka and Gardner[28] listed the pigments on the basis of their strongest IR absorptions and tabulated them according to color. This three-peak fingerprint system allowed the limited number of pigments being examined to be identified after a brief inspection of their IR spectra. This idea is similar to the system devised by Sadtler[3] using up to 10–12 peaks to effect a more positive identification of a very wide range of organic compounds.

Now that sophisticated instrumentation is widely available, it is no problem for the well-equipped organization to analyze unknown organic compounds, including pigments. With mass spectrometry, NMR, IR spectrophotometry, and an efficient backup elemental analysis service, it should be technically feasible to analyze all unknown pigments. However, smaller organizations that do not have access to such expensive equipment and must make the most efficient use of the simple techniques available should be able to identify the more common pigments in commercial use, particularly after a little experience.

By reviewing the techniques discussed above, the analyst should be able to select the system most suited to his own situation, but must always be prepared to modernize his approach to keep abreast of improvements in his facilities as they occur.

REFERENCES

1. J. Lenoir, CSD V, Chapter VI.
2. W. W. Spencer, Am. Paint J., 76 (May 1966).
3. Sadtler Research Laboratories; Dyes, Pigments and Stains, Infra Red Prism Spectra.

4. A. McClure, J. Thomson, and J. Tannahill, *J. Oil Colour Chem. Assoc.*, **51,** 580 (1968).

5. G. H. Rettie and C. G. Haynes, *J. Soc. Dyers Colour.*, **80,** 629 (1964).

6. F. M. Smith and J. D. Easton, *J. Oil Colour Chem. Assoc.*, **49,** 616 (1966).

7. V. C. Vesce, *Off. Dig. Fed. Paint Varn. Prod. Clubs*, **28** (1956).

8. V. C. Vesce, *Off. Dig. Fed. Paint Varn. Prod. Clubs*, **31** (1959).

9. A. Pugin and J. Von Der Crone, *7th Congress FATIPEC*, 61 (1964); *Off. Dig. J. Paint Technol. Eng.*, **37,** 1071 (1965).

10. N. W. Hanson, *J. Oil Colour Chem. Assoc.*, **41,** 203 (1958).

11. Chicago Society for Paint Technology, "Infra Red Spectroscopy—Its Use as an Analytical Tool in the Field of Paints and Coatings," *Off. Dig.*, **33,** Part 2 (1961).

12. L. C. Afremow et al., *Infra Red Spectroscopy—Its Use in the Coatings Industry*, Chicago Society for Paint Technology, 1969.

13. J. Haslam and H. A. Willis, *Identification and Analysis of Plastics*, Illife, London, 1969.

14. J. D. Frazee, *J. Oil Colour Chem. Assoc.*, **57,** 300 (1974).

15. H. Schweppe, *Paint Technology*, **27,** No. 8, 12 (1963).

16. H. J. Sloane, *Anal. Chem.*, **35,** 1556 (1963).

17. P. Rubbi, Congress FATIPEC 673 Milan (1959).

18. Addendum to NPIRI Standard Test Method B-3 (1965).

19. E. Baier, *Farbe Lack*, **80,** 614 (1974).

20. J. C. Brown, *J. Soc. Dyers Colour.*, **85,** 137 (1969).

21. V. C. Vesce, "The Microscopic Identification of Azo Dyes and Organic Pigments," in J. J. Mattiello, Ed., *Protective and Decorative Coatings*, Vol. 2, Wiley, New York.

22. J. Barker, *J. Oil Colour Chem. Assoc.*, **25,** 240 (1942).

23. K. G. Hargreaves, *J. Oil Colour Chem. Assoc.*, **35,** 139 (1952).

24. M. Saltzman and A. M. Keay, *J. Paint Technol.*, **39,** 360 (1967).

25. F. Musik, J. Dobrovolny, and M. Vesely, *Chem. Prum.*, **15,** 151 (1965).

26. A. Bassl, H. J. Heckemann, and E. Baumann, *Plaste Kautsch*, **14,** No. 9, 696 (1967).

27. T. R. Harkins, J. T. Harris, and O. D. Shreve, *Anal. Chem.*, **31,** 541 (1959).

28. S. M. Rybicka and K. E. Gardner, "Infra Red Spectra of Organic Pigments," Paint Research Station Report No. RS/T/77/66 (Oct. 1966).

CHAPTER SEVENTEEN

Analysis of Food, Drug, and Cosmetic Colors

ADRIAN B. LEATHERMAN, JOHN E. BAILEY

SANDRA J. BELL, PERCY M. WATLINGTON,

ELIZABETH A. COX, CHARLES GRAICHEN

AND MANJEET SINGH

1 INTRODUCTION

The first regulation of color additives in the United States of America was the Federal Food and Drug Act of 1906. The Bureau of Chemistry of the U.S. Department of Agriculture was responsible for the administration of the Act, and through the work of Dr. Bernard C. Hesse, a list of seven color additives acceptable for food usage was issued. Ten additional colors were added to the list between 1916 and 1929.

Voluntary certification of color additives was provided in the 1906 Act. The Food, Drug, and Cosmetic Act of 1938 changed the voluntary certification to mandatory for the 15 colors on the list at that time. It created three categories of certified colors: food, drug, and cosmetic; drug and cosmetic; and external drug and cosmetic. It also placed the certification of color additives under the jurisdiction of the Food and Drug Administration.

Section 406(b) of the 1938 Act stated: "The Secretary shall promulgate regulations providing for the listing of coal tar colors which are *harmless* and suitable for use in food . . . ." Chronic toxicity studies were undertaken, and a number of color additives were shown to be toxic at high levels. The United States Supreme Court ruled that FDA, under the 1938 law, did not have the authority to set quantity limitations on the use of colors, and held that the term "harmless" in the law meant harmless per se. Therefore, no color could be certified or listed unless it was harmless regardless of the quantity used.

This led to the Color Additive Amendment of 1960, which permitted safe use of all colors in foods, drugs, and cosmetics without the inflexibility of the 1938 Act. Under the new Act (1) FDA was authorized to set safe limits, or tolerances, on the amount of color permitted in foods, drugs, or cosmetics; (2) all colors, whether synthetic or natural, for addition to foods, drugs, and cosmetics were brought under safety clearance provisions; and (3) FDA was authorized to require that previously permitted colors be retested for safety.

The regulations covering the new law were published in the *Federal Register* in 1963. These regulations outlined the safety data requirements of chemical and biological identity, methods for determination of the color in the finished product, animal testing, manufacturing processes, stability, etc. June 1, 1964 was set as a target date for the completion of the testing. This date has been extended, however, because petitioners needed additional time to gather data required for listing under the Color Additive Amendment of 1960.

2 SYNTHETIC COLOR ADDITIVES

In the United States there are (*a*) certified color additives and (*b*) colors that are exempt from certification. Those exempt from certification are largely natural colors obtained from mineral, vegetable, and animal sources. This chapter deals with the analysis of the certifiable colors permitted in the United States; some of these are listed in Table 17.1. The certified color additives may be the purified chemical colors, frequently called "straights" or "primaries," or lakes, which are straight colors extended onto a substratum by adsorption, coprecipitation, or chemical combination. FD&C straights and lakes may be used in foods, drugs, and cosmetics; D&C straights and lakes may be used in drugs and cosmetics; External D&C straights and lakes may be used in external drugs and cosmetics.

For the purpose of this chapter, organic colors have been classified into a number of groups, according to their chemical structures. Representatives

Table 17.1 Synthetic Color Additives Permitted in Foods in 24 Countries[a]

CI	CI Food	Australia	Austria	Belgium	Canada	Denmark	France	Germany	Greece	Holland	India	Israel	Italy	Japan	Mexico	Norway	Poland	Spain	Sweden	Switzerland	Taiwan	Thailand	Turkey	United Kingdom	United States
19140	Yellow 4	X	X	X	X	X	X	X	X	X	X	X	X	X	X	X	X	X	X	X	X	X	X	X	X
14270	Yellow 8	X	X			X	X	X	X			X													
47005	Yellow 13	X	X			X	X	X	X	X		X						X	R	X	X	X	X		
13015	Yellow 2	X	X	X		X	X	X	X				X					X		X					X
14330																									
18965	Yellow 5	X				X																			X
15985	Yellow 3	X	X	X	X	X	X	X	X	X	X	X	X	X	X	X	X	R	X	X	X	X	X	X	X
15980	Orange 2	X	X	X		X	X	X	X				X												
11920	Orange 3													X						X					
16230	Orange 4													X						X	X				
19235																									R
14720	Red 3	X	X	X		X	X	X	X	X	X	X	X	X				X		X	X		X		
16185	Red 9	X	X	R	X	X	X	X	X	X	X	X	X	X	X	X	X	X	X	R	X	X	X	X	X
16255	Red 7	X	X	X	X	X	X	X	X	X	X	X	X	X	X	X	X	X	X	R	X	X	X		X
14815	Red 2	X	X	X		X	X	X	X				X					X		X					
16290	Red 8	X	X			X	X	X	X				X							X					
45430	Red 14	X	X	X	X	X	X	X	X	X	X	X	X	X	X	X	X	X	X	R	X	X	X	X	X
16045	Red 4	X													X					X					
14700	Red 1	X			R										X									X	
18050	Red 10																								X
18055	Red 11																								
14780	Red 13	X	X																						
42685			X																						
45435		X												X											
45100														X											
16035	Red 17					X									X										X
15850					R		X	R		R		R												R	
12156					R										X										R
69800	Blue 4	X	X			X	X	X	X	X		X		X	X						X				X
42051	Blue 5	X	X			X	X	X	X				X		X		R	X			X				X
73015	Blue 1	X	X	X	R	X	X	X	X	X	X	X	X	X	X	X	X	R	X	X	X	X	X	X	X
42090	Blue 2	X		R	X			X	X					X	X							X	X	X	X
44090	Green 4	X					X	X	X				X	X		X								X	X
42053	Green 3							R						X	X			R			X	X			X
28440	Black 1	X	X	X		X	X	X	X	X			X		X					X					X
27755	Black 2	X	X			X	X	X	X	X			X					X	R	X					X
	Brown 1																								X
	Brown 2	X																							X
20285	Brown 3	X																							X
42580	Violet 3	X																							
42640	Violet 2														R										

[a] X = permitted;
R = restricted usage.

of each class from the permitted list are as follows: azo, FD&C Yellow No. 6; pyrazolone, FD&C Yellow No. 5; triphenylmethane, FD&C Blue No. 1; anthraquinone, D&C Green No. 5; indigoid, FD&C Blue No. 2; xanthene, D&C Orange No. 5; quinoline, D&C Yellow No. 10; and polynuclear, D&C Green No. 8. The dyes range from very soluble to insoluble in water, depending on the type of substituents and the type of salt. An increase in the number of SO_3H or COOH groups increases water solubility. Addition of Cl, NO_2, or Me groups increases the dye's solubility in organic solvents. The alkaline earth salts or lakes of the acid dyes are insoluble in both water and organic solvents.

3 COLOR CERTIFICATION ANALYSES

Analyses are performed by FDA on each batch of color additive submitted for certification to assure that the color meets the specifications set forth in the Code of Federal Regulations. Analytical techniques such as IR, visible and UV spectrophotometry, titrimetry, X-ray fluorescence, spectro-densitometry, and column chromatography, GC, TLC, and HPLC are used to determine total color, intermediates, subsidiary colors, inorganic salts, heavy metals, etc. From the analytical results it is determined whether the batch should be certified or rejected. For each batch certified a certif-icate bearing the lot number and total color content is issued. This certif-icate gives authority to market the product for the stated use.

Table 17.2 lists the color additives subject to certification with their titration factors, absorptivities, and wavelength maxima in the visible region used in the determination of the total color. With the listed titration factors, the formula given in Section 4.2 for the calculation of the total color must be used. The absorptivities listed are approximate when used with instruments other than those on which they were determined. More satisfactory results are obtained if standards of the colors are available.

4 LAKES

Straight dyes color by dissolving in a solvent, whereas pigments and lakes, being insoluble, color by dispersion. Lakes of the FD&C colors, extended on a substratum of alumina hydrate (aluminum hydroxide), have been permitted as food color additives since 1959. The *Code of Federal Regula-tions*[8] defines an FD&C lake as "any lake made by extending on a sub-stratum of alumina, a salt prepared from one of the certified water-soluble straight colors—combining such colors with the basic radical aluminum or calcium." FD&C lakes must be made from previously certified batches of straight color additives.

D&C Lakes are prepared by extending on a substratum of alumina, blanc fixe, gloss white, clay, titanium dioxide, zinc oxide, talc, rosin, aluminum benzoate, calcium carbonate, or any combination of two or more of these, one of the permitted straight colors or its Na, K, Al, Ba, Ca, Sr, or Zr salt.

4.1 Spectrophotometric Analysis of Lakes

FD&C Lakes except Red No. 3. To a 50-mg sample add $\sim$15 g sodium tartrate and 100 ml water. Heat to boiling. Cool, make to volume, and determine spectrophotometrically.

FD&C Red No. 3, D&C Orange No. 5 and 10, Red No. 19, 21, and 27. To a 50-mg sample add 100 ml water and 5 ml 50% sodium hydroxide. Heat if necessary. Make to volume and determine spectrophotometrically.

D&C Red No. 6–13, 31, 34. To a 30–40 mg sample add 5 ml conc. sulfuric acid. Using a stirring rod, break up any lumps and mix well to ensure complete solution. Dilute with $\sim$150 ml ethanol–water (1:1). If any undissolved color remains, heat till sample is in solution. Cool; make to final volume with 50% ethanol. Determine spectrophotometrically.

D&C Orange 17. To a 30–40 mg sample add 200 ml chloroform. Boil. Cool, make to volume, and determine total color spectrophotometrically.

4.2 Calculations of Total Color in Straights or Lakes

$$\frac{A \times 100 \times V}{\text{Std} \times 1000 \times W} = \text{Total color by spectrophotometry}$$

where A = absorbance; V = volume in ml; Std = standard absorbance/ mg/l 1-cm cell (absorptivity); W = weight in mg.

$$\frac{(T - 0.1) \times N \times 100}{F \times W} = \text{Total color by titrimetry}$$

where T = titer in ml; N = normality of the $TiCl_3$; F = factor; W = weight in g.

Table 17.2 Permitted Synthetic Color Additives

Color	CI	Titration Factors	Absorptivity of Standards[a]	Absorbance Max. (nm)
FD&C				
Blue No. 1	42090	2.52	0.164	630
Blue No. 2	73015	4.29	0.0478	610
Green No. 3	42053	2.47	0.156	625
Red No. 2[f]	16185	6.62	0.0436	522
Red No. 3	45430	—	0.110	527
Red No. 4	14700	8.33	0.054	502
Red No. 40	16035	8.06	0.052	500
Yellow No. 5	19140	7.49	0.053	428
Yellow No. 6	15985	8.84	0.054	484
Orange B	19235	6.77	0.0355	437
Citrus Red No. 2[b]	12156	12.94	0.070	515
D&C				
Blue No. 4	42090	2.55	0.170	630
Blue No. 6[b]	73000	7.63	0.079	603
Blue No. 9	69825	—	—	—
Brown No. 1	20170	17.84	0.0935	430
Green No. 5	61570	3.21	0.0213	610
Green No. 6[b]	61565	4.78	0.0392	648
Green No. 8[c]	59040	—	0.051	454
Orange No. 4	15510	11.42	0.0653	484
Orange No. 5[c]	45370	—	0.163	503
Orange No. 10[b]	45245	—	0.131	510
Orange No. 11	45245	—	0.122	510
Orange No. 17	12075	—	0.077	480
Red No. 6	15850	9.29	0.0615	511
Red No. 7	15850	9.42	0.0572	511
Red No. 8	15585	10.03	0.0522	486
Red No. 9	15585	9.00	0.047	486
Red No. 10[d]	15630	9.99	0.0685	494
Red No. 11[d]	15630	10.06	0.069	494

Table 17.2—*Continued*

Color	CI	Titration Factors	Absorptivity of Standards[a]	Absorbance Max. (nm)
Red No. 12[d]	15630	8.97	0.059	494
Red No. 13[d]	15630	9.50	0.0651	494
Red No. 17[b]	26100	22.70	0.094	514
Red No. 19	45170	—	0.236	554
Red No. 21[c]	45380	—	0.150	518
Red No. 22	45380	—	0.140	518
Red No. 27[c]	45410	—	0.129	537
Red No. 28	45410	—	0.122	537
Red No. 30[e]	73360	5.08	0.0248	496
Red No. 31	15800	12.85	0.080	518
Red No. 33	17200	8.56	0.0662	530
Red No. 34	15880	8.69	0.0655	526
Red No. 36[b]	12085	—	0.084	490
Red No. 37	45170	—	0.154	545
Red No. 39	13058	12.14	0.0758	433
Violet No. 2[b]	60725	—	0.0363	588
Yellow No. 7[c]	45350	6.02	0.247	489
Yellow No. 8	45350	5.32	0.228	489
Yellow No. 10	47005	—	0.096	413
Yellow No. 11[b]	47000	—	0.135	420
Ext D&C				
Green No. 1	10020	13.66	0.0217	720
Violet No. 2	60730	4.64	0.0244	570
Yellow No. 1	13065	10.66	0.064	436
Yellow No. 7	10316	33.50	0.049	430

[a] Absorptivity = absorbance/mg/l in 1-cm cell.

[b] $CHCl_3$-soluble.

[c] Basic.

[d] Red 10, 11, 12, and 13 are Na, Ca, Ba, and Sr salts, respectively.

[e] Using xylene instead of chloroform as in the modification of Hobin.[7]

[f] Delisted Dec. 2, 1976.

5 PROCEDURES FOR THE ANALYSIS OF SUBSIDIARIES, ISOMERS IN SOME COLORS

5.1 Higher Sulfonated Subsidiaries in FD&C Yellow No. 6, FD&C Red No. 40, and Ext D&C Violet No. 2

5.1.1 Apparatus and Reagents. (*a*) *Chromatographic column:* 22 × 250 mm with sealed-in coarse fritted disk. *Tamper:* Machined to fit the column. (*b*) *Solvent System:* in a separatory funnel add 100 ml *n*-butanol, 100 ml carbon tetrachloride, and 100 ml hydrochloric acid (1 + 4). Shake for 3 minutes. Allow to stand until layers separate. The bottom layer is the stationary phase (organic) and the top layer is the mobile phase (aqueous). (*c*) *Adsorbent:* Silane-treated Celite 545 (Johns Manville). Fill a large wide-mouth jar ∼$\frac{3}{4}$ full with Celite 545. Place a beaker containing ∼50 ml of General Electric SC-77 Dri-Film on top of the Celite. Seal the bottle and allow to stand in fume hood for several days.

5.1.2 Procedure. Mix thoroughly 15 g treated Celite with 7.5 ml stationary phase. Transfer the mixture to the column and pack firmly with the tamper. Wash column with ∼15 ml mobile phase before adding the color. Weigh ∼50 mg color and dissolve in 10.0 ml mobile phase. Add a 1.0 ml-aliquot of this solution to the column. Elute with the mobile phase. The higher sulfonated colors are eluted ahead of the main color. Collect the subsidiary color or colors, measure the volume, and examine spectro-photometrically.

Standard	Absorptivity (Absorbance/mg/l in 1-cm cell)
Higher sulfonated in FD&C Yellow No. 6	0.0423 at 488 nm
Higher sulfonated in FD&C Red No. 40	0.0494 at 505 nm

5.2 Isomeric Color in FD&C Red No. 2

5.2.1 Apparatus and Reagents. (*a*) *Chromatographic column:* 22 × 400 mm with sealed-in coarse fritted disk. (*b*) 5% sodium chloride solution; (*c*) 10% sodium chloride. (*d*) *Absorbent:* Solka-Floc BW-40 (Brown Corp., Berlin, N.H.).

5.2.2 Procedure. Prepare a slurry of BW-40 in 5% sodium chloride. Pour the slurry into the column and continue filling until the adsorbent forms a column within 3–4 in, of the top. Weigh ∼40 mg FD&C Red No. 2 and dissolve in 4.0 ml water; add 4.0 ml 10% sodium chloride solution.

Place 2.0 ml color on the column, allowing the solution to settle into the absorbent bed. Rinse sides of the column with a small amount of 5% chloride solution, allowing it also to settle into the absorbent bed. Elute the color with 5% sodium choride. The orange-red color preceding the main band is the isomeric color. Collect the isomeric color. Measure the volume and examine spectrophotometrically.

Absorptivity of isomer (absorbance/mg/l in 1-cm cell): 0.0436

5.3 Isomeric and Monosulfonated Subsidiary Color in FD&C Blue No. 2[9]

5.3.1 Apparatus and Reagents. (a) *Chromatographic column:* 22 × 250 mm with sealed-in coarse fritted disk. *Tamper:* machined to fit column. (b) *Adsorbent:* Celite 545 (Johns Manville). (c) *Solvent:* Hexane. (d) *Solvent system:* to a 2-l separatory funnel add 450 ml n-butanol, 450 ml chloroform, 100 ml conc. hydrochloric acid, and 800 ml 2.5% hydroxylamine hydrochloride. Shake for 3 minutes. Allow the layers to separate. The bottom layer is the mobile phase and the top layer is the stationary phase.

5.3.2 Procedure. Mix 12 g Celite and 7 ml stationary phase. Pack all the Celite mixture except ∼1 g into the column.

Prepare a 0.1% solution of the color in the stationary phase. Transfer a 5.0-ml aliquot of the sample to 10 g Celite. Mix thoroughly and pack in the column. Rinse the beaker with the reserved Celite from the column preparation, adding the rinse to the column. Pack firmly. Elute with the mobile phase. The monosulfonated fraction elutes first, followed by the isomeric color. Collect each band separately.

Transfer each to a separatory funnel, add an equal volume of hexane, and extract the colors with several small portions of water. Measure the extracts and determine spectrophotometrically.

Standard	Absorptivity (Absorbance/mg/1/in 1-cm cell
Monosulfonated	0.0513 at 615 nm
Isomer	0.0478 at 620 nm

5.4 Lower Sulfonated Subsidiaries in FD&C Colors

5.4.1 Apparatus and Reagents. (a) *Chromatographic column:* 22 × 250 mm with sealed-in coarse fritted disk. *Tamper:* machined to fit column. (b) *Solvent system:* in a separatory funnel add 100 ml n-butanol, 100 ml carbon tetrachloride, and 100 ml dilute hydrochloric acid (1 + 19) for FD&C Red No. 2 and Yellow No. 5; (1 + 49) for Red No. 4, Red No. 40, and Yellow No. 6. Shake the mixture for 3 minutes. Allow to stand until layers separate. The bottom layer is the mobile phase (organic) and the top layer is the stationary phase (aqueous). (a) *Adsorbent:* Celite 545 (Johns Manville). (d) *Solvent:* hexane.

5.4.2 Procedure. Mix 5 g Celite 545 and 2.5 ml stationary phase. Reserving a small amount, put the mixture into the column and pack firmly with the tamper.

Weigh ∼40 mg of color and dissolve in 5 ml of the stationary phase. For examination of Red No. 2, mix a 2.0-ml aliquot with 5 g Celite. For Yellow No. 5, Yellow No. 6, Red No. 4, and Red No. 40, mix the entire sample with 5 g Celite. In each case transfer the dye–Celite mixture to the column and pack firmly. Rinse the beaker with the reserved Celite and pack in the column. Elute with the mobile phase. The lower sulfonated colors are eluted first.

Transfer the eluent containing the lower sulfonated subsidiary color to a separatory funnel. Add an equal volume of hexane and extract the color with several small portions of water. Measure the volume and examine spectrophotometrically.

Standard	Absorptivity (Absorbance/mg/l in 1-cm cell)
FD&C Red No. 2	0.0413 at 505 nm
Red No. 4	0.054 at 502 nm
Red No. 40	0.0644 at 508 nm
Yellow No. 5	0.064 at 432 nm
Yellow No. 6	0.0533 at 484 nm

5.5 Ethyl Ester in Halogenated Fluoresceins

5.5.1 Apparatus and Reagents. (a) *Chromatographic column:* 2.5 × 25 cm with sealed-in coarse fritted disk. *Tamper:* machined to fit column. (b) *Solvent system:* in a separatory funnel add 800 ml 0.4% sodium carbonate solution, 160 ml *n*-butanol, 400 ml chloroform, and 160 ml ethanol. Shake for several minutes. Let stand until layers separate. The top layer is the stationary phase and the bottom layer is the mobile phase. (c) *Adsorbent:* Celite 545 (Johns Manville).

5.5.2 Procedure. Mix 10 g Celite and 5.5 ml stationary phase. Retaining ∼2 g, transfer the Celite mixture to the column and pack firmly with the tamper.

Transfer a 2.0-ml aliquot of a 2% solution of the color to a beaker containing 4 g Celite. Mix thoroughly. Transfer dye–Celite mixture to the column. Pack firmly. Rinse the beaker with the 2 g reserved from the column preparation, adding the rinse to the column. Pack firmly. Elute with the mobile phase. The ethyl ester is eluted with the solvent front. Collect the ethyl ester, measure the volume, and determine spectrophotometrically.

Absorptivity (Absorbance/mg/l in 1-cm cell): 0.122

5.6 Subsidiary Colors in FD&C Red No. 3 by Column Chromatography

5.6.1 Apparatus and Reagents. (a) *Fraction collector:* 200 fractions of 20-ml capacity. Protect from light. (b) *Chromatographic column:* with sealed-in coarse fritted disk fitted with device to regulate sequence of eluents; see Figure 17.1. (c) *Cellulose powder:* Whatman CF-11. (d) *Absorbent:* Solka-Floc BW-100 (Brown Corp., Berlin, N.H.). (e) *Ethanol:* 95%. (f) *Alcohol wash solution:* ethanol–water (3:1, v/v.) (g) *Eluent 1:* 350 ml 25% sodium chloride containing 5 ml ammonium hydroxide/l. *Eluent 2:* 500 ml 2% sodium sulfate solution containing 5 ml ammonium hydroxide/l. *Eluent 3:* 1000 ml 1% sodium sulfate solution containing 5 ml ammonium hydroxide/l. *Eluent 4:* 600 ml 0.5% ammonium hydroxide (v/v). *Eluent 5:* 400 ml 60% ethanol solution containing 5 ml ammonium hydroxide/l.

5.6.2 Procedure. Prepare a chromatographic column, using 16 g of BW-100 Solka-floc in ∼150 ml water. When most of the water has drained, wash with 100 ml (f) followed by 100 ml Eluent 1. Allow the liquid to drain to ∼2 cm above ths surface of the column. The support material must have a level surface.

Transfer a 5.0-ml aliquot of a 0.1% solution of the color into the tube, mixing the color with the salt solution, but taking care not to disturb the level surface of the support material. Allow all the solution to drain. Protect the column from light and position it over the fraction collector.

Add carefully ∼20 ml Eluent 1 and ∼3 g Whatman cellulose powder. When the cellulose has settled to form a protective cap over the color, fill the column with Eluent 1. If there is an excess of the eluent, place it in a flask and connect to the glass tube ending at the highest level (Tube 1, Figure 17.1). Place Eluents 2–5 in suitable flasks and connect to the appropriate tubes as shown in Figure 7.1. Invert the flasks and mount above the top of the tube. Collect fractions of ∼20 ml.

Combine the fractions of each band of subsidiary color. Measure the volume and absorbance, using a 5- or 10-cm cell where necessary. Using

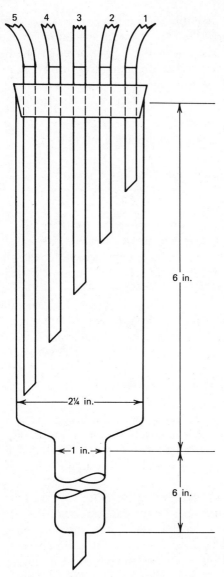

Figure 17.1 Chromatography Column for Subsidiary Colors.

these data, calculate the composition of the sample from the following tabulation, which gives the order, identity, and absorptivity of each band:

Eluent 1
    Band 1   Unidentified color (calculate as FD&C Red No. 3)
    Band 2   Fluorescein

Eluent 2

Band 3   Mixture of 2- and 4- monoidofluoresceins

Band 4   Mixture of 2,4-, 2,5-, and 2,7-diiodofluoresceins

Eluent 3

Band 5   Mixture of 4,5-diiodofluoresceins
          and 2,4,7-triiodofluoresceins

Band 6   2,4,5-Triiodofluorescein

Eluent 4

Band 7   2,4,5,7-Tetraiodofluorescein

Eluent 5

Band 8   Unidentified color (calculate as FD&C Red No. 3)

Standard as Na Salt	Absorptivity (absorbance/mg/l in 1 cm cell)
2-Iodofluorescein	0.193 at 502 nm
4-Iodofluorescein	0.154 at 498 nm
2,5-Diiodofluorescein	0.145 at 510 nm
2,7-Diiodofluorescein	0.179 at 512 nm
4,5-Diiodofluorescein	0.122 at 508 nm
2,4,5-Triiodofluorescein	0.116 at 518 nm
2,4,7-Triiodofluorescein	0.140 at 518 nm
2,4,5,7-Tetraiodofluorescein	0.110 at 527 nm

5.7   Subsidiary Colors in D&C Red No. 21

5.7.1   Apparatus and Reagents. See Section 5.6.1, (a)–(f). In addition, (g) *Eluent 1:* 450 ml 25% sodium chloride solution (w/v) containing 5 ml ammonium hydroxide/l. *Eluent 2:* 2000 ml 10% sodium sulfate solution (w/v) containing 5 ml ammonium hydroxide/l. *Eluent 3:* 600 ml 0.5% ammonium hydroxide solution (v/v). *Eluent 4:* 400 ml 60% ethanol solution containing 5 ml ammonium hydroxide/l.

5.7.2   Procedure. See Section 5.6.2 for the procedure. The order of elution is as follows:

Eluent No. 1

Band 1   Unidentified color (calculate as D&C Red No. 21)

Band 2   Fluorescein

Eluent No. 2

Band 3   Mixture of 2- and 4-monobromofluoresceins

Band 4   Mixture of 2,4- and 2,5-dibromofluoresceins

Band 5   4,5-Dibromofluorescein
Band 6   2,4,5-Tribromofluorescein

Eluent No. 3
Band 7   2,4,5,7-Tetrabromofluorescein
Band 8   Unidentified color (calculate as D&C Red No. 21)

Eluent No. 4
Band 9   Unidentified color (calculate as D&C Red No. 21)

Absorptivities of standards: see D&C Orange No. 5, Section 5.8.2.

5.8   D&C Orange No. 5

5.8.1   Apparatus and Reagents.   See Section 5.6.1, (a)–(f). In addition,
(g) *Eluent 1:* 350 ml 25% sodium chloride solution (w/v) containing 5 ml
ammonium hydroxide/l. *Eluent 2:* 1000 ml 15% sodium sulfate solution
(w/v) containing 5 ml ammonium hydroxide/l. *Eluent 3:* 800 ml 5%
sodium sulfate solution (w/v) containing 5 ml ammonium hydroxide/l.
Eluent 4: 500 ml 3% sodium sulfate solution (w/v) containing 5 ml ammonium hydroxide/l. *Eluent 5:*500 ml 0.5% ammonium hydroxide solution
(v/v). Eluent *6:* 500 ml 60% ethanol (v/v) containing 5 ml ammonium
hydroxide/l.

5.8.2   Procedure.   See Section 5.6.2, for the procedure. The order, identity,
and absorptivity of each band follow:

Eluent 1
Band 1   Unidentified fraction (calculate as D&C Orange No. 5)
Band 2   Fluorescein

Eluent 2
Band 3   Mixture of 2- and 4-monobromofluoresceins
Band 4   Mixture of 2,4- and 2,5-dibromofluoresceins

Eluent 3
Band 5   4,5-Dibromofluorescein

Eluent 4
Band 6   2,4,5-Tribromofluorescein

Eluent 5
Band 7   2,4,5,7-Tetrabromofluorescein

Eluent 6
   Band 8   Unidentified fraction (calculate as D&C Orange No. 5)

Standard in Color Acid	Absorptivity (Absorbance/mg/l in 1 cm cell)
Fluorescein	0.258 at 492 nm
2-Bromofluorescein	0.231 at 500 nm
4-Bromofluorescein	0.206 at 498 nm
2,4-Dibromofluorescein	0.190 at 504 nm
2,5-Dibromofluorescein	0.186 at 507 nm
2,7-Dibromofluorescein	0.214 at 507 nm
4,5–Dibromofluorescein	0.163 at 504 nm
2,4,5-Tribromofluorescein	0.151 at 512 nm
2,4,7-Tribromofluorescein	0.182 at 513 nm
2,4,5,7-Tetrabromofluorescein	0.149 at 518 nm

5.9   Lower Sulfonated Subsidiary Colors in FD&C Blue No. 1 and FD&C Green No. 3 by Extraction

5.9.1   Reagent.   *Salt acetate solution:* 250 g sodium chloride, 24 ml glacial acetic acid, and 27.2 g sodium acetate, made up to 1000 ml.

5.9.2   Procedure.   Prepare a 0.2% aqueous solution of the color. To a 5-ml aliquot of the sample add 45 ml salt acetate solution and extract by shaking successively in three separatory funnels, each containing 50 ml isoamyl alcohol. Wash the extracts with 50-ml portions of the salt acetate solution until washings are colorless, passing each wash portion successively through the three funnels in the order used for the original extractions. Dilute the alcohol with one to two volumes of petroleum ether. Remove the color from the alcohol by washing with several 10-ml portions of water, passing each portion through the three funnels in the reverse order to that previously followed.

Combine the aqueous extracts, measure the volume, and examine spectrophotometrically.

Absorptivity of lower sulfonated (absorbance/mg/l in 1-cm cell): 0.0126

5.10   Sodium Chloride in FD&C Red No. 3

Dissolve 2.5 g color in ~200 ml H_2O. Add 15 ml 1.5 N nitric acid. Transfer the mixture to a 250-ml volumetric flask, make to volume with water, mix, and filter through dry paper. Refilter the first 50–100 ml to eliminate the small amount of precipitated color present. Carry a blank through the procedure. Titrate a 100-ml aliquot of the filtrate with 0.1 N silver nitrate solution to the potentiometric end point. Calculate the results as sodium chloride.

$$\% \text{ NaCl } = \text{ Volume of AgNO}_3 \text{ used } \times \text{ Factor (0.584)}$$

5.11 1-p-Tolylazo-2-naphthol-3-carboxylic Acid in D&C Red Nos. 6 & 7

Boil a 0.100-g sample gently with 100 ml glacial acetic acid and 75 ml of 8 N hydrochloric acid until the color has dissolved. Cool and transfer to a 1-1 separatory funnel, washing any residual dye into the funnel with a few milliliters of acetic acid. Extract the solution with 150 ml ether, and separate the miscible solution formed by adding 150 ml water. Transfer the lower layer to a second funnel, and extract with another 100 ml of ether.

Combine the ether extracts and wash with 100-ml portions of water until the washings are colorless, then twice more. Remove the subsidiary dye from the ether layer by extraction with 20-ml portions of 2% sodium hydroxide. Warm to expel dissolved ether. Make to 100 or 200 ml with 2% sodium hydroxide, depending on the intensity of the color. Determine spectrophotometrically.

Absorptivity of standard (absorbance/mg/l in 1-cm cell): 0.032 at 505 nm in 2% NaOH

5.12   1-Phenylazo-2-naphthol in D&C Red No. 31[10]

Extract a 0.100-g sample in a Soxhlet extractor with benzene until the leachings are colorless or have a slight persistent bleed. Transfer the extract to a separatory funnel and wash with 1% sodium hydroxide until the washings are colorless. Remove the excess sodium hydroxide solution with water, and evaporate the benzene solution to dryness. Dissolve the residue in alcohol and make to 100 or 200 ml, depending on the intensity of the color. Determine spectrophotometrically.

6   HEAVY METALS BY X-RAY FLUORESCENCE

X-ray fluorescence is used routinely as a qualitative and quantitative analysis for the determination of heavy metals in batches of color additives submitted for certification. The straight color additives are pelleted by applying ~20,000 psi with a hydraulic press. This improves the surface exposure and increases the density of the elements.

The pellet is positioned in such a manner that the primary X-ray beam passes through the thin Mylar window and impinges on the sample exciting each element to its characteristic X-ray spectrum. To excite fluorescence, the primary radiation must have a wavelength shorter than the absorption edge of the spectral lines selected for the analysis. The fluorescence photons pass through a primary collimator to a crystal that serves as a dispersing monochromator. The crystal lattice acts as a three-dimensional grating, having a spacing of the distance between parallel atomic planes from which the X-rays are diffracted. All X-ray spectroscopy is based on the simple relationship known as Bragg's equation:

$$n\lambda = 2d \sin \theta$$

where λ = wavelength, θ = angle between X-ray beam and the reflecting crystal surface, and d = grating constant (distance between atomic layers parallel to the reflecting surface). For any particular angle of incidence θ, only those wavelengths that fulfill the Bragg equation can be reflected from the crystal. The diffracted rays emerging from the crystal pass through a secondary collimator to a detector, which rotates through an angle 2θ when the crystal is rotated through angle θ. The detector permits amplification and counting of the radiation emitted. The intensity signal is proportional to the concentration of element in the sample.

Standards of the element of interest are prepared in the same or a similar matrix as the unknown and in suitable concentrations so that they bracket the unknown. The quantitative determination of an element is made by comparing the intensity of the unknown to the intensity of the known.

$$\text{Concentration of unknown} = \frac{\text{Standard Concn} \times \text{Net Counts Unknown}}{\text{Net Counts Standard}}$$

NOTE: Net count = sample count − blank count.

An alternative technique is to use a lithium-drifted silicon [Si(Li)] diode. An X-ray photon entering the diode generates charge carriers which are collected in ~10^{-9} seconds by an applied bias voltage giving a current pulse, the height of which is linearly proportional to the photon energy. The pulse height thus becomes characteristic of the element emitting the X-ray. After amplification, these pulses are sorted out by a minicomputer-programmed multichannel analyzer on the basis of their heights, and a complete spectrum of peaks is built up, each corresponding to an emission from an element in the specimen. A quantitative measurement is made by integrating the total number of pulses within a peak. In more recent instruments, this method of detection and analysis is preferred because it is fast, all the elements are analyzed simultaneously, the losses associated with diffraction are absent, and no delicate alignment of moving crystals is involved.

This technique is not used in our laboratory, but is included for information.

7 SOLUBLE BARIUM IN SOME LAKES

Rub 10 g color into a paste with a little water and 4–8 drops of ethanol. Add 150 ml water and 40 ml hydrochloric acid (1 + 249). (On a separate aliquot, test the pH of the suspension with Metacresol Purple indicator. It should be pH 2.0 ± 0.1.) Warm on a water bath for 30 minutes, stirring frequently. Cool, transfer to a 250-ml volumetric flask, make to volume, mix, and filter on a dry filter. To 200 ml filtrate, add 20 ml conc. hydrochloric acid and heat to boiling. Add 5 ml sulfuric acid (1 + 3), also heated to boiling, and allow to settle for 30 minutes on a water bath. Filter, wash, the precipitate with hot sulfuric acid (1 + 199), ignite, and weigh as $BaSO_4$.

$$BaSO_4 \times 0.8923 = BaCl_2$$

8 SUBSIDIARY COLORS

Since most synthetic color additives are made from technical rather than reagent-grade chemicals, it is probable that subsidiary colors will be present in the finished product. As an example, in the sulfonation of 2-naphthol to produce 2-naphthol-3,6-disulfonic acid (R-Salt), other sulfonic acids such as 2-naphthol-6-sulfonic acid, 2-naphthol-6,8-disulfonic acid, and 2-naphthol-3,6,8-trisulfonic acid may be formed in small amounts. In the manufacture of Amaranth, R-salt is coupled with diazotized naphthionic acid. If any of the other sulfonic acids are present, they will also couple with the diazotized amine to produce subsidiary colors.

Subsidiary colors can also arise as a result of decomposition of the dye during manufacture or purification. This is particularly true of the triphenylmethanes, halogenated fluoresceins, and Orange B.

The subsidiary colors in certified color additives are determined by column chromatograph, extraction with immiscible solvents, and TLC using extraction or densitometry for quantitation.

All the FD&C, and a number of the D&C and Ext C&D, colors have a specification as to the amount of subsidiary colors permitted in the finished product. This particular specification along with all the specifications on color additives subject to certification and those exempt from certification can be found in the *Code of Federal Regulations.*[8]

8.1   Procedure for TLC of Subsidiaries

Using a microliter syringe, spot as a band the prescribed amount of sample solution on a TLC plate (20 × 20 cm; 0.25-mm layer; silica gel, except for FD&C Red No. 40, Orange B, D&C Green No. 5, and Red No. 8 and 9, where cellulose is used). Allow the plate to dry. Develop the plate (see Table 17.4) until the solvent front nears the top of the plate. Remove the plate and allow to dry. Scrape off each band and extract the color with the prescribed solvent. Filter the extract through a sintered glass funnel, measure the volume, and examine spectrophotometrically.

Table 17.3 lists the certified colors for which TLC procedures are available, together with the sample size, elution pattern, and standard absorptivity values of the subsidiary colors. The solvent systems are listed in Table 17.4.

9   UNCOMBINED INTERMEDIATES BY COLUMN CHROMATOGRAPHY AND HPLC

9.1   Apparatus, Reagents, and Standard Spectra

(*a*) *Chromatographic column:* see Figure 17.2. (*b*) *Ammonium sulfate:* reagent-grade, free of UV absorbers. (*c*) *Eluent:* see Table 17.5. (*d*) *Powdered cellulose:* Whatman CF-11 or equivalent. (*e*) *Standard spectra* of the intermediates in the solvents listed in Table 17.5.

9.2   Chromatographic Isolation

The method described here is a revision of section 24.046, *Official Methods of Analysis of the AOAC,* 12th Ed., 1975.

Stir 10–20 g cellulose powder with ∼200 ml water. Allow the mixture to settle. Decant the liquid. Repeat the wash and decantation. Add ∼100 ml eluent to the washed cellulose, mix, and pour the slurry into the chromatograph column. When the liquid has drained, wash with an additional 100 ml eluent.

Wash 5 g cellulose as above. Add 100 ml eluent to the washed cellulose, stir, allow to settle, and decant.

Combine the 5 g washed cellulose and color additive sample, and add 10 g ammonium sulfate. Stir thoroughly. Transfer the slurry to the column.

Table 17.3 Certified Colors Determined by TLC

Color	Quantity of Color Spotted on Plate (mg)	Solvent	Solvent System[a]	Location and Identification of Subsidiary colors	Standard Absorptivity[b]	Extraction and Spectral Solvent
FD&C Colors						
Blue No. 1[11,12]	2	H_2O	1	Lower sulfonated—all bands above main band	0.126 at 620 nm	Ethanol
Green No. 3	1	H_2O	1	Lower sulfonated—two top bands	0.126 at 620 nm	Ethanol
				Isomer—third band	0.156 at 625 nm	Ethanol
Red No. 2	1	H_2O	2	(Naphthionic acid →2-naphthol-3,6,8- trisulfonic acid)—above main band	0.0377 at 515 nm	H_2O
				(Naphthionic acid→2-naphthol-6-sulfonic acid)—below main band	0.0413 at 505 nm	H_2O
Red No. 4	4	H_2O	3	2-(5-Sulfo-2,4-xylylazo)-1-naphthol-4-sulfonic acid	0.0603	H_2O
				2-(2,4-xylylazo)-1-naphthol-4-sulfonic acid	0.0541	H_2O
				FD&C Red No. 4	0.0333	H_2O

Color	No.	Solvent	No.	Component	Absorptivity	Solvent
Red No. 40	1	H_2O	4	2-(4-Sulfo-2,5-xylylazo)-1-naphthol-4-sulfonic acid	0.0466	H_2O
				2-(3-Sulfo-2,6-xylylazo)-1-naphthol-4-sulfonic acid	0.0256	H_2O
				(Cresidine→2-naphthol-6-sulfonic acid)—above main band	0.0597 at 508 nm	H_2O
				(2-Methyl-5-methoxy-sulfanilic acid→R-acid)—below main band	0.0494 at 513 nm	H_2O
Yellow No. 5	1	H_2O	2	3-Carboxy-5-hydroxy-1-phenyl-4-(p-sulfophenylazo)pyrazole—above main band	0.066 at 427 nm	H_2O
Yellow No. 6[13]	1	H_2O	5	1-Phenylazo-2-naphthol-6-sulfonic acid—above main band	0.0533 at 482 nm	H_2O
				1-p-Sulfophenylazo-2-naphthol-3,6-disulfonic acid—below main band	0.0501 at 490 nm	H_2O
Orange B[14]	3	H_2O	6	2-(4-Sulfonaphthylazo)-naphthionic acid—below main band	0.035 at 482 nm	H_2O
				Followed by Orange K (COONa in CI 19235)	0.046 at 458 nm	H_2O

Table 17.3 (*Conitnued*)

Color	Quantity of Color Spotted on Plate (mg)	Solvent	Solvent System[a]	Location and Identification of Subsidiary Colors	Standard Absorptivity[b]	Extraction and Spectral Solvent
Citrus Red No. 2	2.5	$CHCl_3$	7	[2,5,2',5'-Tetramethoxy-benzidine→2-naphthol (2 mol.)] below main band	0.0851 at 555 nm	$CHCl_3$
				(2,5-Dimethoxyaniline→ 2,5-dimethoxyaniline→ 2-naphthol)—below the the benzidine dye	0.087 at 570 nm	$CHCl_3$ $CHCl_3$
D&C Colors						
Green No. 5	1	H_2O	8	D&C Green No. 6 with the solvent front Lower sulfonated Ext D&C Violet No. 2	0.0392 at 648 nm 0.0283 at 650 nm 0.0258 at 570 nm	$CHCl_3$ DMF Ethanol–H_2O (1:1)
Green No. 6	1	$CHCl_3$	9	D&C Violet No. 2 below main band	0.036 at 588 nm	$CHCl_3$
Orange No. 5[15]	1	H_2O	10	Ethyl ester Tetrabromofluorescein Tribromofluorescein Dibromofluorescein	(See section 5.8)	15% NH_4OH

			No.	Description	Value	Solvent
Orange No. 17	0.25	$CHCl_3$	7	1-(4-Nitrophenylazo)-2-naphthol—above main band	0.095	$CHCl_3$
Red No. 8 and 9[16]	1	DMF	11	4-(4-Chloro-2-sulfo-5-tolylazo)-1-naphthol	0.052 (Red No. 8) / 0.47 (Red No. 9)	DMF / DMF
Red No. 10–13[17]	1	DMF	12	(2-Naphthylamine-6-sulfonic acid→2-naphthol)—below main band / (1-Naphthylamine-2-sulfonic acid→2-naphthol)—below main band		DMF / DMF
Red No. 17[18]	3	$CHCl_3$	13	1-Phenylazo-2-naphthol—above main band	0.066 at 505 nm	$CHCl_3$
Red No. 19[19]	1	H_2O	14	Triethylrhodamine—above main band / Followed by other fluorescein-type colors	0.236	Ethanol–NH_4OH (99:1)
Red No. 21[15]	1	H_2O	10	Same as Orange No. 5		
Red No. 27 and 28	1	H_2O	15	Lower halogenated—below main band / Ethyl ester—above	0.127	15% NH_4OH

Table 17.3 (*Continued*)

Color	Quantity of Color Spotted on Plate (mg)	Solvent	Solvent System[a]	Location and Identification of Subsidiary Colors	Standard Absorptivity[b]	Extraction and Spectral Solvent
Red No. 36	0.5	$CHCl_3$	16	Descending order: Red-1-naphthol color (Red No. 36)	0.084 at 490 nm	$CHCl_3$
				4-Nitrophenylazo-2-naphthol	0.095 at 492 nm	$CHCl_3$
				2,4-Dinitrophenylazo-2-naphthol	0.077 at 480 nm	$CHCl_3$
				Yellow-1-naphthol color	0.009 at 452 nm	$CHCl_3$
Violet No. 2	1	$CHCl_3$	9	D&C Green No. 6—above main band	0.0392 at 648 nm	$CHCl_3$
Yellow No. 10[20]	1	Ethanol–H_2O (1:1)	2	D&C Yellow No. 11—at solvent front	0.135 at 420 nm	$CHCl_3$
				Disulfonated—below main band	0.084 at 413 nm	H_2O

[a] Numbers refer to solvent systems listed in Table 17.4

[b] Absorbance/mg/l in 1-cm cell.

488

Table 17.4 Solvent Systems for TLC (parts)

1. 10 Isoamyl alcohol
   10 Acetonitrile
   3 Methyl ethyl ketone
   1 H_2O
   1 NH_4OH
2. 10 Isoamyl alcohol
   10 Dioxane
   4 H_2O
   1 NH_4OH
3. 55 Ethyl acetate
   20 Ethanol
   10 Diethylamine
   10 H_2O
4. 10 Isoamyl alcohol
   10 Dioxane
   10 Acetonitrile
   10 Ethyl acetate
   10 H_2O
   2 NH_4OH
5. 10 Acetone
   13 Isoamyl alcohol
   4 H_2O
   1 NH_4OH
6. 45 Dioxane
   25 Isoamyl alcohol
   1 Acetic acid
   20 H_2O
7. $CHCl_3$
8. 10 Butyl acetate
   5 DMF
   1 H_2O

9. 6 Hexane
   2 Trichloroethylene
   1 Diethylamine
10. 95 Actone
    25 $CHCl_3$
    10 Butylamine
    10 H_2O
11. 0.02 N KOH
12a. 14 Dioxane
    10 Benzene
    5 Ethanol
    2 H_2O
    1 NH_4OH
12b. 20 Dioxane
    10 Benzene
    4 DMF
    1 NH_4OH
    1 H_2O
13. Toluene
14. 30 Acetone
    45 $CHCl_3$
    5 Triethylamine
    1 H_2O
15. 88 Acetone
    12 $CHCl_3$
    9.5 Butylamine
16. Benzene
    Redevelop in $CHCl_3$

Rinse the beaker with ~25 ml eluent, adding the rinse to the column. When all the solution has drained, add ~400 ml eluent. Collect eight 50-ml fractions.

9.3 Sample Treatment

The sample of color additive is treated in one of the following ways: (a) Dissolve 1.0 g in 50.0 ml water. Transfer 5.0 ml to the 5 g washed cellulose. (b) Slurry 0.1 g with 5 ml ethanol. Add the 5 g washed cellulose to the

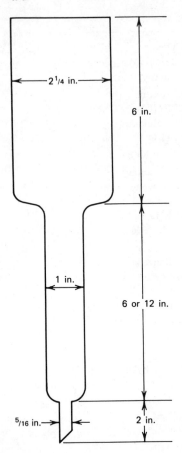

Figure 17.2 Chromatography Column for Uncombined Intermediates.

sample. (*c*) Dissolve 1.0 g in 49.5 ml water + 0.5 ml ammonium hydroxide. Transfer 5.0 ml to the 5 g washed cellulose. (*d*) Slurry 0.1 g with 2.5 ml water + 2.5 ml ammonium hydroxide. Add the 5 g washed celluose to the color. (*e*) Dissolve 1.0 g in 50 ml hydrochloric acid (1 + 99). Transfer 5.0 ml to the 5 g washed cellulose.

9.4 Spectrophotometric Determination

The sample, prepared as in Section 9.3 and chromatographed as in Section 9.2, is submitted to one of the following procedures: (1) Examine each fraction spectrophotometrically from 350 to 210 nm. (2) Divide each 50-ml fraction into two, adding 0.25 ml conc. ammonium hydroxide to one and

0.25 ml conc. hydrochloric acid to the other. Proceed as in (1). (3) Add 0.5 ml ammonium hydroxide to each fraction. Proceed as in (1). (4) Divide each 50-ml fraction into two, adding 0.25 ml conc. hydrochloric acid to one and nothing to the other. Proceed as in (1). Calculate as follows:

$$\frac{A \times V \times 100\%}{Std \times 1000 \times W} = \% \text{ Intermediates}$$

where: A = absorbance; V = volume (50) in ml; Std = absorbance/mg/l of the intermediate in a 1-cm cell (absorptivity); and W = weight in mg (100).

9.5   Pyrene–Trisulfonic Acid in D&C Green No. 8

9.5.1   Apparatus and Reagents.   (a) *Chromatographic column:* 26 × 650 mm with sealed-in coarse fritted disk. *Tamper:* machined to fit column. (b) *Absorbent:* Celite 545 (Johns Manville). (c) *Solvent system:* to a 2-l separatory funnel, add 500 ml *n*-butanol, 500 ml chloroform, 750 ml water, and 250 ml conc. hydrochloric acid. Shake for 3 minutes. Allow the layers to separate. The bottom layer (organic) is the mobile phase and the top layer (aqueous) is the stationary phase.

9.5.2   Procedure.   Mix 75 g Celite and 75 g of stationary phase. Add $\sim\frac{1}{3}$ of the Celite mixture and pack with the tamper. Repeat the process until all but $\sim$2 g of the Celite is packed in the column.

Weigh $\sim$50 mg D&C Green No. 8 and dissolve the color in 5 ml of stationary phase. To the color sample, add 5 g Celite, stir, and transfer the mixture quantitatively to the column. Rinse the beaker with the 2 g remaining from the column preparation. Add the rinse to the column and tamp.

Elute the Celite under moderate vacuum with the mobile phase. Discard the first 250–350 ml, which contains one or more subsidiary colors. Change to a clean collection flask and collect all the eluent up to the time the main band (D&C Green No. 8) is about to be eluted.

Transfer the eluent to a large separatory funnel. Add 10 ml 50% sodium hydroxide and shake. The solution should now be basic. Add a volume of hexane to the separatory funnel equal to the eluent collected, followed by the addition of 150 ml water. Shake for 2–3 minutes. Allow the layers to separate. Draw off the aqueous layer. Repeat the extraction with three 100-ml portions of water. Combine the aqueous extracts. Measure the volume and examine spectrophotometrically.

Absorptivity of standard (absorbance/mg/l in 1-cm cell): 0.0785 at 282 nm

Table 17.5 Data for Determination of Uncombined Intermediates

Color	Column Support Size	Sample Treatment[a]	% $(NH_4)_2SO_4$ in Eluent	Spectrophoto. Detn.[b]	Intermediates and Standards	Absorptivity
FD&C						
Blue No. 1	20	a	35	2	Benzaldehyde-2-sulfonic acid	0.44 at 252 nm
					N-Ethyl-N-(3-sulfobenzyl)-sulfanilic acid	0.047 at 274 nm (Basic)
					N-Ethyl-N-(3-sulfobenzyl)aniline	0.047 at 252 nm (Basic)
Blue No. 2	10	a	25	1	Isatin-5-sulfonic acid	0.089 at 244 nm
					5-Sulfoanthranilic acid	0.053 at 260 nm (Basic)
Green No. 3	20	a	40	2	Benzaldehyde-3-sulfonic acid	0.0495 at 246 nm
					4-Hydroxy-2-sulfobenzaldehyde	0.090 at 335 nm (Basic)
					N-Ethyl-N-(3-sulfobenzyl)aniline	0.04 at 252 nm (Basic)
Red No. 2	10	a	35	1	2-Naphthol-3,6-disulfonic acid	0.237 at 235 nm
					Naphthionic acid	0.036 at 320 nm
Red No. 3	20	a	25+ 10% EtOH	2	Sodium iodide	0.091 at 223 nm
					Phthalic acid	0.045 at 228 nm (Acidic)
					2-(2',4'-Dihydroxy-3',5'-diiodobenzoyl)benzoic acid	0.047 at 348 nm
Red No. 4	10	a	25	3	NW-acid	0.074 at 247 nm
					m-Xylidine-6-sulfonic acid	0.039 at 237 nm
Red No. 40[21]					Cresidinesulfonic acid	0.047 at 250 nm
					2-Naphthol-6-sulfonic acid	0.285 at 232 nm

					2,2'-Dinaphthyl ether 6,6'-disulfonic acid	0.174 at 240 nm
					2,2'-Dimethoxy-5,5'-dimethyl-diazoaminobenzene 4,4'-disulfonic acid	0.046 at 383 nm
Yellow No. 5	20	e	30+ 1% HCl 5% EtOH	2	Sulfanilic acid	0.0856 at 249 nm
					Phenylhydrazine-p-sulfonic acid	0.073 at 253 nm (Basic)
					3-Carboxy-1-(4-sulfophenyl)-5-pyrazolone	0.064 at 257 nm (Acidic)
Yellow No. 6[22]					Sulfanilic acid	0.0856 at 249 nm
					2-Naphthol-6-sulfonic acid	0.285 at 232 nm
					2,2'-Dinaphthyl ether 6,6'-disulfonic acid	0.174 at 240 nm
					Diazoaminobenzene-4,4'-disulfonic acid[22]	0.076 at 360 nm
Orange B	20	e	30+ 1% HCl 5% EtOH	2	Naphthionic acid	0.27 at 223 (Acidic)
					Phenylhydrazine-p-sulfonic acid	0.073 at 253 nm (Basic)
					3-Carboxy-1-(4-sulfophenyl)-5-pyrazolone	0.064 at 257 nm (Acidic)
Citrus Red No. 2	10	b	10	1	2-Naphthol	0.49 at 223 nm
					2,5-Dimethoxyaniline	0.026 at 290 nm (Basic)
D&C						
Blue No. 4	20	a	35	2	Same as FD&C Blue No. 1	
Blue No. 6	10	b	10	2	Isatin	0.161 at 242 nm or
						0.031 at 367 nm (Basic)
					Anthranilic acid	0.059 at 240 nm (Basic)

Table 17.5 Data for Determination of Uncombined Intermediates—(Continued)

Color	Column Support Size	Sample Treatment[a]	% (NH₄)₂SO₄ in Eluent	Spectro-photo. Detn.[b]	Intermediates and Standards	Absorptivity
Blue No. 9	10	b	10	2	2-Aminoanthraquinone[24]	0.124 at 249 nm in isooctane[21]
Green No. 5	10	a	25	2	Quinizarin	0.134 at 280 nm or 0.0396 at 240 nm (Basic)
					p-Toluidine-m-sulfonic acid	
Green No. 6	10	b	10	3	p-Toluidine	0.079 at 232 nm
					Quinizarin	0.124 at 249 nm in isooctane[26]
Green No. 8	10	a	40	1	Pyrenetrisulfonic acid	0.094 at 281 nm (See Section 9.5)
Orange No. 4	10	b	25	2	2-Naphthol	0.49 at 223 nm (Acidic)
					Sulfanilic acid	0.086 at 250 nm (Basic)
Orange No. 5	25	c	25	2	Phthalic anhydride	0.045 at 228 nm (Acidic)
					2-(3',5'-Dibromo-2',4'-dihydro-xybenzoyl)benzoic acid	0.059 at 345 nm (Basic) 0.069 at 223 nm (Acidic)
Orange No. 10	20	c	25	2	Same as FD&C Red No. 3	
Orange No. 17	10	b	10+ 10% EtOH	1	2-Naphthol	0.49 at 223 nm
					2,4-Dinitroaniline	0.076 at 347 nm
Red No. 6	10	b	10	4	3-Hydroxy-2-naphthoic acid	0.29 at 234 nm or 0.282 at 237 nm (Acidic)

Red No. 7	20	b	10	4	p-Toluidine-m-sulfonic acid	0.0396 at 240 nm
Red No. 8 and 9	10	b	10	4	Same as D&C Red No. 6	0.49 at 223 nm
					2-Naphthol 3-Amino-6-chlorotoluene-4-sulfonic acid	0.041 at 247 nm or 0.011 at 305 nm
Red Nos. 10–13	10	b	10	4	2-Naphthol 2-Naphthylamine-1-sulfonic acid	0.49 at 223 nm 0.22 at 242 nm or 0.014 at 342 nm
Red No. 17	10	b	10	2	2-Naphthol Aniline 4-Aminoazobenzene	0.49 at 223 nm 0.09 at 230 nm (Basic) 0.077 at 319 nm (Acidic) 0.033 at 240 nm (Basic)
Red No. 19	10	d	35	2	m-Diethylaminophenol Phthalic anhydride	0.049 at 253 nm (Basic) 0.045 at 228 nm (Acidic)
Red No. 21	10	c	25	2	Same as D&C Orange No. 5	
Red No. 22	10	a	25	2	Same as D&C Orange No. 5	
Red No. 27	10	c	30%+ 4% NH$_4$OH, 2% EtOH	2	Tetrachlorophthalic anhydride 2-(3'-5'-Dibromo-2',4'-dihydro-xybenzoyl) benzoic acid	0.018 at 220 nm
Red No. 28	10	a	30%+ 4% NH$_4$OH, 2% EtOH	2	Same as D&C Red No. 27	0.059 at 345 nm (Basic) 0.069 at 223 nm (Acidic)
Red No. 30	10	b	10	1	4-Methyl-6-chloro-thioindoxyl	

Table 17.5 Data for Determination of Uncombined Intermediates—(Continued)

Color	Column Support Size	Sample Treatment[a]	% (NH₄)₂SO₄ in Eluent	Spectrophoto. Detn.[b]	Intermediates and Standards	Absorptivity
Red No. 31	10	b	10	2	3-Hydroxy-2-naphthoic acid	0.294 at 234 nm (Basic)
						0.282 at 237 nm (Acidic)
					Aniline	0.09 at 230 nm (Basic)
Red No. 33	10	a	25	2	H-acid	0.117 at 240 nm (Acidic)
						0.128 at 237 nm (Basic)
					Aniline	0.09 at 230 nm (Basic)
Red No. 34	10	b	10	1	3-Hydroxy-2-naphthoic acid	0.29 at 234 nm
					2-Naphthylamine-1-sulfonic acid	0.226 at 240 nm
Red No. 36	10	b	10+ 10% EtOH	1	2-Naphthol	0.49 at 223 nm
					2-Chloro-4-nitroaniline	0.074 at 374 nm
Red No. 37	10	b	10+ 10% EtOH	1	Same as D&C Red 19	
Red No. 39	20	b	35	2	Anthranilic acid	0.050 at 240 nm (Basic)
					N-Phenyldiethanolamine	
Violet No. 2	10	b	10	2	Same as D&C Green No. 6	

Yellow No. 7	20	c	35	2	Phthalic anhydride 2-(2,4-Dihydroxybenzoyl)benzoic acid	0.045 at 228 nm (Acidic) 0.1 at 338 nm
Yellow No. 8	20	a	35	2	Same as D&C Yellow No. 7	
Yellow No. 10	10	a	25	2	Quinaldine 8-Sulfoquinaldine Phthalic anhydride	0.070 at 315 nm 0.048 at 318 nm (Acidic) 0.045 at 228 nm (Acidic)
Yellow No. 11	10	b	10	2	Quinaldine Phthalic anhydride	0.070 at 315 nm 0.045 at 228 nm (Acidic)
Ext. D&C						
Green No. 1	20	a	50	1	2-Naphthol-6-sulfonic acid	0.285 at 232 nm
Violet No. 2	10	a	25	2	Same as D&C Green No. 5	
Yellow No. 1	20	b	10%+ 1% NH$_4$OH	1	Metanilic acid Diphenylamine	0.044 at 237 nm (Basic) 0.087 at 280 nm[27]
Yellow No. 7	10	a	35	1	1-Naphthol-2,4,7-trisulfonic acid	

[a] See test Section 9.3.
[b] See test Section 9.4.
[c] Absorptivity = absorbance/mg/1 in 1-cm cell.

9.6   Alternate and/or Latest Instrumental Analysis

A number of methods have been developed that are no longer used in the day-to-day certification procedures. As newer methods have been developed utilizing the latest instrumentation, the older, more time-consuming methods have been abandoned. A number of those methods are included in this chapter since some are classified as the official methods of analyses and used as backup procedures for samples not meeting the specification.

Included with the group of older methods are those utilizing the latest instrumentation in the FDA Division of Color Technology, namely, X-ray fluorescence for the determination of heavy metals and HPLC for the determination of intermediates.

Since the time of publication of the original method for the determination of intermediates in FD&C color additives by HPLC, there have been some modifications in the apparatus and reagents. The modifications were necessary to determine the presence of diazoaminobenzene-4,4'-disulfonic acid in FD&C Yellow No. 6 and 2,2'-dimethoxy-5,5'-dimethyldiazoaminobenzene-4,4'-disulfonic acid) in FD&C Red No. 40. The triazenes are thought to be present in most diazo colors and their possible presence will be further investigated.

9.7   Operating Parameters for the Determination of Uncombined Intermediates by HPLC

9.7.1   FD&C Red No. 40.[28]   Primary solvent: 0.01 M sodium tetraborate solution. Secondary solvent: 0.01 M sodium tetraborate + 0.1 M sodium perchlorate solution. Liquid chromatograph: Du Pont Model 830. Strong anion exchange (SAX) column: Du Pont No. 830950405 (no heating or conditioning of the new column necessary). Column pressure: adjust to give 1 ml/min flow rate. Temperature: ambient. Attenuation: 0.04. Gradient: 0–70 at 5%/minute linear. Equilibration time: 6 minutes.

9.7.2   FD&C Yellow No. 6.[29]   Primary solvent: 0.01 M sodium tetraborate solution. Secondary solvent: 0.1 M sodium tetraborate + 0.1 M sodium perchlorate solution. Liquid chromatograph: Du Pont Model 830. SAX column: Du Pont No. 830950405 (no heating or conditioning of the new column necessary). Column pressure: adjusted to give 1 ml/min flow rate. Temperature: ambient. Attenuation: 0.02. Gradient: 0–90% at 3%/minute linear. Equilibration time: 10 minutes.

9.7.3   FD&C Yellow No. 5.[30]   Primary solvent: 0.01 M sodium tetraborate solution. Secondary solvent: 0.01 M sodium tetraborate + 0.2 M sodium perchlorate solution. High-pressure liquid chromatograph and accessories: Du Pont Model 830 equipped with gradient-elution accessory and a detector sensitive at 254 nm, as well as a Du Pont Model 836 multiwavelength detector with a wide band pass filter (325–385 nm). *Two-pen recorder:* with one pen driven by the 830 detector and the other pen by the Model 836 detector. SAX column: Du Pont No. 820950005, 1 m × 2.1 mm i.d. Column pressure: adjust to give flow rate 3.5 ml/2 minutes. Temperature: ambient (23–26°). Attenuation: 0.01 × 4 for the 830 detector; 0.01 × 1 for the 836 detector. Gradient: 0–100% at 4%/minute nonlinear exponential 5. Equilibration time: 10 minutes. Injection: Inject 5µl 2% solution of FD&C Yellow No. 5 on-stream.

10   DETERMINATION OF FD&C COLORS IN FOODS

The method described below, employing a combination of ion-exchange and adsorption chromatography, is used routinely by the FDA for the determination of colors in food products.

The food is finely ground with Celite and one of three aqueous phases, and the mixture is packed into a column. Fats and oil-soluble carotenoid-type colors, if present, are eluted with chloroform. The water-soluble colors are eluted with solutions of a liquid anion-exchange resin (Amberlite LA-2) in hexane and butanol. The colors are extracted from the resin solutions into water. FD&C Red No. 3 is isolated by extraction into ether. The remaining colors are separated by chromatography on cellulose columns using principally two alcohol–water–salt solutions. A few color separations require the use of dilute ammonium hydroxide–salt solutions. The separated colors are identified from their visible absorption spectra.

Method I uses a dilute acetic acid aqueous phase, a resin in hexane solution to elute the sulfonated azo colors, and a resin in butanol solution to elute the triphenylmethane colors. The resin solutions are equilibrated with the aqueous phase before use. FD&C Blue No. 2 fades in this acidic medium. FD&C Red No. 3 is not quantitatively eluted.

Method II is used if the colors include FD&C Blue No. 2 or FD&C Red No. 3. A pH 7.5 buffer is used as the aqueous phase, and the resin in butanol solution is equilibrated with this buffer. All colors are eluted. The FD&C Blue No. 2 has reasonable stability under these conditions. The quantitative datum for this color is always taken from this resin solution spectrum.

Method III uses a 0.1 N hydrochloric acid aqueous phase, a resin in butanol solution equilibrated with 0.1 N hydrochloric acid, and a delayed elution step, which is required if the Al lakes of the colors have been used.

All colors elute. The recovery of FD&C Red No. 3 Al lake may be a little low, but will be much better than by Method I or II.

The procedure, described in three publications,[31-33] was recently updated and submitted to a collaborative study. The report[34] includes some of the changes made in the updated procedure and indicates further changes to be made before another collaborative study is undertaken.

11 DETERMINATION OF CERTIFIABLE COLORS IN DRUGS

Many drugs contain FD&C color additives, and the procedure for FD&C colors in foods is usually applicable. Reactive drug ingredients may bind with a color and alter its properties. Some colored drug ingredients could be extracted with certifiable colors and thus be mistaken for a nonpermitted synthetic organic color. It may be necessary to design the procedure for a particular drug.

The procedure for FD&C colors in foods has not been systematized for the determination of D&C and Ext D&C colors in drugs. It is usually applicable, but the analyst must determine the proper choice among the three extraction steps and among the several chromatographic systems to separate the colors from each other.

12 DETERMINATION OF CERTIFIABLE COLORS IN COSMETICS

FD&C, D&C, and Ext D&C colors, as well as many color additives exempt from certification, are permitted for cosmetic use in the United States. Some of the restrictions set forth by the 1940 Color Regulations are that Ext D&C colors may not be used on the lips or other mucous membranes, and that coal tar colors are not permitted in the area of the eye.

The large number of permitted dyes, together with the diversity of possible cosmetic ingredients, has made it difficult to incorporate all the variables into a single analytical method applicable to the analysis of every cosmetic. The group of cosmetics that present the most complicated mixtures of dyes includes the highly colored lipsticks, nail enamels, and blushers or rouges.

Lipsticks may contain up to 6% color, which is usually present as a mixture of two to six different dyes. Other types of cosmetics, such as lotions, creams, and shampoos, usually have fewer than three dyes, and at much lower concentration levels. The most widely used method in the United States for the analysis of dyes in lipsticks, nail enamel, and blushers involves a direct application of the product to a warm thin-layer plate containing an adsorbent layer of silica gel G.[35] Oil-soluble colors are separated first by development with methylene chloride. This solvent also elutes fats and oils to the top of the plate, preventing them from interfering with the subsequent separation of the water-souble dyes, which remain at the base line. A second development of the plate, using a solvent system of ethyl acetate–methanol–30% ammonium hydroxide (15:3:3) separates the water-soluble dyes from one another. The colors are individually extracted from the silica gel and identified as well as quantitated spectrophotometrically. This method was originally designed for the analysis of 15 certifiable colors usually found in lipsticks, although other dyes, if present, may also separate under these conditions. Perdih[36] has published another thin-layer method for the analysis of cosmetic colors in lipsticks. He gives a series of selective solvent systems of increasing polarity, a combination of which allows the separations of more than 150 dyes by TLC. These colors include those certifiable in the United States, as well as many other dyes permitted for cosmetic use in other countries.

There are general guidelines, rather than a specific method, for the analysis of dyes in other types of cosmetics. Very highly colored products, whether in solid, crayon, or gel form, can be slurried with the appropriate solvent, applied to a thin-layer plate, and treated in the same manner as a lipstick. Cosmetics that are clear solutions containing only one dye can be analyzed directly by obtaining spectrophotometric curves and comparing them with curves of standard dyes at the same pH. Other products, such as creams and lotions, which usually contain a lower concentration of dye, require separation of the dye from the substrate. This can usually be accomplished by extraction; precipitation of the interfering material with acids, bases, or solvents; ion exchange, as in the separation of dyes from foods; or any combination of these. Once removed from the cosmetic, mixtures of dyes can be easily separated from one another by TLC and identified spectrophotometrically, using the methods cited above.

REFERENCES

1. *Official Methods of Analysis*, 12th ed., AOAC, Washington, D.C., 1975, sections 34.019; 34.020; 34.024–34.033; 34.084; 25.006; 34.103.

2. C. Graichen and J. E. Bailey, *J. Assoc. Off. Anal. Chem.*, **57**, 356 (1974).

3. J. E. Bailey and C. Graichen, *J. Assoc. Off. Anal. Chem.*, **57**, 353 (1974).

4. J. Dantzman and C. Stein, *J. Assoc. Off. Anal. Chem.*, **57**, 963 (1974).

5. J. A. Wenninger, *J. Assoc. Off. Anal. Chem.*, **48**, 826 (1965).

6. L. Moten, *J. Assoc. Off. Anal. Chem.*, **53**, 916 (1970).

7. N. Hobin, *J. Assoc. Off. Anal. Chem.*, **54**, 215 (1971).

8. *Code of Federal Regulations*, Title 21, Parts 8 and 9, U.S. Government Printing Office, Washington, D.C.

9. M. Singh, *J. Assoc. Off. Anal. Chem.*, **53**, 250 (1970).

10. L. Koch, *J. Assoc. Off. Anal. Chem.*, **25**, 948 (1942).

11. C. Stein, *J. Assoc. Off. Anal. Chem.*, **52**, 34 (1969).

12. S. Bell, *J. Assoc. Off. Anal. Chem.*, **56**, 747 (1973).

13. *Ibid.*, **58**, 717 (1975).

14. *Ibid.*, submitted (Orange B).

15. *Ibid.*, submitted (Red No. 21, Orange No. 5).

16. C. Stein, *J. Assoc. Off. Anal. Chem.*, **53**, 534 (1970).

17. *Ibid.*, **53**, 240 (1970).

18. J. Molitor, *J. Assoc. Off. Anal. Chem.*, **50**, 1198 (1967).

19. S. Bell, *J. Assoc. Off. Anal. Chem.*, **57**, 961 (1974).

20. C. D. Ritchie, J. A. Wenninger, and J. H. Jones, *J. Assoc. Off. Anal. Chem.*, **44**, 733 (1961).

21. Ref. 1, section 34.059.

22. Ref. 1, section 34.053.

23. J. E. Bailey, and E. A. Cox, *J. Assoc. Off. Anal. Chem.*, **58**, 609 (1975).

24. S. Bell, *J. Assoc. Off. Anal. Chem.*, **52**, 831 (1969).

25. E. Hoskins, *J. Assoc. Off. Anal. Chem.*, **54**, 1270 (1971).

26. C. Stein, *J. Assoc. Off. Anal. Chem.*, **50**, 1297 (1967).

27. J. Dantzman, *J. Assoc. Off. Anal. Chem.*, submitted (Yellow No. 1).

28. M. Singh, *J. Assoc. Off. Anal. Chem.*, **57**, 219 (1974).

29. J. E. Bailey and E. A. Cox, *J. Assoc. Off. Anal. Chem.*, **58**, 609 (1975).

30. M. Singh, *J. Assoc. Off. Anal. Chem.*, submitted (Yellow No. 6).

31. R. N. Sclar and K. A. Freeman, *J. Assoc. Off. Anal. Chem.*, **48**, 797 (1955).

32. M. Dolinsky and C. Stein, *J. Assoc. Off. Anal. Chem.*, **45**, 767 (1962).

33. C. Graichen and J. C. Molitor, *J. Assoc. Off. Anal. Chem.*, **46**, 1022 (1963).

34. C. Graichen, *J. Assoc. Off. Anal. Chem.*, **58**, 278 (1975).

35. R. Silk, *J. Assoc. Off. Anal. Chem.*, **48**, 838 (1965).

36. A. Perdih, *Z. Anal. Chem.*, **260**, 278 (1972).

CHAPTER EIGHTEEN

Analysis of Hair Dyes

JOHN F. CORBETT

1 INTRODUCTION

The analysis of hair dyes deserves separate treatment by virtue of the fact that, except for a few important cases, the materials employed find use as dyes only in the dyeing of furs and of human hair. Corbett[1] has recently reviewed the technical and patent literature on hair dyes over the period 1945–1970, and a compilation of dyes patented for use on hair, up to 1930 has been published by Charle and Sag.[2] Fortunately for the analyst, only a relative few of the hundreds of compounds mentioned in these reviews are in wide current use. Furthermore, present-day standards for product safety testing necessarily restrain the use of new dyes in hair coloring products unless they show a marked superiority over those presently in use, thus meriting extensive biomedical testing.

There are four broad classes of hair dyes, which differ to a marked extent in their method of application, type of result, and lastingness, as well as in the nature of the dyes employed.

The so-called "color restorers" or metallic dyes are readily distinguished as colorless solutions having application instructions indicating a gradual build-up of color by frequent and simple application. These products usually contain lead acetate or, more rarely, a bismuth salt. Analysis is performed using conventional inorganic analysis methods; e.g., qualitatively, hydrogen sulfide shows the presence of lead as a black precipitate or bismuth as a brownish black precipitate.

Temporary hair colorants, or color rinses, are generally sold as aqueous solutions of dyes containing a small amount of a resin. The product produces a light coloration of the hair by rinsing the hair with the solution. As the name implies, these dyes have poor lasting qualities and are generally removed by shampooing. Occasionally these products are sold as powders with instructions to dissolve in water before application (such products should not be confused with powder dyes of the permanent type, which require an oxidizing agent to develop the color, as discussed below). The temporary hair colorants employ high molecular weight dyes such as textile dyes, FD&C, D&C, and Ext D&C colors. The identification of the dyes in these products presents a particularly difficult problem for the analyst in that they may be acid, basic, or disperse dyes chosen from a wide range, including premetallized dyes.

The semipermanent hair dyes are generally marketed as shampoo-in products giving a coloring that withstands four to six shampoos. These products normally comprise a solution of relatively low molecular weight dyes in a simple shampoo system or in an emulsion shampoo system. The dyes employed are generally from the narrow group of nitroanilines, nitrophenylenediamines, nitroaminophenols, and amino- and aminohydroxyanthraquinones.

Finally, there are the long-lasting "permanent" or oxidation dyes. These normally comprise a dye solution containing a mixture of diaminobenzenes, aminophenols, and polyhydroxybenzenes in an ammonium oleate soap or ammonia-containing synthetic surfactant solution. This solution is mixed with a hydrogen peroxide solution or a solid oxidizing agent such as urea peroxide, melamine peroxide, or sodium perborate immediately prior to application. The color develops, mainly inside the hair fiber, by oxidation of the p-diamines and p-aminophenols to quinoneimines which couple with other amine and phenolic components to give a variety of indoaniline and indamine dyes. These dyes are relatively stable under dry conditions and, by virtue of their high molecular weight, are not readily leached from the hair during shampooing. Although a large number of intermediates have been patented for use in oxidation dyes,[1,2] it is probable that fewer than two dozen of these are in use in the United States today. In addition to the colorless intermediates employed in oxidation dyes, it is not unusual to find nitrophenylenediamines, particularly in warm, auburn, or golden shades, because the available intermediates can produce brown, greenish brown, magenta, violet, and blue indo dyes, but not red or yellow compounds.

In the analysis of hair dyes, it is necessary to consider both the assay of raw materials and the analysis of the finished product—in the latter, both chemical composition and performance require attention. We discuss the methods separately since, in general, there is little overlap between the techniques employed.

2 ASSAY OF RAW MATERIALS

Techniques for the assay of color strength of textile dyes and certified food colors are discussed elsewhere (Chapters 19 and 17). Essentially, this is done by comparison with a standard using visible colorimetry or spectroscopy. It is of course essential to confirm the identity of the dye by one or more techniques that are more discriminating. Such techniques would normally be m.p. determination, IR spectroscopy, and TLC. It should be remembered that although the IR spectrum is characteristic of a compound it is not necessarily sensitive to the presence of impurities even at the 5–10% level. In view of this it is worthwhile to examine samples from each batch by TLC.

A knowledge of the method of manufacture of the dye can often aid in the choice of the appropriate method of analysis. For example, 4-nitro-*o*-phenylenediamines can be made by "selective" reduction of the appropriate 2,4-dinitroaniline. However, the method is not absolutely selective and in assaying it is important to examine for the presence and amount of the isomeric 2-nitro-*p*-phenylenediamine

The nitrophenylenediamines are the only example of raw materials in which the presence of isomers is known to occur. GC methods have been described for the examination of isomeric diaminotoluenes as their trifluoroacetyl derivatives on neopentylglycol succinate or on six-ring *m*-polyphenyl ether.[3] The isomeric phenylenediamines have been separated on Triton X-305[4] and on Apiezon L–alkali[5] columns. Goldstein et al.[6] have separated the amine components of hair dyes on a 10% UCON 50HB-5100 plus 5% sodium hydroxide column, using *N*,*N*-diethyl-1-naphthylamine as an internal standard. To my knowledge, all studies of phenylenediamine, toluenediamine, and aminophenol raw materials used in hair colorants have shown them to be free of isomers at limits of detection below 0.1%.

Some of the dyes used in temporary or semipermanent hair colors are not completely soluble in the dye base and are used in dispersions. In such cases, the advisability of making a laboratory-scale batch of product and testing its dyeing properties on hair swatches should be considered.

The oxidation dye intermediates, being colorless and, in some cases, sensitive to oxygen, present special problems in assaying. A list of the intermediates used in the United States is given in Table 18.1. As raw materials, the amines are used both as the free bases and as the hydrochlorides or sulfates. Assay for total amine content can be accomplished by titration.

The free bases of amines can be assayed by titration with aqueous acid to an end point of pH $\sim$2. Aminophenols can be determined similarly, but it is usual to employ perchloric acid and nonaqueous conditions, such as solutions in acetonitrile. If the materials are in the form of their salts, particularly sulfates and chlorides, titration of the acid with alkali can be employed. In most cases the raw materials employed assay greater than 96%. An exception is 2,4-diaminoanisole which, owing to its hydroscopicity, may assay as low as 80%.

Advantage can be taken of the ability of these compounds to undergo oxidative coupling reactions to give colored products.[7] The general reaction is shown in Figure 18.1. The reaction involves oxidation of the *p*-diamine or *p*-aminophenol to a quinoneimine by ferricyanide, followed by coupling of the imine with a *m*-diamine, *m*-aminophenol, or phenol to give a leuco indo dye, which is then oxidized by ferricyanide to an indo dye. *p*-Diamines give 2-aminoindamines with *m*-diamines, 2-aminoindoanilines with *m*-aminophenols, and indoanilines with phenols. *p*-Aminophenols give N^1-

Table 18.1   Methods of Assay for Important Permanent Dye Intermediates

Compound	Methods
p-Phenylenediamine	Titration, oxidative coupling
2,5-Diaminotoluene	Titration, oxidative coupling
2,4-Diaminoanisole	Titration, oxidative coupling
p-Aminophenol	Titration, oxidative coupling
m-Aminophenol	Titration, oxidative coupling
o-Aminophenol	Titration
m-Phenylenediamine	Titration, oxidative coupling
N-Methyl-*p*-aminophenol	Titration
2,4-Diaminophenol	Titration
N-Phenyl-*p*-phenylenediamine	Titration
Resorcinol	Bromination
Hydroquinone	Iodimetry
Pyrogallol	Colorimetry
1-Naphthol	Oxidative coupling
1,5-Naphthalenediol	Oxidative coupling
2-Nitro-*p*-phenylenediamine	Colorimetry
4-Nitro-*o*-phenylenediamine	Colorimetry
5-Nitro-2-aminophenol	Colorimetry
2-Nitro-4-aminophenol	Colorimetry

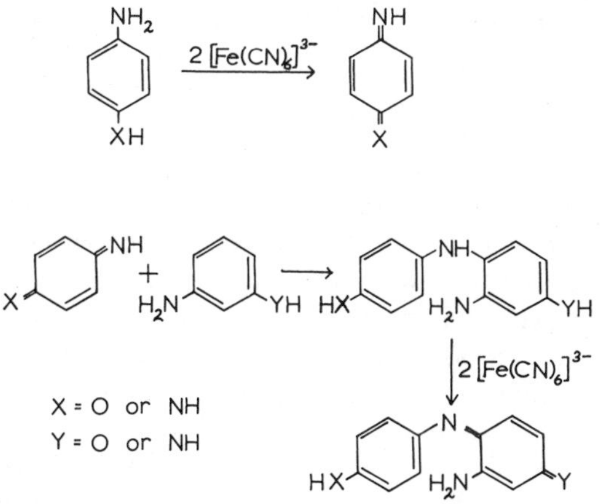

X = O or NH
Y = O or NH

Figure 18.1 Reaction involved in assaying by oxidative coupling.

(*p*-hydroxyphenyl)-2-aminobenzoquinone diimines with *m*-diamines, N^1-(*p*-hydroxyphenyl)-2-aminobenzoquinone monoimines with *m*-aminophenols, and indophenols with monohydric phenols. Konrad[8] has recommended the use of a spray comprising *m*-phenylenediamine, ammonia, and hydrogen peroxide for the detection of *p*-aminophenols on chromatograms, which make use of the pH sensitivity of the particular indo dye as contrasted with those formed from *p*-diamines and *m*-phenylenediamine.

It has been pointed out elsewhere[7] that, in using oxidative coupling as an assay method, great care should be taken in the choice of conditions. In particular, the choice of pH is critical because it affects the position of equilibrium in the imine formation, the rate of hydrolysis of the imine, and the rate of the coupling reaction. Since the last two are competing reactions, the conditions should be chosen so as to avoid significant hydrolysis of the imine. Additionally, the concentrations of the reactants are important. Thus, although a slight excess of ferricyanide is desirable, too large an excess can result in destruction of some of the *meta*-compound or the phenol.

In general, it has been found best to use stock solutions such that the concentrations during the coupling reaction are about 10^{-4}–10^{-3} M, employing at least 25% excess of the component which is not being assayed, and 5-molar equivalents of ferricyanide (based on the amount of *p*-diamine of *p*-aminophenol). In all cases, the ferricyanide should be added last and sufficient time for full color development allowed to elapse before diluting with water or ethanol for determination of the absorbance.

p-Diamines are best assayed using 2,4-diaminoanisole as the coupler, carrying out the reaction at pH 8, and determining the absorbance at 511 nm. Conversely, *m*-diamines can be assayed using stock solutions of *p*-phenylenediamine. The latter is preferred to *p*-toluenediamine because it reacts faster. Similarly, 2,4-diaminoanisole is more reactive than other readily available *m*-diamines.

m-Aminophenol can be assayed by coupling with *p*-phenylenediamine at pH 8 and determining the absorbance at 511 nm. *p*-Aminophenol can be determined by coupling with *m*-diamines, but the sensitivity of the spectrum of the product to pH makes the method difficult. A better method[7] involves coupling with 2,6-xylenol at pH 11–11.5. For this assay, dilution with ethanol before measuring the absorbance is recommended since a small amount of water-insoluble biphenoquinone is formed.

1-Naphthol and 1,5-naphthalenediol are highly reactive couplers and can readily be assayed by oxidative coupling with *p*-phenylenediamine at pH 8. Again, dilution with ethanol is advised since the resulting indoanilines are only sparingly soluble in water.

Oxidative coupling has been found unsuitable for the assay of polyhydric phenols, *o*-aminophenols, and *N*-methyl-*p*-aminophenol.

Resorcinol is assayed by a bromination procedure. Bromine is generated by acidifying a known quantity of Koppeschaar's solution (bromate plus bromide) in the presence of a known quantity of resorcinol. The excess bromine is determined by adding potassium iodide and titrating the liberated iodine with thiosulfate.

Because of the detrimental effect of iron on the oxidation dye process, it is usual to examine raw materials for the presence of trace iron. The material is ashed and the residue is dissolved in hydrochloric acid. The iron content of the resulting solution is then determined spectrophotometrically, using *o*-phenanthroline, or by atomic absorption spectroscopy. Acceptable limits range from about 15 ppm in resorcinol to 200 ppm in 2,4-diaminoanisole, and are chosen, bearing in mind reasonably achievable limits in the particular raw material, to give less than 5 ppm in the finished product.

3 ANALYSIS OF DYES IN HAIR COLORANTS

3.1 Temporary Dyes

There are no references in the literature to the analysis of this class of dyes; they represent the most difficult, and probably the most unrewarding area, for the analyst. Separation can of course be achieved by the various chromatographic techniques but, apart from revealing the colors of the dyes present, this does not give much useful information on the nature of the dyes. Further information for the purpose of classifying the dyes can be obtained using electrophoresis—neutral, acid, and basic dyes being identified by their direction of migration, if any.

The temporary dyes can sometimes be distinguished from the semipermanent dyes by dyeing, for 30 minutes at room temperature, on a standard multifiber cloth containing acetate, wool, nylon, cotton, silk, and viscose. The semipermanent dyes strike on acetate, wool, nylon, and silk to give colors characteristic of their shade on hair, and give little or no staining on the cotton or viscose. Under similar conditions, the temporary colors strike heavily on the silk, moderately on the wool and nylon, and little if any on the acetate, and stain the cotton and viscose to the same extent.

3.2   Semipermanent Dyes

In semipermanent hair color products, the most important dyes are the nitrophenylenediamines and nitroaminophenols and N-substituted derivatives. These dyes provide the yellows, oranges, reds, and violets from which, with the aid of blue anthraquinones, natural and even colors can be produced by blending from two to about 12 different dyes in a shampoo base. These dyes, and their colors on chromatographic paper or plates, are listed in Table 18.2.

Table 18.2   Commonly Used Semipermanent Dyes

Dye	Color of Spot[a]	λ_{max}[b]
2-Nitro-p-phenylenediamine (NPD)	Orange-red	471
4-Nitro-o-phenylenediamine (NOD)	Orange-yellow	408
4-Nitro-m-phenylenediamine	Greenish yellow	389
N^1-substituted NPD[c]	Red	495–498
N^4-substituted NPD[c]	Red	490–492
N^1,N^4,N^4-trisubstituted NPD[c]	Violet or purple	500–535
N^1-substituted NOD[c]	Orange	425–435
N^1,N^1-disubstituted NOD[c]	Orange	396
2-Nitro-4-aminophenol	Yellow-orange	446
Picramic acid	Yellow	380
N-Methylisopicramic acid	Violet	530
1,4-Diaminoanthraquinones[c]	Blue	600–650
1,4,5,8-Tetraaminoanthraquinone	Blue	590, 624

[a] Color of spot on silica gel plate.

[b] For solution in 95% ethanol.

[c] The N-substituents on these dyes are generally methyl and/or 2-hydroxyethyl.

There is little in the published literature on the separation of these dyes. Newberger[9] has described a method for the extraction and quantitative determination of 2-nitro-*p*-phenylenediamine by spectroscopy. This dye is also widely used in permanent hair color to produce warm brown and auburn shades. Corbett and Fooks[10] reported that whereas they found 2-nitro-*p*-phenylenediamine and 4-nitro-*o*-phenylenediamine difficult to separate by PC, they were able to separate five isomeric nitrophenylenediamines quickly and clearly by electrophoresis on paper using 1% aqueous acetic acid as the electrolyte.

NHR'

NO$_2$

NR^{2}R^3

(1)

Most workers with whom I have talked confirm that although there is still a paucity of published methods, the nitro dyes are most readily separated by TLC methods. In one recently completed study,[11] the TLC behavior of the series of nitro dyes represented by formulas (1), where the substituents were the same or different and chosen from H, Me, or 2-hydroxyethyl, it was found that, except for isomeric pairs, all the compounds were separable using Quantagram LQD® silica gel plates (Quantum Industries, Fairfield, N.J.) developed to 5 cm with methanol–methylene chloride (5:95) and twice to 17 cm with methanol–isopropanol–methylene chloride (3:2:95). In fact, it was found that the presence of a methyl substituent in compound (1) increased the R_F by 0.04, whereas the presence of an hydroxyethyl substituent decreased the R_F by 0.17. From Table 18.3 it can be seen that the effects are additive for the polysubstituted compounds for which $R_F = 0.70 + 0.04x - 0.17y$ (± 0.05), where x is the number of *N*-methyl groups and y is the number of 2-hydroxyethyl groups. Although isomeric pairs are not separated well by this technique, they are usually distinguished by the color of the spot. Further studies along these lines will probably lead to excellent methods for the chromatographic analysis of semipermanent hair color products.

3.3 Permanent Dyes

Most of the published literature on the analysis of hair dyes pertains to the chromatographic separation of the intermediates employed in permanent hair dyeing. The materials commonly empoyed in the United States are listed in Table 18.1. Many of the lists in published methods of analysis of hair dyes contain a wider variety of materials, but it is probable that many of these would not normally be encountered in commercial hair colorants.

Table 18.3   Chromatographic and Spectral Data for Some
2-Nitro-p-phenylenediamines

Compound (1)[a]					λ_{max}
R^1	R^2	R^3	R$_F$ value[b]	Color of spot	(95% ethanol)
Me	Me	Me	0.81	Orange	502
Me	Me	H	0.80	Purple	519
H	Me	Me	0.78	Yellow	478
H	Me	H	0.76	Orange	492
Me	H	H	0.75	Red	497
H	H	H	0.70	Yellow	471
Me	he	Me	0.68	Red	525
he	Me	Me	0.63	Orange	501
H	Me	he	0.60	Red-brown	500
he	Me	H	0.59	Red	516.5
Me	he	H	0.58	Purple	515
he	H	H	0.48	Red	495.5
H	he	H	0.47	Red	490
Me	he	he	0.42	Violet	535
he	Me	he	0.38	Purple	524
H	he	he	0.33	Red-brown	509
he	H	he	0.28	Red	513
he	he	he	0.16	Purple	532.5

[a] Me = methyl; he = 2-hydroxyethyl.
[b] For solvent system, see text.

Because of the susceptibility of oxidation dyes to oxidation by air, it has been recommended that sodium sulfite or sodium bisulfite be added to the sample[12–14] or to the eluent[15] if optimum separation and spot size are to be achieved. Oxidation is also slowed down by the use of acidic solvents; it is noteworthy that the solvents recommended for PC or for TLC on silica gel plates (Table 18.4) are generally acidic or neutral.

In view of the number of dyes involved, it is not surprising that none of the systems reported in six papers on PC and 13 papers on TLC give entirely satisfactory results. The problem is further complicated by the presence of surfactants in the commercial preparations. To overcome this, Cavallaro and Rossi[12] recommend adjusting the pH of the hair dye to 4 and extracting the dye intermediates with ether, chloroform, or benzene. Pinter and

Table 18.4   Solvents for Permanent Dyes

Solvent System	Ratio	Ref.
For PC		
1. BuOH–conc. HCl–H_2O	7:2:4 (upper phase)	16, 17, 18
2. BuOH–AcOH–H_2O	4:1:5	19, 20, 21
3. n-BuOH–EtOH–H_2O–AcOH–Na_2SO_3	50:10:40:1:1	15
4. BuOH–EtOH–H_2O	4:1:5	19, 22
For TLC on silica gel G		
5. $CHCl_3$–C_6H_6–BuOH–AcOH	40:10:7:1	12
6. BuOH–EtOH–H_2O–AcOH	50:10:40:1	12, 23
7. $CHCl_3$–polyglycol–AcOH–H_2O	60:20:5:25	12
8. BuOH–glycol–AcOH–H_2O	10:2:1:10	12
9. MeOH–C_6H_6	35:65	24
10. $CHCl_3$–EtOH	10:1	14
11. i-PrOH–Me_2CO–i-Pr_2O	1:1:10	14
12. Et_2O–MeCOMe	98:2	6
13. Et_2O–MeCOMe	98:5	6
14. MeOH–AcOH–Et_2O	10:2:88	6
15. $CHCl_3$–AcOH	8:2	6
16. $CHCl_3$–AcOH–H_2O	50:45:5	25
17. $CHCl_3$–EtOAc–MeOH–AcOH	30:50:20:1	25
18. C_6H_6–C_6H_{12}–MeOH	85:10:5	25
19. BuOH–HOAc–Et_2O	10:10:80	13
20. Me_2CO–Et_2O	2:98	13
21. EtOAc satd. with 1:1 C_6H_6–H_2O	—	13

Kramer[5] suggest saturating the commercial preparation with sodium chloride and extracting with ethyl acetate. In the case of emulsion products, freezing followed by extraction with dilute acetic acid has been suggested.[23] Oleate soaps can be removed by filtration after acidification of the product with hydrochloric acid–sodium chloride.[19] Turi[26] has suggested a selective extraction procedure: the hair coloring preparation is acidified, boiled, and saturated with sodium chloride; the filtered solution is then extracted with ether (to separate the polyhydric phenols), made alkaline and again extracted with ether (to separate the amines and nitroamines), then adjusted to pH 7 and again extracted with ether (to separate the aminophenols and nitroaminophenols). A similar procedure is given by Deshusses and Desbaumes[18] for separation and identification of the amine components of hair dyes. Even after such a separation they found it necessary to prepare four chromatograms and different visualizing agents to distinguish the 14 amines studied.

Shupe[27] has described a number of selective extraction procedures for the preliminary separation of hair dye ingredients. Thus mixtures of diamines and aminophenols may be separated by rendering the solution alkaline with sodium hydroxide, adding sodium sulfite, and extracting the diamines into ether. These diamines may be isolated or converted to their diacetyl derivatives before isolation. The solution from which the diamines have been extracted is rendered slightly acid with hydrochloric acid, sodium bicarbonate is added, and the aminophenols are extracted into ethyl acetate. Recoveries of 96–102% for the diamines and 94–98% for the aminophenols are reported. For mixtures containing soap, diamines, aminophenols, and resorcinol, Shupe[27] recommends preliminary removal of the soap by acidification and extraction with chloroform. The soapfree solution is then extracted with ether to separate the resorcinol. The diamines are then extracted with chloroform after rendering the solution alkaline. Finally the remaining solution is neutralized and the aminophenols are extracted. The use of a continuous extractor, rather than a separatory funnel, is recommended in order to minimize oxidation. Shupe[27] further describes the separation of 2,5-diaminotoluene from 2,4-diaminoanisole by selective precipitation of the former, from alcoholic solution, as its sparingly soluble sulfate.

Kottermann[17] obtained moderately good separation of 30 dye intermediates using two-dimensional TLC. The two developers were concentrated ammonia–water–50% aqueous hypophosphorous acid–petroleum ether (30–60°)–chloroform–n-butanol in the ratio 20:63:2:50:250:25 (lower layer) and chloroform–ethyl acetate–ethanol–acetic acid in the ratio 350:100:60:20. The procedure required 8–10 hours and gave a good separation of most of the major hair dye intermediates. A similar two-dimensional procedure has been described by Turi.[19]

Goldstein et al.[6] have made an extensive study of single-dimension TLC for the separation of 28 hair dye intermediates, and give details for 17 solvent systems on silica gel G, five on alumina, four on cellulose, four on cellulose impregnated with formamide, five on cellulose impregnated with Dow Corning 555 Fluid–phenylmethylpolysiloxane, and one each on cellulose and on kieselguhr G, each impregnated with Carbowax 1000. In general, better results were obtained using silica gel G and Solvents 12–15 of Table 18.4. They give details of the best chromatographic system for the separation of each of the 28 compounds from the others. These results are summarized in Table 18.5.

Table 18.5   Recommended Separations for Related Compounds[13]

Compounds	Recommended Separation
p-Phenylene- and toluylenediamines	Chloroform on alumina
Phenylenediamines (o, m, p)	Solvent 19[a] on silica gel
Toluenediamines (o, m, p)	Solvent 21[a] on cellulose[b]
Aminophenols	Solvent 20[a] on silica gel
Nitrophenylenediamines	$Me_2CO-HOAc-CHCl_3$ (1:2:7) on silica gel
Nitroaminophenols	$MeOH-CHCl_3$ (5:95) on alumina

[a] From Table 18.4.
[b] Satd. with formamide.

Ortega[28] has examined the electrophoretic behavior of phenylenediamines and aminophenols using a variety of buffer systems, and has described the optimum conditions for the detection of the presence of p-phenylenediamine in hair dyes. This is of particular importance in those countries where p-phenylenediamine is not permitted in hair dyes. It has also been reported[22,29,30,31] that the presence of p-phenylenediamine, as opposed to p-toluenediamine, in hair colorants car be detected by use of a spot test in which a spot of the colorant on a filter paper is treated with an acidified solution of vanillin in isopropanol. p-Phenylenediamine is shown by the formation of a red ring and p-toluenediamine by a yellow ring. In this test, 4,4'-diaminodiphenylamine gives a violet-brown ring.[30]

Seguin[21] has described details for the examination of permanent hair dyes, with particular reference to the quantitative determination of aminophenols, toluenediamines, resorcinol, pyrogallol, and diaminophenols, all of which are permitted only up to a certain maximum percentage under French law. Other quantitative methods described in the literature[5,16,24,32,33] generally involve chromatographic separation of the ingredients, followed by extraction of the spots and spectrophotometric determination. Few claim an accuracy better than 10%. It thus seems likely that these tedious methods offer no better accuracy than comparison of the color developed in situ with that of a suitable series of concurrently run standards.

The somewhat tedious titrimetric method for analysis of hair dyes using p-benzoquinone dichlorimide, described by Shupe,[33] does not appear to have found acceptance.

Since most of the intermediates in permanent hair colorants are colorless, it is necessary to use spray reagents to locate the spots. The most versatile reagent is p-dimethylaminobenzaldehyde which, under acidic conditions, forms colored anils with the amine constituents. These are generally red with p-diamines, orange with m-diamines, and yellow with aminophenols. Also useful is a solution of diazotized p-nitroaniline, which couples with most of the intermediates to give azo dyes.[35] Sodium 1,2-naphthoquinone-4-sulfonate in acetic acid also gives colors with most intermediates.[15] Ammoniacal silver nitrate is reduced by many of the intermediates to give gray-black silver spots.[6,15] Smyth and McKeown[15] give the times for these spots to develop (Table 18.6, column D); in general the easily oxidized intermediates ($para$ and $ortho$) develop within 5 seconds, whereas the remainder take 5–30 minutes to develop. Goldstein et al.[6] recommended the use of a solution of sucrose in hydrochloric acid as specific for resorcinol, with which it gives a red color. Other sprays reported in the literature include ferric chloride,[35] dilute nitrous acid followed by 1-naphthol-4-sulfonic acid (for amines),[18] and Griebel's reagent[35] (vanillin in acidic isopropanol).[18,30] Because of the carcinogenicity of benzidine, the use of tetrazotized benzidine[17] should not be considered.

Finally, mention should be made of some methods for detecting specific ingredients in hair colorants. Tanase et al.[36] describe a method for determining o-phenylenediamine based on its reaction with benzil to give diphenylquinoxaline. When oxidized with ferric chloride, in the presence of acidic sodium sulfide, p-phenylenediamine gives Lauth's violet, which can be determined by its absorption at 620 nm.[37] o-Phenylenediamine and p-aminophenol are reported not to interfere. p-Aminophenol can be determined by indophenol formation on reaction with o-cresol in alkali in the presence of air.[38] Joiner[39] has described a method for determination of pyrogallol.

Newburger and Jones[40] have described a method for the determination of resorcinol in hair dyes involving selective extraction by the method of Shupe[27] and quantitation by UV spectroscopy ($\lambda = 273$ nm) in 0.1 M hydrochloric acid. These authors[41] also describe a spectrophotometric method for analysis of mixtures of p-phenylenediamine and 2,5-diaminotoluene by conversion to the diacetyl derivatives and measuring the absorbance at 250 and 270 nm.

4 QUALITY CONTROL

Thus far we have considered the assay of raw materials and the analysis of unknown dye compositions. Of equal importance to the manufacturer is quality-control analysis to ensure batch to batch reproducibility of shades. Quantitative analysis of intermediates in hair dye compositions is, as indicated in the preceding section, extremely difficult. For this reason it is

Table 18.6   Color-Developing Reagents Useful for Detecting Hair Dye Ingredients on Chromatograms

Ingredient	Reagents[a]			
	A	*B*	*C*	*D*
p-Phenylenediamine	R	R–P	G–Y	5 sec
p-Toluenediamine	R	P	G–Y	5 min
N-Phenyl-*p*-phenylenediamine	B–R	Bl	G–Y	5 sec
m-Phenylenediamine	O–Y	P	R–O	30 min
2,4-Diaminoanisole	O	P	O–Y	5 min
o-Aminophenol	Y	O	Y–O	5 sec
m-Aminophenol	G–Y	P	O–Y	5 min
p-Aminophenol	Y	P	B	5 sec
N-Methyl-*p*-aminophenol	Y	P	Y	5 sec
2,4-Diaminophenol	B–O	Bl–P	B–P	5 sec
Resorcinol	—	—	Y	5 min
Hydroquinone	—	—	—	5 sec
Catechol	—	—	R	5 sec
Pyrogallol	P	P	B–Y	5 sec
1-Naphthol	—	—	O–Y	?
1,5-Naphthalenediol	—	—	R–O	5 sec
2-Nitro-*p*-phenylenediamine	O	P	B–O	5 sec
4-Nitro-*o*-phenylenediamine	B–Y	B	Y	5 sec
2-Amino-4-nitrophenol	Y	O	Y	5 sec

[a] *A*   1 % *p*-Dimethylaminobenzaldehyde in 0.1 *M* HCl.
    B   Sodium 1,2-naphthoquinone-4-sulfonate in dilute acetic acid.
    C   Diazotized *p*-nitroaniline.
    D   Ammoniacal silver nitrate.
    Colors: Y = yellow, B = brown, O = orange, R = red, G = green, P = purple, Bl = blue, — = none, ? = not reported.

generally found convenient, for quality-control purposes, to compare a new batch with a standard control batch when determining dye content.

For semipermanent dyes, TLC of the batch alongside a control can give both a qualitative and quantitative (± 5–10%) assessment of the dyes present. Some success has been achieved with densitometric measurements on TLC plates, but the method is not absolute and gives only relative concentrations of the component dyes.

Similar considerations pertain to the examination of permanent hair colorants, where it is necessary to run two or three chromatograms for spraying with various reagents.

In addition to chromatography, quality control of hair colorants usually involves a laboratory dyeing of a swatch of hair, which is then compared with a standard. Obviously, such a technique requires an expert colorist, particularly if correction of a batch by addition of a further quantity of one or more of the color components is to be achieved. An additional problem is to obtain suitable samples of hair. In general, large batches of blended hair are employed to make up the swatches and a new standard must be prepared when a new batch of hair is to be used.

In an attempt to overcome these difficulties, Callison et al.[42] have described an instrumental technique for the evaluation of dyeings. More uniform and reproducible dyeings are attained when a standard tightly woven wool worsted test fabric is used instead of hair swatches. Evaluation of the dyeings is performed by tristimulus colorimetry. The authors point out that it is still necessary to produce new standard dyeings from time to time, owing to the spontaneous fading which occurs with both oxidation and semipermanent hair dyes. Storage of the standard at 0% relative humidity would undoubtedly increase its useful life.[43]

REFERENCES

1. *CSD* V.
2. R. Charle and G. Sag, *Manufacturing Chemist and Aerosol News*, **33** (1967).
3. F. Willeboordse, Q. Quick, and E. T. Bishop, *Anal. Chem.*, **40**, 1455 (1968).
4. W. H. Bryan, *Anal. Chem.*, **36**, 2025 (1964).
5. I. Pinter and M. Kramer, *Parfuem. Kosmet.*, **48**, 126 (1967).
6. S. Goldstein, A. A. Kopf, and R. Feinland, *Proc. Joint Conf. Cosmetic Sci.*, Toilet Goods Assoc., Washington, D.C., 1968, p. 19.
7. J. F. Corbett, *Anal. Chem.*, **47**, 308 (1975).
8. E. Konrad, *Parfuem. Kosmet.*, **48**, 32 (1967).
9. S. H. Newburger, *J. Assoc. Off. Agr. Chem.*, **37**, 519 (1954).
10. J. F. Corbett and A. G. Fooks, *J. Soc. Cosmetic Chem.*, **18**, 693 (1967).
11. J. F. Corbett and U. Caterbone, unpublished work.
12. A. Cavallaro and G. Rossi, *Boll. Chim. Farm.*, **109**, 25 (1970).
13. A. Cavallaro and G. Elli, *Boll. Chim. Farm.*, **109**, 427 (1970).
14. M. Nanjo, E. Isohata, S. Kano, and A. Kobayashi, *Eisei Shikenjo Hokoku*, **85**, 90 (1967).
15. R. B. Smyth and G. C. McKeown, *J. Chromatogr.*, **16**, 454 (1964).
16. I. Pinter and M. Kramer, *Elelmiszeruissgalati Kozlemeny*, **11**, 305 (1965); *Parfuem. Kosmet.*, **46**, 61 (1965).

17. C. M. Kottemann, *J. Assoc. Off. Anal. Chem.*, **49**, 954 (1966).

18. J. Deshusses and P. Desbaumes, *Mitt. Gebreite Lebensmittelunterschum*, **49**, 335 (1958).

19. C. J. Turi, *Rend. ist. Super. Sanild*, **21**, 748 (1958).

20. C. J. Turi, *Ann. Chim.*, **49**, 459 (1959).

21. L. Seguin, *Am. Fals. Exp. Chim.*, **59**, 265 (1966).

22. T. Brouwer, *Chem. Weekblad*, **55**, 325 (1959).

23. K. Zelazna and B. Legatowa, *Rocz. Panstw Zakl. Hig.*, **22**, 427 (1971).

24. I. Pinter and M. Kramer, *Elelmiszeruissgalati Kozlem*, **12**, 193 (1966).

25. J. Vigek, R. Floriani, and C. Berner, *Mitt. Gebriete Lebensmittelunterschum*, **59**, 107 (1968).

26. C. J. Turi, *Rend. ist. Super. Sanild.*, **20**, 570 (1957).

27. I. S. Shupe, *J. Assoc. Off. Agr. Chem.*, **24**, 871 (1941).

28. M. Ortega, *Anales Real Acad. Farm.*, **28**, 99 (1962).

29. F. W. Lange, *Siefen-Ole-Fette-Wachse*, **92**, 751 (1966).

30. S. Fregert, *Hautarzt*, **23**, 393 (1972).

31. C. Griebel, *Apoth. Zig.*, **45**, 318 (1930).

32. I. Pinter and M. Kramer, *Parfum. Cosmet. Savons*, **10**, 257 (1967).

33. B. Legatowa, *Rocz. Panstw. Zakl. Hig.*, **24**, 393 (1973).

34. I. S. Shupe, *J. Assoc. Off. Agr. Chem.*, **23**, 747 (1940); **26**, 116 (1943).

35. R. Gwiazda and A. Pobudejska-Piotrowska, *Rotz. Panstw. Zakl. Hig.*, **20**, 427 (1969).

36. Y. Tanase, S. Shimomura, A. Kise, and Y. Masuda, *Tokushima Daigaku Yakugaku Kenkyu Nempo*, **15**, 15 (1966).

37. Y. Tanase, S. Shimomura, A. Kise, and A. Ishihara, *Tokushima Daigaku Yakugaku Kenkyu Nempo*, **15**, 19 (1966).

38. Y. Tanase, S. Shimomura, A. Kise, and S. Suga, *Tokushima Daigaku Yakugaku Kenkyu Nempo*, **15**, 23 (1966).

39. C. R. Joiner, *J. Assoc. Off. Agr. Chem.*, **30**, 512 (1947).

40. S. H. Newburger and J. H. Jones, *J. Assoc. Off. Agr. Chem.*, **34**, 787 (1951).

41. *Ibid.*, **33**, 374 (1950).

42. J. Callison, C. Schmidt, R. Piel, S. Grant, and W. Holland, *J. Soc. Cosmetic Chemists*, **13**, 449 (1962).

43. J. F. Corbett, *J. Soc. Cosmetic Chem.*, **24**, 103 (1973).

CHAPTER NINETEEN

Quantitative Analysis

ERIK KISSA

1 QUANTITATIVE METHODS FOR DYE ANALYSES

1.1 Introduction

Quantitative analyses of dyes are of theoretical and practical significance. In research, quantitative analyses of dyes, dye solutions, or dispersions and dyed fabrics are useful for evaluating new dyes, developing dyeing processes, and studying dye fastness or mechanisms of dyeing. For dyeing studies it is often more convenient to use an analyzed commercial dye than to work with the pure active ingredient. If a dye is hygroscopic, e.g., by forming a hydrate, it is preferable to work with the hydrated dye and use analyses to make corrections.

In dye manufacture, analyses are required to control the dye concentration in a commercial product at the desired level. In the dyeing industry, quantitative analyses are valuable for quality control, especially in automated dyeing processes.

Successful development of efficient dyeing and printing processes requires a quantitative knowledge of dye utilization and a thorough understanding of the mechanisms involved. During a dyeing process a dye is adsorbed on and in the fiber, or is unutilized; in exhaust dyeing a fraction of the dye remains in the dyebath. Studies of dyeing processes are more meaningful when each of these quantities is measured.

Dyes in *solid samples* and in *solutions* are usually determined by spectrophotometric methods (see Chapter 6), although other physical methods and elemental and functional group analyses are useful and may be needed, e.g., with reactive dyes, to complement spectral data.

The *dye content of dyed fibers* is usually determined by spectrophotometric methods using reflected light or transmitted light. Determination of dyes by X-ray fluorescence has also been suggested.[1]

Although measurement of the reflectance spectrum is of great importance in color matching and production control, the determination of dye content in fiber by reflected light is complicated. The reflectance of dyed fabric or yarn is not solely a function of dye concentration, but depends also on the distribution and physical state of the dye in the fiber, e.g., aggregation and dye–fiber interactions. Therefore, reflectance data can be used to estimate the dye content only when these factors are considered.

Conversely, the relationship between the absorption of reflected light and the dye content of the fiber indicates the tinctorial efficacy of the dye in the dyed fabric and/or the efficiency of the dyeing process. Therefore, for complete evaluation of a dye or a dyeing process, reflectance data are needed as well as the actual dye concentration in the fiber.

To determine dye content in a fiber by transmitted light, the dye has to be dissolved in a suitable solvent, either by dissolving both fiber and dye, or by extracting the dye from the fiber. Both methods are used extensively, because both have advantages and disadvantages. The choice between the two methods depends on the dye, the fiber, and the availability of a suitable solvent for dissolution or extraction.

Analytical methods can be used for quantitative estimation of *dye fastness* and to study mechanisms involved in dye fading, migration, etc. For example, the dye content of fibers has been determined as a function of exposure time in kinetic studies of dye lightfastness.[2] Since dye molecules near the fiber surface fade before those in the interior of the fiber and aggregation effects are possible, the fraction of the dye faded cannot be estimated quantitatively from the visible effect or reflectance data. For the same reasons, measuring dye fading in transparent films by transmitted light is not adequate; the dye content should be determined by dissolving the fibers or extracting the dye from the fibers.

Dye analyses have been used in studies of dye migration into finishes and in laminates.[3–5]

Methods for quantitative analyses of dyes and dyed fibers have been reviewed by several authors.[6–12]

1.2 Solid and Liquid Dyes

Most commercial dyes are not sold in a pure form, but are diluted with adjuvants such as salts, sugar, dextrin, urea, boric acid, dispersants, or wetting agents. The dye content ("active ingredient") of commercial dyes, dye crudes, laboratory preparations, etc. can be determined by dissolving a sample of the dye and comparing its absorptivity to that of the pure dye. By using either the Beer-Lambert law (if applicable) or a calibration curve, the dye content of the product can be calculated. Effects of variables such as the solvent, ionic strength, pH, and temperature have to be controlled. Complications due to photochemical or nonphotolytic fading, photochromism, complex formation, micelles of surfactants, fluorescence, turbidity, adsorption on glass surfaces, etc., must be avoided or minimized.[11] The success of the analysis depends on the sampling procedure. Sampling techniques, as described in analytical literature,[13] are essential for obtaining a representative sample. Some dyes are hygroscopic and attention should be paid to the water content of the dye sample. Procedures for measuring the absorptivity of the dissolved dye are discussed in more detail in Chapter 6.

When commercial dyes are used in studies of dyeing processes and mechanisms, it is convenient to base calculations on the absorptivity of the commercial dye, instead of using the absorptivity value of the pure dye, which sometimes may not even be known accurately. Dyeing studies usually involve determination of the amounts of dye remaining in the dyebath or pad-bath, adsorbed on the fiber surface and sorbed in the fiber. The analytical scheme is greatly simplified by using a solvent that is suitable for all analyses to be performed. For example, both chlorobenzene and stabilized DMF are effective extractants for disperse dyes in polyester fiber.[14] However, DMF is a much more useful solvent since it is miscible with water and dissolves dye diluents and dyeing adjuvants insoluble in chlorobenzene. Determination of absorptivity of commercial dyes is possible with DMF, at least after adding a small amount of water, but difficult or impossible with chlorobenzene. DMF can be used to determine dye fixation in continuous dyeing, but chlorobenzene does not dissolve or penetrate water-soluble gums and pad-bath adjuvants on the surface and does not, therefore, extract the unfixed surface dye at ambient temperatures. When an exhaust dyebath is sampled, DMF can be added to the dyebath to dissolve water-insoluble adjuvants, but chlorobenzene is not miscible with an aqueous dyebath.

Some water-insoluble dyes are used in the form of aqueous dispersions (*pastes*). The paste should be thoroughly stirred before sampling to make sure that a representative sample is obtained. The sample should be weighed in a closed vessel to prevent evaporation of water. The solvent used for diluting the sample should be miscible with water.

Liquid dyes, which are dye solutions or dispersions, can be analyzed after dilution with a solvent miscible with the solvents in the liquid dye.

Although spectrophotometric methods are usually the most convenient, they relate absorptivity of the sample to a standard. They can therefore be used for absolute quantitative analyses only when the absorptivity of the pure dye is known. Otherwise, other chemical or physical methods have to be used. Classical chemical methods have included (see *CSD* II, p. 1345 and ref. 6) (*a*) reduction with titanous chloride; (*b*) oxidation with ceric sulfate or potassium dichromate in acid medium; and (*c*) precipitation or titration of anionic or cationic dyes with a cationic or anionic compound, respectively.

The dye absorptivity is not always a valid indication of dye purity. For example, spectrophotometric analyses cannot distinguish between the fiber-reactive dye and the unreactive hydrolyzed dye. Analyses to determine the reactive functional group are necessary to determine the purity of fiber-reactive dyes.

1.3   Dye Content of Dyebaths and Pad-Baths

The determination of water-soluble dyes in an aqueous dyebath poses no problems as long as variables affecting dye absorptivity (e.g., pH, ionic strength) are controlled. When the dyebath contains water-insoluble dyes and/or water-insoluble dyeing adjuvants, a water-miscible solvent, such as acetone, methanol, pyridine or DMF, has to be added to the dyebath to obtain a homogeneous sample.

The dye content of a dyebath is customarily determined as a measure of dye exhaustion from the bath to the fiber. This is not an entirely satisfactory procedure, since the decrease of dye concentration is not solely a function of dye sorption in the fiber. Some dye may be deposited on the fiber surface and some dye may be lost owing to hydrolysis or degradation by heat in the dyebath. The amount of dye lost owing to hydrolysis in the dyebath cannot be accurately determined by measuring the dye content of a control dyebath heated the same way, but without yarn or fabric fiber. The dye sorbed in the fiber is less vulnerable to hydrolysis or decomposition than the dye in the bath. Thus the loss of dye in a control dyebath without the fiber is usually larger than that observed in a normal dyeing.

Instruments have been designed for continuous and automatic recording of dye concentration in dyebaths.

1.4   Dye on the Fiber Surface

The amount of dye deposited on a fiber surface is determined by extracting the dyed fibers with a solvent that dissolves the dye, but does not swell the fiber to the extent that the dye sorbed *in* the fiber becomes extractable. The surface dye is determined to estimate the amount of dye absorbed on the fiber surface during exhaust dyeing, to measure dye migration from the fiber into the finish layer on the fiber surface, to determine dye fixation in continuous dyeing operations, etc.

Dye fixation is best determined by extracting the unfixed and the fixed dye from the same sample. This eliminates errors caused by unlevelness of the dyeing and uncertainties of the sample weight owing to dyeing adjuvants on the unscoured sample. For example, the unfixed surface dye on polyester fiber can be extracted from an unscoured dyeing with stabilized DMF[14] at room temperature for 3 minutes. The extraction is repeated until the extract (usually the second one) is colorless. The same sample is extracted at 140° with stabilized DMF to determine the dye *in* the fiber. The dye contents of the extracts are measured spectrophotometrically.

If the unscoured fabric contains considerable amounts of dye dispersants or pad-bath thickeners (gums), addition of water (10% by vol.) to the extractant facilitates the removal of the surface dye occluded in water-soluble dyeing adjuvants. This also suppresses light scattering and aggregation. In order to keep the dye absorptivity constant, the same amount of water is also added to the extract containing the fixed dye and to the reference solution (extract of undyed fibers).

1.5   Determination of Dye in Fiber by Reflected Light

Quantitative analyses of dyes in fibers by reflected light is rapid, nondestructive, and similar in principle to visual estimation. However, interpretation of reflectance data in quantitative terms is complicated because a simple linear relationship does not exist between reflectance and dye concentration. This difficulty has been overcome to a large extent by using eomputers, and reflectance methods have proved useful in routine industrial production control, color matching,[15,16] and automated process controller systems.[17−19]

The experimental procedures for reflectance measurements have been described in AATCC reports[20,21] and in a monograph.[11] Fabric samples must be folded until one more fold does not cause a change of reflectance. Each sample is measured in four different areas using magnesium oxide, barium sulfate, or white tile as the reference standard. Staple or raw stock is formed into a pad with cards or a webber. Yarn is wound from the original package on to a metal card.

The theory of color measurement by reflected light has been thoroughly discussed in several monographs.[11,22–26]

Several equations have been proposed to relate the reflectance of a dyed fabric to the concentration of dye in the fiber.[11] The equation of Kubelka and Munk,[27] which is widely used in color measurement, relates reflectance to absorption and scattering. Since the relationship between reflectance values and the amount of dye in the fiber depends on dye distribution, which is usually undefined, variations and modifications of the Kubelka–Munk equation have been of little help. The limitations of reflectance methods in computer color matching have been reviewed by Brockes,[28] who concluded that the accuracy is most severely affected by differing dyeing conditions and textile substrates. Most factors related to optical theories are much less significant.

Stearns[11] has noted that the accuracy of determination of dye in solution by transmitted light is twice that obtained for determination of dye concentration on fiber by reflected light. This is based on the accuracy of the spectrophotometric measurement only. In addition, measurement of dye in solutions or extracts of the fibers is not complicated by uniformity of dye distribution in the fibers. Therefore, reflectance methods are useful mainly for measurement of *color* and comparison of color differences, whereas the *amount of dye* in the fibers is best determined by transferring the dye from the fiber into a solvent.

1.6 Determination of Dye in Fiber by Dissolution Methods

Dyes in polymeric substances such as films or textile fibers are usually determined spectrophotometrically by either (*a*) dissolving the dye-containing polymer in a solvent for both the dye and the polymer, or (*b*) extracting the dye from the polymer with a solvent which dissolves the dye but not the polymer. The dissolution method is applicable also to dyes that cannot be extracted from the fiber, e.g., covalently bonded reactive dyes, and is relatively simple, when a suitable solvent for dissolving the dyed fibers can be found.

Ideally, a solvent for dyed fibers should (*a*) dissolve the fibers without heating, because some dyes may decompose in a hot solvent. If it is necessary to heat the solvent to accelerate fiber dissolution, it may be preferable to extract the dye from the fiber instead of dissolving the fiber. Decomposition of the dye being extracted can be minimized by extracting the fiber repeatedly with small portions of hot solvent and keeping the extraction time short, e.g., 2–3 minutes. The extracts can be cooled immediately, so that the dye solution is heated only for a very short time. It usually takes a longer time to dissolve a sample of dyed fiber, and the risk of dye decomposition is therefore greater when the fibers are dissolved in a hot solvent. The solvent should (b) dissolve the dye. Usually the dye is soluble in the solvent that dissolves the fiber because the dye and fiber are compatible, with notable exceptions. Dyes that undergo chemical reactions during dyeing, e.g., vat dyes, may be insoluble in solvents used to dissolve the fiber. Insoluble dyes are sometimes determined as dispersions in the solvent used to dissolve the dyed fibers. Moreover, the solvent should (c) be colorless and form a colorless solution with undyed fiber; (d) form stable dye solutions and not react with the dye; (e) be stable, nonhygroscopic, and commercially available in a degree of purity adequate for dye analyses without purification; (f) have low volatility for convenient handling; and (g) be nontoxic, noncorrosive, and nonflammable.

Unfortunately, solvents that meet all these requirements are rare. Many solvents used for dissolving fibers do not meet one or more of the requirements listed, and most of the solvents used are toxic (see Section 1.9).

To find a solvent that can dissolve the fiber, the solubility parameter, which is defined as the square root of the cohesive energy density, can serve as a useful guide.[29] According to the solubility parameter concept, a fiber is soluble in solvents whose solubility parameters are similar to that of the fiber-forming polymer, assuming that the polarity of the solvent and polymer are similar. An amorphous polymer and a solvent that dissolves the polymer are miscible in all proportions. Extensively cross-linked or highly crystalline polymers do not dissolve, but may only swell. Many synthetic fibers have a high degree of crystallinity and do not dissolve unless heated to break the forces between the polymer chains.

The most frequently used solvents for dissolving dyed fibers are listed in Table 19.1.

The procedure for dissolving dyed fiber is usually quite simple once a suitable solvent is found. A weighed sample (usually 0.1–0.3 g) is placed into a volumetric flask (25–100 ml) and covered with the solvent (about $\frac{2}{3}$ the final volume). The fibers are allowed to dissolve with occasional shaking and the volume adjusted to the marked volume with the solvent. An undyed sample or, better, a "mock dyed" sample, in an amount equal to the dyed sample, is dissolved and its solution used as the reference solution (blank).

The dissolution method has the disadvantage that the dye solution is turbid when the fiber contains a delustering agent. The delustering agent, e.g., TiO_2, can be removed by centrifugation or by precipitation.[30] However, Kissa[31] has shown that a high degree of accuracy and reproducibility can be achieved without separating the delustering agent when a solution of the same quantity of undyed ("mock dyed") fiber is used in the reference beam of a double beam spectrophotometer.

Table 19.1   Solvents Used in Quantitative Analyses of Dyed Fibers

Solvent	Acrylic	Aramid	Cellulose	Cellulose diacetate	Cellulose triacetate	Nylon	Polyester	Polyethylene	Polyvinyl chloride	Polyvinylidene chloride	Wool
Acetone				S							
Cadoxen			S	S							S
γ-Butyrolactone	S			S							
Chlorobenzene						E	E				
Chloroform						S	E				
o-Chlorophenol			E	S	S	S	S				E
m-Cresol					S	S	S				
Cyclohexanol								S			
N,N-Dimethylacetamide (DMAC)	S	S	E	S	S	E	E				
DMF	S		E	S	E	E	E				
DMSO	S	S		S	S						
Dioxane				S						S	
Formic acid	E			S	S	S					
1,1,1,3,3,3-Hexafluoropropanol						S	S				
Methylene chloride						S	E				
Phenol						S	S				
Pyridine				E*			E*				E*
				E			E				
Sodium hydroxide, aq.											S
Sulfuric acid, conc.	S		S								
Trichloroethylene					E						
TFA							S				
Toluene or xylene									S		

a Code: E, extraction method; S, dissolution method; *, aqueous pyridine.

1.7   Determination of Dye in Fiber by Extraction Methods

The extraction method is applicable to nonionic and ionically bonded dyes soluble in the extractant. Covalently bonded reactive dyes cannot be extracted from the fiber, and their resistance to extraction has been used as evidence of a covalent dye–fiber bond. The dye extraction can be combined with a chemical reaction to convert the dye into a soluble form.

Requirements for the solvent to be used as the extractant are the same as for the solvents used for dissolving the fiber in the dissolution method, except that the extractant swells the fibers but does not dissolve them (Table 19.1). The extractant should not dissolve or disintegrate the fibers even partially, because the fragments of the fiber cause turbidity and interfere with the spectrophotometric determination of the dye in the extract.

Extraction of a dye from a polymer is the reversal of the dyeing process; it is a desorption process of a nonionic dye from a polyester or polyamide fiber. The diffusion of the dye from its location in the fiber to the solvent in contact with the fiber is facilitated by the mobility of polymer chains. The chain mobility can be increased by (a) thermal energy and/or (b) a solvent which swells and plasticizes the fiber. The efficiency of an extraction solvent depends on (a) the diffusion rate of the extractant into the fiber and swelling of the fiber by the extractant, (b) the partition ratio of the dye between the solvent and the polymer swollen or in contact with the solvent, and (c) the diffusion rates of the dye in the polymer and in the solvent. The ability of a solvent to swell the polymer, which is a prerequisite for effective dye extraction, is indicated by the solubility parameter of the solvent. According to the cohesive energy density concept, maximum swelling occurs when the solubility parameters of the polymer and the solvent are equal. The solubility parameter is also an approximate indication of the ability of a solvent to dissolve dyes. It has been estimated[32] that the solubility parameters of most disperse dyes are within ± 1.4 hildebrands of that (10.7) of poly(ethylene terephthalate) (PET). Consequently, solvents that have a solubility parameter in the 9–12 range should swell polyester and dissolve disperse dyes in the fiber.

The efficacy of some solvents with a solubility parameter in the 9–12 hildebrand region is shown in Table 19.2 by the amounts of nonionic (disperse) dyes extracted in 3 minutes.[14] DMF, N,N-dimethylacetamide (DMAC), pyridine, and chlorobenzene are the most efficient solvents listed.

It is interesting to note that dimethyl o-phthalate, which has a solubility parameter (10.7) equal to that of polyester (PET) fiber, and a somewhat related chemical composition, is the least effective of the solvents listed in

Table 19.2. This suggests that the solubility parameter of the polymer indicates only the range of solubility parameters of solvents where the effective extractants can be found. It appears also that the viscosity and effective cross-section of the solvent are important, because the effective extractants have a relatively small molecular cross-section and a lower viscosity than the ineffective solvents, at least at or near ambient temperatures.

It is well-known that the diffusion rate of a dye in a fiber increases abruptly above the glass-transition temperature T_g of the fiber-forming polymer. The extraction rate increases accordingly with increasing temperature. Figure 19.1 illustrates the extraction of two disperse dyes from two PET dyeings with DMF stabilized with a free radical inhibitor.[14] The temperature of the extractant increases as the extraction flasks are heated in a 140° bath. The extraction from the fabric becomes rapid as the temperature of the extractant rises above 90–100°.

Table 19.2 Efficacy of Solvents in Extracting Disperse Dyes from Polyester Fibers[14]

Solvent	Solubility Parameter $(cal^{1/2}/cm^{1/2})$	% Dye Extracted in 3 Minutes at 140° (or in Boiling Solvent)	
		CI Disperse Red 65[a]	CI Disperse Blue 56[b]
Chloroform	9.3	13	71
Chlorobenzene	9.5	98	96
o-Dichlorobenzene	10.0	86	72
Tetraethylene glycol dimethyl ether	10.6	51	
Methoxypolyethylene glycol (Carbowax 350)		51	
Dimethyl o-phthalate	10.7	15	
Pyridine	10.7	99.8	99.2
Dimethylacetamide	10.8	99.0	99.0
DMF	12.1	99.8	99.3
DMF (78 ml) + water (20 ml) + phosphoric acid (2 ml)		64	83
Acetic acid	12.6	74	73

[a] Dyed by the Du Pont Thermosol process (1.9% owf dye).

[b] Exhaust dyed with a carrier (1.0% owf dye).

Courtesy *Textile Research Journal*.

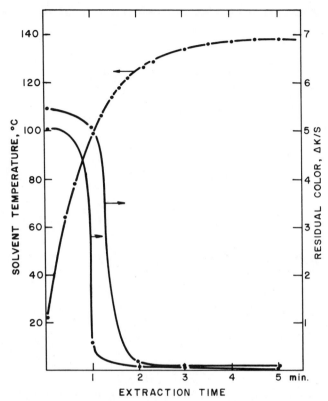

Figure 19.1   Residual color ($\triangle$ K/S, where K = absorption coefficient and S = scattering coefficient)[27] of extracted polyester fabric and temperature of the extractant (DMF) as a function of extraction time (CI Disperse Blue 56 and 65).[14] Courtesty *Textile Research Journal*.

Dyes that are bonded to the fiber by ionic forces, e.g., cationic dyes in copolymer polyester fiber with sulfonate dyesites, cannot be extracted from the fiber with a nonionizing organic solvent, e.g., chlorobenzene. The extractant has to provide a counterion to which the dye ion can be attracted by an ion-exchange reaction. The extractant also has to provide an ion to replace the dye at its ionic site. This is illustrated in Table 19.3 with extraction of a cationic dye from copolymer polyester fiber with various organic solvents.[33] Carboxylic acids which can dissociate to provide a proton and an anion are more effective extractants than the other solvents listed in Table 19.3. However, even with the most powerful extractant in the group, formic acid, the extraction rate is slow and the extraction incomplete.

Kissa[33] has developed a method which effectively extracts cationic dyes from polyester fiber. The method utilizes ion exchange between the dye

Table 19.3   Extraction of a Cationic Dye (0.98% owf CI Basic Blue 3)
With Various Solvents at 140° or at the Boil from Copolymer Polyester[33]

Solvent	% Dye Extracted	Number of Extracts Containing Color	Extraction Temp. (°)
Hexanol	0	0	140
Cyclohexanol	0	0	140
Chlorobenzene	1	2	132
Cyclohexanone	10	3	140
DMF	22	1	140
Pyridine	48	5	116
Acetic acid	63	5	118
Formic acid (91%)	93	5	101

Courtesy *Textile Research Journal*.

cation D^+ held by ionic forces at the dye site and a salt MX or acid HX dissolved in DMF or DMAC to extract the dye from the fiber:

$$\text{Fiber-SO}_3^-\text{D}^+ + \text{MX} \rightleftharpoons \text{Fiber-SO}_3^-\text{M}^+ + \text{DX}$$

The salt or acid can dissociate to solvated ions or form complexes with the solvent. The effectiveness of the acid or salt depends on the extent of dissociation and interaction with the solvent among other factors; strong acids and their salts are most effective.

In comparison with a dissolution method, an extraction method can offer the following advantages: (1) The solvents used for extraction may be less toxic and corrosive than those that dissolve the fiber, e.g., chlorobenzene or DMF as an extractant for disperse dyes in PET, vs. *o*-chlorophenol or 1,1,1,3,3,3-hexafluoro-2-propanol (HFIP) as fiber solvents. (2) The dye extracts are clear and do not contain a delustering agent, in contrast to solutions of dissolved fiber. Correcting for a blank by extracting undyed fiber is nevertheless a good practice, since some fibers contain whitening agents and dye adjuvants which may interfere with the spectrophotometric dye determination. (3) Dye extraction usually requires a high temperature; at room temperature dye extraction is very slow. This makes it convenient to determine the amount of dye on the fiber surface, the "unfixed" dye, by extracting the sample first with cold extractant. This removes only the surface dye and does not extract a significant amount of dye from inside the fiber. (4) In a proper extraction procedure the dye remains in the hot solvent for only a short time. Dissolution of a fiber in a hot solvent requires more time and increases the risk of dye decomposition. (5) The extraction method eliminates degradation of the fiber in some solvents needed to dissolve the fiber (e.g., cotton and wool) and subsequent yellowing of the dye–fiber solution.

1.8 Extraction Techniques

Usually the weighed sample is extracted successively with small amounts of solvent. Dye decomposition in the hot solvent can be minimized by heating the solvent rapidly to the extraction temperature, keeping the extraction time short (2–3 minutes), and cooling the extract immediately with ice. Conventional extraction apparatus does not permit this, and is therefore not suitable for this use. For example, the Soxhlet extractor heats the extract at the boil during the entire extraction involving several cycles, and the dye in the hot extract may decompose. Each cycle requires considerable time and the procedure is therefore relatively slow. It is also difficult to adjust the temperature of the solvent in contact with the fiber. Solvents that are not stable at their boiling point cannot be used in such equipment, and the use of solvent mixtures as the extractant is limited to azeotropic mixtures.

The simplest procedure is to extract the sample once with a large volume of the solvent. The sample and the solvent are placed into a volumetric flask and heated at the extraction temperature, and the extract is diluted to the marked volume after cooling.[34] This procedure eliminates a quantitative transfer of the extract from the extraction flask to the volumetric flask, but has several disadvantages. First, the whole extract has to be heated until extraction is completed; this exposes the entire extract to the danger of dye decomposition if the extraction requires more than 3–4 minutes. Second, it is difficult to follow the progress of extraction by observing the residual color of the sample immersed in the colored extract. Third, partition of the dye between fiber and solvent dictates that a single extraction cannot remove the dye from the fiber as completely as can repeated extractions, although the amount of dye retained may not always be significant.

It is, therefore, better to extract the sample repeatedly with a small amount of extractant until all the dye has been removed from the fiber. A simple apparatus (Figure 19.2) for this purpose has been described by Kissa.[14] About 0.10–0.30 g of dyed fabric or yarn is placed in an Erlenmeyer flask with a spout and covered with 10 ml of the extraction solvent. The flask is loosely stoppered and placed for the specified time (2–3 minutes) into the oil bath heated at 140°. The extract is poured into a 100-ml volumetric flask cooled in ice. The contents of the extraction flask are rinsed once with the solvent squirted from a wash bottle and the washings are collected in

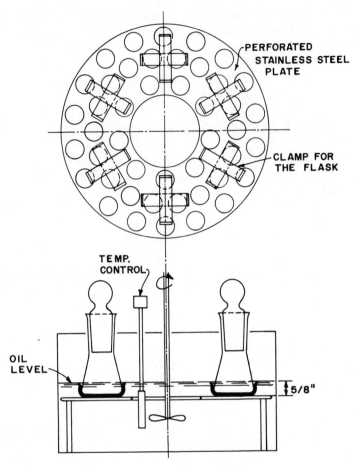

Figure 19.2 Extraction apparatus.[14] Courtesy *Textile Research Journal*.

the same volumetric flask. The extraction is repeated until the sample is colorless. Usually one to three extractions remove all the dye. Two or three extraction flasks can be heated simultaneously by starting the extractions at staggered time intervals.

An elaborate apparatus for dye extraction has been described by Baumgarte (see Chapter 15). This procedure is more complicated and time consuming than the technique described by Kissa,[14] but has the advantage that hot solvent vapors are contained within the apparatus and do not escape during the transfer of the hot extract to the volumetric flask. Although this does not create insurmountable problems when dye extraction is carried out in a hood (as it should be), the option to work in an inert atmosphere (nitrogen) may be helpful for the extraction of air-sensitive dyes, e.g., reduced vat dyes from cotton.

1.9 Safety

The solvents used in dye analyses (Table 19.1) are toxic and/or corrosive,[35] with a few exceptions, e.g., acetone or DMSO. The toxicity of DMSO has been studied recently and found to be relatively low. However, DMSO can penetrate the skin and carry harmful substances into the body. DMF and DMAC are toxic. All workers, especially females of child-bearing age, should avoid contact with these solvents. γ-Butyrolactone, phenol, and o-chlorophenol, applied to the skin of a mouse, have produced tumors. Dioxane and chloroform, administered orally, have produced carcinogenic effects. Cadmium oxide, which is used to prepare cadoxen, has produced cancer in a rat when applied subcutaneously.

Considering the toxicity of most solvents used in dye analyses, it is advisable to work in a well-ventilated hood and avoid any skin contact with the solvents.

2 SPECIAL METHODS FOR DYE IN FIBER ANALYSES

2.1 Dissolution Methods for Acrylic Fibers

Dyes in polyacrylonitrile fibers can be determined conveniently by dissolving the dyed fibers in DMF,[8] DMAC,[31] DMSO[31,36] or γ-butyrolactone,[37] which are good solvents for both fibers and dyes. DMF and DMSO dissolve acrylic fibers quite rapidly, whereas DMAC is considerably slower (Figure 19.3). Dissolution in γ-butyrolactone is very slow (about 12–16 hours) at 25°, but rapid (about 15 minutes) at 100°. Agitation increases the dissolution rate markedly; with constant stirring, less than 10 minutes is needed to dissolve a sample of dyed polyacrylonitrile fabric in DMSO at 25°.

Solutions of cationic dyes in these solvents are not always stable; some dyes, e.g., Malachite Green, fade rapidly in DMF or DMAC. Fading is slower in DMSO or γ-butyrolactone, but nevertheless considerable. Stabilization of cationic dyes in these solvents is therefore a prerequisite for accurate analyses.

Kissa[31] has shown that the solvent acidity is a critical variable determining the absorbance and stability of cationic dyes. Accurate results can be obtained by acidifying the solvents to an apparent pH of 1.4–4.0.

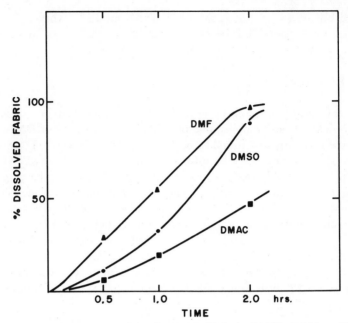

Figure 19.3   Dissolution rates of acrylic (PAN) fabric in DMSO, DMF, or DMAC at 25° (no agitation).[14] Courtesy *Textile Research Journal*.

Cationic dyes consist of a colored organic cation and a colorless anion, inorganic or organic. The fading of cationic dyes in organic solvents is usually caused by (*a*) conversion of the dye to a leuco base or loss of a proton caused by a pH shift, (*b*) nonphotolytic degradation of the dye, or (*c*) photochemical degradation of the dye. Fading of cationic dyes in solvents in the absence of acid is accelerated by traces of water in the solvent.

The effect of acidity of the solvent on dye absorptivity in DMSO is illustrated in Figure 19.4. A similar relationship exists in solutions of acrylic fibers dissolved in DMSO. The absorptivity maximum of Malachite Green, a triarylmethane dye, is at an apparent pH of about 3.2 and drops sharply above pH 6.0. Although some cationic dyes, e.g., Basic Violet 16 and Basic Yellow 11, are less pH sensitive than Malachite Green, their absorptivities are affected considerably by pH changes.

Some of the color changes are caused by photochemical fading. Cationic dyes are more lightfast in DMSO than in DMF containing the same amount of *p*-toluenesulfonic acid or having the same initial pH. The fading of dyes in DMF is accompanied by a marked pH increase caused by photochemical

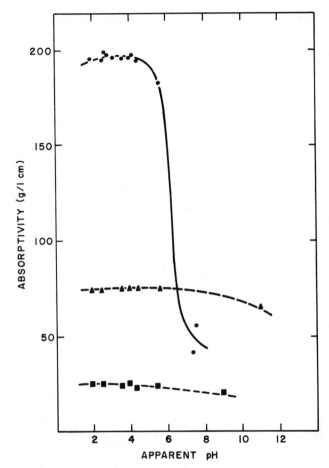

Figure 19.4   Effect of acidity upon absorptivities of of cationic dyes dissolved in DMSO. ● CI Basic Green 4; ▲ CI Basic Violet 16; ■ CI Basic Yellow 11.[31] Courtesy *Textile Research Journal*.

hydrolysis of the solvent. Thus fading of dyes in DMF is not solely a photo-chemical destruction of the dye, but involves also an absorptivity decrease due to a pH shift[31].

In acidified DMSO, DMF, or γ-butyrolactone cationic dyes are adequately stable. No significant decomposition of CI Basic Yellow 11, CI Basic Violet 16, CI Basic Blue 3, or CI Basic Green 4 was observed in 2 days; in 4 days dye decomposition was less than 2% rel.[5] With an anti-

Table 19.4   Accuracy of the Dissolution Methods for the Determination of Cationic Dyes in Acrylic Fiber[33]

Dye (CI Basic)	Calc. (% owf)	Found by the DMSO Method[a] (% owf)	Found by the ZnCl₂/HCl/DMF Method[b] (% Avg.)
Yellow 11	0.79	0.76	0.76
Blue 3	0.80	0.79	0.81
Violet 16	0.80	0.80	0.79
Green 4	0.16	0.16	0.17
Green 4	0.80	0.80	0.82

[a] DMSO acidified to pH 3.0 with p-toluenesulfonic acid.[31]
[b] DMF containing 55 g/l zinc chloride, 0.8% by vol. hydrochloric acid and 20 g/l DBMP.[33] This reagent is used also for extracting cationic dyes from polyester fiber (see 19.2.4.).
Courtesy *Textile Research Journal*

oxidant [5.0 g/l 2,6-di-(t-butyl)-4-methylphenol (DBMP)] no significant dye decomposition occurred in 4 days.

The accuracy of the dissolution methods is shown in Table 19.4 with cationic dyes and DMSO and DMF as the solvents. Similar accuracy can be obtained with γ-butyrolactone containing zinc chloride,[5] if the solvent is not heated excessively, when dissolving dyed fibers.

Disperse dyes in acrylic fibers can also be determined accurately by dissolving the fibers in DMSO[31] or stabilized DMF or DMAC.[14]

The precision of the determination of cationic dyes in acrylic fibers has been examined with acidified DMSO as the solvent.[31] The precision of the absorbance measurement of solutions containing only a dye is excellent (standard deviation 0.0011 absorbance units or 0.18% rel.). The precision is impaired slightly when undyed fiber, in the amount corresponding to the usual sample size, is dissolved in the dye solutions (standard deviation 0.0018 or 0.29% rel.). The slight decrease of precision is apparently caused by light scattering of delustering agents in the fiber, although the solution in the reference beam contained the same amount of dissolved fiber. The precision of the actual determination of a dyed fabric is lower (standard deviation 0.013 absorbance units or 1.6% rel.) than that of solutions containing a measured amount of dye. Since this is caused by fluctuations of the dye concentration in the dyed fabric the precision can be increased by multiple random sampling of the dyed fabric.

2.2 Extraction Methods for Acrylic Fibers

Although acrylic fibers are soluble in several solvents suitable for the dissolution method, dyes in acrylic fiber have also been determined by the extraction method. Mayer[38] extracted cationic dyes from acrylic fibers with 85% formic acid heated to a temperature at which the dyed fibers shrunk. The sample was then rinsed with cold formic acid and the washings and the extract combined and diluted with water. Sand[39] extracted cationic dyes from acrylic fiber with formic acid (85%)–DMF (60:10) at about 100°. Pacifici[34] extracted disperse dyes from acrylic fiber with chlorobenzene–acetic acid (1:1). Carbonell[3] used a mixture of 60 g DMF, 1 g formic acid, 39 g water, and 0.4 g ammonium sulfate. It has been reported that the latter extractant did not extract some cationic dyes completely from "Orlon" 42.[33]

2.3 Extraction Methods for Nonionic Dyes in Polyester Fibers

Disperse (nonionic) dyes have been extracted from polyester fiber with chlorobenzene,[40] pyridine,[41,42] methylene chloride,[43] chloroform,[44] and DMF.[45]

Mixtures of DMF with phosphoric acid (78 ml DMF, 20 ml H_2O, and 2 ml H_3PO_4)[46] and with glycol and formic acid (40 ml DMF, 50 ml ethylene glycol, and 1 ml formic acid)[47] have also been used. Decomposition of some disperse dyes has been reported to occur in both mixtures. However, Kissa[14] has obtained accurate and precise results by extracting dyed fabric or yarn with DMF or DMAC containing a free-radical inhibitor (5–20 g/l DBMP) and a nonvolatile acid (p-toluenesulfonic acid) to lower the apparent pH of the solvent to 4.0. One extraction with this solvent at 140° usually removes more than 90% of the dye in 2–3 minutes. Most dyes are completely removed from the fiber by three extractions. The method is also applicable to quantitative determination of disperse dyes in polyamide, acrylic, and acetate fibers and DMF-soluble nonionic dyes in cellulosic fiber.[14]

DMAC, when stabilized like DMF, is also an effective extractant for nonionic dyes. It has the advantage of being the least volatile of the four effective extractants (DMF, DMAC, pyridine, and chlorobenzene), but is more expensive than DMF. Pyridine appears to be a very effective extraction solvent, but its odor, volatility, and flammability (flash point 23°) limit its practical usefulness. It has also the lowest threshold limit value (5 ppm in air) of the four effective solvents. Chlorobenzene is considered to be less toxic than either DMF or DMAC, but this is, at least in part, offset by its higher volatility. The relative toxicity of the four effective solvents is not of great practical consequence, however, since they are all toxic enough to require a hood for dye extraction. Of the four solvents most frequently used as extractants for nonionic dyes in polyester fiber, DMF and chlorobenzene appear to be the most practical extractants. DMF may be preferable to DMAC because of its lower price. DMF also has important advantages over chlorobenzene: (a) DMF is a better solvent for disperse dyes than chlorobenzene, especially for standardized commercial dyes, which facilitates the measurement of dye absorptivity. (b) At room temperature DMF extracts unfixed dye occluded in adjuvants used in continuous dyeing and printing, e.g., gums and thickeners. This makes the determination of dye fixation possible in the same sample. (c) DMF extracts nonionic dyes soluble in the hot extractant quantitatively from cotton. This makes it possible to extract nonionic dyes quantitatively from polyester–cotton blends, including dyes which have been designed to dye both fibers in PET–cotton blends. (d) DMF extracts disperse dyes at 140° more rapidly and more completely from PET fiber than does chlorobenzene at the boil (132°).

Extraction of dyes from PET fiber requires an extraction temperature above 100°, preferably 130–140°. However, a high extraction temperature can cause decomposition of the dye and solvent. Most disperse dyes are stable in boiling chlorobenzene (132°) or pyridine (116°), at least during the time required for multiple extractions. DMF and DMAC are not adequately stable at 140° and the color of some dyes can change during extraction, causing a significant error in the determination of dye concentration. Kissa has shown[14] that extraction with hot DMF can give erroneous results unless a free-radical inhibitor is added and the acidity of the extraction solvent is controlled to stabilize the solvent and the dye. Without the stabilizers, DMF or DMAC can give erroneous results because of (a) partial decomposition of the dye causing low results or (b) a change of the dye spectrum which may increase or decrease the absorptivity of the dye.

The partial *decomposition* of some dyes may involve peroxides in the solvent, probably $HCON(CH_3)CH_2OOH$ in DMF. Free-radical inhibitors, such as phenols and nitro compounds, are very effective in preventing dye decomposition.[14] The commercial antioxidants found to inhibit dye decomposition include 2,6-di-t-butylphenol, DBMP, 4,4'-bis(2,6-di-t-butylphenol), 4,4'-methylenebis(2,6-di-t-butylphenol) and 4,4'-methylenebis(6-t-butyl-o-cresol). However, some of the commercial products are unsuitable because of their yellow color.

An error resulting from a *change of dye absorptivity* can be caused by a pH shift of the solvent on heating. As an example, CI Disperse Yellow 54 has three peaks in DMF, but only two peaks and higher absorptivity in acidified DMF (Figure 19.5). The acid–base equilibrium may involve

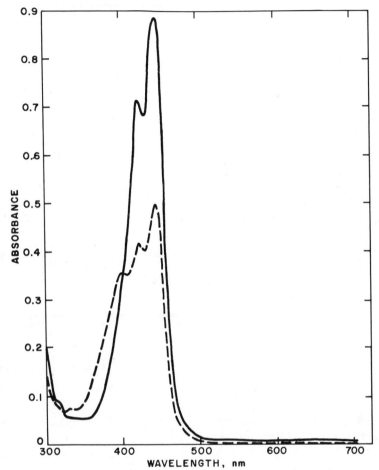

Figure 19.5 Absorption spectra of CI Disperse Yellow 54 in DMF (– – –) and in DMF acidified with p-toluene sulfonic acid (——).[14] Courtesy *Textile Research Journal*.

tautomerism, hydrogen bonding, etc. When a solution of the dye in DMF is heated, the absorbance may decrease when the dye decomposes or increase when the absorptivity increases owing to a pH shift (Figure 19.6). As a consequence, extraction with DMF can give unpredictable results unless the pH is controlled and the solvent is stabilized.

In some cases acidification of DMF with a sulfonic acid is sufficient for accurate results and the free-radical inhibitor may not be needed. However, the pH of acidified DMF in the absence of the inhibitor changes rapidly

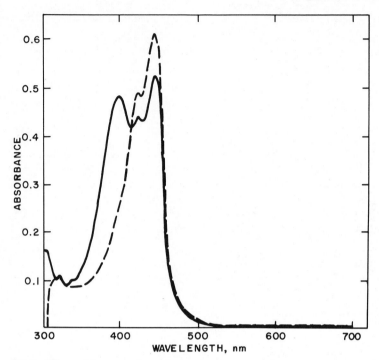

Figure 19.6 Effect of heat on absorption spectra of CI Disperse Yellow 54 in DMF (————) at 22°, pH 10.4; (– – –) after heating for 10 minutes at 140° and cooling to 22°, pH 9.48.[14] Courtesy *Textile Research Journal*.

on heating (Figure 19.7) and may cause an error if the dye absorptivity changes also. In DMF stabilized with both the sulfonic acid and the free-radical inhibitor, the dye is stable and its absorptivity does not change during the extraction.

2.4 Extraction Methods for Cationic Dyes in Polyester Fibers

Cationic dyes are bonded to anionic dye sites in copolymer polyester fiber by ionic forces and cannot be readily extracted from the fiber with a non-ionizing organic solvent such as chlorobenzene. The extractant has to provide an anion to which the dye cation can be attracted by an ion-exchange reaction and a cation which can displace the dye cation at its dye site. The extraction medium has to be acidic and its pH constant to prevent variation of the dye absorptivity.[31]

Carbonell et al.[3] extracted cationic dyes with an extraction solvent consisting of 60 ml DMF, 39 ml water, 1 ml formic acid (85%), and 4 g/l

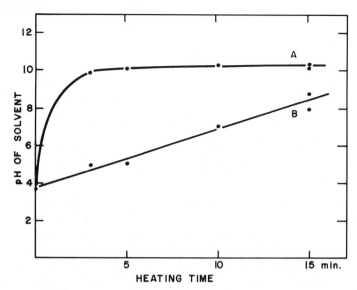

Figure 19.7   Effect of heat on the apparent pH of the extractant[14]: *A*, DMF acidified with *p*-toluenesulfonic acid; *B*, DMF acidified with *p*-toluenesulfonic acid and stabilized with 5.0 g/l DBMP. Courtesy *Textile Research Journal*.

ammonium sulfate. This reagent extract has been reported to extract cationic dyes satisfactorily from polyamide fiber,[33] but incompletely from polyester and acrylic fiber.

Kissa has shown that cationic dyes can be extracted rapidly and quantitatively from polyester fiber with solutions of strong acids and salts of strong acids in a polar solvent, such as DMF and DMAC.[33] Suitable strong acids are hydrochloric acid and sulfonic acids, including *p*-toluenesulfonic acid, 2,5-dimethylbenzenesulfonic acid, *p*-nitrobenzenesulfonic acid, *p*-chlorobenzenesulfonic acid, 2-chloro-5-nitrobenzenesulfonic acid, and 2,4-dinitrobenzenesulfonic acid. The efficacy of the sulfonic acids is, at least in part, related to the formation of solvent-soluble ion pairs with the dye cation.

The extraction rate increases with increasing acidity of the extractant (Figure 19.8) and increasing concentration of the ions involved in ion exchange. The useful acidity of the extractant is limited by dye decomposition and fiber disintegration at excessively high acid concentrations. Additional ions needed to increase the extraction rate are provided by a salt which can participate in the ion exchange and form a solvent soluble ion pair with the dye. Of the inorganic salts known to be soluble in DMF, lithium chloride and zinc chloride form powerful extractants with acids in

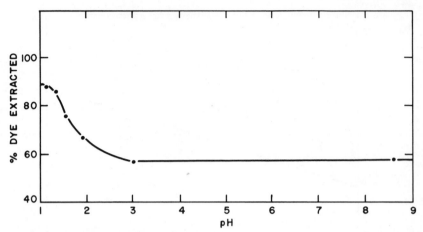

Figure 19.8 The amount of CI Basic Blue 3 extracted in 2 minutes at 140° with DMF containing 0.1M ZnCl$_2$ and 20 g/l DBMP as a function of the apparent pH of the extractant.[33] Courtesy *Textile Research Journal*.

DMF. Zinc chloride may be used with hydrochloric acid and lithium chloride with a sulfonic acid, e.g., *p*-toluenesulfonic acid.

Hydrochloric acid and zinc chloride in DMF are individually not satisfactory extractants for cationic dyes in polyester fiber. Their mixture in DMF is very effective. Cationic dyes are extracted rapidly and quantitatively from polyester fiber at 140° with DMF containing 0.4M zinc chloride, 0.8% by vol. conc. hydrochloric acid, and 20 g/l DBMP.[33] The accuracy of the method is very good (Table 19.5).

Extraction of a cationic dye from polyester fiber requires a high extraction temperature (140°) and a free-radical inhibitor to stabilize the dye in the extract. Without the inhibitor some cationic dyes are almost completely destroyed in less than 10 minutes at the extraction temperature (Figure 19.9).

As a further, although usually superfluous, precaution against dye decomposition the extraction time is limited to 2 minutes (first extraction) or 3 minutes (subsequent extractions). The dye solutions obtained with the stabilized extractant can be stored for several days at ambient temperature without significant dye decomposition. With most dyes no loss of dye was detected after 2 weeks' storage; with some dyes the loss was barely significant in 2 weeks.

2.5 Dissolution Methods for Polyester Fiber

Dissolution methods for determining dyes in polyester fiber are not as convenient as the extraction methods, but are nevertheless widely used.

Table 19.5   Effect of Extractant Composition on Cationic Dye Extraction from Polyester Featuring Anionic Dye Sites

Dye (CI Basic)	Calc. (% owf)[a]	Found (% owf)	% Dye Extracted in 2 Minutes	% Dye Remaining in the Extract After 2 Weeks at 20°
Lithium Chloride Method (4.0 g/l LiCl, 1.0 g/l p-toluenesulfonic acid, and 20 g/l DBMP in DMF)				
Violet 16	1.11	1.10	96	92
Blue 3	1.98	1.94	94	98
Green 4	0.78	0.77	96	97
Zinc Chloride Method (54.5 g/l ZnCl₂, 8 ml/l conc. HCl, and 20 g/l DBMP in DMF)				
Violet 16	1.11	1.10	97	100
Blue 3	1.98	1.96	96	100
Green 4	0.78	0.76	97	98

[a] Not corrected for slight loss of dye during dyeing.
Courtesy *Textile Research Journal*

Solvents used for dissolving polyester are more toxic and corrosive than those used for extraction. Phenols used as solvents for polyester fiber are not stable and have a pungent and adhering odor, which makes working with them unpleasant. For analyses of dyed fiber blends it may be necessary to dissolve polyester fiber, and the dissolution methods are therefore useful.

For determination of disperse dyes in polyester fiber samples have been dissolved in o-chlorophenol,[48] phenol (80%) or m-cresol at 80°,[8] phenol–chloroform (3:2),[49] phenol–chlorobenzene (1:1),[50] and HFIP. The last solvent is especially suitable for separating polyester fiber from dyed polyester–cotton blends.[51]

Janoušek used 3 ml chlorobenzene–phenol (1:1) to dissolve 0.1 g polyester fiber dyed with disperse dyes.[30] The sample was dissolved by careful heating and, after cooling, the solution was diluted with acetone to 50 ml. The addition of acetone precipitates polyester fiber with its delusterant, leaving a clear solution for spectrophotometric measurement.

2.6   Extraction Methods for Nylon

Disperse dyes can be extracted from nylon by the methods used to extract disperse dyes from polyester fiber: with chlorobenzene[52] or stabilized DMF.[14]

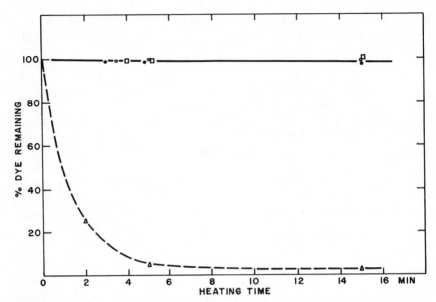

Figure 19.9 Effect of a free-radical inhibitor (DBMP) on the stability of a cationic dye (CI Basic Violet 16) at 140° in DMF containing 0.4 M ZnCl$_2$ and 0.8 % (by vol.) conc. HCl. (- - -) No inhibitor; (———) inhibitor added (● 10 g/l; ○ 20 g/l; □ 30 g/l).[33] Courtesy *Textile Research Journal*.

Acid dyes can be extracted from nylon with hot aqueous pyridine.[53] Back and Zollinger[54] extracted metal (Cr or Co) complex dyes from nylon with an aqueous azeotrope of pyridine (57 % water) in a specially designed extraction apparatus. After five or six extractions (30 minutes each) the extraction was complete. The extract was diluted with a buffer solution and the absorbance was measured.

Cationic dyes can be extracted from nylon with an extractant of 60 ml DMF, 1 ml formic acid, 39 ml H$_2$O, and 0.4 g ammonium sulfate.[3] The effectiveness of this extractant has been confirmed with mono- and dicationic dyes.[33] The extractant containing zinc chloride and hydrochloric acid in DMF, used by Kissa[33] to extract mono- or dicationic dyes from polyester, extracts monocationic dyes completely from nylon featuring anionic dye sites, but the extraction of dicationic dyes is incomplete.

Convalently bonded reactive dyes on polyamide fibers can be determined only by dissolution of the dyed fiber; unfixed dyes, if any, can be determined by extraction (cf. *CSD* VI, p. 398).

2.7 Dissolution Methods for Nylon

Solvents used for dissolving dyed nylon 6 and nylon 66 can be divided into four main classes: (*a*) organic or inorganic acids, e.g., formic acid, hydrochloric acid; (b) phenols; (c) mixtures of alcohols with inorganic salts; and (d) aliphatic halogenated hydroxylic compounds, e.g., HFIP.

The ability of carboxylic acids to dissolve nylon increases with their strength. Acids with a dissociation constant less than about 10^{-4}, corresponding to a pK_a value of greater than 4 at 25°, do not dissolve nylon. Thus formic acid (pK_a 3.75) dissolves nylon, but acetic acid (pK_a 4.76) does not. Formic acid is frequently used to dissolve dyed nylon because it is adequately stable and commercially available in a sufficiently pure form.[55,56] Greider[57] dissolved nylon 66 dyed with acid dyes in DMF–formic acid (1:9), and separated the delustering agent by centrifugation. The dye solutions were stable for at least 20 hours. Brody[58] used a small amount of TFA to dissolve nylon 66 and nylon 6T [poly(hexamethylene terephthalamide)] dyed with acid and disperse dyes. Solutions were diluted with a 91:9 (v/v) mixture of methylene chloride and methanol before determining the dye spectrophotometrically.

The mechanism by which phenols dissolve nylon is probably the rupture of intermolecular hydrogen bridges between the polyamide polymer chains, since the solvent power of phenols has been correlated with their hydrogen-bonding ability. Phenols are not as stable as formic acid, but they are weak acids and the characteristic absorption of a dye is changed to a much lesser degree in phenols than in formic acid. Vickerstaff[6] used o-chlorophenol to dissolve nylon 66 dyed with disperse, acid, and reactive dyes. Remington and Gladding[59] used also "liquefied" phenol (phenol without stabilizers added), but found that the absorbance of some dyes changed in solution and therefore preferred an o-chlorophenol–pyridine mixture. However, aqueous phenol (phenol–water 3:10) was used by Peters and White[60] and Warwicker[61] to determine acid dyes in nylon. m-Cresol has been used to dissolve nylon dyed with Cr complexes.[53] Wimmers[62] dissolved nylon 6 and McGregor et al.[63] dissolved nylon 66 dyed with acid dyes in a solution of $CaCl_2$ (20%) in methanol or ethanol and removed the delusterant by centrifugation. The latter solvent is the least toxic of the solvents used to dissolve nylon and probably the most convenient to work with.

Lautenberger[51] used HFIP to dissolve nylon in fiber blends. Although highly toxic, this solvent effectively dissolves nylon without extracting dyes from cellulosic fibers in the blend.

2.8 Cellulose Acetate

Cellulose diacetate (sec-cellulose acetate) is soluble in solvents suitable for the determination of disperse dye in the fiber by the dissolution method; such as acetone,[6] methylene chloride–ethanol (60:40),[64] stabilized DMF or DMAC,[14] DMSO, γ-butyrolactone, methyl ethyl ketone, dioxane, formic acid, and o-chlorophenol. Cadoxen, a cadmium–ethylenediamine complex, which saponifies and dissolves cellulose diacetate, has also been suggested for the determination of disperse dyes.[65]

Cellulose triacetate is not soluble in all solvents for cellulose diacetate, but dissolves in some solvents not capable of disssolving the diacetate. Solvents for the triacetate fiber include chloroform,[66] methylene chloride or methylene chloride–ethanol (60:40),[64] phenol–chlorobenzene (1:1),[50] formic acid, DMAC, DMSO, dioxane, m-cresol, and o-chlorophenol.

Disperse dyes have been extracted from cellulose triacetate with trichloroethylene[67] or with stabilized DMF.[14]

2.9 Dissolution Methods for Cellulosic Fibers

Dissolution methods are very valuable for the determination of dyes which cannot be extracted from cellulosic fibers, e.g., reactive dyes, insoluble vat dyes, or vat dyes in their leuco form which are not adequately stable for extraction. Cellulosic fibers are soluble in sulfuric acid and in cadoxen, and both solvents are extensively used for dye determination.

The sulfuric acid method is probably the oldest of all dissolution methods for the determination of dyes in fibers.[6] The dye is usually determined as (a) a solution in sulfuric acid, (b) a dispersion in diluted sulfuric acid, or (c) the leuco compound of the vat dye, reduced after dissolving the dyed fibers. Waters[7] determined the dye spectrophotometrically after dissolving the dyed fabric in cold 80% sulfuric acid. Yakanina and Lapkina[68] used conc. sulfuric acid to dissolve viscose rayon mass-colored with pigments. A method that minimizes yellowing of dissolved cotton has been described in detail by Kissa for reactive dyes.[69] Disks cut from the dyed fabric were covered with 70% sulfuric acid at 4° and allowed to dissolve with occasional shaking at room temperature for 3–4 hours. The flask was kept overnight in a refrigerator at 4° to complete dissolution of the fabric. The solution was allowed to warm to the ambient temperature and diluted to the marked volume. A solution of the same amount of undyed cotton was used as the reference solution for absorbance measurement.

Wegmann dissolved cellophane dyed with vat dyes in cold 80% sulfuric acid, neutralized the acid, and reduced the dye with alkaline sodium dithionite, adding a nonionic surfactant.[70]

The use of cadoxen for dissolving cellulose was suggested by Jayme and coworkers.[71,72] The solvent power of cadoxen for cellulose was increased by adding 0.35 M sodium hydroxide.[73] The amount of alkali was increased to 0.5 M by Achwal and Gupta[74] to facilitate dissolution of cross-linked cellulose at 30°. Cadoxen has been used to determine direct, reactive, azoic, and vat dyes in cellulose.[65] The dyed sample (15–25 mg) is dissolved in 25 ml of cadoxen by shaking at room temperature for 2 hours. A longer time (up to 24 hours) is needed to dissolve cotton dyed with dichlorotriazine and dichloroquinoxaline dyes. Cotton dyed with reactive dyes featuring a trichloropyrimidine group is insoluble in cadoxen, and Achwal and Vaidya[65] had to pretreat the dyed sample with 4% sodium hydroxide at 60° for 4 hours to render the sample soluble in cadoxen. The alkali treatment stripped some dye from the fiber, so that the alkali solution had to be added to the cadoxen solution of the sample. Although Achwal and Vaidya reported accurate results with all reactive dyes, it appears that the sulfuric acid method is simpler for the determination of trichloropyrimidine dyes.

Cellulosic fibers (cotton and viscose rayon) dyed with vat dyes dissolve readily in cadoxen, but vat dyes are insoluble in the solvent which complicates calibration. Achwal and Vaidya[65] dissolved samples in cadoxen and reduced vat dyes with sodium dithionite using a dispersant.

No published data are available to indicate the accuracy of the cadoxen method for the determination of nonionic dyes, such as azoic dyes, in cellulosic fibers. Some disperse dyes have a limited stability in cadoxen. In comparison with sulfuric acid this is not a serious drawback and the cadoxen method is certainly more convenient to use, although the reagent is more expensive and toxic.

2.10   Extraction Methods for Cellulosic Fibers

Direct dyes can be extracted from cellulosic fibers with aqueous 15–25% pyridine.[6] Although extraction of many direct dyes with aqueous pyridine is complete, a trace or even a significant amount of some dyes resists extraction. Brody[75] found that Chlorazol Sky Blue FF could not be completely stripped from viscose rayon, apparently because of a "skin" on rayon. It was necessary to dissolve the rayon by immersing 20 mg of the dyed sample in 5 ml 10% sodium hydroxide and freeze this in a Dry Ice–alcohol solution with constant stirring. This process was repeated until the fiber dissolved on melting. The solution was diluted with water and the dye determined spectrophotometrically. Haberthür et ai.[76] extracted CI Direct Red 2 from cotton poplin with DMF at 100° and this procedure should be generally applicable.

Nonionic dyes such as azoic dyes, novel dyes designed to dye both cellulosic and polyester fibers and vat dyes, can be extracted with a nonaqueous organic solvent if the dye is sufficiently soluble and stable in the hot solvent. Kissa[14] extracted nonionic dyes with tri- or tetraethylene glycol stabilized with a phenol, but found DMAC and DMF to be more powerful extractants. Repeated extractions (3 minutes each at 140°) with DMF or DMAC containing a nonvolatile acid (*p*-toluenesulfonic acid) to control pH and a free-radical inhibitor effectively remove nonionic dyes from cotton, and its blends with polyester, polyamide, or acrylic fibers. Cellulose diacetate and acrylic fibers dissolve during the extraction. Preswelling with hot water or steam facilitates extraction of cellulosic fibers, but this is usually not necessary. However, some durable-press finishes hinder the dye extraction from cotton and require a modification of the method or dissolution of the dyed cellulosic fiber in cadoxen or sulfuric acid.

Michie and Fowler (see ref. 6) extracted vat dyes with o-chlorophenol in a Soxhlet extractor for several hours. The completeness of extraction varied with the dye structure; some dyes were difficult to remove. During extraction the solvent oxidized and undyed cotton was extracted as a control to correct for the color change of the solvent. Michie and Fowler also used DMF containing 1% acetic acid to extract vat dyes at the boil (two extractions, 10 minutes each), but preferred o-chlorophenol as the extractant.

Vat dyes that are not soluble in a suitable solvent for extraction can be extracted after reduction. Most methods used now are modifications of the method of Abramovich (see ref. 6). The dyed fiber is treated with 50% aqueous cellosolve containing 1% sodium dithionite and 0.4% sodium hydroxide at 70–75° for $1\frac{1}{2}$ hours.

Plaksin and Loginova[77] extracted a fabric dyed with vat dyes at 70–75° with a solution made by dissolving 5 g thiourea dioxide in 150 ml hot water, adding 10 ml 45% NaOH, then adding 100 ml of a 0.5% solution of a dispersant (OS-20) and making the volume up to 500 ml. The extractant is said to be more stable than sodium dithionite in an aqueous alkaline solution of pyridine. Golomb and Zabotina also reduced vat dyes with thiourea dioxide, but extracted the reduced dye with mono-, di-, or triethylene glycol, ethyl cellosolve, or glycerol.[78]

2.11   Dissolution Methods for Wool

Wool is soluble in sodium hydroxide, alkaline solutions of sodium hypochlorite, cadoxen,[79] and zincoxen.[80] None of the solvents is entirely satisfactory and the stability of alkali-sensitive dyes is limited in these solvents.

Giles and Shaw[8] heated dyed wool with boiling 10% sodium hydroxide for 2 minutes and extracted the turbid alkaline solution with pyridine to get a clear solution for spectrophotometric dye determination. Some dyes, e.g., some mordant dyes, are not extractable with pyridine and have to be determined in the alkaline wool–dye solution against a blank solution of undyed wool.

Odvarka et al.[81] used a similar method for determining disperse dyes in wool, but used ethyl acetate to extract the dye from the alkaline (5% NaOH) solution.

Delmenico and Peters[82] dissolved wool dyed with acid dyes (10–40 mg) in $3N$ (1 ml/10 mg wool) sodium hydroxide at room temperature (20 hours). The solution was diluted with o-chlorophenol at 25 ml, and diluted further, if necessary, with o-chlorophenol containing 1 ml $3N$ sodium hydroxide per 50 ml. A loss of dye was observed owing to reduction during the dissolution step. The loss depended on the relative amounts of dye, wool, and sodium hydroxide, and was often within an experimental error, but increased considerably if the solutions were heated. For this reason, dye absorbances were calibrated with solutions containing different amounts of dye and wool. After addition of o-chlorophenol, the dye solutions were stable for several days.

Achwal and Mohite[79] have reported that the dye content of wool dyed with direct, acid, metal-complex, and reactive dyes can be determined after dissolving wool in cadoxen or zincoxen.[80] The solutions of wool in zincoxen are colorless, an advantage with yellow and orange dyes, but the dissolution time is long: 3 days for Australian Merino and Indian Nali wool, and some types of wool did not dissolve completely even in 6 days. The dissolution time in cadoxen containing 5% Cd varies from 4 to more than 24 hours, depending on the type of wool. Since the solutions of wool in cadoxen are yellow, a solution of undyed wool in cadoxen is needed as a reference solution.

Cadoxen dissolves Bombay mori silk in about 72 hours,[79] yielding a colorless solution. This suggests that the cadoxen dissolution method may also be applied to silk. Direct, metal-complex acid, most acid dyes, and reactive dyes are stable in cadoxen or zincoxen, but most basic dyes are decolorized by the alkaline solvent.

2.12 Extraction Methods for Wool

Acid dyes can be extracted from wool with 20–50% aqueous pyridine at the boil.[7] Although extraction of the dye is usually complete, decomposition of some dyes, presumably due to reduction, has been reported.[83] Chrome dyes have been extracted with pyridine after a treatment of dyed wool with oxalic acid, but the method is not very satisfactory.[79]

Nonionic (*disperse*) dyes have been extracted with either 64 O.P. alcohol or 62.5% aqueous pyridine.[84]

Khachoyan[85] determined indigo in wool after extraction with o-chlorophenol for 1–2 hours at 100°.

Reactive dyes can be held on wool by covalent and ionic bonds. To determine the covalently bonded reactive dye in wool, the dyed wool must be extracted to remove the hydrolyzed (unreactive) dye and the reactive dye that has not reacted with wool but is capable of doing so. As Cockett,

Rattee, and Stevens pointed out,[86] the following side effects can lead to incorrect results: (a) incomplete removal of hydrolyzed dye; (b) cleavage of the covalent dye–fiber bond; (c) reactive dye not covalently bonded is induced during extraction to react with the fiber; (d) degradation of wool resulting in removal of covalently bonded dye attached to soluble breakdown products of wool.

The extractants used to remove the dye not covalently bonded to wool fiber, by three or four successive extractions for 2–3 minutes each, include (a) an aqueous solution of urea (50%) containing a surfactant (1% Dispersol V), at the boil or at 60°[87]; (b) pyridine, either 25% v/v or an aqueous azeotrope, at the boil[88]; (c) boiling DMF; (d) an acidic solution of pyridine containing 10% v/v pyridine, 90% formic acid (20% v/v), and water (to 100% vol.), at the boil[86]; or pyridine (49.9% v/v), water (49.9% v/v), and 37% hydrochloric acid (0.2% v/v) at 70–95° for 30–60 minutes.[89]

Cockett, Rattee, and Stevens[86] have shown that (a) DMF and DMF–water (1 : 1) are not effective extractants for the dye not bonded to the fiber. (b) A urea-dispersant solution degrades wool; as a result, covalently bonded dye is removed together with the degradation products soluble in the extractant. (c) Aqueous pyridine removes the hydrolyzed dye effectively, but promotes the reaction of the reactive dye left on the fiber with wool; this extractant also causes degradation of wool. (d) Acidic solutions of pyridine effectively remove hydrolyzed dye and unreacted dye completely from the fiber; some fiber degradation occurs, but to a lesser extent than with constant-boiling pyridine.

2.13   Other Fibers

Polyvinyl chloride fibers have been dissolved in cyclohexanol, polyvinylidene fibers in dioxane, and polyethylene in toluene or xylene.[8] Disperse dyes in polypropylene have been determined by extraction of the dyed hanks with successive portions of carbon tetrachloride at 40–50°.[90]

Cationic dyes in "Nomex" (Du Pont's aramid fiber) have been determined by dissolving the fiber at 60–80° in either N-methyl-2-pyrrolidone or calcium chloride in DMAC (2%, w/w).[91] "Nomex" aramid is also soluble in DMSO.

2.14   Separation of Dyes and Fibers

The dye content of components of a fiber blend can be determined by dissolving one component in a solvent which does not dissolve the other component or extract dye from it. The dye content of the dissolved fiber can be determined in the solution obtained or by difference between the dye amounts in the blend fabric and the skeleton fabric. The dye content of the skeleton fabric can be determined by conventional methods. The cotton or rayon component of polyester blend can be dissolved in cold sulfuric acid.[69] The polyester skeleton is neutralized with ammonia or sodium bicarbonate and washed. On the other hand, the polyester or nylon component in cellulosic blends can be dissolved in HFIP.[51] The fabric must be dried before component separation; otherwise HFIP may extract substantial amounts of dye from the cotton component.

Instead of separating fibers, dyes can be separated by selective extraction. Kissa separated disperse and cationic dyes in polyester fibers or blends of homopolymer polyester fiber with cationic dyeable polyester fibers.[92] The disperse dye is extracted with dry chlorobenzene, followed by the extraction of the same sample with DMF containing zinc chloride and hydrochloric acid to remove the cationic dye from the fibers.[33]

REFERENCES

1. K. Hoffmann, *Melliand Textilber.*, **50**, 210 (1969).

2. E. Kissa, *Text. Res. J.*, **41**, 715 (1971).

3. J. Carbonell, et al., *Text.-Prax.*, **27**, 622 (1972).

4. H. Gerber and F. Somm, *Textilveredlung*, **6**, 372 (1971).

5. E. Kissa, to be published.

6. T. Vickerstaff, *The Physical Chemistry of Dyeing*, Oliver and Boyd, Edinburgh; 2nd ed., Interscience, New York, 1954.

7. E. Waters, *J. Soc. Dyers Colour.*, **60**, 200 (1944).

8. C. H. Giles and I. S. Shaw, *J. Soc. Dyers Colour.*, **69**, 481 (1953).

9. C. H. Giles and J. J. Greczek, *Text. Res. J.*, **32**, 506 (1962).

10. W. Titterington, *Chem. Ind.*, 746 (1966).

11. E. I. Stearns, *The Practice of Absorption Spectrophotometry*, Wiley-Interscience, New York, 1969.

12. C. A. Horstein, *Galaxia*, **57**, 16 (1974).

13. I. M. Kolthoff, P. J. Elving, and E. B. Sandell, *Treatise on Analytical Chemistry*, Part I, Vol. 1, Interscience, New York, 1959.

14. E. Kissa, *Text. Res. J.*, **45**, 290 (1975).

15. J. Kurz and W. Lebensaft, *Text. Ind.*, **68**, 300, 679 (1966).

16. G. Horstmann and K. Jeltsch, *Textilveredlung*, **10**, 56 (1975).

17. O. W. Hempel, *Melliand Textilber.*, **53**, 86 (1972).

18. J. Dufour, *Teintex*, **39**, 579 (1974).

19. J. Carbonell, R. Hasler, and R. Wallner, *Textilveredlung*, **10**, 61 (1975).

20. W. L. Matthews, *Am. Dyest. Rep.*, **57**, 30 (1968).

21. C. E. Garland, R. F. Hoban, and R. C. Kuehni, ISCC Problem Committee 25 Report, *Text. Chem. Col.*, **6**, 104 (1974).

22. W. D. Wright, *Ciba Rev.*, No. 2, 2 (1961).

23. D. B. Judd and G. Wyszecki, *Color in Business, Science and Industry*, 2nd ed., Wiley, New York, 1963.

24. A. Berger, A. Brockes, and N. Dalal, *Color Measurement in Textile Industry, Bayer (Verona) Farben Revue*, Special Ed. No. 3 (1964).

25. K. Thurner, *Colorimetry in Textile Dyeing–Theory and Practice*, BASF Colors and Chemicals, 1965.

26. F. W. J. Billmeyer and M. Saltzman, *Principles of Color Technology*, Wiley-Interscience, New York, 1966.

27. P. Kubelka and F. Munk, *Z. Tech. Physik.*, **12**, 593 (1931).

28. A. Brockes, *Text. Chem. Col.*, **6**, 98/21 (1974).

29. C. Hansen and A. Beerbower, Kirk-Othmer *Encyclopedia of Chemical Technology*, 2nd ed., Supplement, Wiley-Interscience, New York, 1971, p. 889.

30. J. Janoušek, *Text. Res. J.*, **40**, 192 (1970).

31. E. Kissa, *Text. Res. J.*, **44**, 997 (1974).

32. E. Cianakwalam Ibe, *J. Appl. Polym. Sci.*, **14**, 837 (1970).

33. E. Kissa, *Text. Res. J.*, **45**, 488 (1975).

34. J. G. Pacifici and G. Irick, Jr., *Text. Res. J.*, **38**, 876 (1968).

35. (a) N. I. Sax, *Dangerous Properties of Industrial Materials*, 3rd ed., Van Nostrand-Reinhold, New York, 1969; (b) H. E. Christensen, T. T. Luginbühl, and B. S. Carroll, *The Toxic Substances List*, 1974 ed., U.S. Dept. of Health, Education, and Welfare, Rockville, Md.

36. R. J. Harwood, R. McGregor, and R. H. Peters, *J. Soc. Dyers Colour.*, **88**, 218 (1972).

37. R. H. Blaker et al., *Discuss. Faraday Soc.*, **16**, 211 (1954).

38. U. Mayer, W. Ender, and A. Würz, *Melliand Textilber.*, **47**, 772 (1966).

39. H. Sand, *Kolloid Z.*, **218**, 30 (1967).

40. M. J. Schuler and W. R. Remington, *Discuss. Faraday Soc.*, **16**, 201 (1954).

41. C. J. Bent, T. D. Flynn, and H. H. Sumner, *J. Soc. Dyers Colour.*, **85**, 607 (1969).

42. S. H. W. Buchholz, *Am. Dyest. Rep.*, **54**, P 545 (1965).

43. H. D. Weigmann, et al., TRI Progress Report No. 20 (1974).

44. J. C. Brown, *J. Soc. Dyers Colour.*, **76**, 536 (1960).

45. J. Keaton and D. T. Preston, *J. Soc. Dyers Colour.*, **80**, 312 (1964).

46. E. Merian, J. Carbonell, U. Lerch, and V. Sanahuja, *Am. Dyest. Rep.*, **53**, 1106 (1964).

47. J. Andriessen and J. Soest, *Textilveredlung*, **3**, 618 (1968).

48. E. Waters, *J. Soc. Dyers Colour.*, **66**, 609 (1950).

49. T. G. Majury, *J. Soc. Dyers Colour.*, **72**, 42 (1956).

50. P. Grüner and J. Janoušek, *J. Soc. Dyers Colour.*, **85**, 4 (1969).

51. W. J. Lautenberger, *Text. Res. J.*, **41**, 78 (1971).

52. J. G. Blacker and D. Patterson, *J. Soc. Dyers Colour.*, **85**, 599 (1969).

53. X. H. Modlich, *Z. Ges. Textilindustr.*, **65**, 111 (1963).

54. G. Back and H. Zollinger, *Helv. Chim. Acta*, **41**, 2242 (1952).

55. E. H. Daruwalla and H. A. Turner, *J. Soc. Dyers Colour.*, **69**, 442 (1953).

56. H. R. Hadfield and H. Seaman, *J. Soc. Dyers. Colour.*, **74**, 392 (1958).

57. K. Greider, *J. Soc. Dyers Colour.*, **90**, 437 (1974).
58. H. Brody, *Text. Res. J.*, **35**, 895 (1965).
59. W. R. Remington and E. K. Gladding, *J. Am. Chem. Soc.*, **72**, 2559 (1950).
60. H. W. Peters and T. R. White, *J. Soc. Dyers Colour.*, **77**, 601 (1961).
61. J. O. Warwicker, *J. Soc. Dyers Colour.*, **86**, 304 (1970).
62. D. Wimmers, *Z. Ges. Textilind.*, **65**, 115 (1963).
63. R. McGregor, A. E. Nounou, and R. H. Peters, *J. Soc. Dyers Colour.*, **90**, 246 (1974).
64. T. G. Majury, *J. Soc. Dyers Colour.*, **70**, 442 (1954).
65. W. B. Achwal and A. A. Vaidya, *Text. Res. J.*, **39**, 816 (1969).
66. J. Cegarra, P. Puente, and J. Carbonell, *Textilveredlung*, **4**, 107 (1965).
67. M. K. Gokhale, L. Peters, and C. B. Stevens, *J. Soc. Dyers Colour.*, **74**, 236 (1958).
68. E. V. Yakanina and Z. S. Lapkina, *Khim. Volok.*, **3**, 61 (1969).
69. E. Kissa, *Am. Dyest. Rep.*, **56**, (106) 23 (1967).
70. J. Wegmann, *Melliand Textilber.*, **48**, 183 (1967).
71. G. Jayme and K. Neuschäffer, *Naturwissenschaften*, **44**, 62 (1957).
72. G. Jayme and K. K. Hasvold, *Melliand Textilber.*, **48**, 446 (1968).
73. D. Henley, *Svensk Papperstidn.*, **5**, 143 (1960).
74. W. B. Achwal and A. B. Gupta, *Text. Res. J.*, **36**, 939 (1966).
75. H. Brody, *J. Soc. Dyers Colour.*, **82**, 15 (1966).
76. H. Haberthür, R. Kaiser, and F. Hügli, *Textilveredlung*, **3**, 350 (1968).
77. S. A. Plaksin and L. E. Loginova, *Tekstiln. Prom.*, **25**, No. 7, 55 (1965).
78. L. M. Golomb and E. A. Zabotina, *Tekstiln. Prom.*, **26**, No. 10, 49 (1966).
79. W. B. Achwal and V. P. Mohite, *J. Soc. Dyers Colour.*, **88**, 435 (1972).
80. V. P. Saxena, H. L. Bhatnagar, and A. B. Biswas, *J. Appl. Polym. Sci.*, **7**, 181 (1963).
81. J. Odvarka, J. Krystufek, and J. Rais, *Textil.*, **17**, 462 (1962); *CA*, **58**, 6960 (1953).
82. J. Delmenico and R. H. Peters, *Text. Res. J.*, **35**, 14 (1965).
83. C. L. Bird, C. M. Nanavati, and C. B. Stevens, *J. Soc. Dyers Colour.*, **66**, 283 (1950).
84. C. L. Bird and J. M. Firth, *J. Text. Inst.*, **51**, T 1342 (1960).
85. I. Khachoyan, *Teintex*, **22**, 93 (1957).
86. K. R. F. Cockett, I. D. Rattee, and C. B. Stevens, *J. Soc. Dyers Colour.*, **85**, 113 (1969).
87. H. R. Hadfield and D. R. Lemin, *J. Textile Inst.*, **51**, T 1351 (1960).
88. D. M. Lewis and I. Seltzer, *J. Soc. Dyers Colour.*, **84**, 501 (1968).
89. H. K. Rouette, J. F. K. Wilshire, I. Yamase, and H. Zollinger, *Text. Res. J.*, **41**, 518 (1971).
90. C. L. Bird and A. M. Patel, *J. Soc. Dyers Colour.*, **84**, 561 (1968).
91. H. E. Ulery, *J. Soc. Dyers Colour.*, **90**, 401 (1974).
92. E. Kissa, *Text. Res. J.*, **46**, 483 (1976).

CHAPTER TWENTY

Analytical Techniques for Ecological and Toxicological Monitoring

M. S. YLLO

1 ENVIRONMENTAL CONSIDERATIONS

1.1 Introduction

The deterioration of environmental quality and the disturbance of the ecological balance have aroused international concern in recent years. The problems of air and water pollution have received extensive (and sometimes unjustifiably alarming) publicity. Incidents of severe mercury poisoning occurring in Japan and Sweden made headlines in the 1960s.[1-3] Widespread mercury contamination prompted the industrialized countries to investigate the possible adverse effects on the environment of other heavy metals in trace quantities.

In most cases little is known about the imperceptible physiological changes caused by minute amounts of certain metals and their synergistic action. Sprague in his review paper, "Measurement of Pollutant Toxicity to Fish," concludes that it is now possible to predict toxicity of mixtures of two or more pollutants on the basis of chemical measurements.[4] Some trace metals in small doses are essential to sustain life, but can be toxic in higher concentrations; selenium is a prime example of this double nature.[5] Research continues worldwide to resolve the complex problems of the vital and toxic functions of trace elements.

At present there are neither comprehensive data nor suitable tests available to define precisely the effect on aquatic life of residual dyes in plant effluents from dye production or application.

Chemical carcinogens are of increasing concern to the dye industry.[6] A few aromatic amines used as dye intermediates have been classified by governmental agencies as cancer-suspect agents. In 1895 the German physician Rehn reported four cases of bladder cancer in a group of 45 men working in the manufacture of fuchsin.[7,8] During the next five decades several long-range clinical investigations and experiments with animals produced evidence to confirm bladder cancer as an occupational disease among workers in dye manufacture. Benzidine and 2-naphthylamine are now recognized as two of the most potent human carcinogens.

1.2   Investigatory and Regulatory Agencies

The International Agency for Research on Cancer (IARC) has launched a program of international scope "to achieve and publish a balanced evaluation of data through the deliberations of an international group of experts in chemical carcinogenesis and put into perspective the present state of knowledge with the final aim of evaluating the data in terms of possible human risk, as well as to indicate the need for research efforts to close the gaps in our knowledge."[8]

The UICC (Union Internationale Contre Le Cancer = International Union Against Cancer) is a worldwide organization with member organizations in 71 countries.[9] The goals of the UICC include exchange of information, standardization of nomenclature, classification, and analytical methodology. They have considered several classes of compounds including aromatic amines.

Regulatory agencies in a number of countries have issued regulations designed to improve or preserve our ecology. Guidelines have also been established to protect public health in general and industrial workers in particular. It is beyond the scope of this chapter to attempt to cover existing regulations in every country. Some regulations, however, are discussed to point out the demanding task confronting the analytical chemist owing to requirements for determining chemicals at progressively lower detection limits.

The U.S. Environmental Protection Agency (EPA), in an effort to assure uniformity, has established test procedures for the analysis of certain pollutants.[10] Effluent standards have also been issued for a number of designated pollutants.[10a] To protect the receiving waters over a period of time, the total maximum weight of a discharged chemical per day is regulated by a permit system, taking into consideration the size and flow of the receiving body, as well as the rate and volume of the effluent flow. The EPA has issued standards for Hg and Cd and plans to cover As, Pb, and Ni.[10a]

The U.S. Occupational Safety and Health Administration (OSHA) has designated 14 organic compounds as carcinogens and requires compliance with safety measures in the handling of products which contain more than the maximum allowed amount of a known carcinogen.[11] In Japan, the Harmful Chemical Substances Control Law requires toxicological tests for each new dye imported into the country.[12,13] The Carcinogenic Substances Regulations of 1967 now imposes prohibitions or restrictions on 10 organic compounds in the United Kingdom.[6]

The regulatory standards are not uniform from country to country, and new legislation is passed periodically. A recent report of environmental regulations and their impact on international economy is available from the American Association of Textile Chemists and Colorists.[14]

1.3 Dye Ecological Groups

Major dye manufacturers have recognized the need for additional information concerning toxicological, ecological, and analytical problems common to synthetic dye industries. Some manufacturers have pooled technical efforts to avoid duplication of effort in characterizing common environmental problems. The Ecological and Toxicological Association of the Dyestuffs Manufacturing Industry (ETAD), composed of representatives from Europe, Japan, and India, is attempting to gain a better understanding of the effects of dyes on health and the environment.[12,13] Working independently, the Ecology Committee of the American Dye Manufacturers Institute (ADMI) has conducted studies of the environmental impact of dyes and dyeing assistants.[16] The Association of British Chemical Manufacturers sponsored a study on industrial papilloma in the bladder in 1947.[15]

1.4 Biological Studies for Ecological Impact

The Ecology Committee of the ADMI selected the following 55 commercial dyes and CI Fluorescent Brightening Agent 28, which were submitted to a number of research institutions for an assessment of the effects of dyes on the environment: 11 CI Acid Dyes (Yellow 17, 38, 151; Orange 7, 24; Blue 25, 45, 113; Green 25; Black 1, 52); 15 CI Basic Dyes (Yellow 11, 13, 37; Orange 2, 21; Red 2, 18; Violet 1, 10, 16; Blue 3, 9, 21; Green 4; Brown 4); 13 CI Direct Dyes (Yellow 4, 11, 28, 50, 106; Red 23, 81; Blue 6, 86, 218; Brown 95; Black 38, 80); 7 CI Disperse Dyes (Yellow 3, 11, 42, 54; Red 60; Blue 3, 7); one CI Mordant Dye (Black 11); one CI Sulfur Dye (Black 1); and 7 CI Vat Dyes (Yellow 2; Orange 1; Blue 6, 43; Green 1, 3; Brown 3). Detailed information on the techniques used, the data acquired, and the conclusions reached concerning a number of biological systems are assembled in the two volumes of *Dyes and the Environment.*[16] The fathead minnow (*Pimephalis promelas*) was used to study detrimental effects on fish. Ninety-six-hour TL_{50} (concentration of 50% survival) values were determined by testing a series of five concentrations in conformity with the American Public Health Association (APHA) method.[17] The data indicate that many of the dyes are not likely to present a practical fish toxicity problem because the dye threshold values are far above concentrations that are likely to be acceptable in streams from the standpoint of color.[16–18] This may not be true for cationic dyes, which appeared to be the most toxic class, at least with respect to the fathead minnow. The relevance of this static test to the actual situation in nature has not been established. In addition, all tests were carried out with neutral dye solutions without any allowance for any waste water treatment processes, which could substantially lower the dye concentration of the effluent.

Tests on a green alga (*Selenastrum capricornutum*) disclosed a strong correlation with the earlier fish study. In general, basic dyes were inhibitory to algal growth in various degrees. In an activated sludge system only eight dyes appeared to produce inhibitory effects at the concentrations studied. In anaerobic systems only two anthraquinone dyes (Disperse Blue 7 and Acid Blue 45) had inhibitory effects strong enough to cause process failures in the digesters.

In addition to dyes, a group of dye carriers has been tested for detrimental biological effects and biodegradability.[19]

2 ANALYTICAL TECHNIQUES FOR TRACE METALS

2.1 General Considerations

The remarkable growth in sophisticated analytical instrumentation in the last decade has greatly facilitated the determination of metals in low concentrations. The availability of sensitive and rapid analytical methods has, in turn, generated considerable interest to probe into ecological systems more deeply.

In this chapter the discussion of suitable analytical techniques is limited to As, Cd, Cr, Co, Cu, Pb, Hg, and Zn, which were selected by the ADMI because they are most likely to be present and have been cited for special concern.[16] The sources for metal contaminants in dyes are residual catalyst, corrosion of equipment, raw water, raw materials, and intermediates.

The ADMI has collected a wealth of analytical data (1298 dyes) to establish a concentration range for tramp metals in various classes of commercial dyes.[16] Heavy metal concentration, according to the ADMI report, usually does not exceed 100 ppm. Metallized dyes contribute metal to the extent of the dye not being absorbed by the fabric. Considering the volume of process water used for washes and rinses in the textile mills, the dilution factor may reach 10000, producing effluents at a level of a few parts per billion.[16] Recent analytical studies concerning heavy metal content in mill effluents used untreated samples from exhausted dyebaths.[20, 21] The ADMI Analytical Subcommittee selected Cd, Cr, Cu, Pb, Hg, and Zn to be measured in dyebath wastes from 20 dyeing systems. Only 3% of the values for the individual metal concentration exceeded 1 mg/l and only 2 out of 20 systems showed more than 1 μg/l mercury. Significantly lower concentrations are found in textile mill effluents, since these bath wastes are diluted by other operations 100–1000 times and treated in a waste water treatment plant before the final discharge.[20]

In selecting the most satisfactory methodology for a modern trace metal laboratory, one should consider a number of variables: capability of the instrument, sensitivity, detection limits, accuracy of the measurement, flexibility, speed of the system, and technical skills required to operate and maintain the instrument. In general, it takes more than one technique to solve all the trace analytical problems. The cost to equip an up-to-date trace laboratory varies with the choice of the analytical instrumentation from a low-cost atomic absorption spectrophotometer (AAS) to the most expensive system for neutron activation analysis (NAA). AAS has been recommended by regulatory agencies for trace metal analysis[22, 23]; the technique has also found extensive use in most industrial analytical laboratories. Because of the wide interest in AAS, this technique is reviewed more thoroughly in Section 2.6. Other equally applicable methods are summarized; refs. 24–27 provide detailed information, including tables comparing the detection limits for metals by assorted techniques. Most tables represent a composite of data extracted from other publications. In order to judge the actual value of the quoted detection limits, one should revert to the original paper for vital parameters of the experiment (sample sizes, volumes, optical path lengths, sensitivities).

2.2   Samples, Standards, Contamination

Procedures for the collection of representative effluent samples have been outlined by the APHA[17] and by the ASTM.[22] Instructions are also given for preparation of sample containers. It may seem contradictory, but even waste water samples can be contaminated if they are not handled with proper care. Samples must be properly treated to preserve the initial metal concentration. Usually the sample is acidified with nitric acid to delay the loss of metals by precipitation or absorption on container walls.[17,23]

If a container surface (Pyrex glass) has been stripped too clean with nitric acid, it can cause negative contamination (decrease in sample metal concentration) problems in nanogram ranges. Teflon (Du Pont's fluorocarbon resins) seems to offer the most inert container material for storage of standards and samples. In the case of nanogram amounts of mercury in an aqueous acidified (HNO_3) solution, it is necessary to saturate the walls of volumetric flasks by treating the flasks overnight with a dilute mercury solution (10 ng/ml) and then rinsing the flask with deionized water (no acid) just before use. The same type of negative contamination occurs in the cold vapor technique for Hg; it requires two or three runs to saturate the walls of a newly assembled or cleaned apparatus before maximum and reproducible peak heights can be obtained.

The potential contribution of a positive contaminant from reagents used can be substantial; blank runs containing all reagents (including deionized water) should always precede standards and samples. In order to avoid positive contamination from chemicals, ultrapure reagents should be used. Zief and Speights have described the continuing advancements in the preparation, handling, containment, and analysis of ultrapure chemicals.[28] Tölg presents a detailed account of recovery problems and errors concerning nanogram range methods.[29] Standard solutions for calibration also suffer from both negative and positive contamination, and the same precautions must be exercised as for samples. An often neglected factor with standards is stability during storage. Nanogram range standards must be prepared daily. Recently the U.S. National Bureau of Standards (NBS) issued a nanogram range Hg standard stabilized with Au. Stability is certified for 1 year.[30] Standard solutions purchased from various suppliers usually contain 1000 μg/ml of the element, and stability is guaranteed for 1 year.

2.3   Destruction of Organic Matter

Most AAS procedures for determination of trace metals, with the possible exception of the graphite furnace technique (provided there are no chelated metals), require decomposition of organic matter before the procedure can be successfully applied. Organic compounds in sample matrices can also cause interference (color, functional groups) with the following techniques: colorimetry, polarography, and specific ion electrodes. The oxidation of organic matter must be performed without any loss of the trace metal, which can occur either through volatility or formation of an insoluble compound.

For most metals in effluents a beaker digestion with nitric acid on a hot plate is sufficient.[17,23] To retain more volatile metals (Hg, As) a reflux system is preferred. In the case of As a strongly oxidizing medium should be used during the digestion. If any charring occurs, As is volatilized as AsH_3. Gorsuch describes a reflux-recycle apparatus that has gained wide popularity.[31,32] Using this apparatus the condensate can be redigested from the trap or the condensate can be analyzed separately to determine if losses are occurring.

Dyes may be digested with the conventional sulfuric–nitric acid digestion using micro Kjeldahl flasks, except for the volatile metals, which should be digested under reflux.[31] Perchloric acid digestions are noticeably faster, but require a special fume hood or other equipment and an analyst with considerable experience to avoid any possibility of an explosion.[31,33]

In my laboratory the following method is used. About 1 g of dye is charred by heating in a Kjeldahl flask with 1 ml conc. sulfuric acid; more sulfuric acid may be added if necessary. To the cooled, completely charred sample, 3 ml nitric acid is added. The solution is heated to destroy the carbonaceous matter. The nitric acid treatment is repeated, if necessary, for complete digestion. After cooling, small portions of hydrogen peroxide and deionized water are added to remove any residual nitric acid detrimental to several analytical techniques.

2.4 Preconcentration and Separation

In order to achieve lower detection limits and more reliable analyses, various preconcentration methods can be employed. An effluent sample may be concentrated simply by starting with a high volume of sample (100 ml or more) for the beaker digestion with nitric acid and taking it almost to dryness (baking could result in insoluble residues); the residue is then dissolved and transferred to a small volumetric flask (e.g., 10 ml). A concentration factor of 10:1 has been achieved.

If higher concentration factors are desired, ion-exchange[34] and chelating resins such as Chelex-100[35] may be used. 8-Hydroxyquinoline on porous glass beads[36] and other chelating functional groups immobilized by silylation have been introduced.[37,38] Either the heavy metals collected on resins can be eluted with a minimum volume of a suitable eluent, or the resins can be submitted directly to analysis via appropriate physical methods, e.g., X-ray fluorescence spectrometry (XRF).[38] Passing large effluent volumes through relatively small resin beds produces a significant preconcentration factor with the stipulation that the metal of interest should be in the ionic form in order to be retained by a resin.

In most cases where a separation from a high salt matrix is required after a digestion procedure, various complexing agents are used to extract the desired metal into a suitable solvent.[39,40] Colored metal complexes may be used for spectrophotometric determinations.[41] In general, the metal in the extract can be most conveniently determined by AAS, XRF, and other techniques.[17,23,26,42] An assortment of metals complexed in a mutually favorable medium can be extracted together. Kinrade and Van Loon have extracted eight metals simultaneously (Cd, Co, Cu, Fe, Pb, Ni, Ag, and Zn) using two chelating agents, ammonium pyrrolidinedithiocarbamate (APDC) and diethylammonium diethyldithiocarbamate (DDDC).[43]

Precipitation or coprecipitation is an old tool used in separation and concentration of trace metals. Buono et al. report a fast separation of trace metals from a highly concentrated salt solution using poly(5-vinyl-8-hydroxyquinoline) alone or with oxine to precipitate nine metals.[44]

2.5 Survey of Techniques

Spectrophotometric methods (see Chapter 6) have been long-time favorites in trace metal analysis. It is obvious that the application of any colorimetric method for determination of metals in dyes and exhausted dyebath liquors can only follow a complete digestion of the organic matter. Since most color-forming agents react with several metals, a preliminary separation from concurrent interferents is absolutely essential. Quite often a masking agent or a pH adjustment can eliminate the competing color.[45] Reliable procedures for colorimetric metal analysis are found in standard textbooks.[17,22,23,41,46,47]

Compared to spectrophotometric methods, polarographic methods[24,48,49] have advantages in certain cases: they are more specific and, provided that the polarographic waves ($E_{1/2}$) are sufficiently separated, several metals may be determined simultaneously. A classical polarographic method[17] allows the determination of Cd, Co, Pb, Ni, and Zn at the same time. An acid digestion or other treatment to convert the metal to ionic form should usually precede any polarographic technique to eliminate interference by functional groups unless proven otherwise with known compounds in the same matrix.

Classical polarography, voltammetry with a dropping mercury electrode, is rapidly being replaced by more advanced techniques providing significant improvement in resolution and sensitivity. One of the most sensitive techniques available for trace metal analysis is the differential pulse anodic stripping voltammetry (DPASV), a successful combination of anodic stripping voltammetry (ASV) and differential pulse voltammetry.[50-52] Commercially available polarographic equipment is simple and easy to operate.[53,54] As with conventional polarography, simultaneous determinations of several metals in the same experiment may be made. Separation of Cd, Cu, Pb, and Zn has been reported.[55,56] Beyer and Bond have compared polarographic methods with AAS.[55] Detection limits for As by both DPASV and ASV for As, the effects of acid concentration, and interferences have been reported.[57] Polarographic methods have been used to determine metals in waste waters.[58]

Ion-selective electrodes[59-61] operate similarly to pH electrodes measuring ion activities; these electrodes are currently available only for a selected number of heavy metals. The electrodes are usually not completely specific for the ion of interest and may be subject to possible interference from other ions. Matrix effects are minimized by adding a noninterfering salt to eliminate differences among samples in total ionic strength. The logarithmically responding electrodes are both accurate and sensitive over a wide concentration range. This last capability makes these chemical sensing electrode systems most attractive for automatic monitoring, although interferences may cause considerable difficulties. The chemical sensing electrodes are commercially available for the following metals: As, Cd, Cu, Hg, and Zn. New ion-selective electrodes are being developed continually.[62,63]

Neutron activation analysis (NAA) is a powerful tool for both qualitative and quantitative analysis, but the equipment is exceedingly expensive. NAA is a most sensitive nuclear technique for a wide range of metals; the sample is bombarded with suitable nuclear particles to produce radioactive isotopes, which are then identified and measured quantitatively. The technique is applicable to both liquid and solid samples.[24] A simple and rapid multielement method for the determination of trace elements in water by NAA is presented by Salbu et al.[64]

Conventional X-ray techniques do not offer the required sensitivity for trace metal analysis in concentrations below 1 ppm. Satisfactory detection limits have been achieved with X-ray fluorescence (XRF) techniques preceded by a concentration step. Cation-exchange papers, ion-exchange resins, and (for more selective preconcentration) chelating ion-exchange resins (Chelex-100) have been used. A preconcentration step combined with proton-induced X-ray fluorescence analysis has recently received recognition as a well-established method with adequate accuracy.[25,38,42,65-68] Most of the ADMI analytical data on trace metals on dyes were obtained by XRF.[16]

Emission spectroscopy is a useful tool for determination of trace metals[17]; it can be applied to solids directly, eliminating the need for digestion or dissolution. All detectable elements are determined in one run. For improved sensitivity, a large volume of a water sample is usually evaporated to dryness. By the plasma jet method trace metals in the parts per million range can be measured in water samples without preconcentration.[24]

The use of spark source mass spectrometry (SSMS) for trace metal analysis is steadily expanding. An overall coverage of almost all elements in the periodic table is obtained in a single analysis and matrix effects are almost nonexistent.[24, 25] Crocker and Merritt give a detailed discussion of the technique for the determination of trace metals in natural waters using freeze drying for sample preconcentration.[69] SSMS was also used to characterize sludge samples at a water-treatment plant.[70]

2.6   Atomic Absorption Spectrometry

2.6.1   General Considerations.   AAS has enjoyed unprecedented growth and wide acceptance as an accurate tool for the determination of trace metals ever since Alan Walsh developed the analytical technique and designed the components for instrumentation in the early 1950s.[71] A great selection of AAS instruments with varying degrees of capability and sophistication is now on the market.

The sample is heated to a high temperature to break up chemical bonds between molecules, enabling individual atoms to float freely in the sample reservoir. In this condition atoms can absorb either UV or visible radiation at specific wavelengths. The absorption of radiant energy is measured at resonance analytical lines involving only the ground-state atoms. High flame temperatures are not generally advantageous for elements with low ionization energies; an increase in ionic population results in decreased atomic population. The quantitative relationship of the absorbed radiation with the metal ion concentration in the sample offers the means for calibration with a standard and determination of an unknown concentration.[24, 26, 72–74]

Two types of atomic absorption instruments are commercially available: the simpler, less expensive single-beam and the double-beam system. In the double-beam system, Figure 20.1, light from the source is passed alternatively through the flame (sample beam) and past the flame (reference beam), and the ratio of the two intensities is measured. The reference beam compensates for any changes in the lamp intensity and electronic gain, resulting in improved detection limits and better precision. Double-beam instruments offer the option of placing a background corrector in the reference beam; a deuterium arc (D_2 lamp) is the usual choice. When the

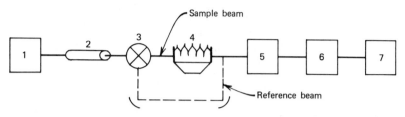

Figure 20.1. Simplified schematic of AAS double-beam system. 1, Power supply for radiation source; 2, hollow cathode lamp (source); 3, chopper; 4, flame or another atom reservoir; 5, monochromator; 6, detector; 7, electronics and readout.

D_2 lamp is introduced into the system the reference beam is replaced with an emission continuum from the deuterium arc. The light from the source and that from the D_2 lamp pass alternately through the flame. The metal of interest absorbs only the light from the hollow cathode lamp at its characteristic wavelength, whereas background absorption affects both beams equally. When the ratio of the two beams is measured electronically, the effects of background absorption are eliminated unless the nonspecific absorption is unusually high. As schematized in Figure 20.1, the instrument functions as follows: the radiation source, a hollow cathode tube, emits the line spectrum of the metal to be determined. The particular metal in the standard or sample is transferred into the flame or some other type of atom reservoir, where it absorbs energy at the resonance line. The monochromator isolates the resonance wavelength (unless overpowered by molecular absorption from background) and rejects all other line absorption. The photodetector sees only the resonance line emission decreased by sample absorption, which is measured electronically by the detector-readout system. Excellent texts are available on the theoretical aspects of atomic absorption and related techniques; they also cover flame emission and atomic fluorescence.[72-74]

Hollow cathode lamps capable of emitting sharp spectrum lines are generally used as radiation sources for commercial instruments. For some elements, however, electrodeless discharge lamps provide better intensity and stability, e.g., As and Pb.

The preceding discussion of instrumental components should serve only as a guide to detailed accounts found in texts previously referred to. All major instrument companies offer a selection of models with optional attachments providing the desired versatility. It does not seem feasible to describe the choices in commercial AAS systems in view of the phenomenal speed at which new technology is enabling advanced models to be put on the market.

2.6.2 Interferences. The introduction of the first commercial AA instruments was greeted by many as the panacea for trace metal analyses: a spectroscopic technique with no interferences. The fact is that all AA techniques are susceptible to interferences from a number of sources,[72,74] although there are relatively few spectral line interferences.[26] The more complex the matrix, the more possibilities for interferences, which can either enhance or suppress the absorbance. If we define an interference as any factor that causes a signal to deviate from the signal produced at the same concentration under standard conditions with previously established optimum parameters, the list would be quite long. Some trouble from changing instrument parameters can be avoided by careful calibration with standards in the same matrix before and after the unknowns are run. If the sample matrix is unknown or cannot be reproduced, a standard addition technique should be used to compensate for chemical interferences. The standard addition technique does not eliminate interference by molecular or scatter absorbance due to salt concentration. If a D_2 lamp is not available the correction for nonspecific absorption should be made by measuring the absorbance on the resonant line and on a nonresonant line (nonspecific absorption) adjacent to the resonant line. The difference between the two signals is proportional to the actual metal concentration. Some metals with low ionization energies are very sensitive to any change in the ionic concentration in the sample; this phenomenon is usually remedied easily by adding a more readily ionizable metal to the solution. Anions (e.g., PO_4^{3-}) can suppress the signal by forming molecules, which are reluctant to yield free atoms in the flame. To overcome this difficulty an excess amount of another metal which has greater affinity for the interfering anion is added to free the desired metal for atomization (e.g., La for PO_4^{3-}). The same response should not be expected from a metal at different acid concentrations or in different solvents.[75] In most cases mineralization of the sample is mandatory unless the composition of the sample is known and standards can be prepared with the same matrix. If a complex matrix cannot be simplified by usual means, it is advisable to isolate the metal of interest by a suitable technique (extraction, coprecipitation, ion exchange).

2.6.3 AAS Flame Techniques. The acetylene–air flame (2300°) is one of the most widely used vehicles to produce a cloud of free atoms; other chemical flames are used for specific purposes.[72] Refractory elements require the use of a strongly reducing (red cone) nitrous oxide–acetylene flame (2955°) to prevent oxide formation.[76–78]

Although the fuel and oxidant flows are adjusted by fine controls, minute changes in their ratio affect the signal, necessitating a new calibration once a flame is started or adjusted. Premix or laminar flow burners are generally used for commercial AAS. The advantage of the less turbulent laminar flow outweighs the disadvantages (memory effects, harder to handle) compared to the total consumption burner used in earlier flame emission techniques. Several special-purpose burner heads are available for the premix burner: the regular one-slot, Boling burner (three-slot, less noisy flame) and a special high-temperature burner head for nitrous oxide.

For safe handling of a selected fuel–oxidant mixture the manufacturer's instructions should be strictly followed. It is good practice in general to select instrument settings according to the manufacturer's instruction manual for a particular metal. Modified conditions should be used only after the analyst is thoroughly familiar with the equipment. Special caution should be observed when working with the nitrous oxide flame.

In order to determine trace metals in waste water, 100 ml of the sample is digested as described earlier, diluted to a convenient volume (25 ml), and submitted to AAS analysis. A calibration for each metal has to be performed with standards at the same acid concentration and a matched matrix, if excess salts are known to be present. Acetylene–air flame is suitable for all the metals of our concern; only the determination of chromium is subject to less interferences when the nitrous oxide flame is used. The optimum flame composition varies from metal to metal and a fine tuning of small differences in the oxidant–fuel ratio can be significant, the blue flame being the oxidizing (excess oxidant) and the luminous flame the reducing (excess fuel) flame.

The capability of the AAS technique for the determination of trace metals is presented in Table 20.1.[20] The ADMI data represent an interlaboratory study by the Analytical Subcommittee; "spiked" samples were analyzed by participating laboratories under routine conditions.

2.6.4 Graphite Furnace. Although high-temperature flames are still the most popular devices in use as atom reservoirs, other forms are rapidly gaining popularity.[79–85] When better detectabilities are required, one can employ a graphite furnace, thus improving detection limits without the time-consuming preconcentration techniques. With a graphite furnace detection limits are lowered as much as 1000 times compared to the conventional flame techniques. Most samples can be handled in situ, eliminating the need for prior mineralization. Extremely high sensitivities with an optimum working range of 1–10 picograms are obtained for most metals with a number of elements reaching 10 femtogram limits. At this level impure reagents, high blanks, and the quality of the laboratory environment become serious considerations. Morgenthaler very appropriately calls the graphite furnace an "instrument that suffers from hay fever."[83] A given

Table 20.1   Accuracy and Precision[a]

	EPA Data			ADMI Data		
	Added	Found	S.D.	Added	Found	S.D.
Cd	0.078	0.074	0.018	1.00	1.00	0.09
				0.10	0.09	0.03
Cr	0.407	0.380	0.128	1.00	0.96	0.06
				0.50	0.48	0.04
Cu	0.332	0.324	0.056	1.00	0.82	0.21
				0.50	0.52	0.02
Pb	0.367	0.377	0.128	1.00	0.95	0.12
				1.00	0.96	0.10
Zn	0.310	0.308	0.114	1.00	0.95	0.09
				5.00	5.22	0.83
Hg	9.6	9.1	3.57	10.0	7.8	1.7
	3.40	3.41	1.49	2.00	1.5	0.9

[a] All data in mg/l, except for Hg, which is in μg/l.

amount of metal transferred into the furnace (1–100 μl) gives a much higher signal than in the conventional burner owing to nearly 100% efficiency on atomization. Also, the residence time of an atom in the furnace is considerably longer than in the flame. Several variations of the original Massmann design[79] are on the market. Our laboratory has found that one of these with an improved flow pattern (opposed gas flows) to eliminate condensation problems substantially reduces background absorption by sweeping out most of the vaporized salt, when dealing with samples of a high salt concentration.[86]

A typical graphite furnace is a 50-mm-long carbon cylinder (5-mm i.d., 6-mm o.d.), provided with a 2-mm hole at the top for liquid sample introduction; solid samples are introduced through the open ends with a special sample spoon. A controlled electric current is passed through the cylinder to provide three stages of heating for drying, charring, and atomizing. Temperature and time dials facilitate the selection of optimum operating conditions for every type of sample, taking into account the composition of the sample and the parameters for the metal to be determined. In order to avoid oxidation, the carbon tube is constantly swept with an inert gas (argon or nitrogen). For most elements argon atmosphere produces higher sensitivities, eliminating the possibility of suppressing the atomic population by possible nitride formation when nitrogen is used. The pyrolysis temperature has to be very carefully controlled; at this stage a fractionation takes place. The optimum temperature should produce 100% charring of organic matter and volatilize a high salt matrix (e.g., seawater) without any loss of the particular trace metal to be determined. In case the charring stage has to be conducted at a temperature at which a higher amount of residue is left in the tube, a high nonreproducible background reading at the atomization stage can be expected. A background corrector (D_2 arc) is required with a graphite furnace to correct for any molecular absorption contributed by the residue after charring.

When dealing with an exceptionally high salt concentration the D_2 lamp cannot correct for all the nonspecific absorption, and chemical means have to be used. Ediger has suggested ways for matrix modification to produce both more volatile compounds for the undesired salts and less volatile compounds to retain the metal to be determined.[87] Matrix interferences resulting in possible chemical reactions are quite prevalent at the high temperatures of the graphite furnace. The official EPA manual[23] states, "Methods of standard addition are mandatory with these furnace techniques to insure valid data."

2.6.5 Cold Vapor Technique, Mercury. The analysis of Hg by the conventional AAS flame atomization procedure has insufficient sensitivity and the number of free atoms produced is related to the initial oxidation state of the Hg. High sensitivity is achieved with the cold vapor technique in which the exceedingly strong line absorption by the monoatomic Hg vapor at room temperature is measured at 253.7 nm. The metallic Hg has such high vapor pressure at room temperature (0.001 torr at 20°) that cold Hg vapor in high concentration is easily obtainable. The technique was used by Woodson in 1939 for the determination of Hg in air.[88] The cold vapor technique was used during the following 30-year span until the pollution abatement of streams and lakes induced the development of more or less officially acceptable standard methods, the Hatch and Ott version being the most popular one.[17,22,23,89,90]

Broadly, the technique is quite simple; the ionic Hg in a mineralized sample is reduced with stannous chloride to metallic Hg (in a reaction vessel) and subsequently aerated into a long (10–18 cm) optical cell, which is placed in the path of the Hg hollow cathode emission lamp. The absorption measured is proportional to the number of Hg atoms in the cell. The Hg vapor may be measured either in an equilibrium system,[89] where a continuous signal reading is obtained, or an "open end" system, where a peak reading is recorded.

Kalb's adaptation of the cold vapor technique includes amalgamation of the metallic Hg by passing it through a silver foil packing while other volatile compounds are swept out of the system.[91,92] Using an induction furnace the Hg is vaporized from the amalgam instantaneously, and a concentrated Hg cloud is swept into the optical cell, producing a sharp symmetrical peak with substantial increase in the signal compared to the equilibrium system. The amalgamation technique eliminates interference from volatile substances which show a broad band absorption around the Hg resonance line and would therefore cause erroneous results. Obviously, if the determination were preceded by a total mineralization, the mentioned UV absorbers would not be found in the solution. A digestion is mandatory if the analysis is to report total mercury and not only inorganic Hg, since most organic mercurials do not respond to the reduction step. The official U.S. EPA digestion procedure for waste water[17,23] calls for treatment with a mixture of conc. sulfuric acid, potassium permanganate, and potassium persulfate for 2 hours at 95°. A complete digestion for dyes may be performed with a sulfuric–nitric acid digestion using the Gorsuch recycle–reflux apparatus to avoid loss of mercury by volatilization.[31]

2.6.6 Hydride Evolution Technique, Arsenic. The conventional continuous flame technique offers very poor sensitivity for As. The As resonance line is in the lower-wavelength portion of the UV spectrum (193.7 mm), and is greatly obscured by the high background absorption of the conventional flame gases. The problem is eliminated when argon or nitrogen-(entrained air)–hydrogen flame is used,[93] but the sensitivity still remains unsatisfactory for low As concentrations, thus requiring some form of preconcentration to meet the standards for pollution control. Arsine gas (AsH_3), the product of the classic Gutzeit reduction, provides a highly useful vehicle for the isolation and concentration of As. Schematics of typical hydride generators may be found in standard texts[26]; the apparatus is also commercially available. Better sensitivity and well defined peaks are usually obtained when the arsine is first collected by some technique and then instantaneously swept with a stream of nitrogen (argon) into a hydrogen–nitrogen(argon)–entrained air (low UV-absorbing) flame.[94–96] Some workers make use of a balloon for collecting the evolved gas[94]; others use cold traps[97] in liquid nitrogen. To achieve high efficiency in condensing and vaporizing AsH_3 gas a 22-ft, $\frac{1}{8}$-in. i.d. stainless-steel coil in a bath of hot water (60–80°) is used in our laboratory.[98] With this technique the sensitivity of the determination of As has been increased 1000-fold over the conventional method.

In order to have the As available for reduction a complete digestion of organic matter is mandatory.[99]

3 ANALYTICAL TECHNIQUES FOR AROMATIC AMINES

3.1 General Considerations

3.1.1 The Safe Handling of Carcinogens. In the United States safe handling procedures for certain chemical carcinogens are specified for industrial plants and laboratories in the Occupational Safety and Health Act of 1970 as amended in 1974.[11] Special provisions for laboratory activities in laboratories of the U.S. Department of Health, Education and Welfare are given in "Laboratory Operations Involving Chemical Carcinogens."[100] Generally, good housekeeping habits should be observed when handling cancer-suspect agents. All transfers of pure chemicals as well as mixtures containing more than 0.1% (1% in certain cases)[11] of a carcinogenic contaminant should be handled in a hood with adequate draft or a glove box. Protective disposable clothing should be worn by any person handling these compounds. Preassignment medical surveillance and periodic examinations by a physician are also considered necessary for employees handling carcinogens in significant concentrations.

3.1.2 Carcinogen-Suspect Agents in the Dye Industry. Some intermediates for important dyes have been declared to be carcinogens by regulatory agencies.[101,102] The Carcinogenic Substances Regulations (No. 879) in the United Kingdom prohibit the manufacture, presence, and use of 2-naphthylamine, benzidine, 4-aminobiphenyl, and 4-nitrobiphenyl; they also control the employment of personnel in the manufacture and uses of 1-naphthylamine, dichlorobenzidine, o-tolidine, and dianisidine, and the employment of personnel in the manufacture of Auramine and Magenta.[6] The 1974 OSHA regulations in the United States contain safety standards for 14 key chemicals termed carcinogens, which include the first six in the United Kingdom list plus 4-dimethylaminoazobenzene.[11] The techniques available for determining these compounds, including applications and limitations of the methods, are now discussed.

3.2 Isolation of Aromatic Amines

Aminoaromatic contaminants are usually isolated from dyes or waste waters by solvent extraction from an alkaline aqueous sample. Working with the extract offers two advantages: a strong matrix effect of a dye can generally be eliminated and the concentration of the amine is increased. Some basic constituents or other extractable components in dyes, however, complicate the separation, giving highly colored extracts with broad absorption peaks. These extracts cannot be handled by spectrophotometric methods. Extractions may be carried out manually at room temperature or at elevated temperatures using a continuous liquid–liquid extractor. Longer extraction periods obtained with continuous extractors are, as a rule, more effective than manual extractions. Solid samples of deposits, clothing, etc., may be extracted in a Soxhlet apparatus after pretreatment with alcoholic potassium hydroxide.[103]

Recovery of amines at low levels may not be 100% (70% in our experience); thus calibration of the method includes the extraction step.

Once the primary amines have been extracted into a suitable solvent (ether, ethyl acetate, chloroform), there are several optional techniques for their final determination.

3.3   Spectrophotometric Methods

3.3.1   Oxidative Procedures. Colored oxidation products of aromatic amines are frequently used for their identification as well as for their quantification. Although a number of oxidants produce colored solutions or precipitates,[104–108] chloramine-T (CH_3—C_6H_4—SO_2NNaCl) seems to offer the most convenient means for a rapid quantitative determination.

Chloramine-T has been used by industrial hygienists to determine occupational exposure to benzidine and some of its analogues.[103,109,110] In 1975, EPA adopted the chloramine-T method as official for benzidine.[10b,111] The free amine is extracted manually from a previously obtained solvent extract into dilute hydrochloric acid. The benzidine is oxidized with chloramine-T to produce a yellow product, which is extracted into a suitable solvent (ethyl acetate or chloroform) and measured spectrophotometrically. Since the product is very unstable and photosensitive, timing is a most important factor. The color increases to a maximum intensity in a matter of minutes, but the solution becomes colorless in 20–30 minutes.[98] This method is subject to positive interference by o-substituted diaminobiphenyls; *meta* isomers do not react as readily.[110] Reproducible color complexes are formed by o-dianisidine, o-tolidine, and 3,3'-dichlorobenzidine under the same conditions as for benzidine. These amines may be determined individually, provided there is enough resolution between the absorption maxima to separate coexisting amines; e.g., the λ_{max} for benzidine is 445 nm and for o-dianisidine is 482 nm, both in $CHCl_3$. It is advisable to look at the spectra with a recording spectrophotometer to detect interfering absorption. If other primary aromatic amines or phenols are known or suspected to be present, the degree of interference should be evaluated by reacting them with chloramine-T. The accuracy of the method is $\pm 10\%$ or better in the 2–10 μg amine range.[110,112] Neither 1- nor 2-naphthylamine reacts with chloramine-T to produce any color interference in the benzidine determination. They are readily determined as yellow products obtained by hypochlorite oxidation in acidic solution.[103,113] 2-Naphthylamine produces a color with a significantly higher intensity than the 1-isomer, which can still cause erratic results in mixtures containing less than 25% 2-naphthylamine. The method cannot be used in the presence of other color-forming amines: benzidine, o-tolidine, o-dianisidine, o-, m-, and p-toluidine, and aniline. 2-Naphthol and naphthylaminesulfonic acids interfere and should be removed prior to the test.[103]

Florea has described conditions for the determination of benzidine and o-tolidine with sodium hypochlorite, which give products with λ_{max} 429 and 440 nm, respectively. The sensitivity is claimed to be remarkable, and the method is applicable in presence of 2-naphthylamine and the toluidines.[108]

3.3.2 Diazotization and Coupling.

A technique frequently used for the determination of aromatic amines is the spectrophotometric determination of a soluble azo dye, produced by diazotization and coupling. A number of couplers have been tested and compared from the standpoint of the following pertinent criteria for the color: stability, molar absorptivity, λ_{max} (resolution of λ_{max} from other amines present).[114,115]

Butt and Strafford used 2-hydroxy-3-naphthoic acid in 1 M sodium carbonate to couple tetrazotized benzidine or diazotized 2-naphthylamine.[103] The method is subject to interference by other unsulfonated aromatic amines; the test can then be used to determine the total amine content.

N-Ethyl-1-naphthylamine has been used as the coupling component in acidic solution for the determination of benzidine, o-tolidine, and o-dianisidine; coupling was carried out in 2% ethanol to speed up the reaction and to increase the solubility of the dye.[114] A similar method was developed in our laboratory; N-(1-naphthyl)ethylenediamine was coupled to the tetrazotized aromatic diamines under optimum pH conditions.[98] The color is stable for 24 hours in the range 0–0.2 μmoles/50 ml solution; the dye precipitates at higher concentrations. The blue dye formed by coupling is extremely sensitive to a change in acid concentration affecting both the molar absorptivity and the λ_{max}. The maximum intensity was reached in 0.09 N hydrochloric acid; decreasing the acidity to 0.04 N caused a 20% decrease in absorbance. Benzidine, o-tolidine, and o-dianisidine may be determined using N-(1-naphthyl)ethylenediamine as the coupler. Unfortunately, the resulting blue dyes have overlapping spectral curves with the following λ_{max}, respectively: 635, 450–650, and 605 nm. The molar absorptivities range from 152,000 to 29,000, requiring individual calibrations. Monofunctional primary aromatic amines, if present, interfere. Aniline and o-toluidine produce colors with broad absorption curves in the visible spectrum which overlap the curves obtained from benzidine or o-dianisidine. Separation based on spectral differences did not appear attractive; separations via paper chromatography are discussed later. The measurement of the mixed color gives an estimate of total primary aromatic amines present.

3.3.3 Other Reagents. Other color-forming reactions have been used to identify and determine primary amines. Sawicki et al. use 3-methyl-2-benzothiazolone hydrazone[116] and 4-azobenzenediazonium fluoroborate[117] for the spectrophotometric determination of primary amines, including 1- and 2-naphthylamine. Wavelength maxima and molar absorbance values are tabulated and interferences are discussed. The yellow color developed with p-dimethylaminobenzaldehyde has been used for the colorimetric determination of benzidine, o-dianisidine and o-tolidine in the air of factories.[118]

3.4 Chromatography

3.4.1 Paper Chromatography and Spot Tests. The principles of these techniques are described in Chapter 3. The purpose of this section is to indicate their utility for the separation of aminoaromatics. Hais and Macek recommended a method in which benzidine and its analogues, as well as 1- and 2-naphthylamine, were chromatographed on formamide impregnated paper using cyclohexane as the mobile phase.[119] The spots were then developed by suspending the paper in a cylinder saturated with nitrogen oxide fumes and spraying with a solution of N-(1-naphthyl)ethylenediamine or some other coupling component. Ghetti et al. separated aromatic amines (benzidine, o-tolidine, dianisidine, dichlorobenzidine, 1- and 2-naphthylamine) in various substrates using isobutanol–acetic acid–water (3:1:1) as the developer. The paper was bisected: half was used to locate and identify the amine bands with p-dimethylaminobenzaldehyde; the amines from the other half were individually eluted with 1 N hydrochloric acid, diazotized, and coupled to N-(1-naphthyl)ethylenediamine, and the color was measured spectrophotometrically.[120]

A flat-plate PC method has been developed in our laboratory to separate the difunctional aromatic amines from monofunctional amines such as aniline and p-toluidine. The colored coupling products of N-(1-naphthyl)-ethylenediamine from the previously discussed spectrophotometric method are chromatographed from 0.09 N hydrochloric acid–1% ethanol and developed with 1% pyridine in ethanol.[98] The presence of the difunctional aromatic amine is identified by a pink to purple center; the depth of color and size of the spot can be easily correlated with the amount of the amine present comparing with standardized spots (0.5–5 μg amine). The dyes from monofunctional amines are eluted as blue or green circles, which can be eluted completely; however, we were unable to differentiate between the difunctional amines (benzidine, o-dianisidine, o-tolidine).

Another PC separation of benzidine and its isomers is achieved, using paper pretreated with formamide, cyclohexane as solvent, and the characteristic colors formed with p-dimethylaminobenzaldehyde.[121]

p-Dimethylaminobenzaldehyde is also used as one of the visualization reagents for the selective detection of carcinogenic amines in working environments.[122] 2-Naphthylamine can be detected in a spot test with pyridine-2-aldehyde in the presence of 1000-fold 1-naphthylamine.[123] Spot tests for amines are also discussed by E. Sawicki et al., using the reagents previously mentioned under spectrophotometric methods.[116,117]

3.4.2 Thin-Layer Chromatography. Since Chapter 2 describes the techniques of TLC, only procedures pertinent to detection of amino-aromatics are discussed here. The separation of primary arylamines on TLC plates after diazotization and coupling with 2-naphthol in aqueous alkali is documented with R_F values by Jones.[124] The loadings were about 200 μg of each amine and the colors ranged from orange-yellow to purple; the R_F for 1- and 2-naphthylamine is reported as 0.65 and 0.59, respectively. Thielman[125] lists a number of R_F values for substances capable of coupling using commercially available plates impregnated with 4,4′-diazido-stilbene-2,2′-disulfonic acid (Silufol UV 254). He achieved a remarkable separation of 1- and 2-naphthylamine using a mixture of benzene–glacial acetic acid (70:30) as the mobile phase, reporting R_F values of 0.52 and 0.39. After development of the chromatogram, the plate was subjected to UV radiation, causing the reagent to decompose to the corresponding azo compound, which was then coupled to the test substances. A separation of amines using Silufol UV 254 in a different solvent system was also obtained by Mikolanda.[126]

Ligand exchange has been shown to expedite the separation of aromatic amines by TLC using silica gel and aluminum oxide thin layers impregnated with Zn, Cd, Ni, and Mn ions.[127,128] Zn and Cd ions retard different amines to different extents and thus greatly improve the separation between them. For example, the R_F values of 1- and 2-naphthylamine on aluminum oxide with carbon tetrachloride–methanol as solvent are quite close (0.68 and 0.62); if the same system is used with Zn ions, the resolution improves remarkably (R_F 0.73 and 0.46).

3.4.3   Gas Chromatography.   In 1969 Masuda et al. published a quantitative GC method for the determination of 1- and 2-naphthylamine in cigarette smoke.[129] The amines were reacted with pentafluoropropionic anhydride and the resulting pentafluoropropionamides (better than 95% yield) were analyzed by GC with an electron capture detector, with a sensitivity limit less than 1 ng. Experimental conditions and retention times are tabulated for 22 primary amines; ^{14}C-labeled amines were used as internal standards.

Trifluoroacetyl derivatives have been used in our laboratory for the separation of the monofunctional aromatic amines (eluted with solvent) from diamines (benzidine, o-tolidine, o-dianisidine) which were determined using a flame ionization detector.[130,131] Trifluoroacetyl derivatives were also employed for the determination of 1 ppm 2-naphthylamine in 1-naphthylamine using a "tail trap" method.[132,134]

3.5   New Developments

Kissinger et al. have described a simple liquid chromatograph with an extremely sensitive electrochemical detector for routine work at 5–10 ng levels of biogenic amines.[135,136] There is every reason to believe that the same technique could be used for the determination of other amines. The technique should warrant a study with difunctional amines; in a scouting experiment by Adams, o-dianisidine was determined with excellent sensitivity using the same detector system as was used for the catecholamine work.[137] If the free amine is extracted into 10 ml solvent from 100 ml waste water, the detection limit would be 0.1 μg/l.

REFERENCES

1. G. Westöö, *Acta Chem. Scand.*, **20**, 2131 (1966).
2. J. M. Wood, F. Scott Kennedy, and C. H. Rosen, *Nature (London)*, **220**, 173 (1968).
3. S. Jensen and A. Jernelöv, *Nature*, **223**, 753 (1969).
4. J. B. Sprague, *Water Res.*, **4**, 3 (1970).
5. D. L. Klayman and W. H. H. Günther, *Organic Selenium Compounds: Their Chemistry and Biology*, Wiley, New York, 1973.
6. C. E. Searle, *Chem. Br.*, **6**, 5 (1970).
7. J. H. Weisburger and E. K. Weisburger, *Chem. Eng. News*, 124 (February 7, 1966).
8. *IARC Monographs*, Vol. 4, World Health Organization International Agency for Research on Cancer, 1973.
9. UICC Technical Report Series, Vol. 4, *The Quantification of Environmental Carcinogens*, Geneva, 1970.
10. *Federal Register*, (*a*) **38**, 28758–28760, 35388–35395 (1973); (*b*) **40**, 24535–24539 (1975).

11. *Ibid.*, **39**, 3756–3797 (1974).

12. *Colourage*, **22**, 44 (1975).

13. *Am. Dyest. Rep.*, **63**, 78 (September 1974).

14. *Text. Chem. Color.*, **7**, 117, 120 (1975).

15. *Papilloma of the Bladder in the Chemical Industry, A Study of its Cause and Prevention*, The Assoc. of British Chemical Manufacturers, London, 1953.

16. *Dyes and the Environment*, Vols. I and II, American Dye Manufacturers Institute, Inc., 1973, 1974.

17. *Standard Methods for the Examination of Water and Wastewater*, 13th ed., American Public Health Association, New York, 1971.

18. *A Literature Survey of Colored Wastes*, American Dye Manufacturers Institute, Inc., 1971.

19. J. M. Haas, H. W. Earhart, and A. S. Todd, *Am. Dyest. Rep.*, **64**, 34 (March 1975).

20. *ADMI Analytical Subcommittee Report*, American Dye Manufacturers Institute, Inc. To be published.

21. A. Netzer, H. K. Miyamoto, P. Wilkinson, *Bull. Environ. Contam. Toxicol.*, **14**, No. 3, 301 (1975).

22. *Annual Book of ASTM Standards, Part 31, Water*, American Society for Testing and Materials, Philadelphia, 1975.

23. *Methods for Chemical Analysis of Water and Wastes*, U.S. Environmental Protection Agency, Office of Technology Transfer, Washington, D.C., 1974.

24. G. H. Morrison, *Trace Analysis*, Wiley-Interscience, New York, 1965.

25. W. W. Meinke and B. F. Scribner, *Trace Characterization*, National Bureau of Standards Monograph 100, 1966.

26. D. C. Burrell, *Atomic Spectrometric Analysis of Heavy-Metal Pollutants in Water*, Ann Arbor Science Publishers, Ann Arbor, Mich., 1975.

27. R. A. Minear, *J. Am. Water Works Assoc.*, **67**, 9 (1975).

28. M. Zief and R. Speights, *Ultrapurity*, Marcel Dekker, New York, 1972.

29. G. Tölg, *Talanta*, **19**, 1489 (1972).

30. *National Bureau of Standards, SRM No. 1642*, U.S. Dept. of Commerce, Washington, D.C.

31. T. T. Gorsuch, *The Destruction of Organic Matter*, Pergamon, Oxford, 1970.

32. P. O. Bethge, *Anal. Chim. Acta*, **10**, 317 (1954).

33. G. Frederick Smith, *Anal. Chim. Acta*, **8**, 397 (1953).

34. J. Korkisch and A. Sorio, *Anal. Chim. Acta*, **76**, 393 (1975).

35. L. R. Hathaway and G. W. James, *Anal. Chem.*, **47**, 2035 (1975).

36. K. F. Sugaware, H. H. Weetall, and D. G. Schucker, *Anal. Chem.*, **46**, 489 (1974).

37. D. M. Hercules et al., *Anal. Chem.*, **45**, 1973 (1973).

38. D. E. Leyden and G. H. Luttrell, *ibid.*, **47**, 1612 (1975).

39. J. Starý, *The Solvent Extraction of Metal Chelates*, Macmillan, New York, 1964.

40. Y. A. Zolotov, *Extraction of Chelate Compounds* (translated by J. Schmorak), Humphrey Science Publishers, Ann Arbor, Mich., 1970.

41. E. B. Sandell, *Colorimetric Determination of Traces of Metals*, Interscience, New York, 1961.

42. B. Armitage and H. Zeitlin, *Anal. Chim. Acta*, **53**, 47 (1971).

43. J. D. Kinrade and J. C. Van Loon, *Anal. Chem.*, **46**, 1894 (1974).

44. J. A. Buono, J. C. Buono, and J. L. Fasching, *Anal. Chem.*, **47**, 1926 (1975).

45. D. D. Perrin, *Masking and Demasking of Chemical Reactions*, Wiley-Interscience, New York, 1970.

46. F. D. Snell and C. T. Snell, *Colorimetric Methods of Analysis*, Vol. IIA, Van Nostrand, New York, 1959.

47. M. Pinta, *Detection and Determination of Trace Elements* (Translated by M. Bivas), Ann Arbor Science Publishers, Ann Arbor, Mich., 1966.

48. S. M. Kolthoff and J. M. Lingane, *Polarography*, Vols. 1 and 2, Interscience, New York, 1952.

49. G. J. Hills, *Polarography*, Interscience, New York, 1966.

50. J. B. Flato, *Anal. Chem.*, **44**, 75A (1972).

51. H. Siegerman and G. O'Dom, *Am. Lab.* (June 1972).

52. A. M. Bond and R. J. O'Halloran, *Anal. Chem.*, **47**, 1906 (1975).

53. Princeton Applied Research Corp., Princeton, N.J.

54. Environmental Sciences Associates, Inc., Burlington, Mass.

55. M. E. Beyer and A. M. Bond, *Anal. Chim. Acta*, **75**, 409 (1975).

56. S. T. Cosmun and J. A. Dean, *Anal. Chim. Acta*, **75**, 421 (1975).

57. G. Forsberg et al., *Anal. Chem.*, **47**, 1587 (1975).

58. G. Piccardi and P. L. Cellini, *Ann. Chim. (Rome)*, **64**, 1 (1974).

59. G. A. Rechnitz, *Chem. Eng. News*, **45**, No. 25, 146 (1967).

60. K. Cammann, *Das Arbeiten mit Ionenselektiven Electroden*, Springer, Berlin, 1973.

61. G. J. Moody and I. D. R. Thomas, *Selective Ion-Sensitive Electrodes*, Merrow, Watford England, 1971.

62. Analytical Methods Guide, Orion Research, Inc., Cambridge, Mass., 1975.

63. Bentley, *Dependable Electrodes*, Bentley Laboratories, Inc., Irvine, Calif., 1975.

64. B. Salbu, E. Steinnes, and C. Pappas, *Anal. Chem.*, **47**, 1011 (1975).

65. C. H. Lochmüller, J. W. Galbraith, and R. L. Walter, *Anal. Chem.*, **46**, 440 (1974).

66. J. L. Campbell et al., *Anal. Chem.*, **47**, 1543 (1975).

67. L. R. Hathaway and G. W. James, *Anal. Chem.*, **47**, 2035 (1975).

68. *X-ray Spectroscopy, Practical Spectroscopy Series*, Vol. 3, Marcel Dekker, New York, 1976.

69. I. H. Crocker and W. T. Merritt, *Water Res.*, **6**, 285 (1972).

70. C. R. Schmitt and J. E. Hall, *J. Am. Water Works Assoc.*, **67**, 40 (1975).

71. A. Walsh, *Spectrochim. Acta*, **7**, 108 (1955).

72. G. D. Christian and F. J. Feldman, *Atomic Absorption Spectroscopy*, Wiley-Interscience, New York, 1970.

73. J. A. Dean and T. C. Rains, *Flame Emission and Atomic Absorption Spectrometry*, Vols. 1 and 2, Marcel Dekker, New York, 1969, 1971.

74. J. Rubeška and B. Moldan, *Atomic Absorption Spectrometry* (translated by B. T. Woods), Chemical Rubber Company Press, International Scientific Series, 1969.

75. G. Buttergereit, *Z. Anal. Chem.*, **267**, 81 (1973).

76. J. B. Willis, *Nature (London)*, **207**, 715 (1965).

77. M. D. Amos and J. B. Willis, *Spectrochim. Acta*, **22**, 1325 (1966).

78. G. F. Kirkbright, M. K. Peters, and T. S. West, *Talanta*, **14**, 789 (1967).

79. H. Massmann, *Spectrochim. Acta*, **23B**, 215 (1968).

80. H. L. Kahn, *Int. J. Environ. Anal. Chem.*, **3**, 121 (1973).

81. G. Torsi and G. Tessari, *Anal. Chem.*, **47**, 839 (1975).

82. M. R. Sensmeier, W. F. Wagner, and G. D. Christian, *Z. Anal. Chem.*, **277**, 19 (1975).

83. L. Morgenthaler, *Am. Lab.*, 41 (April 1975).

84. W. K. Robbins, *Am. Lab.*, 23 (August 1975); 38 (September 1975).

85. W. H. Gries and E. Norval. *Anal. Chim. Acta*, **75**, 289 (1975).

86. *Technique and Applications of Atomic Absorption*, Perkin-Elmer Corporation, Order No. AA 322F, Norwalk, Connecticut,

87. R. D. Ediger, *At. Absorpt. Newsl.*, **14**, 127 (1975).

88. T. T. Woodson, *Rev. Sci. Instrum.*, **10**, 308 (1939).

89. D. C. Manning, *At. Absorpt. Newsl.*, **9**, 97 (1970).

90. W. R. Hatch and W. L. Ott, *Anal. Chem.*, **40**, 2085 (1968).

91. G. W. Kalb, *At. Absorpt. Newsl.*, **9**, 84 (1970).

92. *NIOSH Manual of Analytical Methods*, U.S. Department of Health, Education and Welfare, U.S. Government Printing Office, Washington, D.C.

93. A. Ando et al., *Anal. Chem.*, **41**, 1974 (1969).

94. J. F. Fernandez and D. C. Manning, *At. Absorpt. Newsl.*, **10**, 86 (1971).

95. E. F. Dalton and A. J. Malanoski, *At. Absorpt. Newsl.*, **10**, 92 (1971).

96. D. C. Manning, *At. Absorpt. Newsl.*, **10**, 123 (1971).

97. W. Holak, *Anal. Chem.*, **41**, 1712 (1969).

98. M. S. Yllo, unpublished.

99. Y. Talmi and D. T. Boslick, *J. Chromatogr. Sci.*, **13**, 231 (1975).

100. DHEW Toxicology Subcommittee for Carcinogen Standards, *The Department of Health, Education, and Welfare Safety Standards for Laboratory Operations Involving Chemical Carcinogens*, January 8, 1975.

101. *Am. Dyest. Rep.*, **63**, 68 (March 1974).

102. *Chem. Eng. News*, **52**, 12 (February 11, 1974).

103. L. T. Butt and N. Strafford, *J. Appl. Chem.*, **6**, 525 (1956).

104. R. G. Rice and E. J. Kohn, *Anal. Chem.*, **27**, 1630 (1955).

105. K. C. Khulbe and S. P. Srivastava, *Z. Anal. Chem.*, **208**, 427 (1965).

106. K. R. Manolov and V. T. Stamatova, *Mikrochim. Acta*, 222 (1970).

107. R. C. Gupta and S. P. Srivastava, *Z. Anal. Chem.*, **257**, 275 (1971).

108. I. Florea, *Revue Roum. Chim.*, **17**, 915 (1972); **19**, 157 (1974); *CA*, **77**, 83306 (1972); *CA*, **80**, 127901 (1974).

109. J. W. Meigs, R. M. Brown, and L. J. Sciarini, *Arch. Ind. Hygiene*, **4**, 519, 533 (1951).

110. L. J. Sciarini and J. A. Mahew, *Arch. Ind. Health*, **11**, 420 (1955).

111. *Method for Benzidine and its Salts in Waste Water*, Methods Development and Quality Assurance Research Laboratory, National Environmental Research Center, USEPA, Cincinnati, Ohio.

112. J. K. Piotrowski, W. Bolanowski, and A. Sapota, *Medy. Pr.*, **22**, 307 (1971); *CA*, **76**, 21034 (1972).

113. O. L. Evenson, J. A. Kime, and S. S. Forrest, *J. Ind. Eng. Chem. Anal. Ed.*, **9,** 74 (1937).

114. V. Kratochvíl, M. Matrka, and J. Marhold, *Collect. Czech. Chem. Commun.*, **25,** 101 (1960).

115. J. W. Daniel, *Analyst (London)*, **86,** 640 (1961).

116. E. Sawicki et al., *Anal. Chem.*, **33,** 722 (1961).

117. E. Sawicki, J. L. Noe, and F. T. Fox, *Talanta*, **8,** 257 (1961).

118. P. Engelbertz and E. Babel, *Zentr. albl. Arbeitsmed. Arbeitsschutz*, **7,** 211 (1957).

119. J. M. Hais and K. Macek, *Paper Chromatography*, Publishing House of the Czechoslovak Academy of Sciences, Prague, 1963.

120. G. Ghetti et al., *Lav. Um.*, **20,** 389 (1968); *CA*, **71,** 24552 (1969).

121. J. Gasparic, J. Petranek, and M. Večera, *Mikrochim. Acta*, 1026 (1955).

122. R. J. Weeks, Jr., B. J. Dean, and S. K. Yasuda, National Am. Chem. Soc. Meeting, August 24–29, Chicago, Ill., 1975. U.S. Energy Research and Development Administration Contract W-7405 Eng. 36.

123. F. Feigl, E. Jungreis, and S. Yariv, *Z. Anal. Chem.*, **200,** 38 (1964).

124. G. R. N. Jones, *J. Chromatogr.*, **77,** 357 (1973).

125. H. Thielman, *Z. Anal. Chem.*, **262,** 286 (1972); *Microchim. Acta*, 578 (1972).

126. F. Mikolanda, *Chem. Prum*, **23,** 414 (1973); *CA*, **80,** 13710 (1974).

127. K. Shimomura and H. F. Walton, *Sep. Sci.*, **3,** 493 (1968).

128. K. Yasuda, *J. Chromatogr.*, **72,** 413 (1972); **87,** 565 (1973).

129. Y. Masuda et al., *Anal. Chem.*, **41,** 650 (1969); *Nature (London)*, **221,** 254 (1969); *J. Chromatogr. Sci.*, **7,** 694 (1969).

130. J. H. McClure, private communication.

131. A. L. Linch et al., *J. Am. Ind. Hyg. Assoc.*, **32,** 802 (1971).

132. R. J. Troy, unpublished.

133. L. J. Papa and A. J. Varon, *J. Gas Chromatogr.*, **6,** 185 (1968).

134. N. Mellor, *Analyst*, **96,** 164 (1971).

135. P. T. Kissinger et al., *Anal. Letters*, **6,** 465 (1973); **7,** 791 (1974); *Clin. Chem.*, **20,** 992 (1974).

136. R. N. Adams, *Electrochemistry at Solid Electrodes*, Marcel Dekker, New York, 1969.

137. R. N. Adams, private communication, December 4, 1975.

Index

Numbers in *italics* are Colour Index Generic Name numbers.